COMPUTER ENTREPRENEUR

ROBERT H. MORRISON

Library of Congress cataloging in publication data
Main entry under title:

COMPUTER ENTREPRENEUR

PUBLISHED BY:
COMPUTER INFORMATION, LIMITED
P.O. BOX 60369
SAN DIEGO, CALIFORNIA 92106

ISBN #0-9614906-0-8

ACKNOWLEDGEMENTS

Below are listed people who are very special to me—for their support, time and understanding. My warmest thanks and appreciation to everyone of them for each of their individual efforts to make this project a success.

Judy Bausch
D. P. Beguelin
Dyan Beguelin
Henry Beguelin
Joan Beguelin
Richard Beguelin
John J. Bohannen
Eileen M. Burkart
William F. Burkart
Leonard Diamond, PHD.
Millicent P. Diamond
Lynne M. Ebenkamp
Theodore L. Ebenkamp
Edward N. Elton
Santina Elton
Leon Fine
Phyllis A. Fine
Jeri Lyn Fink
Robert E. Fink, Jr.
Joseph J. Fonzo
Hank Garfield
Spencer Garrett
George Greenspon
Walton R. Held
Stuart W. Heller
Shirley Hulett

L. R. Jackson
Alexandra Marquette
Teri Jackson
Toni Michael
Al Mogilner
Kaye Morrow
Lewis Morrow
Richard J. Oberholzer
Nello Panelli
E. James Perry
Jenifer F. Peterson
Rebecca L. Peterson
Richard E. Peterson
Robert E. Peterson
Linn L. Redelsperger
Robert Redelsperger
David Rice
Drew Robinson
Guy Rosati
Joyce Sperber
Stephen Sperber
Thad Stevenson
Wally Wang
Harold C. White
Linda Wood

Special thanks to *Dian Schaffhauser* for her patience and fine editing job, to *Sherry Russell* for many hours of computer time and her loyalty to me and the project. Last but not least, my wife, *Tricia*, and sons, *Jim* and *Shawn*, whose support cannot be measured.

Cover design: *Tom Strutton*

FORWARD

Would a second income of $1,000 a month, $2,000 a month, or even $5,000 a month come in handy?

If you answered yes to any of those figures, then you are already on your way to turning dreams into reality. All it will take are a few hours of your spare time and the use of your personal computer.

No matter if your computer is a bare bones Atari or an IBM PC with all the goodies on it, you can use it to provide enough second income to live life on the leading edge or, if you prefer, just plain, old laid-back lazy. Either way, you can make life fun again.

The concept of this book is to show you how to make money by operating your own small business. It is designed to show you how to run a computer business successfully and how to maximize your personal income from your ventures.

Over seven years in research and development, this book has 100 fully detailed business plans for you to choose from. They range from a traditional local bookkeeping service for small businesses to a far-out program for handicapping horses that generates a substantial income. And there are 98 other businesses in between.

This book is NOT another one of those "One hundred and one ways" books that contain only a paragraph or two of information about each business. In this book, each business plan is fully-detailed, including such information as: how to start up, how to operate, how to market the service, how to keep the books, what to charge, where to locate it and how many hours it will take to make it a success. The book even includes a quick and simple method for determining the best business for your own interests and experience.

You don't have to be a computer whiz to start or operate these ventures. Nor do you need any programming skills or fancy materials. Almost all of these businesses can be operated simply by using off-the-shelf software that you probably already have.

Before you get started in reading about the particular businesses included in this book, there are a couple of things I'd like to pass on to you from my own experience as a small-business operator.

The first thing to do is clear up in your mind what you want personally from your new business venture. Too many small business owners don't have a clear concept of what they want from their business, other than to put meat on the table and a roof over their heads.

What you need to do is set precise goals for your business operations and then set about to obtain them. That is how I have always worked. And it is what has made me successful in my many ventures. I set my goals in terms of bank balances in my personal accounts and in material possessions I own free and clear. My businesses are the means to those ends and not ends unto themselves. From the beginning I made those possessions my particular goals to reach, and by setting my sights high, I succeeded in my efforts.

In order to be successful, you must have a beginning and an end to a journey. There is an old saying: "If you don't know where you are going, any road will take you there." The business journey should not turn out to be all lifetime of meandering through the economic thicket. It should be a series of trips up the mountainside. Each goal should be set forth and reached before proceeding to the next one. You can set terms you want and any goals you want, but have them. A clear and precise concept of just what you want to achieve and obtain in each step of the way is important.

This book is going to give you many ideas on how to make money in a small computer business. It is also my desire to show you how I made my own fortunes. I did it, not by putting all my eggs in one basket and watching the basket, but by keeping my eyes open for opportunities of any kind and then moving in on them as quickly and profitably as I could.

This is a book for small business entrepreneurs who intend to survive and prosper. It is not a book about serving your fellow human with selfless devotion or whistling past the graveyard with unfounded optimism that the Lord will provide. It is a book about the real world of business—a rigged economic system created to benefit institutions and penalize individuals. It is a book for eagles who fly alone to make their living, and not for turkeys who run in flocks.

You won't find the simplistic concepts of business as presented by professors who have never been in the game but who write and talk about serving the community and giving time and treasure for the betterment of mankind. Nor will you find a book written by self-appointed experts who deal in hypocrisy and platitudes about self-motivation or being a saint among sinners and how it can bring you inner contentment and success.

It is a book written by a small businessperson who is a winner, who recognizes the system for what it is, and uses that knowledge to succeed, who doesn't buy the power structure, but who uses it to gain his own ends.

The Computer Entrepreneur is your guide to playing the business game and winning at it. It shows you how to use the rules as they are set forth, but to your own advantage. It will direct you through your planning and perserverance, to build your income, and get what you want and need.

So read on!

R. H. MORRISON
CORONADO, CALIFORNIA
MAY, 1985

YOUR 7 STEPS TO FINANCIAL INDEPENDENCE

This chart explains the seven steps you'll need to follow in order to gain financial independence. Each step will also take you to a different section of the book. To further understand what is involved in each step, read on.

STEP 1

If you are unsure where to begin reading in this book, you might want to take the Business Qualification Test in Section 1. This test will ask you questions and, based on your answers, will guide you to those businesses included in the book that best fit your interests and experience.

STEP 2

The Brief Business Outlines that make up Section 2 are one-page explanations of every business included in this book. Each outline gives a brief description of what the business entails, as well as information about what computer equipment you will require, what methods you can use to market the business, whether you can operate it part-time or full-time, what kind of location and market base it is best suited for, and how much start-up capital you should have to get the business started.

STEP 3

Once you have read the Brief Business Outlines for those businesses you'd like to know more about, it is time to take the third step and read the Complete Business Venture Plan. You will find these in Section 3 of the book. Each Venture Plan gives you the details you actually need in order to get your own business up and running. It will explain what the business consists of, what kinds of skills and information you'll need to operate it, how to get started, potential costs, how to market it and what unique business approaches that will give you success.

STEP 4

Once you have an understanding of what business you want to succeed at you will want to read Section 4, the Business Structure and Plan. This section will explain to you the special details you'll want to know about in order to set your business up. These include what kind of operating name to choose, what type of structure is best suited for the business, how to insure it, and other operation details involved in opening up any new business.

Business Promotion
and Marketing

STEP 5

Not only will you want to read about setting up your business, but you'll also want to know how to properly promote and market it. These subjects are covered fully in Section 5, Business Promotion and Marketing. Not only will you learn the difference between advertising and promotion, but you'll learn how to get the most from both with the least amount of money. You'll also read about how to write display and classified ads that work, how to get free publicity from local newspapers, how to handle direct mail, and how to use the telephone to get potential customers interested in your service.

Where and How
To Get Money

STEP 6

Another important element to any business venture is obtaining start-up capital. This subject is covered in Section 5, Where and How To Get Money For Your Business. Even if you do have enough start-up capital, there may come a time when you want to expand your business, in which case you'll need to read about where to go for your money, what bankers will require, how to put together a solid business plan and financial statement, who to try if the banks turn you down, and how to know when to expect your business to turn a profit.

STEP 7

Of course, one important element to any computer business is the software that you use to carry it out. In Section 7, you will find a Reference Section that lists software products and manufacturers for any business you've decided to try. A list at the beginning of the section will refer you to those kinds of software that are most appropriate for your new venture, running all the way from accounting packages to travel and transportation programs, and everything that falls between.

Reference Section

TABLE OF CONTENTS

Section 3   **COMPLETE BUSINESS VENTURE PLANS**

Section 4   BUSINESS STRUCTURE & PLAN

SECTION 1

If you are unsure about just what business you want to try in this book, you are in luck. We have included this test in order to direct you to those money-making ventures that best fit your interests and experience. All it will take from you is a few minutes of your time to answer some of the questions in the test. Each business in the book has its own number. Once you've found the areas that most interest you, simply refer to those numbers that the questions refer you to. After that, you're already on your way to making money with the use of your computer.

SECTION 1

YOUR BUSINESS QUALIFICATION TEST

Do you prefer working with: (circle one)

1. PEOPLE
2. NUMBERS
3. WORDS
4. COMPUTERS
5. NONE OF THE ABOVE

If your answer:
Equals 1 go to A
Equals 2 go to B
Equals 3 go to C
Equals 4 go to D
Equals 5 go to E

As a person who prefers working with people, you'll find a multitude of businesses in this book that will give you that opportunity. Not only will you be able to assist them in a number of ways, but you'll be able to make a nice income for your efforts.

If you want to be directed to those businesses that best suit you, answer the following questions.

Does your experience or interest include:

1. TEACHING
2. MANAGING
3. HEALTH AND FITNESS
4. WORKING WITH FOOD
5. RESEARCH
6. REAL ESTATE
7. TRAVEL PLANNING
8. PERSONALITY ANALYSIS

If your answer:

Equals 1 go to 1
Equals 2 go to 2
Equals 3 go to 3
Equals 4 go to 4
Equals 5 go to 5
Equals 6 go to 6
Equals 7 go to 7
Equals 8 go to 8

1. If the idea of teaching appeals to you, do you prefer:

WORKING WITH KIDS? Check businesses 145, 153, 165, 195.
WORKING WITH ADULTS? Check businesses 106, 143, 161, 162, 195.
WORKING OUT OF YOUR HOME? Check businesses 162, 165, 195.
WORKING IN A RECREATIONAL SETTING? Check business 144.

2. If you enjoy managing and organizing people, do you prefer:

ORGANIZING KIDS? Check business 203.
ORGANIZING ADULTS? Check businesses 149, 170.
ARRANGING SCHEDULES? Check businesses 110, 112.
INSPIRING ENTHUSIASM IN OTHERS TO WORK? Check business 108.

3. If you enjoy working in the health and fitness field, do you prefer:

ARRANGING DIETS? Check businesses 102, 134.
ARRANGING EXERCISE PLANS? Check business 103.

4. If you relish the thought of making money with food:

Check businesses 102, 133, 180.

5. If you enjoy researching for people, do you enjoy:

TREASURE HUNTING? Check businesses 111, 126, 132, 149.
TRACING FAMILY TREES? Check business 164.

6. If you enjoy real estate:

Check businesses 123, 146, 147.

7. If travel planning appeals to you, do you prefer:

LOCAL AREA PLANNING? Check business 127.
LONG-DISTANCE PLANNING? Check businesses 142, 167, 198.
SMALL PILOT FLIGHT PLANNING? Check business 167.

8. If you enjoy personality analysis, do you prefer:

COMPATIBILITY TESTING? Check businesses 101, 107, 113.
HELPING OTHERS UNDERSTAND THEMSELVES? Check businesses 119, 120, 121.

As a person who enjoys working with numbers, you'll find plenty of opportunities in this book that "add up" to making money for you.

If you want some direction in finding those businesses that best suit you, answer the following questions.

Does your experience and interest include:

1. BOOKKEEPING
2. MARKETING
3. ANALYSIS
4. INVENTORY
5. PRICING
6. SPORTS

If your answer:

Equals 1 go to 1
Equals 2 go to 2
Equals 3 go to 3
Equals 4 go to 4
Equals 5 go to 5
Equals 6 go to 6

1. If you are experienced in or want to learn bookkeeping, would you prefer:

WORKING WITH OTHER BUSINESSES? Check businesses 105, 129, 150, 155, 204.
BOOKKEEPING FOR INDIVIDUALS? Check businesses 105, 106, 16, 175.

2. If you enjoy marketing:

Check out businesses 109, 114, 118, 151.

3. If the idea of numbers analysis appeals to you, do you prefer:

INVESTMENT ANALYSIS? Check businesses 154, 187, 189, 199.
BUSINESS ANALYSIS? Check businesses 104, 125, 128, 130, 136, 137, 139, 158, 178.
PERSONAL ANALYSIS? Check businesses 125, 130, 154, 178, 179, 189.

4. If you have ever dealt with inventory or learning about the field appeals to you, do you prefer:

WORKING WITH BUSINESSES? Check businesses 122, 197.
WORKING WITH PEOPLE? Check businesses 181, 184.

5. If you have ever handled price controls and pricing or have wanted to learn the business:

Check businesses 114, 131, 173, 193.

6. If you enjoy sports and the numbers involved with sports, do you prefer:

KEEPING STATISTICS? Check businesses 192, 194.
ANALYZING OUTCOMES? Check businesses 140, 190.

As a person who enjoys the thought of making money with words, this book contains many businesses that will suit you well. To find out which businesses would best suit you, answer the following questions.

Does your interest or experience include:

1. RESEARCH
2. PUBLISHING
3. WRITING
4. SECRETARIAL SERVICES

If your answer:

Equals 1 go to 1
Equals 2 go to 2
Equals 3 go to 3
Equals 4 go to 4

1. If the thought of research appeals to you, do you prefer:

LEGAL RESEARCH? Check businesses 124, 158, 186.
BUSINESS RESEARCH? Check businesses 104, 134, 163.

2. If publishing is your interest, do you prefer:

WRITING WHAT YOU PUBLISH? Check businesses 138, 196, 206.
COMPILING INFORMATION TO PUBLISH? Check businesses 116, 152.

3. If you enjoy writing and want to learn how to make money doing it, do you prefer:

CREATIVE WRITING? Check businesses 168, 169, 174, 196, 206.
COPYWRITING? Check businesses 115, 117, 157, 171.
INFORMATIONAL AND HOW-TO WRITING? Check businesses 115, 168, 206.

4. If you enjoy secretarial services:

Check out businesses 110, 112, 141, 148, 195.

As a person who really enjoys working with computers, any business in this book could suit you, since all require the use of computers. Yet several also require a certain love of the magical things only a computer can do. All can make money with your special interests.

To find out what these unique computer-oriented businesses are, answer the following questions.

Does your experience or interest include:

1. PROGRAMMING
2. SELLING OR CONSULTING
3. TRAINING
4. GETTING OTHER COMPUTER-LOVERS TOGETHER

If your answer:

Equals 1 go to 1
Equals 2 go to 2
Equals 3 go to 3
Equals 4 go to 4

1. If your interest in is programming:

Check businesses 153, 160, 161, 183, 206.

2. If your interest is in selling computers or consulting, do you prefer:

WORKING WITH BUSINESSES? Check businesses 145, 168, 202.
WORKING WITH INDIVIDUALS? Check businesses 145, 156, 168, 170, 172.

3. If you enjoy training others:

Check businesses 10 6, 143, 144, 170, 203.

4. If you prefer getting other computer-lovers together:

Check businesses 144, 159, 170, 203.

E

As a person who doesn't necessarily enjoy working with numbers more than words, or computers more than people, you have several options. You can simply go through the Menu and see what businesses appeal to you. The variety and number of money-making opportunities is large and several will probably spark your interest.

You may also choose to go through the test and see if any of the questions catch your eye. Answer the questions and check the businesses they refer to.

Or, you might consider answering the following questions. These will direct you to several businesses that don't necessarily fit any of the categories we've set up, yet which might fit you to a "T".

DO YOU ENJOY:

MUSIC?
Check business 160.

ART?
Check business 171.

CHEMISTRY?
Check business 111.

CONSTRUCTION?
Check businesses 135, 193, 200.

SPORTS?
Check businesses 140, 190, 192, 194.

AGRICULTURE AND GARDENING?
Check businesses 183, 196.

BOOKS?
Check businesses 132, 184.

COINS AND STAMPS?
Check business 152.

PREDICTING THE FUTURE?
Check businesses 104, 118, 120, 121, 140, 154.

ASSISTING OTHERS IN STARTING AND OPERATING A SMALL BUSINESS?
Check businesses 124, 125, 128, 136, 137, 139, 158, 178.

KEEPING LISTS?
Check businesses 101, 109, 112, 116, 118, 146, 147, 149, 156, 172, 184, 185, 197, 200.

MAKING BIG MONEY?
Check businesses 101, 104, 105, 108, 116, 118, 124, 125, 126, 137, 140, 145, 154, 155, 156, 157, 163, 186, 202.

SECTION 2

We have included this section to save you time. Each page in the Brief Business Outlines gives you a brief description of one business included in the book. It will also tell you about what computer equipment you'll need to operate the business, how best to promote it, whether it can be operated part-time or full-time, what kind of location and market base it is best suited for, and how much start-up capital you should have to get the business going.

No. 101

EXECUTIVE RECRUITING AND EMPLOYMENT SERVICE

DESCRIPTION:

$100,000 per year is where it's at with this service, and with your computer it's a one-person business. Ever since the early 70's when Dartmouth college students started matching jobs with people on their computer, this has become an easy-to-operate, big-dollar business. It seems that in good times as well as bad, this service prospers, as indicated by the many new firms that have opened up over the past two years. So get your share of the pie.

INCOME LEVEL RATING:
High

MARKETING METHODS
1. Direct mail
2. Display ads
3. Telephone sales
4. Direct sales

EQUIPMENT REQUIRED
1. Computer with disk drive
2. Printer

PART TIME:
Yes

FULL TIME:
Yes

LOCATION:
City or country

MARKET BASE:
5,000–50,000

START UP CAPITAL:
$1,000 To $5,000 (Includes computer costs)

No. 102

COMPUTER CUSTOM DIET SERVICE

DESCRIPTION:
With half of the population always on a diet there is no end to the number of clients you can get. With this plan you can develop low-calorie diets for people using only the foods they enjoy. And because it is all on your computer, you can change and customize their diet programs as their tastes change, collecting a fee each time. This computer business plan requires little time to operate and comes complete with all sample forms and questionnaires. So slim them down and fatten your bank account.

INCOME LEVEL RATING:
Medium

MARKETING METHODS:
1. Display ads

EQUIPMENT REQUIRED:
1. Computer with disk drive
2. Printer

PART TIME:
Yes

FULL TIME:
Yes

LOCATION:
City or country

MARKET BASE:
5,000–50,000

START UP CAPITAL:
Under $1,000

No. 103

COMPUTERIZED CUSTOM EXERCISE PROGRAMS

DESCRIPTION:

Exercise programs in gyms, YMCAs and corporations are the fastest- growing businesses in America today. And everybody needs a plan—whether it's a training program for a marathon or just to get their blood pressure down. With this computer business there are no limits to the parameters you can plug into their custom programs. So each client will have a personalized plan to follow and a specific goal that they can reach by sticking to the program you provide.

INCOME LEVEL RATING:
Medium

MARKETING METHODS:
1. Display ads

EQUIPMENT REQUIRED:
1. Computer with disk drive
2. Printer

PART TIME:
Yes

FULL TIME:
Yes

LOCATION:
City or country

MARKET BASE:
50,000–200,000

START UP CAPITAL:
Under $1,000

No. 104

ECONOMIC FORECASTING

DESCRIPTION:

Every day you hear on the news about the unemployment rate, money supply, gross national product, etc. But these figures never give the local businesspeople any insight into what's happening in their town. With the instructions and ideas presented in this computer business plan, you will be able to obtain all of the pertinent information to sell to local business. This localized service has made several small operators very wealthy because it changes all the time. The need for the service never ends.

INCOME LEVEL RATING:
High

MARKETING METHODS
1. Display ads

EQUIPMENT REQUIRED:
1. Computer with disk drive
2. Printer
3. Modem
4. Plotter
5. Graphics

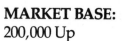

PART TIME:
Yes

FULL TIME:
Yes

LOCATION:
City

MARKET BASE:
200,000 Up

START UP CAPITAL:
$1,000 To $5,000 (Includes computer costs)

No. 105

COMPUTER TAX SERVICE

DESCRIPTION:
This service has been around in one form or another ever since Uncle Sam started collecting income taxes, but never has it been so simple for a non-accountant type to get into the business. For only 15 weeks of work you can make a year's wages with our business plan and your computer. This can be done in your home or your client's home. Some of our computer business operators even set it up in their vans and travel to new locations every year.

INCOME LEVEL RATING:
High

MARKETING METHODS:
1. Direct mail
2. Display ads
3. Telephone sales

EQUIPMENT REQUIRED:
1. Computer with disk drive
2. Printer
3. Modem
4. Plotter
5. Graphics

PART TIME:
Yes

FULL TIME:
Yes

LOCATION:
City or country

MARKET BASE:
5,000–50,000

START UP CAPITAL:
Over $5,000 (Includes computer costs)

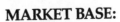

No. 106

I WANT YOURS

TAX SERVICE RENTAL PLAN

DESCRIPTION: As stated in our computer business plan number 105, never has it been so easy to figure out how to do your taxes with the help of home computers. Here is a business plan that shows you how to set up a small space in a well-traveled area of town where with 10 to 15 minutes of instruction a person can sit down and fill out his or her tax return with complete privacy — and you collect while they're doing it. It will make you a lot of money for only 15 weeks of work a year.

INCOME LEVEL RATING:
Medium

MARKETING METHODS:
1. Display ads

EQUIPMENT REQUIRED:
1. Computer with disk drive
2. Printer

PART TIME:
No

FULL TIME:
Yes

LOCATION:
City

MARKET BASE:
50,000–200,000

START UP CAPITAL:
Over $5,000 (Includes computer costs)

No. 107

COMPUTER DATING SERVICE

DESCRIPTION:
I'm sure you've heard all the standard jokes about computer dates, but what you do not hear is how this business is growing and how much its operators are making. With over 10-million singles in this country you never run out of potential clients. We will show you how to find the clients and how to get them to use your program. And because this is done on your home computer, the companies can't compete.

INCOME LEVEL RATING:
Medium

MARKETING METHODS:
1. Display ads

EQUIPMENT REQUIRED:
1. Computer with disk drive
2. Printer

PART TIME:
Yes

FULL TIME:
Yes

LOCATION:
City

MARKET BASE:
5,000–50,000

START UP CAPITAL:
Under $1,000

No. 108

MULTI-LEVEL COMPUTER SALES

DESCRIPTION:

Multi-level selling is going big again, and a couple of companies in Texas are combining computers with this unique marketing technique and are reportedly moving over 5,000 computers per week. With this computer business plan you can break into the market in a small way and let it grow at whatever rate you want it to. Complete instructions are included in this report, so get in while this concept is still hot.

INCOME LEVEL RATING:
High

PART TIME:
Yes

MARKETING METHODS:
1. Direct mail
2. Display ads
3. Telephone sales
4. Direct sales

FULL TIME:
Yes

LOCATION:
City or country

EQUIPMENT REQUIRED:
1. Computer with disk drive
2. Printer
3. Modem

MARKET BASE:
5,000–50,000

START UP CAPITAL:
Over $5,000 (Includes computer costs)

No. 109

SELL COMPUTERIZED SALES LEADS

DESCRIPTION:
Every city has salespeople. It's a way of life. But did you ever consider that they all need to find people to sell their wares to? We will show you how a few minutes of your time everyday will develop sales leads you can sell over and over. Some sales lead operators have had to specialize in only one type of lead, because the demand was so high. This is a great business for working at home in your spare time.

INCOME LEVEL RATING:
Medium

MARKETING METHODS:
1. Direct mail
2. Display ads
3. Telephone sales

EQUIPMENT REQUIRED:
1. Computer with disk drive
2. Printer
3. Modem

PART TIME:
Yes

FULL TIME:
Yes

LOCATION:
City

MARKET BASE:
5,000–200,000

START UP CAPITAL:
$1,000 To $5,000 (Includes all computer costs)

No. 110

TYPING BROKER

DESCRIPTION:
Have you ever noticed how many secretarial services there are in your city or how many part-time secretaries there are working? These both represent how much business is available for this unique middleman business that you can control using your home computer. We will show you the simple ways of obtaining business and equally simple ways of obtaining workers. You just arrange the completion of the work and get a piece of every deal.

INCOME LEVEL RATING:
Medium

MARKETING METHODS:
1. Direct mail
2. Display ads
3. Telephone sales
4. Direct sales

EQUIPMENT REQUIRED:
1. Computer with disk drive
2. Printer

PART TIME:
Yes

FULL TIME:
Yes

LOCATION:
City

MARKET BASE:
50,000–200,000

START UP CAPITAL:
$1,000 To $5,000 (Includes computer costs)

No. 111

COMPUTERIZED FORMULA MIX SERVICE

DESCRIPTION:

Ever wonder what perfume, soap, face cream, plant food, etc. were made from? Well, with this report not only will you know what they are made from, but how much it takes and where to buy it. Now as a service, this can't be beat. You can supply complete formulas in any quantity to your clients, and they can produce almost anything they normally buy at the store for pennies on the dollar. There's no end to the number of items you will be able to supply formulas for.

INCOME LEVEL RATING:
Medium

MARKETING METHODS:
1. Direct mail
2. Display ads
3. Telephone sales

EQUIPMENT REQUIRED:
1. Computer with disk drive
2. Printer

PART TIME:
Yes

FULL TIME:
Yes

LOCATION:
City or country

MARKET BASE:
5,000–50,000

START UP CAPITAL:
$1,000 To $5,000 (Includes computer costs)

No. 112

COMPUTER REMINDER SERVICE

DESCRIPTION:
How many times have you forgotten an important anniversary, birthday or special event? With this report you'll see how many home computer operators are making a lot of money on other people's bad memories. With a simple mailer you can obtain all of the business that you can handle, and with your computer you just call up each day and see who needs to be reminded of what. This keeps them out of trouble and you counting your money.

INCOME LEVEL RATING:
Medium

MARKETING METHODS:
1. Direct mail
2. Display ads
3. Telephone sales

EQUIPMENT REQUIRED:
1. Computer with disk drive
2. Printer

PART TIME:
Yes

FULL TIME:
Yes

LOCATION:
City

MARKET BASE:
5,000–200,000

START UP CAPITAL:
Under $1,000

No. 113

COMPUTER ROOMMATE SERVICE

DESCRIPTION:
Almost every town has people looking for a place to share living expenses with another person. With your home computer you can match these people up, covering all of their individual needs, and with a simple ad you can have them running to you for the best and most complete service in town. You'll be collecting dollars in both directions. This is a business that requires little actual time—the computer does all the work.

INCOME LEVEL RATING:
Medium

MARKETING METHODS:
1. Display ads

EQUIPMENT REQUIRED:
1. Computer with disk drive
2. Printer

PART TIME:
Yes

FULL TIME:
Yes

LOCATION:
City

MARKET BASE:
50,000–200,000

START UP CAPITAL:
Under $1,000

No. 114

COMPUTERIZED ADVERTISING COST NEWSLETTER

DESCRIPTION:

If you are a small businessperson and you want to start an ad campaign, how are you going to get the best "bang for your buck"? Well, here's a service that you can spend about two hours a week doing and make hundreds of dollars on a regular basis by just compiling the ad rates for radio, tv and newspaper by length or size of ad. Print it out on a monthly basis and collect your money. Who else is going to do it?

INCOME LEVEL RATING:
Medium

MARKETING METHODS:
1. Direct mail
2. Display ads
3. Telephone sales
4. Direct sales

EQUIPMENT REQUIRED:
1. Computer with disk drive
2. Printer

PART TIME:
Yes

FULL TIME:
Yes

LOCATION:
City

MARKET BASE:
200,000 Up

START UP CAPITAL:
$1,000 To $5,000 (Includes computer costs)

No. 115

COMPUTERIZED PRESS RELEASE SERVICE

DESCRIPTION: Everybody who sells products or services wants their name in front of the public every chance they can get. Here's a report that will show you how to use your home computer to get free publicity for these people on a regular basis. As soon as you make all of your contacts as explained in this book, businesspeople all over town will be begging you to put them on your service, and this becomes a regular gravy train.

INCOME LEVEL RATING:
Medium

MARKETING METHODS:
1. Direct mail
2. Display ads
3. Telephone sales
4. Direct sales

EQUIPMENT REQUIRED:
1. Computer with disk drive
2. Printer

PART TIME:
Yes

FULL TIME:
Yes

LOCATION:
City

MARKET BASE:
200,000 Up

START UP CAPITAL:
$1,000 To $5,000 (Includes computer costs)

No. 116

LOCAL WHO'S WHO DIRECTORY

DESCRIPTION:

Everybody wants to feel important, and here's a way to make them important. With the application of your home computer, this project becomes one of the easiest home computer businesses we have come across. Before computers, this was so time-consuming that only the biggies were in the market. Now, you can not only compete, but run the local biggies right out of business while counting your money all the way to the bank.

INCOME LEVEL RATING:
High

MARKETING METHODS:
1. Direct mail
2. Display ads
3. Telephone sales
4. Direct sales

EQUIPMENT REQUIRED:
1. Computer with disk drive
2. Printer

PART TIME:
Yes

FULL TIME:
Yes

LOCATION:
City or country

MARKET BASE:
5,000–50,000

START UP CAPITAL:
$1,000 To $5,000 (Includes computer costs)

No. 117

COMPUTERIZED COLLECTION LETTER SERVICE

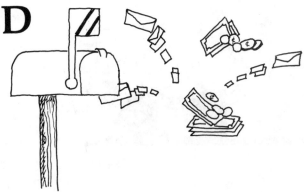

DESCRIPTION:
Here is a very costly part of doing business that most small businesses would like to get rid of. We will show you what methods work and how to have all of the small businesses running to you with their collection problems. And the beauty of this system is that you get paid no matter how the collection turns out. So what have you got to lose? Start doing your own collecting of dollars now!

INCOME LEVEL RATING:
Medium

MARKETING METHODS:
1. Direct mail
2. Display ads
3. Telephone sales
4. Direct sales

EQUIPMENT REQUIRED:
1. Computer with disk drive
2. Printer

PART TIME:
Yes

FULL TIME:
Yes

LOCATION:
City

MARKET BASE:
50,000–200,000

START UP CAPITAL:
$1,000 To $5,000 (Includes computer costs)

No. 118

LOCAL MARKET SURVEY SERVICE

DESCRIPTION:

If you've ever taken a basic business course, you know that nobody should start a new business or expand an existing one without a proper local market survey. This report tells you how to get all of the information together on a local level and how to compile an accurate local market survey on any product or service. And after you have gotten the information together once, you can sell it over and over until you have to revise it for a market change.

INCOME LEVEL RATING:
High

MARKETING METHODS:
1. Direct mail
2. Display ads
3. Telephone sales
4. Direct sales

EQUIPMENT REQUIRED:
1. Computer with disk drive
2. Printer

3. Modem
4. Plotter
5. Graphics

PART TIME:
Yes

FULL TIME:
Yes

LOCATION
City

MARKET BASE:
200,000 Up

START UP CAPITAL:
OVER $5,000 (Includes computer costs)

No. 119

COMPUTER HANDWRITING ANALYSIS SERVICE

DESCRIPTION:
Many articles have been written lately about the use of handwriting analysis for employee selection by large corporations. We will show you how to do it on your home computer with the same accuracy as the experts who are charging as much as $500 for each analysis. This service can also be sold for individual analyses with a less complex printout, where you charge less but deal in greater volume.

INCOME LEVEL RATING:
Medium

MARKETING METHODS:
1. Display ads

EQUIPMENT REQUIRED:
1. Computer with disk drive
2. Printer
3. Plotter
4. Graphics

PART TIME:
Yes

FULL TIME:
Yes

LOCATION:
City

MARKET BASE:
200,000 Up

START UP CAPITAL:
Over $5,000 (Includes computer costs)

No. 120

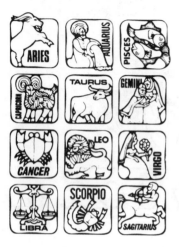

COMPUTERIZED ASTROLOGICAL CHART SERVICE

DESCRIPTION:
Pick up any newspaper and you will see the popularity of this service. Now with your home computer we will show you how you can become a practicing astrologist in your commmunity. The current rate for a full natal chart runs from $10 to $25 each, which by hand takes from one to three hours to prepare—but with our report and your computer you can make these $10 to $25 fees in a matter of a few minutes. So start charting your way to big bucks.

INCOME LEVEL RATING:
Medium

MARKETING METHODS:
1. Display ads

EQUIPMENT REQUIRED:
1. Computer with disk drive
2. Printer
3. Plotter
4. Graphics

PART TIME:
Yes

FULL TIME:
Yes

LOCATION:
City

MARKET BASE:
50,000–200,000

START UP CAPITAL:
Under $1,000

No. 121

COMPUTERIZED BIO-RHYTHMS SERVICE

DESCRIPTION:
This service has been around ever since computers made their debut on the market. We will show you a different approach at cornering a local market by not only doing personal bio-rhythms but also by doing event bio-rhythms and special occasions. This attracts a broader interest group, and makes everybody aware of the service you have to offer. This has been very successful in many areas of the country and is easy to promote as well as to get a lot of repeat business.

INCOME LEVEL RATING:
Medium

MARKETING METHODS:
1. Display ads

EQUIPMENT REQUIRED:
1. Computer with disk drive
2. Printer

PART TIME:
Yes

FULL TIME:
Yes

LOCATION:
City

MARKET BASE:
50,000–200,000

START UP CAPITAL:
Under $1,000

No. 122

ORDER PROCESSING-CATALOGUE AND MAIL ORDER SALES

DESCRIPTION:
Almost every business that sells products is a potential customer for this unique way of using your home computer as a tool to expand already existing retail business into catalog sales and mail order. You can do this by eliminating the biggest drawback that retailers see, and that's product and customer control. We will show you all of the tools to have these retailers begging you to set up their business to handle mail orders. This usually increases their gross sales by over 40 percent. So get your piece of that 40 percent now.

INCOME LEVEL RATING:
Medium

MARKETING METHODS:
1. Direct mail
2. Display ads
3. Telephone sales

EQUIPMENT REQUIRED:
1. Computer with disk drive
2. Printer

PART TIME:
Yes

FULL TIME:
Yes

LOCATION:
City

MARKET BASE:
200,000 Up

START UP CAPITAL:
$1,000 To $5,000 (Includes computer costs)

No. 123

REAL ESTATE LISTING SERVICE

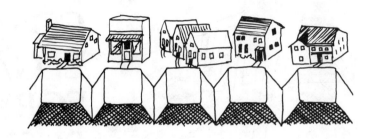

DESCRIPTION:
Most cities have a multiple listing service for realtors, but where this service falls short is where the big money is. Buyers waste a lot of time contacting agents when they really only want to know what's available. With this unique service buyers, through you, can pinpoint what their special interests are and get an overview of what's available in a few minutes. Then they can go to an agent and see exactly what they want. This service gets money for all three legs of the deal—buyer, seller and agent.

INCOME LEVEL RATING:
Medium

MARKETING METHODS:
1. Direct mail
2. Display ads
3. Telephone sales
4. Direct sales

EQUIPMENT REQUIRED:
1. Computer with disk drive
2. Printer

PART TIME:
Yes

FULL TIME:
Yes

LOCATION:
City or country

MARKET BASE:
5,000–50,000

START UP CAPITAL:
$1,000 To $5,000 (Includes computer costs)

No. 124

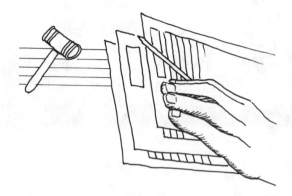

COMPUTERIZED LEGAL FORMS BUSINESS

DESCRIPTION:

You know what happens when you go to a lawyer and ask him to make out a lease, purchase agreement, will or almost any legal contract. He pulls out a book or looks at an old one he did for somebody else, changes the names and dates, retypes it and charges you $200. Now here is a service that is making its operators rich. By having these forms on your home computer and running small ads, you will get all of the business you can handle.

INCOME LEVEL RATING:
High

MARKETING METHODS:
1. Direct mail
2. Display ads
3. Telephone sales

EQUIPMENT REQUIRED:
1. Computer with disk drive
2. Printer

PART TIME:
Yes

FULL TIME:
Yes

LOCATION:
City

MARKET BASE:
5,000–200,000

START UP CAPITAL:
$1,000 To $5,000 (Includes computer costs)

No. 125

COMPUTERIZED LOAN PACKAGE SERVICE

DESCRIPTION:
How many people do you know that go to any lending institution, whether it is a bank, savings and loan or credit union, and never have enough information to satisfy the loan officer they are dealing with? We have developed a loan package you can put on your home computer that will blow the socks off any loan officer. And unless your client is a real deadbeat, they get the money. People are paying from $20 to $50 for these packages, and there doesn't seem to be any shortage of customers. So get on the bandwagon now for your share of this market.

INCOME LEVEL RATING:
High

MARKETING METHODS:
1. Direct mail
2. Display ads

EQUIPMENT REQUIRED:
1. Computer with disk drive
2. Printer

PART TIME:
Yes

FULL TIME:
Yes

LOCATION:
City

MARKET BASE:
5,000–200,000

START UP CAPITAL:
$1,000 To $5,000 (Includes computer costs)

No. 126

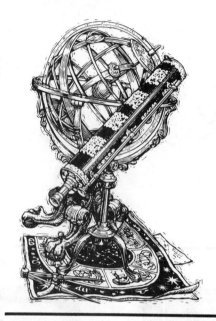

SPECIALTY LOCATING SERVICE

 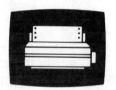

DESCRIPTION:
Have you ever heard your friends say, "I sure would like to find a 1902 Ford" or "I'd really like an old violin like Bill has"? Well, here is a service that makes finding specialized items for people easy. All you need is your home computer and a little research time. The finder's fees are very high because of the uniqueness of this service. In some cases, this is a world-wide service, operated completely from your home, using your home computer as your staff.

INCOME LEVEL RATING:
High

MARKETING METHODS:
1. Direct mail
2. Display ads

EQUIPMENT REQUIRED:
1. Computer with disk drive
2. Printer
3. Modem

PART TIME:
Yes

FULL TIME:
Yes

LOCATION:
City

MARKET BASE:
200,000 Up

START UP CAPITAL:
$1,000 To $5,000 (Includes computer costs)

No. 127

COMPUTERIZED MAP SALES

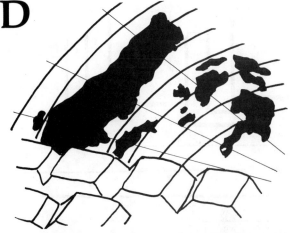

DESCRIPTION:

This is a unique service that requires only your home computer and a remote printer that you hook up through your phone line. Some operate this at their local airport. As incoming passengers arrive, they see big signs telling them to call this number for exact directions to anyplace in the city. Then you print them out a map through the remote printer and guide them to their destination with the minimum amount of time. Your money is waiting for you in the remote coin-operated printer for you to pick up when you feel like it.

INCOME LEVEL RATING:
Medium

MARKETING METHODS:
1. Display ads

EQUIPMENT REQUIRED:
1. Computer with disk drive
2. Printer
3. Graphics
4. Plotter

PART TIME:
Yes

FULL TIME:
Yes

LOCATION:
City

MARKET BASE:
200,000 Up

START UP CAPITAL:
$1,000 To $5,000 (Includes computer costs)

No. 128

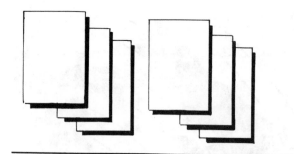

PRO-FORMAS FOR NEW BUSINESSES

DESCRIPTION:

When a person or persons decide to start a new business, they generally make an estimate of their sales and expenses and from that go ahead and start. With this service you can break all of the areas of their particular business down in great detail so they have a realistic understanding of what they can expect to achieve. Some of our customers use this plan in conjunction with Plan No. 118 to give their clients the very best chance of success in their new venture.

INCOME LEVEL RATING:
Medium

MARKETING METHODS:
1. Direct mail
2. Display ads

EQUIPMENT REQUIRED:
1. Computer with disk drive
2. Printer
3. Plotter
4. Graphics

PART TIME:
Yes

FULL TIME:
Yes

LOCATION:
City

MARKET BASE:
200,000 Up

START UP CAPITAL:
$1,000 To $5,000 (Includes computer costs)

No. 129

PAYROLL PREPARATION SERVICE

DESCRIPTION:
This service is on the increase because so many businesspeople just don't want to spend the time learning about every change the government makes regarding payroll taxes. We will show you how to obtain clients and how to set your computer up. Each week, month or day you just transcribe the employee information into your computer and provide all of the statements, forms and reports that are necessary for your client. This is a steady business and makes a good income for the little time spent.

INCOME LEVEL RATING:
Medium

MARKETING METHODS:
1. Direct mail
2. Display ads
3. Telephone sales
4. Direct sales

EQUIPMENT REQUIRED:
1. Computer with disk drive
2. Printer

PART TIME:
Yes

FULL TIME:
Yes

LOCATION:
City

MARKET BASE:
200,000 Up

START UP CAPITAL:
Over $5,000 (Includes computer costs)

No. 130

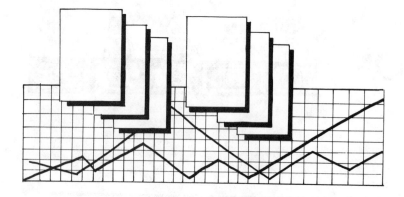

LEASE OR BUY ANALYSIS REPORTS

DESCRIPTION:
By running a few ads in the right places, you can make as much money as you have time to spend. Everybody wants to know if they should lease or buy, but they never spend the time or effort it takes to figure it out. Instead, they let some salesperson decide for them. Now, with your home computer you can offer this service on cars, houses, equipment or anything else. And once customers see the results, they will send you all of the business you can handle.

INCOME LEVEL RATING:
Medium

MARKETING METHODS:
1. Direct mail
2. Display ads

EQUIPMENT REQUIRED:
1. Computer with disk drive
2. Printer

PART TIME:
Yes

FULL TIME:
Yes

LOCATION:
City

MARKET BASE:
200,000 Up

START UP CAPITAL:
$1,000 To $5,000 (Includes computer costs)

No. 131

COST ESTIMATES FOR PRINTERS

 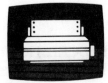

DESCRIPTION:
Here's a little-known business that works very well for home computer operators. The one thing small and medium-sized printers want to do less than anything else is to figure out estimates on potential jobs. All printers know their time is more valuable selling or running presses, so the need is certainly there. We will give you complete information on how to set up programs to run cost estimates for any size shop.

INCOME LEVEL RATING:
Medium

MARKETING METHODS:
1. Direct mail
2. Display ads
3. Telephone sales
4. Direct sales

EQUIPMENT REQUIRED:
1. Computer with disk drive
2. Printer

PART TIME:
Yes

FULL TIME:
Yes

LOCATION:
City

MARKET BASE:
200,000 Up

START UP CAPITAL:
$1,000 To $5,000 (Includes computer costs)

No. 132

RARE BOOK LOCATOR SERVICE

DESCRIPTION:
This is a business that has an international flavor but can be run out of your home. There are over 1,000 rare book specialty shops, but the one thing they all lack is a system for rare book buyers to compare cost and condition of the books they're looking for. Here's where you can step in with your home computer and offer a service that makes both the buyers and the sellers happy, and you can collect both ways.

INCOME LEVEL RATING:
Medium

MARKETING METHODS:
1. Direct mail
2. Display ads

EQUIPMENT REQUIRED:
1. Computer with disk drive
2. Printer

PART TIME:
Yes

FULL TIME:
Yes

LOCATION:
City

MARKET BASE:
50,000–200,000

START UP CAPITAL:
Under $1,000

No. 133

RECIPE SERVICE FOR GOURMETS

DESCRIPTION:
How many times have you been out to dinner and wondered how they prepared the delicious meal you just ate? Here's a service that makes the secret available. Not only do you make the restaurants happy to give them, but you also make the customers happy. With this unique marketing plan you can collect from both sides of each deal and sit back to enjoy the "fruits" of your labor.

INCOME LEVEL RATING:
Medium

MARKETING METHODS:
1. Direct mail
2. Display ads

EQUIPMENT REQUIRED:
1. Computer with disk drive
2. Printer

PART TIME:
Yes

FULL TIME:
Yes

LOCATION:
City

MARKET BASE:
50,000–200,000

START UP CAPITAL:
Under $1,000

No. 134

VITAMIN REQUIREMENT SERVICE

DESCRIPTION:
With the vitamin business growing in leaps and bounds, this service can only get bigger as time goes by. Most of us take some kind of vitamins, but which ones and how much do we really need? We will show you how to set up a vitamin plan for anybody, either on an individual basis or as a service through doctors, pharmacies or vitamin stores. This business has unlimited growth potential with little time investment. Get started now and become the "computer vitamin king!"

INCOME LEVEL RATING:
Medium

MARKETING METHODS:
1. Display ads

EQUIPMENT REQUIRED:
1. Computer with disk drive
2. Printer

PART TIME:
Yes

FULL TIME:
Yes

LOCATION:
City

MARKET BASE:
50,000–200,000

START UP CAPITAL:
Under $1,000

No. 135

COMPUTERIZED ENERGY SURVEY SERVICE FOR HOMES AND OFFICES

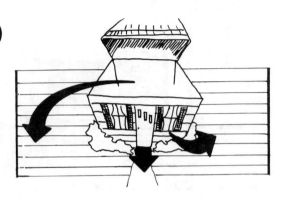

DESCRIPTION:

Everybody is energy-conscious now with the cost of utilities as high as it is. Here's a great home computer service that lets you operate direct or by mail with our unique "energy survey questionnaire." You take the information, enter it into your computer, and make accurate recommendations to improve energy use in homes or offices. There's a sideline to this that turns it into a real money-maker with no additional work.

INCOME LEVEL RATING:
Medium

MARKETING METHODS:
1. Direct mail
2. Display ads
3. Telephone sales

EQUIPMENT REQUIRED
1. Computer with disk drive

2. Printer
3. Plotter
4. Graphics

PART TIME:
Yes

FULL TIME:
Yes

LOCATION:
City

MARKET BASE:
50,000–200,000

START UP CAPITAL:
Under $1,000

No. 136

SBA FINANCING PACKAGE SERVICE

DESCRIPTION:
Here's a business that has been great without computers, so you know how big it could be with computers. Operators using computers report one-third the turn-around time and half the cost, so you know who everyone will be taking their business to. We've discovered the inside track on obtaining new clients, and it's all here just waiting for you to get started.

INCOME LEVEL RATING:
Medium

MARKETING METHODS:
1. Direct mail
2. Display ads

EQUIPMENT REQUIRED:
1. Computer with disk drive
2. Printer

PART TIME:
Yes

FULL TIME:
Yes

LOCATION:
City or country

MARKET BASE:
5,000–50,000

START UP CAPITAL:
Under $1,000

No. 137

ESTABLISHING BUSINESS VALUES FOR BUYERS AND SELLERS

DESCRIPTION:

If you have ever bought or sold a business opportunity, you know that if you don't know more than the seller or broker, you're at their mercy. Well, those days are over with this unique analysis program. You can value any business for either the buyer or the seller (for establishing price). This is a great service for opportunity brokers to use with their clients. It sure stops the con artist from selling a lemon at steak prices.

INCOME LEVEL RATING:
High

MARKETING METHODS:
1. Direct mail
2. Display ads
3. Telephone sales
4. Direct sales

EQUIPMENT REQUIRED:
1. Computer with disk drive
2. Printer
3. Modem

PART TIME:
Yes

FULL TIME:
Yes

LOCATION:
City or country

MARKET BASE:
50,000–200,000

START UP CAPITAL:
$1,000 To $5,000 (Includes computer costs)

No. 138

COMPUTERIZED NEWSLETTER

DESCRIPTION:
The problem with the newsletter business has been solved with the introduction of home computers and word processing programs. Now you can write one newsletter and adapt it to several different markets. We will show you many different applications of this technique in our report on computer newsletters. You are only limited by how much time you want to spend preparing each newsletter. The prices can range from $1 to $50 per issue, and sometimes with slight changes, the same newsletter can get both prices.

INCOME LEVEL RATING:
Medium

MARKETING METHODS:
1. Direct mail
2. Display ads

EQUIPMENT REQUIRED:
1. Computer with disk drive
2. Printer

PART TIME:
Yes

FULL TIME:
Yes

LOCATION:
City or country

MARKET BASE:
5,000–200,000

START UP CAPITAL:
$1,000 To $5,000 (Includes computer costs)

No. 139

NEW BUSINESS PLAN START-UPS SERVICE

DESCRIPTION:
Everybody who wants to start a new business and has no money will be rushing to you for this service. By getting some basic information from your clients, you can prepare a start-up package that will cover everything required for them to satisfy city, state and federal regulations. You can do this for any business at a fraction of the time and cost they would have spent without this inside information.

INCOME LEVEL RATING:
Medium

MARKETING METHODS:
1. Display ads

EQUIPMENT REQUIRED:
1. Computer with disk drive
2. Printer

PART TIME:
Yes

FULL TIME:
Yes

LOCATION:
City

MARKET BASE:
200,000 Up

START UP CAPITAL:
$1,000 To $5,000 (Includes computer costs)

No. 140

SPORTS FORECASTING BUSINESS

DESCRIPTION:
With over 100-million dollars being waged every week on sport events you know this market is strong. With this report you can pick your favorite sport or do them all. Some operators are doing $100,000 per season with this service, and all they need is their home computer, a telephone and our book. How much simpler can you get? If you like sports, here's a natural for a full-time or part-time business. The big bucks ae there!

INCOME LEVEL RATING:
High

MARKETING METHODS:
1. Direct mail
2. Display ads

EQUIPMENT REQUIRED:
1. Computer with disk drive
2. Printer

PART TIME:
Yes

FULL TIME:
Yes

LOCATION:
City or country

MARKET BASE:
50,000–200,000

START UP CAPITAL:
$1,000 To $5,000 (Includes computer costs)

No. 141

SECRETARIAL SERVICE

 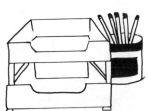

DESCRIPTION:
With computers, anybody can be a secretary. Between word processor, spelling, grammar and punctuation programs, all you need to be able to do is run the programs. This has opened up a whole new way for people working out of their homes to provide a service that pays well, but also allows them to work at their own pace and in their own surroundings. Our report gives you complete details on setting this up for yourself.

INCOME LEVEL RATING:
Medium

MARKETING METHODS:
1. Direct mail
2. Display ads
3. Telephone sales
4. Direct sales

EQUIPMENT REQUIRED:
1. Computer with disk drive
2. Printer

PART TIME:
Yes

FULL TIME:
Yes

LOCATION:
City

MARKET BASE:
50,000–200,000

START UP CAPITAL:
$1,000 To $5,000 (Includes computer costs)

No. 142

TRAVEL PLANNING SERVICE

DESCRIPTION:

With the data bases that are available for personal computers, you can set yourself up to check out almost any airplane, train or bus schedule, as well as hotels, motels and many events. With this service you can plan trips for people and find the best buys, and you won't be prejudiced by commissions, like travel agents are. Some operators are even telling their clients to let a travel agent redo the plan, and then splitting the savings with them, which usually is in the hundreds of dollars for each.

INCOME LEVEL RATING:
Medium

MARKETING METHODS:
1. Display ads

EQUIPMENT REQUIRED:
1. Computer with disk drive
2. Printer

PART TIME:
Yes

FULL TIME:
Yes

LOCATION:
City or country

MARKET BASE:
50,000–200,000

START UP CAPITAL:
$1,000 To $5,000 (Includes computer costs)

No. 143

COMPUTER SCHOOLS

DESCRIPTION:
You probably are among the 96 percent of people who learned how to operate your computer on your own, so you know how great it would have been to have some instruction and how much faster you would have progressed. We will show you how to set up and organize schools, both large and small, and how to get others to run them for you. Most operators of this service work one month and take off the next, or have somebody else alternate with them to avoid getting burned out.

INCOME LEVEL RATING:
Medium

MARKETING METHODS:
1. Direct mail
2. Display ads

EQUIPMENT REQUIRED:
1. Computer with disk drive
2. Printer

PART TIME:
Yes

FULL TIME:
Yes

LOCATION:
City or country

MARKET BASE:
200,000 Up

START UP CAPITAL:
Over $5,000 (Includes computer costs)

No. 144

COMPUTER CAMPS

DESCRIPTION:
Here's the ideal computer business. Check these benefits: work only four months per year, and when you do, work it in some exotic place or tranquil surroundings; the rest of the year travel around finding new camp sites and write it off as a business expense. We will show you all of the secrets of success that have been developed for this business by trial and error, so start now for a l2-month vacation very year.

INCOME LEVEL RATING:
Medium

MARKETING METHODS:
1. Direct mail
2. Display ads

EQUIPMENT REQUIRED:
1. Computer with disk drive
2. Printer

PART TIME:
No

FULL TIME:
Yes

LOCATION:
City or country

MARKET BASE:
200,000 Up

START UP CAPITAL:
Over $5,000 (Includes computer costs)

No. 145

COMPUTER CONSULTING

DESCRIPTION:
This is becoming one of the fastest-growing computer businesses we know of. Projections are that over one-million personal home computers will be sold this year and over 200 new computers will be introduced–and that is only this year. There will always be a need for personal computer consultants to help people look for and evaluate what will be the best programs for their use and the best computer for their needs at the best price. We will show you how you can become an expert almost overnight.

INCOME LEVEL RATING:
High

MARKETING METHODS:
1. Direct mail
2. Display ads
3. Direct sales

EQUIPMENT REQUIRED:
1. Computer with disk drive
2. Printer
3. Modem

PART TIME:
Yes

FULL TIME:
Yes

LOCATION:
City or country

MARKET BASE:
5,000–200,000

START UP CAPITAL:
Under $1,000

No. 146

APARTMENT LOCATING SERVICE

DESCRIPTION:
The people who are looking for apartments are generally a different type than those looking for houses to rent, and we have found that their special needs can be fulfilled. With this report and your personal computer you can tailor-fit an apartment to your client with a minimum amount of time being spent by either of you. This is another one of those businesses where you collect from both ends of the deal.

INCOME LEVEL RATING:
Medium

MARKETING METHODS:
1. Display ads

EQUIPMENT REQUIRED:
1. Computer with disk drive
2. Printer

PART TIME:
Yes

FULL TIME:
Yes

LOCATION:
City

MARKET BASE:
50,000–200,000

START UP CAPITAL:
Under $1,000

No. 147

HOUSE RENTAL LOCATING SERVICE

DESCRIPTION:
The people who are looking for houses to rent are generally a different type than those looking for apartments. That is why we have prepared two different sections. Although some operators combine the two, it has been our experience that if the market will handle it, you're better off specializing in one so you can handle more clients in a more efficient way. Remember, this is one of those both-end dollar deals.

INCOME LEVEL RATING:
Medium

MARKETING METHODS:
1. Display ads

EQUIPMENT REQUIRED:
1. Computer with disk drive
2. Printer

PART TIME:
Yes

FULL TIME:
Yes

LOCATION:
City

MARKET BASE:
50,000–200,000

START UP CAPITAL:
Over $5,000 (Includes computer costs)

No. 148

TYPESETTING SERVICE

DESCRIPTION:
With the new communication equipment now available for hooking up to existing typesetting machines, you can operate a typesetting service right in your own home without the expense of owning typesetting equipment. We will show you where the business is and how to get it, and how to make your computer talk to typesetting equipment anywhere in the country. So get started today in this new and profitable service.

INCOME LEVEL RATING:
Medium

MARKETING METHODS:
1. Direct mail
2. Display ads
3. Telephone sales
4. Direct sales

EQUIPMENT REQUIRED:
1. Computer with disk drive
2. Printer
3. Modem

PART TIME:
No

FULL TIME:
Yes

LOCATION:
City or country

MARKET BASE:
50,000–200,000

START UP CAPITAL:
Over $5,000 (Includes computer costs)

No. 149

BARTER CLUB SERVICE

DESCRIPTION:
One of the biggest problems in the barter exchange business has been the mass of products and services that have been available with no way to connect them to the people who need them. We will show you how to set up your personal computer to make the barter process easier for everybody that belongs to one of these barter groups, and you'll get your share in the process.

INCOME LEVEL RATING:
Medium

MARKETING METHODS:
1. Direct mail
2. Display ads

EQUIPMENT REQUIRED:
1. Computer with disk drive
2. Printer

PART TIME:
Yes

FULL TIME:
Yes

LOCATION:
City

MARKET BASE:
200,000 Up

START UP CAPITAL:
Under $1,000

No. 150

MULTI-LEVEL MARKETING AND RECORD-KEEPING

DESCRIPTION:

Those who are involved in multi-level sales know that keeping track of who gets what from whom is a complex and frustrating problem. We will show you how to find your clients and how to set them up on your personal computer, so they can keep their downline people happy and give the main distributor an accurate check on how the source company is doing with their money. Most operators have been making a lot of money with only one or two clients.

INCOME LEVEL RATING:
Medium

MARKETING METHODS:
1. Direct mail
2. Display ads

EQUIPMENT REQUIRED:
1. Computer with disk drive
2. Printer

PART TIME:
Yes

FULL TIME:
Yes

LOCATION:
City

MARKET BASE:
200,000 Up

START UP CAPITAL:
Under $1,000

No. 151

SELL LOCAL MAILING LISTS AT $1 PER NAME

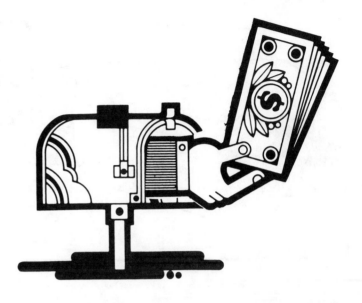

DESCRIPTION

Every city has requirements for names and addresses of residents, businesses, etc. The great part about this business is that once you compile the names, they are rented over and over. The national average is eight to 10 times per year and at six to 10 cents per name, that adds up fast. In this report you'll learn how to get good names and how to keep those names sellable, plus, how to let the people who use names know you have them.

INCOME LEVEL RATING:
Medium

MARKETING METHODS:
1. Direct mail
2. Display ads
3. Telephone sales

EQUIPMENT REQUIRED:
1. Computer with disk drive

2. Printer
3. Modem

PART TIME:
Yes

FULL TIME:
Yes

LOCATION:
City or country

MARKET BASE:
50,000–200,000

START UP CAPITAL:
$1,000 To $5,000 (Includes computer costs)

No. 152

COMPUTERIZED CLASSIFIED NEWSPAPER

 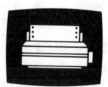

DESCRIPTION:
With this unique plan and your personal computer you can produce specialty classified newspapers for people who aren't interested in going through the local newspaper every day. With your service they will be able to subscribe only to the things they're interested in, and in this way they won't miss anything. This service is limited only by how many you want to produce and how many clients you want to service, so get in on this unique opportunity now.

INCOME LEVEL RATING:
Medium

MARKETING METHODS:
1. Direct mail
2. Display ads
3. Telephone sales
4. Direct sales

EQUIPMENT REQUIRED:
1. Computer with disk drive
2. Printer

PART TIME:
Yes

FULL TIME:
Yes

LOCATION:
City or country

MARKET BASE:
50,000–200,000

START UP CAPITAL:
Over $5,000 (Includes computer costs)

No. 153

PROGRAMMING GAMES FOR MARKET

DESCRIPTION:
Every day you see another new or better game that's available for your computer. Who do you think comes up with these games? Well, our research has determined that the successful programmers of home computer games are not gifted, rather, they are ordinary people with a pre-conceived plan. We have found many of the secrets that these people use and included them in our book. So, if you want to get in on those six-figure royalties that you hear about, get started.

INCOME LEVEL RATING:
Medium

MARKETING METHODS
1. Direct mail
2. Display ads

EQUIPMENT REQUIRED:
1. Computer with disk drive
2. Printer

PART TIME:
Yes

FULL TIME:
Yes

LOCATION:
City or country

MARKET BASE:
5,000–50,000

START UP CAPITAL:
Under $1,000

No. 154

SELL STOCK MARKET ADVICE

DESCRIPTION:

You've probably seen all of those stock market programs that promise you riches beyond your wildest dreams. Well, we can show you how to turn those dreams into reality by selling your services to others. We will show you how you and your home computer can prepare stock predictions just like the big brokerage houses, but the key here is to supply them on a local level where the big boys don't read. So get into the stock market, where the money is in selling "services," not buying and selling stock.

INCOME LEVEL RATING:
High

MARKETING METHODS:
1. Direct mail
2. Display ads

EQUIPMENT REQUIRED:
1. Computer with disk drive
2. Printer

3. Modem
4. Plotter
5. Graphics

PART TIME:
Yes

FULL TIME:
Yes

LOCATION:
City

MARKET BASE:
50,000–200,000

START UP CAPITAL:
$1,000 To $5,000 (Includes computer costs)

No. 155

BOOKKEEPING SERVICE

DESCRIPTION:
Here is a business where the computer age has produced many small operators with five-figure earnings who only spend a few hours a week at it. The problem nowadays is not whether you can do bookkeeping, but how you get clients. We have solved that problem, as well as how to process your client's bookkeeping needs in a way they have not seen before. You actually eliminate all of the competition. There are big dollars here with minimum effort.

INCOME LEVEL RATING:
High

MARKETING METHODS:
1. Direct mail
2. Display ads
3. Telephone sales
4. Direct sales

EQUIPMENT REQUIRED:
1. Computer with disk drive
2. Printer

PART TIME:
Yes

FULL TIME:
Yes

LOCATION:
City

MARKET BASE:
50,000–200,000

START UP CAPITAL:
$1,000 To $5,000 (Includes computer costs)

No. 156

USED PERSONAL COMPUTER BROKER

DESCRIPTION:
For the last several years used-computer brokering has been big business for the large units. Now you can get in on the ground floor and share in the same success that the big computer brokers have. With your personal computer you will learn how to set up a network of both buyers and sellers, with you acting as the middle-man and collecting as each deal is made.

INCOME LEVEL RATING:
High

MARKETING METHODS:
1. Direct mail
2. Display ads
3. Telephone sales
4. Direct sales

EQUIPMENT REQUIRED:
1. Computer with disk drive
2. Printer

PART TIME:
Yes

FULL TIME:
Yes

LOCATION:
City

MARKET BASE:
50,000–200,000

START UP CAPITAL:
$1,000 To $5,000 (Includes computer costs)

No. 157

CUSTOMIZED SALES LETTERS FOR SALESPEOPLE

DESCRIPTION:
Most good salespeople don't have the time to contact as many people or businesses as they would like. We will show you how to find the salespeople that need and will use this service and how to give them an edge in their business that they never had before. This is a steady business and has made some operators financially very comfortable.

INCOME LEVEL RATING:
High

MARKETING METHODS:
1. Direct mail
2. Display ads
3. Telephone sales

EQUIPMENT REQUIRED:
1. Computer with disk drive
2. Printer

PART TIME:
Yes

FULL TIME:
Yes

LOCATION:
City or country

MARKET BASE:
50,000–200,000

START UP CAPITAL:
$1,000 To $5,000 (Includes computer costs)

No. 158

COMPUTERIZED CORPORATION FILING SERVICE

No: 158

 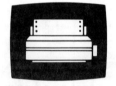

DESCRIPTION:
With over 250,000 new corporations being formed each year, you can see that this service has unlimited potential. This plan will give you everything you need to start this fast-growing service business, and the only tool required is your personal computer. Some operators have been specialists in just one state and others cover them all. You'll even learn how to get the local lawyers to use your service and be more than happy to turn their business over to you. So get started now.

INCOME LEVEL RATING:
Medium

MARKETING METHODS:
1. Direct mail
2. Display ads

EQUIPMENT REQUIRED:
1. Computer with disk drive
2. Printer

PART TIME:
Yes

FULL TIME:
Yes

LOCATION:
City

MARKET BASE:
50,000–200,000

START UP CAPITAL:
$1,000 To $5,000 (Includes computer costs)

No. 159

CUSTOM ELECTRONIC MAILING SYSTEM

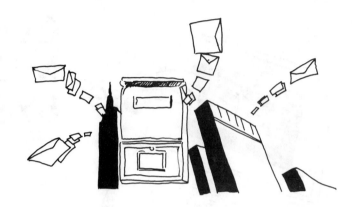

DESCRIPTION:
You have heard about express mail next-day service. Well, here is a next-hour service you can offer local businesses that maintain branch offices too far away for quick service. This is just like a private Western Union, only you can offer the service at half the rate charged by Western Union. You will learn how to set up a network of operators all over the country. This has the potential of becoming a million-dollar-a-year business.

INCOME LEVEL RATING:
Medium

MARKETING METHODS:
1. Direct mail
2. Display ads
3. Telephone sales

EQUIPMENT REQUIRED:
1. Computer with disk drive
1. Printer
2. Modem

PART TIME:
Yes

FULL TIME:
Yes

LOCATION:
City

MARKET BASE:
50,000–200,000

START UP CAPITAL:
$1,000 To $5,000 (Includes computer costs)

No. 160

COMPUTERIZED MUSIC SYSTEMS

DESCRIPTION:
Computerized music has been around for a long time, but try to find somebody that knows anything about it! We have found out everything there is to know about it and have put it into this book. If your flair is for music, all you need is your personal computer and our book to start a school, be a personal consultant, or put together special programs for local clubs and businesses. So, music buffs, get in on this unique business.

INCOME LEVEL RATING:
Low

MARKETING METHODS:
1. Display ads

EQUIPMENT REQUIRED:
1. Computer with disk drive
2. Printer

PART TIME:
Yes

FULL TIME:
Yes

LOCATION:
City or country

MARKET BASE:
5,000–50,000

START UP CAPITAL:
Under $1,000

No. 161

SELL CUSTOM EDUCATIONAL PROGRAMS

DESCRIPTION:
Everywhere you look, there are educational programs. The problem is there are very few programs that deal with specialized markets, such as real estate, construction, ham radio operation, etc. We have found through our research that there are literally hundreds of specialized programs just waiting to be designed and marketed. We will show you the who, where, why and how of this unlimited business.

INCOME LEVEL RATING:
Medium

MARKETING METHODS:
1. Display ads

EQUIPMENT REQUIRED:
1. Computer with disk drive
2. Printer

PART TIME:
Yes

FULL TIME:
Yes

LOCATION:
City or country

MARKET BASE:
50,000–200,000

START UP CAPITAL:
$1,000 To $5,000 (Includes computer costs)

No. 162

FOREIGN LANGUAGE INSTRUCTION SCHOOL

DESCRIPTION:
Here is a business no one thought would ever come around, until the computer made its entry. You can teach almost any foreign language and not know a word of anything but English. We will teach you how to obtain the best programs for your home computer and then how to go about getting people to take your course of instruction. Your computer does all of the work! You can't beat that.

INCOME LEVEL RATING:
Low

MARKETING METHODS:
1. Display ads

EQUIPMENT REQUIRED:
1. Computer with disk drive
2. Printer

PART TIME:
Yes

FULL TIME:
Yes

LOCATION:
City or country

MARKET BASE:
50,000–20,000

START UP CAPITAL:
Over $5,000 (Includes computer costs)

No. 163

INFORMATION RESEARCH SERVICE

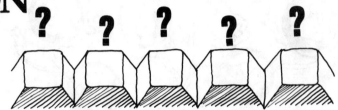

DESCRIPTION:

We have found a lot of home computer operators making a fortune in this business. With the increasing number of data bases becoming available, this is where the future is in the research field. We will show you where all of the information is and how you can tap this great resource and then sell it to others. You will also learn a well-guarded secret on where the people are who use this service and are willing to pay big money for it.

INCOME LEVEL RATING:
High

MARKETING METHODS:
1. Direct mail
2. Display ads
3. Telephone Sales

EQUIPMENT REQUIRED:
1. Computer with disk drive
2. Printer
3. Modem

PART TIME:
Yes

FULL TIME:
Yes

LOCATION:
City

MARKET BASE:
200,000 Up

START Up CAPITAL:
Over $5,000 (Includes computer costs)

No. 164

GENEALOGY AND FAMILY TREE SERVICE

DESCRIPTION:
It is estimated that 25-million Americans are involved in learning about their family roots. So, the size of the market proves you won't run out of clients very soon. We will show you how to set up your home computer to not only work out the charts, but also to tap into the data bases that have complete details on genealogy, allowing you to offer a complete service to your clients.

INCOME LEVEL RATING:
Medium

MARKETING METHODS:
1. Direct mail
2. Display ads

EQUIPMENT REQUIRED:
1. Computer with disk drive
2. Printer

PART TIME:
Yes

FULL TIME:
Yes

LOCATION:
City or country

MARKET BASE:
50,000–200,000

START UP CAPITAL:
Under $1,000

No. 165

HOME TUTORING FOR CHILDREN BUSINESS

DESCRIPTION:
With the availability of self-teaching programs for personal computers, this home business becomes a gold mine. Some of the operators we have interviewed are specializing in certain subjects, and others cover the whole field. Using computers as teachers has proven to be one of the most effective ways for students to retain what they have learned. We give you complete plans on how to get the programs and how to get the students that need the help. So don't let this slide by.

INCOME LEVEL RATING:
Low

MARKETING METHODS:
1. Display ads

EQUIPMENT REQUIRED:
1. Computer with disk drive
2. Printer

PART TIME:
Yes

FULL TIME:
Yes

LOCATION:
City or country

MARKET BASE:
50,000–200,000

START UP CAPITAL:
$1,000 To $5,000 (Includes computer costs)

No. 166

PERSONAL FINANCIAL STATEMENT SERVICE

DESCRIPTION:
If you have ever tried to make a major purchase, like a home, you have had to go up against those tight-fisted, beady-eyed bankers. Well, this service turns those tight-fisted bankers into pussycats. By applying the techniques in our book, you can prepare personal financial statements for anybody and give them a lot better chance of getting the loan they are after. This service can also be operated through referrals from banks and financial institutions.

INCOME LEVEL RATING:
Medium

MARKETING METHODS:
1. Display ads

EQUIPMENT REQUIRED:
1. Computer with disk drive
2. Printer

PART TIME:
Yes

FULL TIME:
Yes

LOCATION:
City or country

MARKET BASE:
50,000–200,000

START UP CAPITAL:
$1,000 To $5,000 (Includes computer costs)

No. 167

PRIVATE PILOT TRIP PLANNER

DESCRIPTION:
Any good pilot will file a flight plan before going anywhere, but because conditions change very rapidly when it comes to weather and airports, this personal computer service is a welcome sight to the harried pilot. This business can be run out of your home with the use of a phone line and a remote printer. You can deliver an accurate flight plan right into the hands of the pilot in a matter of minutes. If you're a pilot or weather buff, you'll like this service.

INCOME LEVEL RATING:
Medium

MARKETING METHODS:
1. Direct mail
2. Display ads

EQUIPMENT REQUIRED:
1. Computer with disk drive
2. Printer

PART TIME:
Yes

FULL TIME:
Yes

LOCATION:
City or country

MARKET BASE:
5,000–50,000

START UP CAPITAL:
$1,000 To $5,000 (Includes computer costs)

No. 168

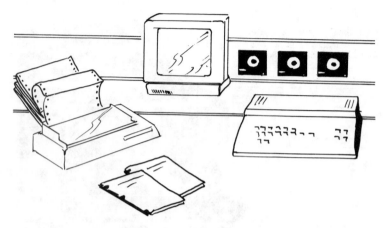

COMPUTER KITS

DESCRIPTION:

If you're an electronics buff as well as a personal computer operator, you will like this business. A lot of people would rather build their personal computer than buy one that has limitations built into it. This way they can fill all of their computer needs using parts of several different packages. You can put together all compatible components on your personal computer and in a few minutes mix and match to get exactly what your customer wants.

INCOME LEVEL RATING:
Medium

MARKETING METHODS:
1. Display ads

EQUIPMENT REQUIRED:
1. Computer with disk drive
2. Printer

PART TIME:
Yes

FULL TIME:
Yes

LOCATION:
City or country

MARKET BASE:
5,000–50,000

START UP CAPITAL:
Over $5,000 (Includes computer costs)

No. 169

POETRY-MADE-EASY VERSE BUSINESS

DESCRIPTION:
If you have a flair for writing poetry, this might be just the business for you. With your personal computer and some of the new programs that are now on the market you can literally turn into a factory of verse for any and all occasions, customized for your clients. We have devised a formula for constructing verse for almost any event you can think of, and you sit back while your personal computer does the majority of the work.

INCOME LEVEL RATING:
Low

MARKETING METHODS:
1. Display ads

EQUIPMENT REQUIRED:
1. Computer with disk drive
2. Printer

PART TIME:
Yes

FULL TIME:
Yes

LOCATION:
City or country

MARKET BASE:
5,000–50,000

START UP CAPITAL:
Under $1,000

No. 170

START AND OPERATE A COMPUTER CLUB

DESCRIPTION:

Being the operator of a computer club for profit is not a new concept, as we teach you in our plan. All kinds of clubs are run for profit, such as health, game and travel clubs. Some operators have made fortunes just by starting these clubs and getting them running, and then they turn around and sell them as soon as they show a profit. Then they go on and set up another club. With one-million new personal computer buyers this year, there will be no shortage of potential members. So act now!

INCOME LEVEL RATING:
Low

MARKETING METHODS:
1. Direct mail
2. Display ads

EQUIPMENT REQUIRED:
1. Computer with disk drive
2. Printer
3. Modem

PART TIME:
Yes

FULL TIME:
Yes

LOCATION:
City or country

MARKET BASE:
50,000–200,000

START UP CAPITAL:
$1,000 To $5,000 (Includes computer costs)

No. 171

CUSTOM COMPUTER POSTER SERVICE

DESCRIPTION:
Here's a simple business that takes only your personal computer and a printer to operate. There are enough special occasions and stores with specials to keep your printer running night and day. We will show you how to find the users of this service, and you will learn there is no competition, because nobody can compete with your prices and obtain the same results.

INCOME LEVEL RATING:
Low

MARKETING METHODS:
1. Direct mail
2. Display ads

EQUIPMENT REQUIRED:
1. Computer with disk drive
2. Printer
3. Plotter
4. Graphics

PART TIME:
Yes

FULL TIME:
Yes

LOCATION:
City or country

MARKET BASE:
50,000–200,000

START UP CAPITAL:
Under $1,000

No. 172

SOFTWARE EXCHANGE SERVICE

DESCRIPTION:
Here is a big-dollar business that will do nothing but grow. With our report you will learn how other operators are making hundreds of dollars per week. And all they're doing is following our business plan and putting themselves in a tollgate position for every user of programs in their city or town. This business is very efficient with the use of your personal computer, and as it grows, the work becomes less and the dollars more. You can't beat that!

INCOME LEVEL RATING:
Medium

MARKETING METHODS:
1. Direct mail
2. Display ads

EQUIPMENT REQUIRED:
1. Computer with disk drive
2. Printer
3. Modem

PART TIME:
Yes

FULL TIME:
Yes

LOCATION:
City

MARKET BASE:
200,000 Up

START UP CAPITAL:
Over $5,000 (Includes computer costs)

No. 173

RESTAURANT PRICING SERVICE

DESCRIPTION:
Here is a unique business that the restaurants in your city or town won't be able to do without. We will show you how to get all of the restaurants as clients, or just as many as you want to handle. The secret to this business is rapidly-changing wholesale food prices and their effect on the prices charged on menus. The clients that take advantage of your service will always operate at a profit no matter what happens to food prices.

INCOME LEVEL RATING:
Medium

MARKETING METHODS:
1. Direct mail
2. Display ads
3. Telephone sales
4. Direct sales

EQUIPMENT REQUIRED:
1. Computer with disk drive
2. Printer

PART TIME:
Yes

FULL TIME:
Yes

LOCATION:
City

MARKET BASE:
200,000 Up

START UP CAPITAL:
$1,000 To $5,000 (Includes computer costs)

No. 174

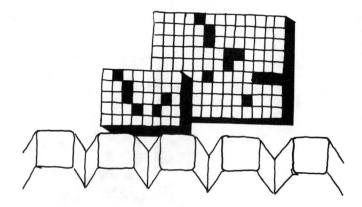

CROSSWORD PUZZLE DESIGN BUSINESS

DESCRIPTION:

If you like crossword puzzles and word games, this business will appeal to you. We will show you how to adapt many of the new programs that are now available to create any kind of crossword puzzle or word game you want, and the computer does most of the work. This is a great syndication deal, and we'll show you how to tap into that market as well as many others. So start changing those words into dollars now!

INCOME LEVEL RATING:
Low

MARKETING METHODS:
1. Display ads

EQUIPMENT REQUIRED:
1. Computer with disk drive
2. Printer

PART TIME:
Yes

FULL TIME:
Yes

LOCATION:
City or country

MARKET BASE:
50,000–200,000

START UP CAPITAL:
Under $1,000

No. 175

CHECKBOOK BALANCING SERVICE

DESCRIPTION:
How many people have you heard say, "I hate to balance my checkbook"? Now you will be able to provide the solution to their problems. We will show you how to get clients. And once you get started with them, the work becomes easier and the dollars become greater. We will also show you how to get referral clients from financial institutions and money managers as well as business consultants. So you can bet the market that is out there is ripe for the picking.

INCOME LEVEL RATING:
Medium

MARKETING METHODS:
1. Display ads

EQUIPMENT REQUIRED:
1. Computer with disk drive

PART TIME:
Yes

FULL TIME:
Yes

LOCATION:
City or country

MARKET BASE:
50,000–200,000

START UP CAPITAL:
Under $1,000

No. 178

CUSTOM LOAN, ANNUITY AND INTEREST CALCULATIONS AND ANALYSIS SERVICE

DESCRIPTION:

This service can be sold to both the consumers and the retailers. When people buy or sell anything on terms, the question is always, "how much will I owe in two years, or in five months?" And the only way to find out is to do a long series of calculations to come up with the answer. With this report you will find out how easy it is to sell this service, and it's a snap to do with your personal computer. Remember, people will never quit buying and selling, so the market is yours, if you want it.

INCOME LEVEL RATING:
Medium

MARKETING METHODS
1. Display ads

EQUIPMENT REQUIRED:
1. Computer with disk drive
2. Printer

PART TIME:
Yes

FULL TIME:
Yes

LOCATION:
City

MARKET BASE:
200,000 Up

START UP CAPITAL:
Under $1,000

No. 179

PERSONAL BUDGET MANAGEMENT CONSULTING

 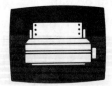

DESCRIPTION:
Here's something everybody needs but few will spend the time to sit down and work out. Using our plan you can put together a workable budget for people with just a few minutes of your personal computer time. This business can be started with a few classified ads written like the ones we show you in the book, and you can get referrals from several sources by using our special referral letter. This business can be just as big as you want it to be, so get started now.

INCOME LEVEL RATING:
Medium

MARKETING METHODS:
1. Direct mail
2. Display ads

EQUIPMENT REQUIRED:
1. Computer with disk drive
2. Printer

PART TIME:
Yes

FULL TIME:
Yes

LOCATION:
City

MARKET BASE:
50,000–200,000

START UP CAPITAL:
$1,000 To $5,000 (Includes computer costs)

No. 180

LOCAL STORE MENU PLANNING SERVICE

DESCRIPTION:
This unique business has great potential for growth. We will show you how to obtain the weekly specials from your local markets and design menus using those specials so they can run them in the local papers to entice people to come into their stores. We have devised a system for your personal computer to take the specials and do all of the work for you to produce the menus. This is making big dollars for some operators even in small towns.

INCOME LEVEL RATING:
Medium

MARKETING METHODS:
1. Direct mail
2. Display ads
3. Telephone sales
4. Direct sales

EQUIPMENT REQUIRED:
1. Computer with disk drive
2. Printer

PART TIME:
Yes

FULL TIME:
Yes

LOCATION
City

MARKET BASE:
200,000 Up

START UP CAPITAL:
$1,000 To $5,000 (Includes computer costs)

No. 181

COIN AND STAMP COLLECTION INVENTORIES AND VALUES SERVICE

DESCRIPTION:

If you are a collector of either coins or stamps or both, I'm sure you would like to maintain an accurate inventory and current value of your collection for your own information as well as for insurance purposes. We will show you how to get other collectors to use your service. Once you get them set up, you can sell this service on a monthly, quarterly or semi-annual basis as values change. And once they get started using this service, our experience has shown, they do not want to give it up.

INCOME LEVEL RATING:
Low

MARKETING METHODS:
1. Direct mail
2. Display ads

EQUIPMENT REQUIRED:
1. Computer with disk drive
2. Printer

PART TIME:
Yes

FULL TIME:
Yes

LOCATION:
City or country

MARKET BASE:
50,000–200,000

START UP CAPITAL:
Under $1,000

No. 183

DESIGN AND SELL COMPUTER PROGRAMS FOR FARMERS

DESCRIPTION:

This is an area that is just beginning to grow. Farmers and ranchers have unique problems that most of them keep in their heads. The more experienced do better. Now you will learn how to get this experience into the hands of less-experienced operators and at a fraction of the cost that they would pay in the school of hard knocks. We will show you how easy it is to have your personal computer put out reports that are invaluable to both farmers and ranchers.

INCOME LEVEL RATING:
Medium

MARKETING METHODS:
1. Direct mail
2. Display ads

EQUIPMENT REQUIRED:
1. Computer with disk drive
2. Printer

PART TIME:
Yes

FULL TIME:
Yes

LOCATION:
City or country

MARKET BASE:
50,000–200,000

START UP CAPITAL:
$1,000 To $5,000 (Includes computer costs)

No. 184

PERSONAL LIBRARY CATALOGUING SERVICE

DESCRIPTION:
It is estimated that there are over 10-million people with personal libraries having 1,000 books or more. We will show you how to find these customers, and then how to set up cataloguing systems complete with index cards and a cross-reference system, and all on your personal computer. People who have had this service done for their libraries say it's the best system they have ever seen. So get started in this interesting service today.

INCOME LEVEL RATING:
Low

MARKETING METHODS:
1. Direct mail
2. Display ads

EQUIPMENT REQUIRED:
1. Computer with disk drive
2. Printer

PART TIME:
Yes

FULL TIME:
Yes

LOCATION:
City or country

MARKET BASE:
50,000–200,000

START UP CAPITAL:
Under $1,000

No. 185

COMPUTER CARPOOLING SERVICE

DESCRIPTION:
This service got started during the gas shortage days, but it has continued to grow ever since. We will show you how to contact large and small businesses in a concentrated area to get names of people who commute from specific areas. Then, after compiling this information on your personal computer, we will show you how to set up carpools that are convenient to everybody. Both employees and employers will pay for this service—the employees because it will save them money, and the employers because it saves them lost production time. So start carpooling today, and get your share of the revenue.

INCOME LEVEL RATING:
Low

MARKETING METHODS:
1. Display ads

EQUIPMENT REQUIRED:
1. Computer with disk drive
2. Printer

PART TIME:
Yes

FULL TIME:
Yes

LOCATION:
City or country

MARKET BASE:
50,000–200,000

START UP CAPITAL:
Under $1,000

No. 186

LEGAL RESEARCH SERVICE

DESCRIPTION:

This report shows you how with your personal computer you can do legal research through several different data bases. This service business is just coming into its own, now that lawyers have learned you don't need to have a law degree to do legal research—just a computer. With our plan you will learn which data bases to use and how to use them effectively. We will also show you how to get as many lawyers as you want and can handle with a simple mail campaign.

INCOME LEVEL RATING:
High

MARKETING METHODS:
1. Direct mail
2. Display ads
3. Telephone sales
4. Direct sales

EQUIPMENT REQUIRED:
1. Computer with disk drive
2. Printer
3. Modem

PART TIME:
Yes

FULL TIME:
Yes

LOCATION:
City

MARKET BASE:
200,000 Up

START UP CAPITAL:
Over $5,000 (Includes computer costs)

No. 187

ESTATE PLANNING SERVICE

DESCRIPTION:
This system has been around a long time using manual techniques. Now with your personal computer you can produce complete estate planning packages in a matter of minutes. We will show you how to set these up and make them so anybody can understand them. We will also show how you can get clients for this service - the kind of clients that will come back over and over. Insurance brokers and lawyers are not the only ones to offer this service.

INCOME LEVEL RATING:
Medium

MARKETING METHODS:
1. Direct mail
2. Display ads
3. Telephone sales

EQUIPMENT REQUIRED:
1. Computer with disk drive
2. Printer

PART TIME:
Yes

FULL TIME:
Yes

LOCATION:
City

MARKET BASE:
200,000 Up

START UP CAPITAL:
Over $5,000 (Includes computer costs)

No. 189

PROPERTY ANALYSIS SERVICE

 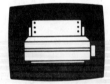

DESCRIPTION:
When people buy income property, most have little idea of how to analyze the potential income, investment and tax advantages that are there or not there, as the case may be. They usually rely on a real estate salesperson to give the information to them, which may not be accurate. We will show you how to prepare reports that are accurate and understandable, and you'll see how a small ad placed in the right publication will produce a good client flow.

INCOME LEVEL RATING:
Medium

MARKETING METHODS:
1. Direct mail
2. Display ads

EQUIPMENT REQUIRED:
1. Computer with disk drive
2. Printer

PART TIME:
Yes

FULL TIME:
Yes

LOCATION:
City

MARKET BASE:
200,000 Up

START UP CAPITAL:
$1,000 To $5,000 (Includes computer costs)

No. 190

HORSE RACE HANDICAPPING SERVICE

DESCRIPTION:
If you're a horse racing fan, this will assure you of winning—if not at the track, at home where you will be selling this service. We will show you how to set up handicapping systems for all the variables. Some operators just follow the circuit around with their personal computer in their trailer or motor home and enjoy the racing as well as the money they make selling their services.

INCOME LEVEL RATING:
Medium

MARKETING METHODS:
1. Display ads

EQUIPMENT REQUIRED:
1. Computer with disk drive
2. Printer

PART TIME:
Yes

FULL TIME:
Yes

LOCATION:
City or country

MARKET BASE:
50,000–200,000

START UP CAPITAL:
$1,000 To $5,000 (Includes computer costs)

No. 191

ACCOUNTS PAYABLE SERVICE

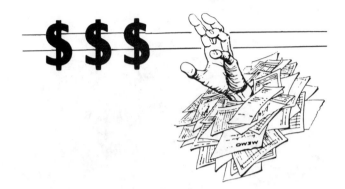

DESCRIPTION:

One of the problems that small business operators have is keeping up with their accounts payable. Not only do they forget to pay on time, which hurts their credit, but they lose hundreds of dollars every year by not taking discounts. Here's a service that is needed by many. We will show you how to get clients for this business, and once you start taking care of their accounts payable, they won't want to let you stop.

INCOME LEVEL RATING:
Medium

MARKETING METHODS:
1. Direct mail
2. Display ads
3. Telephone sales
4. Direct sales

EQUIPMENT REQUIRED:
1. Computer with disk drive
2. Printer

PART TIME:
Yes

FULL TIME:
Yes

LOCATION:
City

MARKET BASE:
50,000–200,000

START UP CAPITAL:
$1,000 To $5,000 (Includes computer costs)

No. 192

KEEPING STATS FOR LITTLE LEAGUE TEAMS FOR PROFIT

DESCRIPTION:
With all of the sports going on for kids now and the great interest by coaches, parents and the kids in how they are doing, this business is a natural for any area of the country that supports kids' sports. We will show you how your service will be as valuable to each team as the uniforms they wear. And the income sources are from everybody – coaches, sponsors, parents and local newspapers, just to name a few.

INCOME LEVEL RATING:
Low

MARKETING METHODS:
1. Display ads

EQUIPMENT REQUIRED:
1. Computer with disk drive
2. Printer

PART TIME:
Yes

FULL TIME:
Yes

LOCATION:
City or country

MARKET BASE:
50,000–200,000

START UP CAPITAL:
Under $1,000

No. 193

REMODELING AND NEW CONSTRUCTION COST ESTIMATE SERVICE

DESCRIPTION:
Everybody who wants any new construction done has the problem of getting estimates from several different builders and then getting bugged by their salespeople until they do something. Here's a service that takes that pressure off of homeowners who just want to get some idea of how much it will cost to get something done. We will show you how to get this service started with a few ads and with the help of local building supply houses.

INCOME LEVEL RATING:
Medium

MARKETING METHODS
1. Display ads

EQUIPMENT REQUIRED:
1. Computer with disk drive
2. Printer

PART TIME:
Yes

FULL TIME:
Yes

LOCATION:
City or country

MARKET BASE:
50,000–200,000

START UP CAPITAL:
Under $1,000

No. 194

BOWLING TEAM STATS SERVICE

DESCRIPTION:
Have you ever checked to find out how many bowling teams there are in your area? You will be amazed if you're not already involved. We will show you how to provide weekly printouts for all leagues and how to collect from not only the leagues but from the bowling alleys and the league players. With your personal computer you can spend a few hours each week and make a good living.

INCOME LEVEL RATING:
Low

MARKETING METHODS:
1. Display ads

EQUIPMENT REQUIRED:
1. Computer with disk drive
2. Printer

PART TIME:
Yes

FULL TIME:
Yes

LOCATION:
City or country

MARKET BASE:
50,000–200,000

START UP CAPITAL:
Under $1,000

No. 195

TEACH TYPING FOR PROFIT

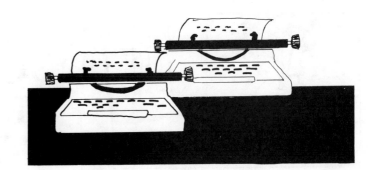

DESCRIPTION:
Here is a little known business that is making a lot of operators a good second income with little or no effort. We will show you how to multiply your stations without costing you an arm and a leg. Also, you will learn how to get the local schools to refer students to you. This is a real sleeper, so get in on it now.

INCOME LEVEL RATING:
Low

MARKETING METHODS:
1. Display ads

EQUIPMENT REQUIRED:
1. Computer with disk drive
2. Printer

PART TIME:
Yes

FULL TIME:
Yes

LOCATION:
City or country

MARKET BASE:
50,000–200,000

START UP CAPITAL:
Under $1,000

No. 196

LOCAL GARDENERS' PLANTING TIMES NEWSLETTER

DESCRIPTION:
If you're a garden buff, you know every different kind of vegetable, fruit, flower, tree and bush has its own specific planting time, and it usually is based on the first freeze along with other factors. Most information available is for general areas of the country. But the factors that determine the final success or failure are based on local green thumbs as well as the professionals' information not available anywhere else. Our report gives you all of the tools to start right up.

INCOME LEVEL RATING:
Low

MARKETING METHODS:
1. Display ads

EQUIPMENT REQUIRED:
1. Computer with disk drive
2. Printer

PART TIME:
Yes

FULL TIME:
Yes

LOCATION:
City or country

MARKET BASE:
5,000–50,000

START UP CAPITAL:
Under $1,000

No. 197

SELL INVENTORY CONTROLS FOR SMALL BUSINESSES

DESCRIPTION:
One of the hardest jobs for any small businessperson is keeping up with their inventory so they will know when to buy and how much they are making on what they have sold. We will show you how to set these small businesses up and keep them current on a monthly basis, thereby saving them time and lost revenue from shortages. All it takes is some of your time and your personal computer. A good, steady income can be provided from this service.

INCOME LEVEL RATING:
Medium

MARKETING METHODS:
1. Direct mail
2. Display ads
3. Telephone sales
4. Direct sales

EQUIPMENT REQUIRED:
1. Computer with disk drive
2. Printer

PART TIME:
Yes

FULL TIME:
Yes

LOCATION:
City

MARKET BASE:
200,000 Up

START UP CAPITAL:
Over $5,000 (Includes computer costs)

No. 198

AUTO TRIP PLANNING SERVICE

DESCRIPTION:

Here's a service that is being supplied by auto clubs around the country. But if you've tried them, you know the results are anything but acceptable. We will show you how to put together an auto trip plan giving your clients a thousand times more information than is being offered by the auto clubs. With your personal computer you will be able to show the best routes, mileage, cost, time, etc., and all of this in only minutes.

INCOME LEVEL RATING:
Low

MARKETING METHODS:
1. Display ads

EQUIPMENT REQUIRED
1. Computer with disk drive
2. Printer

PART TIME:
Yes

FULL TIME:
Yes

LOCATION:
City

MARKET BASE:
50,000–200,000

START UP CAPITAL:
$1,000 To $5,000 (Includes computer costs)

No. 199

INVESTMENT ANALYSIS ADVISOR

DESCRIPTION:

How many times have you wanted to ask someone, "how much should I invest in real estate, stocks, metals, mutual funds, etc."? Well, now we will show you how you can give people a percentage breakdown of where their investment dollar should go, and you can let them choose what they want to do, whether it's being conservative or going after a larger return with more risk. With this unique plan you can become an investment advisor, simply with the use of your personal computer.

INCOME LEVEL RATING:
Medium

MARKETING METHODS:
1. Direct mail
2. Display ads
3. Telephone sales

EQUIPMENT REQUIRED:
1. Computer with disk drive

2. Printer
3. Modem
4. Plotter
5. Graphics

PART TIME:
Yes

FULL TIME:
Yes

LOCATION:
City

MARKET BASE:
50,000–200,000

START UP CAPITAL:
Under $1,000

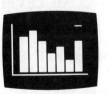

No. 200

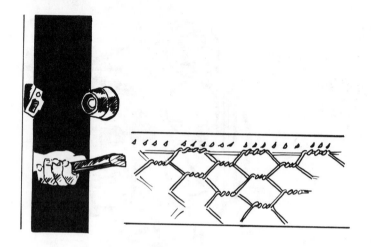

HOME SECURITY SYSTEMS ANALYSIS SERVICE

DESCRIPTION:

With home burglaries now at an all-time high, more people are becoming aware of the need for a home security system. But when they call a security systems company to get an estimate, usually it's a lot more than anybody can afford. Yet the products that make up the systems can be purchased at a fraction of the cost and installed by the homeowners themselves. We have developed a system using your personal computer to determine what your customer needs to protect their home, and then they can do it themselves; you get your fee, and you are both happy.

INCOME LEVEL RATING:
Medium

MARKETING METHODS:
1. Direct mail
2. Display ads
3. Telephone sales
4. Direct sales

EQUIPMENT REQUIRED:
1. Computer with disk drive
2. Printer

PART TIME:
Yes

FULL TIME:
Yes

LOCATION:
City

MARKET BASE:
50,000–200,000

START UP CAPITAL:
$1,000 To $5,000 (Includes computer costs)

No. 202

LOCAL COMPUTER SHOWS

DESCRIPTION:
We will show you how to put together a local computer show with a minimum of problems and a maximum of profit. We will explain how to get sponsors, show space and free publicity. Some operators are putting one of thse shows on every month and making enough to take two weeks of each month off and still live very well. So get your share of this market in your area.

INCOME LEVEL RATING:
Medium

MARKETING METHODS
1. Direct mail
2. Display ads

EQUIPMENT REQUIRED
1. Computer with disk drive
2. Printer

PART TIME:
No

FULL TIME:
Yes

LOCATION:
City

MARKET BASE:
200,000 Up

START UP CAPITAL:
Over $5,000 (Includes computer costs)

No. 203

COMPUTER CLUBS FOR KIDS FOR PROFIT

DESCRIPTION:
If you haven't guessed already, more than half of the personal computer market is made up of kids under 18 years of age. With this report you will learn how to organize a local club for every different type of computer being used in your area. With these clubs not only will you collect dues and fees, but you will have buying power with the local suppliers who will also give you finder's fees, so you can profit both ways.

INCOME LEVEL RATING:
Low

MARKETING METHODS:
1. Direct mail
2. Display ads

EQUIPMENT REQUIRED:
1. Computer with disk drive
2. Printer

PART TIME:
Yes

FULL TIME:
Yes

LOCATION:
City

MARKET BASE:
200,000 Up

START UP CAPITAL:
Under $1,000

No. 204

ACCOUNTS RECEIVABLES AND STATEMENT-MAILING SERVICE

DESCRIPTION:
Most businesses and professional services that have accounts receivables would like to have this part of their business done outside because of cost and aggravation. We will show you how to find these customers and get this system up on your personal computer. Some operators have found that only one or two accounts make them all the money they need and still give them a lot of free time.

INCOME LEVEL RATING:
Medium

MARKETING METHODS:
1. Direct mail
2. Display ads
3. Telephone sales
4. Direct sales

EQUIPMENT REQUIRED:
1. Computer with disk drive
2. Printer

PART TIME:
Yes

FULL TIME:
Yes

LOCATION:
City

MARKET BASE:
200,000 Up

START UP CAPITAL:
$1,000 To $5,000 (Includes computer costs)

No. 206

SELL COMPUTER PROGRAMMING COURSES

DESCRIPTION:
With one-million units being sold this year and a large percentage of the buyers wanting to develop their own programs, the market for simple programming instructions on their personal computer is huge. The income here could easily be in the six figures. We will give you a basic guide for developing computer programming instructions on your personal computer and marketing the instructions—both locally and through the mail. So, if you lean towards programming, here's a wide-open market.

INCOME LEVEL RATING:
Medium

MARKETING METHODS
1. Direct mail

EQUIPMENT REQUIRED:
1. Computer with disk drive
2. Printer

PART TIME:
Yes

FULL TIME:
Yes

LOCATION:
City or country

MARKET BASE:
50,000–200,000

START UP CAPITAL:
Under $1,000

SECTION 3

In this section you'll find complete descriptions of the computer businesses you most want to know more about. Each Complete Business Venture Plan gives you the details you actually need in order to get the business up and running. It will explain what the business consists of, what kinds of skills and information it requires, how to get started, potential costs, how to market it, and what unique approaches to follow to ensure success.

No. 101

EXECUTIVE RECRUITING AND EMPLOYMENT SERVICE

Ever since the early 70s, when Dartmouth college students started matching jobs with people on their computers, this has become an easy-to-operate, big-dollar business. It seems that in good times as well as bad this service prospers, as indicated by the many new firms that have opened up over the past two years. So start recruiting today and earn your share of the pie.

CONCEPT

The concept of this business is to match companies who need skilled employees with the people looking for a new or different job. You make your money on both ends of the deal by charging both the company and the employee for the match-up.

Experienced people are always needed, and all you have to do is tap into this market with your personal computer.

SKILLS YOU WILL REQUIRE

You certainly don't need to be an expert in corporate relations or human relations to operate this business. All you'll need is the ability to organize your information with your computer. If you enjoy working with people and the idea of helping them find their dream career appeals to you, you will do well with this business. An employer doesn't care if you are 90 years old, live in Hawaii and operate out of a phone booth, as long as you can prove you know how to match up people with the openings they have.

INFORMATION REQUIRED

There are two types of information required to operate this business. The first is what you'll need to know to run your computer and the second is what you'll need to know to recruit clients and fill job openings.

First, you will want to choose software for your computer that will enable you to sort through the qualifications of your employee-clients and come up with recommendations to give your company-clients.

A data base will allow you to plug in the same information under a number of different categories, then pull out the information as you need it. For example, if you have an employee-client who has skills in marketing, engineering and sales, you can list the information about his experience once, then have it designated under a number of categories. That way, if a company comes to you wanting an engineer, the computer will produce your employee-client's name. Likewise, if another company is looking for a marketing expert, your client's name will appear under that category as well.

A data base is also useful for cross-referencing. Using the same example, if a company comes to you needing an engineer who is skilled at marketing as well, your computer can sort through its listing of people possessing both skills to produce the names you need to provide the company.

The other type of information you need concerns the jobs to be filled. The more information you have about the positions companies possess, the greater your chances of making a successful match. Likewise, the more you know about your employee-client's experience, the easier it will be to find a position for which he is qualified.

One way for you to garner this information is by preparing two questionnaires, one to be filled out by the company with the opening and the other to be completed by the potential employee.

For the first questionnaire, questions might include:

Name of company:
Address:
Phone number:
Contact name or personnel director:
Job title:
Responsibilities:
Experience required:
Number of years required:
Salary range:
Special licenses or qualifications required:
Date job will be open:

The questionnaire for employees might include:

Name:
Address:

Phone number:
Currently employed at:
Position sought:
Salary desired:
Area of country where job is sought:
Job experience:
Special licenses and qualifications:
Education:

This questionnaire can be supplemented with the information on the resume of the employee to get a detailed understanding of qualifications and experience.

Once you have this information, you can plug it into your computer and file it under the appropriate files, to be called up as job positions become available.

GETTING STARTED

Once you have designed questionnaires for your clients, you are ready to get business. You can do this by following the recommendations in Marketing Methods.

Once you begin compiling a list of client companies and employees and inputting the pertinent data into your data base, you are ready to start matching up.

One of the secrets to this business is that you can recruit both employees and positions. Say you get a company needing an expert in direct mail copywriting. With a little research in the field, you should be able to determine some of the top direct mail companies in the nation, then contact the people at these companies to learn whether they are interested in moving to a different company. This is where the recruiting comes in. If you can offer the potential employee a job in a more desirable part of the country or at a higher salary, you may convince him to consider the position you are trying to fill. This also works in reverse. If you have a top-notch direct mail copywriter, you may be able to locate a company that will consider employing your client.

Your recruiting skills will be honed with experience, so don't fret if the idea of negotiating with either companies or employees makes you nervous. Soon enough you'll get the methods down.

THE COMPETITION

There is no end to competition in this field. Yet the sheer number of recruiting firms should give you a good idea of how lucrative this business can be. The way you can eliminate your competition is by working just a little harder, using your computer to keep up on demands and by presenting a polished appearance in your work that will impress both employees and companies that may use you.

Generally, once a client has used your service to satisfaction, he will continue using you. That means that once you've convinced a company to rely on you to fill openings, your work will come steadily and can only grow with time.

POTENTIAL INCOME

The income you can earn with this business is limited only by how much effort and time you want to give it. Many recruiting firms charge upwards of $5,000 to place a single employee in a large corporation. Figure it out for yourself; how many would you have to place to get the extra income you want?

The beauty of this business is that you have a number of ways to make your money. Basically, you won't charge anybody anything until a successful match is made and an open position filled. For example, if a company wants to hire three new computer programmers, you don't collect a cent from them until you have found the employees they need. This makes the service easier to market, since there is no obligation on the part of your clients. Likewise, you don't charge an employee-client until you've found the career of his dreams.

Once you have completed a match, you can usually collect a percentage of the annual salary as your fee. If a company pays $35,000 to those programmers it needs, and you find two that fit the bill, you may consider charging the company 2% of that salary. That equals $1,400 for your efforts.

To estimate what to charge, calculate your business expenses, including a salary for your time and a profit for the business.

Basic Costs

1. Cost of data base software
2. Cost of advertising
3. Cost of long-distance phone calls
4. Cost of time spent preparing questionnaire
5. Cost of time spent with company and employee clients
6. Cost of time spent making matches
7. Cost of materials used

Since this is basically a low-cost business to operate, aside from the equipment you use and long-distance phone calls made, you can estimate a fairly high profit margin into your fee.

MARKETING METHODS

Direct mail, display ads, telephone sales and direct sales are the best ways to market this service.

You can run display ads in the business and classified sections of your local news-paper or in local business publications. The ad should make clear that your service costs absolutely nothing until a job match-up has been completed.

You can use telephone and direct sales by contacting the major companies in your area and speaking with the personnel directors. Explain your service succinctly, offer to do a match-up to prove the reliability and effectiveness of your service, and point out that the company won't have to pay a cent unless the match-up is successful. What company wouldn't want to try a no-obligation service that helps them?

You can most effectively use direct mail by targeting major companies in your area and offering to fill their positions. You can obtain a list of these companies the same way you do to make direct and telephone contact, by using either a list service that will supply you with company names and addresses or by relying on a contact book that most areas have listing company names, sizes and addresses.

Here is an example of a direct mail letter you can try to market this service:

DEAR EMPLOYER:

Do you need qualified workers? Even if you don't now, wouldn't it be more cost-effective for you to know who is available for positions that may come open in the future? Exec Finders can put you in touch with all the qualified people you need to keep your company up and running without a lot of lag time in doing your own recruiting.

We can provide you with several people who are not only specially screened and qualified for your openings but want to work in the kind of job environment you offer.

Plus, we don't charge you a cent until your match is made.

Interested? Call now for details about our unique, low-cost service that can save you time and money in filling those positions you may have open on a moment's notice.

Your own variation of this letter should bring you inquiries for more information. And you can follow up the letter with a phone call to the personnel director. Be prepared to answer questions, such as give them an idea of how long you will expect to spend finding employees for them and how much your service will cost.

UNIQUE BUSINESS APPROACH

There are several approaches in this field that will make your business succeed by leaps and bounds.

The first is to offer to match up companies the first time absolutely free. This means you gain the potential of gaining them as steady client, which in the end will make money for you. You can offer this bonus in your direct mail letter or other sales techniques, and even put a deadline to it. For example, say "if you respond within 10 days, your first job match-up will be absolutely free." Sweetening the pot can only bring you business.

The second approach you can try is to contact companies listed regularly in the classified job openings section. Offer to save them the cost of advertising for employ-ees by supplying them with all the workers they need. Since they appear to have a steady turn-over of workers, they will probably be amenable to listening to what you have to say.

Another approach you can take that will reach both companies and workers is to hold a job fair. You can charge companies to appear at the fair to solicit employees in specialized fields. You can also get speakers to hold seminars about how to write winning resumes or handle interviews, to attract potential employee-clients. This will cost money in terms of renting a space to hold the seminar, organizing and advertising it, etc., but it can pay off in a big way when you get a large list of well-qualified customers.

The final approach you may consider is specializing in one field, such as advertising, engineering, computer programming, etc. This will make you an expert on who the people are in the field, as well as who the big employers are.

LOCATION and MARKET BASE

This business would best be suited for operation in either the city or country with a population base of from 5,000 to 50,000 people. Since much of your work can be handled by phone, you aren't necessarily limited by the number of companies in your own area or by the number of potential well-qualified workers.

TO SUM UP

An executive recruiting and employment service is a business with many money-making opportunities. No matter how you decide to operate it, you can lead the flexible life you desire while earning a sizable income at the same time.

With the use of your computer to organize your data, you can tap into the thousands of job openings in this country today and fill them to the satisfaction of both companies and employees.

To put the value of this service into perspective, look at it this way: finding qualified job applicants can cost a company thousands of dollars every year. And finding the job of one's dreams can take a lifetime, if it is ever found at all. Yet with your single-handed drive, you can match up dream jobs with employees and take a cut of the profit. All it will require is for you to recruit yourself into this business opportunity.

SOURCE MATERIAL

For source material, refer to Section 7.

No. 102

COMPUTER CUSTOM DIET SERVICE

This is an opportunity for you to cash in on the growing awareness of the health benefits of proper diet. Not only is half the population constantly dieting to lose weight, more and more people want to tailor their diets for weight training and body building. With off-the-shelf software, you can provide custom diets that meet all the nutritional requirements for individuals, and include the kinds of foods they most like to eat.

CONCEPT

The concept of this business is to develop custom diets, tailored to lose weight or add muscle mass while meeting individual nutritional requirements. A wide variety of off-the-shelf software is available to meet this need.

Virtually all the software for diet planning requires you to enter data about the person's present weight, height, type of body build, physical activity and weight goal. You'll need to prepare a questionnaire for your clients. Some diet planning software includes a questionnaire already prepared. You can just adapt it for your own business. Or you can design your own questionnaire to collect the information you need.

When you receive the completed questionnaire with an order, you enter the information into your system and a custom diet is printed out quickly and easily.

Once your clients reach their weight goal, they can come back to you for updated maintenance diets. Or if their tastes change and they want different kinds of foods on their diets, you can easily update their custom diets.

SKILLS YOU WILL REQUIRE

More important than any particular skill is a commitment to healthy eating habits and good nutrition. Personal interest and dedication will go a long way toward creating a successful business of this kind.

The main technical skill you'll need is the ability to use your diet planning software package. The documentation that comes with the software should provide everything you need to know to use it effectively. Get some practice by planning diets for yourself and your own family.

INFORMATION REQUIRED

You don't have to be an expert on nutrition before you get started in this business. If you are genuinely interested in improving your own diet to maintain peak health and physical condition, while satisfying your tastes for good food at the same time, then you will naturally pick up more and more information on the subject.

As you get into the topic, you'll find that dozens of books are available on nutritional needs appropriate to every kind of activity and health goal. The U.S. Department of Agriculture provides numerous pamphlets on nutrition and diet, at little or no charge.

OPERATING NAME

You'll probably want an operating name that includes the concepts of nutrition, diet and personalized service. An obvious example is "Personal Nutrition Planners." You might decide to concentrate on either weight loss diets or body-building diets, according to your personal interests, and choose a name that conveys that idea. Some examples are: "Personal Weight Loss Planning" and "Body Designs."

An alternative is to use your own name for your business, with an appropriate phrase, such as the names suggested above, as a motto which explains your business. Jack LaLaine and Eileen Feather are two names that have become household words closely associated with the concepts of diet, nutrition and health.

See Section 4 for more information and considerations about choosing a business name.

GETTING STARTED

To get started, first you should practice with your diet planning software to become familiar with how it works. Once you feel confident about preparing effective custom diets with it, you're ready to start on the business.

Then prepare your questionnaire to be filled out by your clients.

If your diet planning software package comes with a questionnaire, be sure to modify it somewhat to avoid problems of copyright violation. If your software package doesn't have a separate questionnaire, design your own using the items that have to be completed for data entry.

What you will be supplying your clients is a list of menus they should follow each day. These menus will include the foods they want to eat, along with other foods they need to meet their daily requirements. You may choose to prepare a month's worth of daily menus that they can vary in the coming months or for as long as they want to follow their diets. The software you choose to use will direct you in how you will present your diets—whether monthly, weekly, etc.

The next step is to prepare advertising materials—display ads, flyers, magazine ads, and so on. See Marketing Methods and Unique Business Approach, for more information about suitable ads.

You want to get your name out there and get it known. You want your potential customers to know about your service. So start telling people about it. Have business cards printed and give them to people. Explain your service. To meet more potential customers to give them to, go to fitness centers or weight loss groups. Involve yourself in the market you want.

THE COMPETITION

While it's true that a lot of off-the-shelf software is available for custom diet planning, most of it is being sold to home computer enthusiasts for their own personal use, rather than as the foundation for a business. Some of this software is also being used by health professionals.

But as far as consulting for the general public, the field is wide open. The best way to get ahead of the competition in this field is to start early. Carve out a solid market share for yourself before everybody else gets in the race.

POTENTIAL INCOME

You'll have to charge a flat fee for this service, but you want to make sure that you earn a reasonable amount for the time you spend on it. When you're working on your practice diet plans, figure out how long each one takes, so you can set an appropriate flat rate for the service, based on the hourly rate you want for your work.

If you charge a rate of, say, $50 for the initial diet plan, you can earn $500 a week with only 10 clients. Since each client's plan will require at most two hours of your time, this will generate a handsome hourly income for you.

To estimate your fee accurately, add up all the costs of the program and include a salary for your time, as well as a profit for the business.

Basic Costs

1. Cost of software
2. Cost of time spent organizing questionnaire
3. Cost of advertising
4. Cost of brochure, business cards, reproduction of questionnaire
5. Cost of time spent creating diet plan
6. Cost of materials used

Aside from your initial investment in equipment, your day-to-day operating expenses will not be very great. In addition to the cost of your office, utilities and phone, your primary expenses will be for supplies, paper, printer ribbons, diskettes and advertising costs. Be sure to calculate these overhead costs before you get started and figure them into the rate you charge.

MARKETING METHODS

Several different methods are appropriate for marketing this service—display ads, flyers, even magazine ads, once you've developed an operating base big enough to support them. After all, you can perform this service conveniently by mail order, no matter where your customers are.

Fitness centers are good places for your display ads or for distributing flyers. Support groups for dieters, such as Overeaters Anonymous, also present good target markets.

Here's some sample text you might use for a flyer. Also include your questionnaire on the flyer. This will provide a way for potential customers to take immediate action. As a bonus, you only have printing costs for one form.

CUSTOM-DESIGNED BODIES!

What's your ideal weight and body type? Wouldn't you like to have your ideal body without boring diets? Wouldn't you prefer a diet that's custom-designed just for you? One that's nutritionally complete, designed to help you reach your ideal weight and body build with only the foods you like?

Now you can forget about counting up calories, looking up nutritional information in charts, and trying to figure out your own diet plan. Our computer service will create your custom diet plan for you. It will be nutritionally balanced and designed to help you reach your ideal body type—no matter whether you want to lose weight, build muscles or maintain the body you've already worked so hard to attain.

Your custom diet plan lists only foods you like and includes all necessary nutritional elements for you. It takes into account your exercise habits and the goal you've set for developing your body. It's a complete diet plan with actual menus, not just a list of foods with their calorie content.

Just take a few minutes to complete this questionnaire and send it along with your check. In just a few days, you'll recieve your own custom diet plan—your personal road map to your ideal body.

As your business develops, you may want to expand by advertising in magazines. You can target your potential customers very specifically by selecting carefully from the many special-interest magazines, such as Runner's World.

UNIQUE BUSINESS APPROACH

As a way of developing a substantial market when you start out, you can offer a discount to members of groups, such as fitness centers and athletic teams. If you are a member of the group, you'll have a much better opportunity to place your display ad or flyers.

Discounted rates won't cost you anything if you include the discount in your calculations when you're establishing your rates. To the contrary, with an appropriate discount you can establish a profitable list of clients and start making money much sooner.

LOCATION AND MARKET BASE

You can run this business no matter where you are, in the city or in the country. Since it's primarily a mail order business, you don't have to be located near your customers; you won't be depending on people to drop in off the street. An effective market base for this business can be as little as 5,000 people, or it can be over 50,000. You really have a wide open range in this business. It's up to you to develop it as far as you want.

START UP CAPITAL

If you already have your computer, you can get into this business on a shoestring—under $1,000. All you need besides the computer, printer and software is a minimal investment for advertising. See Section 6 for information on how to raise capital for starting a business.

TO SUM UP

If you are interested in developing a healthy lifestyle for yourself and others through well-planned nutrition, this is an ideal business for you. You can live anywhere and you don't need much capital to get started. The main requirements are enthusiasm, a clear vision of your goals and a commitment to making them come true.

People considering a diet want the personal touch. You can provide it with little effort and make good money for your time. So start today, planning your way to your dream income.

SOURCE MATERIAL

Refer to Section 7.

No. 103

COMPUTERIZED CUSTOM EXERCISE PROGRAMS

This business provides a valuable service which can be of great benefit to just about everyone. It can be started almost anywhere with relatively modest capital and if managed properly can produce a good income.

CONCEPT

The concept of this business is to sell health and fitness in the form of customized exercise programs.

Exercise programs in gyms, YMCA's and corporations are among the fastest-growing businesses in America today. But if you've ever joined a spa or gym you know that most facilities aren't able to develop and supervise really personalized exercise programs due to lack of staff and time.

That's where YOU come in.

You provide the customized exercise, fitness and nutrition programs—a weekly or monthly program and a personal log updated on a regular basis to make sure each client achieves his or her special goals, whether it's training for a marathon, working to keep blood pressure down or just keeping fit.

With this computer business there are no limits to the parameters you can plug into a client's custom program. Therefore, each client will have a personalized plan to follow and a specific goal in sight, which can be reached by sticking to the program which you provide. You are selling something everyone wants and needs - wellness and a healthier way of life.

There are a many different personalized programs you can offer. These include:

LIFESTYLES AND STRESS EVALUATION

Many of us are unaware of the ways our habits, lifestyle or family history affect our health. You can change this by gathering and analyzing important lifestyle information which can have an important bearing on your client's present and future health. By gathering and analyzing information which the client himself provides, you can point out key health needs and develop an individualized program designed for his specific requirements. This information has tremendous value if it is gathered and used correctly. It can save lives by computing life expectancy, evaluating stress levels and identifying the most deadly health hazards.

NUTRITION AND EXERCISE

We all know that nutrition and exercise are the cornerstones of a healthy body. But for most of us, keeping track of eating habits and analyzing our food intake for nutrition and calorie content is, at best, a nuisance. Add the task of deciding just how much and what type of exercise is necessary to burn off spare pounds, and the record-keeping task is enough to send you to the refrigerator for another piece of chocolate cake!

A personalized nutrition and exercise program is the answer. You provide a program which helps each client meet his nutritional and/or exercise goals. And to make your program special, you can offer special incentives when he reaches a plateau—a special note, certificate of achievement or perhaps a special food reward.

SPECIAL SPORTS EXERCISE PROGRAMS

Special sports require special exercise programs to let participants know how their fitness, endurance and performance compare with their previous performances, and how they can expect to perform under specific conditions.

Alpine skiers, for instance, will be enthusiastic about a program which analyzes their racing performance on various types of skis, different slopes and snow conditions and also provides specific exercise and diet information.

Serious runners will be knocking down your door to obtain a program which maintains a daily memo and training calendar, provides a series of exercises to obtain fitness levels, troubleshoots aches and pains and provides a special diet for optimum performance. Programs that will let you create such plans are already on the market.

SKILLS YOU WILL REQUIRE

If you have the knowledge and interest in health and fitness, you have what it takes to get started in this business. If you already participate in one or more active sports, that's a big plus. You not only know the basics of the sport, but you also have a built-in source of business contacts.

You will need to know the basics of business, learn some terminology and know where to get information.

If business booms and you need help in a hurry, don't panic. Remember, there are plenty of moonlighters around. Medical students, nurses, nutritionists, physical education students and others will be happy to earn extra spending money. Just tack a notice on the university bulletin board, run an ad in the campus paper, or telephone the dietary departments of local hospitals. You'll have a list of well-qualified associates in no time.

INFORMATION REQUIRED

Do your research before spending a dime. Find out what background material is available at public and university libraries. Magazine articles, books and reports by well-known clinics are available practically for the asking.

And don't overlook hospitals as a source for the latest health, exercise and nutrition information. All hospitals have education departments which develop education and training programs for patients, nurses, physicians and the community. Get to know these helpful professionals. Sign up for courses. Explain your interests. Ask for materials. They'll welcome the opportunity to share information which may ultimately help their patients.

Most hospitals have libraries for both their medical and nursing staffs. Ask if you can use their research material.

GETTING STARTED

Whichever areas you decide to concentrate on, you will have to spend some time researching available software. Read the ads in computer and fitness magazines. Visit your local software store and get demonstrations.

Once you have chosen your software, it will determine what kinds of questions you will have your clients answer about their exercise needs. You might decide to create a questionnaire for them to fill out, or you may simply choose to perform a personal consultation to ask the key questions yourself.

Either way, the computer will do the bulk of your work for you, if you spend time in advance choosing software that suits your needs.

Getting a business off and running depends not only on software, but also on business contacts. If there are professional groups in your area related to health, exercise, marketing or related fields, attend a few meetings. Introduce yourself. Pass out your business cards. The same goes with attending ski club meetings, runs, spas, the YMCA and introducing yourself to local corporate leaders. They can provide you with valuable information which could take years to learn otherwise.

If your budget permits, develop a brochure or flyer explaining your services. If properly distributed, these "leave behind" pieces can increase your business enormously.

THE COMPETITION

Never overlook the competition as a valuable source of information. Use the yellow pages in your area to find out who they are. Also check with hospitals, sporting goods stores, health spas, nutrition stores, etc.

Approach your competitors as a potential client. Find out what services they offer and what they charge. Ask for a brochure. Make note of how they handle your inquiry. Are they courteous? Prompt? What do they send? How do they follow up? All this adds up to a free business education.

Above all, never alienate your competition. They can be a valuable source of referrals. And who knows? Someday you and they may be partners.

To out-distance the competition, consider setting up your own mini marketing service. Offer your service to local physicians, hospitals and health spas at a discount. They, in turn, can provide your services to their patients or clients as a service or means of boosting business. In the advertising game this is known as cross promotion.

POTENTIAL INCOME

Our research indicates that you can expect a medium level of income from this business.

The key to making money is pricing. Generally, pricing this type of service is not complicated. Start by placing an hourly value on your time (be sure to include about 20 percent to cover taxes, social security and benefits). Then add up all costs of the program (you'll find a list following) and add in a profit figure for the service. Now divide by the number of clients you will be able to handle comfortably.

Keep in mind that the hourly rate is not profit; it's what you're paid for working on the project. Profit is what you pay the business after all costs are covered. And it's profit that makes a business grow. You should earn money for your time and a profit for your business on every personalized program.

Basic Costs

1. Cost of business license
2. Cost of stationary, business cards
3. Cost of transportation
4. Cost of educational programs
5. Cost of software
6. Cost of professional meetings
7. Cost of advertising
8. Cost to prepare and produce brochure
9. Cost to prepare client questionnaires
10. Cost of reproducing questionnaires
11. Cost to distribute patient questionnaires
12. Cost to organize and evaluate client data

13. Cost to organize data
14. Cost of envelopes and reply postage
15. Cost of checking questionnaires
16. Cost of organizing and maintaining information
17. Cost of preparing and writing weekly or monthly analysis
18. Cost of developing incentive materials, such as award certificates
19. Cost of mailing reports and incentive certificates

How To Be Paid

Since personalized programs of this kind require regular updates every week or month, it's wise to get the initial payment "up front." From then on, require payment in full at the end of an established period of time, such as at the end of every month.

MARKETING METHODS

Getting started is a matter of getting news of your business to your target market—the people who need your service.

Make a list of the types of people who most need and will use your service on a regular basis. The list might include families, mothers-to-be, senior citizens, corporation employees, members of spas or gyms, college students, runners or skiers—whomever you want to help.

Now, list all of the ways you can reach your potential market. Let your imagination run wild. That's how great ideas are born. How about sky-writing, referrals from doctors, flyers, news stories, endorsements from celebrities, classified or display advertising, billboards?

Narrow down the list to the one or two methods you can afford and that get the job done quickly and most efficiently.

I recommend placing classified ads in publications most read by your target market. Check the yellow page listings for newspapers dealing with health, nutrition, active sports, etc. Then vist several gyms and nutrition stores. Examine what types of materials are available and ask members or shoppers what they read and are looking for in personalized programs. You can learn a lot from what marketing professionals call field research.

Here is an example of a classified ad for a running publication:

> Improve your time and endurance. Personalized running and exercise program by top marathon winner. J. Jamison 213-999-9999

Here is a classified ad for a general-circulation or health publication:

> Stress and lifestyle patterns can shorten your life. It's not too late to change. Personalized lifestyle analysis by J. Jamison 213-999-9999

As I said earlier, flyers or brochures can be a valuable tool for promoting your business. There are a number of good books available in bookstores or at your local library which provide valuable information on writing and designing your own material.

To determine the message, first examine your competitors brochures. What does the brochure say about them? Does it reflect professionalism or is it a "hack" job?

If you are planning a brochure, keep in mind that its content and quality reflect on your professionalism. Do the first draft yourself. Then contact graphic designers and copywriters. Find out what they charge to do a complete brochure. If the price doesn't fit your budget, check with several local typesetters to see if their in-house designers can do the job. And here's another cost-saving method: ask whether these businesses would be willing to trade their services for yours. Bartering can be a great way to save money.

UNIQUE BUSINESS APPROACH

Another way you can build your business visibility and attract clients is through publicity releases. Send releases to publications which use articles on health, wellness, sports, etc. If possible, include background information and quotes from people who have used your service successfully. There are a number of good books in the public or university libraries that can tell you how to write a release and place it with the proper news media. Do this on a regular basis and you're sure to build your business.

LOCATION and MARKET BASE

You can run this business either in the city or country, as long as you have a market base of 50,000 to 200,000 to draw on. There is an enormous need for this service. You can start right where you are and build your business through newspaper ads and word-of-mouth referrals.

TO SUM UP

Personal computerized exercise programs will be the next big boom for exercise-conscious America. Everyone wants to look and feel his or her best. With this business you have an opportunity to join one of the country's fastest growing industries, to provide a valuable and much needed service, and to make money at the same time. Isn't it time you put your own good health to work for you?

SOURCE MATERIAL

Refer to Section 7.

No. 104

ECONOMIC FORECASTING

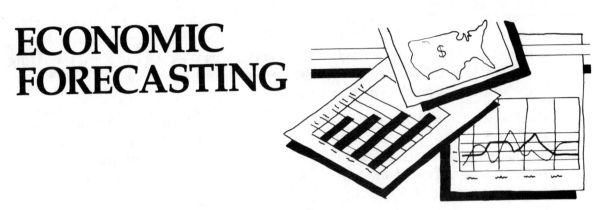

Every day you hear news about the unemployment rate, money supply, gross national product, etc. But these figures never give the local businessperson any insight into what's happening in his or her town. With the instructions and plans presented in this computer business plan, you will be able to obtain all the pertinent information to sell to local business. This localized service has made several small operators very wealthy, because information changes all the time, meaning that the need for the service never ends.

CONCEPT

The concept of this business is to sell predictions. You use numbers from past economic performance to calculate trends. Then you divulge these trends to your clients, enabling them to make decisions regarding projects or business ventures they are involved in or are planning.

What you are actually selling is advantage. The forecasts you provide your clients will enable them to better decide where their money should be spent or invested. It will give them a picture of what is happening on the local economic scene before it actually occurs. The cost of obtaining the information you can provide will turn out to be the best investment they ever made.

This is the reason economic forecasting is one of the best-kept secrets in the world. Insiders want to remain part of a small, elite, well-informed group. The price others will pay to become a part of the group is a small fraction of what they have the potential of earning back with the information you supply them.

SKILLS YOU WILL REQUIRE

Obviously, everybody must do forecasting of one kind or another in life. When somebody takes a job, he or she is forecasting that a new employer will stay in business and be able to pay wages. When a person buys a car, he or she is predicting the ability to make payments. The difference with economic forecasting is that you organize the information you have to discover trends.

If you enjoy strategy games or playing with numbers and statistics, you'll do well in this business. You don't need to be a financier, stockbroker or investment counselor to get started in economic forecasting. You will need to understand the basics of the business, learn some of the terminology and, most important, know where to get your information.

INFORMATION REQUIRED

The information or data you'll need to get started in forecasting economic trends can come from a multitude of resources.

City and county governments are always doing local surveys of housing outlooks, consumer spending habits, business and industry growth and availability of money for investment and loans. To tap into these numbers, all you have to do is contact them. It is their responsibility to provide the public with the information they possess.

Chambers of commerce are filled with members of local business and industry who are experts in their fields. This is an excellent place to get information on what is happening in the community's business sector. They can provide statistics on a wide array of subjects, from how many cars were sold last year to the average amount of money spent by each age bracket.

Contact with the chamber of commerce can also provide you with an opportunity to tap its members for their insider's knowledge.

A businessperson likes nothing better than to project how his business will grow or flounder in the coming decade. Interviews with businesspeople can elicit invaluable information for determining how other fields will do. If a local lumber store is having difficulty finding wood, that means local housing will either cost more or use alternative construction materials. When the money market tightens, loans will be harder to come by, workers are more apt to hang onto the jobs they have rather than switch employers, and local business will be less likely to invest in new ventures or expand their current operations. Business needs to know what to expect, in order to plan for it and stay on top of the game.

When starting a new forecasting business, get what you can locally. Many times you'll find that what you need has already been gathered and organized by somebody else and is available for the asking. Then all you'll have to do is compile the data into your computer and come up with the direction the trends are heading.

Information bases are another source of statistics that can aid you in your forecasting business. With a modem and phone you can tap into any number of financial reports, indexes and listings. Somewhere, right this minute, somebody is feeding data into a computer that you will find useful for forecasting. The gathering of information is the number one business in the world. All you need is assistance in making sense out of it.

There are a multitude of programs, called "number crunchers" by those in the financial world, that will do the sorting for you. They work by asking a series of questions. You plug in the data, then the computer analyzes the information and provides you with evaluations based on its "number crunching."

Statistical software will enable you to save, edit, update and analyze data. Some programs will also allow you to merge several sets of data. Plus, you'll be able to create subsets of data that match the criteria you have established. In this way you can determine what information you'll need in a particular set of numbers or statistics, and have your computer sort it out for you.

With your computer you can also create written evaluations that can be integrated with your statistics, charts and graphs.

GETTING STARTED

Getting business isn't just a matter of what you know, but who you know. Your first step should be to prepare a brochure of the services you intend to offer and a sales letter asking for assignments. These should be sent to businesses and organizations in your area on a regular schedule. The Marketing Methods section will give you techniques for doing this.

To figure out what to say and how it is done, write or contact existing economic forecasters, acting as a potential customer. See how they handle your inquiry, what they send to you, how they follow up, etc. This will provide free training on how you can market your own business.

THE COMPETITION

To handle the competition in this business, let it work for you to get started, then offer your own twist. Let the competition show you how they make money with their economic forecasting, then think up your own area of expertise and sell the concept at a reduced price to a number of clients. In this way you can create your own cash flow.

The need for this field is growing at an incredible rate. And that is because business needs people who can tell them what all the numbers pertinent to their industry mean. You will be limited only by your own imagination. All you have to do is think up an idea and decide whether a group of firms or organizations would pay to find out your results. Then make them an offer by letter. If you get enough response, you'll have the money up front to do the research you need. If not, all you lost was the cost of mailing out a few letters.

The first step is to figure out your concept. Then put together a plan to do the research for it and decide on a list of the benefits for those who could use the information you will provide. Next, write a sales letter to those you think would pay for the information. In the letter, tell them the benefits of becoming your client. You can tell them that the value of your research in terms of added profit to them can equal thousands of dollars. Then say that since the material is currently available, they can have it for $100, or whatever price you pick. Don't forget to ask for the order, and tell them it will take four to six weeks to put the material into report form.

If you get 25 orders from your mailing, you have $2,500 to do the researching. If you only get a couple of orders, return their checks and go on with your next forecasting project.

POTENTIAL INCOME

To figure out a price for your service, you'll need to do a little forecasting. Start by figuring how much your time is worth to you. Then add up the costs of the program (you'll find a list following) and a profit figure for the job. The total is what you should get for the job. Remember that your hourly rate isn't profit. Those are two different numbers. One is what your time is worth and the other is the amount you'll get for your work minus all expenses. You should expect to earn both money for your time and a profit for your business on each project.

Project Costs

1. Cost of writing letters for information
2. Cost of making phone calls for information
3. Cost of using information bases
4. Cost of purchase of any materials to be used
5. Cost of miscellaneous reports or files that aren't free
6. Cost of organizing results

Business Expenses

7. Cost of preparing order letter
8. Cost of reproducing letter
9. Cost of mailing letter
10. Cost of envelopes and reply postage

Final Report

11. Cost of preparation and writing
12. Cost of reproduction and delivery

MARKETING METHODS

Direct mail and display ads are typically the best methods to market this business.

Most economic forecasters deliver their information in the form of newsletters. These newsletters usually run from two to six pages and are sent out to a mailing list of subscribers who pay to receive it.

To get your own mailing list of subscribers started, choose the market you intend to forecast for, then send them a letter like the sample one below. The letter should be accompanied by a brochure outlining your services, or possibly a sample copy of your newsletter. Let them have a small nibble and they'll want to order the whole dinner. The two pieces should be mailed out to all prospects in your area at the rate of 10 or 20 a day.

Here is the letter:

> Dear Business Owner:
>
> Could you increase your profits if you had tomorrow's newspaper today?
>
> Of course you could, and we'll show you how. We can supply you with the information you'll need to anticipate what your marketplace will be tomorrow, or next week, or even next year.
>
> We'll show you what the local trends in business are going to be, allowing you to cash in on the information.
>
> The total market share in this area last year was $50 million. How much of that was yours? Would you like to get a bigger share?
>
> By knowing what your competition doesn't know, you can increase your business potential. And that is exactly what a tailor-made economic forecasting program can do for you.
>
> Give me 10 minutes of your time—I'll prove it.

That letter, or a variation of it, sent to all the right prospects in your area, should bring you results for specific assignments and possibly for your newsletter, if that is what you intend to produce.

It will take time to build your market. Nothing happens overnight. But if you persist in sending letters that show what benefits you can offer, you can turn a prospect into a client.

UNIQUE BUSINESS APPROACH

Of course, there's a well-kept secret in this business that can make all the difference between success and failure. That secret is free advertising. How do you get it? By sending out press releases to create publicity for your business. What it entails is creating hype for your economic forecasting. If people read about a successful forecaster, they'll want to find out more and will bang on your door to get it.

The media like to use stories about local trends. What you need to do is find a creative slant to your findings and package your information effectively. When a local newspaper runs your story, it'll list you as the source. This not only builds recognition, but supplies you with clippings that you can reproduce and add to your other sales materials for potential clients.

Local libraries carry plenty of books that will explain how to write a publicity release. After you have composed one, contact all the newspapers and radio and television stations to find out who the release should be forwarded to. Some newspapers have one editor for a single subject, such as science or finance. So get the name of each, and find out what their deadlines are and how they prefer to receive publicity releases. By following their instructions and guidelines, you can start hitting them on a regular basis. This builds your image and can bring in business. For more information on this topic, refer to Section 5.

LOCATION AND MARKET BASE

This is a business that would be best suited for a city with a market base of at least 200,000 residents. The reason for this is because only a town of this size can afford to support the business and industry that can best benefit from your service.

Keep in mind that presidents of national corporations won't be calling to ask your opinions on financial matters, at least not at first. Instead, the big opportunity lies in helping small businesses, because they can't afford to have full-time economic forecasters working on their staffs. That's where you can make your mark—by providing them with a service they cannot provide themselves. By developing concepts and ideas for small business, you eliminate the major competition and build a nice cash flow for yourself.

TO SUM UP

An economic forecasting business is a great opportunity. You can turn something you enjoy doing into a real money-maker. By starting out with a small business and finding the niche that's right for you, you can dream up all kinds of projects that will get the cash flowing in. Then when you're ready, you can expand by simply deciding to.

You'll be offering an invaluable service to an appreciative clientele. Think of it this way: if you had the ability to prophesy what horse was going to win a race, wouldn't you do what you could to make a large bet on that horse? Each day business bets on that race without any idea of what the finish will be. You can provide them with that insider's knowledge that will turn their investment in business, and in you, into a winning stake.

SOURCE MATERIAL

Refer to Section 7.

No. 105

COMPUTER TAX SERVICE

1984 INCOME TAX

This service has been around in one form or another even before we began rendering unto Caesar his due. But never has it been so simple for a non-accountant type to get into the business. With only 15 weeks of work, plus our business plan and your computer, you can make a year's wages. This can be done in your home or your client's home. Some of our computer business owners even set up portable operations in their vans and travel from one location to another.

CONCEPT

You may be surprised to learn how many people either feel they are too busy to add up their receipts and fill in the tax forms, don't want to spend the time or money on software for their own computers, or are fearful of making a mistake on official-looking papers. For whatever reason, there are people who use a tax preparer, not because their tax return is complicated, but because they simply don't want to be bothered doing it themselves.

The concept of this business is to help bring order out of a jumble of tax forms and a shoebox full of receipts. Your client will watch in wonder as the financial events of the past year are magically converted into neat columns of numbers. A client will come to you with a chaos of papers and go away with a smile on his face, a signed return and, with any luck, the prospect of a refund.

What you are offering is relief from anxiety. By helping your clients organize and record their tax information, you may save the world a few cases of ulcers.

SKILLS YOU WILL REQUIRE

Extensive knowledge of tax laws is not required for this business.

There are computerized information services that you can tap into using your computer and the telephone lines if you wish to familarize yourself with general information. These services are like newsletters that publish the latest tax revisions.

Since the service you offer is really filling out the blank spaces on a tax form, it is not necessary or even legal to give tax advice. The skills you will require are those that have to do with the computer itself and are not difficult at all.

High-level math is not needed—just simple arithmetic. Your computer software will take care of the complex stuff.

INFORMATION REQUIRED

You can get free and low-cost taxpayer information publications from your local IRS office. These will inform and instruct you on how to fill out this year's forms. Familiarize yourself with the rules and regulations and you'll be on your way to making money with this business. Online information services or data bases are services you can subscribe to just as you subscribe to your favorite magazine. But instead of the magazine being delivered to your door, you get information through your computer. You hook your computer to a telephone line through a device called a modem, call up another computer possessing the information you seek, and it is displayed on your monitor and can be printed for future use. Sometimes when you buy a modem, there is a trial offer to subscribe to one of these services free of charge. This will give you a chance to see if you like it.

You can call up information pertaining to tax regulations, filling out forms, etc. This way, when you need help while preparing a client's tax form, you can simply get it right there at your computer.

OPERATING NAME

In the field of tax accounting and related businesses, using the name of the founder is the usual practice. Consider, for instance, Arthur Young or H & R Block. On your letterhead and business cards you can put "John Doe" and then add "and Associates," if you think that sounds more businesslike.

GETTING STARTED

No matter what kind of business you are thinking about starting, the very first thing you should do is sit down and make out a master plan. If you don't have a clear view of where you want to go, you'll probably end up nowhere. A master plan includes your ultimate goal and the route you propose to take to get there. Your goal should be written in concrete and your working plan in sand. It is like taking a long trip and finding road blocks. You don't change your destination, you just change your route. Treat your business like a business. No successful corporation would think of proceeding without having goals and plans written down, and neither should you.

Comb the software stores in your area for all the tax programs that will work on your computer. The time you spend choosing software wisely is time well spent, since your business revolves around the program you choose. It is comforting to know that new tax programs are coming out all the time. Some of the software even allows you to print out the information onto the tax forms themselves.

In selecting a software program, you need to ask yourself some questions about the type of business you want to create, such as:

Am I going to start by doing only very simple returns until I build my confidence?

Am I going to do both federal and state tax returns?

Am I going to include all schedules in my service?

Do I need depreciation capability?

Do I want to retain customer files from year to year and therefore encourage repeat business?

Do I want to buy a program designed for individual use or professional use?

Do I want a program that has a "what if" feature so that my client can see other possibilities before printing the return?

Tax programs run from $50 on up. The more expensive ones usually include the federal and state return ability. The less expensive ones may not include the state tax package. The state package can be bought separately.

Annual updates are important. Tax laws and forms change constantly and responsible software companies provide for this. The updates run between 25 percent and 50 percent of the original cost of the program.

Buying software is not the place to "save money." Select the software carefully. The more it fits your needs, the less hassle you will have with it and the more profit you can realize. Some software manufacturers have a demo system for you to try. Usually this demo is a previous year's package and sells for under $50. If this demo package is available for the program you are considering, the money would be well spent to give the program a try. Usually the price of this kit is deducted from the price of the full current system if you decide to buy it.

Plus, you can find out what software is available by reading magazines catering to your brand of computer. The ads are worth the price of the subscription. They will give you the names and addresses of manufacturers of software and services that could be useful to you. There may even be articles now and then that apply to your new business. The few hours a month spent looking through these publications can save you a lot of time in your business.

THE COMPETITION

Most of your competition is content to be passive about attracting customers. They advertise on television and in newspapers and wait for people to come to them. Since a tax preparing service involves very private financial affairs, potential customers may be turned off by this mass media approach. You can beat the competition by offering more personal contact. You do this by following the Marketing Methods included in this report.

POTENTIAL INCOME

Pricing your services is not difficult. Since you are in a competitive field, call around to others who are doing similar work and see what they charge.

It's important to know your cost of doing business. Go back to the master plan you made and begin adding the costs of everything on it.

1. Cost of equipment
2. Cost of advertising
3. Cost of telephone
4. Cost of postage
5. Cost of travel
6. Cost of software
7. Cost of publications
8. Cost of data bases
9. Cost of any materials used

Your business lasts for about three and a half months every year. Figure out what your time is worth during those months and add that to the above total. Add in a profit figure for the business. This money can be used to make the business grow.

Estimate the number of customers you can handle. You don't want to take on more customers than you can reasonably help. That will only breed dissatisfaction.

Divide the total of your costs and labor by the number of clients you plan to serve. How does that compare to the price other people are charging? The price should come out fairly low, since you won't have the same overhead and labor expenses they have. Any money left over is profit and can be used to update and expand your business.

In the end, what you can charge is a fraction of what the traffic will bear. If you are called upon to work odd hours or after the filing deadline, or if you offer some exclusive service, you can charge a premium. Most people are afraid to charge enough.

It is customary to pay for services at the time they are rendered. Big companies insist on it, and so should you. That's one reason they succeed. Make yours a cash-and-carry business. The cost of billing any other way is burdensome.

Since your business occurs during a few months, that leaves time for you to do what you want the rest of the year. The potential profit from this business is high.

MARKETING METHODS

Flyers describing your business can be mailed to homes in your area or you can pay to have them delivered and tucked in the door. This may sound like a very impersonal method, but it can be very effective if you do it repeatedly. This will keep your name in your potential customer's mind. If you have the capability to personalize the flyer, so much the better. There are mailing lists with names and addresses that you can buy or rent, and address books by area available at libraries. Don't expect too much from a single mail contact. Follow up with another mailing, or even better, a telephone call.

A sample flyer could read:

>Don't waste your valuable time preparing your own taxes!
>
>Our computerized tax service will prepare your federal and state forms at a low cost you won't believe.
>
>Not only are our methods completely accurate and reliable, but we can show you how to get a fatter refund based on this year's regulations.
>
>Call now for more information about our low-cost, up-to-date tax preparation service.

Anywhere you are allowed to place notices, post a flyer with a tear tab for your phone number. Put flyers on parked cars.

The thought of telephone calling may be a little scary to you. Read some of the source material on the subject. Treated like a business call, this can be your richest source of all, because of the personal touch.

And remember to give out your card at every opportunity. For instance, those boring parties someone drags you to can provide a wealth of contacts.

UNIQUE BUSINESS APPROACH

In your area there are some certified public accountants and bookkeepers who do not have a computer. Or they have more business than their computer can handle. Make a telephone call to the tax preparers in your area offering to handle their overflow work for less than they charge their client. They can give you the easier tax preparation jobs they have to do. You both make money on the deal.

LOCATION and MARKET BASE

You are not going to need to rent an office. The information you will need can be obtained at your client's home and the finished product delivered back to them. If you feel you need to have clients come to you, be sure to add the cost of business space to your cost of doing business.

A good location would be one that has a market base of 5,000 to 50,000 taxpayers. You can expand your market base simply by driving to other towns and cities outside of your area.

TO SUM UP

A tax service business can serve every taxpayer. And that's a massive market. Using a computer and good software, you can help people with a job that isn't actually hard but that most people dread.

This service is so flexible that you can take on as little of it or as much of it as you want. Once you get your feet wet, you will probably want to expand.

Not only will you be helping others, but the money you can make with this business will give you reason to shout the next time you fill out your own income tax returns.

SOURCE MATERIAL

See Section 7.

No. 106

TAX SERVICE RENTAL PLAN

Never has it been so easy to figure out how to do your taxes with the help of home computers. Here is a business plan that shows you how to set up a small space in a well-traveled area where, with 10 or 15 minutes of instruction, a person can sit down and fill out his or her tax return in complete privacy—and you collect while they're doing it. It will make you a lot of money with only 15 or so weeks of work a year.

CONCEPT

The concept of this business is to provide a fast, accurate way for people to prepare their own income tax returns in complete privacy. They don't have to reveal any of their personal financial information to anyone except the government.

In addition to providing the computer and the software, your job is to help your customers feel competent and comfortable using a computer. People who have never used a computer before often suffer from computer-phobia and need a patient, friendly person to hold their hand through their first computing experience.

SKILLS YOU WILL REQUIRE

You don't have to be a tax expert for this business, but you do need thorough knowledge of how your tax software package works, whether you create your own program or you buy your software off-the-shelf. You'll need a thorough knowledge of all the package ins and outs and what to do in special cases.

Equally important is the ability to explain how to use your system in simple, concise terms, since this is part of the service you offer your clients.

INFORMATION REQUIRED

There's nothing difficult about the mathematical part of completing tax returns—it's just simple arithmetic. The hard part is putting all the information in all the right places and understanding how all the separate special forms fit in. To complicate matters, tax returns change every year, so you really have to do your homework.

Of course, you can get reams of information on how to complete tax returns from the IRS or your state tax authority. Plus, there are a multitude of annually updated books explaining how to do taxes. You can read them also to become familiar with tax forms.

OPERATING NAME

Since this is a highly specialized business with a short season, your operating name must explain the service you're offering. "Quick 'n Easy Tax Service" or "Tax Service Computer Rental" will tell people instantly what your business is. Refer to Section 4 for more information about choosing a business name.

GETTING STARTED

A critical factor in starting this business is finding an appropriate location. You won't need large, lavish offices, but you will need a convenient location close to parking facilities or public transportation. In addition to the office itself, you'll also need to arrange for the necessary furnishings and utility service.

Once you've taken care of the mechanics of setting up the business, you need to arrange for appropriate marketing. See the Marketing Methods section for information about this.

Before opening your door to customers, you should also have a brief set of instructions for using the system printed. Remember that many of your customers may not know anything about computers. You'll need to spend 10 to 15 minutes with each customer explaining what to do, so the written instructions you prepare don't need to be exhaustive. Just include the most important points, to serve as a reminder. Also be sure to give each customer a copy to take home. This will help you market your service through word-of-mouth advertising.

THE COMPETITION

You probably won't have any competition from identical businesses, at least not during your first year. You also won't be competing against expert accountants who serve clients with really complex, difficult tax returns. Your most direct competition will be from companies that primarily cater to people with simple tax returns.

To compete effectively against these well-known, established companies, start by pricing your service competitively. To gain a competitive edge, stress the privacy and confidentiality of your service. And stress the ease of completing a tax return with your computer service. Take the mystery out of it. Plus, you can add that your service

COMPLETE BUSINESS VENTURE PLANS

will even produce the printed tax return. All your customer will have to do is mail it in.

POTENTIAL INCOME

There are two alternative approaches to establishing the price for your services in this business. You can charge a flat rate for each type of form that the customer completes, or you can charge for the time the computer is actually used. One company in a major city that rents computer time for do-it-yourself word processing charges $10 an hour for the first two hours, plus $6 an hour for additional time. Another company with a big city location charges as little as $4 an hour for use of its computers, with a minimum printing charge of $6.50. Since your service requires highly specialized software, and people probably will not need to use your system for several hours at a time, you could probably charge a higher hourly rate.

If you charge a flat rate for each form completed, check the rates charged by tax preparation services to establish a competitive price. Be sure to find out what they charge for each special form, in addition to the basic forms.

It's important to know your cost of doing business. Estimate what your expenses will be. These include:

1. Cost of equipment
2. Cost of advertising
3. Cost of telephone
4. Cost of postage
5. Cost of travel
6. Cost of software
7. Cost of publications
8. Cost of data bases
9. Cost of any materials used

Your business lasts for about three and a half months every year. Figure out what your time is worth during those months and add that to the above total. Plus, add in a profit figure for the business. This money can be used to make the business grow.

Estimate the number of customers you can handle. You don't want to take on more customers than you can reasonably help. That will only breed dissatisfaction.

Divide the total of your cost and labor by the number of clients you plan to serve. How does that compare to the price other people are charging? The price should come out fairly low, since you won't have the same overhead and labor expenses they have. Any money left over is profit and can be used to update and expand your business.

In the end, what you charge is a fraction of what the traffic will bear. If you are called upon to work odd hours or after the filing deadline or if you offer some exclusive service, you can charge a premium. Most people are afraid to charge enough.

It is customary to pay for services at the time they are rendered. Big companies insist on it, and so should you. That's one reason they succeed. Make yours a cash-and-carry business. The cost of billing any other way is burdensome. The potential profit from this business is high. Since your business comes for a few months, that leaves time for you to do what you want the rest of the year.

MARKETING METHODS

The most effective marketing method for this business is display advertising; you want HIGH visibility. In your ad, stress privacy, ease of use, and personal instruction. A sample ad might read:

DO-IT-YOURSELF COMPUTER TAX SERVICE PRIVACY – ACCURACY – SIMPLICITY

Dreading tax time again? Wishing you could have a computer take care of it all? You don't have to be a major business owner to have your tax return prepared with computer accuracy. You don't even have to own or know how to use a computer. In our office you can rent time on a computer, complete with expert software specifically designed to prepare income tax returns.

In just a few minutes we can show you all you need to know about using a computer in order to prepare your own computerized tax return. You can throw away your calculator. No more tedious adding and subtracting and no more errors. We offer fast, convenient, efficient service that will save you time and money. For more information, call now.

Of course, you'll also include your business name, address and phone number.

UNIQUE BUSINESS APPROACH

Now I'll let you in on a secret that can increase your business tenfold. The most important factor in this business is getting your name out there—letting people know about your service. One way to get the word out is to have flyers printed for distribution in banks, libraries, even shopping center parking lots.

On your flyers you can list the same instructions for the computer system that you'll give to customers when they come in. This will show people how really easy it is to use a computer. Plus, you can stress that the computer will print the actual tax forms they'll be mailing in. This is a technique that can't be beat for this service.

LOCATION and MARKET BASE

For this business you really need to be in a city to have enough potential customers for it to pay off. In order for this to be a profitable business, you need a market base in the range of at least 50,000 to 200,000.

TO SUM UP

This business offers the opportunity to earn a substantial amount of money in a few short weeks. After all, virtually everybody has to file a tax return, regardless of how much or how little they actually paid in taxes. Most people hate doing their taxes, so you'll be offering a valuable service. With this business you'll no longer dread tax time. You can take advantage of it and make it pay for you. What could be smarter?

SOURCE MATERIAL

Refer to Section 7.

No. 107

COMPUTER DATING SERVICE

A computer dating service matches single people with others who share the same interests. With millions of single people in the country today, this business is a sure moneymaker.

CONCEPT

Anyone who has been a part of the "singles" scene would agree that somewhere out there is a romantic match for them—the difficulty is in finding that special one. Most people either settle for less or give up altogether.

It doesn't have to be that way. With your help, thousands of people can find the partners that were meant for them. You can provide the service that will make many lives happier than they thought possible before learning of your service. In fact, in a very real way you are selling happiness. People will flock to your door if you are good at your job, and we will tell you how to be the best. The motivation you need will be a desire to help people realize their dreams.

This is a business that can easily be run part or full time using your home computer. Your financial investment to get started will be minimal, as you can do a large amount of the advertising work with your computer.

SKILLS YOU WILL REQUIRE

Your most valuable skill in this business will be an ability to relate to your customers and understand their frustrations. You will be an important contact to them. They will be looking for hope, and you can give it to them.

The organization of your system will be fairly simple. You will be collecting information by questionnaire, survey, etc., and then categorically looking for matches item by item. This is the kind of task your computer was made for. Your job will be to set up a data base which will contain information about each client. It is then a simple matter to have the computer find the perfect match. Although you can go to outside sources for your advertising, it is a simple matter to design and print very effective display ads and flyers on your computer. Don't worry if you feel you don't have artistic talent—there are terrific computer programs that will make the job easy.

INFORMATION REQUIRED

Formulating a questionnaire will require some research. Go to a library and check out a few books about compatibility. You will find the material you need in the psychology section. In addition, contact some of the other dating services in your area as though you were a potential client. Study the material they send you and look for ways to improve upon it.

Keep in mind that your customers will want to see their concerns reflected in the questionnaires they fill out. You must give them a sense of "somebody understands me" in your advertising and surveys. Ask your friends if they can offer suggestions on what they want to see when they're looking for a mate. You'll probably find the most honest, useful answers from those who are out there looking. You'll find the enthusiasm contagious as word gets out about your service, and you're bound to have customers waiting for you to open for business.

You'll also need to discover where the most effective places to advertise exist. Meeting places such as restaurants, bars, fitness centers, etc. are good places to start.

OPERATING NAME

Use a name that implies favorable results. "Cupid's Arrow" is a good example. There is little doubt about the nature of the business, and the imagery will appeal to the romantic nature of your clients. Remember, you will be trying to reach a fairly cynical bunch, so keep it light—any hint of desperation or self-consciousness will scare people away.

There is a unique kind of psychology going on here. Most people will be a little nervous about resorting to a dating service. The implication of using one is that they must be doing something wrong. It's up to you to transmit an easy-going but competent image and you can do this by choosing a light-hearted name. After all, your customers will be looking for someone to feel at ease with.

GETTING STARTED

As mentioned earlier, your first task will be to do some research. Formulate your questionnaire carefully, using up to 50 questions. Any more than this might discourage some potential customers. Make your questionnaire relate to everyday life—What styles of music do you like? Are you a homebody? Is your family important to you? Do you like to read, go to movies, sail, bowl, etc.? Is romantic love high on your list of priorities? Do you take an interest in social issues?

The best format for questionnaires is probably the "rate by scale" method. For example, on a scale of one to 10, how much do you enjoy parties? Make the questionnaire fun to complete, but also make sure the questions asked have real relevance to the goal—finding a mate.

After your surveys are printed and ready for distribution, put together a simple data base on the computer. It need only consist of name, address and phone number, along with blanks for input of questionnaire results. Upon receipt of results, simply enter each customer's information and then you're ready to match! You will be using the data base to supply output on which of the clients has the most similar answers to the client you are working with. This is a fast, simple task on the computer, and you'll be amazed at how well it works.

THE COMPETITION

With the millions of single people in America today, there should be plenty of business for everyone. However, we want your business to be number one in the field. The fact that you are able to run the entire business on your home computer allows you to undercut any other price. Also, you can do it better, and there will always be a market for quality.

Plan your advertising around this concept: the competition leaves something to be desired. Use statistics of successful matches you've arranged, and endorsements from satisfied customers. Make it clear that you know what it takes to satisfy clients—you ask the right questions and you understand their frustration with other dating services. Most companies will offer a certain number of matches for X amount of dollars—go one or two better, and offer more matches for less money.

POTENTIAL INCOME

Your pricing structure will be competitive, and at the beginning you will want to beat everybody else's price. This is a terrific strategy, because your customer base will climb rapidly. The general approach as far as cost to customers is to offer a few weeks or a month of unlimited access to your service. This gives clients a chance to date several people, and then continue the service for as long as they want, paying for each time period.

Your overhead will primarily be in advertising, and production of questionnaire forms. Once your customers start coming in, and after their information is in the computer, the cost of connecting one person with his or her match will not involve much more than a phone call. As your business becomes established, you can reasonably expect to make $300 to $500 a week.

To price your service, remember to estimate your business expenses. A list is supplied below. Plus, you must add in an amount for your time, and a profit for the business.

Service Costs:

1. Cost of advertising
2. Cost of time spent organizing questionnaire
3. Cost of reproducing questionnaire
4. Cost of mailing supplies
5. Cost of flyers
6. Cost of telephones
7. Cost of software
8. Cost of time spent making matches

MARKETING METHODS

Display ads will be the best way to reach your potential customers. Place them in entertainment sections of the new breed of city newspapers—the free arts and entertainment papers that can be picked up in most stores and meeting places, such as bars.

I'll give an example of an approach that can be effective in bringing in new business. Since you'll be using a computer in your business, why not use that as a marketing approach? For example:

> LET OUR COMPUTERS GET PERSONAL WITH YOU
>
> How often have you wished for help in finding Mr. or Ms. Perfect? If you're like the 10 million single people in this country, you know how hard it can be doing it on your own.
>
> We can help. We're CUPID'S ARROW and our vast data bank of eligible mates is at your service!

Show your potential customers an understanding of their situation, and show them that you can help. Let them know that you will give them fast results. Whenever possible, make flyers available in key locations.

This approach, showing that you understand and can help, will quickly build up a strong customer base.

As in any new business, try to open yours with a bang. Saturate your market areas with advertising and offer an introductory special, such as two months for the price of one.

UNIQUE BUSINESS APPROACH

The concept of computer dating is a new idea, so there are plenty of unique approaches available.

A great way to advertise your service is to emphasize that you are giving your customers first crack at the multitude of eligible people in the area. For every single person, there is a mate, and your vast selection virtually guarantees satisfaction.

Another effective idea is to hire a few people, male and female, for a couple days of work. Pick attractive representatives and station them in high-traffic areas on a weekend, handing out flyers for your business. The obvious implication is that attractive people are associated with your service. It's a simple idea, and it works!

You may even decide to have your assistants pass out the actual questionnaire a potential client would fill out. On one side of the sheet you can have the questionnaire. On the other side, you can place your advertisement, along with the company name, address, etc. This method will save the cost of having to produce your flyers and questionnaires on separate sheets of paper.

When your business expands, you might want to consider incorporating video equipment into your service. Make tapes of your customers and when you've found several matches for one of your clients, let him or her see the tapes. People love being able to see their match beforehand—it will add new excitement to your service.

LOCATION and MARKET BASE

Your strongest location will be in an urban area. The social scene will be most active there, so you'll have plenty of prime places to advertise. Another obvious advantage is the larger number of people in a city. Of course, your business will have no trouble surviving with a market base of as little as 5,000.

TO SUM UP

The 1980's are an ideal time to begin the dating service we've discussed. Millions of single people are looking for some guidance in the frustrating task of finding a mate, or just somebody to spend time with socially.

The single person of today has a higher per capita income than ever before and spends more on entertainment than ever before. With the methods we've suggested you can help make their lives more satisfying. With a little time and effort you can make this business satisfying to you as well—in dollars, that is.

SOURCE MATERIAL

Refer to Section 7.

No. 108

MULTI-LEVEL COMPUTER SALES

Multi-level selling is going big again, and a couple of companies in Texas are combining computers with this unique marketing technique and are reportedly moving over 5,000 computers per week. With this computer business plan you can break into the market in small way and let it grow at whatever rate you want it to. Complete instructions are included in this report, so get in while this concept is still hot.

CONCEPT

Do you know a few people who would be interested in making a couple hundred dollars a month extra? Do those people know three or four more in the same situation? If the answer is yes, you already have the basis for unlimited financial success.

Multi-level marketing is being used by highly successful entrepreneurs in direct sales for everything from diet herbs to crystal. Multi-level marketing is primarily a sales method in which people sell products to other people who, in turn, sell them to others, and so on. Each sale generates income for each seller in the line. Now this method is currently being applied by selling one of the hottest items of this century: computers.

Without having to sell a large volume of computers yourself—in fact, without having to sell anything at all—you can recruit an infinite number of people to generate sales, and recruit more distributors to provide you with income.

The major concept of this business is to recruit other sales personnel. When you do that, you will be able to earn a percentage of their sales, and of the sales from the people they recruit, and so on. As the owner and founder of your business, you will receive a percentage of every sale made by anyone in your company.

SKILLS YOU WILL REQUIRE

This business can be very lucrative for those who can learn how to recruit, train, motivate and control others. It is not necessary to go into this business with these skills. However, you must be willing and able to learn them if you are to make a true success of this business.

The major skill that is really required for this business (and one that can't be taught) is enthusiasm—the idea that you can do it, and so can everyone else in your organization.

Inspiration is as important as perspiration in this business. It is also imperative that you know how to locate, select, recruit and train effective salespeople. Recruitment techniques must be mastered so you can effectively choose those who will do a good job in sales and recruitment

INFORMATION REQUIRED

In most cases, it isn't important in this business to carry around large amounts of information in your head. It is important, however, that you know how to find the answers to your client's questions.

What you will have to know are basics, such as the type of operating system the computer uses and the amount of memory it has, information you will already know just from using your product.

What will probably be much more important is that you can explain the sales plan to your recruits and be able to answer the technical questions about that.

GETTING STARTED

Setting up the basic structure of the company is relatively simple.

To start, you will need to determine what computer equipment you want to market. Don't waste time dealing with the products already sold by hundreds of stores; search out the lesser-known, quality brands that aren't carried in most stores.

Read computer magazines, study their ads, send off for brochures and catalogs, then choose the products you feel have the most potential for this type of marketing.

Contact the companies and discuss with them how you can become one of their main distributors. Once you have shown them your marketing techniques, they'll probably be as enthusiastic as you are about this opportunity.

Then you are ready to start setting up your sales teams. A very successful approach to recruiting first-level sales people is to hold what is called "opportunity meetings." Your contacts with potential distributors are made before the meeting. (Remember those few friends who want to make some extra money?) Simply ask them to come to a meeting. You can reach others by asking your friends to bring another person, or by advertising.

You should never downplay the potential your company has when you recruit people. You must stress what a fantastic business opportunity awaits the potential sales person. However, don't do much more than that. Release a minimum of information before the meeting. It is curiosity that gets people to the meeting.

Selling your company to these people once the meeting is in progress should be relatively easy. The real potential for financial independence, freedom, flexibility and unlimited earnings in multi-level marketing is difficult for anyone to turn his back on.

To actually start the meeting, you might ask the prospects if they have all the money they will ever want or need. An alternative is to have them write down on paper how much they dream about being able to earn. Then ask if they have a few hours a week or month to trade for limitless wealth — far more than they wrote down, far more than they are willing to believe right now at this moment. This is an extremely good approach for upwardly mobile audiences.

A quieter approach is to stress that the business is a wonderful tax shelter. The small independent business is one of the few viable shelters available to middle-class salaried families who need it desperately. After all, how else can their pencils and even vacations become tax-deductible?

At the opportunity meeting describe the plan in detail.

As an independent contractor the salesperson buys computers from you at a price discounted from the company's list price. A first- level distributor resells computers to his own salespeople at a slightly higher price. Therefore, the distributor realizes income from both his own sales and from the sales generated by the people he has recruited. As each recruit sponsors other salespeople, the person at the top and the sales reps in between all receive bonuses from the sales of the various levels under them. Typically, the first-level distributor gets 30 to 40 percent off the retail price. This ranges to 10 percent for the lowest level of recruit.

The most successful programs of the multi-national, multi-level sales organizations are limited to a four-tier pyramid-marketing structure, with the opportunity for every salesperson to move up to become a distributor, or first-level salesperson, himself.

If you choose to use this four-level pyramid, a second-level salesperson moves up to distributorship (first level) when he has three levels below him, and so on. This encourages active recruitment and allows for reasonable profit margins for you and your sales reps.

In addition to straight commission on sales, most companies based on this system offer extravagant gifts, automobiles, diamonds, exotic vacations, fur and cash. The incentive for your salespeople to perform is high, but well-paid-for through their own efforts. Don't let the costs of these bonus programs frighten you. The exotic trips are paid for long before they are ever earned.

Both tangible and intangible incentives for becoming a distributor should be pre-sented at the opportunity meeting, both visually and verbally. If you choose to have a bonus program, the rewards should be graphically displayed, even if the diamond ring is only glass and the Cadillac a photo.

When the prospective sales rep puts down money for the "sales kit," or in another way commits himself to your program, he receives several hours of training on the products. You should also have copies of computer and sales manuals for them as part of their sales kits.

Training on the use of the equipment is important, since the sales people, to be most effective to themselves and you, will have to be able to not only answer the end-client's questions, but be able to train the buyer in the use of the computer.

THE COMPETITION

This business has only been tried by a few, but they are doing very well with it. There are "home party" plans and door-to-door sales. "Home computer parties" are the next big leap in the marketing of computer equipment.

POTENTIAL INCOME

One of the most amazing aspects of this sales system is that there really is virtually no limit to your profit potential. Your income is in direct relationship to the amount of work you put into your organization.

This business is considered to be one of the few that are "recession-proof." If the economy is bad, people begin to look for new ways to make money. That is the time you get your best potential recruits. They, in turn, can often sell the computers to others who are also looking for new ways to earn money.

You make your money in this business by selling computer equipment and taking a cut, and by selling recruits "sales kits" that possess all the samples, brochures, selling techniques, etc. that they need for their end of the business.

Expenses for this business vary depending on how much time and money you spend putting the program together. One expense you'll incur is producing a quality-looking catalog of the products you distribute. This catalog is used by the salespeople, as well as handed out to the customers that want to purchase the products. The manufacturers that supply your inventory may offer to create your catalog of products for you.

MARKETING METHODS

Distributors can hold meetings anywhere. Let them sell them as fund raisers for their churches, in their own or others' homes, or door-to-door. Encourage them to use their imagination. The idea is that anyone, even first-time salespeople, can become computer sales reps and be comfortable and successful doing it.

One very shy woman earned $75,000 last year selling Mary Kay cosmetics at church bazaars. She set up a booth and donated a percentage of her profit to the church. When people approached her in such a "safe" setting, she was not only comfortable selling—she enjoyed it. After all, she was helping support a church. Another successful distributor of cleaning products makes over $100,000 a year just by spending one day a week at a local swap meet.

UNIQUE BUSINESS APPROACH

To be really successful in this business, you will want to carve out a niche for yourself. That is, approach a market that is either under-utilized or ignored by the large computer retailers.

For example, you may wish to concentrate on women, both as salespeople and customers. After all, women make 85 percent of all purchases. Few stores concentrate their energies on female customers, yet women certainly have the money to make expensive purchases.

You may want to concentrate on certain ethnic, minority or professional groups, such as teachers or doctors. Marketing studies show that ethnic minorities buy more educational toys, magazines and books and watch more educational TV than any other group. This means that a concentrated effort at targeting them for computer sales has the potential of doing very well.

It's a good idea to recruit salespeople from inside the ranks of your target group. They understand the needs of the group and already have a "foot in the door." You will find a ready supply of salespeople in almost any group, no matter how fancy they may seem. The American Medical Association regularly carries "second income" and potential small-business articles in their publications. Teachers are being told every day that computer literacy for their students, and for themselves, will be imperative in the years ahead.

Whatever group or approach you choose, remember two guiding rules: (1) Get your salespeople to give "hands on" demonstrations. Psychologists tell us that possession, no matter how brief or fragile, signals ownership. (2) Computers, for all their high price tags, are primarily an impulse item. That's why computer fairs, party plans and similar marketing schemes are so successful in selling computers.

LOCATION and MARKET BASE

People are looking for opportunity, whether in a large town or in a small one. However, if you are planning to keep your executive duties home-based, it's easiest to maintain a living with this type of business in a city. If you are simply looking for a little exta income, a small town may very well do to get started.

Remember that you will reach a saturation point of sales in a small town, while a large city not only offers a larger customer base, but also a changing population. Therefore, you will always have new opportunities for sales and the saturation point may never be reached.

TO SUM UP

If you are a good leader and can recruit, train and inspire others, you are on your way to the top. In addition, if you can identify and work with a viable target group of customers, you and your company can reach heights you may never have dreamed possible.

There is little competition in the independent computer sales field, and virtually no one has developed a successful multi-level sales force in this area. The market is just beginning to open up. We aren't close to saturation point, even in small towns. There are plenty of full and part-time salespeople available to you if you look for them. In other words, the product, market and people to make your business work are there waiting. You are the catalyst. Only you can make it happen. The world is ready to pay for that little bit of magic you can provide, and it is willing to pay dearly.

SOURCE MATERIAL

For source material, refer to Section 7.

No. 109

SELL COMPUTERIZED SALES LEADS

A computerized sales leads business involves accumulating lists of people who have value as potential customers for business. All you have to do is collect and market these lists to the appropriate businesses and collect a nice chunk of money for your time.

CONCEPT

Ask businesspeople what one of their greatest frustrations is and they'll tell you that they wish they had the information needed to develop their market more thoroughly. Whether they are merchants, insurance agents or corporate presidents, they know that there is a tremendous untapped market for their products. Why don't they approach this market? Because they don't have the time or resources to do the research—research that involves pinpointing possible customers.

Your sales lead business can find this market for them. With your computer, you can put together a potential customer list of people who will, for example, be interested in buying household appliances. Such a list could be generated from marriage announcements in recent newspapers. Newlyweds need new appliances. This is just one example of a source for your sales leads. The important point is that these lists are invaluable to the right business. They represent very strong sales leads or likely customers for the products and services they supply.

SKILLS YOU WILL REQUIRE

Accumulating sales prospects will be a matter of locating people with something in common. Therefore, you'll have to know where to look.

Readers of computer magazines, for instance, will be an ideal market for someone selling computer supplies. Magazines will sell or rent you lists of their subscribers. This is a source of extra money for them and you can compile a list of thousands of possible buyers to sell to computer-supply companies. Likewise, you can check the local and regional wedding announcements and compile a list to be sold to furniture dealers. The only limit to the sources of your list-gathering is your imagination. Finding a market for your sales leads won't be difficult either. Simply contact the marketing department, if the company has one. Or just walk in the door of the business and pitch your product. Offering to conduct a test of your effectiveness at no cost to the buyer is a super way to attract clients.

The skill you'll find most useful here is your ability to come up with lists that people want. Lists that go into detail, stating such things as income, sports interests, marital status and other information, are valuable finds for the sales lead business. One method of putting together lists involves the cross-checking of names. You may see one name on seven lists. By putting all the information together you will have a customer profile that is a head above the others. The more information you can gather, the better. Companies will pay top dollar for these carefully researched lists.

INFORMATION REQUIRED

This business is based on names, so names are the primary information you'll need. Magazine subscriber lists, club membership rosters, newspapers, professional organizations, sporting associations, auto clubs and a multitude of other groups will all be sources for your lists.

Keep a data base on your computer that keeps track of your sources for names— organization names, contacts and prices. Then you can regularly keep in touch with them and provide your customers with a steady, updated supply of leads. Knowing what kind of customer a company wants will help too. Sure, a computer company can use lists of computer owners as potential customers. But those companies selling expensive products, like hard disk drives and state-of-the-art equipment, will want their leads to be above a certain income level. This information is not difficult to find. You've probably answered some magazine surveys yourself that asked questions about income. These surveys are used to compile lists about that magazine's readership. And these lists are the same ones you'll rent or buy to sell to your customers.

Learn how to make use of the telecommunications capability of your computer. Using your modem, you'll be able to receive and send information at a rapid pace, and you'll find that this gives you the fast response time most people associate with the biggest companies. Your creative use of the information channels will give you an advantage and professionalism that will enhance your credibility with your clients.

OPERATING NAME

In this kind of business it might be to your advantage to use your own name. There's a certain integrity to the sound of "Robert Smith Research Associates." Plus, you'll be able to use all the phones, bank accounts and other such items already in your own name.

GETTING STARTED

The first step is to contact all the sources you can. Go to the library and get the addresses of magazines that cater to the various markets you want to begin with. Mail out letters requesting information on available subscriber lists and prices. This might take awhile; in the meantime contact clubs, associations and other groups and ask if their membership rosters are available.

As you begin to gather this information, enter it into your "source" data base and begin your purchase of the lists. In the design of your second data base, the sales lead base, allow for qualifying categories, such as income, interests, occupation, etc. Try to think of any key interest that will be a selling point for your clients.

When you're up to speed and ready to make your pitch, the marketing of your service begins. Flood the business community with notice of your arrival. As in all other new businesses, let people know who you are. It's possible to cover the market with direct mail, telephone sales and display ads for a reasonable price. More on this in the Marketing Methods section.

THE COMPETITION

As you start out, expect to have to put your time in for free. Don't worry. This will soon pay off, because you will be able to offer your customers service at a level that the competition cannot beat. Once your customers realize the value of your service, they will stick with you.

Another sure-fire way to beat the competition is to approach markets that they might not have considered—some of the smaller businesses, for example, that have been disregarded by the big companies. With your help, though, what once was a small business can grow quickly, and your service can be a big part of that growth. Your reputation will also be invaluably boosted. After all, one of these small companies may soon grow enough to make you their marketing advisor! Even more important, they will tell others about your service and your business will grow by word-of-mouth.

POTENTIAL INCOME

In this business you will find that you may soon have to narrow your leads down to one specific area because of high demand. Remember that you are offering your customers something that is as good as gold. So expect success dreams to become a reality. As a one-person operation, you may expect to make $300 to $500 a week, and when the time comes to expand, the sky is the limit.

To estimate a price for your service, calculate the costs. Some of these are listed below. Add in a salary for your time and a profit for your business and you're on your way!

Potential Costs:

1. Cost of advertising
2. Cost of buying and renting lists
3. Cost of time spent organizing results
4. Cost of materials used
5. Cost of printing sales leads
6. Cost of data base software

You may find that you'll want to charge your clients by the number of leads you provide. Or you might decide to charge them a flat rate each week or month for your service. This will depend on how much business they are willing to give you. If they will be a steady customer for the coming year, you may choose to give them a break on your rates, by supplying a steady list of leads but billing the same amount each week, no matter how many leads you supply. The choice is up to you. With experience you'll discover the method that best suits your business.

MARKETING METHODS

Direct mail, display ads and telephone sales are the best approaches for your sales lead business.

Direct mail is a powerful tool here. Target your potential clients and offer to show them how you can increase their profits and customer base. Endorsements from satisfied customers are very useful here. It won't take you long to receive positive feedback, so use it to gain greater credibility. Walk into as many companies as you can and let them know that you have thousands of strong leads. Let them know that your supply is limitless. Offer a price break to get in the door. Once you've proven yourself, you'll have a long-term relationship with that company.

In your direct mail approach, try this:

> Are you getting all the business you can handle? If so, congratulations! Throw this away.
>
> If not, why not? Successful business must depend on a constant flow of new customers. We can offer you the carefully qualified leads you need for that new business. Our meticulous research has resulted in the discovery of a large number of potential customers for you—people who fit the profile of the ABC Company market. Give us a few minutes of your time and we'll prove we can increase your business.

UNIQUE BUSINESS APPROACH

Here's a technique that has worked for others and is sure to work for you as well. One of the best ways to prove the effectiveness of your service is to bring business to a company you would like to have as an account.

Upon agreement with a particular business, offer to send, at your own expense, direct mail to some potential customers from the same list of leads you are selling. In your direct mail, ask the customer to mention your firm's name when they deal with the company. This approach will be proof to your potential client that your service is effective. Your willingness to bring him business at your expense will be an example of your commitment to satisfying him. Another method is to offer a week's worth of leads for absolutely nothing. Once your potential client is convinced of its effectiveness, he'll come back to you regularly.

LOCATION and MARKET BASE

This business can be successful anywhere. Much of your work can be done by mail, computer and modem, so you really are not limited to any particular area. On a part-time basis, you'll find that a market base as small as 5,000 will keep you busy. Keeping it as a home-based business, you will find things get hectic when your market pushes the 200,000 level.

TO SUM UP

Information is a premium commodity today. Sales leads are as good as money to any business, and there are still many companies which do not understand and know how to thoroughly exploit their target markets.

In a business like this, you immediately become an invaluable addition to any company you work with. You'll find little competition when you work with the small businesses that the others ignore. Expansion can be inevitable and long-term success a realistic goal. So get started today and "lead" your way to the top!

SOURCE MATERIAL

Refer to Section 7.

No. 110

TYPING
BROKER

A typing broker offers a customer the fastest possible service for customized typing and word processing jobs. You've probably noticed that there seems to be a multitude of secretarial services in your area. That means there are a lot of potential clients for a service like this, and this is could mean money in the pocket for you. Yet you don't have to type a word. You simply act as a broker for typing jobs and get a cut of the profits.

CONCEPT

In this age of information, it seems everyone must have an edge when it comes to written communication. Work performance, school performance and advertising, just to name a few, are dependent to a great extent on the quality and presentation of the work. The typing broker provides benefits to all those involved. Customers get exactly what they need with the fastest possible turnaround, the workers get the business, free of any scheduling mix-ups, and you reap the profits by supplying a much-needed service.

You will be offering your clients a chance to present their work in a polished, professional manner. That might be just the edge they need to be accepted into the college or grad school of their choice. To your business clients, you will be offering an advantage over a competitor whose presentation is not quite as polished or timely. This means more business for your client.

SKILLS YOU WILL REQUIRE

You will neither have to know how to type quickly nor be an expert on the various typing formats. You leave that up to your experts—the workers. Your job will be to bring clients and typists together. There will be an ample supply of both if you understand how to find your market, which in this business is primarily the academic and business communities.

You can find typists by simply looking on bulletin boards in student unions and dormitories and in campus and local newspapers. You'll quickly discover that your typists will heave a sigh of relief when they discover that they can leave the advertising and scheduling up to someone else.

Your data base and time management programs will make the necessary organization painless. Your business will thrive as long as your service is prompt and professional.

INFORMATION REQUIRED

The primary information you will need will be a list of qualified typists and their specialties—whether their strength is in academic formats, business letters, resumes or whatever.

This is where your computer will become really useful. Setting up a simple data base containing typists, names, their specialities, their schedule preferences and their turnaround time will allow you to instantly give a prospective client a proposed completion time. Time will be of the essence to your customers. It's your fast service that will sell your business. Students are always on a deadline and business clients turn to the service that gives fast, accurate results.

This brings up another point. Know what your customer wants. In this case, speed and accuracy are the key. Some of the smaller details are very important. Make sure you know, for instance, what sort of paper your client requires, and whether or not they need the work submitted in a folder. The basic questions you'll want answered are: "When do you need it?" and "How do you want it done?." Don't make assumptions about a client's requirements. If there are any questions, ask.

Know where to find your business. Again, go to local colleges and universities, advertise on bulletin boards and in school papers. Soon, word will get out about your service, and word-of-mouth advertising will be the source of much of your business. The business community will also benefit from your service, so go to them. Lawyers, doctors, and any number of professionals need typing services.

OPERATING NAME

The name of your business in this case should be something catchy. People must see immediately that yours is not a simple typing advertisement. Even something such as "THE TYPING BROKER" is an eye-catcher and will bring people to you. Once you've got their attention, your unique service will sell itself. Refer to Section 4 for more information about choosing an operating name.

GETTING STARTED

As stated earlier, first find your typists and propose your idea. Sell them on the advantage of using your service, i.e., no worries about missed phone calls, getting overbooked and letting quality slip, etc. Enlist as many typists as possible who have access to word processors. Your clients will often demand the multiple "originals" and speed that only a word processor can offer. You will have some customers who want to do mass mailings, so you should be able to make arrangements with your workers to offer that option. Ask your typists about their specialties and look at samples of their work. It's important to be extremely quality-conscious. The future of your business depends on your early work. A real source of typists can also be found in the yellow pages of the phone book for your area. Part-time secretaries will also want to come on board, since it will mean their advertising overhead can be reduced.

Arrange a wide variety of specialties and schedules, including back-up typists in case of emergencies, and set up a simple data base on your computer. The design should not take more than a couple of hours. A scheduling/time management program is also necessary — there are very good ones for under $100. Make sure you have typists who can work on the weekends. You'll need to offer that kind of service.

Find your market. Advertise in college papers, bulletin boards, etc. Your overhead here will be inexpensive. Put advertisements in the business section of local newspapers and in the yellow pages. Have flyers available on college campuses.

When the first call comes, be up to speed and ready to go. You'll find your scheduling software will be invaluable, so be sure to keep it up-to-date.

THE COMPETITION

There are some terrific advantages to having a new business. The primary advantage comes in the first rush of advertising. Make people notice you and impress them with your aggressive, fresh approach. Make the competition's approach look like something that needs improvement. Study their advertisements and incorporate some of the best concepts into your own unique approach.

POTENTIAL INCOME

Typing services tradionally charge a "rate per page" cost, and to be competitive you should stick to these guidelines. The best bet here is to call some similar businesses you find in the newspaper and ask questions as though you were a potential customer.

Make arrangements to pay your workers on an hourly rate. The steady business they receive will at least equal the income they received when they were on their own, but now they have steadier work with less hassle. You'll find that the difference between the per-page rate you're charging and the hourly wage you pay your workers will result in a comfortable margin that will allow you to cover your overhead and advertising costs and recoup your start-up costs.

Basic Costs

1. Cost of hourly wages to workers
2. Cost of advertising
3. Cost of software used
4. Cost of telephone and postage
5. Cost of paper supplies, ribbons, etc.
6. Cost of time spent organizing workers

When calculating what to charge, estimate your expenses, then add in a profit figure. This profit isn't the same as what you make for your time. It is the money your business makes, enabling it to grow.

Once the business gains momentum, you can easily start earning $300 or more a week, depending on how much time and energy you put into your efforts.

MARKETING METHODS

Direct mail, display ads, telephone sales and direct sales are the best methods for marketing your typing broker service. Display ads in yellow pages, newspapers and bulletin boards will be strong sellers for your service. Since the common element in all of your customers' projects will be time, emphasize it! Here's an example of a display ad built around the need for fast service:

YOUR TIME IS UP!

How often have these words sent a chill down your spine? If you have one day to finish putting together your research paper, and all the typing services are overbooked by others in the same boat, WE CAN HELP! We're the TYPING BROKERS and there is no job we can't complete to your satisfaction. We can GIVE YOU THE TIME YOU NEED! Call us now!

Take the same approach in ads for other markets, but tailor the situation to the market, i.e. missed deadlines for business contracts, etc.

Telephone sales and mailings to businesses should also emphasize the time and professionalism of your service. Pinpoint smaller businesses where the cost of hiring full-time secretarial help may be prohibitive. Suggest to these businesses that you can take the pressure off their office workers and give them the time they need to tend to business. In conjunction with your service you can offer a mass-mailing option. Sales letters can be contracted to your firm—typed and mailed.

UNIQUE BUSINESS APPROACH

An introductory offer is an excellent idea for any new business, including this one. Give the customer two pages free, or discount the price for high volume. A sure way to make your commitment clear is to offer a guarantee of completion by or earlier than the due date. Seek endorsements from satisfied customers. Remember, put a lot of effort into the first advertising campaign. You are different than the others; you are the best!

A very catchy idea is to include some statistics in your ad copy. For instance, poll some businesses and colleges. Ask them how the quality of a presentation affects their impression of written work. I'll guarantee they will agree that presentation is important. Use these responses and include some names of colleges and companies who agree with this opinion. Then make your pitch for being able to offer this quality, on time and for a low cost.

LOCATION and MARKET BASE

This is a business that is best suited to a city or college town or ideally, to both. In a city with a medium to large college population you will always find enough customers to keep you as busy as you want to be. Your market, depending on the area, can be productive in a college town of only 50,000. If your city is even larger, great! Business will boom.

TO SUM UP

There is always demand for accurate, fast typing and word processing services. Quality work will never be without a market. The modest investment of capital necessary makes this an ideal opportunity for anyone—either as a part time effort for extra money, or as a full-time investment in a large business. You will have no difficulty in finding typists, nor will your high quality of work go unnoticed. The business is yours to expand as you feel your time and interest allows. Then all you have to do is sit back and watch the dollars flow in.

SOURCE MATERIAL

Refer to Section 7.

No. 111

COMPUTERIZED FORMULA MIX SERVICE

Ever wonder what perfume, soaps, face cream, plant food, etc. were made from? With this business, not only will you know what they are made from, but how much it takes and where to buy it. You can supply complete formulas in any quantity to your clients, and for pennies on the dollar they can produce almost any kind of product they normally buy at the store. There's no end to the number of items you will be able to supply formulas for.

CONCEPT

The concept of this business is to compile formulas for making various products and to sell them to others. You get your formulas out of books that are already on the market, then compile them with the use of your home computer. With a printer you print out the formulas a customer wants.

SKILLS YOU WILL REQUIRE

You don't need to be a chemical engineer to get this business off the ground. All it will require is a little research and organization on your part.

Other than that, you need want to know how to use your computer to sort information. For example, say you have in your computer four formulas to make shampoo. If somebody comes to you wanting a shampoo that doesn't contain a particular ingredient because they are allergic to it, you should be able to call up the shampoo formula that doesn't contain that ingredient.

You can perform this function using something called a data base. The purpose of a data base program is to allow you to file information in a variety of ways without having to input it for each way you want it filed. By using a data base, you can look up any ingredient that might be used and the computer will sort through and supply you with all the formulas that use that ingredient. Likewise, you can use a data base to search for replacements of ingredients. In the example of the shampoo, you may be able to come up with a formula that does the same job with ingredients that will replace the ones in the formula you already have.

INFORMATION REQUIRED

The information required for this business comes primarily from what are called "formulary books." These are volumes that contain lists of ingredients for a particular substance and the amount of each ingredient required. For example, one formula may call for "1 part water, 3 parts sodium tallowate, 1 part chloride and 1 part disodium phosphate." Sound foreign? Only until you've done a little research to learn what these ingredients are—in this case, what goes into making a bar of soap. Although the words used in formula books may sound foreign, they are ingredients that can be purchased from chemical companies and are found in drugstores and health stores.

This business will require that you do a little reading in these formula books to get an idea of how a formula is presented. Then you'll need to do a little library research to locate books that can explain to you what these foreign-sounding ingredients actually are.

Since formula books contain hundreds of various formulas, you may decide you want to become an expert in a particular kind, such as cleaning products, hair care products or skin products. This will turn you into an specialist in your field and heighten the image you create as a formula expert.

Once you have chosen a particular specialty, you can start inputting the data into your computer. The data will consist of the formula ingredients and their measurements. You should set up a method with your computer that allows you to convert the amounts of ingredients into the quantity your customer desires. For example, if somebody comes to you wanting to make up 50 gallons of cleaning material, he will need to know how many gallons of each ingredient will be required. Yet you should also be able to convert the ingredients into the proper numbers for somebody wanting only a single gallon. In other words, you want to be able to convert the amounts of each ingredient into the amounts required for a particular quantity of formula. Many cookbooks do this for recipes by stating that if you want to make four servings rather than the 10 servings the recipe creates, you simply decrease the amounts by three fifths.

You will also want to input information about the resources for getting various ingredients. Your research should lead you to companies that supply chemicals or other ingredients, and you can add their names and addresses into your data base as well. Then when you supply a formula for a customer, you can also provide a list of places for purchasing the ingredients needed.

GETTING STARTED

Getting started in this business is a matter, first, of inputting into your computer the formulas and information you will sell. Once you have that, you are ready to start marketing yourself. You can get ideas for this from the Marketing Methods section.

Then you will have to decide how you want to present your material. Do you want to let customers come to you for any kind of formula they desire? Would you prefer putting together formula guides for particular kinds of products? Or do you want to have a customer come to you with a formula need, then let you do the research for him?

The choice is up to you, but probably you will increase the success of your business by offering a combination of services. You can put out a guide to formulas and also solicit business for formulas themselves as the customer requires them.

Either way you handle it, you will need to prepare a brochure or catalog of the formulas you intend to handle. If you want to concentrate on the consumer market, you'll want to offer formulas for home products, cleaning, personal grooming, etc. If you decide to tackle the business world, you'll want to emphasize your cleaning products and others used in the shop or lab.

In the brochure or catalog, you can give a sample listing of the kinds of formulas you possess and let the reader know that you can supply resources for obtaining the ingredients. You may also consider including your prices. Another technique you may want to try is to list several formulas you possess, along with the prices for putting the substance together. Then you can compare this price with the price it would cost if the customer were to buy a ready-made substances that does the same job. This is a dramatic way to prove how valuable your service is.

THE COMPETITION

This is a business that nobody has tried before, except on a very small scale. Usually these operations will advertise the select few formulas they have in small ads in the back of general-interest publications. And usually the operation is limited and the formulas of very narrow interest.

You can set your own business up to offer several formulas for the same type of product. That way you increase your potential market base. If there is some ingredient a potential customer wants to avoid, either because of allergy, health, etc., you give him the option of using your service because you will supply a formula that doesn't contain that ingredient. If you give the customer a bigger choice selection, you increase your chances of gaining new business.

Your other competition is the large corporations that pre-package their substances—in other words, the off-the-shelf brands. You eliminate this competition by saving people money. You simply prove to them how they can save dollars by making these products up themselves, and they will be interested. The only thing they won't be paying for is the fancy labeling and advertising campaigns.

POTENTIAL INCOME

The income you can make with this business is rated in the medium level. You have several ways to make money here. They include: selling formula guides to people through the mail, and taking orders for special formulas by putting out a catalog of what you have available. If you put out a guide, you can sell it for $10, or whatever you determine. Part of your earnings will depend on how many guides you sell. If you sell 1,000 of them in the coming year, that is $10,000 for your business. You can update your guide once a year to get repeat business from the same customer base. If you decide to put out a catalog of available formulas, you can sell each for $2 or so and sell potentially thousands of them. At that price, a customer would be hard put not to want to order one. If satisfied, the same customer may come back to you for more, in which case you can get $20 or $30 from an order for 10 formulas.

To price your product, you will first want to estimate what your expenses for doing business will be. This should include money for your time in the form of salary, as well as profit for the business.

Basic Costs

1. Cost of data base software
2. Cost of advertising
3. Cost of time spent researching formulas
4. Cost of time spent inputting and organizing material
5. Cost of time spent creating guide or catalog
6. Cost to print guide or catalog
7. Cost of postage and other mailing costs
8. Cost of research materials
9. Cost of other materials used

Once you have an idea of what your expenses are, including the profit figure, you can determine how many catalogs or guides you want to print up, and base your prices accordingly. You may find you can afford to charge less than $10 for your guide and still make a handsome profit. A little experience will tell you what you need to charge for the number of orders you expect to gain. You may find that if you reduce the number of guides you produce, you can still make your profit goal by increasing the price. Either way, this opportunity is open to making a full-time income with only part-time effort.

MARKETING METHODS

The best ways to market this business are with direct mail, display ads and telephone sales.

You can send your direct mail letters to people you feel would most want to know about your service. To establish this, determine whether you want to concentrate on consumers or businesses. For consumers, you can rent or buy lists of names and addresses from mailing list companies. The kinds of lists you'll want to obtain will contain the names of people who like to do things for themselves. These include readers of self-sufficiency publications, how-to guides, home craft magazines, etc. For the business trade, you'll want to send letters to the companies in your area that can use your service. These include automotive centers, electronic firms, janitorial services, restaurants, hotels and motels, and any other type of business that has need for cleaning and workplace formulas.

You can also use telephone sales to reach this last type of customer base. Simply contact potential customers and explain to them how you can save them the thousands of dollars a year they spend on products that you can show them how to create themselves. If they express interest, send them a catalog of your available formulas, or inquire what types of formulas they might need for their particular line. Tell them that you will do the research to obtain these formulas for them. If you are successful, only then will you determine a price for the time you spent. If it is a formula you haven't added to your collection yet, you can call businesses similar to the one that ordered it and market to them as well.

Display ads will work well in the same kinds of publications that have a readership you can try to reach with direct mail. For example, if you want to concentrate on the consumer market, publications geared for self-sufficiency, home crafts and how-to's will be a good place to advertise your service.

A typical display ad could read:

> SAVE MONEY BY MAKING IT YOURSELF!
>
> Our catalog lists dozens of formulas you can buy to create household products. We will show you what the product requires, where to obtain the ingredients and how to do the mixing. Make your own cleaning supplies and grooming products and save money today!
>
> Send for our free catalog now!

Include a coupon with your address on it, as well as a place for the customer to write his own address, and when the inquiries start pouring in, respond promptly.

You can also use this technique to reach the business client simply by running your display ad in publications where he will read it. These include trade publications and business newspapers. You can even include in the ad a price comparison of some off-the-shelf brands compared to what it would cost a customer to make the product himself, based on the information you provide.

UNIQUE BUSINESS APPROACH

The approach you can use with this business that will make for a sure winner is going after the special customer. As we have already discussed, there are a multitude of people out there who are allergic to particular ingredients or must avoid ingredients for health reasons. You can target this market and put out a guide or catalog especially for them. Then you can advertise in the health publications that would reach this audience. You can do several specialty guides, one for each health problem, and increase your market this way. Simply determine what groups have difficulty locating cleaning products or grooming products especially for them. Do some research to locate formulas that they can use, then market these formulas in your guides or catalogs.

LOCATION and MARKET BASE

You can run this business from either the city or the country, with a population base of at least 5,000 to 50,000 people. Since most of your marketing can be done by mail, you don't really need to be where the large metropolitan areas are. If you are in a large metropolitan area, all the better, since you'll be able to make more sales to businesses.

TO SUM UP

A computerized formula mix service is an idea that nobody else has ever thought of presenting in just the way we suggest in this plan. Since it's a new and unique idea, the market is yours if you decide to go after it.

Most people don't realize that the products they use on a daily basis don't have to be purchased from a grocery store. Few know where to get the information that tells them how they can make these products themselves at home to save bundles of money. Yet once you show them how much using your service can save them, they'll want to know more.

You can create a small fortune in the formula business with a little luck, perseverance and forethought. You deserve the profits you can take in with this money-making opportunity. Get started today and formulate your own ticket to success.

SOURCE MATERIAL

For source material refer to Section 7.

No. 112

COMPUTER REMINDER SERVICE

How many times have you forgotten an important anniversary, birthday or special event? With this report you'll see how many home computer operators are making a lot of money on other people's bad memories. With a simple mailer you can obtain all the business you can handle, and with your computer you just call up a calendar each day and see who needs to be reminded of what. This keeps them out of trouble and keeps you counting your money.

CONCEPT

We live in a world where time is of the essence, yet nobody has enough. We have to be here and there, remember this and that, and most of us don't want to take even more time to keep track of it all. But this is exactly the kind of chore a computer is perfect for. Give this device any number of important and "unforgettable" dates, and it will not only remind you of the occurrence, but will also tell you what you need to do or where you need to be. This is an invaluable service for businesspeople.

Once you have customers, you can do your "reminder" work in two ways. You can call them if they are in your area, or even better, you can send them a postcard. On one side of the card you print their name and address; on the opposite side is a message about the meeting, birthday or chore about which they need to be reminded.

SKILLS YOU WILL REQUIRE

The skills you need are probably ones that you already have. You simply need to be more organized than the people you are helping. You will have to set up a program for yourself that ensures that all this information gets out, and gets out to the right person. Also, you will have to set up a mail program that makes this service work for you.

INFORMATION REQUIRED

To operate this business, you need the kind of information people want to be reminded about. Some examples are: birthdays of family members, clients, etc.; anniversaries; meeting dates; and deadlines in business. The list is endless.

Then you can elicit the kinds of dates and times your clients want to be reminded about, by having them fill out a questionnaire. You can then use this questionnaire to add the information to your "computer calendar."

OPERATING NAME

We suggest that you might use your name, or simply the words, "The Reminder." You identify what you are doing up front and get a lot of mileage out of it. You are selling a service based on forgetfulness and you might as well use as many mental hooks as you can.

GETTING STARTED

There are one thousand and one ways to get the word out, but in this case we feel that you need to get started with our old friend, the silent salesman—The Brochure. You can put together a brochure that will act not only as your advertising piece, but also your application form and activity report. It can all be done on a sheet of paper folded over or into thirds. It will all fit in a regular envelope or can even act as a self-mailer. All you have to do is leave one third of the page blank for adding a name and address.

Remember what you are playing on here: the ability of the human memory to forget the "important" things and remember the trivia in a second. Tell prospective clients what your business is and how it can help them. Explain benefits of your service. You can save time, trouble and money. Other people offer wake-up calls to make sure their clients get to work on time. You go one step better and keep them posted about those important times and dates they need to remember. Sometimes, that can make the difference between staying in business and standing in the unemployment line.

On the brochure, you will want to describe the business and its benefits on the front side, then use the other side as a mailer with the information and application form. Look at how other businesses design their brochures. This can aid you in putting your own together.

COMPETITION

We don't know about too many services of this nature currently operating, but we do know of one in particular in the Southwest that at last count had over 1,000 clients. We understand that word-of-mouth hasn't hurt his business a bit.

The opportunity is ripe for you to get in on the ground floor of this business and make a real killing.

POTENTIAL INCOME

The service we are familiar with charges from $50 to $100 dollars per year, depending on how many reminders they have to deliver to the subscribers. They allow 35 reminders on the original form and add from there. It should be fairly easy to figure out a sliding scale to charge.

Remember that you are in the service business, which means the cost of doing business is almost nonexistent. Your time will basically be spent processing orders and inputting a small amount of information into your computer. Much also will depend on whether you intend to do the work yourself or have a helper do the job. You will have to adjust your cost and profit projection accordingly.

Costs

1. Cost of advertising, brochures, etc.
2. Cost of any software used
3. Cost of telephone use
4. Cost of postcards, mailing, supplies
5. Cost of time spent organizing materials

Profit

When figuring out a price for this service, remember to include the costs of your time, and a profit figure for the job. The first goes into your pocket; the second goes into the business to help it grow.

It won't be difficult for you to price this service, since material costs are low. That means the bulk of payment can go into your pocket for "services rendered."

How To Be Paid

This is a cash-on-the-barrel-head operation. Your brochure will have an appropriate box for indicating payment is enclosed. This keeps the cash flowing in the proper direction and doesn't cause you any bookkeeping nightmares.

MARKETING METHODS

The three main methods of marketing I suggest are direct mail, display advertising and telephone sales.

You may want to start out by sending a cover letter and brochure to some of the large companies in your area describing your service and how it can help them. The letter you will want to send out might go something like this:

> Let us jog your memory. Ever forgotten an important client's birthday? Ever missed a filing deadline you just plum forgot? Ever wished somebody could simply tell you when your anniversary really is?
>
> If you answered yes to any of these questions, you're qualified to use our unique service.
>
> "Exec Reminder" will notify you every time an important day in your personal and business life approaches. With our low-cost service you'll never be late again.
>
> Don't wait another minute. Who knows what slipped your mind already about next week's schedule. Call us today for more information!

Your own variation of this letter will elicit plenty of curiosity about your business. Mailed at the rate of 10 or 20 a day, this letter should have you up and rolling in no time.

You can also place display ads in the business section of your local newspaper with the simple statement:

> When was the last time you forgot your wedding anniversary? When was the last time you forgot an important client's birthday?

Almost everyone has blown it on one of these dates and possibly is still paying the price for it. Let them know what the benefit is for them to use your service, and the business will be yours.

The telephone is also your ally in this business. The first time you call to "remind" your client that it's Mom's birthday, you are going to bring a smile to someone's face and "remind" him or her how valuable you have become to a smooth-running life.

UNIQUE BUSINESS APPROACH

We have a couple of angles others have used that will serve you well when promoting your service.

Call up the larger banks, brokerage houses, or department stores in your community and ask to speak to the person in charge of promotion or marketing. Explain to them the service you offer. The idea here is that this particular business can buy your service for their more valued or "high roller" accounts as a small token of appreciation. You might even offer the client a high volume discount or some other inducement to do business with you. By now you will have a pretty good idea of what the service actually costs, and a large contract of this nature could really get the ball rolling.

The name of the game is numbers, and the more, the merrier. Selling this program as an "executive gift" is a sure-fire way to get it off the ground.

The other route is to tell the world what you are doing. Put a news release together briefly describing your business. Send it out to everyone and anyone in television, radio or newspapers. The idea is unique enough that it could get picked up and gain you several interviews, articles and maybe a radio interview or TV spot. You can gain thousands of dollars of free publicity and no doubt quite a few clients in the process. You can promote this service as the gift for the person in one's life who forgets everything, or for that person who has everything but time.

You won't want to miss putting your client's and spouse's birthday on the computer. This way you can send out birthday and/or anniversary cards to them when the time comes. Plus, you'll "remind" your clients in a more graphic way just how valuable your service is. Everyone likes to be remembered on his or her birthday or anniversary and this will be a large feather in your cap when you "remember" to do it.

LOCATION and MARKET BASE

This will work great in any city with a market base of 50,000 to 200,000 people. The larger the base you try to draw from, the better off you are going to be.

START UP CAPITAL

The start-up sum required to finance this business is under $1,000. The actual costs will be up to you and how complex you want to make the business. This is a high-service, low-fixed-cost business. The basic cost other than the computer is going to be finding the program or software that is going to fill your needs. You are going to have to do a good brochure, but don't go overboard in the production and printing costs. Refer to Section 6 for obtaining the capital needed.

TO SUM UP

The keystone of any business is the old theory of "finding a need and filling it." With a computer reminder service, you have at your fingertips such a need, and the method to fulfill it. People move around at a fast pace today and the possibllity of forgetting something important is almost a certainty. You can become the person that these people depend upon to get their lives in order, or at least get the important days down correctly. You are going to be a mental hook they can hang their cares on. If you are the first person in your community to start this project, you can reap the benefits immediately. Start working on this project today. You can then spend the rest of your time "reminding" yourself to head over to the bank. After all, what else can you do with your money?

SOURCE MATERIAL

Refer to Section 7.

No. 113

COMPUTER ROOMMATE SERVICE

Almost every town has people looking for a place to share living expenses with another person. With your home computer you can match these people up, covering all of their individual needs. And with a simple ad you can have them running to you for the best and most complete service in town. You'll be collecting dollars in both directions. This is a business that requires little actual time—the computer does all the work.

CONCEPT

The concept of this business is to match up potential roommates. You do your matching by having customers fill out a questionnaire about themselves and what kind of person they would like to live with. Then you use your computer to sort out the information and match up people who have the most similar wants and needs.

For this service, you collect a fee from both people involved. Most people today don't want to shell out the money to live in their own homes and have to pay not only rent, but also telephone, utility and miscellaneous expenses by themselves. If they can find someone to live with who is compatible with their own lifestyles, then they'll gladly pay a finder's fee. The cost of your service is just a tiny chunk of the money they'll save by having another person help them pay for a place to live.

SKILLS YOU WILL REQUIRE

For this business, once you've figured out a questionnaire to give people when they hire you, you've done most of the work. I'll help you figure out a questionnaire later in this plan.

The only skill you really need is a liking for people, because that's who you will be dealing with—people. And if you like them, you want to help them. That's exactly what a computer roommate service is doing—helping people.

INFORMATION REQUIRED

The information you'll require for this business is questions to ask people about themselves in order to locate a roommate for them. A typical questionnaire might read:

Name:
Phone Number:
Age:
Do you want to live with a man? Yes/No
Do you want to live with a woman? Yes/No
Will you live with either a man or a woman? Yes/No
Area of town you want to live in:
Amount of rent you want to pay:
What furniture do you own?
Do you mind smokers? Yes/No
Do you mind pets like cats or dogs? Yes/No
Do you mind other kinds of pets, like birds or fish? Yes/No
Do you want to share grocery bills with your roommate?
How do you typically spend an evening?
What hobbies, sports, or entertainment do you participate in?
What kind of a person do you prefer for a roommate?
Is there anything special about you that we should know about, such as unusual sleeping hours, preference for loud music, preference for peace and quiet?

Make your own variations of this questionnaire to use when people call up asking for your service. You can have them fill it out over the phone by asking them each question. If you decide to get an office for yourself, you can have your customers come in to fill it out.

OPERATING NAME

You can start this business with a fictitious name, such as "Roommate Finders" or" Roomie Searchers." It will involve some start-up expenses, like registering the name or filing a fictitious name report, getting a new business bank account, etc.

Or you can operate the business under your own name. This will save you the start-up costs and give you as good a name as you need. When you advertise your business, you will be able to explain in the ad what the service is that you're offering. Refer to Section 4.

GETTING STARTED

To get started operating your own computer roommate service, you'll need to write a questionnaire to have your customers fill out. You can do this on your computer, then print out copies. If you don't have a printer, you can put together the questionnaire, then get it copied for a minimal fee. You might consider contacting a roommate service if there is one in your area in order to get a copy of their questionnaire. You can do this by posing as a prospective customer. Tell them you want their application to fill out at home. Then use it as a guide to write your own.

Once you have done that, you are ready to take orders. To get business, you'll need to advertise your services. The best way to do this is probably through display ads. For more information, refer to Marketing Methods, Section 5.

THE COMPETITION

To eliminate your competition, offer a twist that they don't. For example, you can specialize in putting together roommate arrangements for a special group of people, like senior citizens or students. This would work best in a large population area where a multitude of these kinds of people live.

If you are in a smaller town, you probably won't have any competition. Most services like this are located in big cities. So the opportunities are ripe for you to make a killing by offering a big city service in your own corner of the world.

POTENTIAL INCOME

The money you can make from this service comes from two sources: the two people you are matching up as roommates. Each pays, so you get your income coming and going.

If you charge each person only $25 for your service and you match up 40 people in a month, that's $1,000, not a bad amount for part-time work. Since the actual amount of time you'll spend with each customer is very small, the amount of money you make for each hour can easily exceed your expectations.

Plus, the service you offer is continuous. Since roommates split up for a number of reasons—moving to a new city, getting married, etc.—you can expect your customers to come back to you each time they need a new roommate, especially if the match-up you made for them in the first place works out well. You can expect a lot of repeat business with a computer roommate service. The need never ends!

Figuring out what to charge isn't complicated. You start out by placing an hourly value on your own time. Then you add up all the costs of the program (you'll find a list following) and add in a profit margin for the work. Once you know the sum total, you can estimate what to charge each customer. Keep in mind that the cost of the program includes a salary for yourself. Profit is what the business gets after all the costs are covered.

Basic costs

1. Cost of your time
2. Cost of putting together questionnaire & printing
3. Cost of advertising
4. Cost of supplies used
5. Cost of time spent putting together roommates
6. Cost of software

How To Be Paid

You have several choices here. You can charge each customer in advance, when he or she fills out the questionnaire. This ensures that they won't go out and find a roommate on their own, and is fairly standard practice in the field.

Or you can charge a deposit, maybe half of the fee, when they fill out the questionnaire. Then you collect the other half after you have matched them up. If you are unable to satisfy your customer because nobody you find for them is to their expectations, you can always return their deposit as a goodwill gesture. This will ensure that the next time they're looking, they will give you the chance to try it again for them.

Another choice you have is to offer the service free of charge, until you succeed in putting together a match. An advantage of doing this is that you can market the fact that a customer doesn't pay until he or she is satisfied. A disadvantage is collecting the money after the fact. You won't have that income to pay your costs.

MARKETING METHODS

The best way to market this business is with display or classified ads. You can run these ads in local newspapers and magazines. If your area has a weekly shopper mailed to every household in your area, that might also be a good place to market your service.

Here is a typical ad you can run:

> Need a roommate?
>
> We can find the perfect person for you to live with. Give us just a few minutes of your time and we will be able to supply you with a person who matches exactly what you're looking for. The best part is, it won't cost you a cent unless you're satisfied. Save time, trouble and money – GIVE US A CALL TODAY!

A version of this classified ad should bring you all the business you can handle. People would love having somebody help them find a roommate. Without your service, they'd have to run their own ads, screen their own candidates and make their own choices. They'll consider the fee you charge well worth their investment.

Another way to market this business is by placing notices on bulletin boards where people who are likely to want a roommate will see them. This includes laundrymats, college and university bulletin boards, senior centers, etc.

UNIQUE BUSINESS APPROACH

The big secret to this business is offering a service nobody else supplies. That is, the opportunity for a customer to meet a prospective roommate before making the decision to live with him or her.

That is where you come in. When a customer calls for your service, you explain that he or she has the chance to meet the candidates you have selected. If the first person doesn't meet their needs and they don't think the match-up would work, then they can meet another candidate. You tell them that since you have so many candidates that will be right for them, if they decline your first choice, there is no harm done, since there will be a second choice, or even a third choice.

If you want, you can give each person the other's name and phone number and allow them to arrange a meeting time and place, such as a coffee shop. Or you can charge extra and offer to arrange the meeting yourself. Then you call each person and find out if the time and place you have selected is agreeable.

After the meeting, they can call you to say whether the choice you've selected is fine with them. You collect your money, and then they're on their own!

LOCATION and MARKET BASE

This business can best be offered in a city, because that is where most renters live and you'll have a big market base from which to get customers. Plus, if you decide to offer a specialty, such as student roommates, you'll want to be in an area where people of that kind live.

You can run this business in a market base that ranges from 50,000 to 200,000. That means that if you are in a small metropolitan area, you can do it. Chances are you won't have any competition in your small city, because the large companies that offer this service are concentrating on major metropolitan areas.

TO SUM UP

A computer roommate service is a unique and needed business in these days of high rents and impossible mortgage payments. With just a small amount of capital, you can start earning a nice chunk of money in just a little time. When your operation grows, you can start offering it in areas other than your own, maybe even franchising it and letting other people earn your money for you!

To put this business opportunity into perspective, look at it this way: most people are tired of living with strangers that have nothing in common with them, pay the rent late, etc. If they could only find somebody with whom they are compatible, somebody they can share their lifestyle with, somebody to share their meals and good times with, they'll pay a good fee for the peace of mind they will be getting. With your computer roommate service, you will be able to give them the chance to live with a new friend. That isn't just a money-making opportunity. You will be making the world a friendlier place as well.

SOURCE MATERIAL

Refer to Section 7.

No. 114

COMPUTERIZED ADVERTISING COST NEWSLETTER

This business utilizes your computer in one of its easiest, yet least heralded roles: as liaison between those who need information and those who have it. Small businesses need advertising exposure. Newspapers, magazines, and radio and television stations need advertisers. With a minimal expenditure of time on your part, your computerized service can become the "middleman" in your local advertising market.

CONCEPT

The small-business person, like everyone else in business, needs to advertise. Potential ad campaigns are examined for target markets, effectiveness and, above all, cost. The majority of businesses in any area do not have money to throw carelessly or casually into advertising they hope will succeed. They must examine their options at length and select what looks like the best strategy for the money they have budgeted for advertising.

This can be a time-consuming and therefore expensive, process. Information on advertising rates for the different media in an area can usually be obtained only from scattered sources. Even after the information is compiled, it must be sifted and compared.

The concept of your business is to assemble all of this information in one place. You will put out a weekly or monthly newsletter listing the comparative advertising rates of television and radio stations, newspapers and other publications in your area. This will save the small business hours of legwork. Your clients will be able to decide immediately where they want to put their advertising dollars. The time you save them will be well worth the money they pay you.

You can make money in this business from two sources. The business you serve will want the information you provide and will pay for it. Plus, the media you get your information from will also pay to have that information distributed, since your service will certainly bring them more advertising dollars.

SKILLS YOU WILL REQUIRE

This is a business that the computer novice can start up almost immediately. You must be good at assimilating and organizing information, but you need not have any specialized knowledge of the advertising industry, nor of the television, radio or newspaper business. You'll need to know some basics, such as what a column inch is, but the amount of information required is minimal.

The plain truth of the matter is that the advertising rate structure of television, radio and newspapers is not very complicated. There's a good reason for this. The media want to attract advertisers and it is simply not in their interest to scare away potential customers with complicated rate structures. Since your goal is to collect this information and present it in an orderly manner, this works to your advantage as well.

You'll want to organize your newsletter in a simple, easy-to-read style. The faster that businesspeople can put their fingers on the information they need, the more successful you will be. You will want to categorize as much as possible—that is, compare similar markets. A spot on a rock-and-roll station will reach an entirely different audience than a display ad in an interior decorating magazine. If you group your information into a few general categories, you will improve the look and readability of your newsletter and make your service that much more valuable to the people who will be paying for it.

INFORMATION REQUIRED

Generally, newspapers charge by the column inch, while radio and television stations have packages based on the length of the spot and the rotation of airplay. For example, a radio station might charge X amount of dollars for 12 spots per week, randomly distributed over the station's broadcast time, but would charge more for the same number of ads if 10 of them are played during peak listening hours. You will need to familiarize yourself with the different packages offered by different stations.

The first step is to immerse yourself in the local media. Pick up copies of local newspapers and magazines and look at their advertising distribution. Visit the television and radio stations in your area and ask for their rate schedules. A good way to familiarize yourself with this business is to approach a radio or television station as a potential advertiser. You will learn all you need to know.

Once you've become familiar with the advertising market in your area, you are ready to go into business.

OPERATING NAME

Your newsletter needs a title, as does your business.

For the newsletter, almost any name is suitable. "The (name of city) Advertiser's Guide" will do, as will something a little more imaginative. It doesn't matter, except that the title of the newsletter should offer some indication of its purpose.

As far as naming your business goes, it's best to use some form of your own name, such as "Joe Jones Advertising Information Service" or something similar. This eliminates the necessity of opening new business bank accounts and acquiring new business phone lines.

A good strategy for avoiding confusion is to work your name into the title of the newsletter. You could title it, for example, "Joe Jones' Guide to (name of city) Advertising." This way your clients have immediate name identification with you, and all checks you receive will have your name on them.

GETTING STARTED

As mentioned before, the first thing to do is familiarize yourself with the advertising market in your area. The newspapers, radio and television stations will cooperate enthusiastically—anything that can potentially bring in more advertising dollars will be welcomed with open arms.

You must then get the business community interested in your service. To do this, you will have to spend some time publicizing yourself and your newsletter. For more on this, see Marketing Methods.

Once the business community becomes interested, you're on your way. Your goal is to establish a service they will use month after month. Don't expect it to happen overnight—it takes time to establish consistency. But if you do your job, you'll notice your circulation rate climbing steadily as more small-business people climb aboard.

THE COMPETITION

Since this business can be started up so easily, you may find yourself thinking, "What if someone else starts up a similar service before I do?" The only answer to this is to get out and start selling your idea right away. Start with the business community. The newspapers, magazines, television and radio stations will support you once you can demonstrate an adequate audience.

A little research will go a long way once you start publishing your newsletter. Look around at the small businesses that are advertisng in the media you want to cover. Then pick a representative sampling of advertising to use. If you can offer the business community what it wants and are the first to offer it, any potential competition will be eliminated.

POTENTIAL INCOME

The amount of money you can make in this business is directly tied to how much you charge for your newsletter and how often it comes out. Obviously, if you print your newsletter on a weekly basis, you do not have to charge as much per issue as you would if you bring out only one issue per month.

The decision of how often to print depends upon several factors. One is the amount of time you want to spend coordinating information. Another is what the businesses you serve want. As mentioned in the previous section, by doing a little research beforehand, you can tailor your newsletter to your local business community's needs.

Still another factor to be taken into consideration is the sources of your material, the publications and radio and television stations. How often do their rates change? When are special deals announced?

When pricing your newsletter, keep in mind that you have two sources of revenue. The first comes from the media. You are limited in what you can charge a newspaper, radio or television station to appear in your newsletter, because if the price is too high and a fair number of them decline, the publication loses value to the businesspeople for whom it is intended. Your real money has to come from subscriptions.

Still, you should charge a fair and equitable price for listing a media advertiser, since it also benefits. Once you have established your base of media advertisers, this source of revenue will not change substantially, since new publications in any area do not spring up that often. You should keep abreast of any new media ventures, so that you can add them to your base of support.

The real way to increase your earnings is to increase the number of subscriptions. To price your newsletter, determine a minimum number of subscriptions and a minimum level of profit. Add up your cost, including your time, add your profit, and divide by the number of subscriptions. Any increase in subscriptions over your minimum simply adds to your profit.

Here are the major costs you will need to take into account:

1. Cost of your time
2. Cost of postage and circulation expenses
3. Cost of operating your computer and printer
4. Cost of paper
5. Cost of telephone use
6. Cost of miscellaneous expenses, such as travel
7. Cost of software

Let's say that you've decided on a monthly publication. You want to earn $1,500 a month in profit with a minimum of 500 subscribers. You spend 10 hours each month compiling information and pay yourself $10 per hour. Your additional costs come to $400. Add that $400, plus $100 for your time, to your desired profit of $1,500. Divide the result, $2,000, by the number of subscriptions, 500, and you have your per-issue charge—$4, or $48 per year.

This does not take into account the money you will receive from your media sources, so you might want to encourage long-term subscriptions by discounting the annual price slightly while keeping the per-issue charge the same.

MARKETING METHODS

Direct mail, display ads, telephone sales and direct sales are the best methods for marketing this service.

As with any publication, you are dealing here with volume. You are not going to make much money if you get 10 or 50 people interested. Unless you like to talk on the telephone and pay the resulting bills, or unless you have a new pair of shoes that you need to break in with lots of pavement-pounding, I would not recommend direct or telephone sales as your first line of action.

Instead of taking all that time, put your computer to use at something it can do easily and efficiently—mass mailing. A good letter mailed to several hundred small businesses will accomplish more than weeks of telephoning or traveling. If people don't respond, then a follow-up telephone call is appropriate.

A display ad in the business section of your local newspaper will also produce results. It's not as immediate and personal as a direct-mail letter, but it gets you more exposure for your money.

Here is an example of a letter you might send to get businesses interested in your service:

> DEAR BUSINESSPERSON:
>
> Do you spend a lot of time searching for the best and least expensive ways to advertise your business? Could you spend that time more profitably doing something else? Of course, you could! That's why our new "Guide to Advertising" makes sense for the busy executive.
>
> Our newsletter lists the going rates for advertisements of all sizes and lengths in newspapers, magazines, radio, television—all advertising media in the city. So instead of searching for the right deal for you, you can simply glance at our new Guide, and find it right there in front of you.
>
> Now you can get back to your work and leave the running around to us.

A letter such as this one, mailed out on your company stationary at the rate of 30 to 50 a day, will produce results. It will cost you postage, but once your newsletter gets off the ground, you'll recoup that cost in a hurry.

UNIQUE BUSINESS APPROACH

The best way to reach your desired volume of subscribers is to go to them where they congregate. This way, one direct sales pitch can bring in hundreds of clients. Businesspeople gather in organizations like the Rotary Club, the Lions Club and the Jaycees. Get invited to their meetings. It isn't hard—they are always in need of speakers. Offer discounted subscriptions to club members, or give away your first issue for free.

Once they've had that first issue and used it, they'll be hooked.

This approach has the added advantage of generating word-of-mouth advertising. Businesspeople will show each other your newsletter. This will result in additional subscriptions.

LOCATION and MARKET BASE

This business really needs to be run in a city, and the bigger the city the better. Obviously, the more businesses there are in your market area, the more potential subscribers you have. If you live in an urban area with more than 200,000 people, you can make this business work.

TO SUM UP

A computerized advertising-cost newsletter is such a simple idea that no one has really thought of doing it. Yet it can be a boon to a small business that must be frugal with its advertising dollars, and an inexpensive asset to any business at all.

Like much else in American business, making a go of a project such as this one is a matter of being in the right place at the right time with the right idea. If that's where you are, you can start your newsletter publishing career today.

Who else is going to do it?

SOURCE MATERIAL

Refer to Section 7.

No. 115

COMPUTERIZED PRESS RELEASE SERVICE

Here's a business that uses your computer to distribute publicity in your area for those who need it most—the businesspeople who sell products and services. Every business knows that free press is cheaper than advertising, and sometimes more effective. You can use your home computer to tap into the flow of publicity and get the names of local businesses in front of the public on a regular basis.

CONCEPT

A press release service serves as go-between for those who make news and those who report it. And a computer with a good word processing system can make this service easy to perform. While newspapers and radio and television stations must go out and dig up most of their major stories, they are heavily dependent upon press releases to fill out the volume of their news.

News agencies receive press releases from a variety of sources. Political candidates running for office flood newspaper and broadcast offices with press releases, sometimes at a rate of several a day, in order to get their name in front of the public as often as possible. Laboratories and research centers routinely announce new developments through press releases. Often, coverage of local high school sports is dependent upon a public relations person contacting the newspapers with necessary information.

The idea behind most press releases is free exposure. The campaigning politician pays for advertising, but he knows that if anything he says or does can even remotely be considered news and not propaganda, the media will usually run the item for free. Research foundations use the press release and the resulting publicity as ammunition to garner continued funding for their projects.

Generating press releases for business is not much different. Suppose a company comes out with a new product. It has the option of purchasing a large display ad to announce the fact, and paying a rate for each publication in which the ad appears. It has the option of running a radio and television advertising campaign, which is even more expensive. Or it can put out a press release, and reach the same number of people at virtually no cost at all.

An example of this occurs whenever the major airlines get into one of their periodic "price wars." Sure, they advertise the new low rates. But they also show up on the television and radio news and become the subject of prominently displayed stories in major newspapers around the country. Consequently, people everywhere become aware of the new lower prices, even those who don't pay attention to ads.

SKILLS YOU WILL REQUIRE

The most basic skill you will need in this business, obviously, is the ability to write a good press release. It isn't hard. Journalistic writing is one of the easiest types of writing there is. Just keep a few simple rules in mind and you'll do fine.

Rule 1: Put the most important information first. If you look at a typical story in a typical newspaper, you'll see that the gist of the entire story is usually contained in the first two or three sentences. There is no such thing as stylistic suspense. Television and radio news stories are structured this way also. The reason for this? In the case of newspapers, there are so many stories that the average reader will read only a few of them. He usually decides whether or not to read it on the basis of the first sentence. In the case of radio and television, time is usually limited and two or three sentences is all you'll get.

Rule 2: Just the facts, please. Avoid excessive wordiness. You want to get your message across as simply and concisely as possible. The reader or viewer should remember two things: the name of the business, and what it has done to be in the news.

Rule 3: Report, don't advertise. Although I previously compared press releases to free advertising, newspapers, radio, and television stations won't. Remember that they also sell advertising and it is simply not in their interest to run something that is obviously an advertising pitch free of charge. Make it newsworthy. For example, suppose one of your client companies has just come out with a new type of high tensile-strength wire. A good way to begin the press release would be something like this: "Bridges and traffic light fixtures in and around the city may be stronger and last up to twice as long in the future, due to a new product recently unveiled by Jones and Company." Don't start it like this: "Jones and Company's new high-strength wire is now available at prices not much higher than those of wire with half its strength."

A good press release reads like a good news story. The most important information is at the top and subsequent sentences and paragraphs fill in supplemental information.

The further a piece of information is from the beginning of the article, the less important it is. It should read simply and easily, in simple sentences with very little description. And it should not sound like a sales pitch.

Other than the ability to write, you will also need to be able to use your computer, along with a word processing program. Computerizing your operations means that you'll be able to generate your material much faster, as well as your income.

INFORMATION REQUIRED

You need very little outside information to get this business off the ground. All you really need to know is the address and phone number of each media news service in your area. You'll need to find out where to send your press releases, whose attention to direct them to and, most important, what the media look for in the way of news.

Your local yellow pages and your public library are two sources for this information. Most media news services will be listed in the yellow pages, and the library will have copies of most, if not all, of the publications in your area that use press releases.

Spend time looking over your target publications. See how they handle news, especially news from the world of business. Chances are, most of the news items in the business section of the newspapers you see have been generated from press releases. Often, a press release makes its way into print virtually unchanged.

By studying the newspapers in your area, you will have a better understanding of how to write your press releases when you go into business.

You should also spend some time choosing your software carefully for this business. Read reviews of particular word processing programs to get an understanding of what their functions are, how they can assist you, and which packages can best fill your needs.

Then you can visit a computer dealer and test the programs in which you are most interested. This process will save you time, money and headaches once you've started writing press releases for pay.

OPERATING NAME

Your business needs a title. You can name your press release service virtually any name you can think of, provided the name is not already registered in your area to someone else.

The best thing to do, however, is to name your business after yourself. "Joe Jones Press Release Service" or something similar will do quite nicely. The advantage to this is that it saves you the cost of registering a new business name, opening new bank accounts, installing new phone lines, etc. You can simply use all the services you now have in your own name for your new business.

GETTING STARTED

Getting business is a matter of making contacts. In this case, you have two sets of contacts to make: the news media, and the businesspeople who will be your clients.

It's easy to break into the news media. As I mentioned earlier, they receive press releases from a number of sources, and though they receive many, they are always eager for more. Start by compiling an exhaustive list of the media news services in your area. These will be your targets.

Your money will come from the businesses that use your service. For information on how to interest them in your service, see Marketing Methods.

THE COMPETITION

Most press releases come from the source. A politician will hire one or several press liaisons, whose job it is to keep the politician's name in the news. In larger businesses the advertising department also generates press material. There is really no corresponding service for small to medium-sized businesses. They do not have the money to hire their own publicity people, so the only answer is to use someone like you, who has the means to serve many businesses at once.

The best ways to beat the competition are to be there first and to be good at what you do. As in any other endeavor, success breeds success. Once you land a few of your press releases in the local media, you will have documentation to prove to potential new clients that you can produce results.

POTENTIAL INCOME

Pricing this type of service is not difficult. Your object is to guarantee yourself a steady income. You need to come up with a monthly rate for your services that earns you an adequate profit while still being attractive to businesses in your area.

Remember that there is no guarantee that all your press releases will be used. Some will generate a lot of interest, while others will see print in one or two newspapers and be ignored by the rest of the local media. This is not in your control. You need to be paid whether the releases are used or not.

Don't worry. The media will use enough of your press releases to make it worthwhile for the businesses that subscribe to your service. But you will be spending time writing press releases that do not attract wide publicity. It's just part of the business and you need to take that into account in setting your rates.

First, put a dollar value on your time. How much are you going to be paid per hour? Next, add up your monthly costs. Determine the number of businesses you can serve in the hours you have allotted. (Obviously, the more businesses you serve, the more hours you will work.) Then decide on your amount of profit per month. Remember that your time is a cost of doing business, not part of your profit.

Add up the cost of your time over a month, plus your other costs, plus your profit. Divide this total by the number of businesses you plan to serve. The result is your monthly charge for your press release service.

Here are some of the costs you will need to take into account:

1. Cost of your time per hour
2. Cost of postage and mailing supplies
3. Cost of operating your computer and printer
4. Cost of paper
5. Cost of telephone
6. Cost of travel
7. Cost of software

Let's suppose, for example, that you decide you can serve 10 businesses by working 100 hours per month (25 per week) at $10 per hour. Your other costs come to $200, and you want to earn $800 per month in profit for your business. These add up to $2,000. Divide that total by the number of clients (10) and you have your monthly share— $200.

You probably won't have 10 clients right away, and this is simply an example. But set your costs according to your goals, and eventually you will probably surpass them.

MARKETING METHODS

Direct mail, display advertising, telephone sales and direct sales are the best methods for marketing this service.

Since you are entering the business of writing press releases, there is absolutely nothing wrong with a mock press release announcing to your potential clients the launching of your new business. This might, in fact, be a better approach than a simple direct letter, since it will show them the quality of work that they can expect if they subscribe to your service.

Here is an example of a release you might want to consider:

NEW SERVICE FOR BUSINESSES STARTED

(Your City) A new service designed to put your business in the news became a reality here yesterday. Joe Jones of (your city) announced the creation of a business press release service designed to increase exposure in the community at very little cost. Jones plans to market his services to small and medium-sized businesses in the greater city area. "Smaller businesses need publicity too," he said. "Until now, only the big guys with the big bucks got it."

Jones added that the increased exposure from his press release service could be extremely effective for a firm in generating new business. "It's the cheapest kind of advertising there is," he said. Jones can be reached for more information at (123) 456-7890.

Send this release, or an adaptation of it, to businesses in your area at the rate of 20 to 30 per day. After a week or so, you may want to follow up with a straight letter or a phone call. Don't expect a torrent of clients the first week, but if you persevere and are consistent, you will soon have all the business you need.

UNIQUE BUSINESS APPROACH

Every so often, businesses make news without the help of a press release. Either they do something truly noteworthy, or someone in the media stumbles upon them and writes up a feature story. Watch for this—it will happen in your area sooner or later.

When it does, make contact with the manager of that business. Perhaps your service can help him remain in the news. Be prepared for a reluctant reaction, however—they've just gotten exposure absolutely free and may not want to pay for it.

You can, however, ask them to keep records of the increase in business that results from media exposure. This becomes data for you to use in pitching your service to other businesses that have not been so fortunate. You can say, "Look what media exposure did for this business—think what it can do for yours!"

LOCATION and MARKET BASE

This business should be run in a city or urban area of at least 200,000 people. Obviously, the more businesses there are in your market area, the more potential clients you have.

TO SUM UP

Any business that sells products or services wants its name in front of the public every chance it can get. If you get free publicity for your clients on a regular basis, they will consider their investment in your service well worth their money.

Once you have proven yourself by landing several press releases in the media and seeing them turn into news stories that benefit your clients, other businesses will want some of the action too. There's plenty of free publicity to go around, especially in newspapers. All you have to do is tap into it with your computer. Your clients will reward you in a big way.

SOURCE MATERIAL

Refer to Section 7.

No. 116

LOCAL WHO'S WHO DIRECTORY

Everybody wants to feel important, and here's a way to make them important. With the application of your home computer, this project becomes one of the easiest home computer businesses we have ever come across. Before computers, this business was so time-consuming that only the biggies were in the market. Now you can not only compete, but run the local biggies right out of business while you're counting your money all the way to the bank.

CONCEPT

The concept of this business is to sell an idea. You tell your clients that they will appear in a "who's who" directory for their particular line of business, and they in turn will want to purchase your directories to give to their customers, family and friends.

What you offer them is a chance to see their name in print in a publication of importance. Not only can they say that they're in a who's who, but the directory you compile will serve as a valuable guide that works much the same way as yellow page directories. If somebody needs to locate a specialist, your guide will tell them who and where the specialists are.

You can make great money simply by applying your own area of expertise or interest. And you can do it in your area without even leaving the house. The variety of directories that you can put together is limited only by your own imagination. I'll give you help figuring out where to start.

SKILLS YOU WILL REQUIRE

If you like to talk to people, you'll be a whiz at doing this business, because basically that's all it involves. And if you consider yourself shy and unable to think of things to say, you can do this business simply by reading a kind of script over the phone to people who will want to be listed in your who's who directory.

Or if you prefer, you can decide to run this business yourself and hire others to do your work for you. Since your primary tool, besides your computer equipment, is the telephone, you can hire staff to do your research for you. Retirees would be great for this kind of business, since it would give them a little extra part-time income.

Another option you have is to hire a professional telephone solicitor to do your calling for you. The advantage is that this person will have experience in taking orders from people over the phone. A disadvantage is that it will probably cost you more than if you were to hire and train your own staff person. If you decide to go the route of hiring a professional, you might consider paying a small salary plus a commission or bonus for each directory he or she sells. This gives a greater incentive to succeed.

INFORMATION REQUIRED

What you'll need to do is decide what area of business you want to concentrate on for your directory. That will determine what kind of information you'll need. For instance, if you decide to do a who's who of insurance agents and companies in your town, you'll want to know the company's name, its top agents' or owners' names, address and phone number, and specialties such as life, auto or home insurance.

To find out who your likely customers are, you can consult the yellow pages and city directory where you live. These and other resources will probably be available at your neighborhood library for you to use free of charge. Plus, the resources will often give you the name of the person to contact at the business.

OPERATING NAME

You have two choices with this business. You can pick a fictitious company name, such as "Insurance Agent's Who's Who Company," "The Mapleview Blue Book Publishers," etc. There really isn't an advantage to this, and it involves a lot of extra start-up expenses.

The most famous directories around, such as Polk, are all named after the founder. In this case, that would be you. Just use your own name, John Smith, and then add something like "and Associates" under the name. That should do it for you. Your company—and you—will not only become well-known, like Polk, but you'll save start-up costs by being able to use the phones, bank accounts, etc., already listed in your name. Refer to Section 4 for additional information.

GETTING STARTED

The first thing you'll need to do is decide what kind of directory you'll put together. If it's a who's who of accountants, then compile a list of accountants from the sources mentioned before. Keep this list in your computer, because you'll use your computer to sort and coordinate the information you'll be adding later.

The types of who's who directories you might consider are for: attorneys, doctors, accountants, insurance agents, store owners, automobile dealers, or manufacturers. The list is endless, and depends on what kinds of businesses are big in your own area.

Then you'll need to put together a script to use when you call the people whose names you have. You want to emphasize that you are offering a spot in a prestigious directory. Your customers will feel honored when you call to let them know about this opportunity.

THE COMPETITION

The advantage of this business is that you can choose to do a directory that nobody else has done. Consult your local library to find out whether what you have decided on has already been published in your area. If not, it's yours!

Usually you won't even have to worry about competition, especially if you are in a non-metropolitan area. The biggies of the field prefer to work in major cities, which leaves your own small town to you.

POTENTIAL INCOME

You can make a lot of money with this type of business, because the who's who directory you compile can be reissued every year with updates, and you can put out several, one each for a variety of fields.

You make money with a who's who by selling copies to the very people listed in it. Plus, you can make additional income because several of your customers will probably want to advertise in it as well. Or you can sell advertising in it to affiliated businesses that want those listed in your who's who to know about them. For instance, if the directory is a listing of accountants, then office supply stores, computer stores, and local restaurants where businesspeople lunch will want to advertise.

Since you want to put out a good-looking directory that makes people proud to be included, you'll need to hire a printing company to print it for you. Often you can make a deal with the printer to do a "trade-out." This means that you'll offer him advertising in your directory in exchange for a discount on the printing costs. This will save you money and bring in new business for the printer.

To figure out what to charge for each directory, you'll have to add up all your costs for the program and add a profit figure for the job. Then divide the total amount by the number of copies you'll be selling.

If you decide you want to make $5,000 for your time, and the other costs of the project equal $3,000, and you want a company profit of $2000, the sum total equals $10,000. If you print 1,000 copies of your directory, each will sell for $10.

You might also have customers who want to buy dozens of directories to hand out as complimentary copies to their clients. In this case, you can offer them a discount price for each, increase the number of copies you print up and still make your profit.

Primary Costs

1. Cost of printing
2. Cost of staff to make phone calls
3. Cost of direct mail or display advertising
4. Cost of materials and supplies used
5. Cost of time to organize materials, write script, etc.
6. Cost of software

Profit

After you have determined what you want to be paid as a salary, then figure out the amount you want your business to make as profit.

In practical terms, you don't want to make the cost of your directory prohibitive. Nor do you want to undercharge. After all, this is something very elite and prestigious you are offering your customers, and they expect to have to pay for it. If the directory has a quality appearance, people will consider your price well worth the investment.

How To Be Paid

The standard practice should be to take one-half of your fee with the directory order and one-half on delivery. The money you get in advance will give you what you need to do the printing and pay staff salaries.

For your first directory, some customers might decline to pay in advance. They don't want to give out money until they've seen the final product. But after that, when you're working on your second or subsequent directories, you'll be able to use the ones you've already put out as proof that you mean business.

Consider the directories as part of your portfolio, to be added to with time.

MARKETING METHODS

Telephone sales, direct mail, display ads and direct sales are the best ways to market your directories. You can run ads in local publications of interest to the people you'll be including in the directory. Or you can write them a letter explaining that they have been chosen to appear in the directory and that you are taking advance orders to make sure they get all the copies they will need. A third option is to take copies of your book to the people who will want to buy it and get orders from them in person.

But perhaps the most efficient method of marketing this business is to stay in your own home and let the telephone act as your weapon of success. What you'll want to do is call the people whose names you have compiled from the phone book, city directory, etc., and let them know that they have been chosen to appear in a local directory because they have been so successful in their line of work. At the same time that you get information about them to include in your who's who, you can offer them the opportunity to purchase copies of the directory to pass out.

This is an example of what your phone call might sound like:

> Hello, Mr. Jones:
>
> My name is John Smith and the reason I've called is because I am pleased to inform you that you have been chosen to appear in the Blue Book of Accountants.
>
> What I need to do is confirm the information I have about your firm.
>
> You are the president of the firm—is that correct?
>
> Your address is 555 North Avenue.
>
> Do you offer any special services you would like to make sure we include in the Blue Book?
>
> The Blue Book will be out in two months. Would you like to receive copies of it to give to your clients and associates? There will be a minimum charge to cover the cost of printing, handling and shipping.
>
> Thank you for your time and information and, Mr. Smith, one more thing. Congratulations!"

You can write your own version of this script to guide you when you do the calling for your who's who directory. The reason to follow a script is to save time, both your own and that of your client. You'll get the information you need quickly and won't be floundering around for something to say. Also, if you hire people to do your calling for you, they'll have something to follow.

UNIQUE BUSINESS APPROACH

Now I'll let you in on the secret to this money-making opportunity. What you need to do is make your directory sound like the most exclusive thing to be included in since the Encyclopedia Britannica. The way to do it is to get your directory into the collection of local public and university libraries.

Then you can inform your customers that the directory has been chosen to be included as part of the local library's collection. Who wouldn't want to walk into their public library, pull a book off the shelf and find their name listed?

All it'll cost you to do this is a few free directories donated to your local library. To make arrangements, contact the librarian, and tell him or her that you'll be sending material to be included in the reference section. Since libraries are in the business of supplying resource material, they'll be glad to have your who's who directory to add to their collection of information on local businesses.

LOCATION and MARKET BASE

You'll be able to make money with this business whether you live in a large city with millions of residents or a small town with 5,000 residents. The secret is to choose a directory specialty for which your town has lots of potential listings. If you are in an extremely small market base, you can integrate several types of businesses to include in the who's who and make it an all-around listing of important businesspeople.

TO SUM UP

People want to feel important. They want to think they've made a mark on the world in whatever endeavor they perform. With a who's who directory, you offer them the opportunity to show off, to get their name in print, to prove that, yes, they are SOMEBODY!

There are several ways to make money with this enterprise. You can sell the directories, sell advertising in the directories and do annual updates in which you simply add new names and delete the names of those people who have moved elsewhere. With your computer keeping your files, updating is easy.

Somebody famous once said that everybody in the world gets at least 15 minutes of fame in their lifetime, that everybody gets the feeling of satisfaction of being somebody to their friends, family and associates. What you will be offering them is that chance for 15 minutes of fame. It's the stuff of which memories and scrapbooks are made. And it's also the stuff of which fat bank accounts are made—in this case, your own.

SOURCE MATERIAL

For source information refer to Section 7.

No. 117

COMPUTERIZED COLLECTION LETTER SERVICE

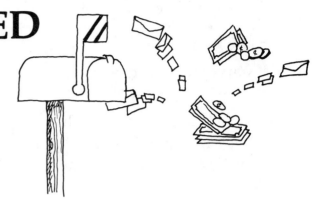

Here is another way for you to get paid for using your personal computer to help the small businessperson. It is very costly in terms of time for the small business to send out collection letters for overdue debts. It is even more costly if a collection agency becomes involved. You can sell your computerized collection letter for a fraction of what it would cost a small business operator to collect unpaid debts any other way.

CONCEPT

The idea behind this business is to develop a stock set of letters to be sent out to debtors at regular intervals. You keep the texts of the letters on file, and plug in the names and addresses as they are supplied to you. It's that easy.

You are not becoming a collection agency. All you are selling is a letter service. Your only task is to make sure the letters get sent out on schedule. You receive money from the business using your service whether the recipient of the letter pays his bill or not.

Businesspeople will use your service because collection is an expensive and time-consuming part of their operation. It's a task they will be happy to be rid of at the low cost you will be able to charge. Most small businesses do not want to waste valuable employee time tracking down delinquent accounts and writing letters. And if a collection agency becomes involved, it usually takes 50 percent of the bill upon payment.

You can offer the letter service at a much lower cost, and with a little creativity produce better results than the more expensive methods of persuading delinquent customers to pay up.

SKILLS YOU WILL REQUIRE

There are really only two skills you will need in order to make this type of operation work: the ability to write a good collection letter and the ability to establish a schedule and follow it.

If you've ever missed payment on a bill, you are familiar with the initial collection letter. It's usually a gentle reminder that your payment is overdue, coupled with a polite request for immediate payment. If this first letter is ignored, more letters follow at regular intervals. A standard interval is 15 days, or half a month. Each letter is tougher than the last, until the final letter relates that the long overdue account is being turned over to the company's attorney for legal action.

There are two basic strategies to follow in a series of collection letters once the "gentle reminder" stage has passed, and these strategies are usually used in some combination. The first is the appeal to the debtor's sense of honor and fairness; the second is the threat of discontinued service and/or legal action. Use threats only as a last resort. A person who feels that he or she is being given the benefit of the doubt is more likely to pay.

I am going to give you some examples of collection letters that can be sent at different stages of the collection process. You will see from these examples how to gradually increase the forcefulness of the appeal, though the actual wording you choose may be slightly different.

When an account becomes 30 days overdue, the following letter is appropriate:

> HI THERE:
>
> In today's busy world, it's easy to overlook things, and our records show that you may have overlooked payment on your account with us, which was due on (date). To avoid additional interest charges, please remit full amount due without delay. Thank you.

If the account is still unpaid after another 15 days, send a letter like this one:

> HELLO AGAIN:
>
> Whether you realize it or not, your account is now 45 days past due.
>
> We have advanced services to you based on your pledge to make your payments on time. We don't think you want to jeopardize your good standing by failing to meet your obligations. We would like to continue to consider you a faithful and valuable customer.
>
> Please remit the full amount shown on your bill without delay. Thank you.

After another 15, the friendly tone might have to be abandoned. Your approach should now be something like this:

> Are you hiding from us?
>
> Your account with us is now seriously past due. Unless you make payment or contact us within the next three business days, we will be forced to discontinue service to you until the account is paid.
>
> We regret taking such action, but we have legitimate interests to protect. We cannot afford to do business with those who fail to meet their agreed-upon obligations.

Finally, when all your other letters have failed to produce results, you must send a letter indicating that it is the final warning before the matter is turned over to legal channels. It is up to you to decide how many letters to send before you reach this point, but chances are, if a person hasn't responded to three letters he isn't going to respond at all without tougher prodding.

In any case, once the account is 120 days past due, the final letter should be sent and the lawyers can take it from there.

The only other skill you will need is the ability to keep track of which letters to send out when. Your computer can handle such a schedule easily. Check the schedule each day and if a letter is due to go out, print it up with the subject's name and address and mail it.

Of course, you must stay in touch with your clients to find out whether or not a subject has paid and can be taken off the list.

INFORMATION REQUIRED

You will need almost no outside information to begin your letter service. This business is simple once you have your stockpile of letters written. Since all you are offering is a letter service, you can leave the legalities of actual collecting to those who practice them.

OPERATING NAME

The best thing to do is to name your business after yourself. "Joe Jones Collection Letter Service," or something similar, will do quite nicely. The advantage to this is that it saves you the cost of registering a new business name, opening new bank accounts, installing new phone lines, etc. You can simply use all the services you now have in your own name for your new business.

GETTING STARTED

Before you can sell something, you need to have something to sell. Start out by writing a sample series of collection letters. You may want to do a few different varieties of letters. For example, one from a service company might differ slightly from one sent out by a department store. It's up to you.

Once you've got your sample letters written, start pitching your service to businesses in the area. Your approach is that you can offer them a low-cost collection letter service that will produce as many results as the more expensive ways of collecting. For more on this see Marketing Methods.

THE COMPETITION

As mentioned earlier in this report, you are not competing with the collection agencies and lawyers who do actual collecting—you are offering a letter service only. You are doing the job previously done by company secretaries or other employees whose time could be spent much more profitably doing something else.

You can effectively eliminate the competition by offering low rates and by being the first in your area to offer the service. It is easy for you to undercut the alternatives. Collection agencies take 50 percent of all payments, and regular employees of any company cannot perform the service you offer in the time it will take you.

POTENTIAL INCOME

It is not difficult to price your service. Remember that you will get paid no matter what the outcome of the collection. Your job is to write and send the letters.

You should charge a flat fee for each collection attempt, whether you need to send one letter or five. When a client turns an account over to you, he is hiring you to facilitate collection of the money due him. If it takes just one letter for the account to be paid, fine. If it takes five letters, the result is the same and payment should be the same.

Besides, the basic letters have already been written before you even go into business. Once you get rolling, almost all of the work is plugging in addresses and mailing out the letters on schedule.

To find a fair price for your service, follow this procedure: place an hourly dollar value on your time. Add up the cost of your service and add the profit you want to make on each job.

The time you spend on each project will vary greatly, but in no case will it be more than a few hours. You've already spent much of your time beforehand, writing the letters. Once you are in business, you will spend time checking your schedule, entering names and addresses of debtors, traveling to and from the post office, and communicating with your clients.

Here are some of the costs you will have to take into account:

1. Cost of operating your computer and printer
2. Cost of telephone
3. Cost of postage
4. Cost of paper and envelopes
5. Cost of any travel time
6. Cost of software

Divide your monthly costs by the number of jobs per month. Add your desired profit, plus your hourly rate of pay, and you will arrive at a figure that is both attractive to you and a bargain for your clients.

Remember that the cost of your time is a part of the cost of doing business and not part of your profit. You are, in effect, paying yourself as an employee of your own business.

MARKETING METHODS

Direct mail, display ads, telephone sales and direct sales are the best methods for marketing this service.

To reach a large base of your target clientele, it's hard to beat a direct mail campaign. I am going to give you an example of a letter that will get businesses interested in what you have to offer. Make a list of businesses in your area you wish to target. Then send your mailing at the rate of 20 to 30 businesses a day, and watch the level of interest climb.

Here is the letter:

> DEAR BUSINESS OWNER:
>
> Are you tired of wasting valuable time keeping after people who don't pay their bills? Do you wish there was a less expensive way to get your delinquent customers to pay?
>
> Well, now there is!
>
> Our new computerized collection letter service will produce results at far less than you pay now. Just turn your overdue accounts over to us, and we'll take care of the constant reminders and notices that seem to take up so much of your valuable time.
>
> Let us show you our unique new service. We guarantee we'll save you money.

Mail this letter, or a slight variation of it, on a regular basis to businesses in your area, and you will get results. Collection letters are something most businesspeople would rather leave to someone else.

UNIQUE BUSINESS APPROACH

One way to attract potential clients to your service is to offer them something they haven't seen before. If your collection letters have a different flair than the run-of-the-mill slips used by most companies and collection agencies, businesses will be even more willing to give your service a try.

If you have any skill at drawing or graphic arts, or know someone who does, you might want to jazz up your letters with a cartoon or drawing, or some other type of visual message. Some printers have fairly advanced graphics capabilities and you might want to give this a try. Such a strategy is certainly an attention-grabber. Similar methods have been used with success.

LOCATION and MARKET BASE

The only restriction on your potential income is the number of potential clients in your area. For this reason, this business should usually be started in an urban area with a population of at least 200,000. Of course, the bigger the area, the more potential clients there will be for your service, and the more money you will be able to make.

TO SUM UP

A computerized collection letter service can save businesses hours of precious time and a substantial amount of money. You can start such a service with minimal prior knowledge and a small investment. Once you get it in gear, the amount of time you spend at it will be well worth the money you will receive from businesses to take care of a part of their operation they would like to live without. And the income you earn will ensure that your own bills always get paid on time.

SOURCE MATERIAL

Refer to Section 7.

No. 118

LOCAL MARKET SURVEY SERVICE

A market survey service supplies a new or existing business with statistics concerning the buying habits of potential markets. Through the use of analysis tools, such as questionnaires and relevant data concerning habits, preferences and other factors that influence buyers, the businessperson can zero in on the most likely market for his products.

CONCEPT

Put yourself in this situation: you've got an idea that you know is a winner, and the financing is there. Production facilities are ready and waiting. What's the next step?

The answer to this is an easy one—who are you going to sell your product to? You've got to know who and where your market is, or you'll be pouring money down the drain before you even get your business started. Sure, you know there will be demand, but that's not good enough. Why spend money advertising on a hit-or-miss basis? Put the money where it's going to work. By isolating your market, you can spend your advertising money much more effectively and make the return on your advertising dollar as high as possible.

A market survey service performs just this function. You survey the buyers in a particular region, using criteria that can be general or specific, depending on the requirements of your client. The data you've gathered will tell your clients who is likely to buy their product. For instance, if your research discovers that females between the ages of 18 and 34 with an annual income under $15,000 are the greatest consumers of glass cleaners, your decision has been made as to where to put the majority of your advertising money.

Obviously, this is invaluable information to any business. To make money in the competitive business world today requires an advantage, and you can offer your clients the edge they need to be a success.

You and your computer have the ability to gather market information and manipulate it into a customized statistical analysis of any potential market. The computer is the perfect tool for this kind of analysis. By following a few simple words of advice and a few rules, you'll find yourself in an exciting, profitable business that has unlimited growth potential.

SKILLS YOU WILL REQUIRE

In the market survey business, your primary need is for tools to gather your information. Samples for questionnaires and surveys can be found in magazines and libraries. Modify them as your demands require. At the same time, you will learn what it takes to formulate your own research-gathering tools.

Learn how the results are broken down. The charts and samples you study will show you that it's a matter of statistics. For instance, what percentage of your overall sample has an income over $50,000? This same group may show a preference for the type of product you are selling. You'll find that the concept of this sort of information-gathering is straightforward, easy and interesting.

The ability to organize will be the most useful skill to you here. The software you use will allow you to break down results according to your demands, but you will want to know how to present the report in it's most understandable form.

INFORMATION REQUIRED

As stated above, you need to know how to create your surveys. The next step is to build your survey around your client's needs. He can give you this information. For instance, if he is selling candy, he'll want to know how well his brand competes with other brands in the areas of flavor, size, price, appearance, etc. He will tell you what he wants, but you will offer good suggestions to him concerning what information is important.

Keep in mind that you are in the business of information- gathering. The required information will be somewhat different every time. One nice aspect, though, is that the information you collect will be useful to more than one client. Simply use the information you've gathered and sell it to firms who find it useful. One way to get the business going initially is to do a few surveys, create reports showing your results, and market them to businesses that need the information. Your business will also work on a contract basis, but a great deal of income can be made by marketing to other companies the information you've gathered for one business.

OPERATING NAME

Your own name will make it easiest to get the new business going. As mentioned in other sections of the book, some of the most successful information operations go by name alone.

This decision is up to you. Some low-key addition to your operating title, such as "Survey Research," always looks good and makes it clear what your business is about.

GETTING STARTED

In the market survey business you'll discover that you have a powerful tool in the statistics you will gather. Use this information to tantalize your potential clients. After you feel comfortable with the research tools (questionnaires, etc.), let people know who you are. Locate appropriate software for your business; there are many programs specifically written for this type of operation. You'll find that you can manipulate your information just about any way you want.

Use this versatility to win customers. Show them how your results paint a clear picture of their market. Send out your advertising literature on a regular basis. You may want to hire some extra help to serve as telephone or street operators to help you gather your information.

One tremendously useful source of information is the U.S. Census Bureau. It is often overlooked as a resource. The Census Bureau can supply you with elaborate demographic data—transportation patterns, growth of particular areas, make-up of the area according to age, race, sex and income, and other factors. The local chamber of commerce can often supply you with valuable census data, and generally their information will be free. State data centers can supply information from census records at a low cost.

Of course, it will also be helpful to you to write or call similar businesses and get information from them. Keep in mind that the more sources you have for your statistics, the better.

THE COMPETITION

To neutralize the competition, use this technique: create your own cash flow. Sell an idea for a market survey to a number of clients at a reduced price. Your imagination is the key here. Put out some feelers and find out what information is valuable. For example, some statistics on computer owners and their habits will be of great use to local computer stores. If you get enough interest, you can offer your clients a bargain rate, get some money up front, and follow through with your idea. Tell them that the going rate for this information will be close to several thousand dollars, but that since you have the material available, you can offer it for less—maybe.

Once your momentum increases, and it will increase quickly, you'll be able to undercut the competition by having established clients for your service.

POTENTIAL INCOME

Place an hourly value on your time and that of your workers. Then add up the costs of your research (a list follows). Your time near the end of your project will be spent in organizing results, manipulating data and designing and presenting reports.

Basic Costs:

1. Cost of advertising
2. Cost of organizing, designing and duplicating questionnaires
3. Cost of hired help, if used
4. Cost of telephone
5. Cost of time spent doing surveys
6. Cost of time spent organizing results
7. Cost of Census Report materials
8. Cost of postage
9. Cost of any materials used
10. Cost of software

Your fee will be the cost of your time and supplies, with a percentage markup for profit. As your operation goes through its early stages, you might want to make some profit concessions in exchange for increased visibility. As business grows, you will be charging the going rate, but since your service has great value above its actual cost, you will soon be able to command a higher amount. Depending on the degree of customization of your project, you'll find that the fee for your work will often be above the standard you set earlier.

MARKETING METHODS

Direct mail, display ads, telephone sales and direct sales are the best methods of marketing in this business.

Consider the following sample of a direct mail approach:

> DEAR BUSINESS OWNER:
>
> How much of your advertising dollar really makes a difference? If you send out direct mail without deciding where it should go, I can tell you where it will go—right into the garbage can.
>
> I can tell YOU where YOUR customers are. I have the resources and expertise to give you SPECIFIC details on who is likely to buy (product name) and who is not.
>
> Give me five minutes of your time and I'll show you what I have done for other successful businesses and what I can do for YOURS!

Blanket the business community with this letter, and you will get enough positive response to give you the momentum you need.

UNIQUE BUSINESS APPROACH

Modern business is information-crazy and this is the key to the high visibility of this service. As we've suggested in other sections that deal with information services, use some of the statistics or trends you've discovered in your research and send out a press release.

Contact all the media who are likely to use the information you have, get a copy of their guidelines for press releases and send out your information. You'll find that the visibility you can acquire here is invaluable, since it is free advertising for your service.

LOCATION and MARKET BASE

Since the source for much of your research will be people, an urban area of at least 200,000 market base is the best location for this business. The more accessible the public is, the faster you will be able to work. Your potential clients also will be easier to find and maintain in this type of area.

TO SUM UP

This is a business that is perfect for these information-hungry times. There are always new marketing angles being tested, and new markets for products appearing daily. The software industry, for example, is still very unsure of exactly who buys games and who buys home and business software. Believe me, there is much opportunity for a new, fresh outlook on the problem. This is the kind of challenge you'll find in a market research business.

There is a terrific chance for creativity in this business. Devising surveys that go a step further in understanding what people think can be one of the biggest thrills of your life, as well as an opportunity to make the money you want.

SOURCE MATERIAL

Refer to Section 7.

No. 119

COMPUTER HANDWRITING ANALYSIS SERVICE

Many articles have been written lately about the use of handwriting analysis for employee selection by large corporations. We will show you how to do it on your home computer with the same accuracy as the experts who are charging as much as $500 for each analysis. This service can also be used for individual analysis, with a less complex printout, letting you charge less but deal in greater volume.

CONCEPT

The concept of this business is to analyze handwriting for the purpose of understanding the personality of the customer. Handwriting analysis, or graphology, is coming into its own as a tool not only for self-analysis, but also for the hiring practices and screening of potential employees. This business allows you to use your computer to take advantage of this trend.

SKILLS YOU WILL REQUIRE

For this business, the skills you are going to have to develop include being able to integrate your computer, the software, plotter and printer to give you the equipment you need for handwriting analysis.

If you enjoy a pioneering use for your computer, you will do well with this business. Since computers haven't been used for this service traditionally, you can take it wherever you want, set new trends in the field and make a killing in the process.

INFORMATION REQUIRED

This is one business opportunity that requires you to do a fair amount of research before opening up. What you'll need to familiarize yourself with is the whole area of graphology. You can start by reading books from the library about the business. Become familiar with the terminology used by the experts and the methods used in analysis.

Handwriting analysis uses as its base the peculiarities of an individual's style of writing. Each loop, slant, curve and dot signals something about that person's personality. And these signals are what you want to study up on.

Once you become familiar with the basics of the graphology field, your real work begins. This will consist of creating a program to use on your computer that will analyze the handwriting. This means you'll be inputting all the possible ways for a person to write, along with a description of what those style peculiarities say about that person. Sound difficult? Not really. There are only about 20 elements in writing that can be studied. These include degree of slant, breadth and height of letters, space between letters and words, etc. Your initial research should familiarize you with these elements enough so that you will feel comfortable in putting your computer to work in analyzing them.

To aid in your research on the topic, you may decide to go to a graphologist yourself, either as a customer or as a researcher. Most enjoy talking about their work with others and may even consider going into business with you to assist in the technical areas about which you are unfamiliar.

GETTING STARTED

To get started in this business, you need to do your research, become familiar with the field, then input the information into your computer in a way that will allow you to use your plotter to analyze the data. What you want to be able to do is take a sample of writing—usually a full page, written in relaxed conditions—and use a light pen or other electronic technique to follow the writing patterns in a way that the computer can analyze the data. You may also choose to have the person who is being analyzed use the light pen himself, in order to prevent inaccuracies from occurring in the copying of the data. The sample text will then be in the computer itself and you can manipulate it any way you need to do your analysis.

When a customer comes to you, you will have him write a page of sample text, make a note of his age, sex and nationality (which all have a bearing on handwriting styles), then let the computer do its work. Once the computer has studied the handwriting, based on what you have fed into it earlier, it can print out the analysis, along with sample handwriting from the text to prove its points.

Your initial set-up work in this business is extensive. But once you have the system running, the actual analysis will only take a few minutes, meaning that your profit will be very high for each job.

THE COMPETITION

Your competition in this business is usually located in major metropolitan areas and all of them use manual methods for their work. You eliminate your competition simply by using computerized techniques, which ensure a greater degree of accuracy, speedier service and a lower cost. You may even consider putting your competition to work for you by assisting you with your initial research in the business.

POTENTIAL INCOME

The income you can earn with this business is astounding. In the beginning you will be working for free, since you will have to do research and set your system up. After that, the sky truly is the limit. For example, if you have 12 corporate job applicants, and you charge each $200 for analyzing, say, 10 employees, you can earn $2,400 in a month simply from these three clients. Likewise, you can charge $25 to individuals wanting an analysis performed. If you get 10 customers in a week, that is $250 for you. Add that to your corporate clientele, and you can write your own ticket. The potential income you can gain is dependent only on how much time and energy you want to give the business.

To figure a cost for your service, you will have to do a little arithmetic. First, add up all the costs of your program (a list follows), then add in a salary for your time and a profit for the business. Estimate how many customers you can handle comfortably, whether corporate or individual, and divide your costs by that number. This will give you an idea of how much to charge each.

With this service, you may try several different pricing options. If you choose to handle corporate customers, you may decide to charge a set amount for each round of job applications you analyze. Or you may charge for each individual analysis you perform. That is, if one job opening gets 25 applicants and the company wants you to look over all of them, you can either charge a flat rate for the entire job or a rate for each applicant. Or you may choose to create a service contract with your corporate customers and charge them a flat rate every month, no matter how much or little they use your service.

Basic Costs

1. Cost of time spent researching subject
2. Cost of time spent inputting data into computer
3. Cost of special software used
4. Cost of time spent on each analysis
5. Cost of time spent compiling and printing results
6. Cost of advertising
7. Cost of telephone use
8. Cost of transportation
9. Cost of special materials used
10. Cost of printer, plotter supplies

You will find with this business that once you get going on it, your expenses will decrease and your profits will increase.

MARKETING METHODS

The best ways to market this service are direct mail and display advertising. You can aim your display ads at both general-interest and business clients, depending on where you place the ads. For example, to attract private customers, you can run ads in newspapers, magazines and other general-interest publications. For business clients, you can run ads in business publications or in the business section of your local newspaper.

A typical ad might read:

> WHAT DOES YOUR HANDWRITING SAY ABOUT YOU?
>
> Better yet, what does it say about potential employees? You know what kind of person you want to fill that new job opening. Let us use our computerized techiques to tell you which applicant best fills the bill for you. Call us today for more information about this low-cost, effective and scientific method of learning about a person through his handwriting.

You can experiment with an ad of this type by running it in several publications to see which draws the most interest and attention.

You may also consider attacking your potential markets by sending out direct mail letters. Compile a list of companies in your area that could most use your services, then send out letters explainig what you can do. An example might be:

> Dear Personnel Director:
>
> Would you like to save time and money finding the right kind of employee for that new job opening?
>
> Of course you would, and with our unique service you can start today!
>
> A simple test can tell you all you need to know about each applicant, what kind of personality he or she possesses, what strengths and weaknesses, and many other factors that could have a bearing on your decision. What kind of test are we talking about? Handwriting. That's right, handwriting analysis, or graphology, is the study of personality as exposed through handwriting.
>
> And now we can put you in touch with the latest technology in this growing field. Our service is effective, low cost and incredibly accurate. To find out more about this fascinating field, contact us today. We'll demonstrate our service and give you a free sample of what handwriting can tell about a person.

Mailed out at the rate of 10 to 20 a day, this letter should bring you plenty of inquiries for business. Reply promptly, and in no time you should begin to get customers with your efforts.

UNIQUE BUSINESS APPROACH

This is a unique business in its own right, but there are several approaches you can try that should prove effective in generating business.

The first approach is to give demonstrations of your service any place where businesspeople gather. This might include service and professional meetings, seminars, conventions, and a multitude of other places. Since the time you spend actually doing an analysis will be very short once you have the initial system up and running, you will be able to give actual analyses for potential clients right at the meeting or convention.

You can use this same technique to sell to individuals. Simply set up a booth at a place where others can pay you to do their analysis, or hire yourself out to companies for their next office party, to civic groups for their next meeting, or any other group where people will pay you to demonstrate your graphology methods.

Another market you might consider tapping is that of employment agencies. This multi-million-dollar field is always in need of new ways to convince clients and companies that the candidates chosen for a position are the right ones. You can hire yourself out to employment agencies to perform handwriting analyses on their clients to ensure they get into the career for which they are best suited. This method of getting business can work into a very profitable line if you have the time to handle the flood of business that could result.

The best way to make money with this business, though, is one we've saved for last. The secret in business is always to come up with an idea and then let others make your money for you. In this case, you've developed a thorough, effective and efficient method of analyzing handwriting; now all you have to do is market it to others as a business opportunity, or in other words, as a franchise operation. If you get others to franchise the equipment and methods you've developed, you can sit back and take a cut of their profits. What could be smarter than that?

LOCATION and MARKET BASE

For this business you'll want to be in a city with a population base of at least 200,000. The reason for this is that any smaller an area won't give you the number of businesses and individuals you'll need to get this project off the ground and running. On the other hand, if you decide to franchise the operation after developing the entire program, it doesn't matter where you live, city or country, as long as you have access to the post office and a telephone.

START UP CAPITAL

You can expect this operation to require more than $5,000 in start-up capital. This will give you the money you'll need for development of the program, as well as for your computer equipment. Refer to Section 6 for information about obtaining the needed capital.

TO SUM UP

A handwriting analysis business isn't for everyone. It will take a little effort and thought, and some work for free in the beginning. But the beauty of this business is that because so few people would ever choose to try it, the ones who do can make a fortune.

Graphology isn't by any means a new science. Discussion of the subject first began surfacing more than 300 years ago. And since that time people have been fascinated by what their handwriting can tell about them. Handwriting experts run columns on their subject regularly in newspapers and magazines, and several books have come out on the subject and have become big sellers.

What is new about the subject is that more and more corporations are turning to graphology to help them find qualified job candidates. This is where you can sweep up. If you take the time to place the analysis process on computer, you will take the least amount of time and offer the most accuracy of anybody. No doubt, your system will get written up in many publications, which will only generate more business for you. Once that happens, all you will have to do is get other people to sign their way to your success. And that's something you can bank on.

SOURCE MATERIAL

Refer to Section 7.

No. 120

COMPUTERIZED ASTROLOGICAL CHART SERVICE

This is an efficient business that can be started in a medium-sized metropolitan area using a small investment. If properly managed and promoted, even a part-time service will reduce your work hours and increase profits.

CONCEPT

The concept of this business is to sell astrological information. After asking a few questions about your clients' birthdays, you can tell them, for example, if their relationship with a Libra will sail on or is headed for troubled waters. Your computer will do your work for you! And why not turn this capability into business?

With a computer printout, you provide information that can guide your clients in all aspects of their lives. With only a little knowledge, you can become a full-fledged astrologist and tell your clients their likes, dislikes, strengths and interests.

What is so attractive about this service is that it is fast, which means you make your money quickly. An astrologist without a computer would need up to three hours to provide a full astrological or natal chart. Your computer can do the same chart in minutes. The printout is clear and understandable, and your clients will admire the quality and professionalism of your service.

SKILLS YOU WILL REQUIRE

You don't have to be Jeanne Dixon to start your business. Basically, the computer will do all the work for you. It will print special reports that are so personalized that your clients will know you are excellent at your job. If you really get hooked on astrology and want to bone up on the subject, libraries, book stores and supermarkets carry a wide assortment of books on the "stars." All you have to do is zero in on your particular audience.

INFORMATION REQUIRED

Probably the biggest obstacle in getting started is simply deciding on what type of astrological information you want to furnish to your clients. There are many different programs to choose from and, of course, they vary in price. You can choose software that will give you information about personality, tastes, strengths and possible weaknesses. Or you can specialize in numerology, which uses name and birthday to show one's destiny, life cycles, and challenges. I Ching is another choice.

Do a little research about the available software. Figure out what your personal interests are in astrology and find a program that fits your needs. Then you are ready to target your market.

GETTING STARTED

Clients are what make this business. Once you have determined what type of astrology you want to specialize in, use marketing techniques that will reach the people you are aiming for. More about this is in Marketing Methods.

Become familiar with your software. Practice it on friends and family. Become confident in its use. Then you are ready to get started.

THE COMPETITION

Remember, you are head-and-shoulders above the competition simply because you can do the same full-scale charts in a fraction of the time. After you have purchased the software, your start-up costs are very low. And once you attract your initial clients, word of mouth will bring more to your door. Even if people don't believe in astrology, millions still read their horoscopes in the newspaper every day. They may not follow the advice or warnings, but they're curious about it all the same. To eliminate your competition will simply take the time necessary to carve out your own slice of the market base.

POTENTIAL INCOME

Most astrologists charge $25 or more for a natal chart. You don't have to charge this much since you won't be spending hours to produce it. If you charge only $15 a customer, you can easily make $100 to $500 a week with only a small amount of time. Since your computer does your work for you, your labor output is minimal.

Pricing your service is not complicated. You start out by placing an hourly value on your own time. Then you add up all the costs of the program (review the following list) and add in a profit figure for the job. The total is what you should get for the job. Keep in mind that your hourly rate is not pure profit; that is what you are paid for your effort. Profit is what the business makes after all costs are covered.

You should earn money for your time and a profit for your business with each client.

Costs To Get Started

1. Cost of writing sales letters and flyers
2. Cost of printing letters and flyers
3. Cost of preparing display advertising
4. Cost to advertise
5. Cost of preparing questionnaires and reproducing them
6. Cost of mailing sales letters
7. Cost of software and computer supplies

Point-of-Service Costs

1. Cost of time to perform service
2. Cost of forecast production
3. Cost to mail/deliver

Profit

Don't undercharge. Just because Madame LaRue is charging $30 for an entire hour of the same service, doesn't mean that you should charge $5 because you spent only 10 minutes. With your computer, you are more efficient at providing the reading. In practical terms, charge what you feel people will pay. You can devise a formula that will allow you to calculate what you must make. If you schedule one appointment every 30 minutes on Saturday afternoons at $25 each, in four hours you will receive $200. That is a monthly income of $800. Just think what you could make if you expanded to two or three days a week.

MARKETING METHODS

Display advertising and flyers are the best methods for marketing this service. Sales letters are also a good approach. If you were providing a service which analyzes love relationships, you might want to draft a letter like the following:

> DEAR ASTROLOGY ENTHUSIAST:
>
> We see something very important happening in your life soon. The picture is cloudy now, but with only a few minutes of your time, you can answer three strategic questions that will clear up the view.
>
> Contact us today for a personal reading that will change the direction of your life.

You have several methods of contacting clients. You can rent or buy lists of astrology magazine subscribers, who will have a natural interest in your service. Or you can mail the letter out at random to people in your area. Establish who visits the astrologists, then target that market. You can get lists of names from local demographic companies for a low fee.

Another route for finding clients is running a display ad in a local newspaper or weekly shopper. Come up with imaginative slogans that will stimulate an interest in astrology. An example of a display ad might be:

You are unique.

Let us show you why.

Helen Jones and Company Astrology—555-1212

UNIQUE BUSINESS APPROACH

Some successful astrologers we know have increased their earnings considerably by offering a free reading. Advertise a free, no-obligation forecast for the coming month. Once a prospective client has tried it and seen what it is about, he or she will return again as a paying customer.

Since each forecast takes only a few minutes of time, your initial investment will eventually pay off handsomely.

LOCATION and MARKET BASE

This business requires a population base of at least 50,000 people. You may wish to promote your business to include the county if your city base is marginal.

Keep in mind that once you have the basics down and are established, you can begin to provide printouts to other astrologists who don't own computers. Using the mail, you can begin a pipeline to astrologists from Maine to Oregon right from your home office in Macon, Georgia. Plus, you can sell the service to individual clients through the mail. Either way, it means more business for you.

TO SUM UP

Astrology charts seem to be a constant attraction to people in this country. We all want to know more about how to face the uncertainty that plagues us each day. The fact that on the day of our birth the solar system was in a particular arrangement, and can affect events in our future, somehow appeals to us.

Aim your computer toward the stars. With a small investment you can become a scientific astrologist. You can pick your own hours. If you provide sound, professional information, your clients will pick you—and send their friends as well. That means money in your pocket any way you forecast it!

SOURCE MATERIAL

Refer to Section 7.

No. 121

COMPUTERIZED BIO-RHYTHMS SERVICE

This service has been around ever since computers made their debut on the market. We will show you a different approach at cornering a local market by not only doing personal biorhythms, but also by doing event biorhythms and special occasions. This attracts a broader interest group and makes everybody aware of the service you have to offer. This has been very successful in many areas of the United States, and it is easy to promote and to get repeat business.

CONCEPT

The concept of this business is to tell people when they are going to have good days or bad days during the coming month. This information is provided by the computer program you use, based on your customer's date of birth.

Many important people use biorhythms to know when they should make major business decisions, when they can look forward to a good period of time and when they should probably avoid major decisions for awhile.

This is the reason biorhythms are so popular. People like to know what kinds of days lie ahead for them, when they should be careful, and when they can take chances. With just a few minutes of time, you can earn a nice income with this business.

SKILLS YOU WILL REQUIRE

You certainly don't need to be able to read a crystal ball for this service. All it requires is a computer program into which you will add a few numbers. The computer does your work for you and supplies you with the product you hand over to your customer.

Have you ever noticed that some days you feel like everything you touch turns to gold, while other days, nothing seems to go right? Some people believe that your life goes through cycles of highs and lows, based on your date of birth. This is what a biorhythm is—a charting of the patterns of your life day by day.

If you have ever worked with biorhythms yourself, you might as well put your interest to work earning income. But even if you have never explored this idea, the biorhythm programs on the market are so easy to use that it won't take much time or effort for you to set up this business.

INFORMATION REQUIRED

The information required for biorhythms has three parts: physical vitality, or how you will feel on a particular day, level of alertness, or how aware you will be, and emotional sensitivity, or whether you will feel happy or sad.

Computer programs are available on the market that will chart these three cycles for the coming week, month, or even year. Sometimes they peak all at once, in which case, according to biorhythm charts, no matter what you do, you seem to be lucky. Other times, each will take its own direction. Your biorhythms will predict that you will be lucky at love, but unlucky at business, or vice versa.

When a customer comes to you for this service, you simply plug his birth date into the program, as well as today's date, and the computer processes the information and creates a chart for you. It will also tell you how to interpret the chart.

This business isn't difficult to operate at all. Once you have customers, they will come back to you time and again, every time they want to know what the coming month holds for them. Since it takes just a few minutes to create a chart, you will amaze yourself with the money you can make.

GETTING STARTED

To get started in this business, you will need to get a computer program for biorhythms. Many cost under $20. Once you have that, it is time to get customers. The Marketing Methods section will explain how to attract business.

The chart you supply your customer can be of two varieties. You can do a chart for the month, telling which days will be good or bad, or you can do one for the whole year. If you have a printer, you can even supply a chart that will show the cycles your client will go through. At the bottom of the chart, you can show the months listed, one after another. At the side of the chart, you will have the three cycles you are measuring— emotional, physical and mental. Three lines will run across the chart showing highs and lows, depending on what part of the month it is. Your computer program will do this work for you. It is up to the customer to use the information you provide as he sees fit.

THE COMPETITION

To eliminate the competition in this business, offer your services at less than they charge. You can find out what they charge by calling and posing as a prospective customer. Ask how their service works, what they give you, what it costs, etc. Since you'll be using a computer to do your work for you, your cost will probably be less than theirs, in which case you don't need to charge as much to pay your expenses, but can still make a profit.

POTENTIAL INCOME

Pricing this service is not complicated. First, you have to place an hourly value on your own time. To do this, you add the cost of your overhead and expenses, plus a profit for the business. The total will give you a good idea of what you can afford to charge.

With a business of this kind, you can easily charge $10 and still make a profit, as well as money for your time. If you have 20 customers in a month, that is $200 for only a few minutes of work on the computer.

You can greatly increase this amount by offering biorhythm charts through the mails. All you have to do is run an ad with a coupon requesting the information you need to do a person's biorhythm chart. A customer will send you a check along with the coupon. Then you do the chart and mail it back.

Basic Costs

1. Cost of computer program
2. Cost of advertising
3. Cost of paper and printer supplies
4. Cost of time spent creating biorhythm chart
5. Cost of any materials used
6. Cost of postage

Overhead

Remember to add in your costs of overhead when calculating what your expenses will be. This will include phone charges, office space, etc.

Profit

Also remember to include a profit figure in your expenses. This isn't the same as the money you earn for your time. That is your salary. A profit is the money your business earns, money that allows it to grow.

How To Be Paid

For this business, you collect your fee as you provide the service. Your customer simply pays you when you create his biorhythm chart for him.

If you choose to operate this business through the mail, you can request payment with the order.

MARKETING METHODS

Display ads are probably the best way to market this business. Run your ad in those publications where people who are most likely to want your service will see it. These include local newspapers, weekly shoppers, etc. If you want to run this business through the mails, you can run your ad in magazines catering to people who might want to use it. Businesspeople are a great market for this, since many use it to know when they should make important business decisions. All you have to do is include a coupon with your ad that can be filled out and mailed in with a check or money order.

Here is a sample of an ad:

> CHART YOUR YEAR NOW!
>
> Biorhythms tell you when you can expect to be on top of the world and when to be cautious—in love, money and health.
>
> In just a few minutes, I'll produce a chart telling you what cycles your life will go through in the coming days and months.
>
> Call now for more information.

Your own versions of this ad will bring responses for more information. Tell them your price and invite them to try your service. Once they have, they'll be back time and time again.

UNIQUE BUSINESS APPROACH

Although you can expect to earn a nice part-time income with this business on a single-customer basis, I'm going to tell you another method you can use to increase your business tenfold.

What you want is a lot of customers, and fast. The way to get them is to offer your service at parties, conventions, meetings and other gatherings where a lot of people congregate and want to have a little fun.

The company or person sponsoring the group meeting can pay you a flat rate to provide a biorhythm chart for each person at the function. For a few hours of time you can make hundreds of dollars.

You can get business this way by making a list of all the party givers and organizations you know that would enjoy having you at their next event. Include groups like senior citizen clubs, business groups, sororities, fraternities, service organizations, shopping centers, conventions, etc. Don't forget local corporations. You'd be a big hit at the next office party.

Contact people in these groups and offer your service for a flat rate for the event. Then you can tote your computer and printer along with you for the evening and chart up biorhythms right on the spot.

The people who use your service at the party or meeting will probably want to come to you on a personal basis once they have seen a biorhythm and how they can use it in their personal lives.

LOCATION and MARKET BASE

If you live in a city or town with a population of at least 50,000, you should have a sufficient market base of people for this business. If you are in a small town, you can make your money by offering your service through the mail. And if you're willing to drive to neighboring towns and cities, you can also perform special events, increasing your potential income dramatically.

START-UP CAPITAL

To get this business started, you'll need less than $1,000 to pay for the computer program and special supplies you'll use. With this small amount of start-up capital, you will quickly be on your way to a nice income that will pay for those extras you want in life.

TO SUM UP

People love speculating about what the future holds for them. Biorhythms won't tell you that you will fall in love with a tall, dark and handsome stranger. But it will inform you about what kind of day you can expect. If you have a major business decision to make in a coming month, you can use your biorhythm to tell you when you will probably be in the best frame of mind to make it. If you are wondering when to make a trip to Las Vegas or elsewhere for gambling, biorhythms will tell you when you will probably be at the peak of your luck.

With a computerized biorhythms service, you can have some fun at the same time you're earning money. People will come to you because they want to know what to expect in the future — when they will be at the top of their form, and when they should stick close to home. They can make whatever they want of your information. It is up to them to interpret the chart. All you do is provide it for them.

With just a few minutes of your time, a little effort and perserverence, you can start predicting your own future, one filled with riches and rewards. With this business, you can be "lucky" all the time. And that's something you can take to the bank.

SOURCE MATERIAL

Refer to Section 7.

No. 122

ORDER PROCESSING- CATALOGUE AND MAIL ORDER SALES

In this business, you handle catalog and mail order sales for existing retail businesses. You don't have to invest your own capital in starting a retail business; you help expand other people's retail businesses and cash in on their increased sales. If you're good at details and like analyzing and organizing quantities of data, this is a good business for you.

CONCEPT

The concept of this service is to help existing retail businesses expand their sales through mail orders. The merchants can use either catalogs or magazine ads. You take over the job of customer contact, keeping track of orders and having them filled. Retail businesses that go into mail order sales usually increase their gross sales by 40 percent; your profit comes out of that 40 percent.

While many different kinds of retail businesses are potential targets for this kind of service, the best ones are specialty shops. Some examples are: clothing in unusually large or small sizes, sporting equipment, gourmet foods, unique jewelry, and bath accessories. The list is endless.

You can help the businesses in publishing their catalogs or placing ads in magazines. Then you develop and maintain a data base of the products each company sells. When orders come in, you match them with the products and prepare shipping documents. If items must be back-ordered, you notify the customer and maintain the records for both the customer and the products.

An additional service that will be invaluable to your customers— the retail businesses—is to develop and maintain a mailing list of customers who place mail orders.

SKILLS YOU WILL REQUIRE

For this business you don't need any particular experience or background in retail sales—orders will come to you. You do need to be good at detail and organizing information. If you like working with numbers, that's even better. And you will need patience.

Accurate typing is a must for data entry. But you don't necessarily have to do that yourself; you can hire part-time help if you need to.

The main skill you'll need is the ability to set up and maintain a data base and retrieve information from it. Before computers came along, order processing involved tediously copying information from one form onto another and maintaining several files of papers—products available, incoming orders, filled orders, back orders and so on. With a computer and good data base management software, you can do an even better, more accurate job in a fraction of the time it would take to do it manually.

INFORMATION REQUIRED

One of the beauties of this business is that your customers—the retail businesses—and their customers will supply almost all the information you need. The retailers will supply you with all their product information—product names, stock numbers, colors, sizes, styles, vendors and prices. The customers who place orders will provide their names and addresses and the kind of merchandise that interests them.

As an asset to getting started, you should know about shipping methods and rates, production methods and costs for publishing and distributing catalogs, and costs for advertising in various magazines. While you could conduct this business without knowing these things, the more information you can provide for the retailers, the more valuable your service will be.

You'll also need to know how to set up and maintain your data base. All the information you'll need to do this should be included in the user's manual for the data base management software you get. A variety of different data base management software is available, with different features and capabilities, and manuals with varying degrees of usefulness. Before you buy this important software, you should investigate the various options thoroughly.

OPERATING NAME

For this business, as in many other cases, you have two choices about an operating name. You can either make up a fictitious name, or you can simply operate under your own name. Since you'll be serving a special market, and not advertising to the general public, a fictitious name that describes your business isn't really necessary. A fictitious name involves extra start-up expenses for filing the business name, a special bank account, business phone rates and so on.

Instead, you can simply use your own name. As you develop a reputation for providing an effective service, your name will become a valuable asset. See Section 4 for more information about operating names.

GETTING STARTED

The first step is to let your potential customers know about your service. Have a professional-quality brochure prepared explaining the service you're offering and how it will benefit the retailers. Stress the size of the probable increase in their sales and what little effort it will require from them. Tell them about the high profit margin for this kind of sales—they don't need more space, they don't need more salespeople, they don't even need to maintain more inventory, because they can order from their suppliers as needed.

Explain what you'll do for them—maintaining their data base of products, maintaining a customer mailing list, processing orders, providing liaison with customers. Show them how effortless this expanded market will be for them.

Once you've prepared your brochure, you have to distribute it, of course. See Marketing Methods and Unique Business Approach for some suggestions on ways to make contact with potential customers and distribute your brochure.

THE COMPETITION

This service is so unusual, you'll probably have very little competition. Large companies that engage in mail order business already have their own in-house order processing departments. Your clients will be smaller businesses that haven't tackled this approach yet. Point out the benefits of having you take over this job for them.

POTENTIAL INCOME

Your fee will be a percentage of the orders you handle, with a flat rate minimum. The total amount you earn will depend on how much time you're willing to devote to the business. As a rule of thumb, you can expect a medium level income from this business.

You can also charge for your services in helping produce a catalog or magazine ads. And once a retailer has established a sizeable number of mail order customers, you can also produce a mailing list to send catalogs to regular customers.

Your day-to-day costs of doing business will be fairly low. If you're doing business out of your home, your operating costs will consist mainly of the cost of supplies—paper, printer ribbon and diskettes. You'll also have the usual overhead costs—office space, utilities, phone, and your own advertising. And, as the business grows, you may want to hire some help and add in salary expenses.

Basic Costs

1. Cost of software
2. Cost of advertising and brochure production
3. Cost of mailing supplies and postage
4. Cost of time spent organizing mail order account
5. Cost of telephone
6. Cost of time spent filling orders

MARKETING METHODS

You can choose among several different marketing methods for this business. Display ads, direct mail and telephone sales are all effective approaches. You can target retail businesses in specific shopping centers, or you can use a directory of retail businesses in your area. This kind of directory is usually available at the public library.

Here's a sample letter that you can use with your brochure if you choose the direct mail approach.

DEAR BUSINESS OWNER:

Would you like to increase your gross sales by 40 percent? Of course you would. With my help you can do it with no additional expense for facilities, sales force, or inventory.

The local market for your unusual line of products is limited. With my help you can extend your business into the profitable mail-order share of the market. I can help you develop a catalog or an ad to place in the right magazines to reach potential new customers. Then when the orders come rolling in, I'll process them for you and make sure your new customers are satisfied with your mail order service.

You won't have the expense of setting up a mail order system and hiring someone to process your orders, because I'll take care of all that for you. I'm so confident of the success you'll have, that I'll only charge for the orders I actually process—there's no monthly maintenance fee.

As an introduction to this new service, I'm offering a special rate for helping prepare your catalog or magazine ad. Don't delay—start increasing your sales now!

Keep a record of your mailings so that you can follow up with a phone call about a week after you send out your letters. The mailing will introduce you and your service, and the retailer will recognize you when you call to clinch the sale.

UNIQUE BUSINESS APPROACH

Here's a special approach that will really help market your services. Contact merchant organizations and offer to give a presentation about this unique new approach to marketing. People usually respond very favorably to seminars. If they're well-designed and informative, they often don't seem like just another sales pitch.

If your knees turn to jelly when you think about standing up and talking in front of a group, have someone else do it for you. But be sure to go to the meeting and meet your potential clients and talk to them yourself. Get yourself known! Networking is one of the most powerful and effective marketing techniques for services that you'll ever find.

LOCATION and MARKET BASE

For this business you really need to be located in or near a city large enough to provide plenty of retail businesses as potential clients for you. On the other hand, you can conduct this business in any state. You're not restricted to any particular region. Your primary interest is in having access to enough retailers to provide a base sufficient for your operations. But the retailers' customers can be anywhere in the world.

You'll need a market base of 200,000 or more to conduct this business effectively. That doesn't necessarily mean your city has to have a population of 200,000. The city itself could be a bit smaller, if suburban towns around it add up to that magic number.

START-UP CAPITAL

You can get into this business with an investment in the range of $1,000 to $5,000, including the cost of your computer. The amount you'll need depends on the features and capabilities of your equipment, and whether you can find a satisfactory computer that comes bundled with the appropriate software.

See Section 6 for information on how to obtain the capital you need.

TO SUM UP

This unique idea offers you an opportunity to develop a profitable business for yourself while helping retailers in your area expand their business. It provides a great boost for the general economy of your community while it boosts your own personal economy!

If you're good at detail and like working with figures, this is a great way to take advantage of your skills to build your own business. You can put in as much time and effort as you choose, to build the business to just the size you want. The only limits are the ones you set yourself. So get started today!

SOURCE MATERIAL

Refer to Section 7.

No. 123

REAL ESTATE LISTING SERVICE

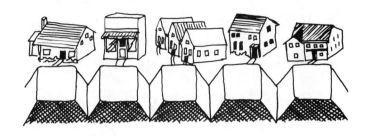

Most cities have a multiple listing for realtors, but it is precisely where such services fall short that the big money is to be made. Most buyers don't have access to the multiple listing book and waste both their time and that of realty agents, just finding out what is available on the market.

With your service the buyer and realtor save time and frustration—and you make the money. In fact, with this business you can make money from everyone—the buyer, seller and agent.

CONCEPT

The idea of this business is to make real estate information easily available to the end buyer. At the same time, you are providing convenience and advertising for the seller and the real estate agent.

To do this, you compile your own version of a "multiple listing" book in the form of a magazine or newsletter. You do this by selling space to those who want to sell real estate, and then selling that information to the buyer.

This service is of great value to your clients on both sides of the bargain. Since it can be done as a one-person operation, or by employing a salesperson on commission, it can generate a very high income-per-hour and per-dollar investment.

SKILLS YOU WILL REQUIRE

First you need the ability to use a word processor, and preferably a data base.

You also need to be willing to sell your service to the real estate community and to sell your product to an outlet that will get your publication to the prospective buyer.

If this type of one-on-one sales is not your cup of tea, you can hire someone on commission to do the selling. However, this approach, while it certainly has its own advantages, cuts down on your profits.

INFORMATION REQUIRED

The information you require is of two types. First you need the names and addresses of those who might be interested in advertising with you. That may include regular real estate agents, commercial brokers, and other companies involved in the realty field, such as banks and title companies. The other type of information is the details of the properties you are listing.

When you sell your services to the first part of this information duo, they will supply you with the information for the second part. Don't just take the information they give you. Be prepared to ask questions. If you get certain types of information, you can dramatically increase your income from this project with virtually no extra work by following a unique business approach, discussed later.

GETTING STARTED

Getting into this business is pretty straightforward. First, you need to choose your market. Don't make your target area too broad. If more than one area interests you, put out separate publications for each one. This is very important because it does two things: it makes you more money. If one listing tries to cover all bases, you'll loose the potential to sell multiple ads and multiple publications. Secondly, your end user won't be as interested in buying your publication. The object of your service is to simplify the buyers' search for the ideal home or property. If a home buyer has to wade through office listings, he or she simply won't buy your product.

Next, make up a "dummy" copy of your publication. This is easy to do. Simply create fictitious listings. Don't forget display ads and other, more expensive listings, using photos, etc. Type them up and paste them onto sheets of paper the size (format) your publication will be. When your "paste-up" is done, have it copied.

With your dummy completed, visit places that might be interested in selling it. Food markets and stores with magazine racks are naturals, as are pharmacies.

Don't let your imagination stop there. Other proven places to sell this type of publication are: gas stations, banks and airport gift shops.

Some places, like the banks, won't sell your publication - they'll give it away. Don't overlook this market. It would make a good gift from businesses such as moving companies or corporations moving people to a new office.

Ask these prospective markets if they would be interested in handling your publication, and how many they could use. When you have found your markets and the number of copies you think you will be able to sell, it is time to approach the sellers.

Be prepared to tell your prospective client several things: how many copies will be printed, how and where they will be distributed, how much different types of ads will cost them, and what special markets you will be able to reach. Go in looking good and sounding confident. Have the answers to their questions and be able to stress how it will help them. If you do that, you'll come out with a sale almost every time.

THE COMPETITION

Many larger cities already have one or more realty publications. To eliminate the competition, create your own unique market. The opportunity here is limited by your own imagination and drive, not the competition.

At the same time, many cities and most small towns have nothing like this available. Resort towns, mountain villages and beach areas are especially good places to start this type of business.

A good example of this type of community is Running Deer, California. The population of this mountain community is 750 people. It has two realtors, a bank, a restaurant, a market, two gas stations and a real estate publication. The realty listings are sold in over half the businesses in town, and the current publishing schedule calls for 3,000 periodicals per month, every month. The publisher tells us that almost every issue sells out.

POTENTIAL INCOME

The costs on this business can be kept low and the profit very high. To study your cost and profit structure, you can use the guidelines that follow. However, you should adapt them to local circumstances (cost of ads and sales price of your publication). This almost always produces a higher profit margin than the example given, because the example uses very conservative figures.

The current average cost of hiring a writer (you) is about $20 per hour throughout the United States. You should base your "hourly" wage on that figure. Then add up all costs of production. That is the cost of putting out your publication. Your hourly rate is not your profit. It is a cost of production. Your profit is what your business clears after all costs are paid.

A rule of thumb is that the end product should sell for four to five times the cost of production. I think you will see that this type of business can easily outstrip that standard. Profits of 1,000 percent to 3,000 percent or more are not uncommon with this business.

1. Printing—four-page digest-sized magazine can currently be produced for about five cents each for 500 copies. The more copies, the cheaper you can produce each copy.

2. Photos of available property, screened and ready to print, should be provided by the advertiser. Since this should constitute the majority of your illustrations, there is little

or no cost here. If you want a special logo, etc., you should be able to get a good one from a clip art book, which sells for about $3.

3. Secondary costs include phone calls, gas to collect advertisements, etc.

Adding up all costs, 500 copies of a four-page pubication will cost you between $20 and $25, plus about an hour of labor and $5 in secondary costs. The total is $50.

Even if you sold each of your publications for 50 cents each, and did not collect one cent from the advertisers, your profit would be $200. You thus have a viable business project.

However, you will also collect from your advertisers at going business rates in your community. If you can sell more than 500 copies, your profit margin can be very healthy indeed.

Two more facts are included here about figuring out your costs and profits. The hourly cost of your time in selling ads should be charged against the amount you collect for your ads, not against publishing costs. You should use the going rate professional salespeople get in your community. Next, be careful not to expand your advertisements too fast. Your new sales must increase to keep your per unit cost down. For example, an eight-page digest will cost you an extra $20 for stapling and folding, and you'd have to sell it for 95 cents (a perfectly reasonable amount, by the way) to make the project viable.

Current publishers of this type of listing service report profits of $200 to $500 per hour of actual work.

UNIQUE BUSINESS APPROACH

1. Sell your Service to Title Companies or Escrow Services

Two areas most real estate publications overlook are escrow and title insurance industries. Title insurance and escrow companies, especially the smaller ones, spend a great deal of money developing realtor and developer clients. Your publication can become one of their most cost-effective forms of public relations.

2. Provide a Search Service

Another unique approach is to optimize your income by using the work you have already done. If you originally enter your client's information into a data base instead of just using a word processing program, you can search for special features a particular client wants. That special search service can be advertised "free" in your own publication.

The hardest part of this approach is knowing what data fields to design into your data base. The answer is to design one in which you can search for the most common asked-for amenities in a home. To do that, talk to several local realtors. They'll be happy to tell you what people ask for.

When you know what most people want, design a questionnaire with those items listed. That questionnaire will save you a lot of work. If you ask an open-ended question like, "What are you looking for?" you'll get all kinds of requests you can't find the answers for. A questionnaire narrows the scope of search and will usually limit their thinking to your questions.

The most commonly asked-for amenities for houses are: fireplace, swimming pool, pantry, family room, electric or gas appliances, solar water, heating, etc., garage, particular neighborhood desired, price range, new kitchen, utility room, lots of storage cupboards. For condominiums, asked-for amenities include: units built on one level, elevators for multi-level buildings, parking for more than one car, clubhouse, pool tennis courts, whether or not children are welcome, units larger than 1,000 square feet, particular location, price range, kitchen, storage area.

3. Concentrate on Investment or Commercial Real Estate

Many cities have housing real estate magazines or newspapers available. Almost all of these concentrate exclusively on homes. However, there is a large field opening up in investment and commercial real estate all over the country. These areas are virtually untouched.

Investment real estate usually consists of "fixer-uppers," estate sales, bankruptcies, or other sales that are either being sold below market value or have a good profit-growth potential.

Commercial properties that are most likely to need your service and have the most end-buyers for your publication are offices and stores that are practical for small businesses.

Listings of investment real estate will require the most work on your part. However, you can probably sell this information as a monthly newsletter publication at a fairly high price. With a regular healthy income, the research is well worth your while— especially when you know how to go about doing it.

First, get on the mailing list of your county assessor's sale announcement. This list will form the backbone of your information. In the United States last year over a dozen houses on full lots sold for as little as $12! Now that's investment property. While that is unusual, it's not uncommon for property to go for a few hundred dollars from these sales.

The minimum sale price is listed in the assessor's announcement. It is usually predicated on the assessed tax value of the property (which is generally well below market value) or the amount the owner owes. Go through the listings and choose the properties most likely to be good investments and list them in your publication. Even people who know about the assessor's publication will be interested in having a listing of the best potential deals, because they won't have to do the research themselves.

Current projections tell us that more and more individuals are beginning to work for themselves, rather than for large companies. During the 1950's and 1960's, 95 percent of the nation's population worked for just five corporations or their subsidiaries. Today, nearly 20 percent of our population is self-employed, and the number is growing every day.

That means that there is a growing demand for shop and office space geared to the needs of the small businessperson. Yet, no one is effectively addressing this area with this type of service.

You can sell your small business real estate listing service to business brokers and commercial realtors, but don't stop there. Look for small, old motels or apartment groups in commercial and tourist areas. The U.S. Bureau of Statistics tells us that 80 percent of tourist-related operations either are renting as office/artist studio/shop spaces or are interested in doing so. Most of them, however, don't know how to go about promoting this use. You have the answer.

LOCATION AND MARKET BASE

One of the really great things about this business is that you can effectively run it almost anywhere real estate changes hands regularly—and that's almost everywhere. In 1980 the average person moved every three years. Big city or small town, this business can work for you.

TO SUM UP

Here is a low-cost, easy-entry business that can provide a good income on a part or full-time basis. You can choose to increase your personal wealth at any time by creating new publications for different target markets. It will also help you become a very real power in the high-powered and important real estate oriented industries.

SOURCE MATERIAL

Refer to Section 7.

No. 124

COMPUTERIZED LEGAL FORMS BUSINESS

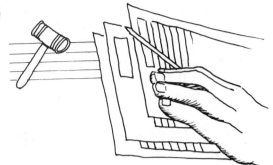

You know what happens when you go to a lawyer and ask him to make out a lease, purchase agreement, will or almost any legal contract. He pulls out a book or looks at a document he did for somebody else, changes the names and dates, retypes it and charges you $200.

Everybody, from individuals to businesses, needs legal documents at one time or another. The business of producing customized legal forms can provide a sizeable income for you by servicing both laypersons and lawyers. By having these forms on your home computer you can do this high-priced legal production work yourself for a fraction of the cost.

CONCEPT

The concept of this business is to sell a client the legal documents he or she needs. Your client tells you what is needed, and you provide the necessary documents specifically tailored for your client.

Essentially, you are selling legal protection. The legal forms you provide your clients allow them to exercise their legal rights.

Customized legal forms are extremely valuable if they are correct and complete. The cost of obtaining a customized legal form from you will be more than offset by the convenience you provide a client. Instead of having to research the legal wording himself or having to consult a lawyer, a client can buy a document from you. Even lawyers can benefit from this service.

For the layperson, computerized legal forms mean understanding legal rights without the expense of a lawyer. For the lawyer, computerized legal forms mean that the headache of producing so many similar documents is reduced, saving enormous amounts of time.

The reason customized legal form businesses have one of the highest profit potentials is because you pay only a one-time cost to obtain the necessary legal forms, then reproduce them to sell to a client. After the initial start-up capital, the only major expenses will be advertising.

SKILLS YOU WILL REQUIRE

You don't have to be a lawyer to get started. You only need to understand your clients' needs and where to get further information.

If you come across a legal problem that you cannot answer, you can talk to various legal clinics that can help you or refer you to someone who knows the answer. If you need a new legal document, you need only check out a book from a library or pay a one-time fee for a lawyer to make one up for you.

INFORMATION REQUIRED

All the necessary legal documents for nearly every possible case have already been written. There are two ways of obtaining legal forms. You can obtain copies of forms by visiting your city law library, or by asking a stationary store for a "Legal Blank Form Catalog" and typing the forms on a word processor. An even easier route is to buy software with all the necessary legal forms already written by lawyers and included.

If you need additional information, look in the yellow pages under "attorneys." Many lawyers are willing to give free consultations. Both the American Civil Liberties Union and the Legal Aid Society can answer questions about legal rights. The Better Business Bureau can answer questions about business law. The Consumer Credit Counselors can provide help with bankruptcy cases. There is free legal information everywhere. Your service is to provide all of it in one convenient package for a client.

GETTING STARTED

Getting business is a matter of contacts. Your first step should be dividing your advertising campaign into three groups: individuals, small businesses and law offices.

For each of the three groups, you will have to prepare a sales letter and a complete list of all the legal forms you have available for that group. For example, homeowners would be interested in mortgage forms, renters would be interested in landlord and tenant forms, and businesspeople would be interested in contracts and business forms. For law offices, look in the yellow pages to see the variety of specialities in law practice. Each type of specialty, such as malpractice or personal injury, requires a multitude of specialized legal forms, which you can offer.

Each of the three groups will need a different sales letter directed towards its own needs. To find out how lawyers treat different types of clients, call or visit a law office that offers free consultations. Ask what types of legal forms are necessary, how they are prepared, and see the response you get. Find out which books the lawyers use and look them up in your city law library. Add the documents to your computer, then get ready to produce them for your own clients.

THE COMPETITION

Eliminating the competition is a matter of selling to the customer before either the client or the competition knows what the client needs. Create a package of related legal forms geared for specific cases, such as small businesses, and market the entire package to a number of clients. In essence, you are selling a client an understanding of the law and his legal rights.

If you enclose a questionnaire with each sales letter, you can determine specifically what potential clients may need.

POTENTIAL INCOME

Pricing your service is not complicated. Start by placing a fee on the time you spend researching legal documents, and add the cost of any software that you purchase. Call several law offices to determine how much they charge to make up various legal documents. Then price your services below their cost and use their quotes in your sales brochure. This will convince people that it would be cheaper to order customized legal forms directly from you than from a lawyer.

Basic Costs

1. Cost of mailing letters to prospective clients
2. Cost of making copies of sales letter and brochure
3. Cost of preparing legal form packages
4. Cost of reproduction and delivery
5. Cost of time spent for research
6. Cost of stationary and business envelopes
7. Cost of preparing client questionnaires
8. Cost of software used

How To Be Paid

Treat your business as if you were selling a product. The standard practice when selling a product is for the client to pay the entire amount up front.

MARKETING METHODS

Direct mail, display ads and telephone sales are the best methods for marketing this service. For more methods and information, refer to Section 5.

A good sales letter should tell how your service can benefit the client, and why he or she should use it. Sales letters should be accompanied by a brochure outlining your services and mailed to prospects in your area at a rate of 10 to 20 per day. Below is a sample letter directed to an individual or businessperson.

> DEAR MR. JONES:
>
> Tired of going to an attorney every time you need a simple legal form created? Let us create them for you at a fraction of the price a lawyer would charge.
>
> John Doe & Associates offers complete legal forms covering most of your legal needs at a cost that can't be beat.
>
> Thinking about improving your home, starting your own business or buying a new car? You need the law on your side and the proper legal forms to help you.
>
> Let John Doe & Associates provide these forms today.

A telephone sales campaign would be effective, especially if you own a modem. Call law offices and offer to have legal forms transmitted to the law office via telephone lines in seconds.

Emphasize the convenience and speed of such a service. No longer will lawyers have to page through law books. All they have to do is use their own computer and modem to access your database of legal forms. In seconds they have the basic form, which they can modify to suit their clients. You can charge your clients on a monthly basis or for each document they access.

Slant your sales campaign to coincide with local or national news. If malpractice or consumer fraud hits the headlines, alter your next sales letter to emphasize the legal rights of patients, doctors and business customers.

The best source of potential clients is the yellow pages. Flip through the various business listings to see which kinds of firms might respond to particular legal forms, such as small business forms, bankruptcy forms, etc. Then slant your sales letters and mail them to those clients.

UNIQUE BUSINESS APPROACH

The way to get this business off the ground is to offer your service free for a month to attorneys and others who will use it on a regular basis. This will prove to them the cost-effectiveness of your service and get you steady clients.

You can also offer the service through nonprofit legal clinics in your area at a discount price. Since the clinics will be sending you business, that saves you the costs of advertising to seek your own clientele. Plus, it helps the people who need the forms you provide, since they'll be saving money.

LOCATION and MARKET BASE

For maximum profit potential, the best location would be a city where you could provide your service to both individuals on a mail order basis and to law offices and businesses on a direct contact basis. The advantage of direct contact is that it is more convenient, since the client can receive the legal forms as quickly as possible.

Another advantage of a city is that it offers more potential clients within a given area. That means more business for you.

TO SUM UP

Computerizing legal documents is a genuine opportunity. If you start by offering your services to individuals, there is little competition. Later, you can go directly to the law offices and provide them with customized legal forms for their clients.

In general, selling to individuals will be a one-shot transaction. Selling to law offices will be a continuous business, since they have many documents that need to be reproduced and you can do that service for them. All they'll have to provide is form type, names, dates and, of course, money to pay your fee.

The time is ripe to start a business like this. So get in on the ground floor and make a killing now.

SOURCE MATERIAL

Refer to Section 7.

No. 125

COMPUTERIZED LOAN PACKAGE SERVICE

How many people do you know that go to any lending institution, whether it is a bank, savings and loan, or a credit union, and never have enough information to satisfy the loan officer they are dealing with? We have developed a loan package you can put on your home computer that will blow the socks off any loan officer and, in almost every case, get your client the money. People are paying from $20 to $200 for these packages, and there doesn't seem to be any shortage of customers. So get on the bandwagon now for your share of this market.

CONCEPT

What you will supply to people who are going to banks, venture capitalists or any other funding institution, is that part of the business plan that is usually missing in most proposals. You will supply the backup financial data that shows the lender two things: what the finances of business are all about, and what the loan seeker figures the business might make in terms of profit over the next few years. Most of the people who approach the money lenders are woefully ill-prepared and totally unknowledgable about this phase of their business.

SKILLS YOU WILL REQUIRE

You need to thoroughly acquaint yourself with the types of business plans now being offered and the kinds of financial information required by the lenders. You can do this by contacting loan officers in commercial loan departments to find out what they look for in a business plan. I would suggest no less than five interviews, and more if you have time. The real value in this is finding out what kinds of questions loan officers ask, and what kinds of answers they feel they need to approve loans.

Generally, these people will more than welcome you because you are in a position to make their jobs easier. You are going to provide them with the types of financial information they have been screaming for, for years. They will probably even give you a copy of a "good" financial plan if you ask, or at least give you an outline of what is required. After several of these interviews, the total picture of what is needed should start to fall into place for you.

The other result of these interviews is that now you can be the "expert" because you have talked to at least four more bankers than your client has. Plus, you have been able to ferret out the data they want most. You have just become a great resource for your client.

INFORMATION REQUIRED

Information is the name of this service. Remember one thing: the people coming to you want help to get their loans. Your job is to provide them with the types of financial data that the banker needs. To do this, you elicit the information needed from your client and put it into a "package" for the banker. The package might consist of the loan application, along with the documents needed to back up the numbers. It must have a neat, professional appearance.

GETTING STARTED

The biggest problem most new businesses have when they get started is letting people know that they are "open for business."

You don't have time or energy to send out a whole crew of salespeople to get your name in the public eye, so we have the next best thing: your brochure. You will want to study the brochures and pamphlets other businesses send out. We recommend that you tell your clients about your business by using a sheet of paper folded over or in thirds. This can handily be put in an envelope with a cover letter.

Let your clients know about the benefits of doing business with you. Let them know that your service can help them deliver to the lender a package that will help them secure the loan. Remind them that this can be a great savings of time and energy for them, as well as make them look like the "pros" they are trying to be. They need you and your expertise to get what they want from the lender.

THE COMPETITION

Few people provide this service to small businesses. Most accountants concentrate on established, large companies, which leaves the field wide open for you to dominate small or brand-new businesses. There are a million people with ideas and no money to get them off the ground. You can help them gather the financial data they need to get their own business rolling.

POTENTIAL INCOME

Using the outline we give you to set this project in motion, this business has no ceiling on earning power. You can get a flat rate of $50 or $100, and make several thousand dollars a month, depending on how hard you want to work. Since your computer handles the financial data and organizes it into a presentable form, you spend your time rousting up new business.

Costs

1. Cost of financial software
2. Cost of brochure and other advertising
3. Cost of time spent gathering, inputting and organizing financial data
4. Cost of time spent meeting with financial lenders
5. Cost of materials used

How To Get Paid

We suggest that you ask for half the money in advance on every job, and the remainder to be paid when you deliver the report. DO NOT, we repeat, do not, do the job for anyone with the idea that he will pay you when he gets the loan. Your fee is not based on the success or failure of the loan application. You are simply ensuring that the financial loan packages you provide your clients is more complete than what they can put together themselves.

MARKETING METHODS

The best way to gain business with this project is by using display ads, followed up with direct phone calls and interviews.

When you decide to advertise in the local business press, you will want to put together an ad that merely centers on the word "HELP!" Let people quickly know what you are doing and how much time and trouble you can save them. You never guarantee that your client will get the loan approved, but you can guarantee that he or she has a better chance by using your service.

We suggest that you might run small ads in the classified sections under the "Money-Wanted" classification. Such an ad might read:

> We can help you get the money you want. Let us organize your loan papers and statements into a package that bankers and lenders will notice. 999-9999.

Small, quick, catchy ads will do the job and you'll be pleasantly surprised by the positive response you can receive.

UNIQUE BUSINESS APPROACH

The single way to get business is for you to have lenders refer their own customers to you. How do you do this?

Contact local bankers and lenders, explain your service to them and offer to put together loan packages for their borderline customers. Bankers love to loan money, since that is how they make money. So if you can improve the chances of their clients getting loans approved, the banker will send business your way. In the end it serves the banker's best interest.

LOCATION and MARKET BASE

Without a doubt, you have to be in a city to make this idea really pay off. Your market base could range from 5,000 to 200,000 people, but the more people there are in your area, the better your chances of making big money. Don't forget the fundamental theory proposed by the infamous bank robber Willie Sutton, when asked why he robbed banks: "Because that's where the money is!"

TO SUM UP

Every day people are turned down for the loans that would make their dreams come true. The reason? They simply didn't know what the banker or lender really required of them.

With a loan package service you can assist people in getting their loan money. Your research into what lenders want from applicants will pay off every time a borderline loan is approved. Word-of-mouth will get your service known around town and bring the business running to you. That means that with the income you'll start earning with this computer business, you can start making your own dreams come true.

SOURCE MATERIAL

Refer to Section 7.

No. 126

SPECIALTY LOCATING SERVICE

Have you ever heard your friends say, "I sure would like to find a 1932 Ford," or "I'd love to have an old violin like Bill has."? Well, here is a service that makes finding specialized items for people easy. All you need is your home computer and a little research time. The finders' fees are very high because of the uniqueness of this service. In some cases, this can be a worldwide service, operated completely from your home using your home computer as your staff.

CONCEPT

The concept of this business is to locate unique items for people who want them. You perform a service that they need, either because they don't have time to do the search themselves, or because they don't know how to go about finding what they want. Much of the time you'll be able to track down collectibles, items that are rare or unique, or things that are valuable for sentimental reasons. Once you have located that much-desired item, your client will consider your fee a worthwhile investment. Repeat clients are common in this business. When customers are satisfied, they'll come back for more. Plus, they'll refer you to friends and family who need to use this service.

SKILLS YOU WILL REQUIRE

You don't have to have your fingertips on the whole world to offer this service. In fact, to start this business, all you really need is to make the decision to do it.

There isn't any special terminology for this business, and that's what makes it easy. All you are doing is acting as a kind of clearinghouse. With your computer doing the coordinating, you hook up buyers with sellers.

INFORMATION REQUIRED

What you are actually doing is simply getting the information about the item your client wants—make, model, color, year, size, or whatever, then advertising for the item. When somebody informs you that they have what you are looking for, you contact the buyer and make arrangements for its purchase. What could be easier? You never have to touch whatever it is you're finding for your client. All you are doing is locating it for them.

If you have a special area of interest, such as coins, cars, stamps or antique furniture, you can concentrate your business on that area. Or you can be a generalist and offer to search for anything. In a way, you are acting as a special kind of detective, tracking down not missing people, but missing objects.

Your computer will not only keep all your information organized, but it can actually aid you in your search as well, through the use of information bases. Information bases have great amounts of information that somebody somewhere has filed for your use, much like the yellow pages helps to group together related businesses. When you need a fact (or company), you simply look up the subject and you'll find a list of resources to assist you.

Similar to data bases are electronic bulletin boards, or BBS's. These are bulletin boards that you can tap into with the use of your modem. Run by computer clubs, stores and private parties, bulletin boards allow you to communicate electronically with other people, leave messages for them, and, even more important, run ads, like classified ads, listing items you have for sale or are looking for.

Bulletin boards are usually free, and currently there are about 25,000 of them being operated in the country. Many computer magazines advertise the bulletin boards as a public service announcement to computer owners.

OPERATING NAME

With a business like this, there is no reason to use any operating name other than your own. For example, "John Smith Locating Service" or "John Smith Specialty Locating" will let your potential clients know exactly what kind of business you run.

GETTING STARTED

Getting started is a matter of advertising your service. Your first step should be to decide whether you want to perform searches for specialty items of one kind, like cars or coins, or to look for anything anybody might want. To learn how to market your business, see Marketing Methods.

You will also want to write up potential ads to use in your marketing. Then it is simply a matter of placing your ads in the correct places and waiting for your orders.

THE COMPETITION

The beauty of this business is that there really isn't any competition. What you will be searching for are one-of-a-kind items. When you receive a request to do a search, you will be seeking something that few other people are looking for.

Another nice thing about this business is that you can let the competition you have work for you. For instance, if you are seeking a rare book for a customer, and your competition is trying to sell that same book for his customer, you can both win by dealing with one another. You both get a finder's fee or commission.

POTENTIAL INCOME

Pricing for your service can be done in many ways. One method is to set a fixed fee for your service, say, $100 a search. Each customer must agree to pay this amount before you'll start your search.

Another method, probably more profitable for you, would be to take a commission on each search you do. The advantage here is that you'll receive money not only from the person who wants the item, but also from the person who has the item to sell. You might charge 10 percent to the buyer and 5 percent to the seller, making a total income on each transaction of 15 percent of the price of the object.

The potential income for this business is rated very high, because the objects you'll be searching for are valuable. If somebody wants a certain kind of car and has $20,000 to spend finding it, your 10 percent portion from the buyer would equal $2,000. Plus, you'd get another $500 from the party selling the car. Of course, this kind of service can also deal in high value items such as real estate. How many times have you read about somebody who wants to buy an island to retire on? There are hundreds of wealthy people in the world who want help finding exactly what would make them happiest. If you were to transact a deal such as the purchase of an island, the amount of money you'd make would be in the hundreds of thousands of dollars.

To get an idea of what would be a good commission or fee to charge for this service, you'll have to add up your costs for the program. Then you add in a profit figure for the job. Remember that your salary for this business should be considered one more expense, just like the cost of paper you use or phone calls made. Profit is the amount of money your business makes above costs.

Besides the costs of the computer equipment you will need for this business, the only other expenses you will have are for advertising your service. Most of the time you can even get that for free by using bulletin board services, discussed earlier, to place your ads.

Other Potential Costs

1. Cost of advertising in specialty magazines
2. Cost of paper supplies
3. Cost of phone time
4. Cost of any other materials used, such as postage
5. Cost of using information bases
6. Cost of your salary

Overhead

Make sure that your fees cover your expenses proportionately. If you spend a year searching for a single item, that search should cost more than another transaction you completed in a week.

Profit

In terms of what kind of profit to expect, charge what the traffic will bear, but still enough to make money. You don't want to charge yourself out of business, nor do you want to undercut yourself too much. A specialty searching business is a unique service, one that people will gladly pay for since they want the object you will find for them.

How To Be Paid

For this kind of business you should probably take a fee in advance as a deposit from your client. If you are searching for a high-priced item, such as a car, charge your client $100 or so to ensure that when the car is found for him, he still wants it. When the final sale is made, you can then charge the rest of your percentage. It will take time for you to establish what amount you should charge in advance, but after a few transactions, you'll get the hang of it.

MARKETING METHODS

Direct mail and display ads are the best techniques for marketing this service.

Bulletin board services that you access by your computer are a good method of advertising. Contact bulletin boards all over the country and place an ad explaining your service. Then when you have something you are seeking for a client, place an ad saying what you are looking for. This will cost you nothing more than the cost of a long-distance phone call. You can avoid even that charge by using the bulletin boards in your own area.

Either a display ad or a classified ad can be placed in a multitude of publications, many of them absolutely free.

One way to place classified ads involves deciding what your specialty will be, such as cars, then placing ads in the places where people who will want to use your service will see them. In the above example, you'll want to direct your marketing to car magazines or car club newsletters. To get information about what publications are available in your specialty, your local librarian can help you. He or she will have indexes listing the publications pertinent to a specific subject.

An example of a display ad might read:

> What are you looking for? An antique? A race car? Write or call us and we'll help you find it!

Another method of marketing this service is to use direct mail. This involves choosing a unique item you'd like to specialize in, then renting a mailing list of customers from others in the same business. For example, if you decide to specialize in rare books, contact the people who deal in rare books to get a listing of their customers. They will charge you a fee for its use, but the investment might bring you more business than you can handle. Then mail letters advertising your service to each name on the list. A copy of a potential letter is below.

> Dear Collector:
>
> Are you getting frustrated searching for that one-of-a-kind item that doesn't seem to exist? We know where it is! Our service will help you search for anything you might want. And it costs you nothing unless we find it for you. Let us prove our reliability. Call or write us with in- formation about your needs and let us take it from there. We have our fingertips on the whole world and we'll make this service available to you for very little money. Call or write now with your needs!

That letter, used with your own variations and mailed to all names on your mailing list, will bring you queries for more information. Explain your service and fees to them, then ask for their order.

Another place you might consider seeking business is through a publication called the Robb Report. What started out as a magazine advertising priceless cars has now become a forum for advertising anything of great value for sale to the ultra-rich. You can use the Robb Report not only to search for items your clients want to buy, but also to advertise your services in a display ad. For a copy of the Robb Report, consult your local library. They will either have copies in their collection or be able to tell you where to subscribe. You can also ask the librarian if he or she knows of any similar publications that you can use in the same way.

For more information about marketing methods, refer to Section 5.

UNIQUE BUSINESS APPROACH

The secret to this business is that you can advertise the fact that a search will cost your customer nothing unless it is successful. When a client comes to you for assistance, you can make an agreement that if the item isn't located in a year, the deposit you charge will be refunded. In the meanwhile, you have the advantage of putting the money into a bank account that will pay you interest. This is a nice little income-producing sideline to a business like specialty-searching.

Another advantage to this line is that you can get a lot of repeat business. When you have a satisfied customer, he or she will come back to you for other searches. Plus, you'll be recommended to business associates, friends and family to fill their needs.

LOCATION and MARKET BASE

This is a business that can be done anywhere, with the use of a modem to handle your communication. Since you don't actually ever handle the item you are seeking or finding, you don't have to be located in a city. It is very easy to promote your service through your computer. With a computer and a modem, you have the world at your fingertips.

START-UP CAPITAL

To start up this business you will need from $1,000 to $5,000. This amount includes the money you'll need to spend for your computer equipment. Other than that, if you decide to start it in your own area by advertising your services on local free bulletin boards, your costs will equal exactly zero. When you get clients who pay you a deposit, you can use the interest from those deposits to cover your expenses. For more information about obtaining capital, refer to Section 6.

TO SUM UP

A specialty locating service is a natural for people who own computers. All you have to do is hook up the buyers with the sellers and take a fat commission for your small effort.

Look at it this way: the service you give to your clients cannot be valued merely in dollars. What you are offering them is the chance to fulfill their dreams, wants and desires. They'll think nobody can put a price tag on that. But you'll know better and be able to collect money for it.

SOURCE MATERIAL

Refer to Section 7 for source information.

No. 127

COMPUTERIZED MAP SALES

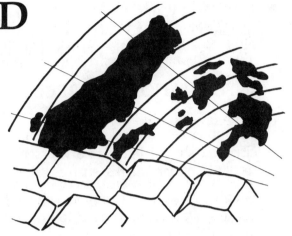

This is a unique service that requires only your home computer and a remote printer that you hook up through your phone line. You can set up the remote printer at the local airport for example. As incoming passengers arrive, they see big signs informing them that there is a service that can tell them how to get anywhere in the city. You provide customized maps, which people pay you for. You collect their money into a coin-operated remote printer and pick it up anytime.

CONCEPT

The concept of this business is to direct people where they're going with as few hassles or hang-ups as possible. When they arrive in the airport, they are directd to one of your remote terminals. They call you up, tell you where they need to go, then deposit money into a printer for a copy of a map giving them easy, time-saving directions. The money is collected much like money in a newspaper machine. When you are ready to pick it up, it's waiting for you.

This service is especially popular with traveling businesspeople and sales representatives who don't know their way around your town, but don't want to put out the money for a taxi to take them there. All they have to do is pick up their rental car, follow your map and they've arrived! When they've used the service once with satisfaction, they will start seeking out your computerized map sale machines, and refer the service to their associates and traveling companions.

SKILLS YOU WILL REQUIRE

If you know your way around town or know how to read a map, this business doesn't require any other special skills. All you need to be able to do is take a location, track it on your own maps, then supply that information to your customer.

INFORMATION REQUIRED

Computerized map sales require that you can give directions based on a map of your city. You should familiarize yourself with major highways, freeways, streets and recognizable landmarks, such as bridges, rivers, stadiums, etc.

Since you want to get your customer where he or she is going with as little trouble as possible, you will also need to know where major road projects are going on that might disrupt or redirect traffic. To get this information, you can contact your state transportation department. They should be able to tell you in advance where road construction will be taking place, how long it will last, and what, if any, effect it will have on traffic flow. With a pencil or plastic overlay you can draw these locations on your own map to help you direct your customers on alternative routes.

For your own reference, you'll want to use a detailed map book that includes not only an index of all streets, but also address numbers to let you know where a particular location will be on that street. One national company that puts out such maps books for most major cities is Thomas Brothers Maps.

You might also want to find out whether any software company sells a program that has a map of your city, as well as a street and address index listing. Then you will be able to plug in the address you're seeking for your customer, find out quickly where it is, along with the major roads to that area and the specific streets he or she will need to make turns on.

The product you are selling can come in two different forms. If you have a plotter, you can have your computer plot out a map for the customer with his route drawn in.

The second option is to use a printer to print out directions in easy-to-read format. For example, if somebody needs to get from the airport across town, your directions might read:

> Turn left at the airport entrance.
> Follow the road for 3 blocks to 1st light.
> This is Main Street.
> Turn right, then right again at Freeway entrance.
> Move left onto far left lane of freeway.
> Drive 5 miles.
> Take 10th Street exit.
> Turn right at stop sign.
> Destination is on left side of road about 1 block down.

OPERATING NAME

For a service of this kind you won't need to use any name other than your own. All you are basically advertising is the location of your map terminal. You aren't trying to get your customers to remember your company name as much as its availability.

If you plan to expand your business to other cities, you might consider using a fictitious name, such as "Location Finders" or something like that, that people can ask for as soon as they arrive at the airport. In this case, you'll have extra expenses, such as filing a fictitious name report, getting a new bank account, etc. For more information, refer to Section 4.

GETTING STARTED

To begin this business you'll first need to arrange with airports, rental car agencies, bus stations, train stations, etc. to install your coin-operated terminal and printer.

When your equipment is installed, you'll solicit business by advertising in the place where it is located. If it is placed in an airport, you'll need to get signs posted instructing customers where to go to find a terminal, or you can have flyers passed out to potential customers as they arrive.

If you intend to do this business part time, you may consider hiring another person part-time to run your computer when you are away from it. The cost will be minimal compared to the amount you can make by being able to offer the map service during business hours, or even 24 hours a day.

THE COMPETITION

Your competition for this business offers a different service than your own. Traditionally, if people don't know where they're going, they'll hire a cab to take them. But you offer them the opportunity to find the places they seek on their own. It not only saves them the cab fare, but it gives them the opportunity to go where they need at their own convenience. If they're driving along following your instructions and decide to stop for a bite to eat along the way or for some other reason, they can do it. They can decide their own schedules and pace of travel.

POTENTIAL INCOME

The money you make from this business doesn't come in large amounts, but it does come steadily. For each location a customer wants mapped out, you charge. When the money has been deposited into your terminal, you give them the product.

To price your service, start out by figuring expenses. Add up all the costs of your program, include your salary and a profit. Then based on the number of potential customers that will arrive in the location of your terminal, estimate how many sales you expect to make.

Typical Costs

1. Cost of special equipment, including coin-operated terminals or printers
2. Cost of advertising

3. Cost of maps you use
4. Cost of any miscellaneous materials to be used
5. Cost of computer supplies, such as paper and ribbons
6. Cost of renting space to place your equipment
7. Cost of part-time help to operate the service in your absence

Overhead

The amount you charge for your service should take into account all overhead, including the costs listed above.

Profit

Do not count your own salary as profit. Profit should be the amount of money your business makes above and beyond the total expenses. This is what you'll use to expand your service, buy new equipment, etc.

How To Be Paid

In this business you want to make the customer feel that for the price of a few quarters he's going to get a nice little service that does away with the headaches of traveling in a strange city. Since your machines will be coin-operated, all you need to do is have a hookup from your equipment to the remote equipment that will inform you when the money has been deposited. Then you can make a weekly trip to the location and empty your coin box. If you have several located in various terminals and stations around town, the money you can make with this service can give you full-time pay with only part-time effort.

MARKETING METHODS

The best way to advertise this business is by large signs or posters displayed in the location of your terminals. Such ads will be able to direct the customer exactly to the place where your equipment is located. A typical poster might read:

NEED DIRECTIONS?

Let us show you how to get where you're going and fast. With our directions you'll avoid detours, traffic hazards and costly taxi bills.

Our map service is conveniently located beneath the big clock in the main lobby of this airport terminal.

Another method would be to pass out flyers to potential customers as they arrive in the airport or wherever. You can hire students to do this work cheaply. You can also have car rental agencies offer your flyer to their customers when they rent a car. If your equipment is placed in the vicinity of car rental agencies, potential customers will already be exactly where they can see your service.

UNIQUE BUSINESS APPROACH

The big trick to this business is that you charge so little for your service that the customer doesn't have to think twice about the value of this purchase.

Typically, an airport in a metropolitan area might have 100,000 people passing through in a week. If you get only one percent of all those people to use your service, that is 1,000 customers. If you charge a dollar for each map they request, that's at least $1,000 dollars a week in your pocket. Actually, since most customers will probably have sales or business appointments at several locations, they'll want to buy more than just one map from you.

LOCATION and MARKET BASE

This business would be operated best in a city with a market base of at least 200,000. The reason for this is that you will make your money in places where a lot of people need directions quickly—primarily large airports, bus stations or other places where people rent cars once they have arrived in town.

TO SUM UP

Las Vegas is a city of one-armed bandits. There is an attraction to people to plug quarters into machines and get something back for their money. Las Vegas has made billions of dollars with their machines that take quarters. You may not be paying off a jackpot to your customers, but you will give them a much-needed service of unique value. You'll be getting them where they need to go quickly and efficiently. With this business you'll be starting your own Las Vegas simply with your ability to know how to get around in your area. And the opportunity is ripe for somebody to become very wealthy on the basis of those quarters. The next time somebody says "Say, can you give me directions," you'll be able to answer "Gladly."

SOURCE MATERIAL

Refer to Section 7.

No. 128

PRO-FORMAS FOR NEW BUSINESSES

A pro forma business service offers a new businessperson a detailed breakdown of expected sales and expenses. This is invaluable information that not only allows the business to prepare for the future, but also is required by lending institutions to secure loans.

CONCEPT

Thousands of new businesses enter the marketplace every year. With competition at such a ferocious level, the new businessperson needs every possible advantage to prepare for contingencies.

You can provide a start-up business with the information it needs to make the business successful, and because this is your specialty, you can offer a very comprehensive evaluation of what to expect. Any new businessperson will realize that this is the best possible investment he can make—you are offering his business a much higher chance of survival.

While your service gathers information for him, the businessperson can spend his time taking action on your recommendations. His intelligent, informed decisions will give him tremendous advantage over other new or already established businesses.

To your clients, the service you can offer is a bargain at any price. You give the business the best possible chance of being successful.

SKILLS YOU WILL REQUIRE

Knowledge of start-up operations will be your guide in this business. These are not difficult concepts to grasp. You will be analyzing the expenses and costs that are necessary to begin any enterprise, and creating graphic and written material that will enable the businessperson to analyze cost ratios, profit margins and sales projections.

One way to analyze sales and expense figures is through the use of spreadsheets or budget programs. With either of these programs you can itemize your expense figures, for example, and then recalculate the figures using a reasonable annual or semi-annual percentage increase. This is the kind of task computers are terrific at—the "what if" analysis of statistics and figures. You'll find this process very straightforward and interesting. You will be dealing with concrete figures based on your own research and experiences of similar businesses. The approach you take is going to be virtually the same for each client. The primary difference will be in the figures and sources you'll utilize to paint the clearest picture each time.

INFORMATION REQUIRED

You'll need to know, of course, what sort of cost outlay is necessary to begin the particular business you're analyzing. Your client can give you some of this information, but you'll find that he will soon be turning to you to find out what to expect.

There are many resources for this information. Other businesses, the local library and area colleges (especially the business library) can give you scores of real examples of the start up process of similar businesses. Study these and decide what information is relevant to your client's situation. The Small Business Administration can sometimes help with this information, but their response time is often slow, so don't expect quick answers.

As far as figures for anticipated sales are concerned, market surveys will be a great help. You can either rely on published figures, do your own surveys (which will make your business that much more valuable and in demand), or subcontract a market survey firm to do the work for you. Again, study some of the recently published figures for similar businesses. In conjunction with market surveys, you'll be able to make intelligent, accurate estimates of potential revenue.

As the cost of services and expenses required to begin a business will constantly change, you'll have to personally contact suppliers, subcontractors, and others to get exact rate figures. A phone call or letter will do the job here.

GETTING STARTED

Review spreadsheet and budget software for your computer and run through several simulations using data you've collected. Make sure the software is suited to the job—for instance, a "windowing" capability on your spreadsheet program makes an impressive presentation. Formulate some attractive report formats that you can use when presenting your pro formas to customers. Make them easy to read and understand. You can even use what you've learned to create a pro forma for your own new business! There's no better way to prepare for your first client than to try it out on yourself.

One of the next steps you'll want to take is to make yourself known. Put together a brochure or direct mail copy and distribute within the business community. Much of your business will come from referrals, so the more people that see your literature, the better.

Consider contacting a firm that sells sales leads and buying a local or regional list of small business owners. Send information to them. Inevitably they will know others who are in the process of starting their own business. Advertise in the business section of local papers.

One great source of customers for your service is property management companies. If they are handling leasing for commercial business districts, shopping malls and the like, they can direct you to new businesses that are preparing to enter the marketplace.

THE COMPETITION

Cost effectiveness is one of the biggest benefits of a business run by you out of your home or office by using your own computer. Your time can be had for a relatively low rate—consider it an investment in the success of your business. Doing much of the data collection yourself will keep your expenses very low, and these savings can be passed on to your customers, undercutting the competition.

After you've completed several jobs, you'll notice that word-of-mouth referral will bring in much of your new business. Make your report presentations easy to understand and thorough and from then on your quality work will sell itself.

POTENTIAL INCOME

Pricing will involve a realistic assessment of your own time and expenses, to which you'll add a profit margin. Your customers should pay a percentage of the fee upon placement of the order - 50 percent is a good figure to start with, but use what you feel comfortable with.

Project Costs

1. Cost of time spent gathering information
2. Cost of telephone
3. Cost of brochures and advertising
4. Cost of travel to collect information
5. Cost of postage and mailing supplies
6. Cost of time spent inputting and manipulating data
7. Cost of time spent creating and delivering reports
8. Cost of software

As your business increases, you can realistically expect a profit of $300 to $500 per week.

MARKETING METHODS

Direct mail and display ads are the best methods for promoting your pro forma business.

Direct mail will probably have the greatest impact on your potential cutomers. The personalized approach, speaking to them about the problems you know they are encountering, will give them the impression that perhaps their new business doesn't have to be as unpredictable as they think.

Let me give you an example of a direct mail approach:

> DID YOU KNOW THAT SIX OUT OF 10 NEW BUSINESSES WON'T SURVIVE MORE THAN TWO YEARS?
>
> Last year 3,300 small businesses filed for bankruptcy. A survey taken of the most successful survivors attributes their success to careful preparation and attention to the future of their business. How did the survivors do these projections? Through detailed analysis of sales and expenses, both present and future.
>
> Robert Smith Business Research offers the most complete pro forma business analysis you can find. We will analyze your new business and make sure that you have the most accurate, realistic appraisal of your business and its chance of survival, and we will suggest methods, tested and approved by successful businesses, that will virtually ensure the good health of your business.
>
> Let us help you plan your business—it's our specialty.

Enclose a brochure or flyer detailing your service and mail it to all your sales leads and local or regional businesses.

UNIQUE BUSINESS APPROACH

Through your leads, contact several start-up operations. A walk-in approach will work best here. Sit down with the owner and offer to discuss his or her preparation for the new business. When possible, have samples of your work—charts, graphs, reports. Make it clear that a new business does not have to be a journey into the unknown. Offer to come back in a few days with a brief overview of your potential client's operation—but remember, don't give him any more than a taste of what you can do.

Show an analysis and a before and after view of another company you've helped. Point out that what you are offering is security and success, and that the return on his investment in you will be the best money he can spend. Stress that he will have a strong advantage over the competition.

One of the most important points you can make here is that you can provide him with the long-term forecast for his business that any loan institution will require before a business loan can be secured.

LOCATION and MARKET BASE

A city of at least 200,000 people is the best location for this type of business. You will need to be near the sources that can supply the data you need—suppliers, contractors, similar businesses and others. You will use your telephone quite a bit, and a central location will keep costs down.

Of course, the primary reason for being in a dynamic area like a city is to have available all the start-up operations that a growing area can support.

STARTUP CAPITAL

Your start up costs, including computer cost, can be as low as $2,000. This will cover all the necessary office supplies mentioned earlier and includes software and other materials.

You'll soon find that most of your overhead, after the business gains momentum, will be the cost of your time.

TO SUM UP

It is a simple fact that the more prepared a new business owner is for any contingency, the more successful he will be. Statistics and survival records for new business make this very clear. Few, however, are conscious of the fact that there are services tailored especially for their particular needs - someone who can make sure that the inherent risk and surprise of starting a new business is diminished almost to the point of disappearing.

A detailed and realistic appraisal of a new business makes a client feel confident and thankful that YOU found HIM.

This is an opportunity waiting to be taken—the information needed to secure a sound future for the new business is there. You only need to organize your operation and start raking in the money!

SOURCE MATERIAL

Refer to Section 7.

No. 129

PAYROLL PREPARATION SERVICE

This service is on the increase because so many businesspeople just don't want to spend the time learning about every change the government makes regarding payroll taxes. We will show you how to obtain clients and how to set up your computer so that each week, month or day you simply transcribe the employee information into your computer and provide all of the statements, forms and reports that are necessary for your client. This is a steady business and makes a good income for the little time it requires.

CONCEPT

The concept of this business is to provide the payroll checks for a business. This service will help your client by freeing up the person presently doing this job, allowing him or her to perform more meaningful activities for the employer. This work is presently being done by hand in most places, which makes the risk of inaccuracy very high. A service that can supply payroll checks, done properly using a computer, can become a valuable ally to a small business. It can also aid in the preparation of year- end reports that are often a nuisance to the business owner but that you can supply with great timeliness and ease.

SKILLS YOU WILL REQUIRE

You don't need any specific skills you can't pick up by doing a little research. You will need to check out a few books if you aren't familiar with the payroll preparation programs used by businesses. The next best thing is to talk with several of your prospective clients to find how they are presently doing their payroll and what complaints they have about their systems. Another piece of research you will need to do is calling people already in the business to find out what kind of system they are using, and what they are charging. You can also ask for a copy of their business brochure. You should talk with four or five of these companies to find out how they operate and how you can improve on the service. After this "initial" research you will clearly see what path you need to follow to be successful.

With several calls and a little face-to-face work you can easily find out almost everything you need to know to make this project work and become profitable.

You will also need to acquaint yourself with the particular computer program you will be using to run the payroll checks.

INFORMATION REQUIRED

Through your friends who have businesses, you will need to find out who normally does this work for most firms. You will need to find out what kinds of reports are expected and when they want them. And you will also want to figure out what program you need to purchase to run the check preparation. There are plenty of them on the market. In your talks with people already in the business you may want to ask what programs they are using to run their checks and what the good and bad points are with each.

When calling your future competition, pose as a prospective client and pick up at least three pieces of information: what they charge for their services, what programs they use, and why they feel they should be the ones to do your payroll checks. After several of these calls, you will get a picture of what you will need to do to become successful in this field.

You will also want to shop the local computer stores to find out about the current programs available. You may even want to look through several of the current business computer magazines to see if you can purchase these programs at better prices through mail-order.

You will find that the more information you get on the front end of this project, the easier the sales and the set-up of the service will be.

GETTING STARTED

You will want to let as many people as possible know about your service. The first thing you will want to do is prepare a brochure describing the services you are offering. Here is where your research comes in handy. You can read the other brochures and decide what the faults and good points of each are. Then prepare your own.

The most important feature you can accent in the brochure is that you are inexpensive, efficient and can always meet your deadline.

With your brochure in hand you can begin to canvass the area, letting people know that you are in business. Remember, this brochure doesn't have to be a "Madison Avenue" effort, but a simple explanation of who and what you are.

THE COMPETITION

There are always going to be competitors in the accounting and bookkeeping field, of which payroll preparation is one aspect. The problem with most of these businesses is that they simply aren't delivering what they promise, when they say they will. Payroll preparation isn't their major line of business.

Anyone can buy a computer to run the program, but your ATTITUDE about this is the one thing that will set you apart from the competition. Payroll preparation will be your specialty, and you can emphasize that fact to your prospective clients.

POTENTIAL INCOME

You have probably figured out by now that the charge for your services has quite a range. You will have to decide what you want to charge, but we suggest you place yourself somewhere in the middle—not too high or too low. You don't want to underprice your service, as people will wonder what it is you are not doing for them.

You should probably charge a monthly or weekly service charge to each customer, based on the number of employees you will be handling. If you charge only a dollar per employee and a company has 100 employees, you'll earn $100 during each payroll period.

Basic Costs

1. Cost of software
2. Cost of brochure and advertising
3. Cost of supplies used
4. Cost of telephone
5. Cost of transportation to pick up and deliver payroll information

Profit

This is the money left over after you have paid all the bills. There are many ways to figure this out, but I suggest you rely on your initial research. What does your competition get for the job? Don't overcharge, yet estimate your costs and include a profit for the business that will enable it to grow.

MARKETING METHODS

Direct mail, display ads, telephone sales and direct sales are the best methods to market this service.

We suggest that you wait until after you have done your research, put together your brochure and done your work on the pricing schedules to go out for business. Then start by calling on your local area merchants and businesses. Don't get too far from home. That'll only eat up time. Call them on the phone, ask what they are doing to prepare their payroll and tell them what you can do for them. Feel them out. We suggest that you pick out businesses in the yellow pages that aren't large advertisers. Make sure you are talking to the owner or someone who can make a buying decision.

Sell your service with the idea of timeliness, and the eagerness you have to work with them. Sell them on the idea that time is money and they can free up an employee to do something more useful for the company by using your service.

In your direct mail piece you will also want to emphasize this whole idea of time savings.

Here is a sample of the type of letter you might want to send to your prospective clients:

> DEAR BUSINESS OWNER:
>
> Tired of wasting employee time on payroll preparation?
>
> Let the experts handle it. We are a service that specializes in payroll preparation. We can deliver checks to you in the form you want, when you want them and with the accuracy you require.
>
> Even if you are already using a payroll preparation service, we can prove to you that we are cheaper and more qualified.
>
> We can prove to you that our service is the one you need.
>
> Call us today!

This letter or a variation, sent to prospects in your area on a regular basis, will bring you calls from people who want to know more about the service you offer. It won't happen overnight, but with a little perserverence and luck, you'll soon be on the way to writing your own paycheck.

UNIQUE BUSINESS APPROACH

The stumbling block to getting new clients in this business is eliminating your competition. Your client will either want to stay with the employees who are currently doing this work or with the service he already uses. The idea of just letting "Alice" keep doing payroll isn't that hard to overcome. It merely means the person doesn't want to take the time to re-organize. Do it for him. Offer to work with the office personnel and set up the program without any cost to him.

Another approach that has been done very successfully is to team up with people who are doing the bookkeeping for businesses. You take over their overflow work. These are people who usually work out of their homes and do the bookkeeping for a number of small businesses. You can team up with them and piggyback your way into several clients by using your instant "in." This type of collaboration can help build your business with "instant" clients, and it can be financially rewarding, not only to you but your bookkeeping partner as well.

LOCATION and MARKET BASE

To become successful at this business, we feel you need to live in an area that has a population base of at least 200,000. This will give you enough businesses in the area to make your service profitable. You will also be able to develop "pockets" of business and cut down on the amount of time spent traveling to your clients by integrating trips to several in the same area.

TO SUM UP

A payroll preparation service can be in described two words: very profitable. Very profitable in the fact that once you have several clients coming to you, you will attract more, with little effort. Very profitable in that, once again, the computer does all the hard work. Very profitable in that it is rewarding to work with people and give them a service they need.

I know of one person in the Midwest who started a payroll preparation service and within 60 days had 30 clients. He went on from there to doing profit and loss and balance sheets for his clients and an entire range of other bookkeeping functions. He had to hire additional people once his clients found out that he was willing to really work with them. The key to this operation is SERVICE. Offer good service and people will beat their way to your door.

SOURCE MATERIAL

Refer to Section 7.

No. 130

LEASE
OR
BUY
ANALYSIS
REPORTS

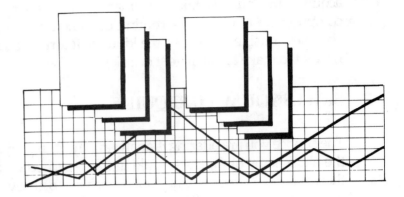

Items like cars, capital equipment, heavy tools, etc. can be acquired in one of two ways—by leasing or by purchasing. Most people do not know the real costs associated with each method and may not even know how to figure them out. Instead, they let some salesperson make the decision about whether to lease or purchase, sometimes without even having been informed of alternative approaches.

By running a few ads in the right places, you can make more money than you thought possible. With your home computer and the appropriate software programs you can satisfy a customer's needs to know about the costs of intended purchases. Once your clients have seen the results, they will refer you to all the business you can handle.

CONCEPT

With very simple arithmetic, most people can figure out the total price that will be paid for an item. All they have to do is multiply the number of months of the contract by the monthly payment. What they don't know is how to compare this total cost of purchasing to leasing costs and benefits.

There are software programs that can figure out payment schedules for almost any rate of interest and term of contract. These programs also work the other way. If you know the payment and the term, they can tell how much interest has been paid. All of these features are important, because there are many kinds of leasing contracts. Some allow the lessee to purchase the item outright for a predetermined price at the close of the contract. Some lease arrangements are for the term of the contract only, with no option to buy at the end. Knowing all the financial facts and how they affect the overall tax picture of an individual or a business is very important and can make a difference in lifestyle or profits.

Your main service is to make people aware of the many alternative approaches to acquisition. You will take information supplied by your client, enter it in your computer, and in a few short minutes come up with the cost of several alternatives. Your new business will give the kinds of information to a prospective buyer that are needed to make an intelligent decision.

SKILLS YOU WILL REQUIRE

The service you are offering is analyzing the facts and then making people aware that the old scheme of things—plunking hard-earned dollars into a down payment and then making payments—may not be the way to go. Even total cash purchasing may be unwise for a business. The skills you will require are those that have to do with the computer itself and are not complex at all.

INFORMATION REQUIRED

In every major community there are companies whose sole business is to finance major purchase items for people and companies that would prefer to lease rather than purchase. Find out everything you can by calling these peple and acquainting yourself with how leasing works.

Find out which finance programs are available for your computer. Understand what each one has to offer. You can use more than one program. Being able to figure depreciation could be very useful to you if you are dealing with people and companies that can use depreciation as tax deductions.

Finance programs are fairly straightforward and are therefore relatively inexpensive.

GETTING STARTED

No matter what kind of business you are thinking about starting, the very first thing you should do is sit down and make out a master plan. If you don't have a clear view of where you want to go, you'll probably end up nowhere. A master plan includes your ultimate goal and the route you propose to take to get there.

Your goals should be written in concrete and your working plan written in sand. It is like taking a long trip and finding road blocks or bad roads. You don't change your destination, you just change your route. Treat your business like a business. No successful corporation would think of proceeding without having goals and plans written down, and neither should you.

Before selecting a software program or programs, you need to be clear about the kinds of information that will be needed to help people make their decision.

You also need to know what kinds of information or graphics will help you promote your new business. A word processor, for instance, could be helpful for advertising and cover letters.

Look for trade magazines that cater to your brand of computer. The ads are worth the price of the subscription. They will give you the names and addresses of manufacturers of software, services and devices that could be useful to you. There may be articles every now and then that apply to you. The few hours a month spent looking through these publications could save you a lot of time in your business. After all, time is money and that's what computers are all about.

THE COMPETITION

The competition is almost nonexistent in this field. Sellers and leasers have their own ax to grind and are not necessarily anxious to review both sides of the picture.

Since you are starting up something most people didn't know existed, the sky's the limit and you can do your own skywriting.

POTENTIAL INCOME

Pricing your services is not difficult. It's important to know your cost of doing business. Go back to the master plan you made and begin pricing out everything on it.

Include:

1. Cost of equipment
2. Cost of advertising
3. Cost of telephone
4. Monthly recurring costs—utilities, rent, printing, etc.
5. Cost of car and travel
6. Cost of your time
7. Costs of miscellaneous expenses, such as postage
8. Cost of software

The investment to get started can be very low, so much of the cost of doing business must come from your evaluation of your own time.

Keep close track of your accounts to be sure you are making a profit. Profit is money left after you pay everything else— including yourself.

In the end, what you can charge is a fraction of what the traffic will bear. If you are performing extra work for a client, you are entitled to charge a larger fee.

Don't be afraid to charge enough for your services. You are saving your clients money either directly or through tax savings. If you undercharge, you won't be in business very long.

It is customary to collect for your service at the time you deliver the information and materials.

Make yours a cash-and-carry business as much as possible. The cost of carrying accounts can be large. If you must carry credit every now and then, carry accounts only for people and firms with good credit. You're not looking for a bad debt write-off on your income tax. It's better to refuse business than to pay for the cost of collections.

You can expect a medium income from this pursuit in the beginning. Like everything else, there's money on the table for those who are creative and aren't afraid to work.

MARKETING METHODS

Your main job is to convince prospective clients that your service is needed. You can show them: alternative ways to acquire new or used items, ways to save money, ways to acquire needed items and still stay in a budget. Your main marketing message is that you can show people how to get more for less.

Flyers describing your services can be mailed to homes and small businesses. Don't be reluctant to send more than one mailing.

A sample ad might read:

> CAN YOU SAVE MONEY BY LEASING?
>
> Did you know that making a large purchase is oftentimes more costly than leasing?
>
> Our service, LEASE-BUY ESTIMATORS, can inform you about your options when considering the purchase of a car, capital equipment and many other high-cost items.
>
> Call now about more information about this low-cost and very unique service. We can save you money today!

Post eye-catching notices everywhere that seems appropriate. Make tear-off tabs on your flyers with your phone number on each tab.

Telephone calling may be a little scary. Read some of the source material on the subject. Calls to businesses could be the richest source of all because of the personal touch. Ask for the purchasing agent and explain what you do. Be prepared to explain the types of lease arrangements he would probably use in his business, as well as how you work and what you charge.

UNIQUE BUSINESS APPROACH

Every businessperson who makes any purchase at all faces the problem that you can help solve. You can build your business by getting to the right people and explaining what you have to offer.

The Soroptimist, the Optimist, the Rotary and the Kiwanis Clubs are business organizations. Their members are the kinds of people you need to meet. One way of getting your information to these individuals is to offer to speak or make a presentation at club meetings. If you feel that speaking for groups is not your bag, contact the local Toastmasters Club or adult education public speaking class and use them as an on-the-job training opportunity. Be sure to have hand-outs that each member can file away until they are needed. If you can get a roster for future mailings, you've hit pay dirt.

LOCATION and MARKET BASE

You are not going to need to rent an office. The information you will need can be obtained at your client's home, office or over the telephone, and the finished product delivered or mailed back to the client. If you feel you need to have business space and have clients come to you, be sure to add that to your cost of doing business.

To assure yourself continuing business, start your service in a city of 200,000 or more. The more, the better, of course.

TO SUM UP

Analyzing the short-term and the long-term costs and the potential tax deductions to leasing versus buying is ultimately the sevice that you are offering. Since most people are unaware that there are lease versus buy options for both the individual and business, your real challenge is education. You need to get to the right people with the right message.

You are creating business as you go, so you can be very time- flexible. You can take on as little or as much as you feel you want. Once you get your feet wet, you will probably want to expand.

The main advice from successful entrepreneurs is "Find a need and then fill it." Here's a definite need just crying out to you. Pick up the baton and start running.

SOURCE MATERIAL

Refer to Section 7.

No. 131

COST ESTIMATES FOR PRINTERS

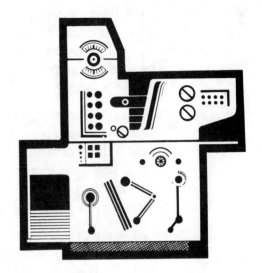

Here is a business that you can easily run out of your home in any sufficiently populated area. Though it won't make you fabulously wealthy, it can be started with very little investment and provide you with a steady source of good income.

CONCEPT

In any medium to large urban area there are literally hundreds of printers. Most of these are relatively small shops with low overhead and only a handful of full-time employees. Their time is most valuable to them when the presses are rolling or when they are soliciting jobs. Figuring cost estimates for potential clients cuts into this time and thus costs them money.

By providing quick and accurate estimates while he does something else, you are selling the printer the resulting savings as well as a necessary service. It is less expensive for him to pay you to do his estimates than it is for him to take the time to do it himself.

Nowhere is the adage "Time is Money" more true than here. If you have the means to produce accurate estimates while the printer is working on another job, you will be well rewarded for it.

SKILLS YOU WILL REQUIRE

You need not have grown up in and around your father's print shop in order to get started in this business. A little knowledge of the basics of printing and some of the terminology will be helpful, but much of that you can pick up as you go along. Since you will be working from lists of services and materials, you will find that the various aspects of the printing trade will soon become extremely familiar.

You will need an estimating program that is both flexible and efficient. The core of your program is the data base, an operations file which lists all possible services to be estimated, and their corresponding rates. Since this will vary from printer to printer, your program will need to accommodate many different rate schedules for different clients. You will also need a library of basic calculations, and an input file to handle the specifications of each particular estimate.

If you are an adept programmer, you may decide to take the time to write a program that works best for you. It is far easier, however, to purchase a software package that suits your needs. There are plenty of them available. Most computer software outlets offer a variety of cost-estimating programs compatible with whatever machine you may own.

If you are shopping for your computer at the same time, and cost-estimating is going to be your primary use for it, shop around a bit and find a system you are comfortable with. In other words, you are buying the computer to suit the software, so find the program or programs you want, then buy a computer that will run it.

INFORMATION REQUIRED

As mentioned previously, you will need price lists from the printers with whom you work. Simply plug this information into your computer program and when a particular estimate comes along, the figures will be there at your fingertips. Once you have completed the first estimate for a particular printer, subsequent jobs are easy. The information is in place and the computer does all of the work.

It won't take long to establish a client base of several printers. You should establish a file for each, listing their services and specifications, so that when you receive a job, you can call up the information you need instantaneously.

You will receive from the printer an estimate input form, detailing the specifications of the job at hand. On it he will list the specifications required by his client, as well as any "judgment" aspects, such as equipment to be used and number of work hours required. It is your job to enter this data into your program, which will produce a quick and accurate estimate for the printer to present to his client.

OPERATING NAME

You can choose any name you want for your new business, but your best bet is some variation of your own name, such as "Joe Jones Estimators" or "Jones and Associates." The advantage to this is that it saves you the expense of registering the new name, opening new bank accounts, installing a new phone system listed under the company name and the like. By using your own name, you can use all of your current accounts, post office boxes and phones for your business at no added expense. Refer to Section 4.

GETTING STARTED

Generating business is a matter of lining up contracts. The best place to start is in your area yellow pages under "Printers." There will be pages of them. From this base you will be able to draw the clients you need.

You should prepare a one-page flyer advertising your services, as well as a business letter offering yourself for hire. Send these out to printers in your area on a regular schedule. See the Marketing Methods Section.

If you want to find out more about the business of estimating printing jobs, approach a printer yourself as a client. You can do this with as small a job as the printing of your stationary. Come up with a design, specify the volume and the type of paper, and get estimates from two or three different printers. See how they do it. If nothing else, this process will aid you in selecting the best approach to use when you offer your services.

THE COMPETITION

The name of the game in this business is speed. You are valuable to a printer because you can save him time. Therefore, you must prove that you can deliver estimates faster than any other method or service the printer might use. Remember that the printer is also serving a client, and the faster his client can receive your estimate, the faster the printer can do his business, thereby increasing both his profit and his reliance on your service.

If you can establish a reputation with several printers as speedy and reliable, they will come to use your service again and again, making you, in effect, their regular estimator. You will know that you have established a successful business when you find the same printers routinely sending you all of their estimating work.

POTENTIAL INCOME

It is important to price your services equitably, so that you make a reasonable amount of money while offering your clients a fair price. To figure out what you should charge, the following criteria should be taken into consideration: the value of your time, the costs of your service (overhead), and your profit margin. You should charge a rate that pays you decently for your time, covers your overhead and makes a profit for your business. Remember that your time is part of the cost of doing business, not part of your profit.

In this case, your time is divided up as follows: time spent working with the printer, including travel time, time spent entering initial data, and time spent entering information for each estimate. Since the first estimate for a new client is going to take somewhat longer than subsequent jobs, you have the option of either charging a start-up fee or charging a slightly higher flat rate.

Here is a list of costs you will need to take into account:

1. All travel-related expenses, including gas, maintenance and parking.
2. Cost of telephone charges
3. Cost of writing and mailing letters
4. Costs of operating your computer
5. Cost of materials, such as paper, business cards, stationary and envelopes
6. Cost of software used

You should be paid in full for each estimate upon delivery.

MARKETING METHODS

The best methods for marketing your service to printers are direct mail, display ads, telephone sales and person-to-person sales.

Of these, direct mail, followed up by a phone call or a visit, is probably the best. I am going to give you an example of a letter that will draw printers' interest and attract them to your service. Mail your letter out to all the printers in your area at the rate of 10 letters per day.

If you are planning to make follow-up calls, wait at least a few days, but no longer than a week or two, so that your letter is still fresh in your potential client's mind.

Here is the letter:

> Dear Printer:
>
> Do you sometimes wish there were more hours in the day? If you could get more use from your presses every day, it wouldn't take long for you to see a substantial jump in your profits.
>
> We can offer you that time, without making your day any longer.
>
> Our fast, accurate, cost-effective estimating service can free you from the chore of figuring estimates and let you get on with the work you need to do. With our computer program, designed specifically for the needs of printers, we can give you an estimate in a fraction of the time you now spend. And you work while we do it. We would be happy to demonstrate our service to you at any time. The few minutes you spend discovering what we have to offer will save you many hours—and dollars—in the future.

If you send this letter or a slight variation of it to all of the printers in your area, you will get results. Don't expect a flood immediately.

People are skeptical and every printer will not want your services. But keep sending letters out, and you will generate interest in what you have to offer.

For more methods and information, refer to Section 5.

UNIQUE BUSINESS APPROACH

Here is a way to interest many printers at once in your service. You can hold a public demonstration for as many printers in your area as you can get to show up. Send out a flyer announcing that you are holding a brief seminar to unveil your new service. This can save you time, but more important, it will get your business discussed among your potential clients.

You can usually rent a room for an hour in a public library or school for a nominal fee. Prepare one or two sample estimates to demonstrate on your system. If you like, you can solicit a fictitious job from one of the printers there, and come up with the estimate as they watch. There is nothing like the immediacy of a live demonstration to impress people.

LOCATION and MARKET BASE

The biggest restriction on the amount of work you can do is the number of printers in your area. Frequent personal contact with your clients is a necessity. For this reason, you will have the most success with this business the closer you are to a large city, one with a population of at least 200,000 people in its market area. The less traveling you have to do, the less your overhead, which will enable you to charge less, and make your services more valuable.

Your targets are the many small and medium-sized printing operations that abound in and around any city. The larger printing houses will either have in-house estimating departments or their own computerized system already in place. For the smaller printer, however, it is much more economical to hire someone like yourself on a per-job basis than it is to make substantial capital investment in a system that would be idle much of the time.

TO SUM UP

Providing quick and reliable cost estimates for printers is a much needed service and one well suited to the personal computer owner. The small printer, especially, has been ignored by mainstream services and can benefit greatly from the service you will provide.

You can enter this business as a novice and within a very short time become a highly valued asset to printers in your area. Once you have established yourself with enough printers to keep you busy, you can find yourself with what amounts to a good, steady job working out of your own home.

SOURCE MATERIAL

Refer to Section 7.

No. 132

RARE BOOK LOCATOR SERVICE

This is a business that has an international flavor but can be run from your home. There are over a thousand rare book specialty shops, but the one thing they all lack is a system for rare book buyers to compare cost and condition of the books they are looking for. Here's where you can step in with your home computer and offer a service that makes both the buyers and the sellers happy, and allows you to collect both ways.

CONCEPT

You may be surprised to know how many people value old books. One man's white elephant may be another man's treasure. Finding the location of these treasures is important. But just as important is their condition. To a collector, a book in good condition is worth many times the price of an identical book in poor or bad condition. Some people, on the other hand, are just looking for out-of-print books for the information they contain. These people may not be willing to pay the price for a book in mint condition. This is where you come in with the information to magically satisfy all parties.

SKILLS YOU WILL REQUIRE

Your main job is to have at your fingertips (literally) information supplied by others. You needn't be an expert on books or authors or publishers.

Since the service you are offering is really being the information link between book "wanters" and books "havers," the skills you will require are those that have to do with the computer itself. They are not hard to acquire at all.

INFORMATION REQUIRED

In every large community there are listings in the yellow pages for booksellers. Visit a few booksellers, especially the rare book specialists, and ask questions. Get information and catalogs of dealers out of town. Keep on looking and adding to your list. This list is a gold mine from which you are later going to pick up nuggets of money.

Before you can select software that will serve you well, a discussion of data bases is in order. A data base is a type of computer program you will need to run your new business. It is like a giant filing cabinet jammed with scraps of useful information. But one of the striking differences is that instead of each being filed under just one heading, each piece of information can be filed under a number of headings, or "fields," as they are called.

An example of fields and field information that might be entered for one book are:

Book title: Love in the South Pacific
Author: C. U. Later
Date of Publication: 1927
Category: Romance novel
Category: Fiji Islands
Category: 1860s
Publisher: E. Z. Reading and Son
Type of Print: Gothic
Type of Cover: Leather
Condition of cover: Good
Condition of Pages: Excellent
Edition: First and only
Cost: What the traffic will bear
Bookseller: Oldies But Goodies
Buyer:
Buyer will pay:
Date Sold:
Remarks: Gold-tooled letters on cover

Back to the example of a filing cabinet. Where would you be likely to file the information about this book if you were running your business by antiquated methods? Probably by the title and the author. If you are very energetic, you could file duplicate copies under both and then laboriously set up a separate cross- referencing index. This entails a lot of work.

The beauty of using a data base to record all this information is that, once information is recorded, you can search in your computer "filing cabinet" for any and all of these headings.

Suppose you find a customer who collects romance novels written before 1940, but only those situated in the Fiji Islands. They must be leather-bound—and most important, they must be in good to excellent condition. Where would you start looking? With your computer and your trusty data base, you could sort for each of these fields. A good program will have a sub-sort feature (sort for more than one field at a time) so you can go directly to only those books that fill all of the needs. What a time saver! It's like having a collection of recipes filed not just under the type of food, but also under every ingredient and every kind of cooking method.

You can see that this would work if you had a buyer looking for a specific book or type of book that you haven't located. You fill in the buyer information and when you do locate the book, presto, you have a ready-made sale.

GETTING STARTED

No matter what kind of business you are thinking about starting, the very first thing you should do is sit down and make out a master plan. If you don't have a clear view of where you want to go, you'll probably end up nowhere. A master plan includes your ultimate goal and the route you propose to take to get there. Your goals should be written in concrete and your working plan written in sand. As in taking a long trip and finding road blocks or bad roads, you don't change your destination, you just change your route. Treat your business like a business. No successful corporation would think of proceeding without having goals and plans written down—and neither should you.

Comb the software stores in your area for all the data base programs that will work on your computer. To look at programs that won't work on your computer is a waste of time no matter how good the program is or how good the "experts" say it is. Time spent choosing software wisely is time well spent, since your business revolves around this purchase.

Before selecting a software program, you need to ask yourself some questions about the type of information you want to store. This is extremely important. Since you will be typing in information (doing data entry), you want to do it only once, so choose the right program in the beginning. If you should change your mind later and want to use another program, it may not be possible to switch all that information you've collected from one program to another without having to re-enter all of it. Questions you should ask yourself before shopping include:

1. What types of information seem to be important to buyers and sellers?

2. What types of information will be important for promoting my business?

3. Based on the information above, how many fields are necessary? (Be generous—you will need more than you think.)

4. How deep do I want to sub-sort?

5. Do I need the ability to add new fields to existing files?

6. Do I want to retain customer files from year to year, therefore encouraging repeat business?

Data base programs run from $75 to several hundred dollars. This is not the place to economize. Get a comprehensive one that will fit your needs and will run on your hardware. The more comprehensive ones will have room for more fields and have lots of other goodies. Select software carefully. The more it fits your needs, the less hassle you will have and the more profit you will realize.

Look for trade magazines that cater to your brand of computer. The ads are worth the price of the subscription. They will give you the names and addresses of manufacturers of software, services and devices that could be useful to you. There may even be articles published every now and then that apply to you. The few hours a month spent looking through these publications could save you a lot of time in your business. After all, time is money and that's what computers are all about.

Write or visit the sellers you have identified and request a written list of their present inventory. If at all possible, include the edition and the condition of the books, as well as the cost. You will need a standardized way of qualifying "condition" of the books so that those doing business with you will be using the same terms to mean the same thing.

Example: Excellent condition—no tears or worn spots—color not faded—looks like new.

Remember, this is just an example.

There are collectors who specialize in just first editions, so knowing the edition could be very important. If there is not an inventory readily available, ask to speak to the manager or owner. Explain that you have some buyers interested in old and rare books and that you run a service that puts buyer and seller together. Booksellers are in business to sell books and will undoubtedly be cooperative.

Data entry and secretarial services are available to help you type in data if you don't wish to do it all yourself.

THE COMPETITION

As I mentioned above, a system for putting buyer and seller together is lacking today. Since you are setting up a service that is virtually nonexistent, you can mold it to fit you and your personality like a glove.

POTENTIAL INCOME

Pricing your service is not difficult. It would be appropriate to take a percentage markup on the sale price.

It's important to know your cost of doing business. Go back to the master plan you made and begin pricing out everything on it.

Include:

1. Cost of equipment
2. Cost of advertising
3. Cost of telephone
4. Monthly recurring costs—utilities, rent, etc.
5. Cost of postage
6. Cost of car and travel expenses
7. Cost of your time
8. Any other costs
9. Cost of software

Keep close tabs on your accounts to be sure you are making a profit. Profit is money left after you pay everything else, including yourself. In the end, what you can charge is a fraction of what the traffic will bear. If you are performing extra work for a client, you are entitled to charge a larger percentage.

There are several ways to be paid for your services. You can sell your lists as a newsletter to buyers and other bookksellers. Or, sell specific books to customers at a markup (but have the dealer do the shipping). Have a standing deal with sellers to receive a finder's fee.

Make yours a cash-and-carry business as much as possible. The cost of carrying accounts can be large. Carry accounts only for people and firms with good credit. You're not looking for a bad- debt write-off on your income tax.

You can expect a medium income from this pursuit in the beginning. Like in anything else, there's money on the table for those who are creative and aren't afraid to work.

MARKETING METHODS

Flyers describing your services can be mailed to homes. If there is a university in your area, or any other area likely to attract bookish people, concentrate your energies there. Personalized direct mail would be useful. Here's where you can use a word processor. Personalizing mail will appeal to those who are potential customers. Don't be reluctant to send more than one mailing.

If you are allowed to post notices in schools and libraries, make tear-off tabs on your flyers with your phone number on each tab.

A typical flyer might read:

RARE BOOK COLLECTORS!

We know where to look for that book you want.

Our computerize book catalog lists thousands of volumes, not only by title and author but by category, condition, price and other elements.

It won't cost you a cent to try us, so give a call today to learn more about our unique, low-cost service.

Tomorrow you could have your hands on just the volume you need to round out your book collection!

Telephone calling may be a little scary. Read some source material on the subject. A business call to institutions and people in search of books could be the richest source of all because of the personal touch.

Seek out and join literary clubs and library associations to become known by these people. Word-of-mouth advertising is very valuable and these circles will spread your name. Remember to give out your card at every opportunity. Those boring old parties someone dragged you to can offer a wealth of contacts.

The yellow pages is the first place local people look to find what they need. You must have a business telephone, however, to have a listing in the yellow pages. Compare the increased costs of a business phone with the increased local business you might expect. Telephone information operators do not look up listings in the yellow pages, so the increase in business you might get would only be from those who have access to the yellow pages.

There are magazines and publications listed in the library's periodical file that have direct interest for you. If these publications take classified advertising, find out the cost and consider taking out an ad to swell your list of potential buyers.

UNIQUE BUSINESS APPROACH

Every service organization, ladies' group, PTA and senior citizens' association are constantly and persistently looking for speakers for their meetings. Work up a presentation with colored slides and show what you have to offer. Explain the benefit of collecting books, what a job it can be, and the investment potential it offers.

You don't have to be a Dale Carnegie to do a great job. Creative preparation is the secret.

If you don't have the time for this or if you just feel you can't, call the local Toastmaster's Club or adult education public speaking class and let them know you have an on-the-job speaking experience opportunity. You just might get a speaker for nothing.

LOCATION and MARKET BASE

You are not going to need to rent an office. The information you will need can be obtained by mail, in person and over the phone.

An area of population between 50,000 and 200,000 people could be considered a good market base. As long as the telephone company and the post office serve your home and you are willing to travel to areas of denser population or areas with more prospective clients, any location would be a reasonable market base.

TO SUM UP

The Rare Book Locator Service may have limited application, but even this limited application can be profitable. Price is sometimes not a consideration for people who collect rare books.

The flexibility of this locator service allows you to take on as little or as much business as you feel comfortable with. Expand as the market leads and your time permits.

This is a service with plenty of room for creativity, especially in the methods of marketing. You're your own boss and that means a lot. If you happen to enjoy books, so much the better.

The world's your oyster, so start shucking!

SOURCE MATERIAL

For source information see Section 7.

No. 133

RECIPE SERVICE FOR GOURMETS

This is a fun business that can be started easily and at low cost. You can begin in your spare time, and with the proper promotion expand it into a profitable and rewarding business.

CONCEPT

How often have you gone to your favorite restaurant, and after savoring an excellent meal, wished that you knew the recipe to try out at home?

Well, many people like you have thought the same thing. That's the basis for this business opportunity.

Most quality restaurants have unique recipes for meals, which keep bringing their customers back for more. By giving out their unique recipes to customers, restaurants actually keep the establishment's name fresh in the customer's mind.

But won't the restaurant lose business by giving out the secrets of their cuisine? On the contrary. The customers who would prepare the meals at home would proudly mention the source of the recipe to their guests. The name of the restaurant would receive continuous exposure.

You would therefore provide a valuable service to both sides. The customers would be happy to get the unique recipes, while the restaurants would benefit from the promotion your service would generate.

SKILLS YOU WILL REQUIRE

This is a very easy business to start without special skills. It doesn't require technical know-how or extensive business experience. It does require the ability to talk with restaurant managers, and a little flair for promotions to create interest among the customers.

Once you have set up the initial contact with the restaurants, the business can almost run itself. The orders will come in to you for additional recipes and you can gradually promote new business.

As will be explained in the following pages, there are computer programs available to help you prepare the listings which you will sell to your customers. As a result, it won't be necessary for you to have programming skills. Once you enter the information into the computer, it will do the rest.

INFORMATION REQUIRED

The information necessary for the business will be supplied to you by the restaurants themselves. They will provide you with all the recipes you'll need. As you build an information base, it will become the lifeblood of your business. As you gradually accumulate more recipes, you will have virtually an encyclopedia of culinary delights for your customers to choose from.

The customers who bought from you before will also become the source of additional business. You will keep records of their names in your computer files. With time, you will accumulate a large number of names, which will become your customer base. You can then use those names to promote additional sales. They should be easier to sell to, since they have already bought from you once. Through special offers by mail, you'll keep them coming back for more recipes. You'll find more ideas on this concept in the Marketing Methods Section.

With time, your computer will become a storehouse of valuable information, consisting of names of customers, restaurants, and your valuable recipes.

The computer programs that will be valuable to you in working with recipes are low in cost and easy to use. A good program will enable you to file recipes by various categories, such as name of restaurant, type of food, and main ingredients. It will also neatly print the full description of the recipe along with a shopping list of the ingredients. It will give out customized listings of portions based on family size. And it will do it all in minutes, a feature which will come in very handy when processing several hundred orders.

OPERATING NAME

You don't have to go right out and spend money on business licenses and recording fees. At the beginning, you can deal with the restaurants as an individual. But often first impressions are most important, and to give yourself a more professional image, you may choose to establish a fictitious name for your business. An impressive company name, along with some attractive literature, may add more credibility to your service, since you'll be dealing with restaurant managers who will want to be assured of the best of care for their customers.

GETTING STARTED

This is an ideal business to start part-time and expand to full-time. The risk is very low since the business requires only a small computer, and because it is based on providing a service, rather than having to manufacture a product.

The best way to get started in this service is to visit the restaurants in person. In talking with the managers, realize that selling them on your idea is one of the most important steps in developing your business, and to do so, you must convey your enthusiasm for the idea.

As the most important thing, stress the additional promotion the restaurant will receive and the satisfaction the customers will derive by trying out the recipes on their own. The customers will, of course, keep coming back, because the atmosphere is always more attractive at the restaurant. Plus, the customer may not be able to duplicate the quality of cooking which the chef can achieve.

Point out how your idea will help to create goodwill for the establishment and as a result make your service worthwhile.

THE COMPETITION

The competition is virtually nonexistent. With hundreds of restaurants to choose from in any metropolitan area, there is plenty of room to establish your business. Eventually some competition may arise, but by then your business will be well-established and can even be expanded to additional services.

POTENTIAL INCOME

The income from this business could be enough to support your efforts part-time or full-time. It all depends on how much time and effort you want to put into it.

You could charge a fee to the restaurant for the service and then collect, for example, one dollar for each recipe listing you sell to a customer. You might give a discount for larger orders.

In determining your potential income, estimate the expenses you'll incur in your business. Fortunately, your expenses will be very low. Your overhead costs will be minimal, since you'll be able to operate the business out of your home. You should keep track of all your expenses, however minimal, for tax purposes.

Program Costs

1. Cost of software

2. Cost of advertising
3. Cost of recipe cards
4. Cost of time spent gathering, processing and inputting recipes
5. Cost of transportation expenses
6. Cost of telephone charges
7. Cost of postage

How To Be Paid

Since collecting an income and making a profit are the main reasons to begin a business, you'll want to make the most of your opportunity. This is a unique situation, one in which you'll be able to collect from both the restaurants and the customers.

The amount you can charge the restaurants will depend on how valuable they consider your service to be. To start with, you can charge them for the brochures or cards you make up with their name on it. You could arrange to print just a few hundred to begin with. First find out your costs and then charge them an amount above that you think is fair. Also, as mentioned at the beginning of this plan, you could charge restaurants a flat fee for the service, which would be enough to cover your costs and to give you a profit.

With the customers, you'll be charging a fee for each recipe listing. A dollar each should be acceptable. You might discount quantity orders to $4 for five recipes and $7 for 10 recipes, for example.

The customers would send orders to you by filling out the coupons they find attached to the brochures in the restaurants. You then promptly fill the orders and mail them to each customer.

MARKETING METHODS

Again, restaurants will be your primary source of business. Through them, you'll generate the customers to sell your recipes to.

You should prepare an attractive brochure or sales leaflet, which you will leave at the restaurants. The customers will pick them up and then place orders with you directly by mail coupon.

The brochures could be placed on tables and at the registers to attract the customer's attention.

You could have cards made up to look like small brochures, with pictures and enticing prose to interest the customers. Attractive cards can be purchased which have a color photograph on the front. You could design an attractive picture or photograph depicting the restaurant, and have a set made for each restaurant with its name on it. The restaurant should be happy to pay for this service, since it will bring them constant promotion.

On the cards that will be left at the restaurants, you could write something similar to this:

Dear Patron:

If you liked our meals here at the restaurant, now there is a way for you to try your hand at making some of these delicious dinners at home.

Send the enclosed coupon indicating which recipes you would like mailed to you. You will very shortly receive a full description of how to prepare our special recipes, along with a shopping list of the necessary ingredients.

Please enclose one dollar for each recipe you would like.

You might refine the wording to fit the type of restaurant you are working with and possibly even experiment with different prices for the recipes.

You could also place small display ads in the restaurant section of your local newspaper, along with ads in the entertainment magazines or city guides available in your area.

Once your customers have ordered from you, they are ideal prospects for follow-up sales. Periodically, you can mail promotional material to entice them to purchase more recipes. You'll store the names on a disk with the mailing list program (see your dealer for one suitable for your computer), and you'll be able to call them up alphabetically or by restaurant preference, to make additional mailings.

UNIQUE BUSINESS APPROACH

You could entice the restaurants to put together some type of contest promotion. For example, the customers could try to guess the ingredients of certain dishes and the winners would receive free dinners.

To really make a splash, you could give a news release to the local newspaper and the city magazine which covers the restaurant scene. These publications are always searching for interesting events to cover in their issues and with the right twist, your business would provide worthwhile news material.

Another good approach would be to take advantage of your recipe listings by combining all the ones for each restaurant together into a special package. You could then sell a restaurant package with all their recipes for a bargain price.

LOCATION and MARKET BASE

Location is not crucial in this business, since the customers will not be coming to your place to purchase the listings. You can operate it entirely through the mail and through personal visits to the restaurants.

TO SUM UP

Thousands of people visit restaurants in your area daily. This business opportunity is a unique way of taking advantage of a source of income which the restaurants have already established for you.

If you have an affinity for good food and like visiting nice restaurants, this could be an ideal business for you. It will be easy to start, has little risk and has the potential to expand. Those attributes are very important to consider in any business, since they allow you to become independent without taking large risks.

SOURCE MATERIAL

You will find reference information in Section 7.

No. 134

VITAMIN REQUIREMENT SERVICE

In this business you use your computer to create custom vitamin plans and cash in on the growing public awareness of specialized nutritional requirements. This business has unlimited growth potential with little time investment. Get started now and become the "Computer Vitamin Czar!"

CONCEPT

The concept of this business is to create custom vitamin plans, tailored to meet your client's unique nutritional requirements. In spite of the fact that the U.S. Food and Drug Administration has established basic "minimum daily requirements" for vitamins and minerals, each person's actual needs vary greatly, depending on physical activity and health conditions. The nutritional requirements for a woman expecting a baby or an athlete training for a marathon are quite different from the well-publicized minimum daily requirements.

A wide variety of software for custom diet planning is available off-the-shelf. Some of this software focuses specifically on nutritional requirements, rather than calorie counting, and can easily be applied to individual clients.

By placing ads in pharmacies and vitamin stores, you can quickly attract a substantial clientele for this service.

SKILLS YOU WILL REQUIRE

The most important skill you will need is the ability to operate your software package correctly. Typically, you'll have to enter specific information about height and weight, physical activity, foods normally eaten and personal health. The software will come with an instruction manual to guide you through it, and you can practice by creating custom vitamin plans for yourself and your family. You may be surprised to find important nutritional requirements you've been neglecting in your own diet.

INFORMATION REQUIRED

You don't have to be an expert nutritionist to get started in this business, but a general knowledge of nutrition provides a solid foundation. A wide variety of books are available to add to your understanding of vitamins and nutrition. You can find these books almost anywhere. In addition to bookstores and libraries, you'll also find them in supermarkets, drugstores and elsewhere.

Pay particular attention to the nutritional requirements for people in unusually stressful situations—athletic training, pregnancy, weight-loss dieting, illnesses. This information will help you in targeting your market and preparing advertisements.

OPERATING NAME

As with any business, you have two choices for an operating name. You can simply use your own name, or you can choose a fictitious business name.

When you do business under a fictitious name, you have to register the name or file a fictitious name report. You also have to have a special business bank account, which is usually more expensive than a personal account. Phone rates for businesses are also higher. In spite of the extra costs, an appropriate fictitous name has the advantage of immediately identifying the nature of your business. For example, you could use a name such as "A to E Vitamin Planning."

Using your own name is a bit easier, and makes it cheaper to get started. You don't have to have a separate business checking account or business phone. On the other hand, your name alone doesn't tell anything about your business. To get around this problem you can try using a slogan that explains the nature of your business on your ads, business cards and letterhead. For example, you could use a slogan such as, "Personalized Planning for Health and Nutrition."

See Section 4 for more information about selecting an operating name for your business.

GETTING STARTED

The first step in getting started in this business is to select the software and learn to use it. Shop carefully for your software and make sure you get the package most appropriate for your needs. Some nutrition planning software is designed specifically for weight-loss diets, but your needs in this case are much broader.

After you have your software, the next step is to prepare a questionnaire for your clients. Your software package may include a questionnaire that you can adapt for your business. Or you may have to design your own questionnaire, based on the information you need to enter for each nutrition plan.

With your questionnaire complete, you're ready for action! It's time to start advertising. See the Marketing Methods section for suggestions on how and where to advertise your business.

THE COMPETITION

In this unique business you probably won't have much direct competition. Instead of competing directly with professional nutritionists, take advantage of them by offering your service to help them plan for their clients!

POTENTIAL INCOME

As a general rule of thumb, you can expect a medium-level income from this business. But exactly how much you make depends on your own commitment to the business and how much time and effort you're willing to put into it.

To set your fees, time yourself when you're preparing your own practice nutritional plans. Once you have a solid idea of how long one takes, you can set your fees based on the hourly rate you want to earn.

Basic Costs

1. Cost of software
2. Cost of advertising
3. Cost of time spent compiling questionnaire
4. Cost of reproducing questionnaire
5. Cost of time spent with clients
6. Cost of materials used
7. Cost of books, pamphlets, etc. purchased for education

To realistically figure your earnings, you have to take your expenses into account. With this business you won't have much overhead for operations—a portion of your rent or house payment for office space, a portion of your utility bills and phone bills, car expenses if you use your car for distributing advertising, and mailing costs for your completed nutrition plans.

Aside from your initial investment for equipment and software, your major expense will be for advertising. You'll need to pay for preparation and printing for display ads or flyers. See Marketing Methods for detailed suggestions on advertising.

How To Be Paid

For this business you have several ways to collect payment. You can request your fee at the same time the customer gives you the completed questionnaire. You may also choose to take half the fee as a deposit and half when you return the vitamin analysis.

If you advertise your service through the mail, you can simply request payment in advance, like any other mail order business.

MARKETING METHODS

For this business you don't want to take a shotgun approach to ads; you want to target your potential clients as specifically as possible. Display ads and flyers are suitable, especially when placed in locations such as pharmacies and vitamin stores. Fitness centers also provide good locations for your ads.

If you use flyers, be sure to include the questionnaire you've drawn up. This way potential customers immediately have the questionnaire in their hands, and can see what kind of information they need to provide and how easy it is to take advantage of your service. Make it simple for them to fill out the questionnaire and mail it to you, along with a check.

In your ads, stress the custom-planning aspect of your service— each person is a unique individual with unique nutritional requirements. Here's an example of a flyer you could use in marketing this business:

> DID YOU TAKE YOUR VITAMIN TODAY?
>
> And even if you did, are you sure it was the right vitamin to take?
>
> Your vitamin needs are unique. What your body requires depends on what you put it through day by day, what you like to eat, how you handle stress, and a variety of other factors.
>
> Now there is a method to calculate exactly what vitamins your body requires. With just a few minutes of your time we will design a vitamin program that fills those needs.
>
> Don't wait. Pick up your phone now and call us about this low-cost and unique service. It'll be the best thing you do for yourself all week.

Your own variation of this copy should bring you inquiries for more information. Prepare yourself in advance so you are ready to answer questions from potential customers.

UNIQUE BUSINESS APPROACH

To get this business off the ground, you need to develop a group of satisfied clients quickly and let them spread the word about your service to their friends and associates.

One effective approach to establishing clients is to offer a discount to members of fitness centers. People who are willing to spend the time and money to join a fitness center are serious about maintaining their health and will provide an excellent target market.

Make arrangements with fitness centers to display your advertising materials. If you yourself are a member of a fitness center, you'll greatly enhance your opportunities to distribute your flyers or place your display ads.

You may also choose to target specific groups, such as runners, swimmers, the elderly, pregnant women, smokers, etc. Simply place your advertising in local publications that have your targeted market as readers.

LOCATION and MARKET BASE

For this business to be successful you should be in or near a city. Even though you'll be handling most of the business by mail, you need to have a market base large enough to provide a sufficient number of clients. Your opportunities for placing display ads and flyers are much better in an urban area than in a sparsely populated area.

The minimum market base for this business is in the range of 50,000 to 200,000 people. You could do well in an even larger city, but you shouldn't try to go much smaller.

START-UP CAPITAL

You can get started in this business on a small initial investment. In fact, you can get started for under $1,000 — not counting the cost of your computer. See Section 6 for information on obtaining the investment capital you need for starting a small business.

TO SUM UP

If you're interested in helping people live fuller, healthier lives, this is an excellent business for you to get into. It requires little start-up capital or expertise and can easily be operated by one person. It can be a part-time or full-time venture, depending on your own interests.

No doubt you'll become a much healthier human being in the process of operating this business, and, of course, a richer one as well.

SOURCE MATERIAL

Refer to Section 7.

No. 135

COMPUTERIZED ENERGY SURVEY SERVICE FOR HOMES AND OFFICES

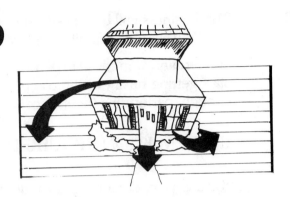

Everybody is energy-conscious now with the cost of utilities as high as it is. Here's a great home computer service that lets you operate direct by mail with our unique "Energy Survey Questionnaire." You take the information, enter it into your computer, and make accurate recommendations to improve energy use in homes or offices. There's a sideline to this that turns it into a real money-maker with no additional work.

CONCEPT

The concept of this business is to show people how they can cut down on their energy consumption. You charge a fee to do an energy-efficiency analysis for their home or office. The money they can save by following your advice will more than cover the amount they pay you for the service.

This business is especially needed at a time when everybody is so energy-conscious and utility bills are so high.

The average home or office uses 50 percent more energy than it should. Most people don't know this fact, yet they constantly complain about utility bills that are "outrageous." Once you show them how they can cut down on their energy usage, they will recommend your service to business associates, friends and family.

SKILLS YOU WILL REQUIRE

This business will be well suited to you if you know anything about home construction. You should be familiar with some of the terminology used in the business.

You certainly don't need to be an expert in energy efficiency for this service. Once you start getting business, the computer program you use will guide you along. Soon enough, performing this service will make you an expert. You will learn as you go.

INFORMATION REQUIRED

You use a computer program to do your energy analysis in this business. A customer comes to you and you have him fill out a questionnaire that asks about his home design and energy usage. His responses are put into the computer, which sorts and processes the information, then gives you the information you need to advise him about ways to make his home more energy-efficient.

The program will ask questions, for example, regarding size of house, number of rooms, doors and windows, building material, the type of attic and wall insulation used, etc.

Usually utility bills can be cut simply by "tightening" the house. This means the owner should check the insulation around walls, where air can leak through. Also, he might need to weatherstrip around windows and doors, or simply add a new burner nozzle to his furnace. With the information you provide, he can judge the cost of various home improvements versus the savings he can expect in his energy bill.

The amount you charge for this service will be well worth the investment to your customer. Yet your computer does your work for you.

OPERATING NAME

With this business you have two choices. You can pick a fictitious name, such as "Home Energy Analysis" or "Energy Efficiency Consultants." Doing this will require extra start-up costs for registering or filing the name, getting a phone installed at business rates, etc.

Or you can start by using your own name, John Smith. You can add "Energy Consultant" after it, then still use the bank accounts, phones, etc. that are already in your own name. Refer to Section 4 for information about choosing a business name.

GETTING STARTED

To get started in this business you will first have to purchase computer software that does energy analysis. Once you have familiarized yourself with that, you're ready to hang out your shingle for business.

You can operate your business in two ways. You can have your customers come to you in person, or you can do it through the mail. Either way, your customers will have to answer questions about their current energy usage. This is the information your computer will need in order to do the analysis.

A questionnaire might consist of this:

How large is your office/home in square feet?
How many rooms?
How many windows?
What kind of building material is it made from?
What types of lighting do you have?
What type of flooring do you have?
How many minutes a day do you use hot water?
How often do you use all rooms of the house?
When was your home last weatherstripped?
What type of heating fuel do you use—wood, coal, electricity or gas?
Do you set back your thermostat during the day when you are not home or during the night when you are sleeping?

These are the kinds of questions your computer will need to do the analysis. Working with the software, you should be able to develop a questionnaire that anybody can read and answer. This will enable you to offer this service through the mail. Somebody can request your service, you mail them a questionnaire, they return it along with a check for your fee, and you do the analysis and send them tips for cutting down on their energy usage.

You can tell them that if they do such and such, they will save X amount of dollars per year. This kind of calculation will show them how much they can save versus how much your fee was. It's an effective way to show how valuable your service is for the cost.

THE COMPETITION

Your competition in this field is the group of energy engineers who do energy analysis. Most of these people work for contractors who are designing and building new homes and need to keep up on new energy building regulations. The language they speak can usually be understood only by other professionals in the construction field.

You, on the other hand, are not the same kind of expert as they. You can speak the same language as your customers, people who want to save energy in their homes and offices.

Plus, there is another difference between you and your competitors. Many of them are affiliated with a solar company or other company trying to sell energy-efficient products. They do their analysis in order to convince customers to buy their product. You aren't swayed by commissions, as they may be. Your product is the analysis. Theirs is the energy-saving device they are selling. If you were a customer, who would you prefer to go to?

POTENTIAL INCOME

You can make a very nice income with this business. To figure out what to charge for your service, simply estimate your costs, add in a salary for your time, and a profit for the business. This will give you a good idea of what people should pay for each analysis.

If you charge only $50 for each analysis and get 10 customers for the month, that is $500 in your pocket. This isn't bad for a part-time effort.

Primary Costs

1. Cost of computer program
2. Cost of advertising
3. Cost of organizing the questionnaire
4. Cost of postage and other mailing expenses
5. Cost of telephone calls
6. Cost of other materials used
7. Cost of organizing analysis

Overhead

Your overhead in this business will be office space, phone, etc. Remember to include these charges into the estimate of costs for this business to give you a truer picture of what to charge for this service.

Profit

When calculating a price for this business, remember to include a profit figure into your charges. This isn't the same as the money you earn for your time. That is considered a salary. The profit goes into the business and is a separate amount.

How To Be Paid

The standard practice with this type of service is payment in advance. If you are selling the service through the mail, then payment in advance is advised. If you are doing an analysis for a customer who comes to you in person, then you can take half the fee in advance as deposit, then collect the remainder when the analysis is delivered.

MARKETING METHODS

The beauty of this business is that there are numerous ways to market it, all depending on what you prefer. You can use direct mail, display ads and telephone sales for this business. All three methods are explained below.

You can use display ads to sell your service locally. Simply run an ad in local newspapers, homeowner and business publications where the people who will want to use your service can see the ad.

You can get customers by using your telephone as well. All you have to do is call prospective customers and explain that you will do an analysis for their home or office that you guarantee will save them at least as much money on their energy bills in the first year as what you charge. If for some reason the analysis you do shows that they are as energy-efficient as they can get, you simply return their deposit. It is better to keep a clean record with your customers, and maintain your business integrity.

You can also sell this business with direct mail. You have two choices here. You can run an ad in publications that cater to homeowners and business owners who might want to use such a service. You can include a coupon that they return to you. When you receive a coupon, you mail back a questionnaire for them to fill out. From there you do your analysis.

The second method of direct mail is to send a letter to those people you think would like to use the service. If you mail them out at a rate of 20 or 30 a day, you should have business in no time.

A typical letter might say:

> DEAR HOME/OFFICE OWNER:
>
> Your energy bills are probably twice as high as they should be. Let us analyze your energy efficiency and advise you on how to cut down on your energy bills.
>
> We are not salespeople. We do not sell products to save your home energy. We do not earn commissions on any energy-saving devices you may decide to purchase. We are independent agents whose only concern is informing you about ways to save on utility bills.
>
> We guarantee that we can save you more money in a single year on your utility bill than you pay for our service. If not, we will return your fee. All it requires is a few minutes of your time to fill out one of our energy efficiency questionnaires. For more information about this unique, money-saving service, call or contact us now!

Your own variation of this letter will bring inquiries for more information. Mail your questionnaire to customers who respond, and in short order you'll be on your way to earning income with this money-making opportunity.

UNIQUE BUSINESS APPROACH

If you're intrigued by this business, you will want to be aware of one approach that can make you a nice extra income. The group of people who can really use this service is senior citizens. Most are on a fixed income and can't afford the incredible utility bills they often have to pay. Many live in rented apartments, which means they can't have insulation added or more energy-efficient flooring put down. Yet there are other ways they can cut down on their utility bills.

You can market this service to seniors by mailing out to them as individuals or by going to senior service centers that cater to them and offering your service at a special rate. They will supply you with customers in exchange for you suggesting energy-saving tips. You might also consider putting on energy-efficiency seminars at senior centers. This method will arouse the curiosity of people and probably bring you more customers.

Since seniors are very energy-conscious, they make an excellent customer base for you to approach.

LOCATION and MARKET BASE

This business can best be operated in a city. This will ensure that with a population base of at least 50,000 to 200,000 people, you will have plenty of potential customers. If you have a large senior population, even better.

START-UP CAPITAL REQUIRED

You will need from $1,000 to $5,000 to start this business. This will give you the money you need for your equipment as well as the software you will require.

TO SUM UP

This is the age of energy conservation. People want to know how they can cut down on utility bills without creating discomfort to themselves. With this service, you'll not only be able to inform them on how to cut down on energy usage, but you will be able to tell them how much money each technique will save them.

It is a simple business that can be done with only a little extra time. What prevents many from trying it is the thought that it is too complicated to perform. Yet computers these days are making everything easier. With the right program directing you, you'll learn just about everything you'll need to know to operate this business.

When your customer receives his analysis, he will see how much he saved simply by going to you. Your fee is just a tiny chunk of his savings. Yet for you, those fees add up to a nice nest egg to buy those extras you've been wanting. And isn't that what success is all about?

SOURCE MATERIAL

Refer to Section 7.

No. 136

SBA FINANCING PACKAGE SERVICE

This is a business that has done very well ever since the need for filling out complex government applications made it a necessity. Now with the help of a computer you can turn this into an easy and profitable business. We've discovered the inside track for obtaining new clients, and it's all in this plan, just waiting for you to get started.

CONCEPT

Most people starting in a new business are not able to fill out a loan package on their own, at least not well enough to get approved by a loan committee. That's where your service becomes valuable. As a loan packager, you will provide a needed service to clients by helping them to present a much more professional loan package than they could on their own.

Many business owners and would-be entrepreneurs are in need of financing to continue or to start a new business. The Small Business Administration (SBA) has been providing funds for many years to small businesses that would have been unable to secure financing from conventional sources.

But as with most governmental programs, correctly answering the questions on each form can be vital in getting an approval. As a loan packager, you assist your clients in preparing a proposal that presents them in the best possible light.

In the past this service was done manually and took hours of effort. But now with the aid of computers it's as simple as entering the information on the keyboard and then printing out the completed forms ready for submission. If needed, you can easily make changes or corrections and then reprint the pages that have been modified. This can be accomplished in a third of the time and half of the cost that it would take manually. As a result, you can provide a more efficient service at a lower cost.

SKILLS YOU WILL REQUIRE

The main skill you will require is the ability to prepare an excellent loan package. Although on the face of it you'll be providing a complex service, with the help of your computer your job will be simple.

After you have set up the format based on the actual application, all you'll need to do is enter the information into the computer. You can enter the questions and answers exactly as supplied by the client, and the computer will give the completed report.

In addition to the questions asked on the actual application, you can improve the package considerably by having your client supply additional information which you can add to the package in the form of an addendum.

Your job will be to guide the borrower in showing his or her best attributes and capabilities, proving how well he can manage the business for which he seeks financing.

The appearance of the proposal will also be very important. Your computer will help you immensely in producing a neatly typed manuscript, free of errors and corrections. Each proposal should then be divided in sections, separated by colored tabs, and bound together with heavy-stock covers. The covers can be bound with the manuscript for just a few dollars at most printers or copy shops.

INFORMATION REQUIRED

The first thing you will need to do is familiarize yourself with the rules and guidelines required by the SBA. Your local bank would be more than happy to assist you in your tasks, since you will be making their job easier. Stop by and talk with a loan officer and request a loan application. Explain your purpose and ask them for assistance.

One of the key reasons many loan applicants are delayed or turned down on their loan is because their application was filled out incorrectly or without enough information. That's where you'll help your client with your expertise.

To help you complete a better loan package, it is helpful to first prepare a preliminary information outline to be filled out by the borrower.

The following are some of the items necessary in making a good proposal:

1. A resume showing business and management experience.
2. A detailed description of the business being planned.
3. An estimate of the amount of money needed and how it will be used.
4. A current financial statement.
5. An estimation of projected earnings for the first year.

For an established business, in addition to the above items, a profit and loss statement for the previous year should be prepared.

The application supplied by the SBA contains about 10 forms. You can use the above information as an addendum to the application itself. In doing so, you will present a more complete and effective proposal.

GETTING STARTED

You must familiarize yourself with SBA applications as well as the financial software you will use to process your client's numbers.

Then you are ready to start advertising for business. Techniques for this are explained in Marketing Methods.

To get started in this business, you should get business cards and letterheads printed up. These should be very professional-looking, since you will use them to correspond with bankers. It will probably pay off to have a professional graphics person do your designing for you.

If you decide to have your computer print out the actual applications to be submitted, you should purchase a quantity of the forms that can be computer-generated. These are available in computer and office supply stores. You may also choose to create your own form, following the same format as the SBA application. Then when you get a customer, all you need to do is have the computer prompt you for each line of information that, when completed, will resemble the application given out by the SBA.

THE COMPETITION

There are people performing this service in most metropolitan areas. Most are using classified advertising to generate clients. Where you differ is in using a computer to process the applications. That means you can do your work faster, more accurately, and for a smaller cost.

POTENTIAL INCOME

The potential income you can earn with this business depends on how much information you want to provide your clients and how much time you decide to spend working with them. In calculating a price for your service, add up all the costs of the program, including a salary for your time, and add in a profit figure for the job. If you figure that each client will require four hours of consulting, and you charge $20 per hour, that will make you $80 for your time. You may also consider adding on a charge for every type of application and form you assist them in filing or even filling out. If they decide to use your business to assist them in applying for loans, you can charge even more for your time.

To get an accurate idea of what to charge, consider your expenses. These might include:

1. Cost of software used
2. Cost of advertising
3. Cost of publications, books used in research
4. Cost of forms, brochures, etc. reproduced for clients
5. Cost of phone charges
6. Cost of travel expenses
7. Cost of time spent consulting with client
8. Cost of time spent organizing client's financial forms, contracts, license forms, etc.

Your computer will assist you in expediting the financial calculations required in this business. And that's what makes it pay off for you. You can demand top dollar for your service, because of the speed with which you can deliver. With your computer, you can instantly have your fingertips on the forms, laws and regulations required to open a particular kind of business. The more information you provide your client, the more information you have fed into your computer in advance and the more knowledgable you are about SBA financing, the higher the fee you can command.

MARKETING METHODS

The traditional and still very effective method of getting clients for this service is through newspaper classified ads.

Your ad could read something like this:

> SBA Loan Packaging. Increase your chances of securing a business loan through a professionally-prepared loan proposal. Call now for more information on how we can save you money in preparing your SBA applications. 676-8989.

You may also consider using direct mail. This would consist of locating people looking for financing on a new or existing business and explaining your service in a letter. You can get lists of these people by following the legal listings section of your local business paper. People opening a new business must first advertise their fictitious name for a certain number of days. Not only will these listings provide you with the business name, but it should also give the owners' names and business address.

You can follow the letter up with a personal phone call to the owners. It can be highly effective in obtaining business, if you choose to go this route.

UNIQUE BUSINESS APPROACH

A very unique approach which will put you way ahead of the competition is based on getting your clients from the commercial loan departments at banks.

In order to apply for an SBA loan the borrower must be rejected by at least two banks. As a result of this, the banks can become a steady supply of new clients.

To be most effective in this approach, you must establish a personal rapport with the bankers. You can introduce yourself to the commercial banker and explain that you provide a service to clients by helping them prepare a loan package for SBA loans.

Some bankers may seem reluctant at first to work with you on this program. But you can point out to them that they will benefit by supplying you with business. They will be able to give a commercial loan guaranteed by the government, making it basically risk-free for them.

If you further explain that through your service the borrower stands a much better chance of getting approved, the banker should be pleased to work with you.

Since bankers like the idea of handing out risk-free loans, it will be to their advantage to refer to you their customers who have been turned down for a bank loan.

LOCATION and MARKET BASE

Any populated area is suitable for this business. If you are located in a large metro-politan area, then you'll have plenty of potential borrowers available for your service. SBA offices are located in most major cities, but even if you don't have an office nearby, you can still submit the applications through the mail.

TO SUM UP

There are an estimated 10 million small businesses in the United States. Thousands more start each year. Most of those businesses need funds to get started and to survive once they get going. Your service can be of great value to the people you help. You will be helping to generate new jobs once those businesses become successful. In the long run it will help the overall economy. But most of all, you'll be securing your own economy. If the thought of making fat profits appeals to you, this business will fit your dreams like a glove.

SOURCE MATERIAL

Refer to Section 7.

No. 137

ESTABLISHING BUSINESS VALUES FOR BUYERS AND SELLERS

If you have ever bought or sold a business opportunity, you are aware that if you don't know more than the seller or broker, you're at their mercy. Well, those days are over with this unique analysis program. You can value any business for either the buyer or the seller and let them use the information to establish a price. This is a great service for opportunity brokers to use with their clients. It can stop the con artist from selling a lemon.

CONCEPT

Thousands of businesses are bought and sold daily. The real problem lies in this fact: did they get bought and sold for a good price or did one of the two parties get a raw deal? You can be the information source that reveals to a buyer or a seller the true value of the business they are interested in. By using an analysis of previously sold businesses, along with several indexes now available, plus an analysis of the balance sheet and profit and loss statements, you can provide a service not presently being operated on a regular basis to our knowledge.

SKILLS YOU WILL REQUIRE

You will need to pick up a firm understanding of buy/sell arrangements and how they are generally put together. You will also have to pick up the jargon of the balance sheet, the profit and loss statement and what they mean, and be able to describe them using accounting reporting terms. You should probably get to the point of grasping the concepts behind the negotiating strategies, and the psychology of buying and selling a business.

And you will have to be able to enter all these key points into your computer so that when you need the information, it is at your fingertips.

INFORMATION REQUIRED

You are dealing with an area that needs a tremendous amount of data to make it a success. You will be the "source." You need to acquire the data to be able to live up to that title. One of the books you should immediately search out is the Robert Morris and Associates book of business statistics regarding profit percentages. This will give you a huge amount of factual data to work with.

You should also begin reading, if not subscribing to, general business magazines and journals. You need to keep up to date on what is happening in the business world and be conversant about it.

Business information is the key here, and the more you have, the more valuable you will become.

OPERATING NAME

Stick to the simple here. Call your business by your name and add the two words "and Associates" to the end. It keeps everything simple and dignified. You need to put up a front as someone who really knows the business.

This will also keep the formation of the business simple in the beginning—no need to change phone or bank accounts.

GETTING STARTED

You are going to need to produce one of the most professional- looking brochures of any business plan we have talked about before. You want to go after the big dollars and you can't do it with a small trap.

You should consider using color, a heavy stock of paper and a great amount of style. You might even want to consult a graphic designer and a good writer to do the job.

In terms of copy, the wording, you will need to present to your prospective clients the service you are rendering, the types of things you can do, and how indispensable you can really be.

Get your brochure completed and you are halfway to contacting the business brokers that are going to make you a lot of money.

THE COMPETITION

There isn't really much competition in this field at the present time, but there is likely to be in the future. Once the word is out about how to get something like this started, the field will blossom. But at present, the people who are involved in the business are "flying by the seat of their pants" and guessing business statistics. The first one in this area is going to "rule the roost" if he or she does it properly.

POTENTIAL INCOME

If we wrote here that the sky is the limit in regards to this program we would not be kidding you. It is a ground floor information-seeking business. It is needed by everyone who is buying or selling a business, and the whole plan can be structured to fit a percentage of the dollar amount of the sale. Or, you can set yourself up with a retainer to several business brokers. The cost of this service is going to be paid by either the buyer or the seller. It shows to both parties that it is a good method of determining the final sale price.

The real cost of the preparation of this project isn't going to be cheap in terms of time and effort, but when you stop to think that your payment will come in $100, $500 or $1,000 chunks, the research can't be scrimped on at any level.

Costs of Program

1. Cost of financial or database software used
2. Cost of books, publications used in research
3. Cost of brochure preparation and printing
4. Cost of advertising
5. Cost of time spent setting up business
6. Cost of time spent performing analysis
7. Cost of supplies, materials used
8. Cost of travel charges
9. Cost of telephone charges

Profit

After your original research is completed and the data is compiled and set up to fit into the evaluations needed, the rest is net profit. You might even come up with such a super program, you can sell it to others for a start-up fee, like a franchise operation.

In terms of your pricing, you will have to talk with the business brokers you will be working with and find out what they would be willing to pay for the service. Once they realize the value of the service, your fee will appear quite small.

Say, for example, that you intend to charge a flat rate per analysis. You can easily charge $100 for each analysis. If a particular buyer is considering five properties, that is $500 for the entire project.

You may also take a percentage of the purchase price if the transaction goes through. For instance, a buyer looks at five operations for purchase that you have analyzed. If he chooses one of these five to buy, you can charge a half of a percentage point of the purchase price. On a $200,000 business, this project would reap you $1,000. Not bad for work your computer does for you.

There is a great chance that your analysis is the reason why the business deal will go through or not go through, thereby saving a client some money. Your analysis will get the credit for both situations.

How To Be Paid

You get paid when you deliver the report. If you are tied to a percentage clause, you get paid when the deal goes through. You may consider charging a deposit of "good faith" in either case. That way, if a client reneges on the entire transaction, you have still recouped money for the work already completed on the analysis.

MARKETING METHODS

There are a number of methods to market this service, but probably the best are direct mail and classified ads.

You will need to put together a cover letter to accompany your brochure and send it out to as many business brokers as you can find. The letter might go something like this:

> DEAR BUSINESS BROKER:
>
> Do you know the value of the businesses you handle? We realize that one of the big problems facing you in buying and selling businesses is the range of incomplete financial information and comparable prices you have for the business opportunities you deal with.
>
> We are a business values and analysis firm that can help you and your clients figure out quickly and accurately what the business is worth and what price is reasonable.
>
> We deal with any size business and work hand-in-hand with your clients to help all parties make the situation work.
>
> We will be calling you within the next week to show you how our service will make your job easier, less time consuming and more financially rewarding.

Send this out and the first bites will probably come in the form of telephone calls or letters.

You will want to stress to the brokers that everything to you is handled in the strictest confidence.

To use display ads effectively, try them in the newspaper classifieds "Business For Sale" section. These might read something like this:

> Are you sure you are getting the right price for your business? Call us today for information about how our business analysis will tell you the real value of what you are selling. 999-9999.

This is another classified ad example:

> Do you know whether you are paying the right price for that business you intend to buy? We'll do an inexpensive business value analysis that will tell you exactly what you can expect for your money. 123-4567.

If the classifieds succeed in drawing clients, consider running display ads in the business pages of the newspaper.

UNIQUE BUSINESS APPROACH

If this business intrigues you, consider this approach: contact one of your business brokers and suggest that his or her office hold a "business opportunity night" and allow you give to a speech on the topic you have come to know and love—the values that must be considered when buying or selling a business. After you have put on a few of these and left your brochures around, people will be coming to you for advice.

Also, if you haven't already arranged a deal with a broker, you may want to offer a finder's fee should any of these deals come through.

If you see the need and want to foot the bill, you may even consider setting up a seminar on your own. This is one way to gather a crowd and keep the profits for yourself. You have become an expert in a field where there are no experts. You have done your homework, so why shouldn't you get the credit for it?

If you can round up a crowd of 75 to 100 people who are interested in buying or selling a business, you ought to be able to snare a few of these people for clients.

The undeniable fact is that these people are going to be paying thousands of dollars for a business. Why wouldn't they want to pay you a portion of that to find out if the business is really sound or if they are being sold a bill of goods? Sell them on the benefit of relying on your service and you'll get all the clients you need.

LOCATION and MARKET BASE

This is a business that is tailored to run in a city constantly on the move and where many businesses are turning over. While the range of population can be from 50,000 to 200,000 people, we honestly feel that you should be in a large metropolitan area to make this project take off.

START-UP CAPITAL

We feel you can enter this market from either a low of $1,000 to a high of $5,000. It all depends on the participation level and the type of computer equipment you want to purchase. Refer to Section 6 for obtaining the capital needed.

TO SUM UP

This business can put you in the $25,000 to $100,000 salary range in a hurry. There is no corner on this market right now and you may be able to design the program that revolutionizes the industry.

Once you have designed your program and done your research, your primary energy will go to running analyses in your computer for each of your clients. This will require little time. Once you've set up your business with several brokers, they will probably keep you as busy as you want to be.

A few bright individuals will understand what a gold mine this could be. Make sure you are one of them.

SOURCE MATERIAL

Refer to Section 7 for source material.

No. 138

COMPUTERIZED NEWSLETTER

This is a potentially lucrative business that takes advantage of the capabilities of a good word processing program. With word processing you can adapt the same newsletter, with slight changes, to several different markets. In this way you can handle small orders that in the past have not justified the expense of printing.

CONCEPT

Thousands of newsletters are published each week in this country. Community organizations, businesses, schools and private clubs are just a few of the examples of groups that circulate newsletters to members concerning their activities.

In general, distributors of newsletters run into two problems. Newsletters take time to put together, even though they often repeat much of the same information covered in other newsletters, and the small circulation of many newsletters does not justify the cost of having them printed.

Let's take an example of the first case. Your local chapter of the Rotary Club holds monthly meetings, and a newsletter is published each month to be picked up by members at each meeting. The newsletter contains a great deal of general information of interest to all Rotarians, and a smattering of news specific to the local club. Within a 100-mile radius there are perhaps a dozen or more Rotary Clubs and much of the information in their newsletters will be identical. A word processing program enables you to type the general-interest news once and plug in the specific information in each different newsletter. With minimal change to the original you can then print out 12 newsletters for a much lower rate than the 12 organizations could do it themselves.

An example of the second case would be a local group with few resources and a small yet dedicated membership. The Committee to Restore Haywood Barnes Memorial School might number fewer than 20 members, and no commercial printer could produce 20 copies of a newsletter cheaply. With a personal computer and a good-quality printer, you can give them a product that they cannot get anywhere else.

SKILLS YOU WILL REQUIRE

You will need to own and operate a good word processing program. There are literally hundreds available and you will need to decide which one best suits your needs. Some features you will need to look for are: an efficient system of "cutting and pasting," one which offers different typefaces you can use within the same document, and, if you want to get fancy, one with the capability of integrating graphics with text.

Cutting and pasting is especially important. Ideally, your program should be able to remove, add or relocate words, sentences, paragraphs and larger sections of text with one or two simple commands. You will need to be able to store multiple variations of the same document and be able to retrieve them readily. Many programs do this. Shop around and make sure to get one that does all the things you want it to do.

The only other skill you will need is the ability to put words together—in other words, the ability to write newsletter material. This is not difficult, and reading a few representative sample newsletters will provide you with all the know-how you need.

INFORMATION REQUIRED

Very little outside information is required to get started in this business. The information you will need for the content of the newsletters you'll be writing will come largely from your clients. Every so often you may get a request such as: "The board is meeting up in San Francisco next Tuesday. If they make any major decisions, put it in the newsletter." Such requests will be rare, but when they do occur, ask for the name and phone number of a contact from whom you can get the necessary information.

Newsletters are more like bulletin boards than newspapers. Their purpose is to keep their readership informed of what is going on in a very general way. The business of writing a newsletter is mostly "parroting" information. Rarely will you be required to have any in-depth knowledge of the subject material. A general familiarity will usually suffice.

You should, however, know your audience. A business newsletter should have a different tone than a newsletter for a neighborhood charity or a sports organization. Find out what you can about your readership—what their concerns and interest are, what they like to read about in the newsletter, etc. As indicated earlier, you can find yourself in the positon of writing several different newsletters for almost identical markets located in different areas. You can then categorize your service and re-use blocks of text within a category.

OPERATING NAME

You can name your new business virtually anything you want, as long as the name is not registered in your area to anyone else. You can create a fictitious name if you like, but there is really no advantage to it. You will have to register the name, get a new business bank account, have a new phone put in at business rates – start-up expenses you can just as well do without.

If you use some variation of your own name, such as "Joe Jones Computer Newsletter Service," you have a perfectly good name for your business, and you can use all the phones, addresses and bank accounts you currently have. For more on this, refer to Section 4.

GETTING STARTED

Getting off the ground in this business is a matter of making contact with the people who will be able to benefit from your service. The first thing you should do is find out who these people are. You should compile lists of organizations and businesses you intend to target. This information is available from a variety of sources, including your phone book and the announcements section of your local newspaper.

You are then ready to begin advertising your service. You might want to send out a variety of direct mail announcements, targeted to different types of organizations, or you might want to use a different approach. For more on how to market your service, see Marketing Methods.

THE COMPETITION

Most newsletters are single, in-house publications. By combining the work it takes to produce multiple newsletters into a time-saving formula, you can provide an organization with a periodic newsletter at a cost far below what an organization ordinarily pays to do it. In a sense, it is nonexistent competition, since you are competing with your own clients and saving them time and money.

Your clients, however, are not in the business of newsletters. They have more important things to do, and once they see that the results they get by using your service are equal or superior to their own methods of production (not to mention less expensive and time-consuming), they will be more than glad to have you take over this sideline of their primary operation.

POTENTIAL INCOME

How much should you charge for delivering a periodic newsletter? There are several factors to be weighed. One, obviously, is volume; the more papers you print, the more it costs. Another factor is length. A one-page newsletter will be less expensive than a five- pager. Still another factor is recycling of content. To use an earlier example, if you do 12 Rotary Club newsletters, it will cost you less per job than if you do three.

Fortunately, there is a relatively simple formula to follow when pricing your services. Start out by placing an hourly value on your own time—pay yourself an hourly wage. Add to this all the costs of operating the program, and add in a profit figure for the job. Keep in mind that your hourly rate is not profit, but an operating expense for your business. Profit is what the business makes after all the costs are covered. You should earn money for your time and a profit for your business on each project.

Here are some of the major costs which you will need to take into account when pricing your service:

1. Costs of operating your equipment
2. Communication costs, such as telephone charges, postage and any electronic communication
3. Cost of paper and ribbons
4. Travel expenses
5. Cost of marketing and advertising your service
6. Cost of software
7. Cost of time spent preparing newsletter

You should ask to be paid in full upon delivery of each edition of the newsletter.

MARKETING METHODS

Direct mail campaigns and display ads are the recommended methods for marketing this service. Given the wide-ranging nature of the newsletter business, your best bet might be to go with a combination of these two strategies.

Community service organizations and the like tend to follow the press closely. They are forever generating press releases and checking up on publications to make sure their message finds its way into print. They are likely to be responsive to an ad in the local newspaper.

Businesses, on the other hand, will more likely respond to direct mail. I am going to give you an example of a letter you might send to businesses in your area in order to drum up interest in your service. Make a list of potential clients and send your letter out at the rate of 20 or so per day. Pretty soon you will start to get inquiries, so be ready to talk up your service.

Here is the letter:

DEAR EXECUTIVE:

What would you say if I told you that you could save money on a part of your operation you need to do every month, but never seem to have enough time for?

If you're like most successful businesspeople, you would probably say, "Tell me more!"

Our new computer newsletter service can turn your company newsletter into a vibrant, informative arm of your business, containing all the information you want employees to know. And we can do it for less than half of what it now costs you.

How? Give me 20 minutes of your time—and I will show you.

This letter, or some variation of it, will give you a foot in the door of the business community. If you like, you can follow it up with a second letter or with telephone calls. Be patient and you will get results.

UNIQUE BUSINESS APPROACH

A good way to get organizations interested in your service is to attend their meetings in person. Make up a mock one-page newsletter about your service. Divide it up into several "items" about different facets of your service and print it up as you would a regular newsletter. If your printer has graphics capabilities, use them. Make your sample newsletter look as jazzy as possible.

Ask for permission to address the organization at the end of its regular meeting. Introduce your service as briefly as possible. Then leave a stack of your mock newsletters for people to pick up as they leave. This method of advertising your service gets samples of your work directly into the homes of potential clients. Once they see what you can do, they'll want to see more.

LOCATION and MARKET BASE

Newsletters are everywhere. Even the smallest of towns has a chamber of commerce and a few community organizations. You will make more money in a larger market, but you can turn your newsletter service into a sucessful venture practically anywhere.

START-UP CAPITAL

You can get your newsletter business off the ground with an initial investment of between $1,000 and $5,000, including the price of your computer equipment. For information on obtaining the capital needed, refer to Section 6.

TO SUM UP

A computer newsletter service can be a diverse and interesting business. There are literally millions of newsletters, covering every imaginable area of commerce, politics, recreation and community service. You can tap into the demand for low-cost newsletter production simply by being able to run a printer and a good word processing program. And you can do it cheaper than anybody else. The service will eventually sell itself. And that means you'll have that much more time to count your earnings. So get started today!

SOURCE MATERIAL

Refer to Section 7.

No. 139

NEW BUSINESS PLAN START-UPS SERVICE

Anybody who wants to start a new business and has no money will be rushing to you for this service. By getting some basic information from your clients, you can prepare a start-up package that will cover everything required for them to satisfy city, state and federal regulations. You can do this for any business for a fraction of the time and the cost they would have spent without this "inside" information.

CONCEPT

Most people who get into business have some basic idea of what they are doing there, but oftentimes the missing parts of the puzzle cause the most problems for them. Whether it's not knowing what to do, not being organized enough, or having a good idea and nothing else, you can give your clients a business plan or outline that will lead them from A to Z and in most cases keep them out of trouble.

SKILLS YOU WILL REQUIRE

There aren't any demanding skills you will have to pick up here, but you ought to have an eye for organization and detail to do well at this project.

Plus, you should have the basics of what it takes to put together a good business plan. And your main expertise should fall in the areas of what it takes to get a business rolling. With this research in hand, you will be able to make some good cash with this venture.

INFORMATION REQUIRED

You are, for the most part, in the information-processing business and ought to set yourself up as a clearinghouse for data on new businesses. The more up-to-date you are with the information being written in this area, the larger those paychecks are going to be. You can't put these people in immediate success situations, but you can help them stay away from the more obvious initial business pitfalls. You, like anyone else in the information business, can develop yourself to become the "expert" if you do the necessary research.

There is plenty of data out there. All you need to do is organize and assimulate it. This is a field where you can't have too much information. The kinds of information you'll need to operate this business comes from a wide variety of sources.

For city, county and federal regulations, contact their information divisions and ask what is needed to start up a new business. They'll supply you with forms, permits, etc. that you can add to your information bank.

Also contact banks and the Small Business Administration for books and pamphlets about how to get business loans.

The local chamber of commerce should also be able to give you stats and resource information about starting a business in your own area.

The U. S. Department of Commerce is an excellent source for business information as well.

Use your local resources as much as possible to save time and money while you educate yourself about business start-ups.

OPERATING NAME

Here is a business where having a good recognizable name should result in business.

You might want to consider "Business Starts," "Business Planners" or "Start-up Facts." Get to the point in a hurry and don't confuse the issues in choosing a business name for yourself.

It may cost you a little more money in terms of obtaining a business license, bank accounts, and telephone service, but this is one business where you don't want to hide your light under a bushel. Refer to Section 4.

GETTING STARTED

Here's one project that lends itself to a brochure format for initially attracting customers. The writing of the brochure will also allow you to further crystallize your thoughts as to what you want to do. There is so much information to be processed when starting a business, it is often overwhelming. Putting the pieces together can lead you to where you want to be.

You can offer this information in bite-sized digestible chunks that will make the start-up easier for your clients. For example, give a small, numbered listing of the services you will provide your customers and include a brief decription of each.

You might even want to use one of the panels of the brochure for a quick questionnaire about some of the things people will have to do to get going. You are setting a trap here, as your ending tag line on this panel will be: "And these are just a few of the things you will need to get started. Give us a call to find out how we can save you both time and money on your start-up."

This brochure will be the introduction to your services, so make sure it is as neat and clean as your final proposals.

THE COMPETITION

We don't know of anyone presently in the market place with this type of service for people wanting to start up businesses. There have been reams of paper written about the idea, but nothing done—at least, nothing to the level we are suggesting.

Any of the people you might consider competition are dealing in only minimal information or just a single aspect of start-ups. They can't even begin to compete with the complete service you will offer.

POTENTIAL INCOME

The potential income you can earn with this business depends on how much information you want to provide your clients and how much time you decide to spend working with them. In calculating a price for your service, add up all of the costs of the program, including a salary for your time, and add in a profit figure for the job. If you figure that each client will require four hours of consulting, and you charge $20 per hour, that will make you $80 for your time. You may also consider adding on a charge for every type of application and form you assist them in filing or even filling out. If they go the whole shot and decide to use your business to assist them in applying for loans, you can charge even more for your time.

To get an accurate idea of what to charge, consider your expenses. These might include:

1. Cost of software used
2. Cost of advertising
3. Cost of publications, books used in research
4. Cost of forms, brochures, etc. reproduced for clients
5. Cost of phone charges
6. Cost of travel expenses
7. Cost of time spent consulting with client
8. Cost of time spent organizing client's financial forms, contracts, license forms, etc.

Your computer will assist you in expediting the financial calculations required in this business. And that's what makes it pay off for you. You can demand top dollar for your service, because of the speed with which you can perform it. With your computer, you can instantly have your fingertips on the forms, laws and regulations required to open a particular kind of business. The more information you provide your client, the more information you have fed into your computer in advance, and the more knowledgable you are about business start-ups, the higher the fee you can command.

MARKETING METHODS

There are lots of ways to market this service, but we will give you a couple and let you decide which ones you wish to pursue.

You can start by placing ads in the classified section of the "Business Opportunities" or "Business For Sale" newspaper. Your ads should simply state the fact that you are a service that can give the inside facts of what a businessperson needs to have or do to get a business off the ground successfully.

Here is a sample of a classified ad:

> Have you gotten all the information you need to get your business started? Call us today to find out what you might have left out. Most business failures occur because people did not get them started correctly. Call us today to keep from making that same mistake!

A second tack you may wish to take is that of contacting all the business brokers and bankers in your area.

You can send the brochure and letter that lets them know what you are doing and how you may be of service.

The letter might read something like this:

> DEAR BUSINESS BROKER OR BANKER:
>
> How many people come to your doors daily with the hope of buying a business or getting started in one themselves?
>
> We are aware of how woefully prepared many clients are.
>
> We are a company called BusinessFacts and our specialty is to provide all the information your clients need to start out in business.
>
> We know you want your client to succeed, because that means more business to you.
>
> So let us direct your clients through the entire process of starting up a business.
>
> We've been there ourselves and we know how it should be done.
>
> For more information, call today!

You can even set up a tally or score sheet of have-to-do jobs in start-ups and sell it or give it away to get your name known and clients coming through the door.

One of the areas you might want to explore once you've gotten this project off the ground is the idea of direct mail.

You have a body of knowledge and you can place ads in the business opportunity magazines telling what you can do. Have customers send for your brochure and give them a price range for some of the services you have outlined.

After all, you have become the business start-up clearinghouse and you are shortcutting the process for people. Time is a valuable commodity for them and they will pay for help in saving it.

UNIQUE BUSINESS APPROACH

Probably the best way to get this business off and flying is to team up with a business broker or banker and put on a seminar relating to business start-ups.

You might also consider speaking at business seminars or setting up your own seminar. This is a natural avenue for marketing.

You will have the opportunity to sit down and talk with from 20 to 30 people who are potential clients, and you might be able to do this two or three times a week. You should obtain several leads from this group.

LOCATION and MARKET BASE

To get to the people who are interested in business, you have to be in a population base that will support those businesses.

You also have to be in contact with the brokers and the banks to make it work. The answer is the city. Your market base should be in the range of 200,000 people and up. You can't make the dollars you ought to for the effort in a smaller area.

TO SUM UP

There has never been a time when this type of business was more needed. Many people are getting into business, only to find out that they have left out an essential ingredient. Not so when they work with you. You won't guarantee success, but you will make sure they don't fail for some needless reason. And you can be there when they need more information and keep collecting on the deal. This is a business of the 1980's that needs to be run by someone who understands the problems of starting a business venture. You can be in the driver's seat and reap the benefits. And the first step is to get started now.

SOURCE MATERIAL

For resources refer to Section 7.

No. 140

SPORTS FORECASTING BUSINESS

With over $100 million being waged every week on sporting events, you know the market is strong. With this plan you can pick your favorite sport or do them all. Some operators are doing $100,000 per season with this service and all they need is their home computer, a telephone and this book. How much simpler can you get? If you like sports, here's a natural for a full-time or part-time business.

CONCEPT

The concept of this business is to offer your informed opinions about the winners, losers and odds of the outcome of a sporting event. For this service people pay you, because they, in turn, can make big money based on your advice.

Betting on sports is a big business in this country, and you have at your fingertips the capability to supply those who want to know with the odds and information they need to make good betting decisions.

SKILLS YOU WILL REQUIRE

If you enjoy sports, you'll be a natural for this business. But even if you're a novice at following point spreads, you can do well with this business simply because there are now programs available for your home computer that will direct you through the information you need.

If you enjoy playing with numbers, giving others your opinion and discussing the relative advantages of the starting line-up, you can turn this business into a very lucrative proposition for yourself.

INFORMATION REQUIRED

The information required in this business is the data relevant to a particular sporting event. If you enjoy a certain sport, such as horse racing or football, then you can concentrate your energies on forecasting in your own area of expertise. Or you may choose to simply handle them all, not unlike Jimmy the Greek.

Whatever you choose to concentrate on, you want to start reading the publications that cover that particular sport. Become familiar with the players' names, past performances, performances under particular conditions, etc. Learn how betting is handled for your sport. Get a working knowledge of the betting rules, payoffs and other information that pertains to gambling.

You must also start shopping for the software that will help you organize your data into a workable system. These days there are programs for your home computer that will help you forecast in just about any sport you're interested in. Read the sports publications, peruse the ads and send off for more information about the computer programs you feel might fit your needs. Most are very inexpensive, usually under $100, which means that if you are forced to order a program that turns out to be a flop for your use, you won't have wasted much money. You may consider integrating a couple of programs for various functions or even creating your own, if you have the inclination.

What these programs will do for you is prompt you for information about the event you will be forecasting, then provide you with projected outcome based on the data. With this information you can make your forecasts, give your odds, and watch customers clamor to you to pay for your opinions.

GETTING STARTED

Once you have a working knowledge of the sport you want to cover, become familiar with the program you've chosen to assist you. Spend a month or so playing the odds of the sport with your software, and see what the results are. Fine tune your forecasting abilities on your own time, so that when you're ready to open for business, you're confident about your skills. The better you get with it, the more confidence you'll project to potential customers. And confidence is what customers want to pay money for.

Study the tout sheets or columns that other forecasters put out and see how they handle their material. Follow their success and failure rates. This will prove to you how you can do as well as they do, and bolster your confidence even more.

After you become familiar with how you think you want to process your data, it is time to consider how you will present it. This business offers you several options. The simplest would be to run a column in the publications that cater to the sport you intend to cover. For example, the Daily Racing Form runs several columns of forecasters, each giving their opinions on the odds and outcomes of various races. If you have spent time performing your own forecasts and tracking their results, you can show this to the person in charge of the publication you want to consider forecasting for. Explain the basics of how you operate, your success rate, and your ability to take a large amount of statistics and work them into probability charts that let you predict the outcomes.

This method of presentation for your forecasting won't pay as much as the other methods I will now explain, but it is a good way to get your name known in the business. It can even work to supplement what you do with these other methods.

The second way you can present your information is in the form of your own publication, like a newsletter or tout sheet. You make your money this way by selling subscriptions to the sheet. The advantages of this method are that you can sell as many sheets as you want, thereby increasing your income, and can present your information in any way you desire. Some tout sheets sell for as much as $300 a season. Sound high? Not really, considering that if your information is valid, people betting on these events can make thousands of dollars in a single event.

The final way you can present your material is by offering telephone service. Somebody calls you to get your opinions on the outcome of a particular event. You discuss it with the customer for a limit of, say, five minutes. Based on your information, the caller can place bets as he sees fit.

You can charge for this last method by taking subscriptions, in which case a subscriber will be granted a certain number of phone calls a month or week, or a certain amount of time to talk to you for the duration of the subscription.

Or you may choose to set yourself up to handle charge card calls. Before you talk to your customer, he gives you his charge card number and expiration date, you write up a charge card slip and charge him for the time he spends on the phone with you. This is how the big money can be made with this business. If you charge $50 for each five-minute call, you can easily earn a thousand dollars in a single day.

You may also choose to integrate any of these methods of presentation. If you put out a newsletter, you can advertise right in it that you will handle phone call inquiries as well. And if you do phone calls, you can put in a plug to the caller to subscribe to your newsletter and save himself some money.

Any way you work it, this business can be a regular gold mine for you with a little planning and thought.

COMPETITION

In this business you can play off your competition by proving how accurate your forecasting is compared to theirs. Simply spend some time regularly keeping up on what the competition predicts. Prove to the potential customer that you have the know-how they lack, so the customer might as well give your service a try. Be bold about yourself, use your personality to sell yourself, and show more style than the competition. Since there's no way you can eliminate competition, you simply have to determine to do a better job and be able to prove it. Once you get this business rolling, your customers will spread news of your success rate to their acquaintances, and word of mouth will increase your business. Once a customer starts relying on you, he'll be hard put to find a reason to change forecasters.

POTENTIAL INCOME

The income you can make with this business is truly unlimited. Even if you decide not to actually bet a dime of your own money on your forecasts, you make your money by selling your opinions to others. All you have to decide is how you want to present your forecasts: columns, newsletters, tout sheets or phone calls.

Pricing this service is simply a matter of deciding how much you want to earn with it. If the sport you concentrate on lasts three months, you want to consider that the income you earn will need to see you through the rest of the year.

The kind of expenses you have here will vary depending on how you decide to present your information. If you put out a newsletter, you'll incur expenses for time spent accumulating and writing up the material, as well as printing and postage costs. If you sell your information by phone, you'll have the cost of time spent waiting for calls, or of obtaining the kind of phone equipment where you can take a call at any time no matter where you are, or even possibly getting yourself a toll-free number to encourage your customers to call.

You may also have travel and lodging expenses if you decide to follow the circuit of the sport you cover. You may consider purchasing a recreational vehicle for yourself, complete with phone and computer, in order to take business on the road.

When figuring a price for your service, take these kinds of expenses into account, to ensure that you end up showing a profit for the business when the season has finally ended. In this kind of business, expenses can easily eat up the profits if you don't spend time keeping on top of them and charging accordingly.

MARKETING METHODS

The best methods for marketing this service are direct mail and display ads. You can run your display ads in publications geared to the sports you want to cover or in the sports section of newspapers. Since this is a business you can sell nationwide, you should research what newspapers and publications are available in all parts of the country, not just your own. These ads don't need to be large, but they do need to list exactly what your service consists of, your proven success rate, and a phone number or address or even coupon where the reader can obtain more information.

If you decide to use direct mail, you must determine who you want to target with your letter. You may consider buying or renting a mailng list from the publications geared to the sport you are interested in.

A typical letter might read:

I'LL HELP YOU PICK THE WINNERS!

My scientific forecasting methods can put you in the winner's circle more often than you ever dreamed was possible. I have a proven track record of knowing what the outcome of your favorite team will be and I'm willing to share my insider's knowledge with you.

Not only do I have my fingers on the pulse of what is happening in this game, but I possess a method that predicts the outcome even before the coaches know.

Intrigued? Act now to get more information about how you too can share in this winner's knowledge at a fraction of what you might think it costs. And at a fraction of what you can turn my knowledge into at the betting window.

Call now!

Your own variation of this letter, geared to the sport you are forecasting should bring you inquiries for more information.

Be prepared to talk with people about your services, the charges, the kind of material you will provide them, etc.

UNIQUE BUSINESS APPROACH

One way to get customers to give you a try is to give them something for nothing. In this business that means mailing out a free newsletter or allowing them five minutes of free time on the phone with you. Once you've proven your success with them, they'll come back as paying customers the next time around.

Another approach you might consider is giving something free away to customers who can outpick you. Simply run a promotion that guarantees you'll beat the odds, and if anybody does better than you, they can have either a free subscription, or an hour of free phone time, or whatever you choose as a prize. The reason for this approach is to generate interest among your potential customers. If you turn it into a game for them, you'll not only catch their interest, but get them to remember your product, and that is the secret to promotion in this business. You want people discussing what you have to say on the subject. Word-of-mouth advertising comes free and works well.

LOCATION and MARKET BASE

The beauty of this business is that you can run it anywhere, city or country. A market base of 50,000 to 200,000 is perfect, since that means you can concentrate your energies on the games played in your own area.

TO SUM UP

Sports are a multi-billion dollar industry that you can become a part of very easily with this business. The information you sell can give gamblers the edge they need to make their decisions pay off. In turn, it pays off for you.

To put the value of this business into perspective, look at it this way: gamblers can easily spend $200 at the track in a single session. What they hope to reap is thousands of dollars. The money you charge to accumulate information with your computer and present it to them in a usable fashion is a small fraction of what they stand to reap by using the information. To use an analogy, they can walk into a dark room with dollars of various denominations lying on the floor and start picking them up, hoping they'll pick up the big bills. Or you can walk into the room, turn on the light for them, and let them see what they are picking up. If you were in that dark room, wouldn't you pay somebody to turn on the light for you?

SOURCE MATERIAL

For source information refer to Section 7.

No. 141

SECRETARIAL SERVICE

The advent of computer technology has had a strong impact on the secretarial profession. Word processing software has made secretarial skills available to anyone who owns a personal computer and has facilitated or eliminated completely many of the time-consuming tasks secretaries had to perform in the past.

Today, anybody can be a secretary. It is no longer necessary to go into the office and sit at a typewriter all day, trying to keep up with the flood of communications. You can earn the same amount of money and more working on your personal computer in your home, setting your own hours.

CONCEPT

The concept of this business is to offer the technology of your personal computer system, and your knowledge of how to operate it, to clients who need your service. The advantage to them is that they pay on a per-use basis; that is, they need not hire a full-time secretary if their business does not warrant it.

The advantages to you are numerous. First, your time is your own—you can schedule your work in the manner that suites you best. Second, you have the luxury of working at home, or in a similar comfortable environment of your choice. Third, and most important you are paid for what you do, not the time it takes you to do it. And with today's word processing technology, you will be able to get more donee in a shorter period of time than ever before.

Almost every business, large or small, needs some kind of secretarial service. Businesses need to communicate, and the written word is still the most powerful means of doing so.

For a small business, it is less expensive to use a secretarial service such as the one you will be starting than it is to hire full-time personnel. This is especially true if the business does not own a computer, and many small businesses don't.

Today, there are many computer programs that will do many of the things secretaries do, and in a vastly shorter time. There are programs available to correct spelling, punctuation and even grammar. There are even programs available that act as a thesaurus, cross-checking synonyms and suggesting alternative wordings. You can make these services available to your clients at rates that will be too good for them to pass up.

SKILLS YOU WILL REQUIRE

You will need to acquire and learn how to use the software required for your secretarial service. Fortunately, the trend in word processing programs, at the insistence of writers, is to programs that can be readily run by anyone, with no prior knowledge of the workings of a computer.

You will need some basic secretarial skills good typing speed is a big help, as is some facility at spelling and grammar. Secretarial software provides a good backup, but you should have an inclination toward this type of work to begin with.

The abililty to use software will give you a big advantage over secretaries using typewriters, but that ability should supplement, rather than replace, the secretarial skills you already possess. Combining your abilities with those of your computer and software will make your service a success.

INFORMATION REQUIRED

Before you purchase your programs, do as much research as you can. Try out several different products at length before deciding on what you want. Remember, the faster you can produce, the more money you can make.

No specialized information is required to get started. Later on, you will probably find it useful to learn a little something about your clients' businesses, if only to help you choose the right word in a certain situation. All the information you will need, you can obtain from the clients themselves. It won't be hard to pick it up in the course of your work.

OPERATING NAME

You have two choices here. You can pick a fictitious name that you think sounds good, such as "Evergreen Valley Secretarial Services," or something else appropriate either to the area, yourself or your potential clients. There is no advantage to doing this and it entails a few extra and unnecessary start-up costs. You will have to make sure the name is not already registered in your area, get a new bank account, a new phone with a business listing, etc.

A better (and less expensive) approach is to use some variation of your own name. There is nothing wrong with your name followed by "Secretarial Service" or "and Associates" as the title for your business. This approach saves you the cost of installing new services in a new name. You can simply use the bank accounts, phones and addresses you now possess.

GETTING STARTED

Getting business in this line of work is a matter of making contacts and then convincing them that your service will save them money.

There are many ways to advertise your service and let people know who you are. These are discussed in some detail in the section on Marketing Methods.

One of the best ways to start is to first familiarize yourself with your software and then find a friend or neighbor who has a moonlighting business on the side. It could be something as simple as someone who sells firewood and needs an ad and a cover letter to be sent to the local paper. This will give you an opportunity to try out your service before committing yourself to it.

THE COMPETITION

Your major competition comes from full-time secretaries at businesses in your community. For this reason, you will have the most success if you target small businesses, new businesses and budget-conscious public organizations. Businesses with well-entrenched staffs of secretaries will be reluctant to change, no matter how good your service.

Public organizations are often short of funds for secretarial and other support services. You can transcribe minutes of meetings, agendas and the like far faster than any system they may currently be using. A glance at your phone book or newspaper will show you that there is no shortage of such organizations.

New businesses and sole proprietorships will be among your most eager clients. A new business has many costs and its owner will be looking to save money any way he can. Hiring a full-time secretary initially is going to be far more expensive than employing a service such as yours. Similarly, someone in business for himself can cut costs all around by paying for secretarial work on a per-job basis rather than adding a full-time employee to the payroll.

POTENTIAL INCOME

Since you are doing more work than a regular secretary (and in the same amount of time), you should be paid more. Most staff secretaries are paid on an hourly basis. You can charge by the hour if you like, but it is a better idea to charge by the quantity of work you do. This takes advantage of your ability to use your computer as a time-saving device.

Charging by the word or by the page is the best way to go. To figure out how much you should charge, you need to take several factors into account. One is the amount of time it takes you. Another is the cost of operating your system. A third consideration is the amount of profit you want to make while still offering your clients a better deal than they can get elsewhere.

Begin by placing an hourly value on your own time. You will find that your rate of production is fairly consistent; that is, you will be able to determine the number of pages per hour that you can produce. Thus, when you get a job, you will be able to estimate quite accurately the amount of time you will have to spend on it.

Next, add up your costs. Every penny you spend on running your service needs to be figured into your rates. For instance, if you drive 10 miles to deliver a job, the gas and auto expenses for that 20-mile trip need to be figured into the payment you receive.

Here is a list of some of the major costs of your service that you will need to consider. Since you are charging by the page based on the volume of work you do, you will need to figure out how these costs breakdown to a per-page or per-quantity figure.

1. Cost of operating equipment, such as electrical and maintenance charges
2. Cost of software
3. Cost of paper and other materials
4. Cost of telephone
5. Cost of advertising
6. Miscellaneous costs, such as travel

Some jobs may cost you more than others. In this case, you have the option of adding special charges to your basic rate. For example, most of your clients may deliver and pick up the work you do for them, but you may have a client 10 miles away to whom you have to travel. It is appropriate to add a special charge for this, and to note that on your bill.

Finally, you must determine your profit margin. Your profit is separate from your hourly rate of pay. Your time is a cost of doing business; your profit is the money your business makes after all expenses are met. You should make money for your time and a profit for your business on each job you undertake.

The easiest way to figure your income is on a monthly basis, since many of your costs will be billed that way. Add up your costs for a month (including appropriate percentages of payments on your equipment), add in your hours and profit for the month, and then divide the total by the quantity of work you do in that time. The resulting figure should be the amount you charge for your service.

MARKETING METHODS

Direct mail, display ads in local publications, telephone sales and direct sales are all effective means of marketing this type of service.

As mentioned previously, your best bets are small and new businesses and area organizations without the resources to hire full-time secretaries. By concentrating your marketing approach toward those most likely to use your service, you will get the most value out of the money you have budgeted for advertising.

For this reason, I would recommend a direct mail campaign, followed up by phone calls and personal visits. A display ad can be very effective, but it represents the "buckshot" approach to advertising. It hits the largest number of people, many of whom are not potential clients, and misses some of your primary targets.

You should make a list of businesses and organizations in your area that are likely to be interested in using your service. Your next step is to compose a letter and mail it out to the people on your list at a regular rate.

Here is an example of the type of letter to use in a direct mail campaign:

> DEAR BUSINESS OWNER:
>
> Would you hire a secretary who was four times faster and 50 percent cheaper than most secretaries?
>
> Of course you would. Speed, efficiency and reasonable cost are the bywords of our new computerized secretarial service. We use the latest in word processing software to enable us to perform all the tasks a personal secretary does, in a fraction of the time. And our rates are within the budget of even the smallest business or organization.
>
> But don't just take our word for it. Let us give you a demonstration. You won't be disappointed.

Mail this letter, or an adaptation of it, to your potential clients at the rate of 20 to 30 per day. Allow some time for the message to sink in and then telephone the ones that don't respond. This approach will produce results, and before you know it, you'll be in business.

UNIQUE BUSINESS APPROACH

The ideal method of operation is to work out of your home or a conveniently located office, and have your clients come to you. A good way of doing this is to work with a system of cassette tapes.

You can have your clients dictate their material onto cassette tapes and drop it off at your home or office at the end of a day. The next day, they can drop by and pick up the finished material. If there are corrections, they can then be handled over the phone, since you will have their letter on the computer's file to work from.

This approach makes things easier on both the client and you. Cassette tapes are infinitely easier to deal with than paper. You don't have to decipher someone's hurried handwriting, and there's no danger of an important note jotted down on a slip of paper getting lost in the shuffle. Using cassette tapes eliminates these kinds of problems.

LOCATION and MARKET BASE

To make money at this business, you must be where the clients are. That means a city. A market base of 50,000 to 200,000 is sufficient for making a go of it.

START UP CAPITAL

It is not expensive to start a computerized secretarial service. For an initial investment of between $1,000 and $5,000, including the cost of your computer and software, you can get your business off the ground. For information on obtaining the capital you need, refer to Section 6.

TO SUM UP

If you have a personal computer and can operate the compatible word processing software, you already have the skills you need to start your own computerized secretarial service. Your computer enables you to out-perform most secretaries still using standard office machinery. The time you save translates into more time available to do more work and make more money.

Think of the work of four personal secretaries combined into a single position. Now think of their combined salaries. The person who holds that position can be you; that combined salary can be yours alone.

SOURCE MATERIAL

Refer to Section 7.

No. 142

TRAVEL PLANNING SERVICE

With the data bases that are available on-line for personal computers, you can set yourself up to check out almost any airplane, train or bus schedule, as well as hotel and motel vacancies, and the dates of many events. With this service you can plan trips for people and find the best buys, and you won't be prejudiced by commissions offered, as travel agents might be. Some operators are even telling their clients to let a travel agent redo the plan. They then split the savings, which usually is in the hundreds of dollars.

CONCEPT

The concept of this business is to figure out the lowest possible trip cost for people who need travel plans made. You do this with your computer simply by tapping into a data base that has all the schedule and pricing information you need.

Worldwide travel is as popular these days as going to the corner store for a carton of milk. Most people go to a travel agent to have them do their travel planning for them. Yet once they hear about your service, they'll come to you because the savings you offer them can often pay for an extra week of vacation. Plus, once they've tried you, they'll refer you to their friends, family and associates for their travel planning. And they'll come back to you themselves time and time again.

SKILLS YOU WILL REQUIRE

You certainly don't have to go to a travel agent's school to learn how to do this business.

You will have to understand some of the terminology of the field though, and know where to get your information.

If you enjoy saving people money, then you'll do well with this business. An extra advantage is that you'll save yourself money as well every time you need to travel somewhere by plane, train, bus or boat.

INFORMATION REQUIRED

The information in the travel planning service is located in computer information data bases. An information base is a stockpile of certain kinds of information. These days, when information is power and money, people are saving all kinds of facts, statistics, tables, etc., that you can call up on your computer with the use of a telephone and modem. Computers are being fed everything mankind knows, and it can be located and used within seconds.

The way an information base works is similar to the card file that helps you locate books in a library. You look up the subject you want, and the card file will tell you the titles, authors, dates of publication, etc.

In this business you'll be relying on information bases that contain flight schedules for airlines, bus schedules, etc., along with the prices they charge for tickets on whatever you want to make reservations for.

Some bases are what is called "interactive." You call up the information you need with your keyboard, then if you want to make reservations or buy tickets to some event, the base will allow you to do it without leaving your home, simply by typing in your "password." A password is given to each person when he subscribes to the data base. You use it to place orders for the products listed in the information base.

When you use an information base to look up information, you pay for the long-distance call made to reach the source computer. You will also pay to subscribe to the information base.

Currently, there are information bases available that consist of travel listings and details, such as departure and arrival times, rates, etc. This is the kind of information base you'll subscribe to for the travel planning service.

OPERATING NAME

You have a couple of choices for operating names. You can create a fictitious name, such as "Travel Services Unlimited" or "Worldwide Travel." This will involve paying to register the name or filing a fictitious name report, getting a new bank account, installing a phone at business rates, etc.

Or you can use your own name, John Smith, and avoid these start-up costs. You can add "and Associates" after your name if you choose. This will allow you to use the bank accounts, phones, etc. that you already have in your own name. For more information, refer to Section 4.

GETTING STARTED

Your first step for this business should be to subscribe to an information base that will supply you with travel schedules, etc., as discussed earlier. These are the same kinds of information bases that travel agents rely on when making reservations.

The only difference between you and the travel agent is that you won't be relying on a commission from the airlines, bus companies, etc. to make your income. This is how a travel agency makes its money. Since it sometimes gets a fatter commission by selling a more expensive product, it tends to arrange higher priced travel plans for its customers.

For example, if you were to travel to a South Pacific island, there might be 10 different ways you could get there, as far as flight connections, etc. A travel agent will tend to choose the arrangement that isn't out of your travel budget, but isn't the cheapest available either. The travel agent will send you on the flights that give him or her the fatter commission.

This is how you'll clean up with this business. You won't be swayed by the commissions that travel agents rely on. And the less your customers have to pay by going to you, all the better, because that is how you'll make your big money.

Once you have subscribed to an appropriate information base, you're ready to get in business. To do this you'll want to advertise your services.

Once the business starts coming, you'll find it multiplying faster than you ever imagined. This is because yours is a service that will grow by word of mouth.

One of the nice things about this business is that you don't actually order the tickets for your client. You simply make travel arrangements, tell him what they will cost, where to get his tickets, etc., then take your fee and send him on his way. It is his job to follow your advice. Car travel planning services offer this same kind of service. They'll arrange your trip, tell you what roads to follow, etc., but it is up to you to follow their advice or not.

THE COMPETITION

Your competition in this business are the travel agencies. But since you aren't doing business like them, you can use this as a selling point. Your customers will gladly return to you over and over when they learn what kind of savings you are offering them if they use your service.

POTENTIAL INCOME

To price your services, you have several choices. You can charge a flat rate for each transaction perhaps varing it depending on how far your client is traveling. For example, if the person wants to go to Europe, you might charge $100. If he wants to travel to the next state, you could charge $10. This is one sure way of not being swayed by the commissions that airlines pay people who arrange travel for others.

Perhaps a better option is to tell a client how much it will cost for you to arrange his travel plans. Tell him to go to a regular travel agent and find out how much the arrangements will cost that the travel agent makes. Then explain that you will split the difference with him that he can save by making his travel arrangements with your advice. This can equal thousands of dollars on long-distance travel. For example, to go to a South Pacific island might cost him $500 through your service. But a travel agent might come up with reservations that will cost $1,500. The difference between the two prices is $1,000. Your share of that would be $500 — not bad for a few minutes worth of work and a long-distance phone call to an information base.

Your costs for this business should include a salary for you, your business expenses, and a profit for the business.

Primary costs

1. Cost of data information data base membership
2. Cost of advertising
3. Cost of your time
4. Cost of long-distance phone calls
5. Cost of any materials used

Overhead

Calculate what you will be putting out for overhead, and estimate that into the amount you charge for your service.

Profit

Remember to allocate a profit into your expenses. This isn't the same as what you get for your time. Your salary is just another business expense. But profit belongs to your business.

Obviously, you won't want to charge more for your service than people are willing to pay. With a little time and practice you'll come upon a pricing method that is both reasonable and profitable.

How To Be Paid

In this business you should probably use a couple of methods. For those jobs for which you are charging a flat rate, get your money in advance. Since you don't actually have to make reservations for your client, you don't have any reason to wait for payment until he purchases his tickets.

If you intend to split the savings he'll get by using your advice rather than a travel agent's, then you can work it this way. Tell him exactly what it will cost if he follows your plans. Send him to the travel agent to get that price. When he returns to you, take his money from him and then give him the actual arrangements you have figured out for him. This method will ensure that you get paid.

MARKETING METHODS

The best way to market this service is with display ads placed in local newspapers, magazines, etc. Any place you will attract the attention of people who travel will be a good place to advertise.

A typical ad might read:

> Hawaii for $100!
> Europe for $200!
> Australia for $400!
> Let us save you money on your travel arrangements. We aren't a travel agency, but we do know what flights and routes you'll want to take to get you where you're going quickly, efficiently and inexpensively. Call now for more information about this new, unique travel planning service!

A variation of this ad should bring you inquiries for more information. Ask these people where they want to go, then tell them how much it will cost if they use the arrangements you make for them. What better way to get business than to offer a nibble?

UNIQUE BUSINESS APPROACH

Now, I'll let you in on the secret to this business that will turn a trickle of customers into a waterfall. Most of the travel done these days is done by businesspeople. This group doesn't have time for unneeded expenses, etc. You can tap into this market by taking on corporate customers. Send them a letter explaining your service, then tell them that they can try a sample arrangement for absolutely nothing. It will cost you a little to do this, but the rewards will be great. Once they've seen how well you can take care of their travel arrangements, they'll be calling daily wanting to know how to get from here to there or from there to here.

You might even consider going on a cost retainer basis with these company clients. Charge them a flat monthly service for all travel arrangements. This will let you have a dependable income and give them a slight discount for the volume of work they give you.

LOCATION and MARKET BASE

This service can be operated both in the city and in the country. All it requires is a customer base of people who like to travel. If you are in a small city, you will probably have less competition from travel agencies. They usually prefer to be located in large metropolitan areas, since they figure that is where they will get the most business. That leaves the field wide open for you to rake in clients. This service is best suited for a market base of from 50,000 to 200,000 people. This will give you more than enough business to keep a steady income coming in.

TO SUM UP

Travel is big business. If you have ever known or experienced the glamour surrounding it, you will enjoy helping people plan their vacations and business trips. With just a minimal amount of time and skill, you can create a service that your customers will turn to time and time again. What that means for you is big money.

If you want to understand the value of this service, look at it this way: people take long vacations maybe once or twice a year if they're lucky. When they travel to someplace foreign and exotic, money is important. It is exactly that that will make you your fortune in this field.

Since you'll be saving them so much money, they won't mind paying you some of what you have so easily saved them. And you won't mind traveling yourself—that is, to the bank to deposit the sums you'll make with this opportunity.

SOURCE MATERIAL

Refer to Section 7.

No. 143

COMPUTER SCHOOLS

Every year thousands of people purchase computers with little or no knowledge of how to operate them. Most of these people will learn "on the fly," wading through a morass of often confusing instruction books or attending overpriced adult-education courses which offer relatively little practical information.

Here is a way for you to offer some practical and low-cost help to the computer beginner. Real hands-on instruction that people can afford is a rarity— you can help satisfy this demand and profit from it.

CONCEPT

Statistics show that ninety-six percent of the people who now own personal computers learned to operate them on their own. Chances are you are one of them, and you know how tedious and time-consuming a process this can be. Imagine how much easier it would have been if you had had someone available to look over your shoulder and provide step-by-step assistance.

This is the concept of a computer school. A mere handful of places nationwide offer direct, hands-on instruction for the new or potential personal computer owner. And yet the demand for such a service is great. The most common complaint from new owners of personal computers is that there is inadequate instructional help available.

If you are familiar with some aspect of personal computer use and can get a small group of people together who are also knowledgeable about different computer applications, you can plug into this hole in the computer education market and start collecting money from people who will be more than eager to pay for your time and know-how.

You can operate a small computer school in two ways. You can offer courses in the areas you know and handle most of the instruction yourself, or you can simply coordinate the project, hire your instructors, and offer a variety of courses based on their experience and expertise. Probably a combination of the two is best. That is, if you know a particular word-processing program inside and out, and you have a partner who is well-versed in several business accounting programs, you can widen your curriculum to attract people who want to learn about either.

SKILLS YOU WILL REQUIRE

Unless you plan only to coordinate and not to instruct, you should be skilled in some facet of personal computer operation. That is, you should have a personal computer on which you can run several pieces of software with ease and confidence, and you should be able to show others how it is done.

You don't need to be a professional educator or have any type of accreditation from your state or local government or from any other source to teach your clients personal computing. Only you know whether or not you have the skills required to be an effective instructor. Some of those skills are: patience, the ability to listen, and the ability to explain things in a logical, easy-to-understand manner.

You will also need to be organized. This is not a one-person show. Whether you have a staff of two or 20, you will need to be able to coordinate course material and schedules so that your operation can operate smoothly and professionally, like a real school.

INFORMATION REQUIRED

Teaching is, at bottom, the imparting of information in a way that the student can assimilate and use. All teachers, therefore, are in the information business. The amount of information you have at hand prior to embarking on this venture will in many ways dictate the limits of your curriculum. As mentioned earlier, you should be familiar with several programs that you can teach and that people will want to learn. You will also need to know the basics of personal computing, so that you will be able to field questions intelligently and accurately. Surrounding yourself with a few people whose knowledge complements rather than duplicates yours is a sound idea. This creates a pool of information from which to draw.

You will need to familiarize yourself with the software most in demand and most widely available. For example, many first-time buyers of personal computers buy them primarily for word processing applications—sending out form letters, updating reports and so forth. You will probably want to have someone at your school, yourself or a partner or an employee, who is able to teach clients how to use Microsoft Corporation's WordStar, since that is the most popular word processing package available.

Accounting and personal finance programs are also in demand, and you will want to be prepared for clients who are eager to learn how to use a computer to keep track of the finances of their homes or businesses. Much of your initial clientele, in fact, is likely to come from managers or employees of small businesses contemplating the purchase of a first company computer. These people can often be good for repeat business, if you offer instruction in several different business programs that are useful to them. The more you can help them out, the more they will help you out by coming to you for their instructional needs.

GETTING STARTED

Starting a private computer school requires a great deal of prior planning. Your first steps should be lining up your team and designing your curriculum. Once that is done, you should prepare a brochure and start advertising for potential students. For more on how to do this, see Marketing Methods.

You should know beforehand the volume of service you will be able to offer. All private instruction programs limit their enrollment, and yours is no different. You will have to figure out the right time and people management strategy for your program. For instance, if you have only three computers and two instructors, you can offer in-house instruction to only three students at any one time. Your course selection is also limited.

It is possible to expand after you get more business, by adding equipment and personnel, but you should not overreach yourself in the beginning. Do some research into what the potential clients in your area want, and gear your services accordingly.

THE COMPETITION

Your competition in this field comes from rudimentary programs offered by distributors of personal computers, and from adult education classes offered by your local high school or university. A little investigation into these services will show you that they are not much competition at all.

Most distributors offer little or no assistance to the new computer owner in learning to operate the machine. They will answer specific questions (if they know the answers) and refer the uses to the manufacturer, which usually means a costly long-distance phone call. Manufacturers are not prepared to offer any kind of structured assistance beyond that in the instruction manual that comes with the machine. These instruction manuals tend to be tedious reading and difficult to understand.

Adult education programs, on the other hand, tend to offer a large dose of computer theory with little or no hands-on instruction. It is nice to have a basic understanding of what makes computers work, but practical instruction for getting a personal computer up and running in a short period of time is often lacking.

There are amazingly few programs that provide the type of instruction the new or potential personal computer operator needs—step-by-step guidance while sitting at a computer terminal. Chances are, there isn't one in your area. And more personal computers are being bought by novices every day. That means the need for this service grows every day.

POTENTIAL INCOME

Before you can begin advertising your new service to the public, you will have to know what to charge. There are several factors to be taken into account here, all of them important.

In general, the way to arrive at an equitable cost figure is to add up the costs of your equipment, services and personnel, and add in your profit, all on a per-student, per-hour basis. In practice, it is a little more difficult. For instance, you will have to determine the time period over which to spread the initial cost of your equipment. How long will it take a piece of equipment to pay for itself? If, at a later date, you wish to add more equipment, do you accept more clients, raise the fee for the service, or both?

To answer these and other questions, it is a good idea to look at what other instruction programs offer and how much they charge. There are a few programs around the country with enough similarities to the one you will be starting to give you a fairly accurate idea of what the market will bear. One such program charges $350 for a 12-hour, four-week course. This figure is given here simply as a guideline. Your equipment and personal needs may enable you to charge considerably less, or force you to charge significantly more.

Aside from the initial cost of your equipment, here are the major costs you will need to take into account in pricing your service.

1. Cost of your time—hourly
2. Cost of your instructor's time—hourly
3. Cost of time of any support personnel, such as secretaries or accountants—hourly
4. Cost of running your equipment
5. Other operations costs, such as electricity
6. Cost of advertising and promotion
7. Rent or payments on the space you use.

You should be paid in full by each student upon enrollment.

Refunds of up to half the course fee for those who cancel at the last minute or after the first class are optional, but I would recommend against them, since you have already budgeted for a certain number of students and priced your courses accordingly.

MARKETING METHODS

Direct mail campaigns and display ads are the best strategies for marketing your service. Since people from all walks of life are now buying personal computers, display ads in a few general-interest publications will probably prove to be a more cost-effective means of getting your new school known than sending out letters to a select group.

Direct mail can work well if you deal with distributors of personal computers. But if you send out letters only to people who already own a computer, you will be missing the healthy share of your market represented by potential buyers.

For this reason, a simple, attractive display ad in a few carefully selected publications is probably your best promotion buy. Don't try to say too much in an ad— just get your potential client's attention. Your brochure is your follow-up. Prominently display an address or phone number where the potential client can order a brochure and learn more about what you have to offer.

Here is an example of what you might want to say in a display advertisement:

> For many people, learning to run a personal computer is like learning to read Braille. But with our service, in 12 hours we will open your eyes!
>
> The Jones & Smith Computer Learning Center will show you what your personal computer can do for you. We offer practical, hands-on computer training, with instructors to assist you every step of the way. We offer courses in WordStar, Lotus 1, 2, 3, Symphony, and a host of other popular and practical programs.
>
> So call us at (123) 456-7890 or write to: P. O. Box 111, Our Town, USA, and we will send you a free brochure outlining our unique and exciting service.

Surround your copy with simple but attractive graphics and you will get inquiries. Have a lot of brochures on hand and send them out promptly.

You should run your ad in a variety of publications. For instance, you might run it in the large daily newspaper in your area, several weeklies, one or two regional magazines, and several business publication—a publication for writers and one or two publications aimed specifically at computer owners and operators. By using a cross-section approach such as this, you cover your potential market more fully.

UNIQUE BUSINESS APPROACH

Suppose you do not want to undertake the initial investment of buying a lot of computer equipment and renting a place to house your school. Or suppose you want to reach a larger geographical market, or you don't have the time to devote to hours of teaching classes. Here is an instruction method that is becoming more and more popular and demands far less of your time on an ongoing basis.

Hook up with a video producer in your area. If he is interested, you can even become partners. You can market a series of instruction programs for novice computer operators on videotape. They can play the tapes at home, at their own speed, rewinding if they need something repeated. Video lessons ranging from how to work out properly, to simulated plane flights, are becoming popular. Why not videotaped lessons on how to operate a personal computer?

The advantage to you is that this makes your business independent of location. All you have to do is make and distribute your tapes. Or you can offer a combination program of live and videotaped instruction. Many different approaches are possible. The only limit is that of your imagination.

START UP CAPITAL

Even if you are planning a very small operation at first, you should plan on an initial investment of at least $5,000 and possibly more, depending upon the amount of equipment you intend to purchase. For ideas on obtaining the capital you need, refer to Section 6.

LOCATION and MARKET BASE

You can operate a computer school in any area where there is sufficient interest in learning how to work with personal computers. This can be in either a rural or urban area. If you are thinking years down the line and want to expand as you go, obviously there are more potential clients in an urban area. On the other hand, computer "camps" for both adolescents and adults are springing up all over rural America. The choice is yours.

TO SUM UP

There is a growing need for simple, easy-to-understand, hands-on computer training for the growing number of people who want to work with personal computers. The need is not going to go away. If you have the capacity to offer this type of instruction now, you can get in before the computer companies realize there is a hole in the market. You can establish a clientele and a reputation and make good money.

Public education isn't going to do it - it is simply too expensive to give each student the computer time he or she needs. The computer companies aren't doing it yet. The demand is there, and the time is right for someone to supply the instruction so many people want.

Are you that someone?

SOURCE MATERIAL

Refer to Section 7.

No. 144

COMPUTER CAMPS

This is an ideal computer business. It allows you to work only four months out of the year; the rest of the time you can spend traveling around the country, scouting for new locations and writing it off as a business expense. This report will show you the key things you need to know to succeed in this exciting business.

CONCEPT

If you are the type of person who enjoys the outdoors and is tired of working in a crowded and noisy environment, then owning and operating a computer camp might be the ideal business for you.

A computer camp was allows you to work in a pleasant environment, and make money while enjoying the better things in life.

The first computer camp started in the late seventies, when very few people could anticipate the popularity of computers. Now there are hundreds of camps around the United States and abroad. Some are large operations, while others are more modest in size, but still bring in a good income. Over 100,000 people attended computer camps last year, and many more will continue to do so in the coming years. This is a huge market with plenty of room for new facilities.

Computer camps provide intensive hands-on training within an environment which allows the students to concentrate on learning. Most computer camps are for kids between the ages of nine and 17, and run for one to two weeks with at least three hours a day of instruction. But many camps are now catering exclusively to adults or entire families. Classes usually alternate between other activities like golf, swimming and tennis.

There are many opportunities for new ideas, and by analyzing the current scene, you can apply some of the more successful methods that other camps are using.

SKILLS YOU WILL REQUIRE

The main skills required to succeed in this business are the ability to manage an operation of this type, and the technical know-how to teach others how to work with computers.

Regarding the instruction, you can teach the courses yourself, or hire someone to do it for you. It isn't necessary to be extremely knowlegeable about computers to teach these courses; the key is simply to be able to stay ahead of beginners. You can hire college students as instructors. This will save you money and they will probably relate well with the younger students.

Depending on how many students you plan to have, you should have an appropriate number of instructors. The right ratio of students to instructors means being able to give individual attention to each student. Also, students will expect to work on the computers themselves, so you will need the proper number of machines to keep everyone occupied.

INFORMATION REQUIRED

You will need to learn techniques that are most successful to run the business. One of the first steps in learning will be to find out how other camps are running their business and simply learn from their success. You can write to them for information and brochures to find out what they offer their clients and what they charge. You may even want to visit some of the camps and participate in some of the programs to really learn the inside workings of the operation.

You will also need to know the latest trends and techniques. The best way to keep well-informed about the computer industry is by reading some of the most popular computer periodicals. They'll keep you up to date on new developments and the things that people want to know about computers. Also, talking to professionals in the field will give you a very good idea of what's happening at all times.

Being aware of what people want to learn, and how they want to go about it, will be very valuable to you.

Another effective way to determine what to offer will be to ask your customers what their preferences are. You may even want to do survey mailings to find out what's needed and wanted. You can send out questionnaires to potential customers, simply asking them what they would like to learn and if they would like your type of facility. This is also a very subtle way for you to get customers, since they won't be intimidated by a forceful sales pitch.

Currently, a good guideline for the type of curriculum to offer is to base it on the basics of learning to operate a computer. Children will be interested in learning program-ming skills to design their own programs for games and graphics. Adults will be more interested in learning skills to apply right away for more practical purposes. They'll want to learn about word processing, accounting packages and spreadsheet applications.

You will also be storing valuable information about your business in the main computer. This information, regarding customers' names and addresses, course preferences, etc., will come in very handy in your marketing efforts. More on this is in the Marketing Methods Section.

GETTING STARTED

The first thing you will need is a suitable location. Most camps are located in peaceful country or mountainous areas. Others, like the Club Med, are exotic seaside resorts. The location you choose may also determine the type of customer you are most likely to attract.

You may choose to purchase a suitable property, or you may hold onto more of your capital by leasing a site.

Once you have found a suitable location, you'll want to make the proper preparations to start your first session of training. You will want to give yourself plenty of lead time between marketing efforts and the start of your sessions. If they are too close, together you may loose a lot of potential customers, since this type of expense may require considerable planning on the part of the students or their families. If you plan your marketing well ahead of time, you should have plenty of students for your first session.

THE COMPETITION

As mentioned earlier, there are quite a few camps operating around the country. At first this may look like a signal that there is no further need for additional camps. This would be true in most other fields. But the computer industry, although it has grown by leaps and bounds in the past decade, still has not reached its full potential. Even in this country, the majority of the population has had little or no experience with computers. That, of course, is quickly changing, as more people realize the importance of becoming computer literate.

In order to compete effectively in this field, it will be necessary for you to be well informed on what the other camps offer, and strive to give at least equal or better service. Then, by keeping up with new trends in the industry and by surveying what your customers want, you can adjust your curriculum and always strive to stay ahead of the competition.

POTENTIAL INCOME

The income from this business could eventually be very high. Some camps are generating in excess of a $1 million per year. You could conceivably build your business to full capacity and then gradually open additional camps.

Proper management will be vital to operating this business successfully.

Accurate accounting records will be necessary to budget the operation properly.

You will need to keep track of your costs regarding the property, including all mortages or lease payments; taxes and insurance costs; equipment and software costs; and payroll wages and taxes.

You may not make a profit for awhile, to be realistic, at least not until you have enough paying students to cover your initial start- up costs and your ongoing overhead and payroll costs.

How To Be Paid

All your students should pre-pay before receiving any training. This will avoid any problems with collections and late payments.

MARKETING METHODS

You should prepare an attractive brochure or sales leaflet. You should be able to get plenty of good ideas by comparing what the other camps offer in the form of advertising literature.

You can leave your brochure at computer stores, high schools, and any other place likely to have people interested in computers.

Once students have gone through your course, they may easily become the source of additional business. You may be able to sell them more advanced classes or they may refer some of their friends and acquaintances to you.

You should develop a mailing list of all your customers, and on a regular basis send them promotional literature describing your services.

You might refine the wording to fit the type of customer, putting more of the emphasis on the fun aspects of the training for youngsters, while more on the practical and relaxing features for adults.

You could also place small display ads in the right publications. By carefully thinking about the type of student you are seeking, you can get plenty of ideas for publications and places to promote your camp.

UNIQUE BUSINESS APPROACH

You could come up with a unique angle by providing special courses to particular groups of people. Maybe you could specialize in business executives, who need fast and intensive training, while giving them the surroundings of a vacation spot. If you have sufficient capital, you could even provide a weekend training session on a boat. This would be very appealing for executives who want to relax while learning. The boat could support a dozen or so students, and go for a short cruise to nearby destinations.

You could provide a course for singles only, giving them a chance to meet other people with similar interests. This would have a strong promotional pull in the right singles' publications.

Many types of special groups of people might be suitable for this business idea. Try to tie your camp in with some special promotion through the media, to get the maximum exposure.

You can also work out an arrangement with a computer store to provide discounts to your customers on equipment and books. The store might also refer to you some of their customers who express interest in your camp. In addition, you may want to stock certain materials, such as books and magazines, to sell directly to your customers. Later, once you have adequate capital, you may want to stock some computer systems to sell to your customers after they complete the course.

Depending on how much you charge for your course, you can also include an inexpensive computer free, as part of the course. If you choose an expandable system, the students can then purchase additional equipment for added capability.

For adults who use the camp as a way to acquire additional business skills, the camp could be used as a tax deduction. You can sell this benefit if your camp specializes in an adult clientele.

EQUIPMENT REQUIRED

The type of equipment that you'll choose for instruction should be based on the students you intend to have.

Kids seem to like the game-playing, type of computer, with good graphic and sound capability. You can write to a company like Atari for questions. They might even give you helpful information on operating a camp, since they also have a few camps in operation.

For adults, you might go with IBM-compatible machines, since many of the business application programs are made for these computers.

Do your own research on this matter to make sure that you are getting the best equipment at the lowest cost. Some camps use several small computers tied to a larger one for added capability and storage. Others use individual systems for each student. Again, check into the advantages and disadvantages of each method.

For each student, you'll need to include access to a keyboard, monitor, disk drive and printer.

Depending on the capital you have available, you may choose to either purchase your equipment or lease it. Check with many dealers and manufacturers for the best deal possible.

For the appropriate software, check with your supplier for educational software available. There are many good programs on the market to aid you in teaching your students.

LOCATION and MARKET BASE

One of the most attractive features of this business is the location. The more serene, exotic and relaxing the surroundings are, the more appealing your camp will be to potential students.

There is virtually no limitation on where you can offer your training. Your camp can be located in a city, in the country, in the mountains, next to a lake, near the ocean, on an island, or even on a cruise ship.

QUESTIONS/CHECKLIST

The following is a list of questions which will most likely come up from prospective camper that you should be able to answer:

What type of computers will you use?
Can you provide one computer for each student?
Can you show good credentials for staff and instructors?
Is the instruction person-to-person or will the student be left mostly on his own?
Can the instructors relate well to the students?
How many hours a day of instruction will you offer?
Will the camp provide food and lodging?
Is there a doctor within easy access?

TO SUM UP

Computers are here to stay, and one of the surest ways of making money in the future will be to provide training to the millions of people who do not yet know how to operate a computer. It is a well-known fact that today's youth feels very comfortable with computers. But more and more adults, out of curiosity or necessity, are feeling ready to take the plunge themselves. By setting yourself up early in the educational market, you can profit greatly from the future of computers.

SOURCE MATERIAL

You'll find reference information in Section 7.

No. 145

COMPUTER CONSULTING

New brands of computers, software and computer accessories are being introduced every day. As more people and businesses start using computers, they will need advice on choosing the right equipment. The business of advising people on choosing a computer system offers an unlimited opportunity, because few people have the time to keep abreast of the latest computer developments.

CONCEPT

The concept of this business is selling advice and guidance. You study a client's needs, recommend the kind of equipment that will fit those needs, find the least expensive price for the equipment, and train the client on usage.

The advice you provide will save your clients time and money because they will be able to use their equipment to become more productive in their work. Essentially, you are showing clients the proper tools for reducing their work.

Not only will your advice save a client time and money in purchasing the right equipment, but you will also save a client from spending money on the wrong equipment or spending too much time looking for the right equipment. Your business is to guide a client to the right equipment as quickly as possible.

The reason a computer consulting business is one of the fastest growing and most profitable computer businesses is because so many types of computers, software and computer accessories are introduced every month. Since many people are afraid of losing money by buying the wrong equipment, they are willing to pay someone to help them make a decision. As more computers are introduced in the market, more people will think about buying one, and the more potential clients you will have.

SKILLS YOU WILL REQUIRE

The fact that you are reading this book shows that you already have the basic skill needed to become a computer consultant. That skill is an interest in the different ways of using a computer.

By knowing what a computer can and cannot do, you will be able to advise a client on how a computer can make his work easier.

Another valuable skill is knowing how to explain what a computer can do for a client. The best way to learn this skill is to give each potential client a questionnaire asking what he will need a computer for, such as accounting or word processing. When you get the questionnaire back, visit your local computer stores and ask the salespeople to show you equipment that will satisfy your client's needs.

By visiting several computer stores, talking to different salespeople, and using different software programs in the store, you will be learning the different types of equipment available for your client, as well as learning from the sales staff the best ways to explain computer equipment to people. If you can understand what a salesperson is telling you, use those same methods for your client.

INFORMATION REQUIRED

Once you know what a computer can do, the next step is learning the differences between different computers, software and computer accessories. Finding this information is as easy as reading the current crop of computer magazines which have reviews on computer equipment. You can even learn from advertisements in magazines, since advertisers often compare their equipment with the "leading brand" to demonstrate how and why their equipment is superior.

One of the best sources for information, besides visiting computer stores, is a local computer users' group. There you can meet people who can recommend various equipment and software, as well as tell you which ones to avoid. Membership in a computer users' group will not only get you in touch with people whom you can turn to for help, but any membership dues will be tax-deductible as well.

OPERATING NAME

You have two choices here. You can pick a fictitious firm name, such as "Computer Decision, Inc." However, a fictitious name involves extra start-up expenses, such as registering the name, opening a business bank account, installing a separate business phone, etc.

A less expensive way to name your firm is to use your own name and add "Consultants." This way, your phones, addresses and bank accounts, etc. can still be listed under your own name.

GETTING STARTED

Getting started as a computer consultant is a matter of advertising your services to computer novices. Basically, there are two types of computer novices: individuals and businesses.

Your first step will be learning the different computers, software and accessories available. You can do this just by reading computer magazines. If you need more information, many computer manufacturers offer toll-free numbers for you to call for free information.

The best way to obtain information on a variety of different products is to fill out the reader service card in the back of major computer magazines such as Byte or Popular Computing Magazine. For the price of a postage stamp you will receive a flood of manufacturer's brochures.

If you contact computer consultants (listed in the phone book) as a potential customer, you can learn how the professionals treat clients and what sort of questions they ask. This way you will also learn what your competition will be charging.

THE COMPETITION

Eliminating the competition is a matter of contacting novice computer buyers first. Send sales letters to businesses and individuals (contact a mailing list firm in the phone book for a list of prospects in your area). Enclose a questionnaire asking if they could become more productive in their careers if they had a computer to help them, and offer to evaluate their needs at no cost. As an added incentive for clients to contact you, you can enclose a coupon for a certain amount of money, to be used only as payment for your services.

Prepare an evaluation for your potential clients, showing how they could get the same job done with cheaper equipment, or increase productivity with more advanced equipment. This is a matter of knowing what the various computer equipment can do at what cost—the same information you can pick up from computer magazine reviews.

Print out a report telling what could be done, omitting the exact names of your suggested equipment. Offer to personally deliver this report to a potential client's office. If the client likes your evaluation, you've got yourself a job. In any case, you will have learned how different organizations use computers in actual working conditions, which is a free education. You will then be better able to determine what future clients may need.

POTENTIAL INCOME

There are two ways to price your services. You can charge by the hour (between $25 to $80 an hour, depending on the job and what the local rates are), or you can charge a flat fee.

A flat fee would be best to charge for a simple job such as helping an individual choose the right computer to teach his children programming, or assisting a small business that needs a word processor.

An hourly rate would be best for a more complicated job involving determining the right computer, finding the right software programs, customizing software and training the client how to use the system.

In addition to placing a value on your own time, you will have to include additional expenses when pricing your services. These additional costs include:

1. Cost of mailing sales letters to prospective clients
2. Cost of buying a mailing list
3. Cost of preparing and reproducing client questionnaires
4. Cost of preparing system evaluation for client, based on client questionnaires

How To Be Paid

The standard business practice is for the client to pay in installments. For a flat fee, the client should pay 50 percent up front, and the other 50 percent after buying the suggested equipment.

If you are charging by the hour, the common practice is to be paid in intervals, determined beforehand at the client's agreement. These intervals should coincide with pre-determined milestones, such as: after the initial evaluation of the client's needs, after the client receives your report recommending certain equipment, etc. You can also charge different rates for past clients who need your services again, such as for emergency "housecalls" or for additional advice if they are planning to upgrade their system.

MARKETING METHODS

Direct mail, display ads and direct sales are the best ways to market your services. For more methods and information, refer to Section 5.

Direct mail marketing would be best for attracting small businesses, while direct sales and display ads would appeal to both small businesses and individuals.

Your main selling point in your sales brochures should emphasize that the cost of hiring a consultant is far less than the cost of buying the wrong equipment. For an individual, buying a computer is a major expense, like buying an automobile, so he or she wants to make sure that the money is spent wisely.

Likewise, small businesses cannot afford to hire the more expensive consultants, rarely have trained people within their staff, and cannot afford to absorb the loss of buying the wrong equipment for their needs.

Your sales letter and display ads should downplay the cost of your services as minimal compared to the cost of an entire computer system. An example of how you should write your sales letter or display ad follows.

COMPUTER CONFUSION?

With so many computers on the market today, and more appearing daily, deciding on which computer system to buy is not easy.

If you're confused about the differences between operating systems, spreadsheets and word processors, then you may need the help of a professional consultant.

Send for your FREE questionnaire today to help us determine your needs. An introductory evaluation fee of $10 will get you a detailed evaluation report listing all the choices of hardware and software that you may need.

Big businesses use consultants all the time; why not you?

UNIQUE BUSINESS APPROACH

The secret to consulting is finding your clients when they need help the most. The best way to do this is to contact several local computer dealers and offer a 5 to 10 percent referral fee for every client they send to you. Since most people who need help choosing a computer will first turn to computer stores, you can contact them before they buy a system. This will also acquaint you with the different dealers in your area, and familiarize you with different computers available in local stores.

Another good source of referrals is computer rental dealers. Make a deal with a computer rental store that you will advertise both the computer rental services and your consulting service. The ads can offer the benefit of professional consultation with the added advantage of being able to rent a computer before you buy. This will generate income for both you and the computer rental store. The old saying "two heads are better than one" describes this kind of business relationship.

LOCATION and MARKET BASE

You can start a computer consulting firm in either the city or the country. If you want, you can do all of your business through display ads and mail. If you live in a large city, you can advertise your services by direct mail, display ads and direct sales. The possibilities are endless.

TO SUM UP

Computer consulting offers you your own business, the opportunity to travel and meet different people, and the chance to earn spare income as well. As long as computers continue to sell, you will always be able to sell your services.

If you enjoy reading about the latest computer developments and like talking about computers, you will love being a consultant. You don't need any college degrees to become an expert. All you need is common sense and a love for computer equipment and software. Judging from the fact that you are reading this book, you already have enough interest to become a computer consultant.

The world of computers is like a jungle to the average person. Think of a computer consultant as a safari guide. He knows where to go, what to look for, and most important, what to avoid. A good safari guide can mean the difference between safety and danger. If you were lost in a jungle, wouldn't you be willing to pay a guide to help you find your way out?

SOURCE MATERIAL

Refer to Section 7.

No. 146

APARTMENT LOCATING SERVICE

People who are looking for apartments are generally a different type than those looking for houses to rent. With this plan and your personal computer, you can tailor-fit an apartment to your client with a minimum amount of time. This is another one of those businesses where you collect from both clients.

CONCEPT

The concept of this business is to sell information about rental apartments to renters. You can provide clients with useful information about particular rental units, enabling them to zero in on what they are looking for. They can narrow their search before they even jump in the car.

Suppose you are looking for a two bedroom/two bath house in a quiet neighborhood. Your first step probably would be to check the newspaper classifieds. You'll find enough ads to stay on the phone all morning. It's frustrating because you have to keep asking different landlords the same questions over and over again.

Isn't there some method that would save you time and effort? Yes! You can start a business that will become the eyes and ears of apartments for rent. By getting the information once from a client and feeding it into a computer, rental addresses can be extracted in minutes. Obviously, the more listings you have registered, the longer the selection of rentals to tell your client about.

Landlords, on the other hand, don't enjoy the constant phone calls asking the same questions. Showing apartments and screening tenants is a headache in itself. You could reduce their bother and successfully rent their apartments. Only serious inquiries would be referred to landlords, leaving them the time to attend to those leaky faucets.

SKILLS YOU WILL REQUIRE

You won't need a real estate license to start up this business. Having been a renter or landlord, or both, is certainly on-the-job training. You know the hassles, and how a service could simplify the apartment search.

INFORMATION REQUIRED

You will need to devise two questionnaires, one for renters and one for landlords. Renters will answer questions that will detail their needs and desires in housing. Be as complete as possible in your questions to them. Number of windows may seem unimportant to some, but others may have numerous plants, and windows could be a major factor in making a choice.

Landlords should also be asked plenty of relevent questions. Are children permitted? Do they have parking facilities for more than one car? By offering such detailed information, you will save your client's valuable time and energy. They need not answer those questions over and over.

You will also want educate yourself on rental agreements and contracts. The major complexes have standards, and it would be worth your while to familiarize yourself with them.

GETTING STARTED

The first step is to recruit landlords to list with you. In the beginning, you'll want to search the newspapers for apartment advertisings and contact those listed one by one. Explain the advantages to using your service. You will be disseminating 100 percent accurate information about their properties, screening prospective renters, and saving them the cost of advertising. Your service will act as a bank of information and a one-stop shop for renters.

Your goal is to contact landlords before they place their ads in the newspaper. To do this, you should consider display advertising.

COMPETITION

There may or may not be another service like yours in your area. Your competition is likely to be "skepticism," because no one else is acquainted with your type of service. It's too new. Landlords may think you are over-ambitious. You'll have to work hard at overcoming their doubts, but you can do it. Your service makes sense. You represent clients like a realtor, but at a lot less cost.

You may want to write a one-page flyer or brochure to have on hand should anyone like to see support materials.

You may decide to offer a one-time free listing for landlords initially to get as many rentals signed up as possible. Or you may decide to simply list those rentals in the newspaper, and find out more information by calling the advertisers yourself.

POTENTIAL INCOME

Pricing your services is not complicated. You start out by placing an hourly value on your own time. Then you add up all the costs of the program (you'll find a list following), and add in a profit figure for when you make a rental connection. The total is what you should get for the service. Keep in mind that your hourly rate is not profit; that is what you are paid for your service to a client. Profit is what the business makes after all costs are covered. You should earn money for your time, and a profit for your business on each rental.

Renter Costs

1. Cost of writing informational material
2. Cost of making phone calls
3. Cost of time answering questions and signing clients up
4. Cost of time to organize data received

Landlord Costs

1. Cost of writing informational material
2. Cost of making phone calls
3. Cost of time answering questions and signing clients up

Other Costs

1. Cost of software
2. Cost of advertising
3. Cost of printing questionnaires
4. Cost of other materials used

Profit

Allocate your profit, not including the costs of your time. The profit is for the business; your time is a business expense, not part of the profit.

In practical terms, you will charge what the traffic will bear. You can and often will get far more than you expect for your work. It takes experience to recognize the pricing opportunities.

How To Be Paid

For landlords, the standard practice should be a small fee (you may want to waive it in the beginning) for listing.

For renters, there should be no obligation until a rental agreement has been signed. Then a fee is payable in full. Or you may choose to charge a renter in advance, then supply the listings.

You must have a binding contract drawn up so that you are sure to collect your rightful payment. Be sure you have renters and landlords sign before you perform any services. If you charge in advance, this won't be necessary, since you'll be getting money up front.

MARKETING METHODS

Flyers and display advertising are the best methods to promote your service. Word of mouth will also carry information on to new clients, so be careful and conscientious in your service quality. The following is a sample sales letter you could distribute to renters and landlords.

DEAR RENTER:

Are you bothered by time-consuming and unpleasant apartment-hunting expeditions?

Your next move could be almost effortless and lead you into a tailor-made apartment. Let us handle your search and take the headache out of renting—we serve both renters and landlords.

In a just a few minutes of your time, we'll get the vital information about your special needs and provide you with a list of only the most acceptable rentals.

For a small fee (to both the renter and the landlord), we've taken all the phone calls, wasted apartment showings and tiresome energy out of your search for a new home. Think of the time you can save!

With an apartment available and waiting for you, the only thing left will be to move in.

Call us today for a consultation, and find an apartment tomorrow!

That letter, or a variation of it, sent to prospects will bring results. It will take time and nothing will get launched overnight, but if you keep sending letters and making contacts, you will get your business established.

UNIQUE BUSINESS APPROACH

Advertising dollars are well spent when the message you want to deliver hits your targeted group. You can find landlords because they advertise their apartments in newspapers, bulletin boards in stores, and weekly shoppers. You can reach them with brochures, flyers or sales letters sent through the mail.

Renters, on the other hand, don't advertise their usual needs. They are your "undercover" clients and to reach them is more difficult.

One marketing strategy you may want to consider is to sponsor a sporting event. One example would be to sponsor a local baseball team. You could furnish their shirts, equipment or both.

This usually costs less than a medium-sized advertisement in a local newspaper. And it will get you a season of exposure aimed directly at a major segment of your client base. Then consider the people who attend these games. There will be brothers, sisters, relatives, friends and spouses rooting from the sidelines. The impact is intensified each time they return to see another game. The constant mention of your service worn on the back of a friend certainly is the kind of positive advertising you won't want to miss.

Other events, like walk-a-thons, bowling leagues, running events and skiing races are excellent ways to get your name before the public.

The best way to initiate this form of advertising would be to call the publicity person who is in charge of the event. Let them know that you are a new business and are interested in donating your advertising dollars to help the players or participants. The more publicized the event, the more money it will cost you, but the contacts and credibility you will receive is worth the price.

Don't overlook the fact that these events are well-publicized and well-attended by all sectors of the community. You will reach a very large number of potential clients.

LOCATION and MARKET BASE

This is a business that could be started in any city with a population base of at least 50,000. You can operate this business almost completely by phone and mail if you wish. It is easy to promote your service and sell it through the mail.

Keep in mind that there are some people who will always pull up to one of the first complexes they see and rent an apartment. They don't intend to spend time or money finding a place, so don't be discouraged. Others, though, will want help finding that perfect place.

START UP CAPITAL

To get this business off the ground, you will need to invest some money. To purchase a computer and printer, stationary and postage, will run you from $1,000 to $5,000. This will get you rolling on an advertising campaign and allow you to "open your doors for business."

TO SUM UP

An apartment rental service is a great opportunity. If there is little competition in your area, you can begin a service that will sew up business in your city.

Think about the value of this service. From a renter's perspective, you spend a few minutes and find out exactly the type of apartment (using the questionnaire) they are looking for. Then with your computer, you can instantly provide them with a list of what is available and what meets their needs. Without your service, the cost of time and money for both the renter and the landlord is high, making this a desirable service to open.

It's up to you to promote and manage this opportunity successfully. You must establish a high-quality service if it is to make strides. Take the time to prepare a business plan, and look for ways to improve your service and ensure client satisfaction. In this business, word of mouth travels fast. The efficient and professional service you provide will make a name for you, and, of course, money.

SOURCE MATERIAL

For source information, refer to Section 7.

No. 147

HOUSE RENTAL LOCATING SERVICE

The people looking for houses to rent are generally a different type than those looking for apartments. That is why we have prepared two different sections about this type of business. Although some operators combine the two, it has been our experience that if the market is large enough, you're better off specializing a business that handles more clients in a more efficient way. Remember, this is one of those both-end dollar deals.

CONCEPT

The concept of this business is to sell information about houses to rent to both landlords and renters. You can provide clients with useful information about houses, enabling them to find "the house of their dreams." They will be able to know all the particulars of the house before they walk in the door.

This business would be a bank of information to both house-renters and landlords. By getting information once from a rental client and feeding it into a computer, the appropriate addresses will pop out in minutes. Obviously, the more houses that you have listed, the better the selection for your client.

This business will save landlords time and effort, since they will only have to answer relevant questions once. Their phones will stop ringing and they will only have to show the house a few of times. You could also run a credit check on clients to qualify them. This capability would appeal to landlords who have been "burned" by renters who skipped town ahead of their bills. A house is a valuable commodity, and it is reasonable to want to know if prospective tenants can afford to live there.

SKILLS YOU WILL REQUIRE

You won't act as a real estate agent, so you won't need a license or have to pass an exam. Having been a renter or landlord will certainly provide you with enough insight to know what is expected of your business. You need to have the ability to simplify a house renter's search. You can also take the worry out of the homeowner's life.

INFORMATION REQUIRED

You will need to devise two different questionnaires, one for renters and one for landlords. Renters will answer questions which will nail down their ideals in housing. Be as complete as possible in your questions. What color carpeting do they desire? How much closet space do they need? Do they have any pets? These are all important questions to ask.

Landlords should also be asked as many relevant questions as possible. The neighborhood, which school children will attend, and what utilities usually run a month, are all important points to cover.

You will also want to bone up on rental agreements and contracts. A property management attorney may be a source to consider. Also check your library for some current information about rental agreements.

GETTING STARTED

The first step is to recruit landlords to list with you. In the beginning, you'll want to search the newspaper for housing rental listings and contact those listed one by one. Explain the advantages of your service, the accurate information you will disseminate, how you will screen prospective renters for them, and how you can save them the cost of advertising. Your service will serve as a bank of information and a one-stop shop for renters.

COMPETITION

There may or may not be another service like yours in your area. Your competition is likely to be "skepticism," because no one else is acquainted with your type of service. It's too new. You'll have to work hard at overcoming their doubts, but you can do it. Your service makes sense. You represent clients like a realtor—but for a much lower fee.

You may decide to offer a one-time free listing for landlords initially to get as many rentals signed up as possible. Or you may decide to list those in the newspaper and find out more information by calling the advertisers yourself.

POTENTIAL INCOME

Pricing your services is not complicated. You start out by placing an hourly value on your own time. Then you add up all the costs of the program and add in a profit figure for when you make a rental connection. The total is what you should get for the service. Keep in mind that your hourly rate is not profit; that is what you are paid for your service to a client. Profit is what the business makes after all costs are covered. You should earn money for your time and a profit for your business on each rental.

Renter Costs

1. Cost of writing informational material
2. Cost of making phone calls
3. Cost of time answering questions and signing clients up
4. Cost of time to organize data received

Landlord Costs

1. Cost of writing informational material
2. Cost of making phone calls
3. Cost of time answering questions and signing clients up
4. Cost of time to organize data received

Additional Costs

1. Cost of reproducing questionnaires
2. Cost of mailing questionnaires
3. Cost of stationary, postage and printing

Profit

Allocate your profit, not including the costs of your time. The profit is for the business; your time is a business expense, not part of the profit.

In practical terms, you will charge what the traffic will bear. You can and will often get far more than a "formula" price for your work. It takes experience to recognize the pricing opportunities.

How to be paid

For landlords, the standard practice should be a small fee (you may want to waive if in the beginning) for listing. For renters, there should be no obligation until a rental agreement has been signed. Then a fee is payable in full.

You must have a binding contract drawn up so that you are sure to collect your rightful payment. Be sure you have renters and landlords sign before you perform any service.

MARKETING METHODS

Flyers and display advertising are the best methods to communicate your service. Word of mouth will also carry information to new clients, so be careful and conscientious in your service quality. The following is a sample sales letter that you could distribute to potential clients.

DEAR RENTER OR LANDLORD:

Are you bothered by the time-consuming and unpleasant tasks of house renting?

The next time you move could be almost effortless and lead you into that tailor-made house especially selected for you.

Let us handle your search and take the headache out of renting— we serve both the renters and the landlords. In a brief consultation, we extract the vital information about your special needs and then provide you with a list of only the most acceptable homes.

For a small fee (to both the renter and the landlord), we've taken all the phone calls, wasted house showings and tiresome energy out of your search. Once you know your house is available and waiting for you, the only thing left will be to move in.

Call us today for a no-obligation consultation and find the home of your dreams tomorrow!

That letter, or a variation of it, sent to prospects will bring results. It will take time, and nothing will get launched overnight, but just keep sending letters and making contacts. You eventually will get your business established.

UNIQUE BUSINESS APPROACH

Advertising dollars are well-spent when the message you want to deliver hits your targeted group. You can find landlords because they advertise their houses in newspapers, bulletin boards in stores, and weekly shoppers. You can reach landlords by a sales letter sent through the mail, telephone calls and flyers.

Renters, on the other hand, don't advertise their needs. They are your "undercover" clients, and to reach them will take some effort.

One marketing strategy you may want to consider is to write a press release to be sent to the local media. This can lead to a lot of free publicity if handled correctly. All media use stories about trends, social change and public opinion. The housing industry at this time is making news. Since mortgage rates are still high and building materials have skyrocketed, masses of people can no longer afford to purchase a home. You need to gather statistics from your chamber of commerce and develop a story to show why your service is so handy.

You might like to provide a survey outcome by randomly calling 100 people in your area to see how receptive they are to your service, how many rent, how many own their own homes, etc. This will show your interest and resourcefulness at dealing with the housing situation.

Find a book at your library that shows you how to write a press release. Then contact the media and find out who to send press releases to on your subject. Various departments have their own deadline and a preferred time and way to receive releases. You can find this out by asking and by following instructions. You can keep sending releases on an ongoing basis to build your image and generate business. Refer to Section 5 for additional information.

LOCATION and MARKET BASE

This is a business that could be started in any city with a population base of at least 50,000. You can operate this business almost completely by phone and mail if you wish. It is easy to promote your service and sell it through the mail.

Keep in mind that there are some people who will always be leery of rental consultants. They don't intend to spend extra money for a job they can do themselves. But don't be discouraged. Time and effort will bring success.

START UP CAPITAL

To get this business off the ground, you will need to invest some money. To purchase a computer and printer, stationary and postage, you should count on about $5,000. This will also get you rolling on a advertising campaign.

TO SUM UP

A housing rental service is a great opportunity. If there is little competition in your area, you can start now and sew up business in your city.

Think about the value of this service. From a renter's perspective, you spend a few minutes and find exactly the type of house (using a questionnaire) he or she is looking for. Then with your computer, you can instantly provide them with a list of what is available.

From a landlord's point of view, you also spend a few minutes gathering the particulars of the house (using a questionnaire) and feed this information into the computer. The landlord need not ever be bothered until it is time to show the property.

Without your service, the cost of time and money for both the renter and the landlord is high, making this a desirable service to them.

It's up to you to promote and manage this opportunity successfully. You must establish a high-quality service if it is to make strides. Take the time to prepare a business plan and look for ways to improve your service and ensure client satisfaction. In this business, word of mouth travels fast. The efficient and professional service you provide will make a name for you. And that means money in the bank.

SOURCE MATERIAL

Refer to Section 7.

No. 148

TYPESETTING SERVICE

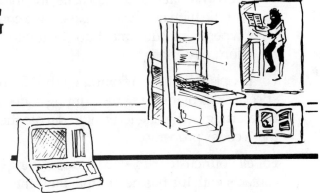

If you're an excellent typist and like the challenge of producing high-quality documents, this may be a good business for you. In this business you don't have to own expensive typesetting equipment. All you do is prepare typed documents on your home computer, inserting the proper codes for typesetting equipment, then transmit the completed file to the typesetter via modem or on a disk.

CONCEPT

In this business, you take advantage of someone else's investment in expensive computerized typesetting equipment. You provide the service of preparing computer files to be typeset. You can either do the original typing yourself, or you can accept disk files already prepared by your customers, then insert the codes for the typesetter. Then you transmit the completed file to the typesetter, either by modem or on a disk.

You can prepare virtually any kind of printing job with this process. Jobs can range from simple business cards to book-size manuscripts, from standard business forms to newsletters and magazines. In addition to businesses, private individuals also need typesetting services, ranging from wedding invitations to resumes.

In this business you're selling specialized skills, knowledge and know-how, and the use of special equipment. You must know the codes that are entered in a computer file to direct the typesetting equipment to print in boldface, or to underline or change to a different typeface. You must know how to enter the codes in the file. You must have professional contact with businesses that own typestting equipment, and if you will be using a modem be able to transmit files over the telephone lines.

This service is valuable to a wide variety of different people for different reasons. For people who don't have a computer, it's a simple question of dollars and cents - you can provide lower rates for the job of keying in the documents than a company that has to support the high overhead of expensive equipment and labor. Many companies with large typesetting equipment don't want to bother with small individual jobs because they don't pay enough.

For people who have a computer and do their own original typing, you provide the special skills of inserting the printing codes. A customer who only occasionally needs typesetting isn't going to want to devote the time and effort necessary to learn to use these codes properly.

For all your customers, you'll be providing the important service of making the right contacts with the businesses that have the typesetting equipment.

SKILLS YOU WILL REQUIRE

Clearly you'll need excellent typing skills and the ability to use various kinds of computer equipment. You'll need to be able to use word processing software to produce and edit text. And in addition to knowing the codes for the typesetting equipment, you'll need to understand and interpret editing marks on copy that's given to you for preparation.

A valuable additional skill is the ability to edit copy for grammar, punctuation and spelling. This is not necessary for running this business, but if it appeals to you and you have a flair for it, you can take advantage of it to enhance your business.

INFORMATION REQUIRED

As a foundation, you'll need the information already described under Skills You Will Require. Your source of information about the typesetting codes comes from the businesses that own the typesetting equipment. Some of them actually prepare their own manuals explaining use of the codes.

Other critically important information about businesses that own typesetting equipment concerns their business policies. What size jobs do they accept? Do they accept small jobs? How small is "small"? Can you access their equipment with a modem? Do they accept completed files on diskette?

How do they charge for their services and how much do they charge? Some companies that operate typesetting equipment charge by the running inch of completed copy; others charge by the number of characters in it.

What's their turn-around time for a job? How quickly will your customers be able to have their completed job to take to a printer?

You'll also need information about the typestyles and special effects available, such as boldface and oversized type for headlines. You'll need to be able to show your customers samples of the different typestyles and sizes available.

You'll need to be familiar with some of the basic terminology of typesetting and printing. For example, "picas," "points," "ems" and "ens" are all terms related to type size. The "font" is the typestyle, which may come in several sizes.

GETTING STARTED

The first step in getting started in this business is to contact companies that operate computer typesetting equipment. You'll find some of them by looking in the yellow pages of the phone book under Typesetting and Printing. Look for clues, such as "telecommunications available," to tell you if the company offers computerized typesetting. In addition to the companies that advertise in the yellow pages, your local newspaper may be a good source of computer typesetting services. Newspapers often provide this service as an additional source of income to offset the cost of expensive equipment.

Take your time and investigate these computer typesetting services thoroughly. To help you evaluate the different services, here are some questions to ask the companies you contact:

What kind of typesetting equipment is used and what are the codes? The degree of complexity of the codes that are used by different varieties of computer typesetting equipment is an especially important consideration for you, because you'll have to learn to use it. Does the company provide a manual explaining how to use the codes, or will you have to wade through a highly technical, incomprehensible manual that comes with the typesetting equipment?

What kind of computers and software can be used to communicate with the equipment? Naturally, this is a vitally important consideration for the business. If you don't already have a computer, this information may help you decide what kind of computer and software to buy.

What kind of modem can be used with the equipment and what is its operating speed? Modem speeds vary widely and you will want to be able to transmit your files as fast as possible.

Are prepared files accepted on diskettes? If so, what diskette size and format is required? Actually, this is a minor issue, since telecommunication over a modem avoids the problems of diskette size and format compatibility. But it's something you should know about in case you have a customer who wants to be able to take a completed diskette directly to the typesetting computer, instead of having you transmit it over the modem.

What is the basis of charges and how much are the charges? This will give you an important clue for setting the rates for your own services. The most expensive part of typesetting is keying in the text, so you'll want to be able to compare how much the company charges for providing that part of the service, compared with how much is charged for typesetting pre-coded text files.

THE COMPETITION

In this business, you'll be competing with both established complete typesetting services and people getting into the same service you'll be providing. The best solution for competing with complete typesetting services is to search out those companies that specialize in computer telecommunications for typesetting. Often they prefer not to do the work of keying in text and inserting codes—some of them don't even want to read the text they're typesetting! You may be able to work out a mutually profitable business referral agreement with companies of this variety.

One way to compete against other people offering the same service you're offering is to get into the business early and establish a reputation for yourself. More important is your approach to marketing and making contacts with potential customers. Don't wait for customers to come to you—go seek them out! See the Marketing Methods and Unique Business Approach Sections for more information about competing effectively.

POTENTIAL INCOME

In general, this service offers the potential for a medium level of income. One small printing company in Virginia has added computer typesetting of business cards alone as a profitable sideline.

The first half of the profit equation—your gross income—will be determined by the rates you charge and the volume of business you attract. In order to attract enough business, your rates will have to be competitive. As your typing skills, and the ability to insert printing codes, improve through practice, your hourly earnings will increase because you'll be able to complete more work in the same period of time.

The second half of the profit equation—your expenses and overhead—will be fairly low once you're established. Your biggest expense will be the capital invested in your equipment and software. If you work out of your home, overhead and operating expense will be low compared to the expenses of setting up shop in a typical business location. In the latter case, you'll have to cover the cost of space, utilities, telephones and advertising.

MARKETING METHODS

You can use a wide variety of different marketing methods for this service. Direct mail, display ads, telephone sales, direct sales and yellow page listings are all appropriate.

In all your ads you should emphasize low cost, speedy service, and professional quality. And all your ads must provide an excellent example of the typesetting service you provide.

Even though some of your business will come from private individuals, most of it will come from businesses, so you should target business firms in your marketing efforts.

Here's an example of a brochure you could send to potential customers.

> DEAR BUSINESS OWNER:
>
> How do your business documents look? Do your forms, brochures and reports look neat and professional? What impression do they create when a potential customer sees them?
>
> For the highest quality and professional appearance, your business documents should be typeset. Up until now, typesetting has been an expensive proposition. Computer typesetting can now dramatically reduce the costs—especially if you take advantage of the service I offer to prepare your text with the proper codes for the typesetter, and transmit it over telephone lines.
>
> I can take over the whole job of typing and preparing your document, or I can take a document already typed on a diskette and add the codes for the typesetter and transmit it for you.
>
> Take advantage of this speedy, convenient and inexpensive service to add that touch of class to all your business documents!

UNIQUE BUSINESS APPROACH

Target your business toward a particular market segment, such as small businesses. Small business needs for typesetting services range from brochures and ads to forms, reports and newsletters.

With the low cost of the kind of typesetting service you provide, even business proposals can be typeset, greatly enhancing their professional appearance and eye appeal.

For an unusual share of the market, target a specific mailing to nonprofit organizations that publish newsletters. Show them how your service can help provide them with a superior-quality publication at a low cost. Do your homework—pinpoint the cost of savings to them.

EQUIPMENT REQUIRED

Your computer must have the ability to communicate over a modem, and it must have at least one disk drive. Two drives for diskettes or hard disk would even be better. See Section 7 for more information about selecting a computer.

You'll also need a printer. Even though you won't be producing the final copy, you'll have to be able to print out your files for proofreading. For this purpose a dot matrix printer is ideal. An average dot matrix printer is not only cheaper than an average letter-quality printer, it's usually about 10 times faster. In this business, speed is much more important than appearance. See Section 7 for more information about selecting a printer.

The third piece of hardware you'll need is a modem. The kind of modem you need will be at least partly determined by the kind of telecommunications the typesetting equipment can handle, so you should thoroughly research the requirements before you buy. An important consideration about modems is their operating speed.

The slowest modem speed is usually 300 baud, or bits per second, which seems agonizingly slow compared to 1200 baud, another common data transmission speed. Remember, time is money and you'll want to be able to transmit your files as fast as possible, so the extra investment for a faster modem is well worth the money. See Section 7 for more information about selecting a modem.

You should also consider installing a separate phone line dedicated to data transmission only. That will enable you to still make and accept phone calls while you're transmitting data. Your local phone company can provide information about phone lines that are specially conditioned for data trasmission.

In addition to the equipment, you'll need software for preparing and editing text. Many different word processing packages are available. Shop carefully for a package that's easy to learn and easy to use, and make sure it provides an option to find and replace text; you'll need to be able to find the right places to insert the codes for the typesetting equipment.

Additional software that will be very helpful is a package to check spelling, and a package to count words or characters. A spelling checker is an invaluable aid to proofreading. Most spelling checkers not only provide a built-in dictionary, they also allow you to add entries to the dictionary. A word or character counter will allow you to estimate the cost of using the typesetting equipment, if the cost of the service is based on word or character count. Or you can use it to establish your own fees, if you choose to base your fees on the length of the document.

LOCATION and MARKET BASE

Since this business relies on data transmission over telephone lines, its location is not restricted. It can be located in the city or the country, as long as it's located close enough to a medium-to-large city to provide both the services of computer typesetting equipment and a sufficient market base.

An ideal market base for this business is in the range of 50,000 to 200,000. This gives you wide latitude in possible locations for the business.

TO SUM UP

This new service offers an opportunity to develop a profitable business providing a valuable service for your community. If you have excellent typing skills, you can turn them into a profitable business of your own, instead of being tied down to a low-paying job working for someone else. Put your skills to work to cash in on the powerful computer publishing technology available today!

SOURCE MATERIAL

Refer to Section 7.

No. 149

BARTER
CLUB
SERVICE

A barter club service is a business that helps keep track of new and used items or services which are traded and bartered by clubs set up for this purpose.

CONCEPT

Do you have "stuff" you want to trade for other "stuff"? Or do you have a service somebody else could use? If you don't, you can rest assured that there are millions of people in this country, of all ages, incomes and trades, who do. Outside of regular merchandising channels, you can find a mass of products and services that people want. With your help, your customers can be put in touch with others who have what they want, and vice versa.

This business, at present, is very unorganized. Since these items are not new or commercially valuable, you have to know where and how to find them. There are barter clubs that meet regularly, perhaps sending out newsletters that serve as the traders and locators, and occasionally holding fairs and swap meets to barter their goods and talk shop. Some of these people also have services to offer in trade for goods.

You'll find that one of the most attractive aspects of the business, and the aspect that holds the greatest promise for you as an entrepreneur, is the fact that people can use their bartering power to get what they need, instead of putting out cash or using credit cards.

With your computer, you can offer these people a needed service—an inventory barter system that keeps track of where items and services are, who has them, and what they need to do to get them. Rather than wait for the semi-annual swap meet to find out that he can't get what he wants, your customer can use your service and get it now.

SKILLS YOU WILL REQUIRE

The setting up of this business is very easy. No special skills are needed other than the ability to organize your data. Most of this data can be solicited from barter clubs around the country, who are only too willing to leave the organizing to someone else.

You'll have to set up a data base that will contain all the information you'll need. This is a very easy task that will allow you to get up and running in no time.

INFORMATION REQUIRED

You'll need to have material for your barter club data base—items, costs, and names and addresses of owners or traders. You'll want to categorize your information into such groups as automotive, kitchen, toys, etc., but that's an easy task.

Locating barter clubs who can help you to find members willing to give you information is simply a matter of looking in your phone book. You can also go to swap meets you see scheduled in your area and look through magazines dedicated to a particular field—antique cars, guns, model trains. A good newsstand or bookstore will have plenty of magazines to help you track down specialties. The personal computer network of user's groups is a great place to find people interested in your service. They often have newsletters you can buy and meetings you can attend. Or better yet, you can use their electronic bulletin boards to advertise your service, as well as what your customers are seeking or trading.

GETTING STARTED

First of all, start gathering information. Go to swap meets, buy the right magazines and, most of all, talk to some of the various local and regional barter organizations. Find out what their members feel would be helpful in keeping track of the mass of products and services they make available.

Many barter clubs will also have a system of credits that allows members to list items they have available and receive working credit toward their own bartering, whether it be local or national. The sources of the hard-to-find barter items will be throughout the country and the world, so this concept of credit allows members to place items into the marketplace without first establishing a direct trade. In other words, a member offers a service or item for credit, then uses credits he gets to gain a service or item in exchange.

With your computer, you can have a comprehensive data base that keeps track of items and owners, and keeps running balance of credits due.

Advertising in magazines and at swap meets will bring in your customers. Advertise yourself as a "listing service" or "broker" for the products and services, and base your fees on a subscription basis. People pay an annual due to use your service. With millions of people involved in barter clubs, you'll find that your "subscription" rates will offer a good profit margin. If you wish, you can eventually enhance your business by putting out an actual newsletter or publication listing your wares.

One good way to show people what you've got and how you operate is to distribute flyers or newsletters that list some available items—items that can only be located through your service. Some sort of code or identification number can be listed with the items. Then people will call you to find out more information.

As is good for all new businesses, make as big a splash as you can when you enter the marketplace. New businesses have many advantages and this is one of the primary ones. Let people know you are new and can offer them something special.

THE COMPETITION

Actually, with this business you turn your competition—the barter clubs—into your customers. You offer them the chance to expand their base of service, and in exchange they supply you with a steady list of clientele.

POTENTIAL INCOME

The rates you charge for your service will probably be low because of the low overhead this business entails. You can offer a discount rate for long-term subscriptions—for instance, 15 months for the price of 12.

Even if you charge each subscriber only $10 a year, you can make thousands of dollars simply by listing the information others supply to you.

You may also charge a fee to the clubs for participating in your service. Most clubs would probably not question paying $50 or $100 a year if they know that your service increases their own value.

Before settling on a fee, estimate your expenses for the program. Add in a salary for your time and a profit for the business. This will give you a better, more realistic guide to pricing your service.

Basic Costs

1. Cost of data base software
2. Cost of advertising
3. Cost of subscriptions
4. Cost of telephone charges
5. Cost of transportation
6. Cost of time spent organizing program
7. Cost of time spent maintaining files

MARKETING METHODS

Direct mail and display ads are the best marketing methods to use here.

You can send your direct mail letters to barter clubs around the country to solicit business, or to the individual members whose names and addresses are provided by the clubs.

A typical letter might read:

> DEAR BARTER CLUB ENTHUSIAST:
>
> Somewhere right now in this country is a person who needs you. And we know who that someone is.
>
> Why limit your bartering to your own area when you can increase your trading by hooking up to other clubs? How can you do this? By belonging to American Barter, the nationwide club that puts you in touch with America.
>
> For one low subscription fee, you can start selling and trading your services at a faster rate than you ever thought was possible.
>
> For more information, fill out and send the attached coupon.
>
> Forget cash: Barter your way to a comfortable lifestyle!

In your ads, make it clear that the biggest advantage to the buyer and trader is that cash or credit have virtually no place in these transactions. You'll be amazed how well people react to this benefit once you have shown them what it is possible for them to get in return.

Most people don't realize what exceptional standards of value and quality barter clubs can offer. Nor do they realize that they can trade their special skills for whatever it is they need.

Bring this to their attention. Encourage people to think about what they have of value to trade. Everybody has something, and they'll appreciate being reminded of that item's "hidden" worth.

UNIQUE BUSINESS APPROACH

The real key to making this business a big success is convincing potential subscribers that they can get what they need without paying a penny.

You can prove it by offering their first "barter" for free. Line them up with what they want—whether it is an item or a service. Once they've tried the system and seen how effectively it works, they'll be back, money in hand.

Emphasize this first free barter in your advertising. Include a coupon good for one barter along with your ad or direct mail letter.

LOCATION and MARKET BASE

As is the case in some of the other businesses in this book, your main resource will be people. Therefore, it is ideal if you work out of an area of 200,000 people or more. In these large areas, you'll find more activity on the bartering scene. If large enough, the area will allow you to make money using just a local market base. If you're not in a city, don't worry. Use your telephone and modem to operate.

TO SUM UP

A bartering club service is a business opportunity that takes a minimum amount of setup and cost outlay, and is interesting and satisfying. People have a different attitude about this kind of business, since it doesn't deal in money.

The potential market for a business that deals not in money, but in products and services, is virtually untapped. One of the services you'll provide is to educate people about how to find the products and services they want but for trade instead of cold cash.

This is a fantastic opportunity to create a virtually "new" business where none existed before. Because of the money-less character of the barter clubs, many people overlook the business possibilities. Yet it's a perfect chance for you to make money with your home computer.

SOURCE MATERIAL

Refer to Section 7.

No. 150

MULTI-LEVEL MARKETING AND RECORD-KEEPING

People who are involved with multi-level sales need to know exactly how much they are selling "down-line" to sales people under them. They also need to keep accurate records for their own distributor (or the company) and the IRS. You can provide this valuable service and tap into your share of the profits from this exciting and lucrative field. This report will show you how to find clients, and how to set up a record-keeping system geared to their needs.

CONCEPT

You may very well be interested in getting in on the great profit potential of multi-level marketing, but feel that your talents are not in the sales and recruiting field. If so, and if you have an eye for details, this business may very well be the answer you are looking for.

For most people in multi-level marketing, sales and recruitment are their calling. Most of these "go-getters" couldn't care less about keeping records and the like—until it costs them money.

The idea of this business is to keep track of everything that is sold down-line in your client's sales pyramid. That way, your client knows exactly how much in profit, bonuses, etc. they are entitled to receive. It also does several other things for the serious businessperson.

It is an excellent inventory control. In every business, most theft occurs on the inside. While we would all like to think that those who work for us are honest, this type of record system helps make sure they are. It does it in a way that is not offensive or accusatory.

Records must be kept for income taxes. The source company needs the information for bonus programs and its own records. Your system will keep up-to-the-minute records for these purposes.

Distributors can actually make more money with your service, than they could without. Your service does more than just keep track of what is owed a distributor; it frees that person's time and talents to make more money.

Even if the multi-level marketer has his or her own computer (and many of them do), your service can still fill a real need. Your computer-owning salesperson may very well not have the temperament for record-keeping, may feel he or she doesn't have time to "keep up" or may just plain not care to do that part of the job.

SKILLS YOU WILL REQUIRE

You do not need to know bookkeeping to operate this business. The real skills you will require include self-discipline, and the ability to do detailed work.

In this job, you must record every sale made to down-line salespeople. You may also be asked to record merchandise your client buys and sells. Without this complete and accurate information, your service will be worthless to your clients.

As for the self-discipline, you must set "office hours" and keep them. Otherwise, it's far too easy to put off recording "those few sales," contacting potential clients and generally running your operation in a businesslike manner. Your clients will need to know where and when they can contact you "at work," even if your office is a desk set up in the kitchen.

INFORMATION REQUIRED

You may wish to refer to Business Plan Number 108 for details on multi-level marketing structures.

Other than that, information you will need is of two types. Primary information is what you collect from your client and his down-line salespeople. Second, you will need to know who the potential businesses and customers are for your services.

If you are just starting the business and don't know any potential clients, you will need the secondary information first. Look for ads in the newspapers and on television for companies in multi-level sales. Even bumper stickers are helpful. Mary Kay, Amway, and Herbalife distributors often advertise the fact on the back of their cars. Large cities often have one or more professional organizations for salespeople. Simply attending one of their meetings can supply you with as many clients as you can handle.

After you get a client or two, the primary information will take care of itself. Different clients, or different types of distribution systems, may require slightly different kinds of information. But after you and your client have designed the system the two of you will use, you simply have to fill in the spaces and keep it up-to-date.

GETTING STARTED

Getting started in this business is fairly easy. Work with someone you know in multi-level marketing, or with one of your new clients, to design a basic form that has the information you will want to collect. That will include: the salesperson's name, the date, items sold, cost of those items, additional supplies needed, and any other information your client will want to know. For your client, that information should include his own purchases and sales.

Different companies may have different needs. However, if you have a basic form, it should be a quick and relatively painless process to add unique information.

It's best to have your clients' down-line salespeople send their merchandise orders, made out in duplicate, directly to you. You then record the data and send one copy of each order to your client, who fills the orders while you take care of the rest.

The alternate method is to have your client send you the duplicate copy of each invoice his people send him. This method can present problems. Since you bill on each invoice, you must insist you get a copy of each invoice, not just a total of sales. Not only that, this method eliminates one of your most powerful sales tools. That tool is the ability to say, "I am offering you a simple, easy record-keeping system you don't even need to touch if you don't want to, at a cost that is based solely on your volume of business. One concern is to keep your client honest with you.

One of the beauties of your service (and multi-level marketing) is that you may pick up clients both above and below your first client. Some pyramids sales organizations have dozens of levels, not just three or four. You may end up with a full-time business, having started with just one person.

THE COMPETITION

While multi-level marketing has been around a long time, this type of service hasn't. To make it really viable, the business needed the right tool—the computer. Few people have put the new tool to work in dealing with the old business. So the field is wide open in most cities.

POTENTIAL INCOME

The potential income from this business is limited only by the time you put into it, and your clients' sales. After you build your business up, you may very well decide that you can only handle accounts with a certain number of sales in order to pay for your time in maintaining your files. Meanwhile you will make money on every sale your client or his salespeople make.

A new client is charged a setup fee. That pays for designing any special needs into the form and setting up a record-keeping system for that person. A typical setup fee is $100.

To encourage salespeople to become clients, many businesses lower secondary setup costs to around $25. That reduction is based on not having to change forms or procedures, and applies only directly down-line from the first client.

After the account is set up for your client, a fee of $1, for example, is charged for each invoice you enter. That is not for each item sold, but for each invoice. It is also not for a tally of total sales. You will need to insist on a duplicate invoice from each salesperson. That is why you have the orders sent directly to you.

The costs of this business are slight if you already own a computer. You'll be doing yourself a great favor if you get a data base software program that allows you to design a form you find easy to use.

Basic Costs

1. Cost of software
2. Cost of advertising
3. Cost of time spent setting up account
4. Cost of time spent maintaining and updating account
5. Cost of materials used
6. Cost of transportation
7. Cost of postage, duplication, etc.

Whether you personally sell your service or it is done by mail, everything must look good. After all, you are selling a detail business. If your own details aren't polished (clothes torn or brochures with mistakes, etc.), how can you expect prospective clients to trust your service?

MARKETING METHODS

Marketing methods for this business cover a wide range. Since one or two clients can provide you with a great deal of income, you can start small without investing a great deal of money in advertising.

Clients can be found by direct mail, specialty advertising, word of mouth, telephone or direct contact. However, direct mail and display ads are two of the best client-getters for this type of business.

In placing display ads, make sure the periodical goes to the people you want to attract. An ad in a direct sales marketing club newsletter can pay for itself many times over. An ad in a drag racing magazine is questionable at best. The moral is—put your advertising money where it will do the most good.

One of the best ways to do that is by using direct mail advertising. You know that every letter you send out will go to someone who is at least a potential client. Whether they buy your service is another matter, but you're at least reaching it to someone who could use your service

. Below you will find a good example of a letter that can bring you all the business you will ever need, without leaving your own home. Send a brochure explaining your service and fees along with the letter to prospective clients in your area.

Dear Multi-Level Marketer:

Would you like the time to be able to sell more and at the same time eliminate the need to keep track of dreary numbers? Do you know what your down-line sales people really owe you, or what bonuses you are eligible for from your source company?

I can help provide the "yes" answer to all of these questions. I offer a simple, easy record-keeping system you don't even need to touch if you don't want to—at a cost that is based solely on your volume of business and designed to meet your personal needs.

By using my service, you can know exactly how much in profit, bonuses, etc. you are entitled to receive, and keep up-to-the-minute records for the IRS or your source company. It will provide excellent inventory control.

In every business, whether it is direct sales or a doctor's office, most "shop loss" and theft occurs from the inside. While we would all like to think that those who work for us are honest, my system assures that they are, and does it in a way that is not offensive or accusatory.

Best of all, you can actually increase your earning power by using my service, because it frees your time and talents for what you are really good at, and what interests you most— making sales.

Give me a call. You can start earning more— with less effort—today.

This letter alone can build all the business you want. A little time, effort and luck can really pay off in using this direct mail technique.

UNIQUE BUSINESS APPROACH

This is one business that can really grow without your having to expend lots of time and energy.

One way to ensure this is by trying an approach that has worked for others.

What you need to do is contact large numbers of clients to show them how efficient your record-keeping system is. This can be accomplished by doing a demonstration at a meeting of salespeople.

Simply contact regional dealers who sponsor sales seminars for their salespeople and offer to be a guest speaker on your specialty—record-keeping simplified.

The secret is to pass on a few time-saving techniques to the audience. If you can impress them with your enthusiasm and knowlege of the subject, they'll most likely be interested in coming to you as a customer.

Have cards and brochures available for potential clients to pick up at the meeting, and you'll be pleasantly surprised at the positive response you get.

LOCATION and MARKET BASE

To do a really good job marketing this service you need to be located in a city. You could conceivably make a go of it by mail, or in a small town where multi-level sales are popular. But in general, to make big money, you need to be where the business is, and that's in a city of 200,000 or more.

TO SUM UP

Your business can be the key to larger profits and fewer problems for a multi-level marketer. At the same time, you'll be in on the best of multi-level marketing—without ever having to sell a single piece of merchandise. What's more, you'll be getting fat commissions from every sale your customer makes, all simply because you are an organized human being. What could be easier?

SOURCE MATERIAL

For source material, refer to Section 7.

No. 151

SELL LOCAL MAILING LISTS AT $1 PER NAME

Businesses in every city have a need for the names and addresses of residents and businesses in their area. With a mailing list business, once you compile the names, the list can be rented over and over. The national average for use is eight to 10 times per year. At six to 10 cents per name, that adds up fast—to as much as $1 a name per year. In this plan, you'll learn how to compile lists of "good names" and how to keep those lists current. You'll also learn how to let the people who use names know you have them.

CONCEPT

The concept described here is to deal with businesses who are trying to encourage growth through direct contact with potential customers. You can facilitate that contact by renting names and addresses of selected types of potential customers already printed out on pressure-sensitive labels, or by renting lists of the names. Selected types could be:

new home owners
newlyweds
new parents
business licensees
business or professional categories
registered voters—by party

The possibilities are endless.

The lists can also include other relevant information, such as telephone number, price of home, age of couple. Since the names are permanently recorded on your disk, you can even contract to reprint the same label to the same customer for second mailing later.

It is important that the lists you rent out are current. No one is interested in spending money on mailings and then getting a large percentage back marked NO FORWARDING ADDRESS. That's money poured down the drain, and will leave you with disgruntled customers who will never buy again or give your name as a reference. Its better that you should make the effort to keep your lists up-to-date. Four ways to do this are:

Lists of this kind deteriorate about 10 to 16 percent every year. In just a few years a list is nearly worthless. A residential list needs updating every six months and a business list once every year. High-transit areas or high-turnover businesses need attention more often.

1.Charge a list rental fee to a customer, then offer to pay postage and any fees on returned mail in exchange for those updated addresses, from the returned mail.

2. Charge a rental fee then offer to pay postage fees plus the price of the advertising material that was returned.

3. Don't charge a rental fee, but ask for all the postal returns. In exchange, supply the list free.

4. Do some sort of mailing yourself on postcards, and request an address correction from the post office.

With first class mail, undeliverable mail is returned free. With postcards, you can ask for an address correction and be charged 25 cents if one is returned. Any of the ideas mentioned will work with either first class mail or postcards.

SKILLS YOU WILL REQUIRE

The skill you will require is really computer know-how. You need to select a data base wisely, and that involves educating yourself. There's plenty of help out there, so start asking questions.

INFORMATION REQUIRED

Before you can select software that will serve you well, a discussion of data bases is in order.

A data base is the type of computer program you will need to run your new business. It is like a giant filing cabinet jammed with scraps of useful information. But one of its striking features is that instead of each piece of information being filed under just one heading, each piece of information can be filed under a number of headings, or "fields" as they are called.

There are programs made just for mailing lists. Be very careful, because some of these allow you to sort for only one or two fields, and that may not be sufficient for what you've planned. Others may not be data bases at all. They may be a kind of word processor with a format set up for lists or labels. These will work for the initial compiling but are woefully inadequate later.

The benefit of a data base will be crystal clear to you when you need to update the mailing list files. With a word processor-type program you will have to read through the list to find the one that needs attention. With a data base, you can go speedily to the name you need to delete or update.

An example of fields and field information might be:

Name: I. Buy Lots
Address: 28 Affluent Street
City: Land of Dreams
Category: New Homeowner
Price: $3,000,000
Telephone: 555-5555
Special appeal to: country club, stock brokers, financial advisors

A good data base would not only print this example as part of the new homeowner list, but would allow you to rent this unusual one to other special-interest buyers—in this case, businesses who are looking for high-rollers.

The beauty of using a data base to record all this information is that, once recorded, any and all of these headings can be searched for in your computer "filing cabinet." Suppose you find a customer at some future date that wants the names of those who live in a certain community which to use the example above, includes Affluent Street. With your computer and your trusty data base, you could sort for streets and come up with this one.

A good program will have a sub-sort feature (sort for more than one field at a time) so you can not only go to those addresses on Affluent Street, but also only to those addresses between certain numbers on Affluent Street. What a time-saver! It's like having a collection of recipes filed not just under the name of the recipe but also under every ingredient and every kind of cooking method.

You can see that this would put each name on several lists automatically and increase the value of each list significantly. Every time you have a new buyer requirement, presto, you have a ready- made sale.

OPERATING NAME

To use a business name that is different than your own, you must spend some time and money publishing your chosen business name. There are papers that make a living publishing this kind of information, although almost any paper can do it. The purpose of this exercise is to publically link your name to that of your business name for identification in case of any future legal matters. Use of a fictitious name (as it's called) also means spending extra money on a business telephone and a business bank account. Both of these are more expensive than accounts held in your own name. You can obtain a business license in your own name as the name of your business. On your letterhead and business cards you can put "John Doe - Marketing" to identify yourself.

GETTING STARTED

No matter what kind of business you are thinking about starting, the very first thing you should do is sit down and make out a master plan. If you don't have a clear view of where you want to go, you'll probably end up nowhere. A master plan includes your ultimate goal and the route you propose to take to get there. Your goals should be written in concrete and your working plan written in sand. Like taking a long trip and finding roadblocks or bad roads, you don't change your destination, you just change your route. Treat your business like a business. No successful corporation would think of proceeding without having goals and plans written down, and neither should you.

Comb the software stores in your area for all the data base programs that will work on your computer. To look at programs that won't work on your computer is a waste of time, no matter how good the program is or how good the "experts" say it is. Time spent choosing software wisely is time well-spent, since your business revolves around this purchase.

Before selecting a software program, you need to ask yourself some questions about the type of information you want to store.

1. Do I want to store more than names and addresses?
2. What types of information would attract buyers?
3. Based on the information above, how many fields are necessary? (Be generous; you'll need more than you think.)
5. How deep do I want to sub-sort?
6. Do I need the ability to add new fields to existing files?

Answering these questions is extremely important. Since you will be typing in information (doing data entry), try to choose the right program in the beginning. If you should change your mind later and want to use another program, it's not the end of the world. You can certainly begin compiling your names on this new software from then on. It's just more handy to have all your information retrieved by one program.

Data base programs run from seventy-five dollars to several hundred dollars. This is not the place to economize. Get the one that fits your needs best, not the least expensive one. A "good buy" will be software that doesn't cause you operating headaches, and retreives with ease the kind of data you want. Select software carefully. The more it fits your needs, the less hassle you will have and the more profit you will realize.

Subscribe to legal newspapers. Their whole purpose is to inform the public of such things as: property going into default, new businesses filing fictitious names, and other such fascinating records. This is the stuff your business is made of.

Some of the online information services have yellow pages. Knowing how important a current and accurate list is, this can be gilt-edged material.

Look for trade magazines that cater to your type of computer. The ads are worth the price of the subscription. They will give you the names and addresses of manufacturers of software and services that could be useful to you. There may even be articles every now and then that apply to you. The few hours a month spent looking through these publications could save you a lot of time in your business. After all, time is money, and that's what computers are all about.

Data entry and secretarial services are available to help you type in data if you don't wish to do it all yourself.

THE COMPETITION

There are companies selling all sorts of mailing lists today. You are looking for local business, so the competition is not so great there. Again, the most important single factor about a mailing list is that it is "clean"—that is, the buyer can expect delivery without returns of a high percentage of his promotional material. Have a plan for updating your lists and emphasize this intent to your prospective renters.

POTENTIAL INCOME

Pricing your service is not difficult. Some clients will be interested in lists on a one-time basis. Others, such as list renters wanting names of new homeowners and new marriages, will contract for lists to be sent weekly or monthly. In the first case, you can simply charge six to 10 cents per name, as has been mentioned. In the second case, estimate the number of names you expect per week or month and charge accordingly.

It's important to know your cost of doing business. Go back to the master plan you made and begin pricing out everything on it. Include:

1. Cost of equipment and software
2. Cost of advertising
3. Cost of telephone
4. Monthly recurring costs such as utilities, rent, etc.
5. Cost of labels and other forms
6. Cost of postage
7. Cost of car and travel expenses
8. Cost of your time
9. Any other costs

Keep close track of your accounts to be sure you are making a profit. Profit is money left after you pay everything else, including yourself.

For those firms that contract your services, arrange payment to be made by a certain day of the month and charge a late fee if the payment is not received within a few days (say five) of that date.

Make yours a cash-and-carry business as much as possible. The cost of carrying accounts can be large. Carry accounts only for firms with good credit. You're not looking for a bad-debt write-off on your income tax.

You can expect a medium income. As you continue to update your lists, you will realize an income on work that was basically completed in the past, and so you see more money for less time spent as you go along.

MARKETING METHODS

Flyers describing your services can be mailed to businesses that would be likely candidates for mailing lists. The yellow pages can be your best friend both in locating customers and in compiling names and addresses for your customers. Here's where you can use a word processor if you choose to personalize your advertising mail. Don't be reluctant to send more than one mailing.

A typical letter might read:

> DEAR BUSINESS OWNER:
>
> Could you increase your business if you had a list of specially-target potential customers?
>
> Of course, you could, and now you can!
>
> John Smith Marketing Services can supply you with mailing lists specifically made up of the names, addresses and phone numbers of the people you most want to reach.
>
> Our service will supply you with lists on a one-time basis or regularly. And since we cater only to local businesses, we ensure that our lists are complete, up-to-date and worth the low prices we charge.
>
> Call today for more information.

Display flyers and posters anywhere in your community that sales or business people are likely to see them.

Telephone calling may be a little scary. Read some material on the subject. A business call to the right people could be the richest source of new customers, and it's something you can easily learn to do well.

UNIQUE BUSINESS APPROACH

This report has concentrated on approaching small businesses, because it's more likely that a telephone call or a letter will get to the right person. There are ways of offering your lists to larger companies also. You can use the modem to go online with information services to get the most immediate and current names of managers and executives of larger firms. There are Dunn and Bradstreet-type information services that supply these names and their positions. In this way you have an avenue of approach to rent your lists to this company. You also have an additional company and contact name for your data base to rent to future customers.

LOCATION and MARKET BASE

You are not going to need to rent an office. The data can be typed into your computer at home either by you or by a person you contract.

Since all of your customer relations can be handled over the phone or by mail, you can be located just about anywhere—city or country.

If there are between 50,000 and 200,000 people in an area you'll be calling, that's people enough to bring you plenty of business customers.

TO SUM UP

Every business that sells products or services to individuals or small businesses is a prospect for your mailing list service. From your base of operations you can target an area of consumers, compile names and then sell those names and addresses either as lists or as labels ready for use.

This service is so flexible that you can take on as little of it or as much of it as you feel able to. Once you get your feet wet, you will probaby want to expand.

The world is your mailing list, so start addressing today.

SOURCE MATERIAL

See Section 7.

No. 152

COMPUTERIZED CLASSIFIED NEWSPAPER

This is a unique plan that allows you to use your personal computer to produce specialty classified listings for people who aren't interested in going through the local newspaper every day. With your service, they will be able to be notified of only the things they're interested in and receive them in a convenient format. It will save them time and ensure that they won't miss anything. This service is limited only by how many listings you want to produce and how many clients you want to service. If it sounds appealing, read on for the details of how to make it work.

CONCEPT

There are many people interested in specialty items who are always on the lookout for bargain opportunities. Others are searching for business contacts, investors and other such things. The list is as varied as the categories of classified ads in the newspaper.

But to these people, it may sometime seem like too much work to go through newspaper classified sections to find what he or she is looking for. In addition, the average person would very seldom look at newspapers from other areas of the state or country to find what they need. It would cost too much and be too time consuming.

That's where your unique service can come in handy. With the help of your computer, you can produce customized listings of certain products or services as listed in newspaper classifieds.

SKILLS YOU REQUIRE

There are only a few skills you need to have success in this business, none of which are too difficult to attain.

First you need to have or develop the ability to do research. This is not very difficult if you know where to look.

Your local library is always a good place to start. Even if you don't know what to look for, the librarians can help you find what you need. You simply describe your purpose, and they are usually very helpful in locating any information you need.

The library will have copies of major newspapers from around the country and the world. From those, you can see which would suit your purpose best and subscribe to the ones you'll need. Or you can use some of them to make copies, if you have a call for something and you don't want to subscribe to that paper just for a one-time use.

Depending on what type of specialty you intend to gear up for, you can subscribe to newspapers of just one state, or you can go nationwide. Some of the opportunities lend themselves well to national exposure, such as real estate, rare automobiles, expensive one-of-a-kind items, and antiques.

In your research, you can also find directories on all kinds of topics. There are, for example, directories for organizations and associations. These are divided by the subject category. You can get plenty of ideas for unique opportunities just by seeing the variety of special interest groups that exist. Many associations might be willing to make available to you the list of their members.

You may also want to consider scanning want ads in magazines. The main difference between magazines and newspapers is that ads are more recent in newspapers.

This could be to your advantage for certain types of items. High-value items will be advertised in magazines, and the seller expects to take longer in finding a buyer for his item or service. And since magazines are geared to special-interest groups, you can even use this as an adjunct to your newspaper listings. That is, when you need additional listings, you can look at magazines that cater to that special-interest group and use those magazines for your promotion.

An additional skill that would be helpful to you is an ability to use some creativity in your matching, or in finding niches in the market.

INFORMATION REQUIRED

First, you need to locate all newspapers from your state. You can resort to the library at first to make copies of pages you need, and type the listings from there. You can then subscribe to certain key papers as you see fit.

When you make up your listings, it is very important to do them to avoid legal entanglement. Since you don't want to infringe on the newspaper's copyright, it is best to treat your service as an information brokerage. The way you do that is by culling only the important facts from each ad. Each of your listings would show only the following information:

The item

The cost

To further protect yourself from any potential problems, you should get permission from the newspapers regarding the use of their ads.

GETTING STARTED

The first step should be to place an ad to test the market and see what kind of response you get. You can then line up some clients and build your business gradually.

Do the research necessary to have easy access to all the information you need. Subscribe to the key newspapers you'll need. Locate the source of the organizations to contact for potential customers and do some mailings describing your service.

Set up your computer to file the ad listings in the appropriate files. Then set up your customer files, describing all vital information on each name. A data base will work well for this purpose, since it will enable you to file each type of item under a number of different headings. Likewise, you'll be able to search for items under a number of different categories.

At the beginning you'll be typing the listings yourself. You can set your own hours and work as long as you like. Once the listing becomes more in demand, you can hire a part time employee to type the listings into the computer for you.

THE COMPETITION

This is a very unique service with little competition. You'll be filling a service that very few people have thought of. But once you make your service known, people will decide that they want to take advantage of the trail you've blazed. The key to eliminating competition will be to supply the information that people are looking for, and establish your niche. Build up a client base before the others get to them.

POTENTIAL INCOME

The income from this business could eventually become quite large. It's all a matter of numbers. The more subscribers you get for your service, the more volume you'll do, and your income will go up accordingly. The only limit you have will be based on how much promotion you do and how aggressive you are in getting new subscribers.

We know of one man who runs a computerized nationwide job opportunities classifieds newspaper. His papers come out once a week and are sold in magazine shops and by subscription. At $2 per copy with 10,000 copies sold per week all over the country, you figure out what kind of income he is probably earning for himself.

To set a price for your classifieds newspaper, estimate all the cost of the program, including a salary for your time and a profit for the business. Then divide that by how many copies you want to print, and that will give you a rough idea of what each copy should cost. For subscription rates, offer a discount.

Basic Cost

1. Cost of software
2. Cost of subscriptions to newspapers, magazines, newsletters
3. Cost of time spent pulling out ads to include in your newspaper
4. Cost of printing and reproducing newspaper
5. Cost of postage and other mailing expenses
6. Cost of time spent keeping records of subscribers, sales, etc.

MARKETING METHODS

The two main methods to promote this business are classified ads and direct mail.

You can place ads in newspapers and specialty periodicals. By targeting business or trade publications, you'll be reaching exactly the type of customer you are looking for.

In the newspaper, you can place the ads in the section of the paper that you want to get business from.

For example, if you were to cater to the real estate market, you could place an ad in that section of the paper to generate interest.

The ad could run something like this:

> Do you want a list of sources for capital or investors? Listings available for what you need. CALL 999-9999.

For other categories you can use this format:

> What are you looking for? Whatever your needs, we can supply you with plenty of sources. For more information, 123-4567.

The advantage of working with newspapers is that the listings are very current. You should therefore mail your new listings promptly so that they are still current when your customers receive them.

Then, when the people call you to find out what your service is all about, you can explain to them the benefits of saving time and money.

The two main sources of orders will be phone calls from local customers, and mail orders from distant ones. For local orders, you can sell the concept over the telephone. If necessary, send them some follow-up literature.

When they place the order through the mail, they can check off on the order form what item or subject they are interested in. They can order two sheets on a trial basis for $5, for example, or they can subscribe for a longer term.

UNIQUE BUSINESS APPROACH

The key to this business is to cater to special groups of people. As in any business, success is based on finding a special niche in the market and filling it.

For example, there are a lot of people who are interested in antique or vintage cars. These people are always on the lookout for others with the same interests, through whom they can find that unique or special item. Since many of the cars are very expensive, these people wouldn't think twice about paying a few dollars for a listing of vintage cars.

The same holds true for other special groups. Real estate, in particular, holds a lot of opportunities for this service. Many of the people involved in buying properties or investing in mortgages are always on the lookout for opportunities. Most are busy people who don't have the time or patience to sort through a lot of classified listings in the papers. That's where your service becomes valuable.

Another excellent example of a specialty group that would be very interested in this service is stamp and coin dealers. They would be very receptive to receiving a regular mailing of potential sources of coins and stamps. Dealers would be happy to pay $5 or $10 per sheet for potential deals as long as they knew the classifieds were current.

If you would like additional ideas on the unlimited potential of specialty groups, look up a copy of the Encyclopedia of Associations at your local library. In it you will find thousands of specialty groups that you can provide your service to. To give you a brief idea of the scope available, the following is a short list of the types of organizations that exist:

Agricultural Organizations and Commodity Exchanges
Educational Organizations
Trade, Business and Commercial Organizations
Hobby and Avocational Organizations
Cultural Organizations

Within each of these major headings there are plenty of specific groups to work on.

As you can see, there is no limit to how far you can take this idea.

LOCATION and MARKET BASE

This is a business that you can conveniently run out of your home. You have the advantage of being able to operate it all through telephone and mail order business. This will help keep your expenses low and allow you to set your own hours. If you set up a post office box, then you simply check it periodically for new orders. This will allow you to conduct your entire operation from your home. Your customers won't really know if they are dealing with a large corporation or a small one-person outfit. You can run this business in the city or the country as long as you have access to classifieds from other publications.

START UP CAPITAL

The capital required for this business is about $5,000 to start. This would include the cost of your computer system. Other expenses will be for advertising and promotion. You should figure the cost for the ads you place, for the mailings you make to special groups, and for the literature you print up to distribute to potential customers. You will also have the cost for newspaper subscriptions and magazines, if any.

Once you get to the point where you have so many listings to process that you can't handle it on your own, you can hire someone to do the data entry for you. If the person is efficient enough, you can train him or her to do additional work, such as processing the orders, stuffing and addressing envelopes, and keying into the computer the accounting and subscription information.

TO SUM UP

This is a business with unlimited potential. Just keep in mind that you are looking for things that people need or want. And if you gear your service toward that goal, you can find plenty of opportunities to profit from. And that's the name of the game.

SOURCE MATERIAL

Refer to Section 7.

No. 153

PROGRAMMING GAMES FOR MARKET

One of the most popular reasons people buy a home computer is entertainment, thus creating a large and constantly growing market for game programs. Programming computer games to satisfy this multimillion dollar market is unlike any other computer-related business, because it can offer you both the fame and fortune of a top celebrity.

CONCEPT

The concept of this business is entertainment. You program a computer to play games with people. The more enjoyable your game is, the more people will want to play it. The more people see and play your game, the more potential customers you will have wanting to buy the same game for their own computer, and the more money you will get.

Essentially, your computer program turns a computer into a toy for people to play with. Your game will pit a person's skill and intelligence against the computer, while challenging people to play again.

Game programs can combine education with play. The market for educational programs is just as large as the market for game programs, so if your game is fun to play while also being educational, the chances of your game's success is doubled.

One of the reasons why the game programming business is so profitable, is that a computer program is like a novel that earns its author royalties. The more people buy your game, the more money you will be earning. Since your game, like a book, could be on the market for years, each day means another day's worth of royalties.

SKILLS YOU WILL REQUIRE

There are basically only two skills you need to become a computer game programmer. The first skill is knowledge of a computer programming language. The most popular programming languages are BASIC, C, and PASCAL. Learning how to write programs in these languages is not difficult. Bookstores are overflowing with self-teaching programming books. Computer languages are like foreign languages; once you know how to use one language, you can easily learn another one.

The second skill necessary for a computer game programmer is playfulness. If you know what kind of games you like to play and why you enjoy playing them, then you will know what makes a good game.

INFORMATION REQUIRED

You need very little information to begin as a computer game programmer. First of all, you will need to know at least one programming language. BASIC is the most common language. The PASCAL and C languages are more complicated. Assembly language is the most complicated language of all, but also runs the fastest on a computer. The language you choose to write your program does not matter. A programming language is like the structure of a building; the structure supports the building, but nobody can see it at work.

Once you have the initial game idea in your head, the next step is learning what kind of games are currently being sold. The reason for this is to study the successful games and determine what makes them successful. If you find your game idea is similar to a game already on the market, you can imitate the best features of that game, improve upon its faults, and create one that is more fun to play.

The most valuable information a computer game programmer needs is what sort of games appeal to different age groups. By studying games aimed at a specific age group, such as children, teenagers or adults, you will have a clear idea of who would be interested in your type of game. Once you know your market, you will know the appeal of the best games for each age group. You can then design your own game to make sure it will be one of the more successful programs on the market.

OPERATING NAME

You have two choices here. You can pick a fictitious name or you can use your own name. Using a fictitious name is good if you plan on publishing and marketing your game yourself, or if you wish to remain anonymous.

The advantage of using your own name is that when you design one computer game, people will remember your name and look for other computer games with your name on it. There are many computer celebrities known only through the games they have designed.

Once you have designed one computer game, your name will be a major selling point for the next game you design. As with novels, the author of a computer game program is almost as important as the name of the computer game itself. If you use your own name for each computer game you design, the chances of success for each game you design increases dramatically, because you will have a proven record of success.

GETTING STARTED

Getting started as a computer game programmer is a matter of playing with your computer. The first step is identifying what kinds of games you would want to play on your computer, and then creating a game to satisfy yourself. Creating a game that you would like to play makes the entire game-designing programming easier and more interesting, because you can look forward to playing the game when it is done.

The next step is to determine the goal of your game, such as exploring a dungeon for treasure and killing monsters. The goal will help focus your thoughts on how to make your game more challenging. Since you will know what players will be fighting for in your game, you can think up creative ways to make the goal difficult to reach.

THE COMPETITION

Eliminating the competition is a matter of knowing the market. An excellent book describing the computer software business is the Programmer's Market, published annually by Writer's Digest Books.

The game market is competitive, but not every game will be competing for the same audience. The best way to make sure your game will sell is to appeal to your target audience at more than one level.

For example, home computer programs can be divided into entertainment programs and educational programs. As a game programmer, your goal is to make your game fit both categories simultaneously. Your game will be fun to play, but if you can also teach people something new, you can capture a large share of the educational software market as well.

Another way to eliminate the competition is to write your game program for a number of different computer brands. Some of the best games can run only on certain types of computers. If your game is similar to a game that works on only one type of computer, people will buy your game if they can use it on their own computer.

Most game programs are written for the major computer brands, but don't overlook the smaller computer brands. There is a large number of the lesser known brand-name computers with little software available for them. By concentrating on these computer owners, you can capture a lion's share of this market.

POTENTIAL INCOME

The profit potential for computer game programs ranges from good to fantastic. Stories abound of individuals making fortunes by selling only one game.

There are two ways you can sell your game. You can either sell it yourself, or you can sell it to a software publishing firm that will take care of the advertising and pay you a percentage of the profits as royalties.

If you sell the game yourself, you will get all the profits. If you sell your game to a software publisher, the software publisher can advertise and distribute your game across the country, and even overseas.

The standard method of payment from a software publisher is a fee plus royalties. Some software publishers offer a flat fee, buying all rights of the game from you. In either case, you will have to sign a contract stating exactly how much you will be paid and what percentage of all profits will be your royalties.

The advantage of a flat fee is that you can make a lot of money in a hurry. The advantage of royalties is that your game will be producing money for you year after year. Some people have retired on their royalty income from game programs they have written, and many more people will do the same in the future. Why shouldn't one of those people be you?

MARKETING METHODS

Direct mail and display ads are the best ways to sell your game program. There are a number of magazines where you can place a display ad for your computer game. First, you can advertise in the various magazines devoted to computer hobbyists, such as Compute or Computer Gaming World. If your game has a science fiction theme, you can advertise in science fiction magazines. If your game is also educational, you can advertise in the education trade magazines. Since computers are becoming more popular every day, you can advertise in almost any magazine and be assured of a response.

The display ad for your game program might read like an excerpt from a novel. Your goal is to grab the attention of the reader and create a fantasy world for the reader to dream about. Briefly describe the goals of the game and challenge the reader to test his game-playing skills. An example of a display ad is shown below.

DATE: THE DAY AFTER TOMORROW

ALIEN INVASION!

As commander of America's last space shuttle, you race against time to save the earth from an alien invasion. Alone and outnumbered, your skills are tested to the utmost to defeat the alien armada. At your disposal are space mines and programmable killer satellites. But will it be enough to stop the determined forces of alien intruders, bent on nothing but complete domination of the universe? Find out if you can stop the invasion by ordering your copy of THE FINAL BATTLE today! (Before the invasion begins.)

Many computer magazines will even offer to publish your game. If you are just starting out as a computer game programmer, you can develop little computer games for these magazines while sharpening your skills for the bigger, multimillion dollar games in your future.

UNIQUE BUSINESS APPROACH

The secret to selling your game to the public or to a software publisher is marketing. The more people who see your game, the more you increase the chances of a sale. Besides direct mail and display ads, you can also attend gaming conventions sponsored by the Game Manufacturer's Association. There are also numerous conventions for people interested in war games. War game magazines, such as The Space Gamer (available in most hobby shops), list dates and places for war game conventions around the country.

The gaming convention will attract game publishers from all over the country who you can show your game to. Selling a game in person is easier than selling a game by mail, since the person can play the game for himself to see if he likes it.

One of the best ways to sell your game is to contact people (through direct mail or display ads) and say that you are developing a new computer game and need people to play it. Offer to sell the game at a greatly reduced price with the option of trading in the test version of the game when the final game is ready.

This way you can earn money before your game is finished, and get valuable feedback from game players, who can offer advice on how to make your game better.

Another method of selling your game is to talk to computer dealers in your area. Offer your game as a demonstration program to run on the dealer's computers. Convince the dealer that your game program will help him sell more computers because more people will want to come to his store to play your game. You can also sell your game program to a dealer who wants to give it away as a publicity stunt to bring people in his store.

If you own a portable computer, you can take your computer and your game to various social gatherings (swap meets, fundraisers, etc.) and charge a quarter for each play. Not only will this earn you extra spending money, it will also give you feedback on how people react to your game.

If your game is fun to play and educational as well, you can sell your game program to local schools. This way, children will see your game, and, if they have computers at home, they will be likely to buy a copy of your program so they can play it outside of school.

EQUIPMENT REQUIRED

If you plan on writing game programs for different types of computers, you will need access to each type of computer you want to write your game program for. Otherwise, you can just sell games for your own particular brand of computer.

The quality and speed of a printer will be up to the individual. Since you will often need to rewrite or debug your program when you are first making up your game, you will need to have a printed copy of the program, because a computer screen can only show a small portion of your program. A dot-matrix printer will not only be cheaper, but faster, as well as able to show the graphics of your game.

LOCATION and MARKET BASE

Perhaps the greatest advantage of computer game programming is that it can be done anywhere, whether you live in the city or the country. If you want to work from your home town or move to a cabin in the wilderness, all you need is your computer, a printer, and lots of imagination, and you're ready to go to work.

TO SUM UP

No other computer-related business offers you the chance for fame, fortune and fun like computer game programming, and no other job in the world has the potential to make someone rich overnight.

Today's computer game programmers are changing the role of computers in the future. They are teaching a whole new generation of people not only how to use and understand a computer, but how to have fun with one as well. Programming games offers you the freedom to live where you want, to set your own working hours, and to retire at any age. And besides, in what other kind of business can you play all day and get paid for doing it?

SOURCE MATERIAL

Refer to Section 7.

No. 154

SELL STOCK MARKET ADVICE

You've probably seen all those stock market programs that promise riches beyond your wildest dreams. We can show you how to turn those dreams into reality by selling your services to others. We will show how you and your home computer can prepare stock predictions just like the big brokerage houses. But the key here is to supply them on a local level, where the big houses don't read. So get into the stock market, where the money is in selling "services," not buying and selling stock.

CONCEPT

One of the biggest problems in working with any stockbroker or investment counselor is that you know they are getting a commission for what they sell. It is a commission built on the idea that the more they sell, the more money they make. And the information they provide you is what will make them, not you, the richest.

Here's a chance to open an information service to show your clients how certain stocks and commodities have performed in the past and what the key indexes say about them. It's completely third-party, so they can make their stock-buying decisions based on the information you provide, not on what you would personally recommend.

SKILLS YOU WILL REQUIRE

You certainly don't need to be a Wall Street bear to make a go of this business. If you enjoy playing with your own stock investments, researching the companies you invest in, and doing number games with the figures they provide in their annual reports, you will do well in this type of business.

Even if you're a novice, though, software programs are now available that will guide you through getting the information you need to research the value of a particular stock investment. The software will also allow you to track your stocks on a daily or weekly basis, and update projected earnings on the investments.

INFORMATION REQUIRED

The kind of information you will need to sell stock market information is, first, a basic understanding of the terminology of the business. You can get this education by reading some of the publications like the Wall Street Journal or Barron's. You might also consider picking up a couple of books on the subject of stocks from your local library. Study these a little bit and you should be halfway to understanding how to run the software you'll need for this business.

The kind of software you use is basically geared for stock market investment. Although you can get software that will analyze all types of investments, you might as well pick a program that will specialize in your own interest, which is stocks only. What you want is a program that will prompt you for information about the stocks you are interested in, past performance, current value, etc. This kind of software will enable you to track the stability of a company for your client.

You will also want to go "on-line" for up-to-date stock information. You can do this by using a modem and telephone line and subscribing to networks, like Dow Jones Retrieval Network, that will give you the latest stock information, as well as multitude of other facts about the companies your customer wants to know more about. The networks allow you to "download" the information they contain to print out on your own printer or show up on your "dumb" terminal. They will cost you the price of the initial subscription, as well as a user's fee each time you go on-line, and possibly a long distance phone call.

You can probably get a demonstration of these networks by visiting your local computer store and requesting to see one in operation. Most will be glad to accommodate you if they think that somehow they are going to make money out of the deal. They should also be able to tell you who to contact for more information about subscribing.

GETTING STARTED

Once you have a working knowledge of the terminology, available software, and available networks, you are ready to start doing research. What you should do is select a group of stocks you want to track, then follow them for a month or two to see how they perform. This will take time, and you won't be earning money with your efforts, but it will pay off in the end, because you are familiarizing yourself with what is required in this business. It will get you comfortable with the formats that the information comes to you in, and probably peak your enthusiasm as the value of your stocks begin to grow or decline. This enthusiasm will work into your ability to convince others that you know what is going on in the stock market business.

When you feel comfortable with the basics of the business, you are ready to sell yourself. Probably what you will want to do is put out a "hotsheet" or newsletter to subscribers, that possesses stock information they want to read. This will be more cost-effective and profitable than dealing with clients on a one-on-one basis, although you may consider operating the business that way as well.

People love to feel they have an "insider's" knowledge of the stock market game, and through your newsletter you will act as that insider. It can be very simple—a regular sheet of paper with printing on both sides. And you want to cram it full of information about various companies and stocks that your subscribers may want to consider investing in.

If you are a person who enjoys telling others your opinion on matters, then this is a great forum for you. Not only will they read what you say, but they'll pay you to read it as well.

As time passes and some of your advice actually pays off for subscribers, you can tout that fact. In this business, the more brazen and confident you are, the more people will be convinced of your worth, as well as the worth of your information.

THE COMPETITION

Your competition in this field is abundant. Stock brokers, investment counselors, financial and business newspapers—you name it, it's out there. The difference is that you will be concentrating on serving local businesses that are on the stock exchange. Most large cities have dozens of these, and if you concentrate on tracking their performance, following their prospects, even profiling them in your newsletter, you can blow the competition away. Few of your competitors concentrate on the local market, either in reporting on it, or in selling to it. If you do, your competition won't be a problem.

POTENTIAL INCOME

You can write your own ticket in a business like this. Should you choose to publish a newsletter, you can get much more than the typical grocery store magazine gets. Many of these newsletters sell for as much as $200 a year for 12 issues. If you sell only 100 subscriptions in the year, that would be $20,000 going to your business. You can make a small fortune with this type of business, and give your subscribers the same opportunity to do it with the information you provide them in your newsletter pages.

To get an idea of what to charge, price out your expenses for each issue, decide how much you want to make for your time, as well as for the business, then multiply that times the number of issues you intend to put out for the year. If the newsletter comes out once a month, multiply your monthly expenses by 12.

Basic Costs

1. Cost of software used
2. Cost of subscriptions to networks

3. Cost of time spent organizing information, researching, etc.
4. Cost of long distance phone calls
5. Cost of producing newsletter
6. Cost of printing newsletter
7. Cost of advertising
8. Cost of postage, mailing, etc.

Keep in mind that with this business, you don't need thousands of subscriptions to stay alive. In fact, the fewer subscriptions you need to sell to make the money you want, the more elite your newsletter will seem and the more people will probably want to receive it. They will consider the high prices you charge well worth their investment.

Should you choose to work with individual clients in providing investment information, your data will be the same, but you will simply charge by the hour or consultation that you provide. The advantage of offering a newsletter is that you can sell the same information over and over again to a larger group of people, but without all the time involved in personal consultation.

MARKETING METHODS

The best methods to market this service are direct mail and display ads.

You can run display ads in your local business publications, the business pages of newspapers and possibly even newsletters that go out to professionals in various fields, such as lawyers, doctors, etc.

The direct mail approach would be most effective by targeting those people in your area with a large income. You can obtain the names and addresses of these people by renting or buying lists from list brokers. Certain ZIP code areas in your city might also supply you with the potential customer base you seek.

Either route you take, whether direct mail or display ads, your advertisement can go something like this:

> STOCK MARKET INVESTORS
>
> You can increase your investment earnings by being better informed.
>
> Our company, Market Finders, provides that up-to-date investment information you need to make those stock market investments of yours pay off the way they were meant to.
>
> We report on local market trends in a way the Wall Street Journal can't touch. If you want to know how local companies are doing on the market, we can help. Our information banks are brimming with performance histories, projections and other pertinent information that can put you on the inside of the market.
>
> Once a month you can receive our privately circulated newsletter, Market Facts, that contains the kind of insider's knowledge you want to know to keep on top of good stock investment potentials. We profile companies on the move, companies on the make and the local movers and shakers that can roll your stocks into a lawn of green.
>
> For more information, call Market Finders now!
>
> P.S. Act in the next 10 days and we won't bill you for your subscription for another three months! Call now!

Your own variation of this letter should bring you queries for more information. Be prepared to answer any questions intelligently. Once those subscription checks start rolling in, you'll have the capital you need to do your research and put together your first newsletter.

UNIQUE BUSINESS APPROACH

A winning technique that will get this project off the ground is offering people a money-back guarantee. And you can do this by mailing out free samples of your first newsletter to the people who want more information, or if budget allows, to everybody on your mailing lists. This will mean you'll need your start-up capital up front, as opposed to relying on subscription checks, but the end result will mean big bucks for you.

Simply compile the information in your newsletter to professional standards, mail it out along with your cover letter, and await the results. Once people get a taste for what their subscription money will be buying, they'll want more.

LOCATION and MARKET BASE

You should be in a city to operate this business, since only a city will offer the opportunity to concentrate on the local companies you can cover in your newsletter. A population base from 50,000 to 200,000 should provide you with a large enough number of potential customers to really get this money-making opportunity to pay off.

TO SUM UP

A stock market advice business can bring big dollars for you if you have a love of the stock market business.

What you will be selling is that "insider's knowledge" that people thrive on. The information you provide can earn them a big return on their investments, and for that, they will consider the charge for your service relatively small.

If the idea of this service intrigues you, get started now, and the dividends you earn will prove to you how right your choice of business was.

SOURCE MATERIAL

Refer to Section 7 for information.

BOOKKEEPING SERVICE

Here is a business where the computer age has produced many small operators with five-figure incomes who only spend a few hours a week at it. The problem nowadays is not whether you can do the bookkeeping, but how you get clients. We have solved that problem, as well as how to process your client's bookkeeping needs in a way he or she has never seen before. You actually eliminate all of the competition.

CONCEPT

The concpet of this business is to handle bookkeeping services for businesses. If you have even a small amount of bookkeeping experience, you know how the old-fashioned methods can take hours of time and effort and reams of paper. Now with your personal computer you can do the same work in just a fraction of the time. This business requires little capital to start up and maintain it, and once you have your clients lined up, you can depend on a steady income for as long as you want the job.

SKILLS YOU WILL REQUIRE

If you have ever enjoyed working with numbers or done bookkeeping services, you already know how to run this business.

All it requires is an understanding of basic bookkeeping practices and an eye for detail. Using your computer, the accuracy of your figures is ensured, and once you've got a bookkeeping system set up for a customer, all you need to do is spend a couple of hours each week or month updating the material.

For this business, you'll want to know how the bookkeeping software your computer runs works and the kind of information it requires. A little practice time with it should teach you all you'll need to know to get this business up and moving.

INFORMATION REQUIRED

The information required for this busisness is of two sorts. The first sort is what you'll need to know to choose software for your computer to run your service. There are lots of bookkeeping software packages out on the market these days, so spend some time reading up on them. Start reading computer magazines that run software reviews and study what the various features are for the kind of software you need. Read ads from these magazines and send off for the literature about the packages. Visit your local computer or software stores and request demonstrations of the programs that can run on your machines.

If you're a novice at bookkeeping, take a class in the subject at a local community college or adult education program. Read a book on the subject. The basics are very easy to pick up with a little study. You'll become familiar with the terminology of the business, as well as the techniques of bookkeeping you will follow. You may even consider taking a course in computer bookkeeping for a particular software package or your brand of computer. This will show you how best to organize your material and work with it using modern technology rather than the old-fashioned ledger books that most bookkeeping classes rely on.

The second type of information you'll need for this business is what you'll get from the customer himself. If his business isn't already computerized, that is probably because the thought of implementing a computer system scares him off. But since you supply the know-how, all he needs to do is supply you with the numbers.

To get this information, spend time with your customer going over his books with him to see how he likes to keep his records. Discuss his needs with him—how he might like to change his present system, how you might be able to save him time or effort. This is time well spent, since it will give you the opportunity to learn exactly what will be required of you. Then you can start thinking up ways to implement the bookkeeping system on the software you've chosen to use for your business.

GETTING STARTED

To get started in this business, first obtain your software and familarize yourself with how to use it. You certainly don't want to waste a customer's time by making mistakes in input or by creating useless or unwanted information. Set up a practice business and create books for the business, along with transactions for a typical month or two. Input the information and see what you come up with. Hone your inputting techniques so that you can save time for yourself when you get your first customers.

Once you feel confident in the use of your computer, it is time to go after business.

Concentrate on small businesses that use a part-time bookkeeper or a bookkeeping service. Chances are, if they have a full-time bookkeeper on staff, they won't need your service.

Get business cards printed up with your name and phone number. Pass these out freely every chance you get. When you stop for gas or to get new tires put on the car, leave behind a card with the proprietor of the shop. If you visit a copyshop, leave behind your card for the manager. When you go to parties, mingle with people and get to meet the ones who operate their own small businesses and might make for potential customers. Don't be shy about spreading word about your business around. The more people know what you do, the more likely they are to consider you when they need bookkeeping services.

Once you get a client and have spent time understanding what his bookkeeping needs are, get to work. Go over his bookkeeping for the previous year or so to ensure that the numbers you will input are accurate. Oftentimes, this isn't the case, so be prepared to do some clean-up work. Once this task is completed, start inputting the bookkeeping materials and updating them regularly. Don't allow your client to get behind in giving you the information you need. Keep on top of him and keep on top of your own work. You don't want to create more problems for him than before he started using your service.

COMPETITION

You'll have plenty of competition in this business, but don't worry. Only a small portion of the competition use computers for their work, a smaller number direct their marketing efforts to the small business, and even a smaller number market their services in the ways we'll show you.

Once you have a customer, keep him by staying timely. Make sure his reports are on his desk when he needs them. Ensure accuracy by inputting the material correctly. Ensure that your reports are easy to read and in an order that makes him understand his business better.

POTENTIAL INCOME

With this business, your price is often determined by how much your competitors charge. Even so, you will have honed your skills to the point where it takes you a lot less time to do the same amount of work, which means you will be earning a greater profit. To determine how to charge for your services, contact several bookkeeping services in your area and pose as a potential customer. Find out their rates, as well as what kinds of services they provide for the money.

Not only will you want to keep within line of your competitions' prices, but you'll want to ensure that you are making enough money to cover your business expenses. This includes a salary for your time, as well as a profit figure for the business.

To estimate your expenses, add up all the costs of your program.

Basic Costs

1. Cost of software
2. Cost of business cards and advertising
3. Cost of time spent with client to set up program
4. Cost of time spent updating bookkeeping data
5. Cost of overhead, such as office space, utilities, etc.
6. Cost of transportation
7. Cost of telephone charges
8. Cost of special bookkeeping materials used
9. Cost of any office materials used

Once you have a general idea of how much it will cost you to do business, you are ready to determine your prices. You may decide to charge a one-time set-up fee to each customer. This will cover your time spent going over his books, bringing them up to date and inputting the data into your computer. This will also cover the time spent with him to discuss how he wants his bookkeeping done. You can then charge him a monthly fee for updating his bookkeeping. If you charge $100 for the set-up and $50 per month to do his books, you can earn $700 per client in a year. If you take on 20 clients, each requiring about two hours a month, that will bring your business an income of $14,000 for the year with less than three months worth of full-time work. In other words, you can earn a full-time income with only part-time effort.

MARKETING METHODS

The best methods to market this service are direct mail, display ads, telephone sales and direct sales.

You can run display ads in local newspapers and publications where the small businessperson will see them. In the copy, emphasize your low prices, computerized methods and complete dependability and accuracy.

If you choose to try direct mail, send lettters out on a regular basis to small businesses in your area. You can locate their names and addresses in the yellow pages or by relying on contact services that provide contact names for businesses of a particular size. A typical letter might read:

> DEAR BUSINESS OWNER:
>
> Are you getting everything out of your bookkeeping that it can provide you?
>
> Do you know as much about the money in your business as you want to?
>
> Bookkeeping Associates can handle your bookkeeping, and teach you more about your business at the same time.
>
> Our methods are completely computerized, which means we save you time and money getting the information you need to run your business better.
>
> We'll show you short cuts in bookkeeping methods and supply you with information you've never considered important before, but that might make the difference between earning a four or a five-figure profit this year.

If you'll give us 20 minutes of your time, we'll prove it!

Call today.

You can follow this letter up with a telephone call. Remind them about who you are and what your service is, then explain the benefits of using your service. Try to set up a direct sales appointment with the owner so that you can present your bookkeeping techniques in person. Try to get him to show you the books in their current status, and be prepared to give him some quick ideas about how you might improve his current system or make it easier for him to keep up on.

You won't need to get too many sales of this kind to make this business worth doing. With a little effort you can quickly line up all the work you want and then settle back for the long haul. Or you may consider hiring somebody to do your bookkeeping work for you while you tend to getting more customers. The choice is yours.

UNIQUE BUSINESS APPROACH

The way to really get this business off the ground is to choose a special business to concentrate on. For example, if you have an understanding of the plumbing business, you can choose to handle bookkeeping for all the plumbers in your area. Or you may decide to work only with gas stations or tire stores or insurance firms or law offices. Whatever you choose, you can become an expert of sorts for this particular line and make that a selling point for your business.

You may even consider going mobile. We know of one man in the northern part of the country who handled bookkeeping only for gas stations. Once a month he would pull up to his customer's station and do the work right from the back of his van. With equipment in place, he'd take his customer's books and do the work in a couple of hours. Then he would drive to his next customer. Even if you don't own a van, you can offer to do this service right in the office of your customer. You'll need a portable computer to operate in this way, but an obvious selling advantage is that the customer's books never leave the premise, except in your computer's memory.

LOCATION and MARKET BASE

The best place to offer this service is in a city with a population between 50,000 and 200,000. This will give you plenty of potential small businesses to convert into customers.

TO SUM UP

A bookkeeping service is an opportunity that is finally paying off with the advent of the personal computer. You can do the work in a fraction of the time it used to take, thereby reaping greater profits for yourself.

Since most businesses find this aspect of their operation a real headache, you alleviate their problems by taking it over for them. In exchange, you'll earn a nice amount of money with just a few hours of time. You'll be able to put your customers' books in better order than they ever imagined was possible, and you'll be able to handle your own books as well. After all, you'll have to do something to keep track of all the money you can make with this computerized business.

SOURCE MATERIAL

Refer to Section 7.

No. 156

USED PERSONAL COMPUTER BROKER

For the last several years, used-computer brokering has been big business for larger computer units. Now you can get in on the ground floor and share in the same success that the big computer brokers have. With your personal computer you will learn how to set up a network of both buyers and sellers, with you acting as the middleman and collecting on each deal.

CONCEPT

The concept of this business is to match up computer sellers with computer buyers. The personal computer has come of age and that means that more and more people are now shopping for used equipment rather than putting out the money for new equipment.

Yet the used personal computer business is a new one. Usually what happens is that a business decides to sell used computers but then finds it must invest thousands of dollars in inventory and repair, as well as setting up a store. Most don't last for long. As a computer broker you'll have staying power simply because you don't actually have to carry any inventory at all. All you do is arrange for sales. This saves on your overhead and business expenses.

SKILLS YOU WILL REQUIRE

To become a used-computer broker, you will want a couple of skills. First, you want to be able to organize your information in a usable fashion that will allow you to call it up as you need it, quickly and efficiently.

The second skill you need is an ability to talk "computerese" with people. You need to know about the various computer components available on the market today, so that when somebody comes to you with a computer to sell, you have an understanding of the value of the merchandise. Likewise, you'll be able to discuss with a potential buyer the kind of system he is looking for. Oftentimes, these customers know what they want their computer to do for them, but they don't know what system is right for their needs. If you have an understanding of the kind of merchandise you will be brokering, you can lead them into a choice that will suit their needs and guarantee you a sale.

INFORMATION REQUIRED

The information required for this business is of three varieties. The first is information about the systems you'll be brokering. If you enjoy reading computer magazines and studying the pros and cons of various computers, you'll do well with this business. That will give you an idea of the value of the merchandise you'll be handling. If you aren't already familiar with several computer brands, you can get this education by studying the magazines, books and ads that come out. Send off for brochures on the popular systems and read reviews of hardware. Become familiar with prices for the systems by perusing classified ads to learn what most people are asking for their used computers. By reading the classifieds, you'll also get an idea of what people list in their ads, ie., that they mention number of bytes in memory, number of disk drives, whether it comes with a printer or a monitor, etc.

The second kind of information you will require for this business is what you'll need to set your brokering service up. You have several choices here. You may decide simply to take the information about the computers people want you to sell for them and put out a weekly listing of what is available. This can be in the form of a classified listing sheet. You can either place the classifieds in your display ads, or circulate it on its own. You may choose to take the information about the computers and simply have your customers phone you to find out what you have available.

The third type of information required to operate this business is what you know about the computers themselves. The best way to get this information is to have both buyers and sellers fill out a short questionnaire. This way you know what the buyer has to offer and what the seller is seeking.

A typical questionnaire would include:
Name:
Address:
Daytime phone number:
Buyer or seller:
Brand name of computer:
Model of computer:
Components included:
Age of computer:
Reason for selling:
Special features, software, etc:
Condition of equipment:
Price sought:

You can have your customers fill this out over the phone or you may include it in your advertising to let them fill out and mail back to you.

GETTING STARTED

To get started in this business, you'll have to design a plan you intend to follow. You'll need to decide how you want to handle the information about the computers and how you intend to present the information, whether by classified listing or other advertising methods in Section 5. You also need to set up a file in your computer to process the information. You may decide that a data base will best suit you. A data base will enable you to file the information under a number of categories. For example, if a customer is looking for a particular brand of computer, your data base can call up all the computers you have listed under that brand name. Likewise, if a customer wants a certain size memory capacity, you might have it filed under that as well, or by price range, components, model, age, whatever you decide is pertinent. Using a data base will give you more flexibility in being able to call up the information under each special requirement the buyer is seeking. Likewise, you can place the buyers requirements in the data base, so that when you do have a computer that fits his needs, your computer can call it up for you.

When you start getting business, you'll have to keep up on putting the information into your computer in an organized fashion. This will ensure that a search calls up the latest information you have about a particular system.

Once you've got a data base started, you have a couple of options about how to present your service. You can advertise the fact that people wanting to buy or sell can contact you for information about what is available. In other words, you get a call, somebody tells you to list their computer, so you collect a fee, then somebody else calls wanting that particular kind of computer, you collect another fee and hook up the buyer with the seller.

Your second option is to offer weekly or monthly listing of what you have "in stock." When somebody contacts you to sell their computer, you add the system into your listing for a fee. When a buyer contacts you after finding a computer that suits his needs, you take a fee and let him know who is selling the system. With a few variations, this is how many used products are sold, from cars to boats to office equipment.

THE COMPETITION

This is a new field in this country, and chances are, you won't have any real competition when you first begin. The only people actually dealing with used computers either buy them, fix them up and sell them or are selling a unit they've outgrown. In the first case, you don't need to worry about the competition because all you are doing is brokering the sales, never actually touching the units. In the second case, a person selling his own computer is only in the business once. Once its sold, he's out of the used-computer business.

POTENTIAL INCOME

This is a business that can bring you a nice income with little effort if you play it right. You increase your earnings from the beginning, simply by charging both the buyer and seller for the information and service you provide.

If you charge $10 for each listing and you get 100 listings for your first month, that is $1,000. On the other hand, if you charge potential buyers the same amount, you have just doubled your money. If you decide to publish a listing of what is available, you can sell it, as well as collect fees from the people who want to be listed in it or want to purchase from it.

You must remember that your accounts may be carried from one month to the next, since one system may take a longer time to sell than another. Soon enough you'll have a good idea of how much business you can expect each month and charge accordingly.

To set your fees, first, you need to add up your expenses of doing business. Then you add in a profit figure, as well as a salary for your time. Then you should estimate how many computers you can comfortably broker. This will give you an idea of how much to charge each customer.

Basic Costs

1. Cost of data base software
2. Cost of advertising
3. Cost of time spent organizing questionnaire
4. Cost of reproducing questionnaire
5. Cost of time spent taking orders
6. Cost of time spent inputting information
7. Cost of time spent making computer matches for buyers
8. Cost of postage, telephone, utilities
9. Cost of materials used

MARKETING METHODS

The best ways to market this business are with display ads and direct mail. You can place classified ads in local dailies under the "Computers for Sale" section, and in computer and business publications. This will reach a wide market and get your service known quickly and cheaply. A sample ad might read:

WE MATCH COMPUTER BUYERS WITH SELLERS!

Jones Used Computer Brokerage has a complete listing of computers for sale. Get your computer listed now for less than it would cost to advertise it yourself. Call now for details. 123-4567.

This ad, along with variations geared specifically for buyers and for sellers, should bring plenty of response. After that, it is up to you to sell your service.

One for buyers could read:

> Want to buy the best used computer equipment? Call us today to learn what we have in stock.

You may also consider running ads about particular systems to generate ads. This will get people calling you for information about the computers, and then you can make your plug about being a broker and being able to find exactly what they are looking for. What you must be careful about, however, is not to run ads for equipment you don't have in stock. Otherwise, you will simply be playing the game of "bait and switch," which is illegal and highly unethical.

You can use direct mail by sending out letters and brochures to lists of people in your own area. You can rent or buy such lists either from computer stores in your area, list brokers or computer publications. Mailed at the rate of 20 to 30 a day, they should start getting you customers in no time.

Emphasize the low cost of your service compared to the price it would cost your potential customers to run their own ads, take or make phone calls, etc. Once customers have tried your service, they'll refer you to friends and associates, especially if they have been satisfied with results themselves.

UNIQUE BUSINESS APPROACH

There are a few approaches you can try that will really make this business pay off for you.

The first is to offer seminars on the appraisal of used computer equipment. You can offer to show people what to look for when buying used computers, how to value them, how to check them over, etc. Since you will have become an expert yourself in this area, a seminar can be a great way to generate new business. You can give talks at computer user group meetings, business seminars or simply open-to-the-public seminars. This last place will require that you run your own ads to generate an audience, but you can charge to hold the seminar and make a sideline income.

You can also work through computer store owners. Say they have a customer who wants to buy a new system, but the hold-up is that he first wants to sell his old system. By working with you, a computer store can offer your service at no charge to the customer. You might consider giving a discount to dealers, since they could potentially supply you with a multitude of listings. And, in exchange, they can make their sale.

Another option you have is to put out a "Blue Book" of computer values. Since you will quickly become an expert in the pricing of used computer equipment, it is a natural to publish a guide for others wanting to know how to appraise the value of their equipment or that which they are considering buying. You can publish quarterly or yearly and sell the book not only locally, but nationally, either through the mail, through bookstores or through magazine distributors. This method of business will take time to get started, but ultimately it can make you more money than any other method listed. You can become the last word in evaluating the price of used computer equipment.

LOCATION and MARKET BASE

The best location to operate this business is in a city with a market base of 50,000 to 200,000 people. This will give you the market you need to make this business a success on a local level.

TO SUM UP

A used computer broker business is a great opportunity right now. Nobody else is doing it yet, and that means the market is yours if you decide to take it.

All it requires is a little organization, and you can quickly become the watchword in valuing used computers. This service has a potential to make you money on many different levels, which means if you want to start small, yet grow quickly, you can.

To put the value of this service in perspective, look at it this way: many people have outgrown the computers they now use. Yet rather than go through the hassle of trying to find their own buyer, they let the equipment gather dust on a shelf. Once they hear about your service, all it will take is a phone call to get that equipment off the shelf and into their wallets—in the form of cash, that is. And you turn the equipment into your own cash as well. What could be easier?

SOURCE MATERIAL

Refer to Section 7 for source material.

No. 157

CUSTOMIZED SALES LETTERS FOR SALESPEOPLE

Most good salespeople don't have the time to contact as many people or businesses as they would like. With this report you will learn how to find the salespeople that will use and need this service, and how to give them an edge in their business that they never had before. This is a steady business and has made some operators quite comfortable financially.

CONCEPT

The concept of this business is to develop customized letters for salespeople. Most good salespeople don't have the time to contact as many people or businesses as they would like to. Customized sales letters are the answer. They provide the "edge" which every professional salesperson needs.

Since each letter is customized to the specifications of the potential buyer, what you are really selling is advantage.

You are providing your clients with a service which has a strong track record of providing high sales returns. These letters have tremendous value if they are accurate and timely. The cost of good sales letters is the best investment a salesperson can make. This is a steady business and it has made some operators very successful.

SKILLS YOU WILL REQUIRE

You don't have to have strong copywriting experience to get started. You will have to know the basics of grammar and punctuation and how to set up a business letter. In addition, you will have to know the basics about any business for which you plan to write sales letters.

It's not necessary to be a touch typist, but if you are, that's a plus, since it means that you have the skill to turn out master letters quickly.

INFORMATION REQUIRED

First off, you'll need to know what kind of businesses use sales letters. You can get a good idea by checking your mailbox. Insurance companies, car dealerships, department stores, banks, credit unions, real estate agents, and charities all use direct mail to obtain leads and solicit sales or contributions.

Next, you'll need to know whether their needs are seasonal or year-round. The easiest way to get this information is to call a few companies in each business area and find out as much as you can.

Insurance companies and real estate agents may need your services year-round, while charities and department stores may send out letters only once or twice a year.

If your business booms, you can get plenty of help from moonlighters. Advertising copywriters and students majoring in communications at local colleges will appreciate the opportunity to earn extra money.

Once you have developed a letter, inserting information from your data base takes only very basic typing skills. If you need extra help with typing, just run an ad in the high school, college or community newspapers in your area.

To get started, begin your marketing by following the techniques recommended later in this plan.

Once you have clients, your paying work begins. This consists of inputting the letter you have written, along with the names and addresses from your client's mailing list, then merging the two to do the mailing.

To do this mail merge, you can enlist the support of a good mail merge program. This software will enable you to use your word processor to put together a sales letter, the merge names and addresses into it to personalize the letter.

Some businesses or salespeople will already have a client list. For others, you'll need to develop one.

You can develop your own client list for customers in one of two ways. You can purchase secondary research from an existing list service, or you can develop your own.

In terms of creating your own list, look to your own community first. Some sources include: county records of home sales, marriages, school enrollment lists, directories, etc.

OPERATING NAME

When it comes to selecting a business name, you have only two choices. You can pick a fictitious name or use your own. We've operated businesses both ways and, quite frankly, we can't see the value of a fictitious name for this type of business.

If you select a fictitious name, you'll have to research it to make sure no one else is using a similar name. Then you'll have to register it, pay for legal advertising, get a new bank account, establish business credit, put in a new phone at business rates, etc.

Just use your own name, then on your stationary add "and Associates" under the name. You will have the best business name you can get, and you can use all the bank accounts, phones, etc., which are already listed in your name. Refer to Section 4.

GETTING STARTED

Now that you have some basic research in hand, your next step will be to develop a list of potential clients. Do this by going through the yellow pages and contacting businesses under each heading you have singled out.

Ask for the name and title of the person in charge of developing sales materials. In some businesses, such as real estate or insurance, this may be a long list, since each salesperson does his own marketing. For others, it may be a single individual, such as the manager or executive director.

If the company has an advertising or public relations agency, talk to the agency as well. Most agencies don't have the staff to produce thousands of customized form letters. They'll be delighted to know about your service.

THE COMPETITION

You can learn a lot from your competition. Contact copywriting or direct mail services as if you were a potential client. Ask what they charge, if they have a mininum, whether they generate their own lists or buy from other sources, etc. Be sure to ask for literature on their firm and copies of several letters they have written.

Another way to find out what to say and how to say it is to analyze the direct mail material which you receive at home and at work. Your instincts will tell which copy is effective and which isn't.

You can eliminate the competition by going after untapped markets. Most big firms prefer to handle large volume accounts. You can make a good living by concentrating on the many small businesses requiring 100 to 500 letters.

POTENTIAL INCOME

Your potential income depends on the number of clients you have, the number of letters you are capable of generating and the amount of repeat business. We know several entrepreneurs who are making high incomes with this service. You can charge to design the master letter as well as to handle the printing and mailing of it.

Pricing is not complicated. Start out by placing an hourly value on your own time. Then add the cost of overhead and expenses, plus a profit for the business. Remember, your salary is not profit. It is a business expense. Profit is what the business earns after all expenses are taken out. Since it is this profit which will allow your business to grow, be sure to pay the business well.

Basic Costs

1. Cost of software
2. Cost of advertising
3. Cost of time spent designing master letter
4. Cost of time spent creating, maintaining and merging mailing lists to letters
5. Cost of renting lists
6. Cost of telephone
7. Cost of postage, mailing supplies
8. Cost of printer supplies
9. Cost of transportation

Overhead

On your overhead list, you'll want to include utilities, business equipment, office furniture, etc. Remember, all fixed overhead should be allocated to each job according to the percentage of time cost. If you generate 3,000 letters a month and one client is responsible for 50 percent of your monthly business, his bill should reflect 50 percent of the monthly overhead as well.

In a practical sense you will price your services based on what the traffic will bear. You will probably want to quote prices based on so much per 100, 500 and 1,000 letters.

One further word—keep in mind that if you use the client's own mailing list or one purchased from another source, legal restrictions and your own conscience should keep you from selling this information to another client in the same business.

If, however, you generated your own data or obtained it from public records, you are free to offer this information to a variety of businesses or salespeople.

How To Be Paid

The standard practice should be one-third paid with the order, one-third when the letter has been completed and one-third when the mailing house and postage have been secured.

We suggest that you collect 50 percent in advance and the balance prior to purchasing postage or sending the material to the mailing house.

MARKETING METHODS

Direct mail, display ads and telephone sales are the best methods of marketing this service.

Your sales letter is your showpiece, so make sure it's a good one. Writing a good sales letter means putting yourself in the recipient's shoes. To do this, just list the services and advantages you can offer which will make his business grow. The rest is easy.

Here's a sample solicitation letter that can bring you inquiries and business. It should be mailed to all prospects in your area at a rate of 10 to 20 per day. And one further word of advice: be sure to mail your customized sales letters and those of your clients by first class mail. A bulk mailing label defeats the personalized approach.

Here is the letter:

> DEAR BUSINESS OWNER:
>
> Could you sell more insurance if you had the time to make more personal contacts?
>
> Sure you could.
>
> But if you're like most agents, you just don't have the time to make as many personal contacts as you'd like.
>
> Mr. Jones, we have the solution: personalized business letters designed to increase your client contact and your "bottom line."
>
> Our letters are more than just sales tools. They provide valuable information and public relations. You can use our service to describe new insurance options, remind a client of an upcoming renewal, wish him a happy birthday, and more.
>
> We can work with your existing client list or develop new sources of business based on the demographics you provide.
>
> We're experienced copywriters who pride ourselves on developing form letters that don't look like form letters. We write bright, zippy, attention-getting copy geared to your special business needs. And because we are small, we can offer you quick turnaround and the best prices in town.
>
> I'll give you a call in a few days to set up a time to meet with you and show you our portfolio of dynamite sales letters. Meanwhile, if you have any questions, I'm as near as your phone.

A variation of this letter, sent on a regular basis to all prospects in your area, will bring results. Be sure to follow up each letter with a phone call. Nothing beats personal contact.

UNIQUE BUSINESS APPROACH

Chances are, if you're just starting out, you won't have anything in your portfolio to show prospective clients. If this is the case, there's a simple solution.

Take several sales letters you have received lately and rewrite them. Make sure your copy is brighter, better written and more sellable than the originals. Once you've done this with several letters, you have "before" and "after" samples. Make an appointment to meet with the businesses or salespeople who sent you the original letters. The chances are good you will make a sale at that first meeting.

Another unique marketing idea is to develop customized letters no one else is offering. One idea we especially like is a line of humorous debt collection letters for various types of businesses. Another is a first-of-the-year letter from a dentist who not only reminds patients of the importance of dental health, but also includes the amount the patient spent on dental services the previous year—for tax purposes.

LOCATION and MARKET BASE

This is the type of business which can be operated just about anywhere. Once you have an established client base and an on- going advertising program, requests will come pouring in from salespeople from out of town as well as from local firms.

If you have an established market base of somewhere between 50,000 and 200,000, your chances of success are better.

TO SUM UP

This business is a genuine opportunity because you're selling something every salesperson and every business needs—increased customer contacts, which lead to increased sales.

There's no limit to the number and types of customized sales letters you can generate. And once a customer uses you successfully, that customer will be yours for a long time. So start today writing your own sales letter to success!

SOURCE MATERIAL

Refer to Section 7.

No. 158

COMPUTERIZED CORPORATION FILING SERVICE

A corporation filing service takes over the chore of wading through and submitting all the paperwork necessary to incorporate a new business. By specializing in this area, a corporation filing system can offer its clients a faster, less costly and more time-efficient incorporation process.

CONCEPT

In this country there are 690 new businesses incorporated every day. With these astronomical figures, new corporations obviously have a tremendous amount of competition. They cannot afford any mistakes, and it is imperative that they pay great attention to detail from the first moment onward.

Often, setting up a corporation gets so hectic that the parties involved find themselves unable to commit themselves promptly to the small details that are so important. When this occurs, the only thing that can happen is that time is lost—precious time that is as good as money.

The laws of incorporation are very clear—there are well-defined rules to be followed in the incorporation process, and any discrepancy will delay the start of business for the new corporation. As each day goes by while details are ironed out, money goes down the drain.

With your home computer, you can offer these new businesses the attention to detail, expertise and prompt efficiency they demand. By being familiar with the steps necessary to incorporate and by having at hand all the tools to get the job done, you can soon be considered a necessity for those new operations that need rapid, precise service.

Your business can either specialize in one state or cover them all. As each state has different incorporation bylaws, there is always room for expertise in any area. By becoming an expert in any one area, you are giving your clients an advantage over the competition.

Much of this business is now handled by lawyers, and we'll discuss how to solicit corporation filing business through them. You'll soon find that there are an endless amount of clients who will appreciate and value your service.

SKILLS YOU WILL REQUIRE

You will have to learn what you need to incorporate a business and how you go about getting it. There are very clear-cut rules and guidelines in each state on how to set up a corporation, so you will find it fairly simple to pick up.

Primarily, you will be collecting information and filling out the proper paperwork, and this is something just about anyone can pick up quickly. As time goes on, you will discover that you have become a valuable resource to your new clients and are educating them about the process.

You should do some reading on the formal procedure of corporation filing. In fact, if you can, buy several texts that deal in the subject. Reference books like this make the job much easier.

Since you will be using a word processor for the majority of your work, you will need to know the ins and outs of some of the more powerful ones. Expect to spend five to 10 hours getting the hang of some of the best ones. It seems like a long time, but the flexibility and versatility you stand to gain are invaluable.

INFORMATION REQUIRED

The first general information you'll need to know is how a corporation is set up. Basically, a new corporation must file Articles of Incorporation with the Secretary of State of the home state. These articles must include name, purpose of the corporation (sales, manufacturing, etc.), number of incorporators, the number of stock shares that will be available, who has authority, who the registered agent is and a number of other things.

The office of the Secretary of State in each state can supply this information to you. There are forms available for all this information, so at the start, gather all the information you can from your state government offices.

Of course, if you are planning on filing for more than one state, you'll have to be aware of the specific requirements for each. Again, you can get this information from each state's Secretary of State's office.

Learn what states are more favorably inclined to the incorporation of new businesses. Nevada and Delaware, for instance, offer tax advantages that make incorporation more attractive. You'll find that this is the kind of information your clients will really appreciate. Even as you receive your information from your clients, you'll find that your specialized knowledge will be a great service to them.

GETTING STARTED

In this business, the first step is to decide whether you will work only in your own state, or also in other states. Whatever you decide, learn what it takes to set up in the states you will work in and get the necessary paperwork in order. Using a word processor, set up boilerplate forms (basic forms which you fill in according to the information you receive from your client) for the information you will need for each state. This will allow you to work fast when your business gets going.

Prepare your advertising (a brochure is always effective) describing your service, and include a sales letter asking for assignments. Stress the time-saving quality of your work, coupled with a guaranteed perfect filing.

Most businesses setting up a corporation will hire a lawyer to do the job. You, however, can do the job more quickly and cost-effectively. Because of this, you should direct advertising toward the law community in addition to the business world. Most lawyers would rather not have to deal with what they consider routine paperwork. Make this your specialty and you'll find that lawyers will be sources of steady work for you.

Once business gets going, much of your work will come from referrals of previous clients and law firms. Contacting firms around the state, and even neighboring states, will bring inquiries and business.

THE COMPETITION

As stated above, much of your competition will be from the legal sector. You can probably soon convince them to give you their business.

As far as other competition is concerned (and you won't find much outside of lawyers), keep yourself flexible. Have as much information as possible about filing procedures in other states and be ready to file there if you get a request to do so.

POTENTIAL INCOME

Your fee scale will be simple—charge a basic rate per job, and if you get some filings that promise to be complicated and time consuming, charge according to an hourly rate you've set for yourself. You probably will have to set your fee according to the state you're filing in, if you work in more than one state, as some of them make it more complicated than others.

If you charge only $50 a filing and handle five or 10 a week, that generates an income of $1,000 to $12,000 a month.

When figuring a price to charge, add up all the costs of the program, a salary for your time and a profit for the business.

Basic Costs

1. Cost of software
2. Cost of advertising
3. Cost of forms, books and publications used
4. Cost of telephone charges
5. Cost of transportation and travel
6. Cost of postage
7. Cost of time spent organizing, writing and filing corporation information

MARKETING METHODS

Direct mail and display ads are the best methods for marketing this business.

Local and area business sections of newspapers and yellow pages are good places to place your display ads. Stress the fact that you are accurate and fast and can handle filing for (here list the states you're qualified for).

Let me show you an example:

> CORPORATE FILING SERVICE
>
> With over 250,000 new corporations being formed every year, your competition is deadly. Every step counts; everything must be in it's place.
>
> With our help, you can rest assured that the all-important job of on-schedule filing will come off without a hitch.
>
> You see, that's all we do. Our entire business is dedicated to seeing that your business gets off on the right foot.
>
> We are qualified to file in every state in the union. Ask the law firm of Smith and Jones—they've turned over all their corporate filing responsibilities to us.
>
> We're here to help you get started. So call today.

Using this as a display ad or direct mail ad will get you the inquiries and business to keep you growing. See Section 5 for more information.

UNIQUE BUSINESS APPROACH

Every corporation must have on file a registered agent who represents the corporation in the event of any sort of outside action involving the corporation. As a means of encouraging your service, offer yourself as the registered agent in your state for the new corporation. Most will welcome the chance to dismiss one more detail, and you can pick up several hundred dollars a year for each business you represent as a registered agent.

LOCATION and MARKET BASE

Location can be an especially important consideration in this business. In any state, a city is the best location, but all states are not equal when it comes to corporate filings.

As mentioned earlier, Nevada and Delaware are two examples of states favorable to corporate filings, so naturally there will be more business there. On the other hand, some other states make it complicated and expensive to file as a corporation, making your service all the more valuable.

If you are working in an urban area, you should have no trouble in a market base of at least 50,000 people, which is an effective minimum for this business.

START UP CAPITAL

Some of your expenses at first will be in gathering information. After you've accounted for the cost of necessary forms and supplies, including cost of advertising, you should be able to get started for between $1,000 and $5,000, including computer costs.

TO SUM UP

Since most new businesses seek out lawyers to do their corporate filing, you'll find that this is a real opportunity for the entrepreneur to take the business away from the lawyers, who are only to willing to leave it to someone else.

There are so many corporations filing every day that this is a tremendous, untapped market in the business world. With your personal computer you have the means to do a thorough, comprehensive job more cost-effectively and quickly than anyone else can. And that means the money you can make will add up quickly.

SOURCE MATERIAL

Refer to Section 7.

No. 159

CUSTOM ELECTRONIC MAILING SYSTEM

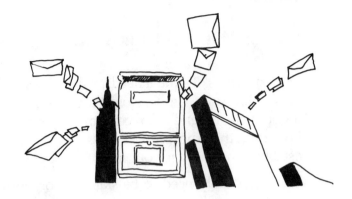

You've heard about express mail next-day service. Well, here's a next-hour service you can offer to local businesses that maintain branch offices too far away for quick service. This is just like a private Western Union, only you can offer the service at half the rates charged by regular telegram offices. You will learn how to set up a network of operators all over the country. This has all the potential of becoming a million-dollar-a-year business.

CONCEPT

In this business you use your personal computer to establish a network of independent operators to conduct an electronic mail service. You use modems and ordinary telephone lines to transmit messages, then deliver them like telegrams, or simply send them locally through the mail.

Electronic mail is a rapidly growing application of computer technology. It takes advantage of word processing software to create and edit the text of messages and uses the old-fashioned technology of telephones to transmit them. Since computers can communicate with each other much faster than people can talk, the messages are transmitted much faster than they could be in an ordinary telephone conversation. Also, they have the advantage of being in the form of printed copy.

You can establish the business in several different forms. In the simplest form, you simply transmit and deliver messages that you either pick up from your customers or have them bring to you.

Or you can accept messages directly into your computer over the phone line and pass it on the same way. In its most sophisticated form, this business is similiar to the computer bulletin boards that are springing up all over the country. Users send messages directly to each other through the medium of the computer network you establish.

SKILLS YOU WILL REQUIRE

The technical skills you'll need are the easiest part of this business. You'll need to know how to use some simple word processing software and how to use telecommunicating software to send and receive messages over the phone lines using a modem. More important than the technical skills, you'll need skill at communicating with people to establish and manage your network of operators and to attract and retain customers.

You'll especially need to be skilled at organization in this business. You'll need to maintain a well-organized network of operators and develop a system of organizing incoming and outgoing messages and keeping track of rates and information to bill customers.

INFORMATION REQUIRED

You'll really need to do your homework in this business and investigate the competition thoroughly. A lot of companies are now offering electronic mail service with a variety of different services and capabilities. Look into the services offered—direct transmissions using electronic mail boxes, courier delivery, postal delivery and international networks. Find out how much they charge—you'll have to be competitive.

GETTING STARTED

This business will require considerable organizational work before you can actually start sending messages back and forth. First, you need to establish a network of operators. The ideal way to find operators is through a computer bulletin board. All the people using a computer bulletin board already have computers and modems, the main hardware needed for an electronic mail service. Post messages on the bulletin boards to attract operators. Your business offers them an opportunity to use their computers to earn extra income.

If you plan to operate the kind of service that allows users to send messages directly to others over your network, you might even start out by offering a computer bulletin board yourself. This will serve several purposes at once. It will give you practice at operating the system, attract many potential operators and gain advance recognition for you and your business.

Once you've established a network of operators, you're ready to start advertising your business and attracting customers.

THE COMPETITION

You'll find quite a bit of competition already in this service, so you'll have to find a special market niche to develop a successful business. The best approach to eliminate competition is to seek out small businesses that won't have a large enough volume of electronic mail to use the larger electronic mail services, which often charge a substantial monthly fee as a base rate.

For example, the U.S. Postal Service offers electronic mail service that requries an initial deposit of $56 for 200 pieces of mail at 26 cents per one-page letter. This service would not be appropriate for businesses that send less than 200 pieces of electronic mail per year. Furthermore, the Postal Service only guarantees delivery of the letter within two days, not within hours.

Charging only on a per-message basis is a big competitive advantage against the large, established businesses that charge a monthly fee. Point this out in your advertising—fast service, low fees, no monthly service charge.

Another approach to help compete against the large, established companies is to concentrate on a regional service—at least at first. Not only is this a special market niche, it will also cost less for phone service, so you can offer competitively favorable rates.

POTENTIAL INCOME

You can expect to earn a medium level of income in this business, depending on the volume of messages you handle. You need to investigate the rates charged by existing companies closely,so you can set your own rates competitively.

When you calculate your expenses, you'll have to include payment to your operators, in addition to overhead and payment for your own time. Since your operators will be independent contractors, not your employees, you'll pay them a percentage of the fee for transmitting a message, not an hourly rate.

Another factor you'll have to take into account when you're setting your fees is the cost of long-distance telephone calls. Your fee for a message that must be sent and delivered in a very short time during the business day will be much higher than your fee for messages that can wait to be sent until late at night when the phone rates are much lower.

MARKETING METHODS

Several different methods are suitable for advertising this business. Direct mail, display ads and telephone sales are all effective marketing methods. Even classified ads in magazines are appropriate if you select the magazines carefully. For this business, special-interest business magazines or a regional magazine would be more appropriate than the popular magazines you find in the supermarket.

If you choose direct mail or telephone sales as a marketing method, regional directories of businesses in your area are an excellent source of potential customers. Here's a sample solicitation letter you could send, along with a brochure explaining all the details of the service you're offering.

DEAR BUSINESS OWNER:

How much time do you waste waiting for the mail to get through? With our new electronic mail service, your mail can be delivered within hours to your employees in branch offices and to your customers.

You don't have to have a computer to take advantage of our electronic mail service. We can do it all for you—from picking up the document you want to send, to hand delivering it.

If you do have a computer, you can send your document to our computer over the telephone and we'll forward it. You don't have to worry about whether the other party has a computer or even whether it's compatible with yours. We'll take care of all that.

No minimum number of messages, no monthly maintenance fees, just fast, efficient service. Give us a call and we'll tell you all about how we can help you join the new age of instant telecommunications.

UNIQUE BUSINESS APPROACH

To establish yourself in this business, you really need to put yourself out. Your potential customers have to know about your service. If you have a flair for getting up in front of people and talking about a subject that interests you, here's an unusual approach to gaining recognition for your business. Design an informative presentation that explains electronic mail and how it's used. Describe the issues to consider — the types of services, charges, etc.

You can send out a special mailing to potential customers, offering to give your presentation to their managers. You can also offer to give a presentation to the members of business clubs, such as the Jaycees or Rotary Club. After a few presentations you'll establish a certain reputation for your knowledge about the field. Groups may come to you and ask you to talk to them. You could even add to your income by charging for giving presentations!

LOCATION and MARKET BASE

You need to be in a city to operate this business. And the city must be big enough to provide a market base sufficient to support the business—in the range of 50,000 to 200,000. Of course, you could operate it in an even larger city. The advantage of being in a smaller city is that you're likely to have less competition.

TO SUM UP

Electronic mail is a fast-growing new service, offering you a golden opportunity to develop an interesting business based on your home computer. Take advantage of existing electronic bulletin boards to establish your own network of independent operators and dial into your own fortune today!

SOURCE MATERIAL

Refer to Section 7.

No. 160

COMPUTERIZED MUSIC SYSTEMS

If you have a flair for music, all you need is your personal computer and this report to become a "music teacher," a personal consultant, or a music customizer for local clubs and businesses. Computerized music has been around for a long time, but few people know anything about it. We have put together some ideas that will expand your mind and give you food for thought and profit. So, music buffs, get in on this unique business.

CONCEPT

Many home computers have the capability to produce musical tones and their harmonics. This possibility opens up all kinds of avenues for creativity and profit. There are software programs that aid a new student of a musical instrument to learn the basics much faster and better than could be learned from an in-person lesson. Instruments like the piano and guitar lend themselves to this kind of tutor. Practice is what most new students dread, and with the right programs even this can be more efficient. The early training in music is not all practice, but is also learning such things as musical notation, rhythms and history. These also can be taught effectively on the computer.

There are composing programs that aid the would-be "Billy Joel" to perfect his skills. You can be the personal consultant to teach the computer skills needed to run these programs. Imagine how you'll feel if your client turns out to be a successful as the real Billy Joel!

Many businesses and groups can use personalized music, especially sales organizations with motivational promotions for their people. You can put together the music and harmony and then record it for later playing. You could also put bits and pieces of various songs together or compose new melodies to suit your client's use. There are even pre-programmed pop hits available for you to use.

SKILLS YOU WILL REQUIRE

Your main job is to focus on the type of business you want to go after and then select software programs that will function in ways that will make it possible for you to satisfy your customer's needs. It will be most helpful for you to have a working knowledge of music and musical terms to be able to make this selection. The other skills you need are simply knowing how to use your computer.

INFORMATION REQUIRED

There's lots of software out there that will turn your computer and printer into a music machine. You don't even need to be an expert musician. Pre-programmed notes and symbols can be put together to print legible sheet music.

There are also programs that will allow you to be even more creative. These utilize light pen technology and writing pads. A light pen stimulates the pixels (those tiny points of light) on the monitor screen to change color by touching the screen. You write music on the screen and then later transfer it to the printer. You do this by running the light pen over the screen and placing notes and notations in the proper place. Then the system works backward from there. Instead of the computer giving instructions to the monitor, the monitor gives instructions to the computer, and finally the printer is told what to print. The pad works very much like this, except that you write or draw on an electronic pad instead of directly on the screen. What you write shows up on the screen so you can see what you are doing before you print it.

Imagine playing a chord and seeing the computer translate that chord into printed notation. Yes, even that is available.

There's hardware available that staggers the imagination—accousticals, rhythm machines, keyboards, synthesized instrument sounds. The industry is bursting with energy and producing some unbelievable innovations. If they're not yet available for your computer, be patient. They probably soon will be.

The printer is very important to you if one of your services includes writing music. If you already own a printer, you must determine whether it is capable of the kind of graphics you have in mind. Perhaps it's one with limited capacity and will do for awhile to give you time to get your feet wet before you invest in a larger or more complex one. If you are considering purchasing another one, always look for software that suits you before you make any decisions about new hardware. The software will lead you to your possible choices of printers. Obviously, speed is important, because unless you have a bank of printers, you can work on only one job at a time.

In many communities there are user groups for your computer. Join one and get on their mailing list. Most of these people are eager to help a newcomer, and in the discussions you'll learn a lot of firsthand information about your hardware and the programs that are out there for it.

OPERATING NAME

To use a business name that is different than your own you must spend some time and money publishing your chosen business name. There are papers that make a living publishing this kind of information, although almost any paper can do it. The purpose of this exercise is to publicly link your name to that of your business name for identification in case of any future legal matters. Use of a fictitious name also means spending extra money on a business telephone and a business bank account. Both of these are more expensive than accounts held in your own name. You can obtain a business license in your own name as the name of your business. On your letterhead and business cards you can put "John Doe—Computerized Music" to identify yourself.

GETTING STARTED

No matter what kind of business you are thinking about starting, the very first thing you should do is sit down and make out a master plan. If you don't have a clear view of where you want to go, you will probably end up nowhere. A master plan includes your ultimate goal and the route you propose to take to get there.

We've already discussed combing the software stores in your area for the programs that will work on your computer. You can use more than one if you find that different ones have application for different jobs. Again, you need to focus on what you want to offer to your customer.

Programs run from $50 to several hundred dollars. Select software carefully. Consider not only the end product but the ease with which the software can be used. There are stores that will allow you to run your prospective program on their computers or will allow you to have a home trial. Take advantage of these opportunities. The store may charge slightly higher prices than discount houses, but they are offering a much-appreciated service. The more that the software you choose fits your needs, the less hassle you will have and the more profit you will realize.

Look for trade magazines that cater to your brand of computer. The ads are worth the price of the subscription. They will give you the names and addresses of manufacturers of software, services and devices that could be useful to you. There may even be articles every now and then that apply to you. The few hours a month spent looking through these publications could save you a lot of time in your business. After all, time is money, and that's what computers are all about.

THE COMPETITION

Your competition is practically, if not entirely, non-existent. Your real challenge is to get to the right people with the right message and you'll have all the business you can handle. Your turnaround time for producing specialized music for groups just can't be matched by old-fashioned methods. A customer can contact you by phone and explain what he wants. With your trusty computer setup, you can have his idea ready for presentation as fast as you can type out what he wants.

POTENTIAL INCOME

Pricing your services is not difficult. It's important to know your cost of doing business. Go back to the master plan you made and begin pricing out everything on it.

Include:

1. Cost of equipment and software
2. Cost of advertising
3. Cost of telephone
4. Cost of monthly expenses such as utilities, rent, printing, etc.
5. Cost of postage
6. Cost of car and travel
7. Cost of dues and subscriptions
8. Cost of your time
9. Any other costs

Start by evaluating your time as an hourly rate and adding a reasonable figure on top of that. Price the competition and see what has been charged for services as close to yours as possible. In the end, what you can charge is a function of what the traffic will bear. If you are performing extra work for a client, you are entitled to charge a larger fee.

Keep close track of your accounts to be sure you are making a profit. Profit is money left after you pay everything else, including yourself.

Make yours a cash-and-carry business as much as possible. The cost of carrying accounts can be large. Carry accounts only for people and firms with good credit. You're not looking for a bad debt write-off on your income tax.

You can expect a low income from this pursuit in the beginning.

MARKETING METHODS

Flyers describing your services can be mailed to homes and small businesses. Many weekly shoppers have a flyer service. They stick your ad in the handout and deliver it along with theirs.

Place flyers wherever you are allowed to post notices. Make tear-off tabs on your flyers with your phone number and a reminder on the type of business on each tab.

The yellow pages of your local telephone company is the first place local people look to find what they need. You must have a business telephone, however, to have a listing in the yellow pages. Compare the increased costs of a business phone with the increased local market you might expect. Telephone information operators do not look up listings in the yellow pages, so the increase in business you might get would only be from those who have access to the local phone book.

UNIQUE BUSINESS APPROACH

Two possible clients for custom music are skating rinks and dance clubs. Skaters need music for special programs, and you can offer faster service than the recording studios now providing traditional music. Dance clubs have the same needs for some of their shows or practice sessions. Get to see the right people and have demos ready to show what you can do. Put flyers on the rink bulletin board.

LOCATION and MARKET BASE

You are not going to need to rent an office. Some of your customer contacts can be made in your customer's home or business. You can set up a studio in your home to have clients for tutoring come to you. Home studios are traditional among music teachers. Even small communities have special musical needs and people who want to learn an instrument.

An area with a population between 5,000 and 50,000 people could be considered a good market base.

TO SUM UP

The flexibility of this service allows you to take on as little or as much as you feel suited for and would enjoy. Expand as the market leads and your time permits.

This is a service with plenty of room for creativity. If you take pleasure in the unusual kind of business, this could be for you. You're your own boss and that means a lot to some people. It's an upbeat business and can be lots of fun. People will come to you for the extras in life, since what you offer is a luxury. The world's your music machine, so go out there and start playing.

SOURCE MATERIAL

See Section 7 for source material.

No. 161

SELL CUSTOM EDUCATIONAL PROGRAMS

Everywhere you look there are educational programs for computers. The problem is that there are very few programs that deal with specialized markets—for example, teaching people the finer points of real estate, construction, ham radio operation, etc. We have found through our research that literally hundreds of specialized programs exist, just waiting to be designed and marketed. We will show you the who, where, why and how of this unlimited opportunity.

CONCEPT

The concept of this business is to sell custom-designed educational programs to independent software publishers, major computer manufacturers, or the general public. By creating new programs, you have the potential to become a software author. The programs you sell will teach people how to fix a car, become a real estate agent, speak a foreign language, or learn whatever they want to.

You can get started virtually anywhere. With a small investment (used primarily to purchase a computer), you can start work today.

The marketing route you choose will depend on the type of program you design, the amount of investment capital you have and if you need additional help to complete the program.

For instance, if you have a limited amount of start-up capital and require help completing your program, you may want to aim your efforts at selling to a large manufacturer. It is not uncommon for a company to advance royalties (for purposes of equipment purchase) to an independent author.

Most major manufacturers are now looking for innovative programs, not deviations to existing software packages. Documentation is also very important. If your instructions are easy to follow, accurate and complete, that will be a point in your favor when it comes time to market the program.

Designing a program is not something that happens overnight. It depends on the individual. Some have spent several months on a program and walked away with thousands of dollars. Who you sell your program to and how informed you are before you sit down at the bargaining table is important. The more you know about marketing and the legalities of selling a software program, the better off you'll be. What sounds like a terrific sum may, in fact, turn out to be a loss of thousands of dollars in royalties.

A consultation with a lawyer may be in order before you start. Or you might read up on the subject in one of the many books now out about the legalities of programming.

Educational programs are one of the fastest-growing areas in software. Professionals and hobbyists represent a large share of consumers, and they will invest in quality software to learn how to do any multitude of jobs or activities.

There is an open market just waiting for specialized programs to appear. You can step into this growing field either full-time or part-time and make a lot of extra cash.

SKILLS YOU WILL REQUIRE

Creativity, originality, discipline and hard work are some of the skills you will need. If you are working in or involved in an area that you feel can benefit from advanced technology, follow it up. As a potential user of the program, you will have a grasp on the need. Consider what your own areas of expertise are. Can you show others how to do home plumbing repair? Can you explain how to write a term paper? Can you demonstrate how to speed-read or sell shoes? Whatever your talents and skills are, there is probably someone else who wants to learn what you know. Since home computers are so popular now, educational software is a burgeoning field.

INFORMATION REQUIRED

Once you've set your course on the type of program you want to write, you'll want to take a trip to the bookstore or library. The more information you know about your subject and its requirements, the better. Talk with potential users of the program. Whether they are realtors, special education teachers, employment counselors or store owners, their views will shed additional light on your work.

Determine what information will need to be included in the software. If you aren't interested in doing the actual programmming, hire a student to handle it for you. That will leave you free to concentrate on the documentation of the software, as well as the business requirements.

OPERATING NAME

As an independent author, using your own legal name is advisable. You may want to use your name and add "Independent Programmer" on your stationary or business card. This will entitle you to use your private telephone, bank account and address for your work. Refer to Section 4 for more information.

GETTING STARTED

You can start today! Begin looking for ideas for programs. Read articles in magazines, trade journals and business publications. Watch for trends and voids that exist.

Some areas you might consider writing educational software for include:
Bookkeeping methods
Remodeling work
Plumbing work
Telephone installation
Automotive repair
Gardening techniques
Spelling improvement
Real estate sales techniques
Retail sales techniques
Sewing methods
Computer maintenance and repair

The list is endless, limited only by your own imagination and areas of interest.

Once you have pinpointed an area of interest and need, don't stop until you strike gold with your program. Ideas evolve, so don't give up!

After your program is basically finished, pass it on to users in the field to do your testing and de-bugging for you. Before you can expect to get top dollar for your work, you must ensure that the program you've done operates properly. By allowing others to test your software, you preclude the possiblity of not recognizing potential problems with it. Potential problems might be the difficulty of use, or with understanding the manual, or functions that don't work correctly. Plan to spend a month or two allowing others to test your program. Although you won't be earning money during this phase of the operation, it will pay off later, once you have made a sale.

Once you've perfected your program and are ready to sell it, lawyers and marketing agents will also be of great value. Solicit advice from them about the best ways to promote and distribute your software.

The first step may be to set up an outline for how you will proceed. Set aside time to work and realistic goals to meet.

THE COMPETITION

The competition definitely exists. An estimate of how many part-time programmers there are would startle anyone. But if you stay tuned into the market and know what is needed, you're one step ahead of the game. An estimated 98 percent of the submissions to major computer manufacturers are deviations on existing games or services. That is not what they are looking for. As leaders in the industry, they want new creations that will accelerate their selling edge.

Don't concern yourself with how many others are spending weekends in the basement working on programs. You've got to believe in yourself and your ability.

Another way to lessen competition is to concentrate on creating programs for lesser-known computer brands. Most programmers try to create software they can sell to only the biggest companies. If you concentrate on smaller markets, not only will you quickly gain an admiring audience, but you'll attain your sale faster and probably get requests for additional programs.

In other words, once you've satisfied a computer manufacturer, he'll come back to you again or listen more attentively to your future plans.

POTENTIAL INCOME

Depending on your type of program and how complete it is, your income will vary. Some have made million-dollar deals, some draw in $100,000 per year. It's impossible to predict what you will make before you even start producing, but the sky is the limit. The potential to become very wealthy certainly exists.

To figure out a profit margin for your work, start by placing an hourly value on your time. Add up all costs of the program (see the list that follows) and include a profit figure. Profit is what you make after costs are covered.

Project Costs

1. Cost of equipment
2. Cost of time producing program
3. Cost of time marketing product
4. Cost of programming materials and references
5. Cost of legal consultation
6. Cost of time spent documenting project
7. Cost of reproduction of software
8. Cost of materials used

You have several ways of making money with this business. You may choose to develop software from your own ideas, then market and distribute it yourself. You can also sell the program to the distributor and get either a flat rate or royalties. You may consider creating a program that can be sold as part of another program. For example, we know of one Texan who created software that will instruct users about the financial advantages or disadvantages of getting married. He sold the program to a software company to include with their package of tax programs.

You may also be able to interest a computer company in buying your program and including it free with their computer systems.

MARKETING METHODS

Direct mail, telephone inquiries and display advertising are the best methods to find customers for your program.

For instance, if you prepare an educational program geared to professional industries, you may choose display ads or direct sales letters to market it.

Place the ads in publications those professionals read. Let them know quickly what your program does, how much it costs, what systems it will run on and where to order it.

A typical ad might read:

> Learn insurance sales on your personal computer! Ten top agents reveal their winning techniques for this high-income profession.
>
> Comes complete with documentation—$24.95.

A direct mail letter should reveal the benefits the user will realize by using your software. Stress the effectiveness of computer-aided instruction, completeness of material covered, cost-effectiveness, etc.

Send letters to prospective clients on a regular basis and be prepared to fulfill the orders you receive.

UNIQUE BUSINESS APPROACH

If you don't want to develop programs in the hopes of finding a buyer, wait until you already have your market. In other words, promote the fact that you can create custom software for any instructional purpose.

If you have a knack for programming, this line can turn into a real money-maker for you. Computer-aided instruction is just now becoming popular. Companies are finally realizing the cost-effectiveness of using computers to educate their employees on subjects ranging from company policy to how to prepare an order for shipment.

LOCATION and MARKET BASE

If you decide to create educational software on a job basis, you should be located in a city with a market base of at least 50,000. In a city this size there will be plenty of companies that can use your service. Creating a program to market by yourself can be done anywhere. You can handle marketing by phone and mail.

TO SUM UP

Designing a new educational program has its rewards. What an opportunity to work independently and creatively! What an impact you can have on the market! There are many potential users of your invention. And there will be plenty of recognition of your work.

The small independent software publishers and the large computer manufacturers are always looking for innovative applications. If you want to create software for companies who order it, the possibilities are unlimited. There isn't any task too large or too small that couldn't be taught by a computer.

This is one opportunity in which you'll have a lot of fun showing others what you know. The fact is, you'll be laughing all the way to the bank. Literally hundreds of educational programs are awaiting discovery. So get started now.

SOURCE MATERIAL

Refer to Section 7.

No. 162

FOREIGN LANGUAGE INSTRUCTION SCHOOL

Many people are interested in learning a foreign language but are not willing to spend the time or money going back to school. However, most people would be willing to learn another language if they could learn at their own pace, in the convenience of their home and at a low cost. The market for learning foreign languages is enormous, and a computerized language instruction business could reap rich rewards in this new and exciting market.

CONCEPT

The concept of this business is convenience. Your business is selling knowledge for people to learn at their own pace. You provide the language lessons and let your customers' computers do the tutoring.

The lessons you provide introduce the foreign language to people. If they want more detailed knowledge, your computerized lessons can provide them with a basic understanding of a new language and refer them to other sources for more detailed instruction.

The main advantage of computerized language lessons is that customers can learn at their own pace and the lessons are relatively inexpensive. By providing only introductory language lessons, you give people the choice of continuing their study of a new language or studying a different language, all at a much lower cost than enrolling in a single class anywhere else.

Think of your language lessons as an aptitude test for aspiring students. If a customer likes the language he chooses, then he can get more detailed instruction elsewhere. If he decides not to continue studying the language he chose, your computerized lessons will have saved him both time and money.

SKILLS YOU WILL REQUIRE

Believe it or not, you don't have to know any foreign language to start your language instruction school. All you need to know is where to get help for each type of foreign language you want to teach, if you should need it.

There are two ways you can offer your business. One method is to offer it as an introductory lesson. The second way is to offer it as a complete foreign language course, but this can be done only if you or someone you know has a good understanding of a foreign language.

The rest of this business plan will concentrate on the first business method and assume that you have no previous foreign language training. If you do know a foreign language and wish to sell complete language lessons, the same principles will apply.

INFORMATION REQUIRED

The information that you need will be knowledge of each type of language you wish to sell lessons for, such as Spanish, French, Italian, Russian, etc. All the information you need can either be found in books or gotten from people, such as foreign language teachers, students, and professional translators.

If you want to get most of your information from books, you can write to the publisher, asking for permission to use the book as a guide for your computerized language lessons. Offer to negotiate a payment for using the book's material.

Another way is to browse through different beginners' language books and study how and what each book tries to teach a beginner. Then use those same methods to make up your own lesson plan. Remember that you are trying to create simple introductory lessons, so you don't have to worry about complex or infrequently used foreign language words or phrases.

Getting information from qualified individuals can be cheaper, easier and more interesting as well. To contact knowledgeable people, you can place an advertisement in the classified ad section of your newspaper, asking for people who know various languages fluently. You can also directly contact foreign language professors, students or professional translators.

Once you have the information-and-knowledge people, the next step will be to create an outline of the lessons you are going to offer. Some language schools start by teaching simple words and phrases, such as how to count from one to 10 and how to say, "I am." Other schools start by teaching the words and phrases that a child would first learn, because in essence, a beginning student is like a child learning to talk.

GETTING STARTED

Getting started means creating your foreign language lessons and advertising your service to potential customers. The advertising of your business will be explained in the Marketing Methods section.

Instead of having all the lessons appear on a computer, you can print most of the lessons in a workbook and have the computer simply act as a teacher, providing the right answers and explanations for each question.

To print out your workbook, you will need a word processor that will let you print foreign language symbols and any special letters, such as are used in Russian. The Source Material section lists several companies which sell such foreign language word processing software.

You can gear your language lessons for adults or children. For children, your lessons should be fun (like a game), colorful (lots of pictures) and easy to use. Adult lessons can be slightly more difficult, but should still be fun and easy to learn.

If you need help in developing your lessons, you can hire the assistance of teachers, translators or students, who will be glad to earn some extra money while you develop your business.

Once you start getting orders, all you have to do is package the diskette you've copies from your "master," along with the workbook you've created, and mail them to your customer.

THE COMPETITION

Eliminating the competition is a matter of reaching potential customers first. Prospective customers include people preparing for a trip to another country, students learning a foreign language, and teachers looking for new ideas for their own lessons.

To reach people preparing for a trip overseas, you can contact travel agencies in your area and arrange for them to hand out copies of your sales brochure to prospective customers. The travel agency benefits because they are able to offer one more service for their clients to prepare them for their trip; the prospective customer benefits because he has the opportunity to familiarize himself with a new language simply and cheaply; and your business benefits by increased exposure and sales to the public.

To reach people who may not be planning a trip in the near future, but who would be interested in learning another language anyway, you can place advertisements in travel magazines, such as the National Geographic Traveler or a similar magazine.

To reach students and foreign language teachers, you can place ads in education magazines, school newspapers and on school bulletin boards. The secret to this business is advertising. The more you do, the more curiosity you will inspire in people and the more contacts you will get.

POTENTIAL INCOME

The income from a computerized language instruction school can grow gradually, the longer you stay in the business. Your initial expenses will be creating your lessons and advertising your business. But once you have created your lessons, your only major expenses will be advertising. You simply copy your lessons on another floppy disk and package it with a workbook.

Once you have paid your initial business expenses, your computerized lessons can provide a steady income. Most educational software programs sell for approximately $30 to $60.

Assume that you sell your lessons for $30 and that you advertise in a monthly magazine with a circulation of 10,000 (a small magazine), with a conservative advertising response rate of 4 percent. Taking 4 percent of 10,000 equals 400. Further assume that only 4 percent of these 400 potential customers decide to buy your lessons (again a conservative estimate, since some people might not own a computer). Four percent of 400 equals 16, multiplied by the cost of your lessons, equals $480 monthly.

Multiply $480 by 12 months and you get a yearly income of $5,760. And that is only a conservative estimate for one magazine! If the profit from one small magazine can bring you that much income, imagine what your profit will be from advertising in several magazines that reach not only travelers but students and teachers as well.

Basic Costs

1. Cost of software
2. Cost of advertising
3. Cost of time spent organizing material
4. Cost of creating and printing workbook
5. Cost of staff salaries
6. Cost of materials used
7. Cost of texts, books and publications purchased for research
8. Cost of postage

Your expenses are largely only the reproduction cost of a workbook, plus the cost of the computer disks. In other words, your profit margin is more than 1,000 percent.

How To Be Paid

In this business you should get a check at the same time you receive an order. If you choose to set up a charge card service, you can either tell people to include their charge card number and expiration date on the order form, or you can have them phone in the order. Either way, you get your money in advance.

MARKETING METHODS

Display ads are the best way to sell this business because you can reach a large audience at a minimal cost. An example of a display ad is shown below. For additional methods and information, refer to Section 5.

COMPUTERIZED SPANISH LANGUAGE INSTRUCTION

Have you ever wanted to learn another language? Does the thought of spending hours in a classroom learning to count backward in Spanish while emptying your bank account in the process turn you off? You've probably told yourself that there must be a simpler way to do it. That "other" way is now available on your home computer.

With Computerized Language Lessons, you learn at your own pace, in your own home, with your home computer helping you every step of the way. It's like having your own private tutor at your fingertips!

Your computer is a powerful learning tool. Why not use it to teach yourself another language?

The above display ad is aimed at a general audience, but by making minor variations, you can direct the ad toward travelers, students, or teachers. Travelers would be interested in learning how a language could help them enjoy their trip more; students would be interested in learning another language quickly and easily; and teachers would be interested in learning how to use your computerized language lessons as a teaching aid.

UNIQUE BUSINESS APPROACH

There are two secrets to this business—knowing people who know other languages, and advertising. One way to do both at the same time at absolutely no cost to you is to reverse your approach and sell English lessons to foreign immigrants and foreign exchange students in exchange for lessons in their native languages.

By publicizing the fact that you are teaching foreigners English lessons by computer, you can generate free publicity and interest in your business. You can work with social organizations that teach foreigners English, and you will be able to write off your costs as a business expense.

In addition, you will be building up a base of people who know many different languages, helping others adapt to their new country and making lots of friends at the same time—and all for free!

Since there are so many immigrants coming to this country, you are assured of a steady source of people knowing other languages. Once you finish writing computerized language lessons for the more popular languages such as French, Spanish, Italian and German, you can expand to include Russian, Chinese and Japanese. The possibilities are endless!

LOCATION and MARKET BASE

Location does not matter since you can do most of your business through the mail. A city location would increase your chances of meeting immigrants to use your service (see the Unique Approach Section), while a country location would allow you to personally contact many students and teachers studying foreign languages.

TO SUM UP

A computerized foreign language instruction school is a unique approach to tapping the foreign language market simply because it takes advantage of the widespread use of computers.

Starting a foreign language instruction school will not only teach other people a foreign language, but will teach you as well. If you have ever seen magazine advertisements offering to teach you another language using cassette tapes, you can get an idea of how lucrative the market is.

If you were ever tempted to teach yourself another language with cassettes, why not start your own foreign language instruction school with computer disks instead? Not only will you learn another language at your own pace and convenience, but you will be making money at the same time. Can any language school offer you that?

SOURCE MATERIAL

Refer to Section 7.

No. 163

INFORMATION RESEARCH SERVICE

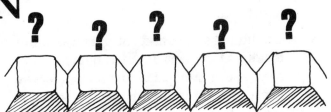

This is an interesting business that can be started anywhere on a small investment, and can produce a sizeable income if it is properly managed and promoted.

CONCEPT

The concept of this business is to sell unknown information. You dig out facts that develop into a body of knowledge that no one else knows. You provide your clients with this information to help them in making decisions concerning projects or ventures they are planning or are involved in.

You are really selling advantage. The information your clients receive gives them an edge in their operations because they know something no one else knows, or learned something others knew but would not reveal.

This information has tremendous value if it is accurate and timely. The cost of obtaining it is the best investment the client can make.

Information research is therefore one of the highest dollar-volume-per-person-employed industries in the world. Price is not important in terms of what it buys. The making or savings of millions of dollars is one area this business can be significant in. Other areas include the ability to do something, get elected to an office or create something that would have been impossible without the information.

SKILLS YOU WILL REQUIRE

You don't have to be an expert researcher to get started. You will have to understand the basics of the business, learn some of the terminology and know where to get information.

If lightning strikes and you get an assignment that requires some real expertise to put together and manage, you can hire to have it done for a percentage of the fee. There is a large supply of qualified moonlighters available everywhere to do this kind of work. Everybody, from librarians to college professors, is happy to pick up some extra money from a research assignment. Notices in college papers, contacts with local library people and ads in the paper for people to do part-time research work will get you a long list of well-qualified people you can call on when needed.

INFORMATION REQUIRED

Information in the research game is classified as either primary or secondary. Primary information is what you gather yourself directly from those you contact. Secondary information is what is published or available from someone else.

When you are starting a new research project, it is best to gather secondary information first. Most of the time you will find what you need has already been done by someone else and is available on a data base.

In terms of using the available sources, you should work from your own community outward. That is, start with what is available closest to home and continue to expand your search until you have what you need. With a little research you will find a lot of data base information without leaving your home or making a long-distance phone call.

Computer data bases are where almost all secondary research will be done. Computers are being fed everything mankind knows, and it can be located and used within seconds if you know how.

There are now data base services available to help you locate information on almost any subject you might be researching. See the Source Material section in this book for more information.

There is some terminology you should understand when you are working with computer-retrieved information. A "data base," first of all, is an index system, like the card file that locates books in a library. A data base locates sources of information, giving you titles, authors, dates of publication, etc.

Another term you will notice when looking at descriptions of data sources is "interactive." This means the data source can supply you not only with the information in its computer, but its computer can call up other computer bases and see what they have to offer. In other words, an interactive source has access to many sources.

When you use a computer terminal to call up another computer, you are "on line." As a rule, you are paying for the long-distance call to reach the computer, plus the charge made by the computer owners to use it. If you find some data you want printed out, you can order it "on line," which means the computer will deliver it through your printer on request. This is expensive. Data travels at the speed of light, but printers run at the speed of a mechanical device. So, it takes time to print what you want. This means you pay phone charges, plus the computer time. If you order the material printed "off line," then the source computer prints it out when it has time in its own office, and the material is mailed to you. This saves a lot of money.

OPERATING NAME

You have two choices here. You can pick a fictitious firm name, such as "Research Associates," the "National Research Service," or something like that. There is no advantage to this, and it involves a lot of extra start-up expenses. You'll need to register the name or file a fictitious name report, get a new bank account, have a new phone put in at business rates, etc.

The best-known firms in the field—Nielson, Roper, Gallup, etc.—are all named after the founder. If you just use your name, John Jones, and then on your stationary add "and Associates" under the name, you have as good a name as you can find. You can then use all the phones, addresses, bank accounts, etc., now listed under your own name. Refer to Section 4.

GETTING STARTED

Getting business is a matter of contacts. Your first step should be to prepare a brochure of the services you intend to offer, and a sales letter asking for assignments. These should be sent to business firms and organizations in your area on a regular schedule.

To find out what to say and how it is done, write or contact existing information research services as a potential customer. See how they handle your inquiry, what they send, how they follow up, etc. This is a free education in how to market your research service.

THE COMPETITION

To eliminate the competition, create your own cash flow. You think up a research project and sell the concept at a reduced price to a number of clients. In other words, you become a research publisher. The only limits of opportunity in this field are those of your own imagination. You can think up almost any idea and decide whether a group of firms or organizations would pay to find out the results, and make them an offer by letter. If enough go along, you have the money up front to do the research. If not, all you lose is the cost of sending out a few letters.

The first step is to figure out your concept. Then organize a plan to do the research for it and decide on the list of benefits. Write a sales letter to those you think would pay for the information, showing them the list of benefits your research offers. You tell them that the cost of such research paid for by an individual firm would be $5,000 to $10,000, but since the material is currently available, they can have it for $100, or whatever price you pick. Ask for the order, and tell them it will take four to six weeks to put the material into report form.

If you get 40 orders from your mailing, you have $4,000 to do the job. If you only get a couple of orders, return their checks and start on your next idea.

POTENTIAL INCOME

Pricing your services is not complicated. You start out by placing an hourly value on your own time. Then you add up all the costs of the program (you'll find a list following) and a profit figure for the job. The total is what you should get for the job. Keep in mind that your hourly rate is not profit; that is what you are paid for working on a project. Profit is what the business makes after all costs are covered. You should earn money for your time and a profit for your business on each project.

Secondary Research Costs

1. Cost of writing letters for information
2. Cost of making phone calls for information
3. Cost of using data bases
4. Cost of purchase of any material to be used
5. Cost of time of moonlighters
6. Cost of time to organize data received

Primary Data Costs

1. Cost of preparing questionnaires
2. Cost of reproducing questionnaires
3. Cost of mailing questionnaires
4. Cost of envelopes and reply postage
5. Cost of moonlighting interviewers
6. Expenses of moonlighters—gas, lunches, etc.
7. Cost of organizing results
8. Cost of checking the questionnaires

Final Report Costs

1. Cost of preparation and writing
2. Cost of reproduction and delivery

Overhead

Allocate costs of all fixed overhead. Each job must pay the percentage of time it costs. That is, if you had 10 jobs in the month and one job took 15 percent of the time, it must pay 15 percent of the overhead.

How To Be Paid

The standard practice is one-third paid with the order, one-third paid when the data has been collected and it is time to prepare the report, and the final third upon delivery.

I would suggest that you change that to 50 percent with the order, and the balance on delivery of the finished report. Some prospects may decline this way, but it is better to walk away than to finance their research for them.

MARKETING METHODS

Direct mail, display ads and telephone sales are the best methods for marketing this service.

I am going to give you an example of a solicitation letter that brings inquiries and business. For more methods and information refer to Section 5. This letter should be accompanied by a brochure outlining your services. It should be mailed out to all prospects in your area at the rate of 10 to 20 a day.

Here is the letter:

> DEAR BUSINESS OWNER:
>
> Could you make more profit if you had tomorrow's newspaper today?
>
> Sure you could—and now you can!
>
> We can find out how you can anticipate the needs and wants of your market and how you can know what will sell best in the future.
>
> You can find out how the market views your business today, and how you can improve their perception tomorrow.
>
> You can learn what ad media, ad message or type of promotion you can plan today for use in the future that will increase your share of the market. The total market share in this area last year was $35,000,000. How much of that was yours? How much of it would you like in the future?
>
> By knowing what your competition does not know, you can build your market share fast; that is what a tailor-made market research program can do for you.
>
> Give me 20 minutes of your time—I'll prove it.

That letter, or a slight variation of it, sent to all the prospects in your area, will bring you results for specific assignments. It will take time, and nothing will happen overnight, but just keep sending letters along that theme and you'll get business.

UNIQUE BUSINESS APPROACH

Now, I'm going to tell you the big secret in this business. You can get a tremendous amount of free advertising by sending out publicity releases with summaries of your surveys or unique information you found, or by making some public opinion polls on your own. The media often like to use stories of public opinion polls. All you need is a creative slant to your information, and you get your name listed in the story as the source. This builds recognition, and you can use reproductions of the clippings in your sales material to potential clients.

Find a book that tells you how to write a publicity release at your library, then contact the media and find out who to send press releases to on various subjects. Some papers have editors for various departments, and each has a deadline and a preferred time and way to get releases. You can find this out by asking. By following instructions, you can start hitting the papers, radio and TV stations on a regular basis. This builds your image and brings in business.

In addition, always send a press release to the media with a summary anytime you do a survey that is not confidential. They will run it as often as not.

LOCATION and MARKET BASE

This is a business that is no better in one place than another. You can start right where you are now and do it all by mail and phone if you wish. It is easy to promote your service and sell it through the mail.

Keep in mind you are not going to get hired by Proctor and Gamble or General Motors when you start out. In fact, there is a very big opportunity in this field dealing with small businesses, because no one is really concentrating on them. By developing concepts and ideas for small business firms, you eliminate most of the competition and build a nice cash flow for yourself at the same time.

TO SUM UP

An information research service is a genuine opportunity. If you start with small businesses, you will have little competition. You can dream up all kinds of projects that will begin the cash rolling in, and expand the service as you wish.

There is plenty of moonlighting help available to make your research valid and well worth what you charge. To put the value of information research in perspective, picture this analogy: every day businesses and organizations go into a room with money scattered all over the floor. Most of the money is dollar bills, but there are some 50's, 100's and 1,000's scattered around as well. Almost all those who enter are blindfolded. They pick up the money at random. But those who have researched the market go in without blindfolds, and they pick up the big money every day.

SOURCE MATERIAL

Refer to Section 7.

•

No. 164

GENEALOGY AND FAMILY TREE SERVICE

Here is a business that is not only interesting, but fun and educational as well. Tracing family histories has become something of a national passion. The process necessitates a lot of record keeping and manipulation of information, tasks for which your personal computer is well suited.

CONCEPT

The concept of this business is to use your personal computer as a tool for the retrieval and sorting of information, and for arranging that information into an ordered family history. Software companies are already marketing products designed to aid you in this process, and information formerly available only in library vaults is now as close as a convenient computer data base.

An estimated 25 million Americans are involved in tracing their family histories. There is a market out there for your service— all you have to do is find it.

Instead of spending hours and hours working out charts for each of your clients, you can use the available software and the capabilities of your computer to structure a family tree system that can be adapted for anyone's family history. From there you have only to gather the required information and plug it in. The end result will be a professional-looking, easy-to-read and complete family history that your clients will pay for with pride.

SKILLS YOU WILL REQUIRE

You don't have to be a seasoned historian to get started at this. You need not even have read "Roots." An interest in historial research and the ability to compile relevant information are the only credentials required.

If you have strong organizational skills, so much the better. More important is your ability to solicit and look for information, and your skill at cross-referencing information sources.

As you get further into this business, you will find that you will pick up many of the skills you need as you go along. You will learn through repeated experience some of the clues to look for when researching a family history, and you will begin to know where to find many of your sources of information. You can use these sources again and again.

INFORMATION REQUIRED

A genealogy business is first and foremost a research business. As with all research, information is divided into two categories: primary and secondary. Primary information is what you gather yourself directly from those you contact. Secondary information is what is published or available from public sources, such as census records.

Start out by getting as much information from your client as he or she can provide. The amount of this information will vary greatly. Some families have long and well-established histories, while others have pasts shrouded in mystery even one or two generations back. You have to work with what is available.

Ask your clients to provide you with a list of all living relatives, accompanied by addresses whenever possible. Even distant relatives, such as second and third cousins, can turn out to be valuable sources of information, often providing names and birthplaces of common ancestors many generations back.

Surnames and birthplaces are extremely important, bcause you can reference the names in census reports and the like, and because birth records are usually kept by municipalities. For instance, it is fairly easy to look up all people with the last name of Applebaum who were born in Chicago between 1860 and 1980.

What you are doing here is gathering all the primary information you can, and then using it to acquire secondary information. A single piece of information can often open up several more paths for you to follow.

Be sure to document your sources carefully, as your client or members of his family (now and in the future) may want this information in order to do further research on their own.

OPERATING NAME

When choosing an operating name for your new business, there are a few things to consider. You can name your business anything you want, provided the name is not already registered in your area to anyone else. If you choose a fictitious name, such as "Majestic Elm Family Trees," or something similar, your sense of poetry may be served, but your pocketbook will be adversely affected. You will need to register the name, get a new bank account, have a new phone installed at business rates – in short, you will incur start-up costs that can be avoided.

The way to avoid these unnecessary expenses is to use some variation of your own name. "Joe Jones Family Tree Service" or "The Joe Jones Genealogy Company" are perfectly good names. This way, you can use all the accounts, addresses, phones and other services you now use, with no extra expense for your business.

GETTING STARTED

Getting into business is a matter of honing your service to the point where it is ready to sell to the public, and finding clients.

As far as learning the ropes, there is no better way to practice than by making yourself the first customer. Do your own family tree. The fact that you are even starting this business means that you are interested, and there is no better way to learn the available sources of information. Besides, you'll learn something about yourself.

This process will give you the confidence you need to open your business to the world. The next step is getting clients and to get clients, you must advertise. For information on advertising services, see the Marketing Methods section.

THE COMPETITION

People can do their own family trees fairly easily. Indeed, some people travel to Scotland, Russia and elsewhere to walk through old graveyards, searching for family names on the worn tombstones. There is some research that the client, if he or she is truly serious, will have to do himself. Your budget does not include airplane tickets for fact-finding tours of the Old Country.

But much of the task of putting together a family tree that would be time-consuming for the individual without a personal computer and genealogy program, is easily and cost-effectively done by your service. This includes the bulk of the research and virtually all of the compilation.

Of course, there is nothing to stop another computer operator from setting up a rival service in your area. But if you are the first to offer such a service, and your clients are pleased with the results you give them, you should have no trouble maintaining a steady flow of income.

POTENTIAL INCOME

When pricing your services, there are essentially three factors which you must take into account. Start by placing an hourly value on your time. Then add up your other costs (a list follows) and add in a profit figure for the job. The total is the payment you should receive.

Keep in mind that your hourly rate of pay is not profit, but a cost of doing business. Profit is what you make after all your costs are covered. You need to be paid for your time, and include a profit for your business.

Here is a list of some of the costs you may incur and will need to figure into your rate schedule:

Primary Research

1. Cost of preparing questionnaires (hourly)
2. Cost of reproducing questionnaires
3. Cost of mailing questionnaires
4. Cost of envelopes and reply postage
5. Cost of organizing and compiling results (hourly)
6. Telephone charges

Secondary Research

1. Costs of letters and phone calls
2. Cost of using data bases
3. Purchases and rentals of materials
4. Cost of organizing results (hourly)
5. Cost of software

Overhead

1. Electrical and other operational charges
2. Cost of work space
3. Cost of materials, such as paper
4. Miscellaneous expenses

The job should pay the cost of your overhead on a per-time basis. That is, if a job takes 10 percent of your time one month, it should pay 10 percent of your overhead.

You should be paid half of your quoted price upon placement of the order, and the remainder upon delivery of the completed family history.

MARKETING METHODS

Direct mail campaigns and display ads are the recommended methods for marketing this service.

Your potential clientele in this business cuts across all social and economic groups. Anyone can become interested in tracing his family history. For this reason, if you elect to market your service with a direct mail campaign, you are operating more or less at random.

This is fine if you want to do it that way, and there are people who will respond to a direct mail letter but not to an advertisement. A display ad in your local newspapers, however, will give you far greater exposure among your potential clients and will cost less than an extensive direct mail drive.

A good display ad should first of all be an attention grabber. Graphic art, borders, one or two words in bold typeface set off from the rest of the copy are good ideas. There are many ways to meet this end. Your message should be short and to the point. You can always use a brochure as a backup to mail to the people who respond. The goal of a display ad is to generate an initial response.

Here is an example of the kind of approach you should use:

> BARE YOUR ROOTS!
>
> Our computerized genealogy service will shake your family tree to its origins. We offer complete documentation of your ancestry, along with an attractive chart you will want to pass along to future generations.
>
> Call today and we will send you a free brochure.

That copy, or a variation of it, coupled with an attractive graphic presentation, will bring inquiries. Once you've done a few family trees, you will begin to benefit from word-of-mouth publicity generated by your satisfied customers.

UNIQUE BUSINESS APPROACH

In doing anybody's family tree, you will come across a great many names. All of us have relatives scattered around the country that we don't know about, some with last names that disappeared from our family trees generations ago.

You can use a direct mail campaign to solicit business from relatives of your clients. This can save you a lot of time, since you have already done some of the work. It is quite easy to obtain from a list broker the addresses of all the Applebaums in California, for example. Some of them will be only distantly related, and some people wtih the same last name may not be related at all. But it's a good place to start when soliciting clients, especially from outside your immediate geographical area.

LOCATION and MARKET BASE

This is a business that can be run virtually anywhere. You can go into business right where you currently live and operate by mail and phone with those clients who do not live near you. Physical proximity to your customers is not required in this line of work.

START-UP CAPITAL

It is not expensive to start a computerized genealogy service. If you have your computer, you can get into business for an initial investment of $1,000 or less. For information on obtaining business capital, refer to Section 6.

TO SUM UP

A computerized genealogy service is an example of how computers can enrich the life of the ordinary person. The painstaking process of searching for roots is immensely facilitated by the quickness of the computer, while the benefits and enjoyment of the search remain.

You can become a computer genealogist with very little prior knowledge of the process. All that is required is your interest and your time. You will find this is a rewarding business for both your clients and for yourself.

In the melting pot culture of modern America the quest for identity has made genealogy a multimillion dollar business. It is ironic to think that by using a computer, you can help people answer that age-old question: "Who am I?"

But it's true. Recognize the value of this service and you're already on your way to making money with it.

SOURCE MATERIAL

Refer to Section 7.

No. 165

HOME TUTORING FOR CHILDREN BUSINESS

With the availability of self-teaching programs for personal computers, this home business becomes a gold mine. Some of the operators we have interviewed are specializing in certain subjects; others cover the entire field. Using computers as teachers has proven to be one of the most effective ways for students to retain what they have learned. We'll show you how to get the programs and the students you need to make this one a winner.

CONCEPT

The concept of this business is to provide a tutoring service to supplement students' educational needs. You can start a service which will help target student's weak areas of understanding.

What you need to do is find a way to tailor your programs around individual needs. Most parents are anxious to keep their children advancing in school. But often they don't have the time to provide personal help with special learning needs.

This is the reason your business will thrive. If you can show demonstrated results by improved test scores, clients will recommend others to you.

And the rewards will be great! You'll know that you've aided the learning process of many young people and helped them overcome obstacles.

The time they spend with your computerized methods will be much more enjoyable than a Saturday afternoon buried in a workbook.

Educational programs are one of the fastest-growing areas in software. For instance, some programs will stimulate students to use their imagination and write creatively. In one example, students can view a graphic scenario that represents a potential story. The computer then prompts them with questions for inventing a story plot based on what they see. It can also offer editorial assistance in structure and mechanics.

There are any number of subjects a student can learn with a computer. Your only problem will be trying to choose which ones you want to concentrate your business on.

SKILLS YOU WILL REQUIRE

You don't need to have a teaching certificate to get started in this business. Obviously, you must enjoy working with young people and feel good about helping them learn. Patience, understanding, good planning and organizational skills, and familiarity with suitable software packages are basic.

If you have taught piano lessons, been a Girl Scout leader or just have children of your own, you probably have all the skill you need to run this operation.

INFORMATION REQUIRED

You'll want to find and read up on what's available in software. Read reviews and analysis reports of what is good and what has problems. Many programs are available that provide different approaches to learning. An informed choice is necessary, so spend time at your local software store trying out available packages.

The next step is to research your market. Talk with teachers at various schools and different grade levels to find out what areas they think most students need assistance in. Also talk with parents and children you know. Get feedback on your ideas. This will save you time and money when you choose which routes you want to cover, since you want to offer a tutoring curriculum your potential students can really use.

GETTING STARTED

Getting business will be a matter of making contact with potential users of your service. Your first step might be to prepare a brochure of the tutoring services you will offer. Since you have already spoken with teachers and parents, you will have a feel for the type of tutoring they need. Design your brochure with photographs (if possible) of children learning by computer. This will give parents a frame of reference to associate your services with.

Start thinking about the structure of your business—the hours you will spend recruiting and teaching, how and what you will charge, what the costs will be, and what your plans for the future are.

THE COMPETITION

Find out exactly what the competition in your area is. You may be the only one who can provide tutoring with a computer. What an edge over Mrs. Marple's one-to-one tutoring!

You really shouldn't run into much competition in home tutoring. This is virtually a wide open market.

POTENTIAL INCOME

Pricing your services is not complicated. You start by placing an hourly value on your own time. Then you add up all the costs of the program and include a profit figure. The total is what you would get for each job. Keep in mind that your hourly rate is not profit—that is what you are paid for your service. Profit is what the business makes after all costs are covered. You should earn money for your time and a profit for your business on each job.

Costs

1. Cost of preparing brochure
2. Cost of time in speaking/sales presentations
3. Cost of a work space for students
4. Cost of software
5. Cost of time with clients and setting up appointments
6. Cost of advertising
7. Cost of preparing and mailing sales letters
8. Cost of time making follow-up phone calls

Overhead

Each appointment must pay the percentage of time it costs. That is, if you had 10 appointments in the month and one took 15 percent of the time, that appointment must pay 15 percent of the overhead.

How To Be Paid

You may decide to meet with the student and parents for a consultation on a no-charge, no-obligation basis. During the interview, you will get an understanding of the special needs of the student. Find out how much time he is able to spend, what hours are good for him, and what goals he needs to set. Then you can accurately plan a program of learning and design a method of study. You may want to prepare a contract for your service for the parents to sign. Either a one-time fee can be paid for a series of appointments, or a plan set up for 50 percent now, and 50 percent when the program is completed. Or, you could decide to use a pay-as-you-go approach and charge each student as he completes his session of tutoring.

MARKETING METHODS

Display advertising would be the best way to gain widespread recognition of your business. Design an ad that clearly defines what you are all about. You may want to use quotes in your advertising which back up your computerized tutoring methods. For example, you might quote teachers who have seen improvements in their students' learning, or kids who are motivated by the idea of spending time on a computer to learn the skills they need.

Another marketing method would be making a presentation. First, you will need to find a group (call the PTA for help on this) and offer to provide a demonstration. Get a mailing list of those who will attend and send an invitation (a brochure with a sales letter attached). Students will get a first-hand glimpse of learning by computer, and parents can witness your programs and see what you offer. Follow up with a phone call.

Here is a sample of the sales letter you could include with the brochure:

> DEAR PARENT:
>
> Could your child do better in school if additional tutoring were available?
>
> Children often balk at the idea of spending their free time with a tutor and a workbook. "Is this some kind of punishment?" they wonder. But what if the experience were enjoyable, almost as enjoyable as playing video games? Of course, they would jump at the chance.
>
> We offer individual programs designed to meet your child's special needs, and that promise to be fun too! With the use of a computer, your child can sit down and work on any problem area in learning.
>
> During a brief consultation (no obligation and no charge), we will create a plan of tutoring which will overcome any areas of weakness your child may be encountering. Improved test results will be your child's rewards.
>
> Within a short period of time we can send your child to the head of the class! I'll prove it!

It will take time to get established, but keep making presentations, sending brochures and letters, and advertising. Your phone will soon be ringing for more information about your tutoring methods.

UNIQUE BUSINESS APPROACH

Product quality and uniqueness of service are especially important to your home business. Since most of your clients will be returning on a continuous basis, it is important to keep them satisfied. Your good service and proven results will get your business off the ground.

Here is an idea that may help you market your service: why not select a student "guinea pig?" In exchange for offering your service, you can use the student's monitored class test scores as an example of how effective your tutoring service is.

First, contact one of the teachers that you feel is receptive to tutoring by computers and ask his or her help in selecting a student who would benefit from some individual help. Contact the student and meet with the parents to make sure they agree to its value. Next, determine a program of study and make appointments for the student.

Be sure to keep a complete record of the student's prior test scores and grades in the area of work he needs help with. As soon as tutoring commences, graph each test score so that you will notice any improvements. Keep this up for at least one month.

You'll want to keep in touch with the teacher constantly and encourage other students to become involved in the student's progress.

After one month, prepare a full-scale study of progress. Exactly what accomplishments has the student made? How much better are grades, attitude and performance? Make this presentation at a gathering where students, teachers and parents are in attendance.

It won't take the parents long to notice just how valuable your tutoring service is.

LOCATION and MARKET BASE

This is a business that can be started right where you are now. You can operate this service right from your recreational room in your house. It is not difficult to promote your service and sell it through the mail.

To begin this business you will need a population of between 50,000 to 200,000 people.

It will take time to get this business off the ground, but don't despair. It is a great idea and has the potential to bring you lots of fulfillment and a nice nest egg as well!

TO SUM UP

Providing a tutoring service for children would be an ideal career for some people. It has plenty of rewards. By helping students overcome any learning shortcomings, your time and energy is well spent.

Your potential clients are all students! You decide if you want to specialize in a particular area, such as math or a foreign language, and decide if you want to work with a particular age group. You can even decide to contact only fourth, fifth and sixth graders, for example.

Individual study programs can be varied week to week, as your students master their difficulties. The service that you provide is customized for each individual.

However you decide to focus your student tutoring business, it is sure to succeed. Since most children today are familiar with video games, they are receptive to learning on a computer. Your client's improved test results will be your most valued selling tool, and new clients will come to your door in droves. So start tutoring today and learn how to make money!

SOURCE MATERIAL

Refer to Section 7.

No. 166

PERSONAL FINANCIAL STATEMENT SERVICE

If you have ever tried to make a major purchase, like a home, you have had to go up against tight-fisted bankers. Well, this service turns those tight-fisted bankers into ready lenders. By applying the techniques in this report, you can prepare personal financial statements for anybody and give them a lot better chance of getting the loan they are after.

CONCEPT

The concept of this business is to create financial statements listing a customer's assets and liabilities. Your customer takes this financial statement to the banks where he wants to apply for a loan for a car, house or other costly item.

What you are actually selling is appearance. A financial statement contains the same information that your customer's tax forms, bank statements, etc., contain. But it is more profesional-looking because it pulls those numbers together and puts them on one sheet to be studied at a glance. This is more impressive than all the loose sheets that make up a financial history. In many cases, it can make the difference between getting the loan and being turned down.

SKILLS YOU WILL REQUIRE

If you enjoy following your own investments or doing your taxes with your computer, or have used an electronic spreadsheet or other financial software for personal or business use, you'll be well-suited for this service.

But even if you're not a financial whiz, you can handle this job with a little understanding of the terminology of the business and a little practice.

With the right program, your computer will guide you through the information you will need to include on a financial statement for your customer.

INFORMATION REQUIRED

A financial statement summarizes all financial transactions that a person has made. Basically, it includes such things as liabilities, income and net worth. It can also list bank information, such as bank name, address, account numbers and balances.

If your customer has stocks and securities or other investments, such as real estate, it will list those, as well as mortgage information.

This kind of information is easy to tally up with financial software. Many of the current programs also allow you to take those numbers and project what their worth will be like in the future—say, for the coming five years.

The computer software will guide you through the information you will need to include on a financial statement. All you have to do is let the computer process it, print it out in a single-page or double-page form, and hand it to the customer. It is up to him or her to take the information to the bank.

OPERATING NAME

With this business you have two choices. You can choose a fictitious name, such as "Financial Statement Service" or something similar. This will involve start-up costs, such as registering or filing the name, installing a phone at business rates, etc.

Or you can simply use your own name, John Smith, then add "and Associates" after it. This will give you a good business name and save the start-up costs involved with using a fictitious name. Refer to Section 4.

GETTING STARTED

Getting started in this business is a matter of making contacts. You can do this by contacting your own banker. Simply ask him what kind of information he would like to see on a financial statement submitted by somebody applying for a loan. This will give you an idea of what to include on the statements you prepare for your customers.

After that, you can get business by following the techniques listed in Marketing Methods.

Once you have customers, you can ensure success by contacting the bankers they are dealing with and asking the same questions you asked of your own banker. Most are willing to talk to you if they think you will be applying for a loan yourself. Simply pose as a customer yourself to get the information you need.

Then you can ask your customers the questions that need to be answered for their individual financial statement, prepare it for them, collect your fee and send them on their way.

THE COMPETITION

The competition in this business is the financial planners people hire to advise them in financial matters. But usually these planners are used only by people who have a lot of money and a very complicated financial picture.

Most people do their finances themselves. Yet they want to get the loan they're after. With your financial statement they stand a better chance. And once they have used your service with success, they'll recommend you to business associates, family and friends, when those people need to apply for loans.

POTENTIAL INCOME

You can make a very handsome income with this service. It is actually a one-shot deal. Your customers come to you, you get the information your computer tells you that you need to do a financial statement, you complete the statement, collect your fee and give the statement to the customer.

Even if the loan is ultimately rejected, the customer will go away with the feeling that he did everything he could do by using your service. If the loan was declined, he may feel it was the bank's fault and not the fault of the person who prepared the statement.

To get an idea of what to charge for this service, calculate your expenses, including a salary for yourself and a profit. You may find that you need to charge only $30 for each statement. With 10 customers in a month, that is $300 you have earned. If people feel that your statement will give them a better chance to get the loan, they will be very willing to part with the amount that you charge.

Your estimated costs for this program should take into consideration several expenses.

These include:

Basic Costs

1. Cost of financial software
2. Cost of advertising
3. Cost of forms and printer supplies used
4. Cost of time spent researching what goes on a financial statement
5. Cost of time spent with customer to get information
6. Cost of time spent organizing information
7. Cost of time spent preparing statement
8. Cost of materials used

Overhead

Remember to include your estimated expenses for overhead. Expenses like transportation costs, telephone use, etc., can add up, and you want to be sure that these costs are part of the fee you charge.

Profit

Also, remember to allocate a profit when calculating your expenses for this business. The profit is for the business. Your time, on the other hand, is another business expense, not part of the profit.

How To Be Paid

The standard practice for this service is to take payment when the financial statement is prepared and either delivered or picked up. Most loan transactions take place in the course of just a couple days, so the work you do will need to be completed quickly. But that also means that you get paid quickly as well.

MARKETING METHODS

Display ads are the best way to market this service. All you have to do is place them in publications where people who will be seeking loans will see them. These publications include local newspapers, home and car buying guides and the like.

I am going to give you an example of an ad that should bring you inquires for more information. For additional methods and information, refer to Section 5.

Here is the ad:

> SEEKING A LOAN?
>
> Our financial statement service can help you get that loan. With just a few minutes of your time, we can prepare a personal financial statement for you that will not only impress your banker or loan officer, but increase your chances to buy that house, car or boat.
>
> And our unique service costs less than you might imagine. Give us a call today for more information.

Write your own variation of this ad, run it on a regular basis in the right publications, and you should get inquiries for more information. Of course, it will take time and a little perserverence on your part. Nothing happens overnight, but with a little luck and effort, you'll get business.

UNIQUE BUSINESS APPROACH

Now I'll let you in the secret market for this service that will guarantee success.

Bankers aren't all bad people. Most really want their customers to get the loans they need. But sometimes bank policy prohibits them from giving loans to borderline cases without having a good reason.

This is where you come in. You can actually get bankers to refer their customers to you when they feel that having a financial statement will help their clients. All you have to do is present your service to the local banks, ask them what kind of information they want on a financial statement, then have them refer their borderline cases to you.

Bankers like to loan money, since it makes them money. This means they want their customers to succeed with loan applications. They will probably be intrigued with your service. And once it works successfully, they won't hesitate to send you customers they think can use your service.

LOCATION and MARKET BASE

This business can be operated in a city or in the country. Even small towns have several banks and financial companies. And there are people who want loans everywhere. So one place is as good as another to offer this service.

You will want from 50,000 to 200,000 people in your area in order to make this service a big success. That will give you the kind of potential customer base you need to get this service up and running.

START-UP CAPITAL

The start-up capital you will require is from $1,000 to $5,000. This will give you the money to buy your computer equipment, as well as the software and other supplies you will need.

TO SUM UP

People hate getting turned down for a loan. Not only do they not get the money they want, but it makes them feel as if they somehow have failed. Using your service, they will feel as if they did everything they could to get their loan. Even if they are turned down, they will feel they did their best.

Since most people don't use a financial planner to provide this service, the market is wide open for you to make a killing in it. The business takes little effort, since the computer will do most of the work for you.

The value of the service you offer people can be measured in this way: when a person goes to a bank to apply for a loan, he usually wants thousands of dollars. For just a fraction of that amount, you increase his chances of success. You put him into the new home or new car he wants. That means a lot to him. Plus, it can mean a lot to you.

The money you earn with this business will make for a handsome income. You will find yourself using your computer just to keep track of your own investments and property. After all, you will want to do something with all the income this business will bring you. And that's something you can bank on.

SOURCE MATERIAL

Refer to Section 7.

No. 167

PRIVATE PILOT TRIP PLANNER

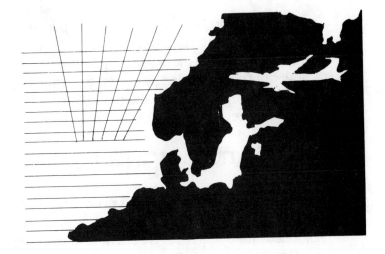

A private pilot trip service provides the private airplane pilot with a hassle-free, up-to-date weather flight plan and pilot's briefing, including printed weather maps. The flight plan can be placed in the pilot's hands and called into the air traffic control tower in a matter of minutes.

CONCEPT

All pilots are required to file a current flight plan to fly anywhere in this country or abroad. This is not always an easy task. It requires data that only airports, FAA Flight Service Stations and weather stations can supply. Weather conditions can change very rapidly, and if the pilot is on a tight schedule, it is often virtually impossible to come up with an up-to-date flight plan on short notice. Needless to say, the FAA frowns on this sort of unpreparedness.

With your home computer, you can supply this needed service to private pilots. While commercial and military pilots have this information gathered for them through their own organizations, the private pilot has no one but himself to depend on.

With a phone line to collect information and a remote printer, you can deliver current flight plans into the hands of a pilot in the shortest time possible. This is a great investment for the pilot to make in terms of the safety of his flight and the best use of his time. You can guarantee an accurate, timely and prompt flight plan to those pilots who don't have the time to do it themselves. By specializing in one service only, you can become familiar with the channels for receiving and distributing this critical information, and you can do it faster than anyone else.

SKILLS YOU WILL REQUIRE

You don't need to be a weatherman or a pilot to know how to provide this service. All you will be doing is collecting data from the appropriate sources and passing it along to your client and to the originating air traffic control tower. Since the data you receive will already be forwarded by printer or terminal, you really only have to make sure it is sent out promptly again to the right place. Your skills will depend on learning where and how to get the flight plan information.

INFORMATION YOU WILL REQUIRE

The information you gather will primarily come from FAA (Federal Aviation Administration) Flight Service Stations across the country. These are federal agencies stationed at key airports throughout the country, and one of their functions is to provide flight plans to commercial military and private aviation. It is a requirement of the FAA that all pilots have an up-to-date flight plan on file with the air traffic controller prior to departure.

Since there is not an FAA station at each and every airport, you will sometimes be receiving your information from local airports who have the information routed to them from Flight Service Stations elsewhere.

Arrange a visit to a local FAA station and see how it operates. The operators will be more than willing to answer questions for you. You will learn exactly where to go for flight plan information, and what a pilot needs to know in his flight plan. One of the determining factors in any flight plan is the kind of equipment the pilot is using. The FAA can help advise you on what to expect from your clients.

You will also be able to make arrangements for flight plan information to be transferred to your home by telephone lines. Sometimes this information comes from the FAA, and sometimes from other sources. In some cities, for instance, pilots (and home computer users) can download weather maps sent through Western Union. You'll find the FAA very helpful in setting up your business, and they will remain a valuable resource for questions you may have.

Another source of information is communications networks such as Compuserve and The Source. They have recent weather maps available for loading into your computer. Then you can simply transmit the maps to your own customers for their use.

GETTING STARTED

As mentioned earlier, visit an FAA Flight Service Station in your area and watch how they operate. Arrange to have someone spend some time with you so that he or she can explain to you the different channels available for transfer of weather information.

Have the FAA station recommend some guidelines for you—how frequently the information is updated, where to call if you have questions, etc. The air traffic control center at the point of origin must have a flight plan filed, so talk to someone there who can tell you what needs to be included in flight plans.

When you are contacted by a client for your service, you will have to find out from him what airplane he is flying and what sort of equipment he is using (pressurized or not, etc.). The FAA can help you devise a checklist of questions for your pilot/client.

Once you have the information about the flight, you'll want to convert it into a flight plan as quickly as possible. After determining departure time, call the flight service station for a current pilot's briefing. Load your weather information into your computer and submit a flight plan containing this information to the air traffic control center. Send (by voice on the phone or by telecommunications lines) the information to your client. In many airports you can leave printed data for him to pick up.

Make sure that when the business begins, you are prepared to receive and transmit data by modem. Know what telephone numbers to call for your information and where to get backup information.

You'll find that soon this routine will become second nature— that's when your efficiency and your customer load can increase!

THE COMPETITION

You won't run into much competition in this business. Most pilots still file their own flight plans, wishing all the while they had someone else to do it.

To get the edge on any competition that does appear, make sure that your information is thorough and complete. If you can supply your clients with printed-out weather maps, for instance, it's going to make an even better impression on them.

One way to keep a steady cash flow coming in is to try to land contracts with some of the pilots who fly enough to justify having you as their permanent trip planner. There are also small flight services that might hire you for all their flight plan preparation. You can offer your service for a lower per-trip rate if you have a long-term agreement.

POTENTIAL INCOME

The only real expenses you'll have, outside of computer equipment, is the cost of advertising and telecommunications fees for sending and receiving your flight plan and weather information. If you use Compuserve or a similar data base, you will also be paying a subscription and use charge.

The fees you charge will be on a per-trip basis, with special rates available when more than one trip is contracted at a time.

To decide what is fair to charge, figure out how much it will cost you, on the average, to gather information (this should be a fairly stable figure). Include a fair price for your own time and add a profit figure. Essentially, what you are doing is adding together costs for an average job.

Say you charge $25 for a single flight plan. If you get 20 customers in one week, that will earn you $500 for your effort.

Basic Costs

1. Cost of the flight plan software used
2. Cost of advertising
3. Cost of information bases used
4. Cost of telephone charges
5. Cost of time spent creating flight plans
6. Cost of printer supplies used
7. Cost of texts, maps, and special equipment purchased for business

MARKETING METHODS

Direct mail and display ads are the best marketing methods in this business.

Most of your advertising should be placed in local aviation publications. Purchase an aviation magazine sales lead list from a firm that supplies sales leads and send your ads to subscribers of these newspapers and magazines.

In this business, a low-key approach is best. Study this example:

> FLIGHT PLANS PREPARED!
>
> We all know that flight plans are not only required aviation tools, but are important to your safety.
>
> But sometimes in the frenzy of getting in the air, your flight plan may not be as accurate or detailed as you would like. Sometimes there just isn't time.
>
> We can offer you the fastest, most complete flight plan service available. We provide weather maps and comprehensive pilot briefings to you on very short notice. We will also advise the air traffic control center of your flight plans.
>
> We can make your business or personal flying easier and safer. Give us a call and let us demonstrate what we can do.

This approach, coupled with an offer to show prospective clients a sample of your work, will bring you business and inquiries. Refer to Section 5 for additional methods.

UNIQUE BUSINESS APRROACH

As part of the service to your first-time customer, offer a free flight plan service. Make sure it is prompt and complete, and follow up with a call to your customer to find out how satisfied he was with your service. Chances are he'll want to try your service again, this time as a paying customer.

Another way to gain attention and business is to offer reduced rates for a long-term agreement. Solicit business from companies in your area that have private planes. Offer a free week's worth of flight planning, then make your pitch for a contract.

LOCATION and MARKET BASE

Either an urban or rural area will suffice as a home location for this business. Since most of your communications will be by voice over the phone or by data lines, any location will allow you to keep the business strong.

The market base can be as low as 5,000 people, since there are airports just about everywhere today. Of course, the larger the population, the more customers you'll have.

TO SUM UP

This business is a terrific opportunity for the right person. Flight plans are required by the FAA for any flight, so the market is there. When pilots realize that they can leave the flight preparation in competent, thorough hands, they will soon make a call to you every time they need flight plans prepared. So start today and begin soaring your way to success.

SOURCE MATERIAL

Refer to Section 7.

No. 168

COMPUTER KITS

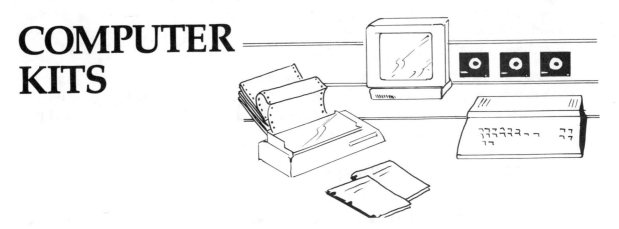

A computer kit business offers the computer buyer the chance to have a personal computer system customized for him. Acting according to a client's needs, the operator assembles the system that will best suit the buyer's applications.

CONCEPT

There are currently many high-quality computer systems and components. The number is so high, in fact, that the newcomer to the world of personal computers is often frustrated by the endless decisions that must be made between components of apparent equal quality. Many potential buyers simply give up rather than try to make choices.

To those who have undertaken such a search, the term "analysis paralysis" brings a nod of recognition.

"If only I could tell someone what I want a computer for, and how much I want to spend," you might hear the buyer exclaim, "and let them do the looking for me!"

With your own home computer you can do just that. Using a data base to keep track of an extensive list of computer equipment, including their compatibilities with other components, capabilities and cost, among other things, you can relieve a client of the trying job of researching, evaluating and customizing the computer setup he needs.

As it stands now, personal computers are sold primarily as manufacturer-specific systems. For instance, if you go to a local computer store, you may find an IBM system, an NCR system or an Apple system. The IBM system may have the keyboard you like, but the NCR has the software you need and the Apple may have the open architecture or accessibility you want.

You can offer the computer-buying public the service that the computer store can't. You mix and match and come up with the perfect system, saving the buyer the time and money it would cost him to make the search himself—a search that might still result in equipment ill-suited for his needs.

SKILLS YOU WILL REQUIRE

You don't need to be a hardware expert to offer this service. If you are an electronics buff or have always found computers interesting, you'll have no trouble. As a matter of fact, this is a job that just about anybody can learn. There will be some things you'll have to know, but once the job begins you'll find the learning comes fast and easy.

For instance, as the business gains momentum, you'll learn what compatibility means in the computer industry. For example, there really is no computer that is completely "compatible" or "incompatible" with the IBM PC. There is operating system- compatibility, hardware compatibility and other degrees of compatibility.

To research this, you will frequently be using information sources, such as the library, manufacturers and software companies. The answers you need are out there. One of the reasons your business will be successful is that the average person on the street doesn't have the time or the resources that you do to find the answers.

INFORMATION REQUIRED

Knowing where to find answers concerning technical specifications and compatibility will be your main information requirement. This is easy to get. Simply write to manufacturers of as many different computers, components, software and peripherals as you can find and request all the literature they can give you. You can get names and addresses from the multitude of machine-specific and general computer magazines. The library will have a complete collection of these magazines, and it will cost you nothing to do your research there.

Find out also how to get in touch with the customer service and support divisions of companies. Many have toll-free numbers, and you'll find that their help will be invaluable when you have compatibility questions.

Another terrific source of information rests in the special interest groups located all over the country. Members of these groups are probably the most knowledgeable group of computer users you'll find anywhere. They love computers and showing others what computers are all about. There are groups for any computer you can name. Local users' groups can also offer a lot of help.

GETTING STARTED

The first step you need to take to get your computer kit business going is to collect and input the data that you'll require. This data will be the information, such as computer, component, peripheral and software information, along with manufacturer— support numbers and any other sources of information such as special interest groups.

Keep your information fresh. Devise a schedule by which you regularly inquire (or are notified) about equipment revisions and updates. The library will always be a strong resource, but you might also want to take subscriptions to some of the more helpful magazines (BYTE magazine is a good resource for this business).

Your data base will consist of records containing information about equipment and specifications, compatibility with other equipment and software, manufacturer and support numbers, comments (including references to reviews, if available) and sources of purchase for the equipment. A lot of your work will be done by phone, so keep careful track of phone numbers, contact names, etc.

After receiving a phone inquiry, you can have your data base do a selective search/sort using the following criteria for example: IBM-type keyboard, 10 megabyte hard disk, UNIX operating system and the ability to run business library accounting software. You will come up with a list of several setups that meet that criteria, along with sources (and perhaps going prices) for the equipment.

Learn where to find your customers. Ads in the same magazines you use as resources, local users' group newsletters, and local newspapers will be the most useful ways to locate clients.

THE COMPETITION

Competition in this field is still virtually nonexistent. There are so many people out there frustrated with the information overload regarding computers, you'll discover you soon have as much business as you can handle.

One source of competition you will encounter is the computer stores tht sell equipment themselves. Most bend over backward to show how they can help a client set up the system right for his needs.

You eliminate this competition simply by emphasizing in your promotions that you don't sell equipment; you simply advise a client on what he can use. Computer stores have a vested interest in proving that their equipment does whatever needs to be done. Your vested interest is in getting the right equipment at the right price and satisfying your customer.

POTENTIAL INCOME

Pricing your services is straightforward. Charge a fixed rate for locating a basic system and alter your pricing depending on the degree of customization. Some clients will simply have you identify the basic components. They will then put everything together, purchasing necessary cables and connectors, software and other items. Others will want you to do everything for them. Adjust your fee accordingly.

If you charge a flat $100 for identifying the proper equipment for your client, you can easily earn $500 and more a week with only a few hours of effort.

Basic Costs

1. Cost of data base software
2. Cost of advertising
3. Cost of phone charges
4. Cost of magazines and publication subscriptions
5. Cost of postage and mailing expenses
6. Cost of time spent doing initial research
7. Cost of time spent assisting each client
8. Cost of transportation
9. Cost of materials used

MARKETING METHODS

Display ads will be your best marketing tool. Make it clear in your ads that you understand the predicament of the computer buyer. You can run the ads in local newspapers and special publications geared to the new computer buyer. Here is a sample ad:

> ANALYSIS PARALYSIS?
>
> BUYING A COMPUTER CAN BE EFFORTLESS!
>
> Don't become paralyzed trying to find the computer that fits your needs.
>
> By now we've all heard stories about the poor guy who bought the state-of-the-art computer for his business and then found out that the only available accounting software did not allow audit trails—the reason he bought the computer in the first place.
>
> Or how about the sales rep who bought a personal computer to keep track of her accounts and discovered that the disk drive she used could not hold all her accounts?
>
> There is no guarantee that what you buy will do the job for you—unless you let us help. We have the time, expertise and resources to find the right computer system for you. And our low fee can save you hundreds of dollars when you make your buying decision.
>
> Don't suffer from "analysis paralysis"—let us do the work for you!

Make it clear that your resources include every available source for any computer equipment, and that your findings must be satisfactory to the customer or no fee will be charged. With your data base, you will discover that you can come up with several alternatives in a few minutes. If you emphasize this point in your promotions, you'll arouse the curiosity of potential clients. Once they learn your service offers guaranteed satisfaction and realize they can't lose, you've made your start in this computer business opportunity.

UNIQUE BUSINESS APPROACH

Put together several systems that would be useful to retail operations, schools, home computer users and others, and send details about these applications out on flyers to the appropriate customers. This will give them a chance to see what your business is about and also will give them new ideas about what is possible.

Remember that most people are not aware that there is anything available other than prepackaged systems. Once you show them how they can save money by mixing and matching, you'll be on your way to winning new business.

LOCATION and MARKET BASE

This business can be operated just about anywhere. You will have some mail and phone requests, but your information-gathering can be done primarily by letter or telecommunications. You'll find that a market base of as little as 5,000, including small businesses, will keep you going.

TO SUM UP

You would be amazed at the number of people who are afraid to enter the personal computer field simply because they feel unprepared. Ask any computer salesperson how often someone comes in the store paralyzed with indecision.

New computer buyers often feel an extreme case of information overload—and you can take the loads off their shoulders. Thousands more personal computers are sold every year, and you can get in on this trend.

Your business is sure to succeed, because you are offering the computer buyer the security of making an intelligent decision on a high-dollar purchase. Your part in this enterprise is simply to find out what the buyer wants, and then offer him several alternatives that suit him perfectly. So start putting together computer kits today and customize your bank account any way you want!

SOURCE MATERIAL

Refer to Section 7 for source material.

No. 169

POETRY-MADE-EASY VERSE BUSINESS

Do you like writing poetry? Have you ever thought about being a professional poet? Now you can use your computer to make a profitable business out of writing personal verse to celebrate special occasions.

CONCEPT

In this business, you write poems to wish somebody a happy birthday, or congratulations on a promotion or any special event. Each poem is unique and personal, a treasure to be cherished by the person being honored. You don't have to have a special gift for poetry for this business. Your secret of success is a computer program that supplies a wealth of rhymes for the words you want to use.

Your clients will supply you with the information you need to compose a poem—the name of the person being honored, the person's age, the occasion, and any special references or items to be included. They'll also tell you the style of poem they want—whether romantic, memorable or humorous.

Then you retire to the privacy of your computer and write the poem. You print it out, using special paper if the client chooses, and present it to the client. And there it is, a unique poem to delight the giver as well as the recipient!

You won't win a Pulitzer Prize for this kind of writing, but you'll have fun, make a nice income, and provide a lot of joy and special memories for many people.

SKILLS YOU WILL REQUIRE

You'll need a flair for writing, especially for rhythmic lines. The computer program can supply rhymes, but you have to supply the meter. You'll also need a creative imagination. Wit and a sense of humor will also be an asset. Many people will want humorous verse.

On the other hand, many people will want elegance and beautiful imagery. For the greatest success in this business, you have to be creatively flexible and able to provide both.

INFORMATION REQUIRED

The bad news is that the information required for this business isn't the kind of thing you can find quickly by going to a reference book. The good news is that you don't need any special education or training to acquire it. It comes from a sincere love of poetry.

Some formal knowledge about poetry would be an asset. You should know what distinguishes a Shakespearean sonnet from an Italian sonnet or a limerick, for example. A standard poetic form gives you a skeleton structure for your verse.

OPERATING NAME

In this business you have two choices for your operating name. You can choose a fictitious name that indicates the nature of your business, such as "Personal Poetics," or you can simply use your own name.

The advantage of a fictitious name is that it spells out clearly what you do. The disadvantage of a fictitious name is that it costs more to get started. You have to file a fictitious name report or register the name, as well as open a business bank account, etc.

The simple alternative is just to use your own name. The problem is that your name alone won't explain what you do. You can avoid this problem by adapting a motto, such as "Personal Poetics" to include on your business cards and promotional material.

See Section 4 for more information about selecting an operating name for your business.

GETTING STARTED

The first step is to get the software you'll need, then to go to work writing some practice poems. Once you feel confident that you'll be able to write poetry on demand for any occasion, you are ready to let people know about your service. Follow the techniques for promotion covered in Marketing Methods.

You may consider creating "Master Poems" into which you can plug names for that personal touch. This way you save time and can keep the masters in your computer to call up and fill in when an order is received.

THE COMPETITION

You'll have very little competition in this business. Not many people have that special creative flair for writing poetry, and even fewer will consider making a business out of it.

People can always buy standard, mass-produced greeting cards for special occasions, but if they want a unique, personal verse and can't write it themselves, they will come to someone like you. Word-of-mouth referrals work wonders in a business like this.

POTENTIAL INCOME

You won't make a fortune in this business. Before you start, you should realize that the income level will be fairly low. On the other hand, you can reap the rewards of great personal satisfaction in doing what you already enjoy and getting paid for it.

You'll need to set a standard rate for a standard poem. Time yourself as you practice using your rhyming software and figure out how long it takes you to complete a poem of a given length and type. Then you'll have an idea of how much to charge for your service, based on how long it takes you.

A good approach is to set a flat rate for poems of a given type. You could charge much more for a lyrical sonnet, for example, than for a humorous limerick.

Once you have your rhyming software and computer equipment, your overhead will be very low.

Basic Costs

1. Cost of software
2. Cost of advertising
3. Cost of time spent creating poetry
4. Cost of telephone expenses
5. Cost of special paper supplies and other supplies used

MARKETING METHODS

Several different methods would be effective for marketing this service. Display ads or flyers would be good, particularly if placed in locations and publications that appeal to people who are gift-shopping.

Your display ads or flyers can include an example of your work. Just like a craftsman who offers handmade lace or pottery, you have to show off your wares. Here's an example of the kind of verse you could write for your display ads or flyers.

Personal Poems for Special People

How often do you find a card in verse
That really says what you want it to say,
A special greeting for a wonderful day?
An ordinary message, whether terse

Or long, can never tell that special way
You feel about a person, come what may.
The searching is enough to make you curse!
Forget those humdrum cards and look around.
A poem can be made to celebrate
Those special moments you remember clear.
A new and different service you have found:
Tell me the subject—we'll collaborate,
Producing special verse, a job to hear!

Personal poems, specially written occasions. Short or long, humorous or sincere.

It's not prize-winning poetry, but it's eye-catching. See what you can come up with that expresses your own individual style. You should probably avoid saying anything about using a computer for this service. Many people think of computers as mechanical and impersonal and would not expect anything unique or personal from one. Let the computer be your own secret.

Another alternative for marketing is classified ads in newspapers. You won't want to advertise in a regular daily paper—the rates are so expensive, they'd soon eat up your profits. But in many areas of the country there are give-away weekly papers that offer free classified ads. If there is such a paper in your area, you should definitely take advantage of it.

UNIQUE BUSINESS APPROACH

As a way to establish an active source of referrals for your service, contact agencies that deliver singing telegrams or balloon-a-grams for special occasions. These companies have become very popular and successful recently, especially with people who are looking for a unique and entertaining way to send a special greeting. Those are exactly the people you want to interest in your business.

In general, these "telegrams" are entertaining productions— delivered by a waltzing bear or a belly dancer. The actual "telegram" is often just an excuse for the event. Take your display ads or flyers to these agencies and offer to take on the challenge of writing unique poems for these special telegrams.

LOCATION and MARKET BASE

You can get into this business just about anywhere, in the city or in the country. This is definitely a business you would operate out of your own home, not from an expensive office. It doesn't matter where you live, as long as you're close enough to a market base big enough to support it.

To be successful at this business you'll need a market base in the range of 5,000 to 50,000. Of course, if you live in or near a large city, that's a bonus for you—you'll have an even bigger audience for your service.

START UP CAPITAL

You can start this business on a very limited budget, once you have your computer and printer. The software, an assortment of special, high-quality paper for printing your poems, and the cost of preparing your promotional materials will cost less than $1,000. See Section 6 for suggestions about obtaining start-up capital for your business.

TO SUM UP

If you are creative and have a flair for writing poetry, this could be an interesting and challenging business for you. It won't pay you a lot of money, but the rewards can be great. Why not set about putting your talents to work earning a nice sideline income?

Poetry writing ain't for everyone;
For others it's a barrel of fun.
From beautiful verse to unrhymed trash,
This is a line that'll bring you the cash.
So start it today,
And you'll get it to pay!

SOURCE MATERIAL

Refer to Section 7.

No. 170

START AND OPERATE A COMPUTER CLUB

This is an idea that can be not only profitable, but fun. Its concept is borrowed from that of other clubs which bring together people with similar interests. You can organize a group of computer enthusiasts in your area, charge a reasonable membership fee, and offer services and items at lower prices than are available in the mainstream market.

Over one million personal computers will be sold during the coming year. For each buyer there are several other people who are interested. That's a lot of potential membership.

CONCEPT

Being the operator of a computer club for profit is not a new concept. There are clubs of all varieties—travel clubs, game clubs, health clubs, you name it—all over the country. Many of these bring in handsome profits for their organizers.

A computer club can offer a lot to its members for a very reasonable membership fee. One thing it can offer is information. Much software is in the public domain and is available at no charge. You can list this information in a newsletter and make it accessible to club members. You can also list available publications, business opportunities, instruction courses and anything else your members want to know about.

Another type of service a club can facilitate is discount distribution software. Suppose your club has 25 members who want to buy a certain program. You can order the software in quantity from a dealer at a greatly reduced price, take your markup, and still sell it to your membership at a price substantially lower than if each person had purchased it individually.

Basically, a computer club can offer its membership any service that a computer can perform, at a group rate. As operator of the club, you serve as the intermediate between the hardware and software companies, and your club's membership. You can also set up instruction programs, referral services and communication networks, which benefit you and your membership alike.

As you can see, running a computer club is a very creative undertaking. The only limit to what you can do is your imagination.

SKILLS YOU WILL REQUIRE

The heart of any computer club is its electronic communications network. Members need to be able to "talk" to one another through their computer systems, in order to exchange information that the club makes available. You will need to know how to set up and operate a modem-based communications network to enable your members to do this.

This is not as difficult as it sounds. There are communications programs available; once you have yours installed, it takes very little effort to maintain it. Your local computer store undoubtedly has literature on the subject that can help you in getting started.

You will need to be a good organizer. A well-organized computer club will thrive and grow; a disorganized one will dissolve into chaos. One of the things you can do is put out a monthly newsletter and mail it to your membership. Electronic bulletin boards are fine, but it's a good idea to keep your membership informed of club activities, whether they are logged on to their computers or not.

INFORMATION REQUIRED

Access to information is one of the major reasons people will want to become members of your club. You will need to keep abreast of many computer-related subjects in order to provide your members with the information they seek. One of the functions of your club will be that of a type of courier service, shepherding information from its primary sources to the large communication network of your club.

There are many publications available that detail new software on the market, and new services and data base information that computer operators can use. You will probably want to budget part of your operation money to subscribe to a few key periodicals, since these are often the first source of information on new material and services.

Find out all you can about existing computer clubs, the services they offer, and their methods of operation before you start your own. The information networks of these clubs are often accessible to non-members, sometimes for a fee. Send away for information on one or two clubs, as a prospective member. This a good way to gain insight into how your computer club might operate.

OPERATING NAME

Something simple is your best bet here. "The (name of your city) Computer Club" is about as simple as you can get, and it will work as well as any other name. Of course, you could name the club after yourself. There are some advantages to this. "The Joe Jones Computer Club" could be run using the phones, addresses and bank accounts now used by Joe Jones. The disadvantage to this is that if you are really successful, the club you start may well outlive your stewardship. A few years down the road, it may be a tremendously profitable operation and you may want to sell the operation and move on to something else. While many clubs are named after their founders, you will want to separate your own finances from those of the club. You can go either way—the choice is up to you.

GETTING STARTED

Starting a computer club is a matter of enlisting members. As previously mentioned, there are several computer clubs already in existence; they are excellent sources of information when you are starting out.

One of the first things you need to do is to decide on the services you intend to offer your membership. You then need to advertise for members (see Marketing Methods). One way to determine what kinds of services computer operators in your community would want from a club is a questionnaire. Most software outlets will cooperate in placing copies of your questionnaire on their counters. From the results, you can find out in advance what kinds of services are in demand and plan your operation accordingly.

Don't be too ambitious at first. It takes time for any organization to build membership, and it is a mistake to break the bank by offering more services than the membership can support. As you add members you can add services. Have a plan. Be able to specify what new features you will offer as certain levels of membership are reached. Not only is this approach an incentive for new members to join, it is an incentive for members who want the extra services to help you in recruiting new members.

POTENTIAL INCOME

There are two ways to make money in this business. One is through membership fees; the other is through sale of software in quantity at reduced prices.

Obviously, the more members you have, the more money you can make. Start out by determining the minimum services you want your club to be able to offer. Determine the cost of providing those services. Next, determine the minimum membership for which you can afford to provide this basic service. Divide the cost of the minimum service by the minimum number of members and the result is what you should charge for membership.

As you expand, you will generate profit from the additional membership fees. As you expand even more, you will begin to be able to provide additional services while keeping your profit margin intact.

Determining your membership fees in this manner means that when you begin buying software in quantity and distributing it to your club members at well below retail value (but above what you pay for it), the money you make in this area of your operation is applied to your profit.

Here is a list of costs you will need to take into account when determining your membership fees:

1. Cost of operating your computer equipment
2. Cost of research and information, including subscriptions, use of data bases, etc.
3. Telephone charges
4. Cost of advertising for new members
5. Cost of generating support material, such as a club newsletter
6. Cost of postage and envelopes
7. Cost of your time

This last item is important. You will want to budget in a salary for yourself as operator of the club. This should be counted as a cost of doing business, not as coming out of the club's profits.

In addition to the costs listed above, you will want to establish a budget category labeled "Miscellaneous." In a business such as this there are always unforeseen expenses and you will want to be prepared for them. You may have to travel across town or further some weekend in order to promote the club. Or you might want to hire a graphic artist to jazz up the masthead of your newsletter. Budget in this extra money at the start of your operation.

Most important, keep in mind the inevitable fact that it is going to take time before you are really making money at this. It may take several weeks just to get your minimum membership. Publicity is the key. Once your club becomes known, there will be no shortage of potential members and you can begin expanding your services. As you expand, a snowball effect begins, with new services attracting new members and the increased membership enabling you to add still more services, which attracts still more new members and so on.

MARKETING METHODS

Direct mail and display ads will be the most effective ways of marketing your new business.

If there is a publication in your area that many computer enthusiasts read, a display ad will bring quite a few inquiries. Failing that, you will still be able to generate some interest with an eye-catching display ad in one or more of your local newspapers.

On the other hand, a direct mail campaign can be aimed more specifically at your target membership. Computer stores and software outlets in your area will be able to provide you with mailing lists of their customers and you can take it from there. Many of these customers will be recent computer buyers, eager to tie in with an organization such as yours for the obvious educational benefits. Others will be relatively skilled computer operators looking for services and materials at a lower cost than they are accustomed to paying.

Here is an example of a letter you might use to promote your club to owners of personal computers. Send these letters out at a steady rate (20–40 per day is manageable) and watch the inquiries pour in.

Here is the letter:

> HELLO COMPUTER ENTHUSIASTS!
>
> Let me be the first to welcome you to the Anytown Computer Club. It is my pleasure to invite you to become a member of our new and growing organization.
>
> For a low monthly membership fee of $2, you gain access to our ever-expanding electronic information network, discounts on popular software and much much more! Our electronic bulletin board keeps you informed on the latest happenings in the world of computers. Plus you will receive our monthly newsletter, which details the services and activities we plan to offer in the future.
>
> Join now—the money you save will be your own.

Give an address and phone number and be ready to answer all questions as completely as you can. You may want to prepare a detailed list of your services and send it out with your letter on a separate piece of paper, or you may opt to send it to people who respond to the initial mailing.

UNIQUE BUSINESS APPROACH

There is nothing like free publicity. A single newspaper story can sometimes do more for a new business than a week of advertisements.

Talk to the media. Newspapers, in particular, are always looking for feature material, and a new business with any novelty at all is considered a ripe subject. A brief press release with your name and phone number on it will usually bring a response.

But don't limit yourself to newspapers. See if you can get yourself on the local television news or local talk show. Computers are hot right now, and the media want to capitalize on this interest. All it will cost you is a little time.

The biggest advantage to media exposure is that it is talked about in a way that advertisements rarely are. "Did you see so and so on TV last night?" is a regular staple of conversation. Even people who don't see you will hear about you, and this factor will give your subsequent advertisements the added value of audience recognition.

LOCATION and MARKET BASE

A computer club can be started anywhere there are computer operators interested in joining one. To make a profit, you should live in an area with at least 50,000 people in the general vicinity. This is probably the smallest market base that can make such an operation profitable.

TO SUM UP

Being the operator of a computer club can be a challenging and enjoyable way to make money. It can also be an education, because it will bring you into contact with computer operators whose knowledge and backgrounds will vary greatly.

You can offer your member access to information and price discounts that would not be available to them under ordinary circumstances. Your club can offer them a valuable network of information on new projects, ideas and moonlighting work available for the personal computer owner. By selling this information to an eager membership at an affordable cost, you can turn your club into a profitable operation for all its members, including yourself.

SOURCE MATERIAL

Refer to Section 7.

No. 171

CUSTOM COMPUTER POSTER SERVICE

Here's a simple business that takes only your personal computer and a printer to operate. There are enough special occasions and stores with special promotions to keep your printer running night and day. We will show you how to contact people interested in this service. You will find there is no competition because nobody else can compete with your prices and obtain the same quality results.

CONCEPT

The concept of this business is to offer layout preparation and speedy printing of posters, flyers and banners with your computer system. Businesses which advertise by mail or that need display signs and posters can use your graphics capabilities. Personalized cards, such as for birthdays, thank you notes and new addresses are a part of the service you can offer. Individuals looking for unique special—occasion gifts would be delighted to know there are places that make up "Happy Occasion" custom banners.

SKILLS YOU WILL REQUIRE

Your main job is to have your computer manipulate information supplied by customers to produce printed materials, posters, banners and the like. The skills you will require are those that have to do with the use of the computer itself and can be learned easily.

INFORMATION REQUIRED

There's plenty of software available that will turn your computer and printer into a graphic arts machine. You don't even need to be an artist. These programs have ready-made letters in a number of styles and sizes. They may have pre-programmed pictures, as well as birthday cakes, Christmas decorations, music symbols, happy faces, etc. You simply select size and placement, and the computer and printer do the rest.

There are also programs that will allow you to be even more creative to design your own graphics. These utilize light pen technology and writing pads. A light pen stimulates the pixels (those tiny points of light) on the monitor screen to change color and design by touching the screen. In other words, you form a letter or picture on the screen by running the light pen over it. The system works backward from there. Instead of the computer giving instructions to the monitor, the monitor gives instructions to the computer, and then the printer is told what to print. The pad works very much like this, except that you write or draw on an electronic pad instead of directly on the screen. What you write shows up on the screen, so you can see what you are doing before you print it.

The printer is very important to you since your product is printed material. If you already own a printer, you must determine whether it is capable of the kind of graphics you will want to create. Perhaps it's one with limited capacity and will do for awhile to give you time to get your feet wet before you invest in a larger or more complex system. If you are considering purchasing another one, things to consider are: speed, width of carriage, and graphics capabilities.

Always look for software that suits your needs before you make any decision about new hardware. The software will lead you to your possible choices of printers. Obviously, speed is important, because unless you have a bank of printers, you can work on only one job at a time. You may want to consider a printer that prints wider than the usual 80 columns. They are available, but are more expensive. There are even printers that print in multicolor. These sophisticated printers can be purchased later on if you find them appealing.

You can purchase colored computer paper and colored ribbons for nearly all printers. For very little investment you can jazz up your product with color and charge a premium price.

In many communities there are user groups for your computer. Join one and get on the mailing list. Most of the members will be eager to help a newcomer, and in the discussions you'll learn a lot of first-hand information about your hardware and the programs that are available for it.

GETTING STARTED

No matter what kind of business you are thinking about starting, the very first thing you should do is sit down and make out a master plan. If you don't have a clear view of where you want to go, you'll probably end up nowhere. A master plan includes your ultimate goal and the route you propose to take to get there. Your goals should be written in concrete and your working plan written in sand. It is like taking a long trip and finding road blocks or a bad road; you don't cancel your trip, you simply change your route. Treat your business like a business. No successful corporation would think of proceeding without having goals and plans written down—and neither should you.

We've already discussed combing the software stores in your area for the programs that will work on your computer. You can use more than one if you find some have applications for different jobs. If you can find a comprehensive one, however, you'll save yourself a lot of time and confusion by buying a single expensive program rather than several cheaper ones.

Programs run from $50 to several hundred dollars. Select software carefully. Consider not only the end product but the ease with which the software can be used. There are stores that will allow you to run your prospective program on their computer or will allow you to take it home for trial. Take advantage of these opportunities. The store may charge slightly higher prices than discount houses, but they are offering a very useful service. The more the software you choose fits your needs, the less hassle you will have and the more profit you will realize.

Look for trade magazines that cater to your brand of computer. The ads are worth the price of the subscription. They will give you the names and addresses of manufacturers of software, services and devices that could be useful to you. There may even be articles every now and then that apply to you. The few hours a month spent looking through these publications could save you a lot of time in your business. After all, time is money, and that's what computers are all about.

THE COMPETITION

Your competition for banners and posters are sign-painting companies. They are very expensive and slow. One of the fabulous things about this business is that your turnaround time cannot be matched by old-fashioned methods. A customer can contact you by phone and explain what he wants. With your trusty computer setup, you can have his idea ready for the printer as fast as you can type out what he wants. While your faithful printer is plugging along at it's assignment, you can be designing your next job or taking a brief siesta.

Your competition for the flyer business is graphic artists, but they work by the hour and are not cheap. Doing lettering the old cut-and-paste way is time-consuming and thus expensive.

POTENTIAL INCOME

Pricing your services is not difficult. It's important to know your cost of doing business. Go back to the master plan you made and begin pricing out everything on it.

Basic Costs

1. Cost of equipment, software, etc.
2. Cost of advertising
3. Cost of telephone

4. Monthly recurring costs—utilities, rent, etc.
5. Cost of postage
6. Cost of car and travel
7. Cost of dues and publications
8. Cost of your time
9. Costs of materials used

Start by evaluating your time as an hourly rate and adding a reasonable figure on top of that for profit. Price the competition and see what has been charged for this type of service. In the end, what you can charge is a function of what the traffic will bear. If you are performing extra work for a client, you are entitled to charge a larger fee.

Keep close track of your accounts to be sure you are being paid promptly and are making a profit. Profit is money left after you pay everything else, including yourself.

Make yours a cash-and-carry business as much as possible. The cost of carrying accounts can be large. Carry accounts only for people and firms with good credit. You're not looking for a bad debt write-off on your income tax.

If you charge a store $10 per poster created and make up 10 posters, you will have earned $100. Since this work will take very little of your time by using your computer, you could easily earn from $300 to $500 a week with a part-time effort.

MARKETING METHODS

Flyers describing your services can be mailed to homes and small businesses. Many local classified ad papers have a flyer service. They stick your ad in the handout and deliver it along with theirs.

A typical flyer might read:

> LET US DO YOUR ARTWORK FOR YOU!
>
> We design posters, flyers, banners, cards and ads at a price that can't be beat anywhere else in town.
>
> We can print up as many copies of your artwork as you need and give you the fast turnaround time only a small business can offer. Contact us today to learn what we can do for you tomorrow!

Place flyers wherever you are allowed to post notices. Make tear-off tabs on your flyers with your phone number and a reminder of the type of business on each tab.

Personalized direct mail would be useful as well. Here's where you can use a word processor. Personalized mail will appeal to potential customers. Don't be reluctant to send more than one mailing to each potential customer. The more they read, hear and see your business name, the more likely they are to consider contacting you when they need a poster created.

The yellow pages of your local telephone company is the first place local people look to find what they need. You must have a business telephone to have a listing in the yellow pages, though. Compare the increased costs of a business phone with the increased local market you might expect. Telephone information operators do not look up listings in the yellow pages, so the increase in business you might get would be only from those who have access to the local phone book.

UNIQUE BUSINESS APPROACH

Every major community has a yellow pages directory crammed with listings under "Singing Telegrams." Your products can form a happy marriage with the festive musical messages delivered by these people. Contact the owners or managers and propose an arrangement that will be mutually profitable. The messenger can not only sing a song but can leave a banner to be enjoyed later. You are expanding the service he can offer. At the same time, you are opening up new avenues for your banner sales without spending advertising dollars.

LOCATION and MARKET BASE

You are not going to need to rent an office. You can conduct your service by mail, in person and over the phone.

An area of population between 50,000 and 200,000 people could be considered a good market base. As long as the phone company and the post office serve your home, any location would be a reasonable market base.

START UP CAPITAL

The cost of starting your business could be under $1,000. A lot depends upon how much equipment you already own.

The capital equipment items are:

Computer
Printer
Software
Monitor
Disk drive
Answering machine as needed

The other expenses could include:

Business cards
Forms, invoices, etc.

See Section 6 for obtaining the needed capital.

TO SUM UP

The flexibility of this printing service allows you to take on as little or as much business as you feel suited. Expand as the market leads and your time permits.

This is a service with plenty of room for creativity, both in the end product and in the methods of marketing. You're your own boss. That means a lot to some entrepreneurs.

This can be an exciting business, because you are dealing with enthusiastic, forward-looking people seeking new and better methods to promote and earn profits. Individuals who use your service are anticipating a happy celebration for friends or family or a whiz-bang store promotion. You are helping to make that special happening something really special. It's an up-beat business that can be lots of fun. The world's your banner, so get out there and start waving it.

SOURCE MATERIAL

See Section 7.

No. 172

SOFTWARE EXCHANGE SERVICE

Software is at the heart of every computer. The most profitable businesses are those related to the growing software market, and one of the simplest and least competitive software businesses is a software marketplace or exchange service. A software exchange service acts like a tollgate; customers do all the trafficking and the exchange service collects a fee from each of them.

CONCEPT

The concept of this business is to match the right people with each other. You provide a market where people can advertise the software programs they want to buy, trade or sell. You print a listing, like a classified ad section from the newspaper.

Essentially, the market is like a bulletin board. A software exchange service offers clients the convenience and influence of major advertising at low cost. A software exchange service can contact far more people than any single person could contact, and in a much shorter amount of time.

As more people use your service, they will tell other people about your business, providing you free advertising.

Software exchange services offer tremendous profit potential because there are few expenses besides advertising. Since you must advertise your services anyway, your own advertisements can also serve to advertise your client's software programs.

SKILLS YOU WILL REQUIRE

Operating a software exchange service requires no special skills. The only skills you need are common business sense and eagerness to make money.

Essentially, operating a software exchange service is no different than operating a used-book store, for instance. You don't have to read (or understand) every product that you sell. You only have to know how to sell your products and at what price. If you are able to organize, then you won't have trouble operating this service.

INFORMATION REQUIRED

There is very little information needed to start a software exchange service besides basic business sense. The most important information you will need is a legal disclaimer as part of your advertising, stating that your service only sells, buys or trades ORIGINAL software programs, not copies of program disks. This is to protect you from responsibility for any violation of copyright laws by individuals using your service.

Since a software exchange service acts mainly as a bulletin board, the only other information you may need you can get from your clients by mailing each of them a questionnaire. In the questionaire, ask the type of software they are selling, the type of computer it runs on and the price value they wish to set for their software.

Basically, the questionnaire lets you organize your listing of available programs in categories. One category can be devoted exclusively to one brand of computer. Another category can be devoted exclusively to word processors. The idea is to increase the visibility of your customer's software to gain a sale for your customer as soon as possible. A satisfied customer will tell friends, and the best advertisement any business can have is word of mouth.

And this job of categorizing is exactly what data base software does best. You can use a data base to organize the same material under a number of headings. For example, if you have a customer wanting to exchange a word processing program for accounting software, you can easily file the information under such headings as "word processing for sale, "accounting wanted," "CP/M" and many others.

Plus, a data base program will simplify the tasks of keeping track of listings, customers and billing information.

GETTING STARTED

Advertising is the lifeblood of this business, so getting started means knowing how to advertise your service to as many people as possible. You will have to prepare a sales brochure describing your services, and also a sample of how you advertise your clients' software. This can be like a small classified ad newsletter or an elaborate catalog listing. The choice is up to you.

The first step is to divide your advertising campaign between direct mail and magazine display advertisements. Your clients will be individual computer owners, and businesses who wish to trade or sell obsolete or unnecessary software. Your advertising should keep this in mind.

For direct mail advertising, you can get a mailing list (look in the yellow pages under "Mailing Lists" or "Advertising Direct- Mail) and send a sales letter and brochure to people who have recently purchased or already own a computer.

Magazine display advertisements would be best in the more popular computer magazines, such as Popular Computing or Personal Computing.

THE COMPETITION

Eliminating the competition is a matter of exposure. Since your business depends on advertising, one of the best ways of wiping out any competition is to reach your potential clients first.

A great way to develop free advertising is to get copies of public domain software (software programs that may be copied free of charge without violating copyright laws). Contact local computer dealers in your area and offer public domain software for the dealers to give away with their computers. Tell the dealers that by offering public domain software, they can increase the chances that a person will buy a computer from them. After all, public domain software will cost neither you nor the dealer any extra money, but will provide an additional attraction for the dealer.

With each copy of public domain software, enclose a certificate offering a free ad in your software exchange service newsletter. The idea here is to tap into the market of bundled software that comes with most computers.

Most people cannot use all their bundled software. Since they consider the software to be "free," they will likely take advantage of your free advertising offer. You will benefit because you will have contacted another potential customer, and the new computer buyer will benefit because he can sell his bundled software, which came with the computer anyway.

If you know how to program a computer, or have a friend who can do it for you, you can program a message on the public domain software disk. This message can be a simple advertisement of your services to remind a potential customer that he can always exchange his software at any time for a minimal cost. By putting your advertisement on public domain software disks, your advertisement will be seen by hundreds of potential clients.

POTENTIAL INCOME

There are two ways to produce income from a software exchange service. First, you can charge a yearly, quarterly or monthly fee (between $30 to $70) for every ad listed in your newsletter. You can let individuals contact each other by themselves, or you can offer an additional service to provide further income.

This additional service would act as a middleman in software exchanges, purchases or sales between two people. By charging a minimal fee, such as $5 or $10 for each transaction your service handles, you will be getting paid twice—once for the advertising fee, and a second time for the transaction fee. Acting as a middleman insures that both parties in a transaction are satisfied with their deal.

There are few expenses to operating a software exchange service. Advertising will be the biggest expense. The next expense will be the cost of reproducing a listing of all your clients and the software programs they wish to trade, sell or buy.

Once you have established the costs of doing business, including a salary for your time and a profit for the business, you are ready to estimate what a reasonable amount is to charge for your service.

Basic Costs

1. Cost of advertising
2. Cost of software used to organize material
3. Cost of time spent organizing and reproducing questionnnaire
4. Cost of postage
5. Cost of time spent processing questionnaires
6. Cost of time spent creating classified listings
7. Cost of time spent putting buyers and sellers together

MARKETING METHODS

Direct mail and display ads are the best methods to advertise your service. For more methods and information, refer to Section 5.

Both your direct mail and display advertisement campaign can be directed at individuals or businesses. An example of a sales letter is shown below.

FREE SOFTWARE!

If your computer came with free software or if you bought software that you no longer need, turn those disks into cold, hard cash through Shop'N Swap Software Services, the new way of buying software at reasonable prices.

Shop'N Swap Software Services reaches thousands of computer owners just like you. With our computerized listing you can sell, buy or trade software for your computer (original program disks only). Why buy software at retail prices when you can trade? Not only will you get the software you really need, but you will get rid of software that only clutters up your desk.

Still interested? Call or write today for more information, or better still, send a blank, formatted disk (specify computer type) and one dollar (postage and handling) to:

Shop'N Swap Software Services
1234 Main Street
Anywhere, U.S.A. 99999

In return, you will recieve free public domain software written exclusively for your computer. If the price of postage can give you access to a whole library of free software, just think how much more software is available to you for the low cost of our services.

The object of the sales letter is to convince a potential customer that there is a wealth of brand-name software available at greatly reduced prices. A sample copy of your latest listing of programs available for sale or trade will further create interest in your business, especially if you list the latest and most popular software programs available at prices much lower than retail value.

UNIQUE BUSINESS APPROACH

Giving away public domain software offers one of the best ways to introduce your services to the maximum number of people at little cost to you. You can give public domain software to churches and other social organizations while gaining free publicity.

Public schools and colleges offer a target for your services. Schools will readily accept free software. By giving away copies of public domain software to schools, you are able to advertise your service to students and teachers at the same time. Since student and teacher computer owners can use various software for their school projects, these potential customers represent a rich source of income.

LOCATION and MARKET BASE

The best location for a software exchange service would be in a high concentration of people. This will increase the number of computer owners you will be able to contact easily by phone.

However, once you get your business going, you can expand across your state and eventually advertise nationwide. You can then do business with your local customers by telephone and with your out-of-state customers by mail.

TO SUM UP

A software exchange business offers you a chance to cash in on the tremendous computer market without having to learn much about computers. Think of the tollgate analogy mentioned at the beginning of this article. The tollgate operator doesn't have to know how cars work or who makes each type of car to stay in business. All he has to know is how to keep this service available and how to collect money.

The increasing use of computers and modems may eventually allow people to work at home instead of commuting to work, and put all the tollgate operators out of business. But if everyone is using a computer to work, they will need software as well. The future of computers seems assured. Why not become the tollgate operator of the future?

SOURCE MATERIAL

Refer to Section 7.

No. 173

RESTAURANT PRICING SERVICE

Here is a unique business that the restaurants in your city or town won't be able to do without. We will show you how to get all of the restaurants as clients, or just as many as you want to handle. The secret to this business is rapidly changing food prices and the way they affect the prices charged on menus. The clients that take advantage of your service will always operate at a profit no matter what happens to food prices.

CONCEPT

Most smart business people have found that a business is run on percentages. If you run outside those percentages, there is often something bad that happens: bankruptcy. You can set up a business that can give restaurants in your area a computer readout on the percentages of what their food is costing them in relation to the prices they are charging for it. They can see in black and white where they need to work with their profit margins.

SKILLS YOU WILL REQUIRE

You need to pick up a good knowledge of how the food business works.

You are also going to have to be able to set up a program that analyzes the menu and food prices of the restaurants that you have for clients and makes the comparisons called for.

The skill level of this project should not cause too many problems, so it is an easy one to get into. You have to have a good working relationship with your computer and know how to extract the data you need from it.

INFORMATION REQUIRED

You should get to work immediately and find out what makes the restaurant industry tick. You might want to begin by reading the industry trade journals to get a feel for the problems it faces. This will enable you to talk with the owners about their individual problems and let them know that you understand what their business consists of.

For research you might want to interview a local fast-food manager or a regional manager to determine how they go about figuring out their food costs. This will give you an appreciation for how chain restaurants keep their cost systems down to a fine science. They are people who know down to the last onion where their food costs are.

Take the time to learn the business and you will be rewarded for the effort.

GETTING STARTED

Make sure that you have done all your research on the food industry as it relates to the restaurant owner. You will also want to do a study of the fluctuations of the wholesale food prices or what the ranges have been over a period of time. These are the prices the restaurant owner has to pay for his food and something you will want to get a working knowledge of. This will give you a picture of the job you will be performing. Without this knowledge, your job is not only useless, but impossible. What you will be doing is taking an inventory of the foods your client purchases, then tracking the cost of those foods. The kinds of information you need to do this include:

Food type
Quantity purchased
Frequency of purchase
Typical amount of waste

Once you have this data, you can begin to track how much those purchases actually cost the restaurant. In other words, if a restaurant buys 50 heads of lettuce a week, pays 50 cents per head and throws out 10 heads that have rotted, that means it is actually paying a higher rate for each head, since only 10 have been used. Yet if menu prices reflect the price of lettuce bought at 50 cents a head, the restaurant is losing money every week on that purchase alone. Such information on a regular basis can keep restaurants in the black, and you gainfully employed, in this needed service.

THE COMPETITION

Here's the good news. We don't currently know of anyone providing this type of service for restaurant owners anywhere. It is a service that is sorely needed for small and medium-sized restaurant owners, due to the fact that they generally don't use the same scientific approaches the large operations do, either because they don't know how or don't have the time.

You can walk in on the ground floor with this one.

As of this writing, there are over 4,000 people who have restaurant licenses in the city I live in. The restaurant business seems to be one of the most popular in the United States and yet people stumble along because of their inability to keep track of their own business. They don't have a handle on the margins; you are going to give it to them. And this should ensure that they stay in business for a long time.

POTENTIAL INCOME

In this business you charge your clients by the week or month, depending on how often you work with them. For their money they get your computerized evaluation of the best buys for their food dollar. You'll also inform them about how well their menu prices reflect their food costs.

If you work with each client only a couple hours a week, you can reasonably expect to charge $20 or $30 a week. The money your client can save will more than cover your fee. This means that with just five to 10 clients, you can earn from $500 to $1,000 a month.

The business will build up overtime, but your customers will supply you with steady work and a dependable paycheck. Your primary costs involved are the start-up expenses, i.e., your time spent researching the subject, doing your advertising, etc.

Basic Costs

1. Cost of software used
2. Cost of advertising
3. Cost of subscriptions to professional publications
4. Cost of telephone
5. Cost of transportation
6. Cost of time spent organizing data each week
7. Cost of time spent with client each week
8. Cost of materials used

MARKETING METHODS

The best way to approach this market is with direct mail and a follow-up telephone call.

You will want to sit down and create a letter for your prospective clients. The following letter will serve as one example.

DEAR RESTAURANT OWNER:

Are you earning enough profit? Do you know your profit?

Wholesale food prices fluctuate, your inventory moves rapidly, and sometimes you don't have time to keep track of where the dollars are going.

These are problems that can be solved by MenuMinders.

We are a firm that specializes in not only inventory control, but the weekly or monthly analysis of your menu prices. By checking your receipts and wholesale food prices, we can give you cost comparisons and food margins and keep you abreast of what your profit is.

All large chains use this type of system to analyze food costs and give out percentages for their food items. Isn't it about time you followed their methods?

Know where your dollars go and whether your prices reflect a profit to you.

Call us today for more information about this low-cost, unique service designed especially for the little restaurant.

Be prepared to do your follow-up work, which will consist of phone calling. And don't forget—do not call these owners between 11 a.m. and 1:30 p.m. or after 4:30 p.m. unless invited to. This is the time of day they start their operations and a call from you tells them immediately that you don't know their business.

UNIQUE BUSINESS APPROACH

You have a computer to do the hard work, and the small restaurants don't. This is the key to your unique approach. The computer allows the small businessperson to do the job of the big businessperson.

In your letter and all the conversations you have with your clients, emphasize the use of large-business methods for the small businessperson and what advantages the use of high-tech equipment can bring.

Since your clients probably will not have the money to get into a point-of-sale terminal that costs anywhere from $20,000 to $40,000, they will be able to spot trends and see where the profit is leaking out of the business by using your methods.

Another idea you can use to market this service is to redesign the customer's menus so that they can change their prices without re-doing the menu each time they have a price shift. They can do this by posting their specialties—the dishes with costs that vary widely from week to week—on a chalkboard. This is a techique many elegant restaurants use.

Show the owner or manager that flexibility is the key to staying in business, or at least the key to making the amount of money he should.

Another means you might want to consider is the business seminar approach. You can send postcards out to a select group of restaurants and invite the managers to a financial reporting seminar at one of your client's eateries. You can call it anything you want, but one thing to bring up is: Are you really analyzing your food costs? Are your food costs a runaway item?. Then explain to the group how you can tame this wild beast.

One other area you might want to consider is to work through a business opportunities broker. These are people who do a lot of work with others wanting to buy restaurants.

Since you are in the business of analyzing the most important feature of this type of business, its food costs, you can help a new businessperson set up your program before they even open their doors.

LOCATION and MARKET BASE

There is no way around it; you have to be where the business is. And the city is the best answer. You have to be in weekly contact with your clients. If you live in the country and don't mind making trips into the city, you can still run this program, since the price and cost analysis can be done at home on your computer any time. Then you simply meet with all your clients on one or two days of the week.

TO SUM UP

A love of the food business, a head for figures and business-building instinct are some of the qualities you should have to start in the restaurant pricing business. But regardless of your motivations, this can be fun and profitable.

But you may want to consider one thing—your waistline. After you have helped some of these food people get a handle on their costs, you may never have to pay for a meal again. They are likely to show their appreciation in the obvious way.

This is a great opportunity for both you and the restaurant owner. You can have the fun of watching a business grow, enjoy the company of some super people and take home a well-earned paycheck in the process. Where else can you get such a combination? Bon Apetit.

SOURCE MATERIAL

Refer to Section 7.

No. 174

CROSSWORD PUZZLE DESIGN BUSINESS

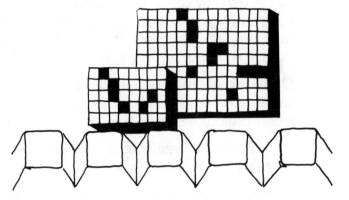

If you like crossword puzzles and word games, this business will appeal to you. We will show you how to adapt many of the new programs that are now available to create any kind of crossword puzzle or word game you want, and the computer does most of the work. This is a great syndication deal, and we will show you how to tap into that market as well as others. So start changing those words into dollars now!

CONCEPT

Hundreds of newspapers carry crossword puzzles and anagrams daily. A great share of magazines also have crossword puzzles. And, interestingly enough, there are quite a few more that would like to have crossword puzzles if they could find someone to build one that fit the theme of the magazine for a reasonable price. There are untold newspapers in this same jam. And we are going to introduce you to the computer program that can furnish this work.

SKILLS YOU WILL REQUIRE

There are no real skills to be developed here.

You merely have to master the program you will use for this venture. Work with it until you are comfortable and then follow your plan for putting together crossword puzzles and anagrams and marketing them.

INFORMATION REQUIRED

You are going to want to start looking at all the magazines and newspapers to find out which have crossword puzzles and which don't.

You should also explore the legalities of syndication for your crossword puzzles. This can be done by contacting syndications listed in writer market books. Ask questions about how they like to receive submissions for consideration, what they pay, etc. You may also find articles about this topic in writing magazines by perusing either the magazines annual index or the Guide to Periodical Literature index.

On the whole there is not a lot to learn here. You need to know how to become conversant with the crossword and anagram software. Then, presto, you have the crossword puzzles and the anagrams needed to make you a few dollars.

By now you are beginning to wonder what this little piece of magic is that we have been telling you about that will produce crosswords puzzles and anagrams.

The software you need is called the Word Plus and is one of the best kept secrets of the software field. This particular piece of software was originally designed as a spelling checker, or what is called an electronic dictionary, but has several other fun aspects. One of them is that of being used as a crossword puzzle-generator. It is available from Oasis Systems, 7909 Ostrow, San Diego, CA (619)279-5711. It will cost you $150. There are several other similar programs that will perform the same functions, so shop around.

GETTING STARTED

After you have done your research on the kinds and numbers of crossword puzzles being published, you'll see that there are plenty of dollars out there for the person who wants to do a little planning.

From this pile of prospects you will want to target some of the local magazines or community papers that don't presently carry any puzzles.

You should put a letter together that describes what you do and the fact that you can put together crossword puzzles that relate to just about any theme they desire, at a price they can afford.

THE COMPETITION

In the larger newspapers throughout the country you will find crossword puzzles. The minute they decide to take them out or move them around, the cards and letters arrive in droves. The editors are swamped. Quite a few of the "city" magazines also feature crossword puzzles, and newstands are filled with books containing crosswords. People love to work on puzzles in their spare minutes.

There is no lack of competition, but since you will cater to community papers and specialty magazines, you will have less competition than you might expect.

One of the real problems in this field is the amount of time it takes to construct the puzzle, and the dollar amount that must then be charged for it.

You are going to remedy this situation since your puzzles will take less time and overhead by being created on a computer. What this means is that you can charge less for your puzzles and still make a profit.

POTENTIAL INCOME

Other than the cost of the program, you will have little or no overhead to speak of—just the computer and time you are going to put into this effort. This is definitely a high profit situation for the person who wants to tackle it.

Your profit margins are going to be a function of how many crosswords you can build and the number of publications you can place your puzzles in. Oftentimes, you'll find you can sell the same puzzle to several publications and triple or quadruple your earnings.

If you can create, for example, a puzzle in two hours, designed for computer users, you might be able to find 15 publications that want to run it. This includes computer newspapers, user group newsletters, professional computer group newsletters and other such forums.

If you charge each publication only $5, you have earned $75 from that one puzzle. The faster you can generate and market your puzzles, the larger your paychecks will become.

Basic Costs

1. Cost of software
2. Cost of time spent creating puzzles
3. Cost of time spent advertising, shipping, etc.
4. Cost of printer supplies
5. Cost of postage
6. Cost of advertising
7. Cost of any materials, books, etc. used

In dealing with these local magazines, you will want to get paid as soon as you deliver the puzzle. Unfortunately, most will pay on publication, which may occur one or two months after they have your puzzle in hand. But once you start the ball rolling, checks will start to arrive to you steadily. Make sure of this by including a simple invoice with each puzzle. This will ensure that the editor will contact the accounting department to pay you.

MARKETING METHODS

By now you should have the list of magazines, newspapers and specialty publications in your area that don't carry crosswords.

Chances are that this "targeted" market knows they need puzzles, but hasn't been able to find anyone to do the puzzles for them. And more important, people who build crosswords don't do it for free.

It is now letter time. You need to send out a letter to the managing editors of these publications. The managing editor is generally the person who makes the decisions as to what goes in the paper or magazines. Find out who he or she is and send off a variation of the following letter.

> DEAR MANAGING EDITOR:
>
> We know that magazines and newspapers are always in the market for new features, articles and ideas that will appeal and attract readership for your publication.
>
> We are in the business of building crossword puzzles and anagrams. We do our own or build ones to fit your specific publication depending on the theme and time of year.
>
> You will be pleasantly surprised at how inexpensive we are. We have priced our product to fit your budget.
>
> We have taken the opportunity to create a puzzle specially-geared for your publication. If you want to see more, please return the enclosed stamped post- card.
>
> Thanks for your consideration.

You should be able to garner some positive response from this approach.

This approach will cost you some research time as well as effort to build a crossword for each of your targeted clients. But the effort will more than pay for itself when you start getting steady customers lined up.

UNIQUE BUSINESS APPROACH

After getting your feet wet with your initial phase of business development, you will begin to see what kinds of puzzles are wanted and which ones will sell the best. You will now have a rudimentary idea of how to deal with the managing editors. But here is where we will ask you to change focus.

Go to the library and get a copy of a reference guide listing all weekly and suburban newspapers. These cannot be checked out, so you will have to work at the library with them. They contain the listing of almost all the paid and free circulation newspapers and so-called shoppers/pennysavers in the United States.

Pick a state or region and write to each one of the owners of these papers, telling them about the service you offer. Let them know that you can do a crossword for only a few dollars each.

The beauty of this program is that, once set up, all you have to do is set up the same crossword puzzles for as many clients as you have and mail them off on a weekly basis.

To give you an idea of how many shoppers/pennysavers there are: you can figure one per county of every state in the midwest, and the same in many states in the east, including New York and Florida. You will have plenty of prospective clients. And these numbers grow every year.

One of the kickers is that most syndicators charge by the circulation figures of the individual publications. We suggest you offer a flat rate.

The reason we suggest this type of publication is that they are starting to look for new material and things that will make their readers pay more attention to them, by offering better gimmicks than the newspapers have. The crossword puzzle will do wonders for them. It will cost next to nothing and chances are that a clever owner or salesperson will sell the crossword to an advertiser to foot the bill for the whole project.

Another field you may want to attack is specialty sports publications. In almost every city that has a major league baseball, basketball or football team there is a publication dedicated to that team or sport. You can put crosswords together for them and probably get a better rate than from the newspapers.

Along with the pro market, you will want to explore the collegiate market, where the same types of magazines and newspapers are cropping up.

You might even want to contact a few large corporations and find out which ones publish a monthly employee newsletter. This would be a great market for your puzzles. You could "theme" this one to reflect the company, time of year, or even to deal with an aspect of the working environment, such as safety.

LOCATION and MARKET BASE

This venture can be worked from the North Pole if the phone service and mail delivery are good enough. It is an ideal situation that requires no set geographical base, just the development of the customers who want to buy what you offer. The market base you'll want to tap is any city or community with a newspaper and magazines.

START UP CAPITAL

This is one business you can get into for under a thousand dollars. If you already own a home computer, you can get into it basically for the cost of the software.

TO SUM UP

The secrets of this one are now out of the bag. While it won't pave the yellow brick road, it can certainly build a substantial part-time business. With a little effort and luck, you'll have your puzzles placed all over the country. And that's money on the gameboard to you.

SOURCE MATERIAL

Refer to Section 7.

No. 175

CHECKBOOK BALANCING SERVICE

Here is a business that can prove useful to just about anyone. Balancing a checkbook is a tedious and time-consuming task that many people would rather have someone else do for them. With your computer you can offer a service that takes a fraction of the time that most people spend on this mundane yet necessary task.

CONCEPT

How many times have you heard people say "I hate to balance my checkbook"? Certainly it is a task that no one looks forward to, yet it has to be done. Most people sit down with a calculator, a ledger, some scrap paper and a few pencils and have at it. A number of hours later, depending on how simple or complex their finances, their checkbook balances, they hope.

With your computer you can set up a simple accounting program that will do the same thing in a matter of minutes. Because of the time you save, you can balance the checkbooks of many clients in the time it would take each of them to balance their own.

Once you get going on this, you will be amazed at the number of people ready to take advantage of your service. You can even branch out into doing the accounts of small businesses in your area, whose proprietors have better things to do than add up figures. A simple task that many people simply do not have time for, can thus become a steady source of good income for you.

SKILLS YOU WILL REQUIRE

Assuming that you know how to balance a checkbook, you already possess most of the skills necessary in order to run this type of service. You will need to be able to operate one of the many programs available to balance checkbooks on any type of computer you might own.

A decent program for your purpose might run anywhere from $20 to $60 — sometimes even less. Super Checkbook III for the Apple II and Checkbook Balancer for Timex and Sinclair computers are two examples of the many programs you have to choose from. Consult your local computer software dealers, or visit your library and check the available computer-related periodicals for more information on this. New software comes out all the time, and the various magazines will run reviews that can serve as a partial guide.

Another skill you will need is salesmanship — the ability to get clients interested in your service. For a business as useful as this one, it isn't hard. For more on this, see Marketing Methods.

INFORMATION REQUIRED

What you are setting out to do is no mystery. You've balanced your own checkbook hundreds of times. You know that the information to do it is contained in your own records — your checkbook ledger, your cancelled checks (if you receive them) and your statements from the bank, which contain any records of automatic loan payments or deductions, service charges, fines, interest payments and the like.

Likewise, all the information you need to run your service, once you've got your program set up, will be in the hands of your clients. Once you have obtained this information, you are ready to go.

OPERATING NAME

You can choose any name you like for your business, provided that the name is not already registered to somebody else doing business in your area. If you like, you can make up a fictitious name, such as "Swiftcheck Accounting," or "Silver Moon Checkbook Service," but there is no point in doing so, and such flights of fancy will cost you extra money. You will need to register the name, get a new bank account, have a phone installed at business rates and listed in the phone book. In short, you will have to shell out money for a lot of start-up costs you could just as easily do without.

If you simply take your own name and add "and Associates," or something similar, you have a perfectly good name for your new business and you can use all the addresses, phone numbers and accounts you currently have. Why make things more complicated than they need to be?

GETTING STARTED

As mentioned earlier, the first thing you will need to do is purchase a program and get it running. You will want to practice and the best guinea pig available is yourself. Run your own finances through your program. When your accounts balance every time, you are ready to run your service for other people.

Your next step is to locate potential clients. This can be done in two ways—advertising and referral. In the section on Marketing Methods we will discuss possible advertising strategies.

Talk up your new service among your friends and acquaintances. Perhaps some of them might want to give it a try. Quite possibly they have contact with others who might be interested. Mention your service to those with whom you do business at your bank or other financial institutions. Chances are, they have many clients who would be interested in finding out about what you have to offer. Have business cards printed up and distribute them freely.

Once you get a clientele established, people will come back to you month after month, because they know that you can save them time, and that's worth their money.

THE COMPETITION

Put you and your computer program next to a person with a calculator, pencil and paper and see who can balance a checkbook faster. It really isn't much of a contest, is it? Legends of John Henry besting a steam drill and the tortoise defeating the hare are nice stories of victory for the underdog, but the fact is that the system with a built-in advantage almost always prevails.

There is no faster or more efficient way to balance a checkbook than on a program specifically designed to do it on a personal computer. Those people whose time is valuable to them will be willing to pay a fair price for the time it saves them.

You can eliminate any potential competition from other computer operators by being the first in your area to offer such a service and by establishing a fair price structure. Once your base clientele is established, you can add new customers as you see fit.

POTENTIAL INCOME

It is not hard to price your service. There are basically three factors to take into consideration: your time, the costs you will incur by running the service, and the amount of profit you wish to make.

Start by placing an hourly value on your own time. Let's say, for example, that your time is worth $20 an hour. Thus, if you spend 30 minutes to balance a client's checkbook, that part of the charge will be $10.

But there are other costs as well, and these costs need to be covered by your business. The electricity to run your computer is not free. You will probably have additional telephone expenses. You need to add up your monthly costs and divide them by the number of jobs you have per month.

Here is a list of some of the costs you will need to take into consideration.

1. Cost of operating your equipment

2. Cost of advertising
3. Telephone and postage costs
4. Cost of accessory equipment and materials, such as envelopes paper, ribbons, etc.
5. Miscellaneous costs, such as travel
6. Cost of time spent on each job
7. Cost of software

In addition, you will need to determine your margin of profit for each job. Your hourly pay is not profit—you are essentially paying yourself as an employee of your own business, and your hourly wage is a cost of doing business. You should earn money for your time and a profit for your business on each job.

Figure out how many clients you intend to serve on a regular basis. Divide your monthly costs by the number of clients. Decide on a monthly profit figure both you and your clients can live with, and divide that figure also by the number of clients. Add in your hourly wage, and the result is the amount you should charge.

You may not reach your desired number of regular clients within the first couple of months of starting out. But once you do have your desired number, you will be making decent money, and any clients you add on after this point mean extra money for you with very litle added time.

MARKETING METHODS

Since this is a service that can be used by just about anyone, you will want to reach as large a segment of your potential clientele as cheaply as you can. The best way to do this is with a display advertisement in your local newspaper or other general-interest publications.

A display ad should, first, be eye-catching. Your primary goal is to attract attention. For this reason you'll want to make use of the services of a graphic artist or someone who can give you the visual edge you are looking for.

Your ad should also be short and to the point. The fewer words you use to get your message across, the better. People perusing the ads in a newspaper for a service they may need do not want to read a lot of copy.

The idea you are trying to get across is a fairly simple one. I am going to give you an example of some sample copy you might want to consider. You will need to decide what is best for your own area and your own purposes, but here is an example of a pitch that will bring inquiries:

HATE TO BALANCE YOUR CHECKBOOK?

Our computerized system can do it in minutes— and at a very balanced price! Haven't you got better things to do with your time? Call Joe Jones and Associates at 123-555-6767 today.

Copy similar to this, coupled with attractive graphics, is bound to draw a reader's attention. Run your ad in the major newspapers in your area and also in the weekly shoppers that are distributed by mail. Many people look at these publications in search of bargains. You can add your service to the list.

UNIQUE BUSINESS APPROACH

Many banks and other financial institutions mail out promotional material with their monthly statements on occassion. Usually this material announces new loan rates, a new type of credit available, the opening of a new branch—something to do with the institution itself. You can print up a flyer on your service—two sides of a piece of good-quality paper the size of a business envelope and, for a price, have one or two financial institutions with a good number of clients in your area include it in their next mailing.

Banks tend to be conservative as a rule and you may encounter resistance to this idea from them, but there are plenty of credit unions, lending institutions and the like that might be willing to enter such a venture. This puts an advertisement for your service directly into the homes of hundreds of potential clients.

LOCATION and MARKET BASE

The larger your market base, the more money you can potentially make. If you intend to do this part-time, then you can run your service in a rural area. If you want to make it your primary occupation, you should be in an urban or suburban setting.

START UP CAPITAL

If you've already got your computer, you can get started in this business for an initial investment of under $1,000. For more on start up capital, refer to Section 6.

TO SUM UP

A checkbook balancing service is the type of low-overhead operation that is perfect for the personal computer. Computer capability turns this formerly tedious job into a routine process that takes minutes to complete. Most people would love to have someone (or something) balance their checkbooks for them.

You can tap into this need and make it profitable, because the amount of time you spend will enable you to charge prices that your clients not only can afford, but will be happy to pay.

SOURCE MATERIAL

Refer to Section 7.

No. 178

CUSTOM LOAN, ANNUITY AND INTEREST CALCULATIONS AND ANALYSIS SERVICE

A custom loan, annuity and interest calculations service provides both retailers and consumers with a detailed report breaking down their loan schedules for intended purchases, including interest and annuity calculations. With this report you'll find out how easy it is to sell this service, and how easy it is to do the calculations with your personal computer. People never quit buying or selling on time, so the market is yours if you want it.

CONCEPT

Whenever anyone is considering buying anything of value, they always want to know beforehand what their options are—whether to go for a three-year loan or a five-year loan, how much interest will be paid annually, how much monthly payments will be for various terms, etc.

Everyone prefers being able to make purchase and investment decisions more intelligently. If you now have a home computer with a loan amortization or mortgage program, you know how much you can use it to speculate on what it would take to buy a new house or car, or what the best loan terms are for making that new large purchase. For instance, people are quite surprised to learn that you should not have to pay more than a $100 per month more when applying a 15-year mortgage to a $100,000 house than if you applied a 30-year mortgage.

When it comes down to it, having this information gives you much more flexibility in your buying decisions. You don't have to simply wonder what the best financial course is. When you don't know the specifics of any transaction you are considering, you're more likely to be cautious and not commit yourself at all. Most people, however, don't have the resources or the know-how to come up with the figures they want or need. Generally, people think that it takes a pencil and paper and a lot of time to do this kind of calculating.

It's not necessary for people to go without this information and not get the most out of their lives and their money. Using your computer, you can supply buyers with detailed reports that will give them all the information they need to make a smart financial decision about a major purchase. Your reports can give them details on the advantages and disadvantages of differing loan repayment schedules, how much their payments will be, how much they should put down, whether to buy or to lease—the list is endless.

To the retailer you can offer a service that will bring him more customers. He can be prepared to give potential buyers specifics on their buying options. As a consumer yourself, you know how nice it would be to have this information offered to you by a merchant when you're out shopping for a large ticket item.

There are software programs out today that will give you answers to any questions a consumer or buyer might have, and there is no reason not to offer as much information as possible to potential clients. These programs can offer advice on savings deposits, deposits needed for future purchase, earning interest on treasury bills, IRA's, variable rate and balloon mortgage payments, refinancing homes, buying, leasing or owning a new or used car and many other financial transactions. Many of these programs go as far as allowing for adjustments for projected inflation levels.

While you won't be recommending any specific course of action, you can make sure your client goes into a situation with his eyes wide open. This is information people will gladly pay for. After all, you are saving them money by allowing them to make intelligent choices!

SKILLS YOU WILL REQUIRE

Although it certainly doesn't hurt if you are familiar with the terms and principles you will be dealing with, it's not at all necessary to know these things to offer this service. Your computer will be doing virtually all the work for you. You will primarily be giving it the information it needs, while it goes about doing the calculations.

You'll soon find that most of the programs you use will give you mini-tutorials about the concepts behind the calculations, so you can learn at the same time you are making money.

INFORMATION REQUIRED

The primary souce of your information will be your customers themselves. It is their data that you feed into the computer to come up with your schedules and analyses.

It will be necessary for you to know the current interest rates and how they are compounded—daily, monthly or yearly. For some of your calculations, you might want to be able to project inflation rates. You might also want to invest in a few reference books to help you understand more thoroughly the terms you'll be using. Again, keep in mind that these are figures that will not be difficult for you to come up with, but your research will simply allow you to work faster.

OPERATING NAME

The easier it is to get your new business going, the better. With this in mind, your own name is the best choice for the name of your business. There is no advantage to a fictitious name and it involves a lot of extra start-up expenses. You'll need to register the name or file a fictitious name report, get a new bank account, have a new phone put in at business rates, etc. Refer to Section 4 for more information.

GETTING STARTED

Do some research and locate the software that will do what you want. Keep in mind that once you get going, you might want to expand your services, so the software should be able to grow with you. As many people have learned the hard way, you should anticipate your needs. If you find that your expanded business now requires new software and it isn't available for your computer, you'll be in a predicament. The best advice here is to make sure your software can grow with you.

Do a lot of sample runs on your computer so you'll get the feel of what people might ask and how best to format the reports.

When you're ready to begin, formulate some display ads (see Marketing Methods) and get ready to bring in the money.

THE COMPETITION

In this business you won't encounter much competition. If you look around, you'll probably not see anyone else doing this type of service, so now is the perfect time to get one going.

Your expenses will be very low. Your reports will generally be going to only one or two people, so you won't have to print out the multiple copies many other businesses demand.

One way to deal with competition is to offer your customer more for his money. It is really no more difficult for you to supply more services; it only requires more information from your client and the extra time it takes the computer to do its calculations— and you know that doesn't take long. You might consider throwing in one of your extra services as a selling tool.

When you're selling your services to retailers, you should be able to negotiate some sort of long-term contract arrangement. This will allow you to drop your per-job fee.

POTENTIAL INCOME

This is an especially easy business to run. Your overhead will be low and advertising costs can be minimal and still generate good results.

Your fee scale can be based on the type of service. Second mortgage analysis can be one price, loan analysis another. You'll find it simple to come up with a good rate structure. As mentioned above, a long-term arrangement with retailers can be charged at a reduced rate.

If you charge only $10 per analysis, you can easily whip out 10 or 20 a day with little effort. This could bring in $500 to $1,000 a week.

To calculate your fee, estimate the expenses of doing business, including a salary for your time and a profit figure on each job. Then estimate how many jobs you can handle and divide the total expenses by this number.

Basic Costs

1. Cost of financial software
2. Cost of advertising
3. Cost of time spent working with each client
4. Cost of time spent preparing each analysis
5. Cost of printer supplies
6. Cost of materials used

MARKETING METHODS

Display ads are the best advertising tools for this business.

Run your ads in the local and regional newspapers. Stress the money-saving quality of your service. Your customers will be making an investment that will be returned many times over when they make a more intelligent purchase. Remember that your target market includes everybody—people will never quit buying or selling.

Let me show you an example of a display ad you can use to advertise your business:

> IF YOU PLAN TO MAKE A MAJOR PURCHASE OF ANY KIND, TALK TO US FIRST.
>
> No, we're not a loan company—we're on your side. Let us give you an example of how we work.
>
> Do you know that you can secure a 15-year mortgage for less than $100 a month more than it would cost you for a 30-year mortgage?
>
> This is the service we offer—we let you know what your options are when making any purchase. According to your needs, we will present to you a detailed loan, annuity and interest calculation report that is customized exactly to your requirements.
>
> Our service doesn't stop there. We can also show you the advantages of buying or leasing a car, buying or renting a home, or securing a second mortgage. We can supply you statistics for virtually any financial situation—statistics customized to your needs.
>
> Don't go into any buying situation without being prepared to make the smartest decision. Call us now and let us show you how we can help you get what you want on your terms.

Place your display ads in local newspapers and weekly shoppers, and send out flyers. If you want to zero in on the most likely buyers of large dollar items, consider the use of a sales lead business or demographic survey. For more methods and information refer to Section 5.

UNIQUE BUSINESS APPROACH

As a means of securing business with your retail market, suggest to your potential clients that they offer interested customers your detailed analysis. This will make their customers happy, as they are getting a tool that helps them make an intelligent decision. The benefits to the retailer are clear—he will bring in business by offering a clever, helpful service to his market.

LOCATION and MARKET BASE

Your custom financial loan analysis service will be strongest in a city, generally, because you have more people with more places to spend money. Plus, you will have more retailers to whom you can market your service.

The market base should be above 200,000 to enable you to get this business up and flying.

START UP CAPITAL

You should be able to start this business for under $1,000, not including computer cost. Your costs will be the standard ones— advertising, software, phones and office supplies. Refer to Section 7 for obtaining the capital needed.

TO SUM UP

People will never quit buying and selling. When anyone is about to make a big purchase, they will always be nervous if they are unprepared. In the average consumer's eyes, the retailer has the advantage—after all, he does this for a job.

You can show people that it doesn't have to be that way. Your clients can go into any store prepared to negotiate from the strongest position—knowing what is and is not possible.

Your clients can easily be convinced of the value of your service. Once you let them know that the things they want may not be out of their reach after all, they will jump at the chance to use your service. You can make it easy for them to realistically realize their dreams, without getting into something they can't handle.

This is a terrific, sure-thing business that no one is really offering. Make it your project to put this one to work making money for you.

SOURCE MATERIAL

Refer to Section 7.

No. 179

PERSONAL BUDGET MANAGEMENT CONSULTING

Here's something everybody needs but few people will spend the time to sit down and work out. With our plan you can put together a workable budget for people with just a few minutes of your personal computer time. This business can be started with a few classified ads, like the ones we show you here. You can get referrals from several sources by using our special referral letter. This business can be just as big as you want it to be, so get started now.

CONCEPT

The concept of this business is to plan budgets for people who don't want to do it themselves. Much like the bookkeeper they go to once a year to prepare their taxes, they'll come to you regularly in order to figure out how to spend their income. You'll keep their information on file, and if their income or spending changes for some reason, they'll come back to you for updates on their budget planning. Each time they do, you make more money.

SKILLS YOU WILL REQUIRE

You don't have to be an accountant or even a bookkeeper to operate this business. You will have to understand the basics of the business, but your computer will even help you with that.

If you enjoy playing with numbers, figuring out how puzzles fit together, or figuring out how to stretch your own budget, you'll enjoy this business as well. You'll be helping people calculate how their money should be spent. Generally, when people don't use a budget, they get to the end of a year and wonder where their money went. With your service, they'll not only know where the money was spent, but probably have some left over, since it wasn't frittered away unknowingly. The fee you get from your clients is just a small fraction of the amount they'll be saving by using what you plan for them.

INFORMATION REQUIRED

There are two kinds of information in this business—that which you'll need to get started and that which you'll need to actually do the budgets.

First, you will want to be aware of the software programs that are available for your computer that do budget analysis. They are simple to use, and they prompt you for information. When you have answered the questions the computer asks, the computer will sort it and give you an analysis of the budget you are designing. This is what you supply to your client in the form of a computer print-out.

The second kind of information you need is what will actually go into making a budget. Each software program is different, but most will need the annual income of your client; monthly bills, such as mortgage payments, insurance, car payment, credit card bills; and expenses, such as gas and car repairs, food, medical costs, clothing, taxes, business expenses, entertainment, etc.

Your customer supplies you with this information when he comes in to get his budget analyzed. You can have your client bring along his bills, payroll statements, etc. to make sure the numbers are accurate.

You key this information into the computer and it will process and sort it. Then the print-out you give your client will tell him what his monthly bills total, what he should put into savings, how much over or under budget he is, and other information he'll want to keep track of.

You can also have clients come in once a month, or every three months or so to update their budgets. In this way you can keep them better on track with how they are following the budget. You'll be able to tell the client if he is $100 over budget for the year or has $50 he didn't account for to put into the bank.

Not only will the budget you manage for your client give a better idea of where his money is going, it will help him at the end of the year when he does his taxes. The numbers he needs will all be in front of him in the form of a computer print-out.

GETTING STARTED

Getting started in this business is a matter of making contacts. Your first step should be to prepare a brochure of the services you will offer. When people respond to your marketing, you can give them a copy of the brochure to answer their questions.

Once business starts, you can consider the way you want to handle it. If you choose, since this is a service that can be done quickly with the use of your computer, you might decide to have the customers come into your office, then do the analysis right then and there.

Or you can have them answer questions over the phone, based on the questions the computer asks you, then do their analysis and mail it to them. The choice is up to you.

Most customers will want to meet with you in person, simply because they're hesitant about giving financial information over the phone. This is all the better, since you'll be able to collect your fees while they are in the office.

THE COMPETITION

Most of your competition in this business will be financial planners. You eliminate your competition simply because you specialize. Most financial planners handle the whole ball of wax for their customers, from budgets to tax planning and investments. You don't offer this. For one low fee you figure out simple, easy-to-follow budgets for your client. Not only will they save money by not paying for a lot of services they don't want, but you make your job easier.

You can explain this difference in the brochures that you send to potential clients. Most financial planners also prefer to deal with clients who have a lot of money to keep track of. Your business will serve the ones who don't have a lot to spend, but still want to keep track of where their money goes.

POTENTIAL INCOME

In this business you'll want to estimate what your expenses will be in order to establish a price for your services. You start by placing an hourly value on your time. Then you add up all the costs of the program and a profit figure for the job. The total is what you should use to figure out what to charge.

If you keep your prices low and charge, say, $25 for a one-time analysis, you can make several hundred dollars a month with only a little bit of effort. And this amount will grow, since your customers will come back to you each year for an updated budget. You'll also be getting new business at the same time.

If you decide to have your customers come in several times a year, you can charge them an initial fee, say $25, then charge slightly less for each visit they make after that. If they come in once a month, you can charge $10. That would equal a sum of about $135 a year for them. The money they save by using your service will be much greater than this.

Basic Costs

1. Cost of software program used
2. Cost of advertising
3. Cost of brochure
4. Cost of materials used
5. Cost of time spent doing analysis
6. Cost of printer supplies
7. Cost of mailings done

MARKETING METHODS

You can market this service in a couple of ways—direct mail and display ads. I will give you an example of a direct mail letter that you can use to get inquiries for more information. If you decide to use display ads, run your ad in those newspapers and publications that will go to the people you want to serve. For example, if a newspaper runs a weekly column about personal money management, you might want to consider running your ad in the same issue, and maybe even on the same page. People who are seeking assistance with their financial planning will see your ad there and, more than likely, consider that it's time they had help like the kind you offer.

If you use direct mail to market your service, you should mail the letters out on a regular schedule to all the prospects in your area.

Here is the letter:

ARE YOU TIRED OF NOT KNOWING WHERE YOUR MONEY GOES?

Let us save you money!

We can help you plan your budget and follow it. Give us only a few minutes of your time, and you'll know exactly where your money is going each month and how you might want to change your spending habits.

If you're the kind of person who has trouble balancing your checkbook, who seems to have only enough to get by each month, who wants to know what luxuries you can afford in the coming year, we can help you.

Our unique personal budget management consulting business is designed to serve families who don't necessarily have a lot of money, but want to know how they can stretch their budgets.

Call or write now for more information about this unique, inexpensive service.

Plan your budget today. We'll help!

Your own variation of this letter should bring you inquiries for more information. It'll take time, but eventually you should have a nice group of customers who will come to you time and time again. For other marketing techniques, refer to Section 5.

UNIQUE BUSINESS APPROACH

If you're intrigued by the possibilities of this money-making opportunity, you'll want to know about an approach you can try that has worked very successfully for others.

People oftentimes overextend themselves with credit cards, high loan payments, etc. They may even have to consider the possibility of filing for bankruptcy. Yet before they do that, they may simply want to arrange lower payments with their creditors until they get back on their feet.

For an extra charge, you can offer to design a letter for your clients that they can mail to their creditors explaining their present financial difficulties. The letter will also explain that they want to send smaller payments for a period of time until they are able to make regular payments again.

A sample letter might read:

> DEAR CREDITOR:
>
> My name is John Smith and my account number is 99-999-9999. I am writing to inform you that due to unexpected medical bills, my finances are under a strain right now. For this reason, I would like to rearrange my repayment schedule with your company.
>
> My current payments are $35 a month. I propose to send you $20 a month instead. I will keep you posted on any change in my finances that will enable me to return to the regular payment schedule.
>
> Thank you for your cooperation in this matter.
>
> Sincerely,
>
> John Smith

A variation of this letter catered to your client's needs will usually keep the wolves at bay. Most finance companies and banks are surprisingly understanding in cases like this. This letter will let them know that your client is sincere about repaying his loan on a regular basis.

This letter is easy to design on a computer. You can print out as many copies as your client needs and charge for each copy you print, as well as for the initial design. Plus, once you have written the first letter, the following ones you do can follow the same format.

LOCATION and MARKET BASE

This business is best suited for a city location. A market base of 50,000 to 200,000 people should give you plenty of potential customers.

TO SUM UP

You don't have to be a financial whiz to help people plan their budgets. Your computer will do most of the work for you. Consider this: many people earn a salary of five figures. They can fritter away hundreds of dollars a year or even a month paying bills before they are due, spending more on groceries than they have to, putting out more in interest charges than they need to. With your service, these expenses will be cut down considerably. The fee you charge for them will probably equal only a 20th or even a 50th of the amount of money they'll save by following your advice.

With this business you can help people regain control of their pocketbooks. In return, you get to make a nice income for yourself. One of the advantages of operating this service is that you can use it yourself to keep control of the money you'll earn by doing it. Get started today!

SOURCE MATERIAL

For source material refer to Section 7.

No. 180

LOCAL STORE MENU PLANNING SERVICE

A menu planning service collects information regarding weekly specials at area food stores and produces customized menus using the items on special. These menus are then used by your clients to entice customers to come into the store.

CONCEPT

Supermarkets count on large amounts of advertising to bring people into their stores. Daily and weekly ads let people know what is on special, whether it is milk, meat, fruit or vegetables.

There is a perfect opportunity for you to use the food stores' advertising practices to make money for yourself. With your home computer, a menu planning program, and lists of the items on sale at any particular store, you can provide your clients with menus built around the items on special to use in their advertising.

The marketing benefit to your client is great. If a store can run ads that not only tell people what is on sale but also exactly how to use it, it will find its advertising will bring in many more people.

There is another way you and your computer can use a menu program to make money. Generating personalized shopping lists for individuals will be very profitable and easy to do. The lists would include only the specific items the customer wants. In conjunction with your menu-planning for supermarkets, you can sort them for the best price and selection around town or the best price for all items at one store. Then you can supply your clients with the sorted lists once a week in time for shopping.

SKILLS YOU WILL REQUIRE

There is no particular skill you will require to make this business a success. All you will be doing, outside of contacting food stores and selling your service (more on this later), is inputting the information you collect about featured specials for each store and sitting back while the computer does it's work.

When you have your information, just present it to the advertising department of the food store and let them do the rest.

The procedure will be about the same with your individual clients. Using your data base of specials and food items, input the items your client is interested in and come up with a where-to-find list.

As is the case with most businesses that you run with your home computer, your organizational skills will be important. However, anyone who can balance a check-book and pay bills can easily provide the menu planner service.

INFORMATION REQUIRED

Your primary source of information will be gathered from the food stores who subscribe to your service. Either you or your helpers will pick up a list of the food items on special at those stores daily or weekly.

As far as your individual shopping list customers go, after the initial consultation the only new information you will require are new suggestions for items to add to the personalized shopping lists.

You'll need to know which software will suit your needs and where to find it (see Source Material). For example, there are programs that will give a nutritional break-down of meals, including things like sodium and cholesterol content. At first glance you may not think you can use this type of information, but it may turn out to be useful to you. One thing you might stress in your menu presentations is the nutritional value of various meals—your grocery store clients will love this chance to offer their shoppers new benefits. It makes both you and your clients look especially good.

GETTING STARTED

The best bet for getting started is to set up a data base or menu program that will do what you want. There are programs that will do the job for just about any computer. Review the available menu-planning software and think about what kind of information you'll want to supply to your clients.

Next, run some sample menus using specials taken from newspapers, flyers or other sources. Contact the stores that you want to work with and show them sample menus generated from very recent ads. If you can show the menus from ads run that very day, they will probably be extremely impressed.

Determine who your clients will be. Both small and large food stores and super-markets are going to be interested in your service. Small ones will like you because you can increase their market share against the tough competition of the supermarkets, and large stores will have the money and flexibility to give your service a try.

Arrange a system whereby you can pick up lists of specials to be advertised as early as possible. The advertising departments will be very helpful here—after all, it will mean increased business for them!

After you've begun working for several stores, consider hiring a part-timer to go to the various stores to pick up the information you'll need. You'll be able to run your business many times more efficiently if most of your time is spent at the computer coming up with customized menus.

For your individual shopping list clients, take the same approach. After contacting potential clients (see Marketing Methods), send out some sample lists. You also might want to offer these people the same type of service—send not only shopping lists, but menus generated from the items on the lists.

THE COMPETITION

Look at the food advertisements in your area newspapers. Do you see anyone else offering this service? Probably not. This is one of those terrific ideas that no one has really put into action yet because it is so obvious.

In areas where you do have competition, you might want to concentrate more on the individual shopping list clients. You can always go one better than the competition, by offering more recipe choices for the dollar, including cooking tips with your menus, adding low calorie diets, etc.

POTENTIAL INCOME

Your expenses will be low. Outside of the investment in the computer and software (virtually all of the software for this purpose will be well under $100) your overhead will be in advertising costs. If you decide to hire some help, you can get one or two people for part-time work. This expense will pay for itself quickly as your efficiency multiplies.

If you charge grocery stores only $10 per week for menu-planning and sell the same menus to several stores carrying the same specials, you can easily generate $100 to $500 a week. Individual clients will probably pay from $5 to $25 a month for your service. This may not sound like much, but remember, you can sell the same menus to many people.

Basic Costs

1. Cost of software
2. Cost of advertising
3. Cost of time spent creating menus
4. Cost of time spent organizing food sale information

5. Cost of transportation
6. Cost of printer supplies
7. Cost of materials used

Your fees can be arranged by several methods—either on a per-job basis, or on a long-term contract basis. To come up with a price for your service, figure out the cost of your time and expense and add a profit margin. Of course, for a long-term contract a selling point should be a reduced price.

MARKETING METHODS

Direct mail, display ads, telephone sales and direct sales are the best marketing methods for this business.

As mentioned earlier, either showing potential clients what you can do by mailing or hand-carrying samples of your work should bring positive results. Display ads will do nicely for generating business for your individual shopping list customers. College students are a great potential market for this service. You can reach them through college newspapers and bulletin board ads.

A very effective approach to make in your direct sales pitch is to show potential clients comparisons—before-and-after samples of their ads. After setting up an appointment to speak to someone at the advertising department of a store, for example, show them their current ad, and then show them the same ad embellished with your menu. Such a graphic sample can make a good impact on potential customers.

Take the same approach with your direct mail and display ads for the indvidual shopping list service. Simply show them what you can do, and how you can make their shopping easier. You'll soon find that this business sells itself very well.

UNIQUE BUSINESS APPROACH

For stores and supermarkets that subscribe to your service, supply flyers that have ingredients broken down according to number of servings. For instance, for any particular weekly special, have four stacks of menus or recipes available in the store— one planned for two people, one for three, one for four and one for six. Use any breakdown you think is best. Virtually all of the menu programs you use will have this capability. It will take only seconds to sort and print these customized menus.

LOCATION and MARKET BASE

This business really should be run in an urban or city area. You will want to have a strong market base, and the larger market your clients have for their advertising, the more valuable you will be to them. Your market base will supply you with adequate business if it is above 200,000.

TO SUM UP

This is a terrific opportunity for anyone willing to put the effort into it. The chances are excellent that there is not an existing service like it in your area, and even if there is, it will be easy to claim your market share.

Shopping for food is something most people don't like to do, and if you can make it easier for them, they'll jump at the chance to use your service. Food stores know this too, and it will be easy for you to show them how they can improve their advertising and win more customers. And that will win you customers as well.

SOURCE MATERIAL

Refer to Section 7.

No. 181

COIN AND STAMP COLLECTION INVENTORIES AND VALUES SERVICE

This is a business that has the flair of an old Sidney Greenstreet thriller. Authors have often made coin and stamp collections the central focus of international intrigues. Here's your chance to have a little of that excitement rub off on you.

If you are a collector of either coins or stamps (or both), you would like to maintain an accurate inventory and current value of your collections for your own information as well as for insurance purposes. We will show you how to get other collectors to use your service. Once you get them set up, you can sell this service on a monthly, quarterly or semi-annual basis for price change reports, as well as other useful reports. Once collectors get started with this service, our experience has shown that they do not want to give it up.

CONCEPT

You may be surprised to know how many people collect coins and stamps. These are not only aesthetically beautiful items to collect, they are in many instances monetarily valuable. Whether a collection is held just for the pleasure of ownership or for the investment, an inventory and an evaluation, as well as other data about the coins or stamps, are "must haves" to bring full joy to the owner. Your home computer can step in at this point, with your help, of course, and provide the necessary reports to please even the most avid of collectors.

SKILLS YOU WILL REQUIRE

Your main job is to have your computer manipulate information supplied by others and produce printed reports relevent to that information. You don't need to be an expert on coins or stamps. The skills you will require are those that have to do with the use of the computer itself and can easily be learned.

INFORMATION REQUIRED

Before you can select software that will serve you well, a discussion of data base programs is in order.

A data base is what you will need to run your new business. It is like a giant filing cabinet jammed with scraps of useful information. One of the striking differences though, is that instead of each piece of information being filed under just one heading, it can be filed under a number of headings, or "fields" as they are called. In this case some of the fields might be: denomination, country, year, description, source, market value, date purchased, price paid, etc. It would be valuble to be able to sort a single field and sub-sort other fields at the same time.

If you were running your business by old-fashioned methods, you'd have to select one heading, say denomination, then laboriously set up an elaborate cross-reference to index the other information. This entails a lot of work. The beauty of using a data base to record all this information is that, once the information is recorded, you can search in your computer "filing cabinet" for any and all of these headings in a matter of seconds.

Of course, all this becomes important when you need to update records. You can search your files electronically and go directly to the file that needs attention.

You will need other capabilities to be of real service in this area. You must be able, with your software, to add up all the values to get a total of the inventory. An ordinary data base will not do this. For many computers there are programs made just for collectors. Of course, this is what you want if they are available. Some of them are pre-loaded with information on the standard coins and stamps and their currealues. Several have provisions for listing collectors' meetings and sources of supply. Some even have periodic pricing update disks sent to you to eliminate the work of individual entries for standard varieties of coins and stamps. They also have room for rarer specimens to be put in. If one of these programs is available for your computer, by all means consider it. If there are no ready-made programs for your particular computer, all is not lost. You can adapt one for your needs. Scour software stores and find a salesperson who is knowledgeable. Ask for help identifying a spreadsheet program or a data base program that can be adapted to your needs. Be bold about poking around and talking to people.

In many communities there are user groups for your computer. Join one and get on their mailing list. Most of these people are eager to help a newcomer, and in the discussions you'll learn a lot of firsthand information about your hardware and the programs that are out there for it.

OPERATING NAME

To use a business name that is different from your own, you must spend some time and money publishing your chosen business name. There are papers that make a living publishing this kind of information, although almost any paper can do it. The purpose of this exercise is to publically link your name to that of your business name for identification in case of any future legal matters. Use of a fictitious name also means spending extra money on a business telephone and a business bank account. Both of these are more expensive than accounts held in your own name.

You can obtain a business license in your own name as the name of your business. On your letterhead and business cards you can put "John Doe—Coin and Stamp Cataloguing" to identify yourself. This means you can use the phones, bank accounts, etc. already in your own name.

GETTING STARTED

No matter what kind of business you are thinking about starting, the very first thing you should do is sit down and make out a master plan. If you don't have a clear view of where you want to go, you'll probably end up nowhere. A master plan includes your ultimate goal and the route you propose taking to get there.

We've already discussed combing the software stores in your area for the programs that will work on your computer. If you are going to adapt a program for your use, look carefully at programs ready-made for this purpose, even though they won't run on your computer. They will give you valuable information. Time spent choosing software wisely is time well-spent, since your business revolves around this purchase.

Before selecting a software program, especially if you are going to adapt a program instead of using a ready-made one, spend some time in the numismatic and philatelict (coin and stamp) stores. If there are clubs in your area, go to some meetings to get a feel for the kinds of things these collectors are interested in. It's a lot easier to know what you want in advance than to have to change horses in midstream.

Programs run from $75 to several hundred dollars. This is not the place to economize. Get the most comprehensive one that will fit your needs and will run on your hardware. The more comprehensive ones will have room for more fields and have lots of other extras. Select software carefully. The more it fits your needs, the less hassle you will have and the more profit you will realize.

Look for trade magazines that cater to your brand of computer. The ads are worth the price of the subscription. They will give you the names and addresses of manufacturers of software, services and devices that could be useful to you. There may even be articles every now and then that apply to you. The few hours a month spent looking through these publications could save you a lot of time in your business. After all, time is money, and that's what computers are all about.

Subscribe to magazines that specialize in information for coin and stamp collectors. As has been mentioned, find out about local collector's clubs. These are your potential customers.

Data entry and secretarial services are available to help you type in data if you don't wish to do it all yourself.

THE COMPETITION

Most people who are cataloguing collections electronically are owners who happen to have a computer available to them. The vast majority of collectors are still cataloguing by the old index card method. There is virtually no competition for the small time collector, and there are plenty of them around.

POTENTIAL INCOME

Pricing your service is not difficult. It's important to know your cost of doing business. Go back to the master plan you made and begin pricing out everything on it.

Include:

1. Cost of equipment, including software
2. Cost of advertising
3. Cost of telephone
4. Monthly recurring costs-utilities, rent, printing, etc.
5. Cost of postage
6. Cost of car and travel
7. Cost of dues and publications
8. Cost of your time
9. Any other costs

Start by evaluating your time as an hourly rate and adding a reasonable figure to that for profit. Remember, once you have a customer on your service, there is continuing business for as long as both of you are satisfied with the arrangement. You can charge an initial fee as a setup charge, and then contract for quarterly or annual reports to be done automatically and sent to the client. Your initial fee may not be the money-maker. You may want to plan to realize your profit on the continuing service, since the time it takes to update files and run reports is minimal compared to the setup time, especially if you have an update service.

MARKETING METHODS

Personalized direct mail would be useful to advertise your service. Here's where you can use a word processor. Personalizing mail will appeal to those who are potential customers. Don't be reluctant to send more than one mailing.

If you are allowed to post notices in schools and libraries, make tear-off tabs on your flyers with your phone number on each tab.

Seek out clubs and organizations that are likely to have collector members. Word-of-mouth advertising is very valuable and these groups will spread your name. Remember to give out your card at every opportunity.

The yellow pages of your local phone company is the first place local people look to find what they need. Look at your telephone book, and if there are numerous listing for coin and stamp sources, you might pick up some business from collectors who are looking in the book to buy. As you increase your customer base you will become a source of contacts for buying and selling coins, and could list yourself in the yellow pages under dealers, even though your real interest is in the cataloguing service. You must have a business telephone to have a listings in the yellow pages though. Compare the increased costs of a business phone with the increased local market you might expect. Telephone information operators do not look up listing in the yellow pages, so the increase in business you might get would only be from those who are local.

There are magazines and publications listed in the library's periodical file that have direct interest for you. The leading publications have feature articles and comments regarding use of the modern-day technology of microcomputers in the ancient world of stamp and coin collection. You might consider a small ad in some of these, because they will go directly to potential buyers.

UNIQUE BUSINESS APPROACH

Every major numismatic and philatelic organization is encouraging the use of computers for both dealers and collectors. Special seminars have been scheduled to acquaint their membership with the usefulness and importance of the personal computer. The market has already been created; you just need to get the word out that you have the service for those that don't have their own computer. Contact these organizations and offer to make a presentation letting them know what you do. You don't have to be a Dale Carnegie to do a great job. Creative preparation is the secret.

If you don't have the time for this or if you just feel you can't do public speaking, call the local Toastmaster's Club or adult education public speaking class and let them know you have an on-the-job speaking opportunity for someone in their group. You just might get someone for nothing.

LOCATION and MARKET BASE

You are not going to need to rent an office. The information you will need can be obtained by mail, in person, and over the phone.

An area of population between 50,000 and 200,000 people could be considered a good market base. As long as the telephone company and the post office serve your home and you are willing to travel to areas of denser population or areas with more prospective clients, any location would serve as a reasonable market base.

TO SUM UP

A coin and stamp cataloguing service may have limited application, but even this limited application can be a profitable market. You are offering a service that is very needed. For the investor who may have financial planning or tax considerations, it's a must. The collector who cherishes his collection for his own pleasure loves to finger through the reports of what he has and dream of what he would like to have. Either way, you're important.

The flexibility of this cataloguing service allows you to take on as little of it or as much of it as you feel suited. Expand as the market leads and your time permits.

This is a service with plenty of room for creativity, especially in the methods of marketing. If you happen to collect coins or stamps, so much the better. So start cataloguing today and inventory your way to the bank.

SOURCE MATERIAL

Refer to Section 7.

No. 183

DESIGN AND SELL COMPUTER PROGRAMS FOR FARMERS

There is more to farming than digging holes and dropping seeds into them. Farming is actually a complex business with its own professional jargon and unique computer program needs. Designing and writing computer programs and reports for farming is an area that is just beginning to grow. This chapter will show you how to tailor programs and produce reports that are invaluable to farmers everywhere.

CONCEPT

Don't think that if you don't live on a farm this isn't a good business for you. If you have skills in commodities trading, farm futures, accounting, oral history, interviewing, or actual farming, this could be a very exciting and rewarding business for you. In addition, many programs you have generated already can be rewritten slightly to fit farmers' particular needs.

A farm is a small business, just like any other small business, and requires a considerable amount of record-keeping. In this area alone the computer is an extremely valuable tool. However, the real future of computer-managed farming is in financial or management decision-making. It is possible to pay for a computer based on the value of one such decision alone.

The big farm (agribusiness) uses computerized techniques in running every area of farm life. A computer in the hands of a small farmer can help him compete with large farms that comprise thousands of acres.

A computer gives the farmer better, more detailed and more accurate information than he had in the past, and its use is growing by leaps and bounds.

SKILLS YOU WILL REQUIRE

Skills you will require vary greatly depending on the type of program you want to market. If you are going to design an interactive computer program on disk for the farmer to use on his own computer or to access in a data bank, you will, of course, have to know how to program in a standard computer language. The most common languages used in this area is BASIC. If, in addition, you want to provide an accounting package for farmers, you will have to know accounting.

If you choose to simply produce reports on how to do some farming operations better, you won't need any specialized skills except research and interviewing.

INFORMATION REQUIRED

Farmers do not think only in terms of debits and credits, inventory, liabilities and assets, but also in terms of bushels, head of cattle and acreage. If you aren't already familiar with their particular jargon, talk to some farmers and read some books and publications on the subject.

You will need some specialized information. You may already have some, if you know accounting or deal in commodities—anything that can be translated to the farmer's advantage. If you are not personally knowledgeable on a subject, you'll have to do some research.

GETTING STARTED

There are two types of products this business can provide. One is a computer program on a disk that is used either on the farmer's own computer or accessed through a data bank. The other is in the form of special reports that give the farmer specialized information on how to do things better, long-term weather forecasts, etc. Depending on your skill, you may choose to do one or both.

One area that really hasn't been touched is selling special reports. Farmers are interested in long-term weather predictions, crop schedules, new research, folklore, how old-timers or large scale agribusiness handles particular problems, or almost anything else relating to their work.

You can also use printed reports to maximize your income from the time and effort you put into researching disk programs, simply by using the information you gain to produce printed reports.

This field has an unlimited opportunity bounded only by your imagination and interest.

Farms have a wide variety of products and customers, complicated assets and record-keeping, and extensive tax considerations. You must keep this in mind if you write programs for farmers to use with their computers. The most important programs will probably be for allocating resources and labor, controlling production, planning, costing and budgeting. Most programs will need to be interactive, with farmers providing specific data, and the program delivering computed results.

The number one need today is farmer-oriented accounting packages. Accounting, herd record and decision aids have been the most popular applications because they meet the urgent need for financial management and requirements of farm lending institutions.

Currently, 75 percent of farm computer use deals with financial record-keeping, but farmers need to track physical transactions, not just financial ones. Farmers must combine inventory control and accounting. The program should ideally encompass all of the separate classifications and departments that make up farming as a whole. They need to know exactly how much it costs to grow a bushel of corn, for example.

Another problem with most commercially available accounting software is that it is based on double-entry bookkeeping. Most farmers keep single-entry books. However, double-entry is acceptable, if you use farmer terminology.

The following types of programs are the most needed by the farmer and have proven a market value:

1. Livestock Programs

Herd records: Herd records are used to plan breeding structures as required by lending institutions and farmers.

Breeding Records: Breeding can be big business. "Semen Shares" are sold in exceptionally good breeding bulls. A bull may make many hundreds of thousands of dollars for its owners over the course of its life.

Dairy or beef cattle least-cost, nutritionally-correct feeding programs: Farmers want to be able to design feeding programs cow-by-cow, or for entire herds. The savings in feed costs are potentially enormous, and increased milk production of up to a ton a cow has been reported.

A program that will supply a printout giving a cow-by-cow breakdown of the milk each gives on a daily basis. It's the best way to find a sick or pregnant cow. The program should include a 10-day production average.

The cost-versus-profit of putting cattle on pasture land.

What to do with barren beef cows.

Raising replacement dairy heifers: This produces a pro forma profit statement that allows the farmer to obtain financing and lets them know if it will be a profitable business for that farm.

Tax Benefits of livestock.

2. Crops

Calculations of net profit using combinations of production and price rental agreements using crop shares.

Irrigation scheduling.

Crop budgeting.

Crop rotation.

Chemical analysis of the soil.

Soil data, crop data and fertilizer specifications to interface with price and availability of fertilizers and result in a list of fertilizer options.

3. Financial Management

Capital-investment programs.

How to rent, buy or custom hire outside help for farm equipment.

Loans: Amortization and discounts for present value of farm loans with all types of payments, interests and repayment times.

Calculator that will allow farmer to print out itemized lists with mathematical calclulations.

Refinancing: True costs of money farmer gets by refinancing to obtain locked-in equity.

Appreciation: Projections of historic rates for commodities trading.

Futures hedging.

THE COMPETITION

The competition here is from university and private industry data bases that can be tapped by telephone, and from a few programmers producing agribusiness disks, such as AG-PC from R. Arthur Steinon of Madison, Wisconsin.

There are a number of things you can do to compete effectively in the market place. First of all, instead of seeing the data bases already out there as competition, think of them as an opportunity. Use their information for your own researching. The other approach is to give the farmer a better value and more user-friendly programs. If you do these things, you will find that there essentially is no competition right now.

Farm programs are currently extremely expensive. A single program can cost $800. If your product goes into the market priced more like word processing or data base programs, you can open up a much larger market and actually make more money because you sell more. You've already done the work. It doesn't matter if you sell one program or a thousand. Except for copying your disk onto proper formats, your work is already done.

Other programs and even data bases are not farmer "user friendly." They aren't written using farm terminology. If you can simply write a bookkeeping program that uses bushels instead of assets, you'll have an enthusiastic audience.

POTENTIAL INCOME

It costs an average of $20 per hour for a farmer to use data banks and current software packages cost from $150 to $1,500. A market base of 50,000 to 200,000 buyers can provide tremendous sales for your product.

The costs involved are in the time researching, writing and producing the reports or disks, the cost of the disks themselves, and the cost of having the programs "translated" into other formats.

The two most popular computers among farmers are Radio Shack and Apple II. If you can produce programs that will fit either one of those computers, you may not have to do anything more than copy your finished disk.

If you decide to put out a farm report, you can get your money with subscriptions. You can even increase income by selling advertising to companies that want to reach the farm market.

Basic Costs

1. Cost of software or time spent in development of software
2. Cost of advertising
3. Cost of research materials, such as data banks, publications, etc.
4. Cost of materials used
5. Cost of time spent organizing information

MARKETING METHODS

Many of the 26 farm data base networks in business today started with clients found by using the subscription list from periodicals they were already publishing. You can tap the same source by simply advertising in these special-interest magazines, or by purchasing their mailing lists and using direct mail. A partial listing can be found under Source Material. You can also find listings at your public library under Periodicals in Print. You can also find samples of some of these magazines in most library periodical sections.

UNIQUE BUSINESS APPROACH

Farmers are accustomed to receiving information from land-grant universities, county extension specialists and private sector production-management consultants. You can save yourself a lot of work and perhaps a good deal of money in advertising by selling your program to one or more of the agricultural networks.

You may sell your program for a much larger sale amount than you would to an individual farmer, and you can also negotiate royalties on the number of times the farmers use the program, just as book royalties are calculated.

This is a particularly good technique for programs that are too large to run on a personal computer or are used too seldom to justify a software purchase.

There are also agents now handling just computer programs. If you don't feel you have the time to market your own work, or just plain don't like advertising, selling, etc., one of these agents may provide just the service you are looking for.

LOCATION and MARKET BASE

This is one business that may be better suited to the country than to the city. If you have access to a farmer's everyday needs, new programs and reports will become apparent to you in an easy and natural manner.

Whether you live in the city or the country, you should have access to a land-grant university or county extension service and a good library with farm reference books; otherwise, research time may be too much of a burden for you.

Only about five percent of small farmers are currently using computers. Large farms are almost fully automated. It is estimated that in only five years 80 to 90 percent of all farm acreage will be farmed with the aid of a computer.

TO SUM UP

Farmers are no longer the agrarian bumpkins pictured in turn-of-the-century fiction. Farming is big business—agribusiness—and a huge sector of our economy is tied to how well it does. Farmers still wear bib overalls, but they often claim a six-figure investment in their farms.

Whatever you choose to wear, a little attention to the details of farm management and the business end of farming can bring you a great deal of money.

Like tractors and irrigation systems, a personal computer is a tool to help a farmer do the work more efficiently. It is a management tool. If you can provide the farmer, small or large, with tools that will help make or save money and time, you have a viable business.

SOURCE MATERIAL

Refer to Section 7.

No. 184

PERSONAL LIBRARY CATALOGUING SERVICE

If you like books, this business is for you. You probably know several people who have upwards of thousand books in their home, or perhaps considerably more. You can use your personal computer to catalog their collections, and the collections of anyone else who wants the service. A personal library can be a source of great satisfaction—or a source of great confusion. With this service, the confusion can be avoided, and you can put money in your pocket.

CONCEPT

The concept of this business is, broadly speaking, to create order out of chaos. While few people who have large personal libraries would describe their collections as chaotic, the fact is that there frequently are times in their lives when they wish to find a particular volume quickly and cannot do it. It is on some shelf in some room, between two or three other books, placed there more or less at random.

Using a computer-sorting system, you can make access to volumes in a personal collection as easy as it is in a public library. You can list books by authors, title, subject, or any way your client desires. You can hand your client a complete card catalog of his or her library, and a computer print-out with a complete cross-referencing system. Locating a book need never be a chaotic process again.

But ease in locating volumes is only one reason that clients will want to use your service. Each year, millions of dollars are lost when personal libraries are destroyed in house fires or other unforeseen disasters. Having a complete and organized cataloguing of one's personal library can be a real savings when it comes to making insurance claims. Just knowing that such a listing exists will allow your well-read client to sleep better at night.

SKILLS YOU WILL REQUIRE

You will need to own and be able to operate a data base management system. Many such programs are marketed for all of the more popular personal computers. They typically run between $300 and $700.

Your data base management system will need to be capable of taking the information typically found on a card in a library card catalog (author, title, subject, publisher, copyright date, etc.) and sorting it by any specified criteria. For example, your client may want his card catalog arranged alphabetically by author, and books by the same author to be listed in order of their dates of publication. Another client may want his books divided into two dozen subject categories and alphabetically arranged by author within those categories. Still another client may want the standard three files arranged by author, by title and by subject. A good data base management system can do any of these things.

Some of the more popular data base management systems include: DataEase, dBase II, dBase III and Condor 3. Shop around for one that works best for you.

INFORMATION REQUIRED

Once you've got your data base system up and running, the only information you will need is your input—that is, a listing of your client's collection. You have two choices here. You can go to the client's home and take an inventory of the collection yourself, a time-consuming process for which the client will pay. Or you can work with clients who bring you the listing themselves.

The advantage to taking inventory yourself is that you are assured of getting complete information. All books have a page at the front which contains the Library of Congress publication data. This all the information you will need in order to sort your client's collection in any way he or she wishes.

Some clients will undoubtedly want to save money by doing the inventory themselves, and this is fine. It is also necessary, if you plan to service a wide geographical area. Make sure beforehand that the client understands how to take inventory of his collection and how to provide you with all the necessary data.

GETTING STARTED

As mentioned earlier, you will need to get your data base management system operating smoothly before you can think about offering your service for sale. If you have a fairly large personal library, catalog it in as many different ways as you can think of. There is no better place to practice, and you will more than likely end up using the results of your labor.

If your library is inadequate, find a friend or associate who owns a large collection of books and offer your services. Perhaps he can return the favor by fixing your lawnmower or taping that television special you have to miss. In any case, a "dry run" is strongly recommended to iron out any problems you may have before you go into business.

Once your program is ready, the next step is to locate your potential clients. There are several ways to do this; they are discussed in Marketing Methods.

THE COMPETITION

To eliminate the competition, you need to come up with a system that is both cost-effective and easy for the client to use.

Most clients, unless they are professional librarians, will not want the Dewey Decimal System installed in their homes. To begin with, most of the collections you will be dealing with are not big enough to warrant it. A client will want an easy referencing system that allows him to find a book in the shortest possible time.

A good way to provide this facility is with a system of stickers. Suppose a client wants two listings, one arranged by subject and alphabetized within each subject by author, the other arranged alphabetically by title. Sort the collection first by subject and author. Assign a number to each book in that order and include the number in the listing of books. Print a series of stickers to be placed on the spine of each volume in the collection. Each subject could get its own set of numbers. For example, all fiction might go by numbers starting with 1000, medical books might go by 2000, and so on. This technique will enable the collection inventory to expand.

Next, sort the collection by title and print out the listing for the second catalog. But keep the original numbers the same. Again, the number of each book will appear in the listing for each book. The numbers in this file will not be in order, but if a client knows the title of the book for which he is searching, he can look it up in this file, check the number and easily find it on the shelf.

POTENTIAL INCOME

Pricing your services is not complicated. You start out by placing an hourly value on your own time. Add to your hourly pay all the costs of operating the program and add in a profit figure for the job. The total is what you should charge for the job. Keep in mind that your hourly rate is not profit, but an operating cost for your business. Profit is what the business makes after all the costs are covered. You should earn money for your time and a profit for your business on each project.

Obviously, if you are going to be doing inventory for a client's personal library yourself, you are going to be spending much more time on the project than if the client presents you with a completed list. And since you are entering the information on each volume into your program, the time you spend will be proportional to the size of the collection. You should therefore come up with a rate structure that reflects the increase in time resulting from increases in library size . You should show side-by-side rates for your service if the client takes inventory, and if you do it.

In addition to your time, here are some other costs you will need to take into account:

1. Cost of operating your computer and printer
2. Cost of materials, such as paper, stickers, ribbons, etc.
3. Cost of advertising
4. Any travel costs
5. Miscellaneous expenses, such as telephone bills
6. Cost of data base software

How To Be Paid

After quoting a price based on the size of the collection to be catalogued, you should probably make it a practice to be paid one-half of the total up front and the remainder upon completion of the job. You can also offer yearly updates which will add books acquired within the last year and delete books sold or discarded.

MARKETING METHODS

Direct mail campaigns and display ads are the best methods for marketing your personal library cataloging service.

Once you've got your program established, the next step is to locate your potential clients. There are numerous ways to do this.

One is to run a display ad in publications that book collectors read. This method, while it can produce results, is essentially hit-or-miss in nature and will reach only a portion of your target clientele.

A better method is to establish a mailing list and send out direct mail letters. The task here is to find people with personal libraries sizable enough to interest them in your service. There are organizations that have mailing lists you can tap into: book-of-the-month clubs, magazines for book collectors, mail order bookstores. There are even mailing list brokers that will sell you a variety of mailing lists for a small fee.

Plug your mailing list into your computer and write up a short sales letter on your service. Send them out in batches of 10 to 20 and watch the inquiries pour in.

Here is an example of a sales letter you might use:

> DEAR READER:
>
> Have you ever wanted to find a poem, a recipe or a piece of useful information you know is tucked away in a book of yours somewhere, and not been able to?
>
> Personal libraries, if not managed properly, can quickly turn into literary jungles. Now, with our new low-cost cataloging system, your book collecton can be as easy to access as the one at your public library.
>
> We offer complete cataloging and cross-referencing. Let us organize your library in whatever way is most convenient for you. Our computerized system can index your collection by author, subject, title, category or any and all of the above methods. Call us today and let us make your reading life a little easier.

That letter, or some variation of it, will produce results. Don't expect a flood of business overnight, but if you keep on top of your potential market, your business will generate a steady income. One factor working in your favor is that people who have large book collections tend to talk to other people who have large book collections, and this word-of-mouth network can help get your business known.

UNIQUE BUSINESS APPROACH

People who collect books tend to frequent bookstores, and you can take advantage of this. Many bookstores distribute bookmarks with each purchase, usually bearing the name of the store. You can work out a deal with one or two bookstores in your area to distribute bookmarks that advertise your cataloging service as well.

You can approach the stores and offer to pay them to print the name, address and phone number of your business on the back of their own bookmarks, or you can ask them to distribute your own bookmarks along with their own. If you are really ambitious, you can approach a bookstore chain and pitch them on the idea.

LOCATION and MARKET BASE

You can operate a library cataloging system anywhere people read books. If you plan on doing most of your inventory work yourself, you need to take travel time into account. A rural, urban or suburban location is appropriate for this business.

START UP CAPITAL If you've already got your personal computer, you can get going in this business for an initial investment of under $1,000. Your major cost, as mentioned previously, is your data base software. For more information on obtaining start-up capital, refer to Section 6.

TO SUM UP

A personal library cataloging service can be a real godsend to someone with a large, poorly organized collection of books. Your computer can organize their collection hundreds of time faster than they ever could and can provide valuable cross-referencing and easy access heretofore only available in libraries.

It is a very simple business to operate once you get started, and the operating costs are minimal. Most important, it is a service people will pay for.

Think of it this way: If you're looking for a needed piece of information, would you rather look for it in a well-ordered file cabinet or in a disarray of books and papers? You know the answer to that and can make money because of it.

SOURCE MATERIAL

Refer to Section 7.

No. 185

COMPUTER CARPOOLING SERVICE

This service got started during the gasoline shortage days, but it has continued to grow ever since. We will show you how to contact large and small businesses in a concentrated area to get names of people who commute from specific areas. After compiling this information on your personal computer, you can set up car pools that are convenient to everybody. So start a car pooling service today and get your share of the revenue.

CONCEPT

The idea behind this business is to set up car pooling schedules for people who work the same basic hours in the same basic area. You get money for the service from the employer who uses it, because it saves him or her lost production time. You also get income from the employees who use it, because it will save them money.

The cost of getting to work is expensive. Not only is there wear and tear on your car, but there are gas and parking expenses. Yet most people still drive themselves to work because they don't know how to get in touch with others who can drive with them and share expenses. With your personal computer, you are able to put these people in touch with one another and let them take it from there. They'll gladly pay for the service, especially after you show them how much they'll save by car pooling with just one other person. Your fee will equal a small fraction of the total savings.

SKILLS YOU WILL REQUIRE

If you enjoy helping people, you'll do well with this business, since that is the primary service you'll be offering. You'll be asking each client a few questions about work schedules and locations. After that, you plug the information into the computer to sort out and put together a list of potential car pooling partners for your customers.

Plus, you'll be dealing with employers who want to set up a carpooling service for their employees. If you are shy, you have nothing to worry about. The service will just naturally sell itself. All you have to do is explain it. After that, it will become second nature to you to talk with people about what you have to offer. Once you're established, you can then hire a part-time person to take your calls for information.

INFORMATION REQUIRED

A computer car pooling service requires that you get certain information from your customers in order to find car pooling partners for them. The easiest way to do this is to set up a questionaire to fill out when they call for your service. A sample questionnaire might ask:

1. Name:
2. Home address:
3. Work address:
4. Days you work:
5. Area of town work is located:
6. Time you need to be at work:
7. Time you get off work:
8. Can you drive your car?
9. Do you prefer to be a passenger?
10. Home phone number:
11. Work phone number:

Your own version of this questionnaire will give you all the information you'll need to arrange carpooling for your customers. With your computer you can sort out the times and places people give you and compile a listing of the people who need to be at the same or nearby place at the same times.

OPERATING NAME

To operate this business you can use your own name, Tom Smith. Under your ads you can add "Car Pooling Arrangements" or "Car pool Schedules Created" to let people know what service you offer. This will avoid the extra start-up costs of filing for a fictitious name, getting a business phone, etc.

If you choose to, at a later date you can always take a fictitious name, such as "Computer Car Pooling Arrangements" or something like that.

GETTING STARTED

To get started with this service, your first step should be to advertise, in order to inform potential customers of the availability of somebody to arrange their car pooling for them. You can also send out letters to employers in your area telling them about your service. (See Marketing Methods below).

Once you get interested potential customers, have them fill out the questionnaire you've designed. Then you can enter the information into your computer and start sorting them out. Once you have a group of two, three, four or more customers who would make likely car pooling partners, print out their names, addresses, etc., to give to each customer. It is up to them to contact each other to make arrangements after that.

Once you have a steady list of clients using your service, they'll keep coming back to you for more partners, as the ones they have been car pooling with change work shifts or move.

THE COMPETITION

The only real competition you have with this business is getting over people's hesitation to rely on your service. They won't think that it's convenient for them or that it will get them to work in a timely fashion. But once you show them how much they'll be saving by carpooling and once they've tried the service, your competition—hesitation—is eliminated.

For example, say a person works 20 miles from where he lives. That means he probably spends three dollars a day for gas coming and going. If he works downtown, he might have to pay $30 or more a month for parking. Plus, he'll be spending hidden dollars on the wear and tear on his car. The total easily equals over $100 a month just to get to work and back. The amount you charge him by supplying driving partners will be just a fraction of the amount he has to pay each month by not car pooling.

Employers will be glad to use your service, because it ensures that employees will arrive to work on time. How many times have you heard that one of the biggest business expenses is workers who arrive late or don't come at all, because of car trouble? With this service, those problems will be eliminated.

POTENTIAL INCOME

In this business, you can make a tidy little profit with little effort. To figure out what to charge is a simple matter. Simply calculate your expenses, add in a salary for yourself and a profit for the business. Then divide that number among the potential customers you have. That should give you an idea of what to charge.

Primary Costs

1. Cost of advertising
2. Cost of time spent organizing questionnaire
3. Cost of materials mailed out
4. Cost of miscellaneous materials used
5. Cost of organizing data from customers
6. Cost of software

Profit

Allocate your profit as something separate from your own salary. The money you make for your time is not profit. That is another business expense. Profit is what goes to the business.

Practically speaking, you don't want to charge more than the traffic will bear. Time and experience will give you an amount that is both reasonable to your customers and profitable for you.

How To Be Paid

To get your money for this service, you can use a couple of methods. Each will depend on who is paying.

Since you will get business from local employers who want to arrange a car pooling program for their employees, you can charge by the number of employees involved. For example, if a company has 100 workers all going to the same location, you can tell the employer that for a one-time fee of $100 you will put together a listing of car pooling partners. This, you can explain, is only one dollar per employee, a small fraction of the amount of money he will be saving by having his workers there on time every day. Then you can offer him a monthly revision to include new employees and to weed out employees who have left, for another $50 or whatever price you decide on. Since the amount of time you will spend on doing the revisions is very small, the amount of money you make for your time increases.

Employees who use your service can pay for a one-time use fee. Say you charge $10, paid in advance. For this money the customer will get a listing of people that he or she can call to arrange for car pooling.

If you set up five employers in a month, that could mean $500 in your pocket. Plus, you make extra money from those customers who come to you on an individual basis.

MARKETING METHODS

The best ways to market this business is with display ads and direct mail. The first method requires that you place ads in local newspapers where people who will want to use your service can see them. You might also consider contacting local companies that put out a newsletter for their employees, to advertise in that also.

Another method is to send out a letter to employers who will want to use the service for their workers. A typical letter might read:

> DEAR EMPLOYER:
>
> Are you tired of losing money, stopping the assembly line, and slowing production because your workers didn't arrive to work on time?
>
> Let us help you get your workers to the job when they're supposed to be there. Let us save your workers money they spend on transportation costs.
>
> Our Computer Car Pooling Service will match your workers to others in their area to share rides with.
>
> For one low fee, we'll compile a list of all employees on your payroll and find them car pooling partners. Call us today for more information!

A version of this letter should bring calls for more information about your service. When you get calls, supply them with the prices you charge and the amount of time it will take for you to do your compiling, based on how large their company is.

To make the most of direct mail, you should mail out 10 or 20 letters a day in your area regularly. You should start with the large companies in your area and work down to the smaller ones. This method will probably bring you more customers than you expected for so little effort.

UNIQUE BUSINESS APPROACH

The people who operate this business know one little secret that you to will want to know before starting out. The secret is to put together your car pooling routes for the customers you already have, then to track down more customers who fall on the same route. For instance, if you have two people who work at company Z, you can probably find workers at companies X and Y right on the way to company Z that will want to use your service as well. What you do is integrate the car pooling of your larger company customers with the car pooling of your smaller company customers. All it takes is to figure out who falls on the same carpooling routes.

Nothing says you have to put together car pooling partners who work at the same company. And nothing's to say you can't increase your income by being smart about your business.

LOCATION and MARKET BASE

With this business, no location is better than another. You can start it right where you are now, with nothing more than a phone and the mails at your service.

If you are in an area that has large companies or other businesses that have a large labor force, this business is particularly well suited to your needs, since that is where your business will come from.

To offer this service, you'll probably want to be in a market base of from 50,000 to 200,000 people. Most large cities already offer a car pooling service to their residents, so the field is wide open to make a killing in smaller population centers.

START UP CAPITAL

To start this service, you'll need less than $1,000. This money will go to buy the software you'll use, plus to put together and mail out letters, and to place advertisements to generate business.

Since your customers, the employers, will be paying you money up front to organize their carpooling programs, you'll have income up front to pay for the materials you'll need.

TO SUM UP

Every day people shuttle back and forth to work alone, grumbling about the cost of commuting, grumbling about congested traffic, grumbling because they're tired of driving by themselves. With a computer car pooling service you rid them of all these problems. First, they'll have somebody to share their commuting expenses with. Second, they won't have so much traffic to battle every morning and afternoon, since carpooling drastically reduces the number of cars on the road. And third, they'll be sharing the driving expenses with somebody else, allowing them to relax on their way to work for a change. They'll arrive on time, with extra money in their pockets and a smile on their face, all because they sat back and let somebody else do the driving.

The money you make with this service comes in small but very steady amounts. Once you've started it, you'll find employers referring their associates in other companies to you. You may even find your face in the local newspaper as the subject of a feature story. Think about it—singlehandedly, you are reducing traffic jams, pollution and driver tension. The handsome chunk of money you make in this business with just a small investment of time is se reward you deserve.

SOURCE MATERIAL

For sources, refer to Section 7.

No. 186

LEGAL RESEARCH SERVICE

Before the age of the computer, the way to do legal research was to go to a law library and surround yourself with stacks of thick volumes. Today, legal information data bases make the job much easier. You can use your personal computer to tap into these data bases and make a substantial amount of money doing research for lawyers in your city.

CONCEPT

The concept of this business is to locate information and sell it to those who need it—in this case, lawyers and law offices. You not only provide an invaluable service to your clients, you save them a lot of time as well.

You are selling advantage as well as time. All lawyers must research countless court cases in search of precedents which will help their clients. You help them to put their hands on the precedent-setting cases they need in a hurry, enabling them to prepare their legal strategies and materials.

Information is a powerful commodity, and the computer is a powerful shepherd of information. Court cases often hinge on a single legal issue, and in providing your clients with the complete range of legal information they need, you are providing a tremendously valuable service—and one for which you will be well rewarded.

SKILLS YOU WILL REQUIRE

You don't have to have a law degree to research legal information, although the present legal system tends to perpetuate the myth that the law is too complicated for the layperson to understand. A surface understanding of some of the less cumbersome legal terminology is really all you will need.

The legal intricacies of what you are researching are not nearly as important as knowing where to look for information. Your clients will handle the interpretation; they need you to locate the information for them to interpret. And as a computer operator you have a great advantage in locating information.

You will need to develop some basic research skills, but those will come as you get more familiar with the business. You will begin to recognize elements that occur in certain patterns, and then be able to search for those patterns. For instance, one of your clients may ask you to research cases involving libel suits against authors. You can search legal data bases for all cases in which the word "author" and the world "libel" occur in the same sentence, or within a certain number of words from one another.

Once you become comfortable with legal terminology and hone your research techniques, you will be able to combine the two and find relevant material in less and less time. The more you do it, the more valuable your legal research business becomes.

INFORMATION REQUIRED

Obviously, you are in the business of information. The advent of the personal computer has made locating information a faster and easier process than ever before. Almost all the information you will need can be found on computer data bases.

Computers are now being fed almost everything mankind knows, and a computer operator can locate and use the information within seconds. There are data base services available to find information on almost any subject anyone cares to research. The law is no exception.

Among the most frequently used legal data bases are Lexis, Westlaw and Juris, and there are many others. These legal libraries give you access to full texts of cases, state case law, citation searches and the Federal Register. They sometimes even provide cross-referencing to other data bases.

Before you embark on this venture, you will need to be familiar with some basic terminology. A data base is a computerized index system, like the card file you use to locate books in a library. It locates sources of information under several different cross-references and is infinitely faster to use than a manual card file.

You may see some data sources described as "interactive." This means that the data base can, in addition to supplying you with the information it has in storage, call up other computer bases and look for additional information. An interactive data base has access to many sources.

When you use a computer terminal to call up another computer, you are "on line." This means that you are paying for the long-distance phone call to the computer's location, plus the charge imposed by the owners or operators to use it. If you find some data you want printed out, you can order it "on line" and the source computer will deliver it through your printer on request. This can be expensive. Data travels at the speed of light, but printers run only as fast as their manufacturers designed them to. It takes time to print what you want, and all the time you are paying computer and telephone charges.

To save money on this part of your operation, you can order the material printed "off line." The source computer prints it up when it has time, and the material is mailed to you. When requesting a lot of information, you will save a substantial amount of money doing it this way.

OPERATING NAME

You have basically two choices when choosing the name of your new business. You can pick a fictitious name, such as "Legal Eagle Research," "American Legal Research Service," or something like that. Such an approach offers no tangible advantage, and involves a lot of extra start-up costs you could just as easily do without. You will need to register the name, get a new bank account, have a new phone put in at business rates, and so on.

A better strategy is to go with some variation of your own name. If you call your business "Joe Jones Legal Research Service" or "Joe Jones and Associates," you have a perfectly good name for your business and you can use all the phones, addresses and accounts currently listed as belonging to you.

GETTING STARTED

Getting your business rolling is a matter of making contacts within the legal profession. Your first step should be to prepare a brochure outlining your service, detailing the research sources you will be using and the areas you intend to serve. Then you need to write a sales letter soliciting assignments. These should be sent to lawyers in your area at a regular rate. For more on promoting your service, see Marketing Methods.

Use all available sources of information in determining your approach. Included in this are professional legal researchers who are employees of some of the larger law firms. Seek these people out and talk to them. Check legal publications to find out what types of research services lawyers are using. The more you know about the needs of your potential clients, the more successful you will be in fulfilling their needs.

THE COMPETITION

Your most serious competition comes from your clients themselves. Most lawyers, if they were so inclined, could do much of their own research using computer data bases in very little time. They already know the key words to look for when researching a case, and for the investment of a computer system, they could save themselves a lot of money.

Fortunately for you, many lawyers do not want to bother to learn the few things you need to know to communicate with computer data bases. This leaves an opening in the market for the independent researcher.

Major legal firms will have the funds to maintain their own research staffs. You will be going after the small firms and independent lawyers. It is these lawyers who will very carefully weigh the cost of hiring researchers against the cost of doing it themselves. With your personal computer, you can make your time worth their money.

POTENTIAL INCOME

Determining what price to charge for your services is a relatively simple process. You need to be paid for the time you spend, the costs you incur, and the profit you want to make.

Start out by placing an hourly value on your own time. Add up your total operating costs for the job, and add your profit to the total of your hourly payment and your operating costs. The result is what you should charge for the job.

Remember that your hourly rate is not profit; it is a cost of doing business. You need to make money for your time as well as a profit for your business on each job.

Here is a list of some of the major costs that you will need to take into account when figuring your rate structure:

1. Cost of your time
2. Cost of using data bases, including long-distance phone bills and subscription fees
3. Costs of operating your equipment, including electrical bills
4. Cost of promoting your service, including postage and telephone bills
5. Cost of materials used
6. Cost of any fixed overhead, such as rental of work space

Any fixed overhead, such as office rental or monthly electrical charges related to operating your service, should be paid for on a per-time basis. In other words, if one job takes 10 percent of your time one month, it should pay 10 percent of your overhead.

As far as the profit goes, only experience will tell you what to charge. As indicated in the beginning of this report, legal research can often be very valuable. Recognize the value to your clients of the information you supply them and don't underprice yourself. As in any business, you should charge what the market will bear.

You should probably be paid half of the agreed-upon price when you are hired, and half upon delivery of the information. This way, your research is financed and you have enough money to operate.

MARKETING METHODS

Direct mail, display ads in legal publications, telephone sales and direct sales are the best methods for marketing this type of service.

You will probably get the best results with either a direct mail campaign or a series of display ads in legal journals. However, the strategy of direct mail allows you to reach 100 percent of your target clientele, and also personalizes your sales approach a little bit. You will have to weigh the costs of each of your marketing alternatives, but remember, you can't do business without customers.

Here is a sample letter for a direct mail campaign:

DEAR LAWYER:

If you are already doing legal research at the speed of light, disregard this letter. Otherwise, our new computerized legal rsearch service can save you a lot of time and money.

You know how time-consuming legal research can be. Not any more! Our fast and reliable service can eliminate those hours of searching and put your hands on the information you need within minutes.

Sound impressive? It is. We would like very much to give you a demonstration of our service. In 30 minutes we can show you how you can save thousands of hours—and dollars—in the future.

That letter, or a similar one, sent to all prospects in your area, will bring you results. Send it out at the rate of 10 to 20 a day. It will take time, and nothing will happen overnight, but if you keep sending out letters on this, you will get business.

UNIQUE BUSINESS APPROACH

Lawyers now advertise and so can you. A good way to catch the attention of lawyers is to place a display ad in the classified section of your local newspaper, adjacent to the often lengthy legal notices section. Not only does this associate your business with the law, it puts your ad in a place where it will be seen by many of your potential customers.

Any kind of free publicity you can get is good for your business. Send press releases to all the local media announcing your founding. More often than not, you will get some free advertising value from doing this.

LOCATION and MARKET BASE

To operate a legal research service successfully, you have to be where the lawyers are. Lawyers tend to congregate in cities. Ideally, you should be located in an area with a population of over 200,000.

Remember that the huge legal firms are not going to hire a fledgling and unproven legal research service. Don't let that discourage you. In any large city, there are hundreds of small legal firms and independent lawyers. By concentrating on them, you can begin building a dependable market base for your service.

START UP CAPITAL

To get your legal research business off the ground, you should plan on an initial investment of at least $5,000, including the cost of your computer equipment. For information on obtaining the capital you need, Refer to Section 6.

TO SUM UP

Legal research is big business. Lawyers will pay good money to someone who can give them a complete information picture in a short time. As lawyer's fees mount, so does the value of research.

By concentrating on the smaller legal firms first, you can create a loyal market base from which to expand your operation as you see fit. Many lawyers don't know how to use computer data bases to locate information. It is a skill for which they will pay handsomely. And the reward will be all yours.

With your personal computer, you can climb aboard this elevator and ride it up to a very comfortable living.

SOURCE MATERIAL

Refer to Section 7.

ESTATE PLANNING SERVICE

This system has been around for a long time using manual techniques. Now, with your personal computer, you can produce complete estate planning packages in a matter of minutes. We will show you how to set these packages up and make them so understandable that anybody can read them. We will also show you how you can get clients for this service very easily.

CONCEPT

The concept of this business is to perform estate planning for your customers. There are no end to people with estate planning problems. Usually, these problems consist of trying to figure out how to allocate their resources. The tragic part is that an unexpected death can really leave an estate in turmoil. With this business, you will be able to set up estate plans that ensure that a lifetime of work won't go down the drain due to poor planning.

What you will be offering people is a number of options for their estate planning. You can use your computer to create several scenarios for how they might want to invest their money. For example, if they put their money into life insurance policies only, their beneficiary will receive one amount. On the other hand, investing in stocks at such a return will pay off another amount. These options can guide your clients into making the wisest or most prudential planning decisions. In return, you will make money for your efforts.

SKILLS YOU WILL REQUIRE

The skills you'll need for this business consist of being able to assist people in understanding what their estates consist of and how they should be managed. If you have ever done insurance work, investment counseling or tax planning, you already have the terminology and basic skills needed to operate this service.

If you are a novice to these fields, do some preliminary research to learn what the whole estate planning arena consists of. You want to gain an understanding of the various options that are available, as well as the forms, terminology and advantages and disadvantages involved in each.

Another source of learning is the software you'll be using. Most of the estate planning software available today will take you through the steps you need to create an estate plan. It will prompt you for information, numbers, projections for the future and other such information that will help you carry out the service.

INFORMATION REQUIRED

The information you'll need to operate this business is of two types. The first type is what you'll need to operate your computer. Before you do this, you'll need to choose your software. Begin by reading reviews of investment and estate planning software in computer magazines. This will get you familiar with what is available, how much it costs, what it can do and how effectively it operates. Once you've narrowed the field down to a few choices, it is time to visit your local software dealer for a demonstration of the packages you are considering.

Once you have made a selection in software, it is time to learn about the second type of information. That is, the data you'll be compiling for the estate plans you do. An effective way to learn not only the software, but also the kind of information that will be required for your service, is to create your own estate plan. You can do this by figuring out what your investment portfolio, pensions, assets and liabilities are, then entering the information into your computer. Depending on what program you use, the software should come up with projected values of your numbers in, say, 5 years, 10 years, 20 years, etc.

After you understand the meaning of these numbers, you can set about putting together an estate plan. This might consist of designating policies in the name of the person who will receive the benefits upon death, creating a will, and researching other such legal and investment information.

An effective method for learning what an estate plan should consist of is to pay a visit to a lawyer, legal clinic or an estate planner. Pose as a prospective client and discuss the kinds of services offered, as well as the prices charged. This will provide you with a low-cost education in the estate planning business. It should also provide you with the types of forms and tax papers used in the business. This will come in handy when you start working with your own clients in creating an estate plan, since you will have before you exactly what your clients will need.

GETTING STARTED

Once you have a working knowledge of the estate planning business, you are ready to open your door for business. By following the ideas listed in Marketing Methods, you should gain a steady clientele in no time.

You might consider putting together a brochure listing your services, as well as the basic advantages and disadvantages of creating an estate plan. This brochure needn't be fancy, but it should look professional. Use a graphic artist and copywriter, if need be, to create art and copy that will impress your prospective customers.

On one side of the brochure you might also consider placing a questionnaire that provides a checklist of estate planning guidelines. Of course, the tag line would read something like, "If you are unsure how to plan your own estate, we can provide the assistance you need. Call today!"

One side to this operation that will make your time more effective is to create a "package" of estate planning tools that your customer can use. This means that you will come up with checklists, financial questionnaires, will forms and other necessary information that you can provide your clients, no matter what their circumstnaces might be. What this does is streamline your operations. Once you have assisted a few people, you will know the kinds of basic data needed by most people, and this is what you can include in your package. When a customer comes to you, you can then plug the numbers he provides into your computer, come up with his options and send him on his way with the necessary paperwork he will need to fill out to make his planning legal.

THE COMPETITION

Your competition in this field is primarily lawyers, investment counselors and insurance agents. How you differ from them is how you can clean up in this business. Since your primary business is estate planning packages, you can churn out your information much faster than they can, and therefore charge less. Plus, you won't be swayed by commissions as some of them might be. To effectively compete, you will need to create estate planning packages that most people can follow easily. All that means is that once you know the necessary forms and information required, you can supply them with quickly created plans that are still customized enough to suit individual needs.

POTENTIAL INCOME

The way you make your money in this business is by charging each customer for his plan. If you intend to create an estate planning packge, you will be able to charge each client less, since the time it takes you to perform the plan is less. If you charge $50 for each customer, which is a very reasonable amount, and you get 10 customers in a week, your business will have made $500. If you get your system down to the point where each plan requires only an hour apiece, then your hourly fee turns out to be $50. What this means is that if you intend to offer this service on a full-time basis, you can pull in several thousand dollars a week.

To accurately price your service, first you will have to estimate all the costs of the program. Then you must add in an hourly salary for your time, as well as a profit for the business. This last item isn't the same as what you earn; it is money that the business earns, enabling it to grow.

Basic Costs

1. Cost of software
2. Cost of time spent researching business
3. Cost of initial lawyer and advisor fees
4. Cost of forms used
5. Cost of brochure
6. Cost of reproducing forms, publications used
7. Cost of time spent organizing package
8. Cost of time spent with each client
9. Cost of advertising
10. Cost of telephone
11. Cost of materials used

MARKETING METHODS

The most effective ways to market this business are display ads, direct mail and classifieds.

The classifieds can be placed in local dailies, under the "Personals" section. You might also consider running them in local publications that go out to the business, senior citizen and investment communities.

You can also run display ads in the same publications. You might consider trying them in the sports pages, business pages or even the obituary pages. Sad as this last method might sound, it would be far sadder if a sudden death were to leave an estate in turmoil.

A typical ad might read:

> Does your estate plan do what it ought to? Our computer analysis of your present plan may offer you additional options. Call today for consultation.

Or it might read:

> Is your money doing everything it should? Call today for an analysis of your estate planning needs.

This approach will reach a wide range of potential customers and should garner you some business.

Another approach can be tried with direct mail. You can rent or compile a list of the people in your area who are, say, over 40, or who earn a particular level of income, or who have taken out life insurance policies recently. What you want to do is reach the audience you need to sell this service to. In most cases, this will turn out to be people who earn at least a medium level of income and who have reached a certain age.

What you can emphasize in your letters is that an estate plan can benefit your client in the long run, how the fee will quickly be recouped from smarter investment planning, and how you will ensure that everything to do with the estate plan is covered, for a fee that can't be matched. You might consider enclosing a copy of your brochure so that your potential customers can read through the checklist you've printed on it.

UNIQUE BUSINESS APPROACH

Now I'm going to let you in on a few secrets that can get this business off and soaring beyond your wildest dreams.

One approach that you should try with this business is to go directly to your competition. This includes lawyers, investment counselors and others who handle estate planning. Since many of these people don't consider routine paperwork or routine counseling very profitable, they can supply you with their estate planning projects. In return, you will get a steady source of work. But instead of working with clients directly, you will be working with their legal counsel, insurance agents, etc. Many of these people may even consider taking you in as a partner for their financial planning business. They supply one kind of service, and you supply another kind. Together, you both can profit.

Another method that can generate business is to give talks on the subject of your service at civic, business, church, social and community meetings and gatherings. Since you will have become an expert in financial planning, you can cover a topic, such as "10 Points to Consider in Estate Planning." If you bring along your brochures and leave them in a conspicuous place, people will have your number on hand when decide to go to such a service. Plus, you will have generated interest and curiosity about a subject that might not otherwise have been considered.

LOCATION and MARKET BASE

You should be in a city to offer this service. The required market base can range from 200,000 up. This will give you a large enough customer base to make this business pay off.

TO SUM UP

An estate planning service is a business that has always been around, yet one that usually cost more than most people are willing to pay. As a result, they let their lawyers, insurance agents or others do their planning for them. With this business, you can offer people the options they want. The fee you charge will be a small portion of the investment income your customers can generate by following the information you've provided. And for your time and efforts, you'll be able to plan your own estate, one that includes all the luxuries you've always wanted but never quite had the money to buy.

SOURCE MATERIAL

Refer to Section 7.

No. 189

PROPERTY ANALYSIS SERVICE

When people buy income property, most have little idea of how to analyze the potential income, investment and tax advantages that the purchase gives them. They usually rely on a real estate person to give the information to them, which may not be accurate. We will show you how to prepare reports that are accurate and understandable, and you'll see how small ads placed in the right publications will produce a good client flow for you.

CONCEPT

With the birth some years ago of the seminar that told people how to buy property with little or no money down, the rage was on for a good buy in real estate. The problem came when it was discovered that so few of these properties maintained a "positive" cash flow, meaning there was actually something left over at the end of the month for the buyer. Many of these properties had been purchased using the "negative" cash flow idea for tax purposes. People wanted to be able to write their losses off on income tax returns. This doesn't work for those who want to make money in the income property market.

With your service you can provide a means for people to understand the numbers behind a potential investment, and show them what kind of returns they can expect by making a particular purchase. The analysis could save your client from financial disaster.

SKILLS YOU WILL REQUIRE

If you have ever owned your own income property, or assisted others in purchasing real estate, you have the skills you'll need to run this business. They consist of knowing the terminology of the real estate field, and having an understanding of the local trends in real estate.

You can get these skills by reading up on the topic. Start paying attention to the real estate sections of your daily newspaper, and subscribe to the local business publications. You might also consider taking a class in the subject at a local community college or adult education program.

Other than that, you will want to know how to operate the real estate investment software you'll be buying for your computer. The software you choose should be geared primarily for real estate analysis. By reading the manuals that come with the software, as well as playing with it, you should get a working knowledge of the kinds of work you will be performing for this business.

INFORMATION REQUIRED

You will have to choose a software package that does your real estate analysis for you. Most will prompt you for information about potential purchases, then supply you with the benefits of each choice. The kinds of information it will probably require include:

Purchase price
Financing terms
Taxes
Income
Expenses
Assumptions about inflation
Depreciation
Potential leases
Creative loan terms

Once this information has been provided, the computer program should produce information such as:

Loan schedules for a variety of loan packages
Depreciation schedules
Pre-tax and post-tax cash flow projections
Information about proposed sale of property
Internal rate of return

Most programs will produce this information in chart form, making it easy to compare the numbers for several properties.

A real estate software package might also enable you to perform such functions as background information, assumption for analysis, cash-flow analysis and return on investment analysis. Some will project these analyses for up to several years. Once you've provided this information to your client, he will be able to negotiate more effectively with the seller about the terms of the price, based on the returns the investor can expect. In other words, your client can work with hard facts rather than guesswork when making a real estate purchase decision.

OPERATING NAME

For this business you can get away with using your own name as the name of your business. If you call it something like "John Smith Property Analysis," you will save the start-up expense of filing a fictitious name report, getting a new phone installed and opening a new business bank account at business rates.

GETTING STARTED

To get started in this business, you will want to become familiar with how your software works, perhaps by setting up a mock set of purchase options and seeing how the figures look for each. Once you feel confident about using your program, you are ready to help others.

You might consider putting together a brochure, outlining your services, that can be mailed out to inquiring potential customers. You can include a listing of the various elements of the purchase they will want to consider, along with the type of information your service can provide. Be sure to include your name, address and phone number.

Once you get a customer, simply garner the information you need to input into your computer, perform the analysis, and deliver the numbers that will guide your client. Make sure that the chart you provide is clean, neat and professional-looking. When you deliver your report, you should plan on spending a certain amount of time explaining what the figures are and how they might affect the purchase decision.

THE COMPETITION

Your competition in this field is the real estate people helping their clients fo find a property. What you offer is a third-party informed analysis of the investment options. And this is how you can effectively compete. You aren't going to make any money on the purchase, aside from the fee you get for doing the analysis, so you can remain unbiased.

POTENTIAL INCOME

To price your service, you will want to figure out the costs of doing business, including a salary for you and a profit for the business. Once you have an idea of what it will cost you to offer the program, you can estimate how many clients you will be able to take on in any one time and price your fees accordingly. Say your expenses come to $1,000 in a month, you want to earn $2,000 for your time and $1,000 in profit for the business. In other words, for a month, you want to take in $4,000. If you figure you will have time to do 40 analyses in that month, you should charge $100 for each. The choice is yours, depending on how much time you want to give the business. If you decide to offer only a few projections rather than a complete analysis, then you can charge less. Likewise, you can raise your fee for complex projects that will require more time.

Basic Costs

1. Cost of software
2. Cost of advertising
3. Cost of time spent on inputting property information
4. Cost of time spent compiling and printing analysis
5. Cost of telephone
6. Cost of materials used

How To Be Paid

With this business, you should be paid when the analysis is delivered. If you choose to handle the analysis when the customer comes to you, you will save the time and expense of either delivering it or mailing it at a later date. You will also collect your fee sooner.

MARKETING METHODS

Direct mail and display ads are the most effective methods for marketing this service.

You can send out direct mail letters to two different customer bases. One is the group of people actually doing the investing, and the other is the group of real estate agents and brokers in your area. This last group should be particularly interested in your service, since they can offer it to their clients to prove how valuable a particular investment will be. If one broker or agent uses you a lot, you can offer a discount on your fees.

A typical letter sent out to these prospects might read:

> DEAR BROKER:
>
> Could you sell more if your customers knew exactly what their purchase would cost them, as well as how much it could make them?
>
> Property Analysis Associates is a company that can provide just that kind of information, and at a rate that can really pay off for you.
>
> We take the guesswork out of income property investment, and provide the hard facts that can turn a maybe-sale into a commission for you.
>
> What we offer is a detailed analysis of your client's investment options. More than that, we offer the competitive edge you need in convincing your client to make that investment.
>
> For more information about this unique, low-cost service, call today!

A variation of this letter, mailed out at the rate of 10 to 20 a day, should generate interest in what you have to offer. You can reply to inquiries by mailing out brochures or even paying personal visits to demonstrate your service.

Classified ads and display ads can be run in local newspapers and business publications to generate business among potential investors. Such an ad might read:

> Are you sure the property you are considering for investment income will give the return you expect? Call today for analysis information.

When a potential customer calls, answer questions and explain your fees. Be prepared for an onslaught of questions regarding "scenarios," in which the customer will ask for your ballpark opinion regarding a couple of properties. Explain that he will have to bring his numbers into your office for an informed opinion. This will prevent you from giving out advice you should be selling.

UNIQUE BUSINESS APPROACH

One approach you might consider for this business is to become a specialist in a particular kind of investment property. For example, you could specialize in rental units, such as apartments or houses, or you might handle only office buildings. What you are doing with this method is finding a niche and becoming an expert in it. This will make your service that much more valuable.

Once you have chosen your specialty, you might consider holding investment property seminars or speaking at gatherings in order to generate interest in your subject. In other words, you'll be bringing back those days of "How To Invest in Real Estate on a Shoestring" seminars. Giving talks is a great way to get your business known among potential clients.

LOCATION and MARKET BASE

The best place to operate this service is in a city with a population over 200,000. This will give you plenty of potential customers and properties to work with.

START UP CAPITAL

The capital you'll need for this business ranges from $1,000 to $5,000, including computer equipment. This will give you the money you need for advertising, software and other expenses involved.

TO SUM UP

A property analysis service is a little-known business that can be performed quickly, accurately and inexpensively with a home computer and the proper software. The fee you charge is just a fraction of the amount of money your clients can generate with their investment decision. In exchange for becoming better informed, your clients can pave your way to riches, and that's definitely one reason to start a business, don't you think?

SOURCE MATERIAL

Refer to Section 7.

No. 190

HORSE RACE HANDICAPPING SERVICE

If you are a horse racing fan, this will assure you of winning—if not at the track, at home where you will be selling this service. We will show you how to set up a handicapping system for all the variables. Some operators just follow the circuit around with their personal computers in their trailer or motor home and enjoy the racing as well as the money they make selling their service.

CONCEPT

The concept of this business is to sell your knowledge of horse racing to others who will use the information to make bets. With the use of your home computer, you can set up a business in the handicapping field to put out your own "tout" sheet. There are several ways you can make money with this operation, and we'll explain some of them.

SKILLS YOU WILL REQUIRE

The skills you'll need for this business certainly aren't difficult to pick up. If you enjoy following the horses, then you're a prime candidate to make money with this venture. You'll already be familiar with the jargon of the track, methods of placing bets, and other elements in the horse racing world.

If the idea of this business appeals to you and you don't already have these skills, then you can acquire them quickly by following race results in your local newspaper, visiting the local track, studying other tout sheets and reading up on the subject in such publications as the Daily Racing Form.

This is a business you can easily set up on your computer with the software already available for it. Most of the software will prompt you for information regarding odds of particular horses, previous performance, condition of track, etc. The software will sort the information and give you a detailed analysis of particular outcomes. This information is what you will be selling to others.

INFORMATION REQUIRED

For this operation, you'll need to obtain information regarding the horses and jockies entered in a particular competition. You can get the data by regularly reading the Daily Racing Form and other publications geared toward the racing crowd. Not only will they keep you posted about what is going on in the racing world, but they'll supply the same type of statistics you need to plug into your software.

Once your computer has analyzed the available data, it will supply you with a ranking of the horses going against one another in a particular race. It will also enable you to forecast the odds regarding certain outcomes.

GETTING STARTED

The first thing you need to do is become thoroughly familiar with your software. Spend several weeks analyzing data and comparing it against actual results of the races. Establish what your success rate is, since this is one way of convincing your customers that you have the "insider's touch" that can turn their bets into gold.

The next thing you'll want to do is determine how you will market your service. Your options are numerous, limited only by your imagination.

Perhaps the easiest way is to run a touter's column in as many newspapers as you can. Since racing is a nation wide sport, you'll be able to market your column to newspapers all over the country. The way to sell your column is to write up several samples to mail to sports editors. Prove your success rate with statistics and give a basic run down on how you gather your results.

Another place you might consider running your column is in track sheets, sold at the track.

You can use your column to generate interest in your other marketing approaches. One of them might be a tout sheet of your own. What this would consist of is a regularly published sheet that lists your opinions about the outcomes of particular races at different tracks. You can sell this sheet either by subscription or at the track itself. The advantage of this over simply running a column in newspapers is that your income is dependent only on yourself. You can sell as many subscriptions as you wish, and you are the one who establishes a price for them.

You may also decide to sell your tout sheets not by subscription but by single issue at the track that is covered. This will get your sheet exactly where you want it, in front of your potential customers.

Any way you decide to operate this business, it can become a nice money-maker for doing something you enjoy—hanging out at the track.

THE COMPETITION

There are probably more tout sheets out than you ever imagined. But there is always room for another one. You can peddle your touts with the confidence that the program you use has given you. It is not the "black magic" of the track that other touters might rely on; it is an analysis of the numbers involved in horse racing.

When you open up for business, you will probably cause a little stir as the "new kid on the block." Let the rest of the "kids" talk about you. It is good for business. Remember, at the track everybody will try anything once. If it works for them, you can expect them to return. And that means money for you.

POTENTIAL INCOME

This venture can probably bring you a medium level of income. What you can expect is based on what you get for either running your columnm or selling a tout sheet. For example, if you publish your own tout sheet, you might sell single issues for $5, a very reasonable amount. If you determine that you want to sell the sheet at five different tracks and you expect to sell, say, 50 sheets per day at each track, that could conceivably add up to 1,750 sales a week. At $5 per sheet, that could bring you $8,750 in a single week. Of course, your expenses for selling in multiple tracks will be increased, since you'll have to pay the track operators for a peddler's permit, as well as pay the sellers you have hawking for you.

To estimate what to charge for your service, add up all the costs of your business, including a salary for your own time and a profit figure for the business. Once this is established, you must figure out how many sheets you intend to publish. It might be more cost-effective for you to sell your sheets at a slightly higher price, yet in a smaller quantity. This will decrease your printing costs.

Basic Costs

1. Cost of software
2. Cost of advertising
3. Cost of time spent accumulating data
4. Cost of analyzing data with computer
5. Cost of time spent writing tout sheet
6. Cost to print tout sheet
7. Cost of paying sellers
8. Cost of track selling permit

9. Cost of attending races
10. Cost of transportation
11. Cost of research, subscriptions, etc.

With this business, you may also accrue expenses by following the horse racing circuit in person. This will cost you the price of getting from track to track, as well as meals, lodging and personal travel expenses. Many operators do this simply because it keeps them in touch with the world of racing and adds that much more authenticity to what they write.

MARKETING METHODS

The best method to market this business is by display ads. You can run these in both the sports section of local dailies and racing publications. Either way, you'll reach the people you want to reach.

If you intend to offer a tout sheet by subscription, that is what you'll cover in your ad. For example, your ad might read:

> START WINNING AT THE TRACK!
>
> Our scientific methods are pulling in an 80 percent success record at the horse track.
>
> Think about what that can mean to you when you visit the betting window.
>
> Others have already won more than they ever dreamed possible simply be reading our weekly letter, the Inside Wire.
>
> Call now to find out how you too can join the winner's circle by subscribing to the Inside Wire.

If you intend to sell your sheets on a single-issue basis, you might try a variation of the ad. Simply inform readers to look for your sheet at the track closest to them.

You might also consider running a display ad about your publication in the schedule put out by the track each day. When people begin losing, they'll try anything to change their luck, and one way is to buy your sheet.

UNIQUE BUSINESS APPROACH

One method you can try with this business is to arrange with the same newsstands that carry racing publications to carry your sheet as well. They get a cut of every issue they sell. Placed next to the stack of Daily Racing Form, your sheet is bound to get noticed. This approach can substantially increase the number of sheets you sell, especially if you get newsstands in all the cities that have tracks you cover in your sheet. If you were to find eight stands in each city and you cover five different tracks, you would have 40 places selling for you. The kind of money you can make this way will add up quickly.

LOCATIONS and MARKET BASE

This is one business that doesn't need to be located in a city to succeed. What it will require is that you are able to cover the tracks, which are usually located in major metropolitan areas. This means traveling from city to city, or at least having a method to obtain information about the races being run at the various tracks you want to cover.

Most tracks are located in cities with market bases that range from 50,000 up. Larger cities will possess more newstands to carry your sheet, and that might determine which tracks you want to cover.

TO SUM UP

If you love the ponies and want to make money with them, this business is a great one for you to try. With your handy home computer, you can turn those statistics and hours spent at the track into more than a "gamble". The secret to winning is not necesarily betting high and winning high, but by selling to others your opinions about how they should bet. People love to feel like they are getting the inside track on whatever they gamble in. With this opportunity you can become the inside track and make a killing by doing it.

SOURCE MATERIAL

Refer to Section 7.

No. 191

ACCOUNTS PAYABLE SERVICE

One of the problems that small business operations have is keeping up with their accounts payable. Not only do they forget to pay on time, which hurts their credit, but they also lose hundreds of dollars every year by not taking discounts. Here's a service that is needed by many. We will show you how to get clients for this business. Once you start taking care of their accounts payable, they won't want to let you stop.

CONCEPT

The concept of this business is to take over that portion of a company's accounting that they may simply not want to do themselves. Accounts payable is keeping track of what the company owes and what needs to be paid when. With this information a business can keep better track of its cash flow by paying some bills early to take advantage of billing discounts and putting off payment of other bills until they are due. The money a business can save by using your service will more than offset your fees.

SKILLS YOU WILL REQUIRE

For this business, you should be familiar with basic accounting methods. You should know some of the terminology used in accounting, as well as the general practices. If you do not already have experience, you can quickly pick it up by taking an accounting class at a community college or by reading up on the subject.

Whereas in some businesses you can acquire an understanding of the subject by reading the documentation that comes with the software you'll be using, the software in this business will probably presume that you already have a handle on what the subject. What that means is that before you begin shopping for software to use in accounts payable, you should understand accounting methods.

When you have the knowledge, you are ready to find a program to do your work for you. There are a multitude of accounting packages available for every computer model. In fact, it is accounting software that compelled the business world to take the personal computer seriously. And although a number of businesses have already implemented their own computerized accounting systems, there are still plenty that could use the services of an outsider to supply this service for them. That is where you step in.

To thoroughly understand what to look for in the software you can use for this business, you should read reviews of available packages in computer magazines, and try out products at your local software store.

Once you have chosen a package, you should play with it by setting up a mock business and handling its typical accounts payable transactions. Some software will provide the transactions for you in its documentation. Study the operations and become comfortable with its use. You certainly don't want to learn on somebody else's time, since that will make them edgy about trusting in the accuracy of your service.

INFORMATION REQUIRED

In the accounts payable business, you will have several things to handle for your customers. Many software packages will allow you to:

1. Record checks written to vendors for materials purchased.
2. Enter hand-written checks write without using the system.
3. Create automatic entry accounts for regular payments, like rent.
4. Distribute information from vendor bill to general ledger accounts.
5. Automatically compute vendor discounts when invoice is paid within discount time.
6. Prevent overpayment of invoice entered into system.
7. Prioritize bills and place information into a cash requirements report.
8. Create any number of vendor accounts and classify them as casual or regular.

Some software will enable you to do all these functions; others will give you only a few features. Research thoroughly and shop carefully before choosing your software package.

Once you have shopped and are familiar with your software, you are ready to go after business. The information involved in this part of the business will be supplied by your clients themselves.

GETTING STARTED

When you get a new customer, your first job will be to put the accounts payable work into your computer. In the beginning you should work closely with your client to get a thorough understanding of what kind of accounts payable method he wants to follow. Study the method already in place, then seek ways to improve on it or make it more efficient. After all, you are the expert and should be able to tell him how he can streamline operations. He will probably also tell you about particular problems he is encountering with the methods currently in place, and you might be able to recommend suggestions for solving them.

Once you understand the material with which you'll be working, it is time to put the data into your system. You should probably place each customer's accounts payable onto its own set of disks. That way, you will ensure that accounts aren't mixed up.

After the system is in place, you will simply obtain the information you need on a regular basis. In most cases, this will be once or twice a week. You can keep your client informed on the same regular schedule by printing out weekly reports telling him what will be paid during that week.

COMPETITION

Your competition in this business is the abundance of bookkeeping and accounting services. The key to beating your competition is to emphasize to potential clients that your expertise is in accounts payable. You can explain that your work is thorough, accurate and timely and will make him better informed about his money matters.

POTENTIAL INCOME

With this business, you can expect to earn a medium level of income. You can charge your clients an initial setup fee for the time spent organizing the system and putting the data into your computer. This could range from $100 to $500, depending on the size of the company. After that, you can charge a regular fee based on the number of transactions you must handle. If you are working with a small company, that might turn out to be about $25 a week. At this rate, you could generate more than $1,500 a year with just a single client. If you handle the accounts payable for five or six clients, you could easily earn enough to make a full-time salary with only part-time hours.

To get an idea of what to charge for your service, the first step is to price out the expenses of doing business. This includes a salary for your time. On top of that, you must add a profit figure for each job. Then you can divide the total by the number of clients you can comfortably handle to get a rough idea of what your fee should be.

Basic Costs

1. Cost of accounting software
2. Cost of advertising
3. Cost of time spent in initial setup
4. Cost of time spent maintaining an account
5. Cost of transportation
6. Cost of phone
7. Cost of materials used

One of the nice things about this business is that one of the accounts you will be tracking payment of is your own. Every time you see your own vendor number pop up in the system, you'll be able to thank yourself for getting into this business. MARKETING METHODS The best ways to market this service are direct mail, display ads and telephone sales.

You can place your display ads in any publication that business people will read. These include newspapers, business publications and professional organization newsletters. A typical ad could read:

> STOP THE HEADACHE OF ACCOUNTS PAYABLE!
>
> Let us handle it for you. Our service, Jones and Associates, specializes in accounts payable bookkeeping.
>
> Our computerized methods will let you know where your money needs to be spent and when. We guarantee that we will save your company money on its accounts payable or you won't have to pay us a cent.
>
> Call now for more details about this unique and low-cost service.

Placed in the right publications, this ad should bring you favorable response.

If you choose to try direct mail, send your letters out on a regular basis to all the smaller businesses in your area. The reason to go after small businesses is that most will not have a full-time bookkeeper on staff. Larger companies won't have as much reason to try you as the smaller companies will. You can get the names and addresses of the businesses either from a list service in your area or by using a contact service that provides business listings on a regular basis. You can contract to receive only those listings of companies that have under, say, five employees.

In your letter, state the benefits of using your service, and make sure you include your phone number and address. A follow-up phone call a week later to the same business is a very effective way of making contacts. When a potential client expresses interest in your service, arrange for a personal visit to show how your system works and to give an idea of what you will charge.

UNIQUE BUSINESS APPROACH

There are a couple of approaches that will get you off and soaring in this business. The first is to "piggyback" your service with one of the same nature. For example, you could approach local bookkeepers and offer to handle only their accounts payable work for them. They can make money on each client you handle for them and you save the cost of getting new clients yourself.

Another approach you can try is to specialize in one type of business. This method is most effective when done in a large city that offers numerous similar businesses. For example, you could decide to handle accounts payable only for gas stations or plumbers. This sets you up as an expert in the kind of system most gas stations or plumbers use and can act as an excellent selling point.

LOCATING and MARKET BASE

For this business, you should be located in a city with a population base of 50,000 to 200,000. This will supply you with plenty of potential customers.

TO SUM UP

Accounts payable is just another headache to most business people. It is a part of their operation that they would probably just as soon do without. Yet, if they don't pay bills on time, they can destroy their credit rating, lose valuable money and create a cash flow nightmare.

You can turn their headaches into a money-making opportunity with a little effort and perserverence. Once they've seen how much you can supply their operations, companies will continue as a client with you. If the thought of steady money and detail-oriented work intrigues you, get started with this business today.

SOURCE MATERIAL

Refer to Section 7.

No. 192

KEEPING STATS FOR LITTLE LEAGUE TEAMS FOR PROFIT

With all the sports going on for kids now and the great interest by coaches and parents about how the kids are doing, this business is a natural for any area of the country that supports kids' sports. We will show you how your service will become as valuable to each team as the uniforms they wear. And the income sources are from everybody—coaches, sponsors and parents, just to name a few.

CONCEPT

The concept of this business is to keep little league statistics for individual players as well as teams. This information is then used by parents, coaches, sponsors and others in the league to monitor the progress of the players.

Since keeping statistics basically consists of recording numbers and doing calculations with them, the home computer is perfect to handle the job. And that is exactly how you can make your money with this business.

SKILLS YOU WILL REQUIRE

If you have ever coached a team, attended a child's game or kept score, you probably have all the skills you'll need for this business. What it will consist of, basically, is preparing performance statistics. Coaches need the information to coach better, league officials need the stats to keep track of team standings, and last of all, parents need to know exactly how little Johnny or Cathy is doing.

There are a multitude of software programs now available that will allow you to do nothing more than keep little league stats. And since they are a one-purpose program, they cost very little. Most probably sell for under $100. Start reading computer maagzines to find ads for the kind of software you want. Send off for brochures and visit local software dealers to see if they carry what you need.

INFORMATION REQUIRED

Once you've purchased a package, play around with it. Most will prompt you for the information you'll need to keep running stats. What this will probably consist of for each player are such things as:

Name of player
Position
Date of game
Times at bat
Hits
Bases
Runs
Strikes
Balls

Once the information is put into the computer, the software will set about analyzing results and calculating total number of bases run, final score, batting averages, etc.

To get the information to input, you are either going to have to attend the games yourself or get somebody else to tally your information for you. Since most teams have at least one or two die-hard fans who attend every game, it should be a simple matter to hire somebody to do your dirty work for you at a very reasonable price.

GETTING STARTED

After you hve learned how to use the software, you are ready to go after business. This will consist of putting together sample league stat sheets and showing them to league officials, coaches, parents and anybody else that might buy the idea.

Tell them that you can provide a weekly sheet to each team that will provide all the stats they'd ever want to know. In most cases, the only ones who can get their hands on these figures are the league officials. Nobody else has the time to keep everybody informed. Since you will be doing the work with your computer, your job will be a cinch, and you can supply the sheets to anybody who wants to buy them.

Since your computer will keep stats for each player, you can even personalize each sheet especially for the player it covers. All you will need to do is pull out the information about that particular player, include stats about the team's performance, print it up and mail it off. If you possess a mail merge program, you can operate this service even more efficiently, since it will allow you to generate mailing list stickers.

When you've completed a sheet, you can simply fold it in thirds, place an address sticker on it and mail it off.

THE COMPETITION

Your competition in this business doesn't actually exist. Usually what happens after a game is that the scorekeeper turns his or her records over the league and that is it. Parents have no way of knowing how their children are doing unless they attend every game and keep their own records or harrass the scorekeepers into sharing the data they accumulate. What this means for you is that the market is wide open.

POTENTIAL INCOME

The income you can generate with this business depends only on how aggressively you intend to market yourself. If you live in a city that has a well organized sports program for kids, you could conceivably keep records on 50 to 100 teams all over town. If you charge parents and others a set rate for the whole season, such as $10, you could easily generate 500 or 1,000 sales. This would produce an income of $5,000 to $10,000 per season, with only part-time work.

To estimate what you need to charge, add up all the costs of your operation, including a salary for your time and a profit for the business.

Basic Costs

1. Cost of software
2. Cost of advertising
3. Cost of payment to scorekeepers hired
4. Cost of time spent organizing data
5. Cost of time spent inputting data
6. Cost of reproduction of stat sheets
7. Cost of postage to mail out stat sheets
8. Cost of any materials used

You can obtain capital to offer your service by selling it at the beginning of the season and collecting money right then. After that, it is simply a matter of producing your weekly sheets and getting them to the people who have subscribed.

MARKETING METHODS

Display ads will be the best way to market this service.

Perhaps the best place to run your ad is on the very same information form that kids get when they intend to sign up for a team. You might even consider going to the league organizers and offering to pay for the reproduction of these forms in exchange for placing your ad in them. Then, when the parents fill the form out, they also see your ad, along with a coupon they can mail in with their subscription check.

A typical ad might read:

> WE SUPPLY LITTLE LEAGUE STATS!
>
> If you want to keep up with how your child is doing during this little league season, you'll want to order your subscription to "League Stats."
>
> "League Stats" will arrive in your mailbox weekly and include all the statistics of your child's performance in the field. Every issue will give you batting average, number of hits, number of bases, and a whole lot more.
>
> Order your subscription today!

This ad should generate response to your offer, and after that, it's just a matter of keeping up on your orders.

UNIQUE BUSINESS APPROACH

The one market for this service that can increase your income are the newspapers. Newspapers, especially community papers, like to run team standings for little league, since it is a chance to print the names of a number of different people and can generate subscribers. With this business you can make their jobs easier by supplying the information they need in a highly organized fashion. In fact, with your computer program, it shouldn't be a difficult matter to pull up such items of news as top player of the week, best batting average for the season, team standings, etc. What this technique will do is generate interest in your stats each week, by getting parents, coaches and kids excited to see if somebody they know is listed.

Although newspapers might not pay much for this service, it will draw free advertising for your business, especially if the newspaper lists you each week as the source of information.

LOCATION and MARKET BASE

This business can best be run in a place where little leagues are popular, whether city or country. If you are in a city, chances are you can expect more business. A market base of from 50,000 to 200,000 will supply you with plenty of potential customers for this service.

TO SUM UP

The time is right to make this operation succeed. Little league has become big business, and you can step into the scene with your computer and generate a nice income for yourself.

With a little bit of effort, you can gain customers who will jump at the chance to see the performance of their teams and kids presented in a professional format. This country is information-crazy, and the enthusiasm about professional sports makes people that much more hungry to have their kids get in on some of the fun. In addition, you'll be having a little fun of your own, counting your earnings with this money-making oppportunity, that is.

SOURCE MATERIAL

Refer to Section 7.

No. 193

REMODELING AND NEW CONSTRUCTION COST ESTIMATE SERVICE

A construction cost estimate service provides homeowners and businesspeople with estimates for remodeling or new construction work they need done. The service gathers the information from several different sources (building supply companies, contractors, etc.) and passes it along to the homeowner.

CONCEPT

The pace and dollar-volume of the construction business in this country surpasses that of any other country in the world. Every year thousands of new homes and businesses are built, and an equal number of expansions are completed. Although the construction business has its ups and downs, dependent on the economic situation, it always seems to rebound and come back stronger than ever.

When construction of new homes and businesses is inhibited by the economy, people turn to other means of expansion—they remodel or add extensions. Whether building anew, remodeling, or putting up extensions, this can often be a frustrating process, because of the time and energy it takes to get several estimates, and the constant pressure from salespeople to begin the construction. Once you begin the whole process, even if you were just getting estimates and didn't necessarily mean to begin right away, it can be difficult to turn back. You might feel as though too much energy has been expended to stop once the momentum has begun.

With your computer you can prove to people that it doesn't have to be that way. You can help home and business owners get the information they need without the hassle of visiting building supply houses and talking to contractors. This gives them the freedom to simply speculate on whether or not remodeling or new construction is even feasible. They have made no commitment to anyone, and have saved their valuable time and sanity.

By establishing contact with building supply houses and individual contractors, you can quickly and inexpensively get the prospective builder the information he needs to make a decision. You'll find that many people who did not want to begin the estimate process will make use of your service, because it's so easy for them to do. This is a service with a tremendous untapped market, waiting for you to take advantage of it.

SKILLS YOU WILL REQUIRE

You won't need to be an expert contractor or construction buyer to make this work. You'll need to learn some of the terminology, and you will need to know how to find your sources (see Information Required) and how to go about getting your estimates. This is all very simple to learn. After all, the businesses that will supply you with estimates are used to dealing with homeowners. In a short amount of time, you will be knowledgeable enough to collect estimates for virtually any home or small business expansion.

As far as the terminology goes, it will make it easier for you if you understand something about what it takes to put an addition on a house or build a new room. I'm going to give you a source that may not seem like much, but that will give you just the education you need and prove to be a valuable resource. Buy yourself one of the books that Reader's Digest or other companies put out about home repair. It will tell you everything from A to Z and in terms you can understand. Take some time to go through some of these books and you will find yourself well—prepared to run this job. Of course, just doing the job will educate you, but these books can get you feeling comfortable and ready to go.

INFORMATION REQUIRED

The source of most of your estimates will be building supply houses, contractors, (electrical, plumbing, etc.) and some retail outlets. Of course, you'll want to know which supply house can sell you what items, so make sure your data base specifies as precisely as possible what items are available at each supply house.

Your clients will be providing you with the details on what they want done. It will simply be your job to simply match up the requirements of the buyer with the products and services of the sellers.

You will have to know the specifications of the proposed construction—for instance, the exact dimensions of that new fireplace, or the price your client will pay for that countertop he wants in the new bathroom. Again, this is all information that your client will give you. Don't forget, though, to ask questions if you feel you don't have enough information to do the job right.

OPERATING NAME

If you choose to use a fictitious name for your business, like "Construction Estimators," you'll find you have a lot of extra start-up expenses. You'll need to register the name or file a fictitious name report, get a new bank account, etc.

It's always easiest when starting a new business to use your own name, adding a tag such as "John Jones Construction Estimates" if you like. This name will let people know what you do, and you can use all the phones, addresses and bank accounts now listed in your name. Refer to Section 4 for more information.

GETTING STARTED

First of all, tend to your computer and software. If you don't have a computer yet, it is best, when buying a computer for a specialized purpose, to shop for your software first. In this business you will be able to use a good data base to store your pricing information and customer files. Outline a trial run estimate and decide what you want your computer to be able to do with the information. For instance, graphs would be a nice touch if you want to show overall comparative pricing levels from one combination of supplier/contractor to another.

Report format is important too. Make sure the program you use is capable of giving you what you want on a report, whether you have to design it yourself or not.

Once your computer and software are ready, get together a list of building supply houses and contractors that you'll use as sources for your quotes. Contact them and find out how long it will take them to quote for their services. This is something your customers will want to know from you—how quickly you can do a job. Get both time and cost estimates, and find out how soon after they're given notice they can start. Some of the contractors will have to see the house to make an accurate estimate, so make an appointment with your client to stop by and look at the area to be worked on. Finally, once you have your figures together, make sure you can clarify any of the information to your client. You will find the contractors will be a big help on this.

Once you begin your operation, all of this preparation will become second nature to you, and your business will just naturally gain momentum.

THE COMPETITION

You won't find much competition in this business. This is one of those great ideas that virtually no one has acted on yet. Look in your yellow pages and you'll see this is true.

To compete with any competition you do run into, create your own cash flow. Offer a reduced rate to your new clients and take a percentage down on the job. This will get you both new customers and money to work with. Just about all suppliers and contractors will offer a low or no-cost estimate as their investment in possible new business.

Last of all, offer your clients a lot for their money. Charts and graphs will cost you a little extra to produce, but you'll find the financial benefits from your resultant good reputation will far outweigh the extra cost.

POTENTIAL INCOME

You will be charging a per-job fee, dependent upon, for instance, the size of the room being remodeled or the size of the house or extension being built. You'll soon be skilled at knowing exactly how much to charge.

Your primary costs will be in supplies, and time to collect your information. Running this business on a part-time basis, you can expect to make $300 to $500 profit per week.

When calculating what you should charge for your service, estimate your expenses, and include a salary for your time and a profit figure for the job. This will enable you to more accurately figure what your fee should be.

Basic Costs

1. Cost of data base software
2. Cost of advertising
3. Cost of transportation
4. Cost of phone charges
5. Cost of books, references, etc., used
6. Cost of printer supplies
7. Cost of materials used

MARKETING METHODS

Display ads are the best marketing method for your remodeling/construction cost estimate business.

The yellow pages of the phone book will probably be the best way to reach your clients. When most people begin to think about remodeling or building, they turn to the yellow pages to decide where to start. This is where your ad catches their eye and they realize how much more sense it makes to leave the footwork up to someone else.

Let me give you an example of an effective display ad:

NEED ESTIMATES FOR REMODELING OR NEW CONSTRUCTION?

Look no further!

We know how confusing it can be trying to decide where to start when you want to remodel or start new contruction.

Also, you might not be ready to build—all you want to do is get a few estimates. Once the estimating process begins, however, you'll find the momentum is hard to stop.

It doesn't have to be that way. We are John Jones Construction Estimators and we can do all the footwork for you. No salesman need ever know your name, and you don't have to waste your valuable time running around getting estimates.

Give us a call and let us show you how we can make the job of building or remodeling much easier.

This type of display ad, placed in yellow pages and newspapers—preferably some of the home sections—will bring you the customers to keep your business going strong. See Section 5 for more marketing methods and information.

UNIQUE BUSINESS APPROACH

Since you'll be using the same group of suppliers again and again, work out a system whereby they give you discount rates on the items being estimated in exchange for the business you bring to them. This will allow you to pass the savings on to your customers. This will obviously also allow you to undercut your competition.

Don't forget about the contractors too. You will probably be able to strike a similar deal with them.

LOCATION and MARKET BASE

Either city location or a more suburban-country location will support this business. You might find that a city will give you more opportunity to grow to full-time operation, but it is not necessary for you to move to a city to make the business a success.

As long as your market base is above 50,000 people, you'll have no trouble. In all parts of the country, you can find building-supply houses and contractors, so that won't be a problem.

TO SUM UP

Billions of dollars are spent every year in new construction, including remodeling and expansion. Even with this amount, there are a lot of people who put off starting any building project because of the hassle of getting it started.

This leaves a perfect opportunity for the enterprising individual to make it easier for both the reluctant builder, and those who have decided to take the step but aren't sure where to start.

For a minimal investment, you can get a business going that will take you as far as you want it to. By helping the homeowners and businesspeople build and expand, you'll be getting your share of that billion-dollar-a-year business. It's an easy business to start, and in a short time the financial investment and time you put into it will be paid back many times over.

SOURCE MATERIAL

For information refer to Section 7.

No. 194

BOWLING TEAM STATS SERVICE

Have you ever checked to find out how many bowling teams there are in your area? You will be amazed, if you're not already involved in bowling. We will show you how to provide weekly printouts for all leagues, and how to collect from not only the leagues, but from the bowling alleys and league players. With your personal computer, you can spend a few hours each week and make a good living.

CONCEPT

The concept of this business is to keep track of bowling records for leagues. This job is usually handled by a league secretary, who spends hour after tedious hour compiling the information, calculating averages, team pin totals, etc., by hand. Yet with a computer this type of information is very simple to work with and takes only a fraction of the time.

With the number of bowling leagues in your own area, you can create a steady income with this business.

You can also offer this service to bowling alleys who handle the secretarial chores themselves, especially for junior leagues. Another customer for this service is the individual bowler who either doesn't belong to a league but bowls regularly, or who belongs to a league but simply wants to keep his own statistics, but without all the work.

SKILLS YOU WILL REQUIRE

To operate this business, you should know how bowling is scored. But you certainly don't need to join a bowling league to learn how that is done. Simply visit your local alley and have one of the desk clerks explain the process to you. It is a simple system that you can pick up in a few minutes.

If you have ever bowled in a league yourself, you'll understand well the need for this service. The stats that abound in a league are mind-boggling. Yet, once a week the league secretary must sit down and do the calculations of the statistics. With the use of a computer, you handle the job in just a small amount of your time each week.

INFORMATION REQUIRED

To find out what kind of information you will need to record, simply visit a local bowling alley and ask to see a league sheet. This will show you what kind of stats a league keeps track of. Remember, this sheet is updated every week to take into account the games bowled during that week. The information includes such things as the weekly averages, weekly series, high series, high game, handicap, cumulative averages, blind scores, lanes bowled, scratches, etc.

Sound overwhelming? Not really, when you consider that all this information can be calculated by the computer simply by plugging in each bowler's scores for the week. You can run through the whole list in just a couple of minutes. Your computer will process the information and give you a print-out that will serve as a weekly league sheet.

The beauty of this business is that there are already several software programs that will do your work for you. Most cost under $50 and will prompt you for the information you need to compile league stats.

OPERATING NAME

For this service you have two choices. You can choose a fictitious name, like "Bowling League Secretary Services" or "Computerized Bowling Stats" or something like that. If you do this, you will have extra start-up costs entailed in registering or filing the name, getting a business phone installed, etc.

You can save these start-up costs simply by using your own name. Call it something like "John Smith Bowling Services." People will understand what your service is because it will be explained wherever they see your name mentioned. See Section 4 for more information about choosing a business name.

GETTING STARTED

Getting started with this business is a matter of making contacts. Your first step should be to compile a list of possible customers. After that, you can start using the ideas in Marketing Methods in order to tell them about your service.

After that, it's a matter of doing your job. First you will have to enter the initial information. This will consist of putting each bowler's name, team, average and handicap into the computer program. After that your chore is simple maintenance work. It involves getting the weekly scores from the leagues for which you work and putting them into the computer. The computer will process the information and give you a print-out that you send back to the league.

THE COMPETITION

Your competition for this service is the league secretary. He or she gets paid to provide the statistics each week. You can eliminate the competition simply by charging less than the league pays its current secretary. Some leagues have a rule that allows only a member of the league to perform the secretarial work. There are plenty though, that don't have this requirement. These are your most likely customers.

To find out what a club is currently paying for the service, simply ask. They have no reason to hide the information. Then you can bid a price that is less than that figure and get their business. Since it takes you a lot less time to do the calculations because you have a computer for a business partner, you can afford to charge less than a regular league secretary does.

POTENTIAL INCOME

You can make a surprisingly large income with this business. For each bowler you keep stats on, you can charge the league about 25 cents a week. If the league has 100 bowlers, that's $25 a week. Multiply that times the number of weeks that league meets—say, 30 weeks for a winter league—and you can earn several hundred dollars from each league. Since there are dozens of leagues at each bowling alley, from junior up to senior leagues, the total can be in the thousands of dollars very easily.

You can also charge individual bowlers who want to use your service a flat rate, such as $50 for the league season. If you take on a bowling alley as your customer, you can charge by the number of bowlers they want you to accumulate stats on, just as if they were a league. Any way you look at it, this is a money-making opportunity.

In order to establish a price for your service, you must first calculate your expenses. A list is below. Plus, you must add in a salary for your time and a profit for the business.

Basic Costs

1. Cost of the computer software
2. Cost of advertising
3. Cost of time spent organizing information initially
4. Cost of time spent each week entering new information
5. Cost of printing supplies
6. Cost of other materials used
7. Cost of transportation to pick up and deliver stat sheets

Overhead

Remember to calculate what your overhead will be each week for this business. That includes your phone time, time spent traveling to and from the bowling alley or wherever you will go to get your score update materials, etc. Including these charges will enable you to more accurately estimate what to charge for your service.

Profit

Remember to allocate a profit in your estimated costs. This is a separate amount from the money you make for your time. That is considered salary and goes into your pocket. A profit belongs to the business.

MARKETING METHODS

The best way to market this service is with display ads. You can run your ad in the sports section of your local dailies, in other local publications around town that bowlers read or, even better, right on score sheets.

Perhaps you've noticed that bowling score sheets often consist of space to keep your score, as well as space for advertising. The usual kinds of ads that run on score sheets are for local restaurants, car washes, and that sort of thing.

If you run your own ad there, bowlers are sure to notice it and want to know more about your service. Plus, league presidents, secretaries and bowling alley personnel will see it there and want to find out how much they can save by using your service.

A typical ad might read:

> BOWLING LEAGUE SECRETARIAL SERVICES
>
> Tired of wasting hour after hour updating all those league statistics week after week?
>
> Let us handle it for you!
>
> Once a week you'll receive a computerized update of your league sheet, listing all the averages, high scores, etc. that your bowlers want to know about.
>
> And it will cost you only a fraction of the price you're paying now.
>
> No more headaches. No more errors. No more wasted hours that you could be spending on the lanes.
>
> Call us today for more information!

Your own variation of this ad will probably bring you more response than you might reasonably expect. And since most score sheets are printed up by a company that sells the same sheet to all the bowling alleys in your area, you can hit all the leagues at one time for a very small expenditure.

UNIQUE BUSINESS APPROACH

There is one approach to marketing this business that is sure to get attention for you and bring in inquiries for more information.

The way to market this business most effectively is to give out free samples at the start of the bowling league season. Do this by obtaining the first week's scores and player information, which you can get by contacting the league president or the bowling alley. Then run the information through your computer and create a sample league sheet. The following week, when the league meets again, provide each bowler with a copy of the sheet. This will get them excited about the prospect of knowing how well they did the previous week. It will also show them how accurate the service is, etc.

Not only will you sell the league on the idea of using your service, but you'll get individual bowlers who want to use it as well. Either way, you'll get business, which will more than offset the cost of this marketing method.

LOCATION and MARKET BASE

You will want to operate this service in an area where there are bowling alleys. This will mean it is best suited for a city. Usually most cities possess a dozen or more bowling alleys, which should supply you with plenty of business.

If your city has 50,000 to 200,000 people, you should consider trying this business. A city of this size will supply you with a ready supply of customers.

START UP CAPITAL

You will need from $1,000 to $5,000 to start this business. This will pay for the computer equipment you need, as well as the software, which is very inexpensive, and your advertising and supplies.

TO SUM UP

A bowling team stats service is a great start-up business. If you don't have a lot of time or a lot of computer knowledge, you can still run this business quite easily. If you run your ads in the right places, the service will practically sell itself.

Bowlers are people who love numbers. They get a thrill each week by poring over the league sheet to see how they compare with the other bowlers in their league. Oftentimes, the information on the sheet, when done by hand, is inaccurate. Even worse, somebody has to spend a good portion of his time compiling the information. With your computer you ensure the accuracy of your numbers and do the work in just an hour or so each week.

The money you are paid is well worth the effort. The fee you charge is just a drop in the bucket for a league of any size. Bowlers like this service because it lets them have more time on the lanes doing what they enjoy most: bowling. Plus, it gives you time to do what you most enjoy—counting your earnings for a job well done.

SOURCE MATERIAL

Refer to Section 7.

No. 195

TEACH TYPING FOR PROFIT

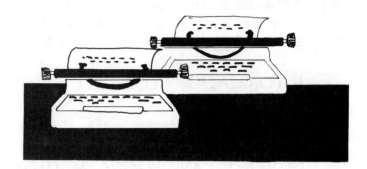

Here is a little business rarely thought of that is making a lot of operators a good second income with little or no effort. We will show you how to multiply your stations without costing you an arm and a leg. Also, you will learn how to get the local schools to refer students to you. This is real sleeper, so get in on it now.

CONCEPT

The concept of this business is to offer a service that just about everybody needs these days. With the popularity of computers, everybody needs to know how to type. If they already know how to type, they need to know how to type faster. So the number of customers you can get with this business is almost unlimited, no matter where you live.

Learning how to type is something that just about every student needs now that computers are so popular in classrooms. Also, you can teach people who want to get a part-time job or become better at the job they now have.

SKILLS YOU WILL REQUIRE

You certainly don't have to be a certified teacher to offer this service. All you need to know is how to type yourself. Since you have a computer with a keyboard, you have probably already mastered the skills needed to do it.

When customers start ringing your phone off the hook to learn where they can sign up for your courses, you bring them into your shop and sit them in front of the computer. It is the computer that does all your work for you. You just sit back and count your earnings.

A big selling point for this business is that you can tell your customers when they call that they won't have to sit in a large classroom while an instructor calls out drill after drill for them to try to keep up with. People enjoy learning new skills on a computer. The available programs for learning how to type are fun and friendly, nonjudgmental, and go at the pace the student wants to follow.

INFORMATION REQUIRED

The information in this business is all contained on the keyboard of your computer. Take a look at it. See that middle row of keys that start with A and end with L? That is called the home group of keys. A student's fingers sit on these keys when reaching for all other keys for all letters in the alphabet. The left hand rests on A-S-D-F and the right hand on J-K-L and whatever key is to the right of L. From these eight keys you can teach all other letters of the alphabet. These keys are the basis of what you'll be offering. Yet the computer will actually be doing the teaching for you.

Many computers today come packaged with a typing program along with the other free software you get with it. You can use that package to offer this service.

If you don't have software like this, you can buy a typing program. Such a program will give your students practice in typing out letters by showing a letter on the screen, then asking the student to find it on the keyboard and to type it. After awhile, the student won't have to look for the key. His finger will naturally find it from habit. Once a student has mastered that, the computer begins to give whole words that the student types out. After that it's complete sentences, then complete paragraphs.

Typing programs will also test students to see how fast they can type and with how many errors. If a customer comes to you and wants to improve his skills—say, increase the number of words he can type in a minute—the computer will drill him until he has reached his goal.

GETTING STARTED

To get started in this business, you simply need to have a student. You can get your customers by following the suggestions in Marketing Methods.

Since you already know how to put a program into your computer, all you have to do is make it available to the student. Set it up for him, sit him down in front of it and tell him to follow the instructions the computer gives him. What could be easier?

THE COMPETITON

This is a service that most people use when they are in high school. They take a typing class and either learn it or don't. But most of the time, schools use old-fashioned typewriters to teach it on. Few can offer what you offer—the opportunity to learn typing on a computer. This is what most people need today—the ability to type on a computer keyboard. Most of the time, therefore, you won't have any competition.

Since most of the people do not want to go back to a regular school to learn this skill, you have a natural selling point for this business. You can offer to teach them during their free hours, which can be in the evening or on weekends or whenever you decide that class will be in session.

Another plus with this business is that you can create your own cash flow to buy the equipment you need. To do this you simply take a teaching fee from the students when they sign up for your course, then purchase the equipment you'll need to teach them with.

POTENTIAL INCOME

Pricing for this business is a simple matter. Since you already have the equipment you'll need—the computer—all you really have are expenses for advertising and the cost of your own time. Since the student is learning how to type simply by following the program you've put in the computer, you are free to do other things.

Since the student is actually paying for the time he spends using your computer, you can get a good idea of what to charge by calling up stores that rent computers. Find out how much they get per hour. It will probably equal from $10 per hour and up. If you charge $10 per hour and get 10 students a week, that's $100 a week for basically doing nothing but turning your computer on and off for students. Plus, if you decide to expand your service and buy more equipment, you can increase the number of students you can handle at one time. With four computers available, you can make $400 a week with only part-time work. That amount can be even higher if you decide to go full-time with this business.

Primary Costs

1. Cost of equipment
2. Cost of advertising
3. Cost of your time
4. Cost of typing program
5. Cost of paper, ribbons, and extra materials to be used
6. Cost of sending letters, etc. for new business

Overhead

Make sure that the amount you charge each student covers a portion of the overhead. If one of your students wants to come in three times a week, his charge should cover three times the amount of overhead of a student who comes in only once a week. Since this is a business in which your customers will come into your home or office, this practice of including overhead in the price is very important.

Profit

When calculating what to charge for this business, remember to include an amount for profit. Your time is considered another business expense, like the cost of paper or advertising. The profit is what the business itself makes. Your salary is for you.

How To Be Paid

The standard practice you should follow for this business is payment in advance. You should follow this practice especially if you decide to offer a package deal, such as 10 hours of typing lessons, say, for $100.

If a student wants to take lessons from you until he feels he has learned enough, you might consider charging him each time he comes in to take another lesson. Since the customer pays in person, you avoid the trouble of having to bill him, wait for his payment, etc.

MARKETING METHODS

The best way to market this business is by display ads. Besides running ads in your local newspapers, you might consider placing them in school newspapers to attract local students, and weekly shoppers that are mailed out free to all the people in your neighborhood. This last marketing method will attract homemakers, unemployed workers and seniors who want to learn a new salable skill.

A typical ad might read:

> Increase your earning power!
>
> You can learn how to type quickly and at your own pace with my simple methods.
>
> If you already know how to type, you can improve your skills and demand a higher salary in today's competitive job market.
>
> Using the latest high technology equipment, you'll learn the basics of typing at a price that can't be beat anywhere.
>
> If you have ever wanted to join the computer age, I can show you how. Call now!

Your own version of this ad will bring customers from schools and business and get you started on your own path to higher earning power. After awhile, you'll learn which newspapers are bringing you the most business. Then if you run it on a regular basis, the newspapers that you decide to place it in will give you an advertising discount. For more methods and information refer to Section 5.

UNIQUE BUSINESS APPROACH

Now, I'll let you in on the big secret to this business that few have ever considered trying. Plenty of people buy computers these days who don't know how to type. What you need to do is tap into this group of people. You have two options. You can go to the local businesses that sell computers in your area and offer a commission to each student they send you. It doesn't cost them anything. When they sell a computer, they can ask their customer, "Do you want to quickly learn how to type so you can be up and operating on this machine as soon as possible?" If the answer is "Yes," the computer dealer can refer his customer to you. In return, you pay the dealer $10 or so for each money-making referral he sends you.

Another option you have is to offer your services to a computer dealer for a charge. Since they can lose hundreds of dollars by not being able to sell a computer to a customer who cannot type, it is worth $50 or more to them to be able to teach that customer what he or she will need to know to use a computer keyboard. You might also consider doing a trade-out with your local computer dealer in exchange for more equipment. Few people realize the value and advantage of barter. Tell your computer dealer that in exchange for giving his customers typing lessons, you would like to get computer equipment at a 50 percent or even 100 percent discount. Most will be willing to listen to your ideas if it means you can help them sell their equipment.

LOCATION and MARKET BASE

Whether you live in the city or the country, you can operate this business. Since people in the country use computers just as much as people in cities, the need is everywhere for your service.

If you are in the vicinity of a school, all the better. Inevitably the school will have failing students that could use a little tutoring on such skills as typing to get by in the rest of their studies. All you have to do is let the school know about your business and let them take it from there. They'll refer their students to you.

This business would probably be best suited for a market base of from 25,000 up. Since few smaller towns and cities will already have anybody else offering this service, it is a natural for these kinds of areas. But if you're in a large metropolitan area, this business can also make you money, since you're offering a unique service – the opportunity to learn typing on the office tool of today, the computer.

TO SUM UP

Teaching typing for profit is a sleeper. Few people have thought of it as a way to make money, yet the ones who have are making a killing. One man we know in the business has converted his garage into a classroom filled with computers to service the number of students he has. For you to do the same, you just have to decide to try the business.

If you want to figure out the rewards of this opportunity, just think about it. How often is your computer just sitting there, turned off, not doing a thing? This business is a way for you to make money when you aren't using the computer for other things. All you need to do is make a schedule of students who want to use it during those off-hours to learn typing. That leaves you free to spend your time going to the bank to make nice fat deposits with the money they'll pay you. You'll be giving your customers the opportunity to hook onto the Computer Age. And you'll be giving yourself the opportunity to buy all those extras this kind of business can offer.

SOURCE MATERIAL

Refer to Section 7.

No. 196

LOCAL GARDENERS' PLANTING TIMES NEWSLETTER

If you're a garden buff, you know every different kind of vegetable, fruit, flower, tree and bush has its own specific planting time. It is usually based on the last freeze, along with other factors. Most information available is for general areas of the country. But the factor that determines the final success or failure is based on local green thumbs and information from professionals that isn't available anywhere else. Our report gives you all the tools you'll need to start right up with this money-making opportunity.

CONCEPT

The concept of this business is to sell a newsletter designed for your own area of the country. With the information you provide in the newsletter, gardeners in your town can get a head start with their plants and gardens.

You are really selling advice. In England, where people take the subject very seriously, some of the most popular radio and television shows are about gardening. Gardners in this country are the same way. If they find out you have a garden, they enjoy spending hours discussing the finer points of it with you, from what types of pesticides you use or don't use, to what variety or strain of tomato you had luck with lately.

With this business, you'll no doubt become a local celebrity. People will seek you out for advice, and you can answer their questions in your newsletter and get paid for it.

SKILLS YOU WILL REQUIRE

This business is best suited for somebody who enjoys gardening. That will give you an added edge on knowing the terminology gardeners use, plus make you familiar with their concerns and desires.

If you have never turned a shovelful of dirt in your life, but the idea of putting out a newsletter appeals to you, you can still give a try at this business, since you'll have several resources for the kind of information you'll need.

INFORMATION REQUIRED

For this business you'll need a basic understanding of the terminology that gardeners use, as well as some basic knowledge of the practice of gardening itself.

As for your "expert opinion," that will come with the aid of software packges that are currently available. Programs have been designed that will prompt you for information about a particular gardening problem, then give you the treatments or solutions you use to take care of it.

With some of the software, you can enter your ZIP code area and have the computer tell you what plants would be appropriate to grow in that area. Software can also inform you about how and when to plant your seeds, as well as how you should lay out your garden by rows.

Since you'll be offering this information in the form of a newsletter, you'll want to consider what kinds of things to include in it. Some of the features you might want to use are:

1. An advice column in which your subscribers write in with questions about their gardening problems and get personalized advice from you.
2. A calendar of what is appropriate to plant for that month.
3. In-depth stories about individual plants, fruits, vegetables, etc.
4. News about new plant strains or gardening techniques, and illustrations of well-laid-out gardens.

You can include whatever you think is necessary. Once your newsletter has come out a couple of times, your readers will no doubt write to you with suggestions for the kinds of things they'd like to see you cover in its pages.

OPERATING NAME

Most newsletters become well-known under the name of the person who creates them. In a way, you are selling your own personality when you sell a newsletter. For this business, it would be very useful to use your own name, such as "John Smith's Gardening Letter." This will get you known and increase your business.

You can also take a fictitious name, like "Northport Gardening Letter" or something like that. This will involve registering the fictitious firm name you choose, getting yourself a bank account using the new name, installing business phones, etc. The choice is up to you, but if you use a fictitious name, it will add to your start-up expense.

GETTING STARTED

Getting started with this business is a matter of getting subscribers. With the money they pay to subscribe, you will have the working capital necessary to put out your first issue.

To get subscribers, use the techniques listed in Marketing Methods.

You will then need to decide what will appear in your newsletter. Once you have it designed the way you would like it to appear, you can type up a copy on your computer and have it reproduced or printed for a very small price. If you have graphics software for your computer, you can even do the illustrations yourself. If you don't have graphics capabilities, the kinds of illustrations you want can easily be done with a regular keyboard. For instance, if you want to show a picture of a garden lay-out, you can use an underlining key to type out the rows and a long series of equal keys to show the plants' locations.

Most newsletters are four pages long, or one sheet folded in half and printed on both sides. At the top is the name and date of the newsletter. It then starts right in with information for your readers.

After your first issue appears, people will write in or contact you with other things they think should appear. Some may even volunteer to write a column for no charge. Most people get a thrill out of seeing their names in print.

This business offers a lot of satisfaction beyond the money. You supply something that people will begin to look for in their mailbox, just as they await the arrival of the latest seed catalogs. And once you have a customer, you'll never lose him unless he moves away.

THE COMPETITION

Your competition in this business is the gardening guides that go out to a national audience. You can beat them simply because you offer something they cannot. Most national gardening guides cover whole regions of the country, as if everybody in that region (which might be as large as several states) has the same gardening needs. You, on the other hand, will offer a guide for your small part of the country.

In fact, if you choose, you can even offer several newsletters, one for each part of your town. You can do this because soil conditions differ from one part of town to another. With a little research you can find out what areas require special attention and gear a newsletter just for those areas. This means you'll be able to increase your income by reaching a wider audience. And you'll be able to eliminate your competition because you specialize, in a way that they can't.

POTENTIAL INCOME

With this business, you can count on a steady amount of income each year. Once you have a subscriber base, it will pretty much remain the same year after year. As your area grows in population, the number of customers you will increase also. To price your newsletter, first you'll want to estimate what your expenses to put it out will be. Since the subscription will probably last a year, you'll want to multiply your monthly expenses by 12. For example, if you get 500 subscribers and each pays $15 for his or her subscription, this will give you $7,500 — not bad for a part-time effort doing something you enjoy.

Primary Costs

1. Cost of advertising
2. Cost of software used
3. Cost of organizing newsletter
4. Cost of mailing newsletter
5. Cost of materials used
6. Cost of reproducing or printing newsletter

Overhead

Your overhead should be included in the estimate you do for your business expenses. This will ensure that it will be covered by what you charge for each subscription.

Profit

Remember to include a profit figure in the estimated expenses. This is above and beyond the amount you allocate for your own salary. Your time is worth money and you should be paid for it. Profit goes to the business, as a separate amount from what you are paid.

How To Be Paid

With this business, the standard practice is payment in advance. This will give you working capital to use when putting together your newsletter. If you choose, you can send out a sample issue of the newsletter to prospective subscribers to give them a little bite of what you offer. Mail it along with a letter explaining that for a small fee they can receive the newsletter in their mailbox once a month. You should get orders and checks from people who want to see more.

MARKETING METHODS

The best way to market this business is with display ads. Placed in newspapers and publications that gardeners read, your ad should bring response for more information and checks for subscriptions.

I'm going to give you an example of a display ad that should bring results. For other methods you can refer to Section 5.

Here is the ad:

> GREEN THUMBS UNITE!
>
> Now you can read a locally produced newsletter that will give you monthly updates on gardening conditions.
>
> The Gardening Newsletter supplies up-to-date planting news, feature stories on topics of interest to you, and even shows you what your garden can look like.
>
> And since Gardening News is produced locally, you know exactly when, why and how you should plant for your own area.

Don't miss out on a single exciting, informative issue! To start receiving your copies, send a check today! This will ensure that for the next 12 months, you'll know exactly what you need to know to make that thumb of yours even greener.

Your own variation of this ad should start the checks rolling in to you. It will take time, persistence and patience, but this business can offer a great amount of personal satisfaction and a nice, steady income to the people who decide to try it.

UNIQUE BUSINESS APPROACH

The approach I'm now going to suggest to you will increase your income with this business and ensure a steady list of subscribers for your newsletter.

People who have succeeded in this business find themselves a sponsor, usually a garden store that sells supplies, seeds, etc. You charge your sponsor for advertising in your publication.

This can increase your earnings with this opportunity by several hundred dollars a month. Plus, you can have your sponsor sell the newsletter on a per issue basis in his or her store. Or you can even charge the sponsor more and allow him to give out your publication free to his customers. This will bring him more business and increase your readership. Either way, you win.

LOCATION and MARKET BASE

You can operate this business in a city or in a country. The beauty is that gardeners are everywhere.

You only need a market base of from 5,000 to 50,000 people to start this business. People garden everywhere, in small towns and big cities. All you have to do is let them know you exist and you'll be on your way to being the editor of your own gardening newsletter.

TO SUM UP

Gardening is a hobby for a lot of people. Others use it to grow the food they put on their table. All gardeners want to know when they should plant to make a successful harvest. All want to know what they should plant for their part of the country. Most of the gardening guides available tell them this information only in general terms, and oftentimes the results are disastrous.

You supply them with information that will help them become successful. In exchange, you'll earn a nice income and become known as a local expert of sorts. When they have a problem with snails, they'll come to you for advice on handling it. When the frost arrives late, you'll be able to use your computer to tell your readers how it will affect their gardening. You'll be paid for your information and perform a service for the people of your town.

With this business you'll be able to turn that green thumb of yours into greenbacks. And that's song you can bank on.

SOURCE MATERIAL

Refer to Section 7.

No. 197

SELL INVENTORY CONTROLS FOR SMALL BUSINESSES

One of the hardest jobs for all small businesspeople is keeping up with inventory so they will know when to buy and how much they are making on what they have sold. We will show you how to set these small businesses up and keep them current on a monthly basis, thereby saving them time and lost revenue from shortages. All it takes is some of your time and your personal computer. A good steady income can be provided from this service.

CONCEPT

The concept of this business is to take care of inventory control for small businesses. Inventory is simply the stock on hand. It can be shoes, books, shampoo, or anything that a small business sells.

Most businesses keep poor track of what their inventory is. They don't order new inventory by any special method, nor do they keep track of how much they have on hand, what their shortages are, either from sales or theft, or what it costs them to carry the inventory versus lowering the price of the product to get it out of the store.

With this service, you handle their inventory worries for them. Since you have a computer that will keep track for you, you don't have to work very hard at all.

SKILLS YOU WILL REQUIRE

This business requires no special skills to operate. All you have to know is how to use your computer. Recently, new software programs have come out on the market just to perform inventory control. With them, you can track the inventory of your customers, plus generate reports listing their inventory changes. Another nice thing about this business is that it is a new one in a sense. Personal computers are only now getting the kind of memory capacity that makes this business feasible. That means the field is wide open for you to make a killing in it.

INFORMATION REQUIRED

The information in the inventory game consists of whatever your customer wants to keep track of. For example, if he runs a store that sells office supplies, he might want you to keep a steady count of what is sold, its selling price, a minimum he wants to have on hand at any one time, who he purchased it from, and what he paid. This kind of information is simple to track with a computerized inventory system.

Your customer will be able to show you what his manual inventory method consists of now and what he would like it to become. From there, you can design an inventory system that meets his needs and requires a minimum of effort from you.

OPERATING NAME

There is little reason for you to choose a fictitious name for this business. If you call your operation something like "Inventory Control Specialists" or "American Inventory Management," you will have to file or register the fictitious name, get yourself a new bank account, and other things that will require extra start-up capital.

You are as well off if you use your own name in the business. For example, you can call your service "John Smith's Inventory Service." This gives you as good a name as you'll need, plus saves you unnecessary start-up costs. For more information refer to Section 4.

GETTING STARTED

Getting started is a matter of getting contacts for work. You can follow the techniques suggested in Marketing Methods.

Once you have customers, you can talk to them about the kind of inventory system they want to use. Then, for a start-up fee, you go into their business and mark all their products with a code sticker. When they sell the product, they take the sticker off, and either place it in a special section of the cash register drawer or onto a sheet of paper. At the end of the month, or however often you perform their inventory update, you take those stickers and record into the computer what was sold, how many, the price, etc. Then you print out a report with an inventory update for your customer. This will inform him about what he needs to reorder, what isn't selling and should be put on sale at a discount, etc.

An advantage of using your service is that the customer can keep track of missing inventory. At the end of the year he has the printed report you gave him in order to make out his stolen inventory reports and to claim the loss on his tax return. This is a great selling point for this business.

THE COMPETITION

Your competition in this business are the large inventory counting services. The difference is that they prefer to handle large customers, such as grocery stores and major department stores. You are going to service the smaller businesses that can't afford to pay what the large inventory companies charge.

Just a few of these kinds of customers will give you a nice steady income.

You will become an expert in inventory for small business. This means your customers will refer you to their business associates and bring you new business by word of mouth.

POTENTIAL INCOME

The income you can earn with this business is steady and quickly adds up to large amounts. You can charge a start-up fee for the initial inventory consultation and marking of items, then a monthly or quarterly fee each time you prepare an updated inventory report. If you charge $100 for the start-up work, then $50 every quarter for an update, you can earn $300 from each business in the first year. The money that a business can save using your service is large in comparison to your fee. Just 10 customers at these rates can bring you $3,000 in your first year of operation. Increase this number, depending on how much time you want to put into it, and the earnings you can get will surprise you.

To price your service, estimate your costs of the program and include a charge for your time as well as a profit.

Basic Costs

1. Cost of computer software
2. Cost of advertising
3. Cost of labels to stick on inventory
4. Cost of time spent for initial consultation
5. Cost of time spent organizing updated inventory report
6. Cost of materials used
7. Cost of transportation expenses

Overhead

Remember to include the cost of overhead for each job. The job should pay for the percentage of time it takes. That is, if you have 10 customers during the month and one customer required 20 percent of your time, that job should cover 20 percent of the overhead.

Profit

Remember to include a profit figure on each job. The profit is for your business. The money you earn for your time is a business expense, not part of the profit.

With a little time you will settle on a good price to quote each customer, based on how large his inventory is.

How To Be Paid

The standard practice with this business should be a pay-as-you-go basis. You can bill the customer for your initial consultation work to prepare his inventory. Then, after you perform each update, you can charge for that service.

You shouldn't have any trouble collecting your fee with this business, since you hold valuable information in your computer. Without his inventory records, a businessperson is lost and will have to spend a lot of time redoing the inventory.

MARKETING METHODS

You can market this business in a number of ways. Perhaps the best methods are direct mail, display ads, telephone sales and direct sales. I'll explain each one of these.

Direct mail consists of sending out letters on a regular basis to the people you think would most benefit from this service. This includes clothing stores, shoe stores, bookstores, office supply stores, camera stores, general merchandise stores and just about any other kind of store. All need this service and all want to save money and make their inventory more efficient.

In your letter you can explain that your charge is lower than they might expect to have to pay, and almost worry-free for them.

A sample letter might read:

> DEAR BUSINESS OWNER:
>
> Proper inventory controls can save your business money.
>
> Ask yourself these questions:
>
> Do you know what you have on hand right this minute?
>
> Do you know what should be sold at a discount just to get it out of your inventory?
>
> Do you know when to re-order stock?
>
> Do you keep control of theft loss?
>
> A smart businessperson knows the answers to these simple questions. Our computerized inventory service will take the worry and expense out of your inventory control needs. Our service will set up the inventory control that is right for your business, plus give you regular update reports to help you run your business better. Call us today for more information and a free estimate.

Mailed out to prospective clients on a regular basis, this letter should bring you calls and inquiries for more information.

You can also market this business by display ads run in local publications where storeowners and small business owners will see them.

Or you can market this business with telephone and direct sales. Simply compile a list of the business and store owners who will best benefit from this service. Start calling each business owner and offer to give a free estimate for handling his or her inventory control. Most will be curious about your service and request that you pay a visit to discuss it further. Once they have seen how little it costs and how much they get in return, you will have a customer for as long as you want.

UNIQUE BUSINESS APPROACH

The secret that will make this business a sure bet is this: offer your services to stores, such as clothing boutiques, that make a high profit margin on each sale.

These kinds of businesses often don't know whether a certain article of clothing has been on the shelf for one week or half a year. Yet for every day that piece of clothing is part of the inventory rather than a sold item, it costs the store owner money.

This means that your customer doesn't really know what is selling and what is sitting. If you offer to perform an inventory that tells him not only what he has in stock, but when he should sell it to make it 50 percent profit when he should sell it to make a 40 percent profit, etc., he will have a hard time refusing you. The fee you charge will be just a small part of the increased profits he can make by having this kind of information.

Plus, you can offer to tell him when he should reorder his stock because a certain line is selling particularly well. If he has something that he sold out in a month, yet he only reorders it every three months, he is losing money. You can keep him updated on a regular basis, perhaps once a week or so, to let him know what is moving quickly and what he should discount just to get rid of it.

You can charge more for this kind of service, since it will require more frequent inventory updates for the storeowner. But you both win in this case. He makes better business decisions and you earn extra money.

LOCATION and MARKET BASE

This business is best suited for a city. That will give you a plentiful supply of stores and businesses that need inventory control assistance. You will probably need a market base of 200,000 people and up for this business. This will provide plenty of businesses that can use your service.

TO SUM UP

Inventory is a headache for busines owners. They realize it is very important to the running of their businesses, yet they don't want to waste their own time in managing it. With just a little of your own time, you can take this effort over for them and make money doing it.

To put the value of your service in perspective, look at it this way: businessowners make money by selling their stock. Some know exactly what their customers are buying, always have it on hand and make a good profit for their smart thinking. Others just flounder around guessing at what they need, guessing at what they should reorder, guessing at what was stolen or is missing. These are the business owners that cannot last for very long. With this service, you keep those business owners in the running.

In exchange, you keep your own business in the running. It requires just a little effort, time and perserverence. But like a horse race, the one who keeps up the pace is declared the winner.

SOURCE MATERIAL

Refer to Section 7 for source information.

AUTO TRIP PLANNING SERVICE

Here's a service that is being supplied by auto clubs around the country, but if you've tried them, you know the results are anything but acceptable. We will show you how to put together an auto trip plan giving your clients a thousand times more information than is being offered by the auto clubs. With your personal computer you will be able to show the best routes, mileage, cost, time, etc.—and all of this in only minutes.

CONCEPT

The concept behind this business is to create personalized auto trip plans for customers. On the surface this may appear to be exactly what automobile clubs do for their customers. Yet what you offer is more customized.

You give your clients the chance to enjoy their vacations on the road in a way that the auto clubs have never offered. And you do this at a better rate than they charge, as well as more conveniently.

SKILLS YOU WILL REQUIRE

You don't even need to have a driver's license to perform this service. All it requires is a desire to help people plan their vacations and other auto trips.

If you have ever known the thrill of the open road, or enjoyed poring over road maps or making your own vacation plans, you'll be especially well-suited to operate an auto trip planning service.

INFORMATION REQUIRED

To operate this business you'll want to be aware of a couple of things. First, there are several programs available that allow you to type in information—such as destination, starting point, type of car being driven, etc.—that will process the information and give you back a listing of the total mileage to be covered. It will also tell how much gas and oil will be used, how long the trip will take, depending on how many miles a day will be driven, and other information that your customer will want to be aware of.

Plus, it will calculate out your customer's budget as well. If he intends to take the whole family and has a certain amount to spend on lodging, meals, entertainment and other vacation expenses, it will tell him what kind of budget he must follow to make his money last as long as his trip.

Another thing that will help you offer this service is something called data bases. You can use your computer, telephone and modem to tap into information about anything you might want to know about. Information can be located quickly without even leaving your home. There are now data base services available to find information on almost any subject you want to research.

When using a data base, you'll want to be aware of some terms. A data base is a kind of catalog system. If you know the subject you want to look up, it will find you information on that subject.

When you use your data base, you are calling up the information contained in the memory banks of other computers. These other computers are located all over the country, and to reach them, all you have to do is make a long-distance phone call with your modem and telephone.

Besides the cost of the phone call, you will also pay a fee to use the data base. Usually it will consist of a membership fee as well as a charge for the minutes you are "on-line" with the data base.

For this business, you will want to call up data bases that give information about hotels, entertainment, restaurants and any other service that your customer will want to know about for his vacation or auto trip. You can get prices, schedules, special information that will be helpful, and if you choose, even make reservations using your computer.

Auto clubs usually supply their members with standard routes they can take and directories that list lodging and restaurants. Usually this listing is very incomplete and includes the higher priced places. You, on the other hand, will be able to give a personalized auto plan based on the interests and budget of your client.

Not only will you make your client's vacation successful, but you'll get a lot of repeat business. When your customer has been satisfied once, he'll return to you year after year for the same service, as well as recommend you to anybody he knows that is planning an auto trip. Your business will grow rapidly, simply by word of mouth.

OPERATING NAME

For this service you have two choices. You can either take a fictitious name, such as "Budget-Wise Auto Plannning" or "Personalized Auto Trips" or something like that, or use your own name, John Smith. The advantage of using your own name is that you will save yourself some start-up costs, like registering your fictitious name, getting yourself a new bank account with the new name, etc. If you choose, you can use your own name, then add "and Associates." You still have the advantage of being able to use the same phone and bank accounts, etc., that you now use. For more information about this, refer to Section 4.

GETTING STARTED

To get started in this business you want to make contacts. After you have the equipment you want to use, your next step should be to put together a marketing campaign for yourself. This is covered in the Marketing Methods Section.

After that, you're ready to start handling that flood of customers who will want to use your service. Imagine somebody comes in wanting to plan a trip for his family during the summer months. He tells you that he has $1,000 to spend and wants to go from point A to point B, and to make stops at all those places in between that offer something for kids to do. You plug the information into your computer and come up with a week-long itinerary for him that he can follow if he drives only 200 miles a day.

You'll be able to supply him with the highways and freeways he'll want to follow, tell him how much gas he'll need to buy, and give him the names of the hotels and motels that offer family discounts. You'll also be able to give him a listing of those towns in between that have amusement parks, historical sites and other entertainment values for families. Plus, you'll be able to inform him about the restaurants that he would enjoy eating at and what kind of weather he can expect along the way. (You'll get this last piece of information by tapping into a data base that has updated weather and temperature reports.)

You can be sure that with the attention and detail you supply him, his vacation will run a lot smoother and he'll be back to use your service again the next time he travels somewhere by car.

THE COMPETITION

With this service you beat the competition by being able to give the kind of information that they can't supply. It isn't that they couldn't get it themselves. The difference is that they have thousands of customers, all wanting the same thing. With this kind of volume they don't have the time to give the personalized and detailed attention that you'll be able to offer.

Once your customers are aware of the advantage of using you to plan their auto trips, they'll more than likely forget about using their auto club for vacation planning and simply rely on them for other services.

POTENTIAL INCOME

In this business, you'll do well by charging less than auto clubs. Whereas they usually charge a yearly membership fee, you'll be making your money on a trip-by-trip basis. Each time somebody wants to plan an auto trip, he pays you a certain amount that you have decided on.

Figuring out what to charge for this service is a matter of calculating what your business expenses are and adding a profit. You may find that your business is more popular during certain times of the year, depending on where you are operating it. If you are in the snow bound North, most of your business will probably come during the spring and summer months. If you are in a warmer climate, the seasons won't dictate your business, but vacation times will. You'll probably get your business during the school breaks, when families usually take their vacations together.

If you were to charge, for example, $25 for each auto trip plan and get 10 customers a week, that's $250 for your part-time effort. During vacation months, you can probably expect a rush of business.

Primary Costs

1. Cost of travel software used
2. Cost of making phone calls for information
3. Cost of maps and atlases
4. Cost of data base membership
5. Cost of advertising
6. Cost of time organizing travel plans
7. Cost of miscellaneous materials used

MARKETING METHODS

Display ads are probably the best way to market this service. You can run ads, like the example given, in any newspapers, magazines and other publications where people who travel by car will see the ads. A particularly effective place to run an ad is in the travel section of the newspaper. When people have vacations in mind, they tend to want to read about exotic destinations and special events or sites that they might want to visit themselves.

I am going to give you an example of an ad that will bring inquiries and business for you. For additional tips and marketing information, refer to Section 5.

Here is the ad:

MAKE YOUR AUTO TRIP WORRY-FREE!

Leave the planning to us. All you'll have to do is enjoy the scenery.

With our special service, we'll work within your money and time budget. We will design an auto travel plan that tells you what routes to take, as well as what hotels and motels, restaurants, entertainment and special events are available to make your vacation worry-free and memorable. We'll even tell you how much gas you can expect to use, what the weather will be like and more!

Call now for more information about this unique auto travel planning service.

That ad, with your own variations, should get potential customers calling you for more information. It will take time to get yourself established, but with a little effort, luck and persistence, you'll be on your own road to success.

UNIQUE BUSINESS APPROACH

Now I'll let you in on an approach for this opportunity that will increase your business considerably. What you can do is market your service to special-interest groups to plan the kinds of trips they would be most interested in. For example, you might consider offering your sevices to disabled people. You can plan auto trips for them that take into account wheelchair access at hotels and restaurants and other places they'll visit. Then, to reach these kinds of customers, you can place ads in the newsletters they receive, or contact the organizations that assist disabled people.

Another example would be a trip planning service for people who are rockhounds. You could direct them to locales that offer the collecting sites and museums that would most interest them.

Other special-interest groups you can cater to are: history buffs, book lovers, movie fans, sports fans, etc. The possibilities are limited only by your own imagination. If you have an interest of your own, even better. You'll increase your knowledge of a subject you like, as well as understand the special needs and desires of the group that wants to take a special kind of trip.

LOCATION and MARKET BASE

This business will work best in a city, since you'll have a larger population base to attract customers.

You'll want a market base of between 50,000 and 200,000 people to operate this business. That should supply you with a steady stream of customers to keep your operation busy.

TO SUM UP

People have a love affair with cars in this country. They love the idea of being able to seat themselves inside a car, turn on the engine and take off down the open road. But oftentimes, they're afraid to take longer than a day trip, simply because they think they can't afford it, that gas will cost too much, or that they won't find anything out there on the road to interest them.

With an auto travel planning service, you allay the fears your customers might have, simply because you can give them the facts about their trip, what the costs will probably run them, what there is to see and do, where they can eat and where they can stay. With just a few minutes of time on your computer you put your fingertips on the facts, data and information they'll need to make their trip a fun one. With this service, you make a nice bit of cash that will enable you to plan your own excursions, not only to those places you've always wanted to see, but down to the local bank where you keep that handsome savings account you've been building.

SOURCE MATERIAL

For source material refer to Section 7.

No. 199

INVESTMENT ANALYSIS ADVISOR

As an investment analysis advisor, you offer your client a detailed breakdown of investment options. These options can either be speculative or based on the client's immediate investment needs. You let them choose what they want to do based on what your personal computer comes up with.

CONCEPT

Interest in the stock market, IRA's, income property, precious metals, mutual funds, etc. in this country has reached new levels, with new and experienced investors clamoring for investment help and advice. There is a tremendous overload of investment information available—so much so that only the professional Wall Street broker seems to be able to give it the comprehensive analysis necessary to actually make money.

In the last few years, however, the advent of the personal computer and on-line investment information services has made it possible to selectively sort and evaluate investment information into something that the average investor can work with.

This runaway interest in the investment market is a perfect opportunity for you to make money with your personal computer. By using any of the dozens of investment software programs available, and going on-line with various investment market information networks, you can offer the investor the detailed analysis he needs to make the right money-making decisons. With your up-to-date information, your client is well prepared for any contingency and able to act quickly.

As is true in so many other computer-assisted businsses, you can offer your client the information he needs to get the advantage—in this case, having the advantage of making more money.

SKILLS YOU WILL REQUIRE

Don't think you have to be a high financier to successfully run this business. As a matter of fact, you will need to steer clear of actually offering direct advice—this is a tricky area legally. Your job will simply be to collect information from various sources and compile it into a form that will help your client make decisions favorable to his investment holdings.

Learning how to collect your information should be easy. One of the qualities of the software you select for your business should be ease of use. Many of the available programs combine terminal programs (these allow you to go on-line and access the investment information services) with financial analysis programs that manipulate the data you've just downloaded.

It will help if you learn the terminology of the investment market. You can pick a lot of this up by simply studying and using the software you choose; it also might be helpful to go to the library and study some financial newspapers and magazines. Get subscriptions to stock market publications as well, to keep up on current stories and trends.

INFORMATION REQUIRED

There are three basic types of financial analysis and investment management programs: portfolio management, fundamental analysis and technical analysis. Portfolio management programs are best used to download information from stock services such as Dow Jones News/Retrieval. The other two types of programs allow you to analyze various investment options, project their potential worth for upcoming years, compare their worth based on interest accumulation, etc.

The programs you use will do a lot of the work for you—you'll just be gathering information. You will, however, have to know what to download. Having a copy of your client's portfolio on your computer will make your job much easier.

GETTING STARTED

As stated earlier, find out what software is available. This is a business that requires software that really can do what you want it to, so choose carefully. If you don't have a computer yet, seriously consider buying the software first and then buying a computer that will run it. The majority of financial analysis programs are going to be configured for IBM and MS-DOS compatibility, so you'll have some leeway in your choice of hardware.

There are alternatives to using prepackaged investment analysis software. A good spreadsheet will allow you to customize your arrangement of data, using formulas and layouts that you design. Do some reading on this (see Source Material) and consider it as an addition to your financial programs.

Part of the consideration in selection of software will be the program's ability to do charts and graphs. Using your printer and plotter, you can put together graphic presentations that will really impress your clients. Although many of the spreadsheet and financial planning packages support graphics, not all do; so shop carefully.

Get everything set up and take as many trial runs as you want, getting the feel of the downloading and analysis procedure. You'll need to subscribe to a few networks to get your information. Many software and computer dealers can give you in-store demos of these, so take advantage of them.

You should put a good amount of practice into doing this efficiently. Offer to help out a friend or two for the sake of experience. This will make you aware of possible problems and situations you might encounter and teach you how to deal with them.

Get your advertising going as soon as you feel you're ready for it (see Marketing Methods). Another good method for gathering information is to call a service doing similar work to yours and pose as a client. This is free and a valuable way to collect information. You can discover how they treat you, the kinds of questions they ask, what they supply you with in terms of brochures, and how they price their services.

THE COMPETITION

Operating on your own, you'll be able to undercut your competition's prices. Also, you'll soon discover that most of the other businesses are full-fledged brokers and financial consultants. Since your business is really just to offer detailed information and not to give direct advice, your overhead and fees will be much lower than these companies.

It should be a simple matter, also, to get on a contract basis with most of your clients, regularly supplying information to them. This will give you a steady income.

POTENTIAL INCOME

Pricing your services is not difficult. After figuring up your operating expenses, decide a fair rate for your time and charge by the hour for your work. Make sure that your costs match your actual overhead. If you have a job that takes 10 percent of your time, for example, then make sure the job pays at least 10 percent of the overhead.

If you charge $100 for the information given to the customer during the course of a year, for example, that may not sound like much money for you. But if you consider that you will be selling the same information to a number of customers, your profit adds up quickly. If you feed investment information to 100 customers a year, your business will have earned $10,000. That's certainly nothing to write off, considering it was produced with only part-time effort.

Basic Costs

1. Cost of software
2. Cost of network subscriptions
3. Cost of network fees and long-distance phone calls

4. Cost of advertising
5. Cost of publication subscriptions
6. Cost of materials used
7. Cost of time spent researching, downloading and organizing information

MARKETING METHODS

Direct mail, display ads and telephone sales are the best marketing methods for this business.

Your service is a moneymaker for potential customers, so make sure you emphasize this in your advertising. Stress that economically speaking, it's far cheaper to use your service than to buy a home computer and do it himself. The financial rewards should be fast coming for him and for you.

Consider this approach for a direct mail ad:

DEAR INVESTOR:

Would your investments be more valuable if you had a clearinghouse of information advising you? Of course they would! And that's what we offer.

Robert Jones Investment Information can fill you in on the most up-to-date information about your investment portfolio.

We won't tell you HOW to invest your money. But we can give you the information that will make your investment decisions easier to tackle.

Try us out. It'll be the best investment you ever made.

Display ads in newspapers and direct mail sent to selected markets (consider a sales lead service to provide you with contacts) will bring the inquiries you need to keep going. Go after the young up-and-coming people, the ones just getting started in their careers. They love the idea of keeping control of their own investment decisions, based on the information you provide. Offer to show potential customers what you can do for them. Set up appointments with interested people and show samples of your work. Include graphs and charts in your presentations. You yourself will be strongly sold on this business once you see what you can do for your clients and, believe it or not, that enthusiasm will be contagious.

UNIQUE BUSINESS APPROACH

As a bonus service to your clients, or as a means of encouraging new business, offer a "what-if" analysis of the customer's stock and investments. For instance, what if you had taken that risk with securities futures, or what if you pulled your investment out of ABC Computers? This will really capture the interest of your clients, as their imaginations will be allowed to run wild and try, at no loss to themselves, what they didn't have the nerve or know-how to try before. The idea here is to show people how much control they can have, based on the information you feed them—so much control that they can afford to experiment.

LOCATION and MARKET BASE

Your investment analysis service is best suited for a city's population. This is where you'll find the largest cncentration of people who invest most heavily in real estate, stocks, metals, mutual funds, etc. A market base of 50,000 or more will be sufficient to make the business go.

TO SUM UP

Few people realize that the only real difference between professional investors and amateur investors is the degree of organization they possess. What once took all an investor's time and concentration can now be done with a personal computer. With access to the right sources and the right programs, the small investor sitting at home has virtually all the tools, time and advantage that only Wall Street used to possess.

With an all-time high of activity on Wall Street today and the millions of investors in this country, there is a huge demand for investment advice. With your home computer, you can help investors make informed, money-making decisions.

By simply collecting information and customizing it according to a client's needs, both you and your business can benefit. He gets a careful analysis that can direct him in the best ways to invest, and you make money by offering this useful service—a service that can only grow as time goes on.

SOURCE MATERIAL

Refer to Section 7.

No. 200

HOME SECURITY SYSTEMS ANALYSIS SERVICE

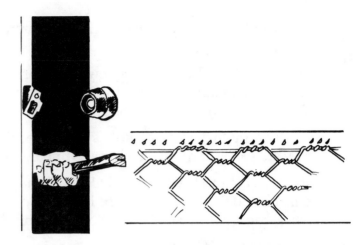

With home burglaries now at an all-time high, more people are becoming aware of the need for a home security system. But when they call a security systems company to get an estimate, its often lots more than is affordable. Yet the products that make up the systems can be purchased at a fraction of the cost and installed by the home-owners themselves. We have developed a system using your personal home computer to determine what your customers need to protect their home. They can then install it themselves. You get your fee, and both you and your customer are happy.

CONCEPT

The whole gamut of security services is wrought with over-priced consulting services, and the costs of installation are such that you almost have to own a bank to get it done. However, you can do a computer analysis for your client, letting them know what they need, how much it costs and possibly even supply it for them, for a fraction of what some high-priced security outfit will charge.

SKILLS YOU WILL REQUIRE

You will have to set up and catalog the types and kinds of security equipment that are now available on the market so you can present them to your client in an orderly fashion.

Obviously, there is no real skill level or large amounts of technical work you will have to gain. Just do the research.

INFORMATION REQUIRED

With a little effort on your part and the research that we suggest you do, you too can become a "security expert."

One of the first places you might want to start is with a trip to the police department and the police's neighborhood watch program. They turn out volumes of material along the lines of preventing break-ins and burglaries. This is fairly solid advice.

A call or trip to the local security systems people might be in order to find out what they are selling and why. You can also find out what their rates are.

You are going to have to do a little work in researching the tools of the trade. Get catalogs and flyers concerning the hardware of the industry; locks, alarms, sirens, the whole bag. Then you will want to organize this data and the prices.

It would not hurt to get copies of the trade journals for the industry. Many libraries will either have copies or be able to tell you where to order copies. Most of these can be obtained free on a monthly basis by sending a letter on your company letterhead. Study the ads in the publications and order brochures and catalogs from those companies producing the equipment you want to know more about.

GETTING STARTED

You need customers, or at least people who know you are alive and well and trying to keep them secure. Nothing is going to help you more in this venture than the preparation of a brochure.

The brochure can serve several purposes—to include with direct mail and the introductory business card, as an explanation of what you are all about, and most of all as a questionnaire to allow people to tell you what kinds of security they want to consider.

Use a strong visual lead-in on the cover panel. A headline should read something like: "YOU ARE A TARGET RIGHT NOW for the people who want to take something you worked hard for: YOUR PROPERTY." This should be in large or boldface type. This headline can be overlaid on a picture of a house or home.

There should also be a short blurb about the numbers of break-ins and robberies that occur daily in your area. You can get these figures from local police statistics. These figures are often a little scary in terms of numbers. Be sure to quote from them and give the source material. According to the figures, there is a good chance that everyone, in his lifetime, will have something stolen.

Next mention what you are going to do about it and what your service can provide.

You will want to ask a series of questions on another one of the panels about what is being secured in your readers' homes right now, and how.

Leave room on another panel for them to draw floor plans that can be used to analyze their security.

And be sure to leave one panel for the mailing label and information.

All this can be done on both sides of a piece of paper that is folded three times. It can be put into a number 10 envelope or used for a direct mail piece.

After getting several brochures from security companies, you will have a good idea of what they are selling and how they do it. But don't forget one thing that many of these brochures miss. You are selling security and safety. Most folks feel a break-in could never happen to them, and when it does, they are devastated. Make your client aware of the fact that most break-ins occur because the homeowner or apartment dweller makes it too easy for the thief.

THE COMPETITION

You are going into competition with people who sell alarms and set up systems for people, for what is often an outrageous sum of money.

Using your computer to develop a security system, you can perform this same service for a fraction of the cost. All you are doing is calling up from your computer the various kinds of equipment and sources for obtaining the equipment. You then allow the customer to order it himself, as well as to install it, thereby saving money.

With this type of program, there is no reason that with a little effort and time you can't compete successfully with security companies and give the consumer more for his dollar.

POTENTIAL INCOME

Pricing your service will not be difficult. First, what you need to do is price out your business expenses. A list follows. Then you should add in a salary for your time, plus a profit for the business. After that, it is a simple matter for you to estimate how many customers you can reasonably handle in the amount of time you want to give the business, then divide your total expenses by that number. That should give you a rough estimate of what you need to make on each job.

Basic Costs

1. Cost of software
2. Cost of advertising, brochure
3. Cost of time spent researching security systems
4. Cost of time spent analyzing customer's security needs
5. Cost of telephone charges
6. Cost of transportation
7. Cost of business start-up expenses, such as bank account, telephone, etc.
8. Cost of materials used

With this service, you can make your money in several different ways. First, you can charge for the home security analysis. If you charge $25 for this service, and you get 10 customers in a week, each requiring about two hours of time, then your business has earned $250.

But the income doesn't stop there. You can also approach the manufacturers who sell the equipment you are advising customers on and request a finder's fee for each system of theirs that you sell. If you do this with enough manufacturers, you will ensure two things: one, that this will provide you with a steady second source of income, and two, that you will not be swayed to recommending only one or two different security systems, just like the companies against whom you are competing. If you go this route and the manufacturers agree to it, your income with this business can be multiplied tenfold.

Another way for you to earn income is to do the home security analysis first if the customer wants you to, you can then purchase the actual equipment they want installed. You can buy it at a wholesale price, then mark it up just enough for you to make money on the sale, but little enough that the customer still saves money from purchasing it at retail cost.

As you can see, this business is loaded with money-making opportunities. The choice is all yours about how you want to get your green out of it.

How To Be Paid

In a word, immediately. You don't have to bill the service. When you deliver it, you get paid for it. You don't want to get caught in an account receivables crunch. The best bet is cash, check or money order.

MARKETING METHODS

You can use the whole gamut of marketing methods here. One is sometimes as good as the next, but we will target both the direct mail and display or classified ad route.

You need to target a group of people who are in the most need of your service. The senior citizen is one you should start with. Send out your direct mail piece to areas of the community that have the highest concentration of the elderly, and follow them up with phone calls using a "reverse" phone directory. This is one that lists addresses, then supplies names and phone numbers. The seniors are the people who are most preyed upon by burglers and hit the hardest when a break-in occurs.

A typical classified geared to seniors might read:

> SLEEP SAFE AT NIGHT!
>
> We can analyze your security needs and advise you about the cheapest, most effective ways to safeguard yourself, home and property. Call today for more information.

Classified ads in the weekly shopper are incredibly cheap. You may want to place a few to see what the results are.

You might also consider branching out to do security analysis for business people. These ads should generate some calls.

A classified directed towards businesses could read:

> DID YOU LOSE MONEY BY THEFT LAST YEAR?
>
> Let us analyze your business security needs and advise you on the most cost-effective methods to protect your inventory and equipment. Don't let your business become the next victim. Call today!

UNIQUE BUSINESS APPROACH

Your research is going to do one thing for you: make you an expert in the security business. Don't stop this research until you feel conversant in this field.

We have two modes of attack for this strategy.

The most reliable is the press release. Send a release out to all the television, radio and newspapers letting them know you are in the security business and that you are using a computer to plot out the best plans for making a home a little harder to break into. You should gain some attention from the release. Then you can embark on part two: the security seminar. You will want to lay some groundwork for this, but the plan goes like this: contact the ministers, priests or rabbis of several of the churches that are in the senior citizen part of the community and tell them what you do, and that you are willing to put on a security safety seminar for the members of their respective congregations, especially the senior citizens. You will get a hall for free, and the attention of people who want to safeguard their valuables. You will also get an instant client list and referral calls. You don't need to sell anything here. Just have plenty of brochures on hand and let people know what dangers they constantly face. You might want to offer as door prizes some dead-bolt locks.

Add to this list all the service clubs you can find. A speech to these people ought to bring in money for consulting.

And finally, round up any senior citizen's groups you can. Make sure seminars for them are held in the morning or early afternoon, as these are the hours most seniors will be available.

The seminar should last no longer than 45 minutes. Leave plenty of time for questions. Make sure you have the facts to back up your statements.

By now your client list will have grown tremendously and you will have picked up lots of names and numbers.

LOCATION and MARKET BASE

In the security business you have to be where the people are, and that definitely is a city with a decent population. You will need the numbers to make this a go.

This is a city game and it ought to be played where the population base ranges from 50,000 to 200,000 to make this one sprout wings and fly.

TO SUM UP

This is another one of those business opportunities that should be looked at carefully. It offers the chance for real growth, but in a steady manner. Crime and criminals and break-ins seem to be a fact of life. They are, unfortunately, the mainstay of this trade.

You can build an excellent business within a year or two and have the satisfaction that you are providing a needed service in the process. It offers some benefits that can't be measured in dollar amounts.

But get in right now if you feel that it is for you. Stop those thieves now and earn a super-hero's reward for doing it.

SOURCE MATERIAL

Refer to Section 7.

No. 202

LOCAL COMPUTER SHOWS

Computers in all their forms are big business today. But it's a fast-changing field with big name corporations going in and out of the business every day. How can you make money without taking the risk of getting stuck with a deadend company? Probably the best answer is not to sell the computer, but to put on the computer show.

This report will show you how to put together a local computer show with a minimum of effort and a maximum of profits. We'll tell you the secret of how to corner the costs of the show ahead of time, find show space, and get free publicity. Here is another business where you can collect from everyone—the buyer, the seller and even computer manufacturers.

CONCEPT

The idea of this business is to provide the potential computer buyer with the best possible chance to find a computer that will fit his or her individual needs. At the same time, you provide the seller with the best possible chance to find new customers for a product without dramatically increasing overhead.

Computer shows bring in lots of people. That means the seller gets a lot of exposure for a very small cost per person. Not only that, computers are a high impulse purchase item. There is a very good chance that computer dealers will be able to sell more units at your show than they could in a month or more at a storefront location. That is why many computer retailers and individuals who handle computers as a sideline are not only happy but eager to pay you to display their wares.

That is also why parent companies are often happy to sponsor even small local shows. That is, they will pay for advertising, guarantee hall rentals and provide other useful services, such as public relations or basics, tables and chairs, or even a place to put it on.

A person interested in computers has a real reason to come to your show. Potential customers often have a difficult time finding the right computer for them. Most stores carry only one or two brands. Cross-shopping is difficult, if not impossible, and there is virtually no access to small company brands that often provide the most computer for the customer's dollar. The computer show is the perfect answer to all of these shopping problems. And that's why the potential customer is willing to pay to attend your show.

SKILLS YOU WILL REQUIRE

Enthusiasm is important. Enthusiasm sells, and this job is primarily a sales job. You must sell the show to the dealer, sponsors and to the people who attend. You must also be able to think on your feet and work well with all kinds of people. You must be an organizer who can see the big picture and be able to either follow through yourself or delegate others to do so.

GETTING STARTED

Getting started in this business takes a little more groundwork than some others. However, once you are up and running, most of the work is in physically producing the show. The contacts you make in this business—computer salespeople, sponsors, etc.—won't need to be "set up" again. In fact, new sponsors and sellers will approach you. That's one good reason to have an "office" set up at each of your shows. A sponsor who likes your show and offers a free site or advertising for your next one is someone you want to talk with now.

What you will need to know includes the following.

1. Where can your show be held?

Make a list of all the possibilities. Ask others for ideas and carry the list with you for several days. Don't jump on the obvious (and expensive) answers, such as a convention center. It could cost you thousands of dollars.

If you are seeking a large, generalized audience, an inexpensive, easy answer can be hard to find. It may take a little imagination, but it can be done. One successful showman uses a large parking lot to great advantage. An airplane hanger or a National Guard armory might also work out very well as a site.

If your target audience is smaller, a hotel with meeting facilities may well suit your needs. Often, if you allow an open bar (and guarantee a certain amount of sales), these rooms can be arranged at no, or low, cost. A large dealer, such as IBM, may also provide a free place for a moderate-sized event. Be careful, though, that the show doesn't look like a "company event" that will turn away both potential sellers and buyers.

2. Who wants to sell at your show?

If you are attracting large crowds, the answer will be: almost all of the home computer brands are potential customers. Don't just contact stores to see if they want to show. You should make a real effort to attract small dealers. The more brands (especially unusual ones) you have, the easier it will be to get publicity and attract an audience. Without the computers you won't have a show.

A really good way to find smaller computer dealers is to place publicity announcements in periodicals that small dealers read thus alerting them to your show. Just remember, your show is news and professional periodicals (and their readers) will want to know what's going on.

3. Who and where are the best customers?

If you don't know the city well, talk to people who do. Don't just ask where the fanciest areas are. You'll want to know a great deal more than that.

If you are putting on a large show, your audience is the upwardly mobile—those who are going from blue collar to white collar. This group, especially those that have a personal identification with minority or ethnic groups, buy twice as many educa and computer-related materials as any other group. Another good audience is the middle-class family that wants to be wealthy.

4. What computer brands will be on display?

When you have a good idea as to what brands will be shown, you should contact each of their publicity and marketing departments. Don't overlook medium to small companies either. They often work with a newcomer more frequently than the big companies because they're new themselves.

Many companies have shared-cost advertising in which they pay half or more of the cost of a display ad if their brand is prominently mentioned. That alone makes your advertising budget go twice as far. But get the agreement in writing before you place your ads so there won't be any misunderstandings.

Other companies won't pay out money, but will provide items such as tablecloths and tables to display on, chairs for your crew, speakers, demonstrations, help with your publicity, even refreshments for small groups. While it's not cash in hand, it certainly saves money you would have spent from your own pocket.

THE COMPETITION

There were about 350 computer trade shows held in this country last year. That is a very small number compared to the potential market. Computers are just beginning. It used to be that four out of five computers sold were for games. Today, three out of five are for business applications. The current market simply isn't touched and there is little or no competition.

POTENTIAL INCOME

Some show promoters put on a computer show one weekend a month, take two weeks off, then start again. After you have your basic information and you've done a couple of shows, you'll probably be earning enough to take that same two-week vacation each month and still live very well indeed.

It is not uncommon for cash flow to reach $100,000 a show. Jim Warren, a northern California show promoter, describes his profit and income simply as "very high." (His last show as of this writing brought in 50,000 people who paid $15 each to view 450 separate display booths.)

Because you want to encourage the small dealer, the display space will probably be moderately priced, say $200 or $300 for a weekend. Actually, that's a very low figure for some companies. IBM estimates that each sales call on an individual business costs about $350. How much of a bargain would your show be if they could reach dozens, even hundreds of potential customers?

It's usually a good idea to charge an admission to the show. While you want a lot of people to attend, you want people who have some real interest in computers and are at least minimally interested in buying one. If the whole city comes, the real customer will not be able to connect with a seller and both parties will go away frustrated. The admission fee will help prevent that from happening.

Not only that, the admission is a very real source of income for you. Admission costs vary from around $5 in the Southern California area, to $15 in Northern California and $25 some places in the East. Even at a low of $5, a show that pulled 5,000 people provides $25,000.

Costs of doing business can be very low or very high. This is one business you can start low and build. Even as you build, however, extra costs are often absorbed by new sponsors.

MARKETING METHODS

The two most effective methods of marketing computer shows to the end-user audience are direct mail and display ads.

For the best direct mail advertising results, buy new "guaranteed fresh" mailing lists of Zip code addresses surrounding the fanciest areas—upper middle-class neighborhoods and better housing tracts with a population that identifies with an upwardly mobile ethnic population. Then, send each of them a flyer about your show.

Display ads work best in the morning newspaper with the local social and gossip coverage. You will also want to use any local periodicals aimed at novice computer users and the curious outsider.

You should also add radio advertising to this group if you can afford it. Don't just buy any radio advertising. Instead, you'll want it directed at the largest audience you can reach at one time who are potential customers.

Very simply, find the radio station that broadcasts news, traffic reports and the time at peak commuter hours. Buy ads specifically on these broadcasts only. To focus even closer, your best audience probably commutes between 8 a.m. and 10 a.m. (early commuters are generally lower on the economic totem pole) and returns home between 3 p.m. and 6 p.m. Placing your ads this carefully will be more expensive, but it will reach the audience you want. Don't be attracted by the inexpensive "as available" rates. If it doesn't reach your potential audience, it's not a bargain.

In placing ads with either radio or print media, ask to talk with the advertising manager. They can often place a "news" story about your event to run in connection with one of your ads. After all, a computer show really is news.

While you're at it, write up your own notices and send them to calendar editors on TV, radio and in newspapers. Short releases written in journalistic style can often be placed in special interest publications or newspapers free of charge. The best way to get them in is to give them a hook (local boy makes good, the grandchild of local resident, the world's most expensive computer, the world's smallest computer, free entertainment, etc.)

UNIQUE BUSINESS APPROACH

Not everything has to be big. Perhaps one of the best ideas to come along is the small, exclusive "luxury" or "private" show. That is, you take a show and market it for special groups. For example, a show aimed at the local American Medical Association would draw enthusiastic sponsors, dealers and buyers.

Doctors are really busy business people, many of whom would like to own a computer but don't have time to shop for the right one. If you could provide this opportunity as part of a regularly scheduled meeting, you would be doing both the doctors and the computer people a great favor. Not only that, but it's easy and inexpensive to set up and can provide a very healthy income for a few hours.

First of all, arrange for a lunch or cocktail meeting at the best local hotel. To do this, talk to the program chairman or board of the local group. Promise them a no-pressure show designed to meet their professional and personal needs.

Then talk to the hotel. The hotel should provide facilities free for a dinner or bar minimum (which should be no problem). A sponsoring computer company may very well provide the doctors with an open bar. The ambience and friendly, familiar surroundings create a wonderful setting for your show.

Because you aren't charging the doctors admission and the market potential is so good, you can charge potential sellers at least as much as you can for a two-day or three-day show.

There you have it. By simply putting the doctors together with the dealers that are most likely to be able to fill their special needs you can collect $200 to $500 from each dealer and make several thousand dollars for a few hours work and no cost.

You can run an entire business this way in a large city, making several thousand dollars a week or a month depending on the number of shows you want to set up. And you can do it without the hassle and competition of the big show.

It's practically guaranteed to be a success, because a wide range of professionals are under a great deal of pressure to computerize or become computer-literate. If you can do the ground work for these groups and promise them an overview of the best machines for their work, you should have no problem booking all the shows you can handle.

Groups such as lawyers, dentists, architects, CPA's, robotics, engineers, bankers, and even educators, are excellent target groups for you to go after.

Another unique idea is to take the computer show abroad. The expo and trade show idea is almost exclusively American. It would translate well, and with no competition, to Europe, Mexico or even Australia. A foreign show could be the best tax-deductible trip you ever had.

There is one lush-budget annual production in Las Vegas that may very well become a standard among professional shows. The promoter's background is in auctioneering top-end decorator and collectors' items and his computer show is based on that system. Its $100 entry fee covers two days of an open bar and buffet lunch along with the show. If you buy a computer system, your $100 is applied to the sale price, but the promoter gets a percentage of the sale (10 percent) from the computer dealer as well as his booth rental. It has done so well, it is an annual event. The promoter won't tell us how much he makes, but he only puts on that one show a year and spends the rest of the time traveling with his wife.

LOCATION and MARKET BASE

One of the few limitations to this business is that it needs to have a city of 200,000 people or more to make it really work.

START UP CAPITAL

The other drawback is that it can cost a good deal of money to get started in this business. If you have contacts and are creative about marketing your show to both sides, you can get in for a moderate investment. However, if you find you must do it in "the usual way" you can expect to spend $5,000 or more.

TO SUM UP

If you like people and lots of them, and have just a little bit of the showman in you, this may very well be business you'll love. It's exciting, glamorous and can make you a very powerful person in the computer industry. It also makes, as show organizer Jim Warren says, "A huge amount of money."

It sounds like an ad in a Sunday magazine supplement—"Make big money in your spare time—" but it's not. If you're willing to put some work into setting up your first computer shows, you can make a great deal of money, and after the first basic ground work is done, you can make that money easier than with just about any other business.

SOURCE MATERIAL

For source material, refer to Section 7.

No. 203

COMPUTER CLUBS FOR KIDS FOR PROFIT

If you haven't already guessed, more than half of the personal computer market is made up of kids under 18 years of age. With this report you will learn how to organize a local club for every different type of computer being used in your area. With these clubs, not only will you collect dues and fees, but you will have buying power with the local suppliers, who will also give you finders' fees. With this business you profit both ways.

CONCEPT

The concept of this business is to organize clubs for kids who have an interest in computers. These days children are spending more and more time in front of the computer. The only problem is that usually they do it alone. You give them the opportunity to share their interest with others their own age. By putting together a club, you can offer them many services, products and club functions that they won't get anywhere else. Their parents will gladly pay a membership fee and dues if they know that their kids are learning and having fun as well.

And since you'll have a natural market for computer games, programs and supplies, you'll be able to get business for local computer stores and national computer companies that sell products to the youth market. For this service, they'll reward you with commissions.

SKILLS YOU WILL REQUIRE

If you have ever led a scout troop, a Little League team or anything similar you'll be a natural for this type of business. You don't even have to own a computer to offer a computer club for kids. All it requires is the ability to organize activities, newsletters, etc. for the membership of your clubs.

INFORMATION REQUIRED

The information you need for this business is the type of computers being used in your area. One way to get this information is to go into local computer stores and look at what brands they sell. You can even talk with a salesperson as if you want to purchase a computer for your own child. Find out what brands are popular with kids and take it from there. Another way to find out what kinds of computers are popular is to contact the schools in your area and ask what brands are being used in the classroom. Most likely these are the same models that parents buy for their kids at home.

You'll use that information to market your service and develop the various clubs for each brand of computer. Since you want clubs for brands that are most popular, this bit of preliminary investigation is strategic to your planning.

OPERATING NAME

For operating this business, there is no reason to use anything other than your own name. By doing this, you save yourself the cost of filing for a fictitious name, putting in a phone at business rates, getting a new bank account, etc.

If you decide you want to call your club something like "Computer Clubs of America" or "Elmville Kids' Computer Club," you'll need to take the necessary steps to register or file the name. For more information refer to Section 4.

GETTING STARTED

The starting point for this business is deciding what kinds of clubs you want to organize. Once you have figured that out, you need to organize the clubs regarding the features you'll be offering in each.

Among the services you can offer kids for joining up are: group activities, such as demonstrations by local computer stores and science museums, computer game contests, programming contests, minicomputer shows with hands-on exhibits, etc.

You might also consider putting out a monthly or bi-monthly newsletter to all the kids. You can even get your members to write it. The kinds of things it could have in it include: short game programs kids can put into the computer themselves, crossword puzzles with computer terms, comic strips drawn by your young members, simple puzzles to be solved with a computer, short articles about local people in the computer business who might be of interest to kids, profiles of members of the club who do unique things with their computers, ways to make money to buy more computer equipment and software, a calandar of upcoming events and television shows of interest to kids, etc.

Another service you can offer your club is a public domain library. In it you can have software of interest to kids that you can copy freely. You can charge them for the cost of the diskette you put the software on, or charge a little extra as a tiny sideline business.

You can also consider putting together a membership package for each child who joins the club. It can include a copy of the latest newsletter, a wallet-sized membership card, a diskette with free public-domain software of interest to kids and a schedule of upcoming events. This will give your club that polished, well-organized look that will impress parents and dazzle the children.

Once you have organized the clubs as far as activities and membership packages, you want to start attracting a membership. To learn how to do this, refer to the Marketing Methods listed later.

If you enjoy working and playing with kids, this is a great opportunity to make money for your time and effort. And the rewards are not just monetary. You'll be offering a service to young people that will entertain, educate and enlighten them, as well as give them something to do with their spare time. The smile on the face of a child who has just learned how to do something he never thought he could can be priceless.

THE COMPETITION

Your competition in this business is computer camps. But even those are usually offered only during school vacation months, cost hundreds of dollars, and don't give the kids the kind of regular weekly fun they thrive on. Whereas kids used to spend their Saturday mornings at the local matinee, now they spend their time and dollars on the computer.

Since you are offering an on-going club, you eliminate your competition, the computer camps, by taking a different approach.

Chances are, if you're in a small city, you won't even have the competition of computer camps. Usually these are offered by local universities on a sporadic basis, or by computer stores that don't have the time, energy or interest to maintain the camps properly. Your competition will be very minor.

POTENTIAL INCOME

Your income with this business comes from many different sources. First, you can charge each child an annual membership fee to join the club, as well as a meeting fee for each meeting or activity he or she attends. Say you decide to organize five clubs for the five most popular computers used by kids in your area. If each club gets 20 members and you charge $10 for each to sign up, you'll get $1,000 from membership fees alone.

If you charge a minor amount for each activity you hold, say $1, that's another $100 for each meeting. For some activities you can increase that price. If you hold a contest, you can charge an entrance fee of $3 and offer prizes which you get donated by local businesses. Or if you put on a minicomputer show, you can charge $2 for each kid that attends and offer the chance to win valuable door prizes, also donated by local businesses.

Another method for making money with this business is through your buying power. If you have 20 or 30 kids with a particular brand of computer, chances are local computer stores will want to tap your market. You can buy computer products and software in bulk rates, getting a discount for the kids in your club. In exchange, the computer store will pay you a commission for each product sold. If you sell $100 software packages and get a 5 percent commission on each, that would equal a $100 commission for doing nothing more than taking orders. Multiply that time the five clubs you organize, and that is $500. The money may come in small chunks, but it adds up quickly.

To figure out what to charge, estimate what your expenses are going to be. Then divide the number of members you expect to have into that amount to get the figure you should charge each child for signing up.

Basic Costs

1. Cost of your time
2. Cost of putting together newsletter
3. Cost of printing up membership cards
4. Cost of mailings done
5. Cost of other advertising
6. Cost of materials used

MARKETING METHODS

This business is best marketed using display ads and direct mail. You can place ads in local newspapers where kids and parents will most likely read about it. Many local newspapers run a kid's page one day a week, and you might arrange for your ad to be on the adjoining page or even on the same page. You might also be able to arrange to have a story written about your club or mentioned in a calendar of events for kids.

The second method of advertising is to send out letters to all the people who can refer kids to your clubs. Among these are schools, computer stores, scout troops, recreation halls, churches, etc. With your letter of explanation (a sample is below), you can include a homemade poster that the school or club can post where the kids will see it.

A typical letter that should bring you business would read:

A COMPUTER CLUB FOR KIDS!

That's right, a computer club for kids. Are you tired of hearing kids say they're bored, there's nothing to do, etc? Now there is! Kids will play games, learn more about their computers, get computer products at a discount and more, all by simply joining the Kids' Computer Club.

Groups are now forming for all types of computers. For more information about memberships and services, call now!

A variation of this letter should bring you more than enough response to get started with your clubs. If you consistently mail them out to the people who have day-to-day contact with kids, they'll let the children know about your clubs. After that, it's time to have some fun!

UNIQUE BUSINESS APPROACH

I'm going to let you in on two secrets to making this business a success for you. The first one has to do with making extra income. Since you'll be selling products to the kids in the clubs, there's no reason why you can't put out a catalog to the membership of products they'll want and need. This will increase your sales and more important, your commissions. Plus, the more you can sell, the less the kids and their parents will have to pay for the product, since you'll be able to get them a better price.

Another little secret to this business is to get others to do your work for you. Your basic job is to organize the club. After that you can rely on helpful parents and volunteers to coordinate the meetings, get demonstrations and speakers arranged, etc. Finding volunteers won't be difficult. All it requires is contacting adult computer clubs, computer stores, etc., where you can meet people who have an interest in kids and computers and wouldn't mind donating a few hours of their time every week to run the club. Consider these volunteers like coaches in your league. They handle the team, while you sit back and count your money.

LOCATION and MARKET BASE

This business would best be suited for a city, since it is there that you will have the large number of kids you'll need to get a sizable membership in each club.

For all practical purposes, you should have a market base of at least 200,000 people to operate this business. This will give you not only the large number of children you'll need for a membership, but it will offer a large number of possible computer brands to center each club around. It will also give you more computer stores to work with as far as selling their products.

TO SUM UP

Computer clubs for kids for profit is an idea whose time has come. Now that kids have taken such a large chunk of the computer products sold, they make a natural market to offer this kind of service to.

Since you'll be getting volunteers to help you run the clubs once you've organized them, there will be very little actual time you'll have to put in on this business. Yet the rewards are great. You'll be giving kids something to do in their spare time that is fun and educational. You'll be preparing them to become part of the computer age they must enter when they grow up. You'll be giving the parents a chance to enjoy some spare hours without having to worry about the kids while they're in their computer club meetings. But most of all, you'll be doing yourself a big favor. With just a little effort and imagination, you'll be rolling in the dough from all sides. The value of what you offer is priceless. Yet at the same time, you know exactly what it's worth. Your bank account will tell you every time you make another deposit with the money you can earn in this business.

SOURCE MATERIAL

Refer to Section 7 for source material.

No. 204

ACCOUNTS RECEIVABLES AND STATEMENT-MAILING SERVICE

Most businesses and professional services that have accounts receivable would like to have this part of their business done by somebody else simply because of the cost and aggravation. We will show you how to find these customers and how to get this system up and running on your personal computer. Some operators have found that only one or two accounts make them all the money they need and still give them a lot of free time.

CONCEPT

Many small and large businesses have one common problem: lack of control in their accounts receivable and inadequate billing procedures.

The concept of this business is to take over these services to free your clients to solve the more major problems of operation. Since steady money coming in on time is a key element to success in business, you can ensure that your clients are still open for business in the coming years. They, in turn, will give you plenty of on-going work.

SKILLS YOU WILL REQUIRE

For this business you should be familiar with basic accounting methods. You should understand the terminology used in accounting, as well as the general practices involved in accounts receivable. If you don't already have experience, you can quickly pick it up by taking an accounting class at a community college or by reading up on the subject.

You will especially have to understand the business in order to adequately assess the various software packages you might use. While in some businesses you can acquire some knowledge of the subject by reading software documentation, the software in this business will probably presume you have an understanding of the subject. So, before you start shopping for software, make sure you understand accounting, especially accounts receivable.

What this means is that if you have ever done accounting work or run your own business possessing accounts receivable, you will do well with this business, since you already have a handle on what you'll need.

INFORMATION REQUIRED

In the accounts receivable and statement mailing service, you will have several things to take care of for your customers. The software you use should do the job for you. Many programs will allow you to:

1. Create customer discounts for payment made by a particular date.
2. Enter orders and point-of-sale functions.
3. Maintain open-order and back-order files.
4. Enter numerous tax codes for your area.
5. Track inventory through billings.
6. Transact commissions and add them to payroll.
7. Call up any customer, along with address, phone number and account information.
8. Create invoices automatically, both on a casual basis and on a regular basis.
9. Provide a gross profit analysis on each statement to pinpoint excessive or incorrect discount levels.

Some software will enable you to do all these functions; others will give you only a few of the features. Research thoroughly and shop carefully before choosing your software package.

Read reviews of accounting software in computer magazines, study ads, and send off for more information about the packages that appear to provide what you need. Try out demonstration software at your local software store. Since this product is what can make or break your business, you want to be very sure that you have found exactly the package that will do the most for you.

GETTING STARTED

To get started in this business you should first become familiar with your software by trying it out on a sample business' accounts or by taking the numbers from a friend's business—anything to get you practice in the use of the software.

Once you are familiar with your software, you are ready to go after business. The information involved in this part of the busines will be supplied by your clients themselves.

When you get your first customer, you will have to work with him to get a thorough understanding of what kind of accounts receivable and statement mailing method he wants to follow. He may be experiencing difficulties in one part of the process. In that case, you might be able to come up with methods that will save him time and trouble. Or you may simply be able to streamline his operations for him. Obviously, using a computer will make your work faster, but you also want to look for ways to make his work faster as well.

After you understand the material you will be working with, it is time to put the data into your system. You should probably place each customer's accounts receivable onto its own set of disks to ensure that accounts aren't mixed up.

When the system is in place, you will simply obtain the information you need on a regular basis, probably once or twice a week. You can keep your client informed on the same schedule by regularly printing out weekly reports informing him about what will be billed that week, what has been received, etc.

COMPETITION

Your competition in this business is the bookkeepers and accounting services who handle the whole ball of wax for their clients. But you can effectively compete, simply because you will be specializing. Perhaps a customer has always handled his own books, but now he wants somebody else to take over the receivables and statement part of it. That is where you can step in. Since that is what you're best at, you'll be able to work faster and probably cheaper than anybody else.

POTENTIAL INCOME

With this business you can expect to earn a medium level of income. You can charge your clients an initial set-up fee for the time spent organizing the system and putting the data into your computer. This could range from $100 to $500, depending on the size of the company. After that, you can charge a regular fee based on how much time you put into the work. If you are working with a small company that requires about one hour a week, you could probably charge around $25 and still make a profit. At this rate, you could generate more than $1,500 a year with just a single client. If you handle the accounts receivable for just five or six clients, you could easily earn a full-time salary with only part-time effort.

To get an idea of what to charge for your service, the first step is to price out the expenses of doing business. This includes a salary for your time. On top of that you must add a profit figure for each job. Then you can divide the total by the number of clients you can comfortably handle to get a rough idea of what your fee should be.

Basic Costs

1. Cost of accounting software
2. Cost of advertising
3. Cost of time spent in initial set-up
4. Cost of time spent maintaining accounts
5. Cost of preparing and mailing statements
6. Cost of transportation

7. Cost of phone
8. Cost of material used

To make sure you get payment for your services on time, make sure that you operate your own accounts receivable to regularly send out statements to your customers. This will ensure a steady paycheck coming in.

MARKETING METHODS

The best ways to market this service are with direct mail, display ads and telephone sales.

You can place your display ads in any publication that business people read. These include newspapers, business publications and professional organization newsletters. Stress what your specialty is and how using you can benefit the reader. Experiment with various publications to learn which ones will draw the most business for you. These are the ones in which you'll want to place your advertising dollars.

Direct mail letters can be sent out to all the business people in your area. You may decide to concentrate on either small businesses that don't possess a full-time book-keeper on staff or the very large firms that have one, but want specialized attention given to its receivables.

A typical letter might read:

> DEAR BUSINESS OWNER:
>
> Do you want to gain better control of your billings? Do you want to understand how your accounts receivable can dramatically improve your cash flow? Do you want to forget about receivables headaches and start running your business again?
>
> If you answered yes to any of these questions, you'll want to know about the services we can offer you.
>
> Accounts Limited is a company that specializes in handling your accounts receivable and statement mailing. Since it is the only job we do, you can bet we do it well. Our computerized methods offer accuracy and timeliness. And since we know the job better than anybody else, we can get it done faster for you. What that means for you is lower rates.
>
> Want to hear more? Call now to get a free demonstration and consultation of what we can do for you.

Include your name and address with this letter. If you do not hear from potential clients, it is time to pull out the telephone and do some personal contact and follow-up. Simply call each customer and remind them of who you are. Offer to come at their convenience to show how you can streamline their operations. Telephone calling is an effective tool when used along with a direct mail campaign.

UNIQUE BUSINESS APPROACH

I will now let you in on a couple of secrets to this operation that can multiply your business quickly.

The first is to offer your services to local bookkeepers. If they can hire you for less money than they earn on a job, then they can give you the accounts receivable and statement mailing portion of their business. This way, the bookkeeper makes money by employing your services at less than he or she earns, and you benefit by not having to generate your own customers.

Another method for getting new business is to specialize. You might consider handling accounts receivable only for lawyers in your city. This sets you up as an expert in the receivables methods of lawyer's offices and can turn out to be an excellent selling point.

LOCATION and MARKET BASE

For this business you should be located in a city with a population base of 50,000 to 200,000. This will supply you with plenty of potential customers.

TO SUM UP

Accounts receivable are just another headache to most business people. It is a part of their operations that they would just as soon do without. Yet, if they didn't keep careful track of what others owe them, they can quickly go out of business.

You can turn their headaches into a profitable opportunity with a little effort and luck. Once they've seen how much you can do for their operations, your customers will continue to use your service. If the thought of having business for as long as you want intrigues you, get started with this business now.

SOURCE MATERIAL

Refer to Section 7.

No. 206

SELL COMPUTER PROGRAMMING COURSES

With one million units being sold this year and a large percentage of the buyers wanting to develop their own programs, the market for simple programming instructions on the personal computer is huge. The income here could easily be in the six figures. We will give you a basic guide for developing computer programming instructions on your personal computer and marketing the instructions—both locally and through the mail. If you lean towards programming, here's a wide-open market that you can make a killing in.

CONCEPT

The concept of this business is to instruct others on how they can create their own programs. You create and publish a small guide that will give them the basics they should follow, while giving them some simple instructions on how they can market their programs.

Another choice you have with this business is to deliver instructions in person. If you enjoy talking to groups of people or have ever taught, you might consider this option instead of, or along with, the guide. You can get people to pay a fee to attend a two-hour or three-hour seminar in which you cover the same basics you write about in your guide. The money will be greater for giving a seminar, but it is limited by the number of people you have in your market base. With a guide, the number of sales you can make is only limited by how many you decide to print up and how you decide to market it.

Or you can do both—hold seminars in your own area and sell the guide to the people who attend. Plus, you can still sell the guide through the mail to people all over the country.

The market for this business is gigantic. Once a person buys a computer, he plays the games and runs the software he gets with it. But then he wants to figure out how he can put it to use for himself, whether at home or in business.

How many times have you heard about somebody who has gotten rich because he designed a program that nobody ever thought of before? For many it can become a road to early retirement. You're not the only one who has heard these rags-to-riches stories. The people who dream of experiencing it themselves are your natural customer. They want to know how they should go about creating a program that will get them millions of dollars. In return for you instructing them, you'll make a nice chunk of money yourself, without writing a single line of programming.

Your audience for this business is all those people who want to create low-end or inexpensive programs. Most large corporations can't afford to create inexpensive programs. So they concentrate on high-end software, the software that will bring them several hundred dollars for each sale. Yet many of the computer owners today just want programs for their home and business that sell for $30 to $100. The people who can create this kind of program have a better chance of succeeding. Perhaps their programs aren't complicated or ambitious, but they serve a purpose. You can tell them how to make money with their ideas, and in exchange you make money yourself.

SKILLS YOU WILL REQUIRE

Even if you're not an expert programmer, you can operate this business. All it requires is a basic understanding of how your computer works and what you like to see in the software that you buy.

After you have created your guide, you get to sit back and relax, while the orders come to you. The kind of income you receive with this business comes in small but very steady amounts.

To run this business you'll want to be familiar with some of the terminology involved in the computer field. For example, you should be aware that programs are written in "languages." These are the words or "commands" that a programmer uses to communicate with the computer. Some of the more common ones are: BASIC, FORTRAN, Pascal, C, and COBOL. With the commands that each language uses, a programmer tells the computer what to do with the information he wants it to process.

"Documentation" is another word you have probably heard. This is the set of instructions that must be included with a program to let the user know how to run it. Documentation comes with just about every appliance you own. For example, when you buy a vacuum sweeper, it comes with instructions that explain how to turn it on, how to change the sweeper bag, how to raise or lower it for various kinds of carpets, etc. Documentation for computer programs are the same kind of instructions. They tell the user how to plug the program into the computer, what the various functions and features are, how to modify material, etc.

If you have ever written your own program, you know the steps you go through to do it. This business is well suited to you if you enjoy programming and want to teach others what you have learned by trial and error.

INFORMATION REQUIRED

The information in computer programming courses consists in knowing a little about your computer and how it works. That is, the fact that it has a memory, that keys on the keyboard are for various functions, etc. The computer is the same tool the programmer will use to create his program.

You will want to know a little about how programs are sold. Usually the story goes that somebody designs a program to fulfill a personal need at home or on the job. His friends suggest he try to sell it in order to be able to write off the costs of the computer and to make a little sideline business for himself. So he runs an ad in a computer magazine, gets a few orders, then takes it to a software distributor. The distributor either buys the software outright or sells it for the software programmer by including it in catalogs or marketing it for him. The distributor makes a profit for his effort and the programmer gets a royalty for every copy of the program sold. This story happens to a lot of people who have built a "better mousetrap." All you need to do is let your customers know what they can expect to go through with their own efforts.

GETTING STARTED

Your first step should be to decide on the way you want to present your instructions. You'll want to put together a guide that lists all the steps a fledgling programmer should follow for creating his own program. If you know a programming language yourself, you can specialize in that and give it even more specific guidelines.

The guide you create shouldn't be complicated. There are already too many manuals and instruction guides in the computer business that nobody can understand. What you create will be simple to follow and easy to read. You don't want to discourage people from following their dreams by making it sound too hard for them. If, after following your instructions, they decide to give programming a try, more than likely they will succeed, simply because they have the desire.

Your guide doesn't have to be long. Twenty pages or so should tell them enough information to get them going on their project. But the guide should have some basic things in it.

A table of contents at the beginning is important, because people can refer to it to find a particular section quickly. Also, you might want to have a small glossary that will explain some of the terminology that you use in the guide.

Some of the subjects you should consider covering in the guide include: where to get ideas for programs, how to write documentation that is understandable, how to debug or get rid of the errors in a program, how to get free publicity in computer newspapers and magazines for the program, how to sell it and how to find a distributor for it.

You want to design the guide so that it is easy to follow and can be read quickly. Label each section in bold or underlined letters. Number each page. If you are an artist, add illustrations to break up the words on the page.

You have two choices in producing the guide. You can either print it yourself, if you have a computer hooked up to a printer, or you can have it professionally printed. The cost of doing this will probably be a lot less than you'd expect and it might give your guide that glossy finish that customers will be impressed with.

After you have created the guide, you'll want to market it. Techniques to do this are covered in Marketing Methods.

THE COMPETITION

Your competition in this business is the whole rack of books on the subject of programming that you find at your local bookstore. Yet you are offering something they don't offer. Most are several hundred pages long and consist of chapter after chapter of technical instruction that can barely be understood by an engineer, let alone a person who does programming for a hobby.

With your simple guide, you give only the essentials somebody will need to get going with this program. Since your guide is small and your overhead is low, you don't have to charge as much for your guide as the major publishers do. Also, you'll be marketing it only to the segment of people who really want to buy a guide like you offer. Book publishers usually try to sell to everybody, thereby wasting advertising dollars and space in the bookstore.

POTENTIAL INCOME

With this business, you want to keep your price low enough so that people don't think twice about buying your guide. Yet you want to earn enough for yourself to cover expenses, a salary for you and a profit for your business.

If you decide to hold a seminar in your own area, you can easily expect to get $25 or $35 from each person. If 10 people sign up, you earn $250 or more for your few hours of work.

If you create a guide to sell, you can charge $4 and get orders for hundreds, maybe even thousands of booklets. This kind of money can bring you thousands of dollars over the course of a little time.

Before pricing your guide, you'll want to estimate what your expenses will be. Below are listed the kinds of costs you will probably have for this business.

Basic Costs

1. Cost of advertising
2. Cost of postage and other mailing expenses
3. Cost of time spent organizing and writing
4. Cost of printing or reproduction
5. Cost of any materials used

Overhead

Include in your estimated costs the amount you put out for overhead. This is essential to get a truer picture of what you should charge.

Profit

Remember to allocate a profit figure for your work. Profit isn't the same as the money you make for your time. Each guide you sell should bring you money for your time, plus money that counts as profit. The first goes into your pocket. The second is what the business makes, enabling it to grow.

MARKETING METHODS

The best way to market this business is with direct mail if you are selling a guide, and display ads if you plan to run a seminar. Run your ads for the seminar in local newspapers and publications where people who want to learn how to program will read about it. If your area has a local computer newspaper, you can probably get them to include it in their calendar of upcoming events.

If you decide to create a guide to sell, you should market it with direct mail. You can place ads in computer magazines and newspapers where aspiring programmers will read about it.

With your ad, you should include an order form that people can cut out, fill in and mail along with their checks. A typical ad is listed below.

> LEARN HOW TO WRITE AND SELL YOUR PROGRAM
>
> This handy guide will tell you everything you need to know to get started creating and selling your own software.
>
> Sections include:
>
> Where to get ideas for programs
>
> How to document your program
>
> How to market your program
>
> How to find a distributor for your program
>
> Join that elite group of people who have become millionaires by building a better mousetrap. With our easy-to-follow tips you can get started right now making your own fortune in this high-growth industry. If you have an idea for a program you think others will want to run on their computers, don't waste another minute – order your copy today!

Your own variation of this ad will be the first step toward those checks coming in, all made out to you. If you want to know how others market their services, look at the ads that run in the magazines where you want to advertise. Chances are, if the same ad runs month after month, it's earning money for the person behind it. Follow their basic format for your own success story.

UNIQUE BUSINESS APPROACH

Now, I'll tell you a little technique to use that will ensure success in this business. Before you have started work on the guide, run ads to generate interest. If you get enough checks rolling in so that you think you can make money with the guide, then you can start putting it together. By doing this, two things will happen. You can deposit the checks in the bank and earn interest on them. Plus, you will have estabished that there is a market for what you are writing.

If for some reason, few people respond to your ads, yet you're convinced that you chose the correct magazine to run it in, you can scrap the project and start it with a different approach. Simply return the checks mailed to you and tell them their order can't be processed for lack of product.

But more than likely, you'll get more business than you could reasonably expect for a simple, inexpensive guide like the one you've created. Since you have priced the guide for only a few dollars, people won't think twice about ordering it, especially if they think it will instruct them about making their own fortunes. In the meanwhile, you sit back and enjoy the fortune your little programming guide has made you.

LOCATION and MARKET BASE

One place is no better than any other to operate this business. If you decide to put out a guide, your orders will be processed through the mail. If you live in a city, you have a larger opportunity to run seminars on the topic of programming instruction. Either way, you can succeed with a little effort, luck and perserverence in this opportunity.

TO SUM UP

Selling computer programming instruction is a genuine opportunity right now. With sales of computers so high, more and more people are looking for ways they can make money with their new toys. You give them this opportunity. With a little planning and effort, you can create something that will bring you income for months to come, even after the work has been completed.

You can do all kinds of variations of this guide to increase your chances to sell. All it requires is a little thought about what advice you have to offer those people who want to know how to write a program.

To put the service you offer in perspective, look at it this way: people all over the world dream of being rich and famous. Those who own computers want to make their fortune by using it to do something new, exciting and creative. But most don't have any idea of where to begin. With your short instructional guide, you get them started on the road to success. Oftentimes, all they need is a little push in the right direction. In return, you have started on your own road to success. And it leads right to the bank.

SOURCE MATERIAL

Refer to Section 7.

SECTION 4

The Business Structure and Plan Section will explain to you the special details you'll want to know about in order to set your business up. We cover how to choose an operating name, what the various business structures are, how to insure your business and many other operation details involved in opening up any new business.

SECTION FOUR

BUSINESS STRUCTURE AND OPERATION

PLANNING YOUR NEW VENTURE

Before you start planning for any venture, you must have a clear idea of what you want from this risk and what effort you are about to undertake. Your concepts of what you want in terms of personal satisfaction, material gain and lifestyle are the keys to the type of computer operation you are going to have. You want to get these personal goals clear in your mind so you can make the business decisions that will bring them about.

In terms of setting personal goals, you will first want to examine what you are bringing to this venture and what you will have to do in order to reach your goals.

First, what experience do you bring to this venture? Have you ever done anything like this before? Do you have a first-hand knowledge of any aspect of running a business? Are you willing to learn what you need to know to be successful? There is a price you are going to have to pay if this venture is going to be on-the-job training. That price is time and the cost of the mistakes you are going to make. The acid test is this: if you owned this business and were going to hire a manager, would you hire yourself?

Many people are frightened by the word "business" and what it connotes. They have an idea of it as some highly complicated and mysterious system of marketing goods and services that is difficult, if not impossible, to master. This is both true and false. You will discover as you use this Business Planner, that there is a great deal to learn— and a lot of decisions to make. But you've got to keep it in perspective. Taken as a whole, it is complicated, but broken down into individual segments, it is not.

As a matter of fact, you have been in business most of your life. I call it the "self business." You have a service or product you sell; you have to sell it at a profit; you have to cover your overhead, pay your taxes and do your personal bookkeeping. It makes no difference whether you are a housewife who manages a family or an executive working for a large corporation. Your product or service is your time and your skills. You market to an employer, who pays you a gross income. From that income you must pay your overhead, food, clothing, shelter, transportation and medical care. Added to that, you must pay for grooming essentials and perhaps some tools or equipment. You could call these expenses "cost of goods sold." Beyond that you need a profit to provide for your family — to give to church and charity and pay your taxes. This "self business" is almost exactly the same economic system used to operate General Motors or the corner gas station.

You can judge your business management potential pretty well by examining how you handle your self business. Do you pay your bills on time? Have you managed to accumulate assets that exceed your liabilities? Can you give up some immediate gratification to invest in a future benefit? Do you have a sound credit rating? Do you have a personal goal to improve your standard of living? Do you have adequate insurance? All of these questions will give you the answer as to how well you are likely to do in a small business of your own.

If you have answered them in the affirmative for the most part, you have an excellent chance of being successful in a computer business venture. If, on the other hand, the answers are negative, I would suggest you either get an associate with management skills, or take some time to get your affairs under control before launching a business venture.

Answer these questions:

When you decide on a course of action, do you follow it through to a conclusion?

Do you face problems head on and solve them?

Are you in good health?

Can you take criticism and handle the hostility of others?

Do you work well under a lot of pressure?

Do you hate to lose?

Do you stick with computer problems until solved?

Those are seven simple questions, and if you answered any one of them no, you should hesitate to get into a computer business. First, you must be willing to follow through on decisions. You can't keep changing your mind or putting off making them. It leads to quick failure.

Second, you must face problems in business at once. You can't let them fester and turn into heavy losses.

Third, you must be in robust health. You are in for a severe test physically and emotionally, and poor health just won't stand up under it.

Fourth, you will get lots of criticism from your customers, your employees and your business contacts—it goes with the territory. Some will be deserved and some won't. If you are thin-skinned and easily upset by it, business may not be your bag.

Fifth, you will have almost constant pressure from many sides in your own computer business. There is seldom enough money, there are late shipments of supplies your computer needs, there are errors, accidents and misunderstandings almost daily. It all puts pressure on you, and you have to handle it and keep going. Finally, you have to be a winner by nature. Losing is not something you do easily. You go into business expecting to succeed and will compete to succeed until the last dog is hung.

There is a serious risk of failure in any business enterprise— big or small. It's like a man-eating tiger prowling the economic jungle waiting to pounce on the careless, stupid or unwary entrepreneurs. Anyone who has ever started a new venture can tell you they have seen him many times, late at night, when they were pouring over their books trying to find a way to stay solvent. The point is that you must consider the consequences of failure from a personal point of view. What will it mean to your family? How will it affect their lives? What do you stand to lose besides the time and money you invested? Can you start over? How will it affect your personal relationships with friends and neighbors? It is only prudent to assess the effects of failure, because in truth, you are more likely to fail than to succeed.

So, consider the other side of the coin before you commit yourself. As you are examining the possibilities and ramifications of failure, keep this point in mind: total commitment to success is the only way you can beat the odds. So, if you find that you are afraid to fail—don't start.

You can't play scared cards in business. You have to take risks, enjoy the action, and when you must place your bets, place them willingly and with the full expectation you are going to win.

CREATING THE NEW VENTURE

The entrepreneur finds the creation of a new computer business venture similar to that of becoming a new parent. First, there is the ecstasy of conception, the thrill of the idea, the moment of creation. Then, the gestation period occurs when the raw idea is formed into an organization. And finally, the day of birth happens, when the business is launched and begins life. The early days of its childhood, when it takes its first stumbling steps, then becomes self-sufficient and can stand alone, are gratifying. This sense of accomplishment is what makes the entrepreneur proud and content.

Money is only the way to keep score, to mark the progress. But it is the pride of the creator and the fulfillment of a dream that is the real reward. This is called the "psychic salary."

THE THREE STEPS TO SUCCESS

Success is achieved in three steps. First, there is acquisition of knowledge. Knowing what you do and why you do it is important. So is knowing what to expect and how to react, learning the methods and skills required to accomplish the tasks that lead to success. When you have the knowledge and know what you are doing, you automatically move to the second step—self confidence.

Self-confidence comes from knowledge. Think about the first time you got behind the wheel of a car: you were certainly nervous, possibly frightened and perhaps terrified. You had to maneuver a ton of metal at relatively high speeds in a confined space without hitting anything. Your first attempts were clumsy, but as you learned how to control that car, and acquired the skills to do so, you became confident, and now you can jump into your car and go anywhere without any problem. Self-confidence then creates the psychology for the third and final step—perseverance.

There is an old and true saying, "winners never quit and quitters never win." Overnight success is luck—and rarely happens. The only way to be sure of success is to persevere—to hang in there and do what needs doing each day. Everything we do that's worth a damn has a price. You want to understand that before you start a small business. No matter how carefully you plan, things will not work out the way you expect they will. There will be mistakes or even disasters over which you have no control. There will be fraud and deceit practiced on you, and setback after setback will happen. You will have to operate under Murphy's Law: "Anything that can go wrong, will," and Murphy's second law: "Anything that goes wrong will go wrong at the worst possible time."

So perseverance is the final step, and backed with knowledge and self-confidence, it will bring you the success you seek.

SETTING PERSONAL GOALS

You must take some time to consider what you want from this venture. First, list the personal satisfactions you seek:

1. To be a winner
2. To be free to choose your own way in life
3. To be recognized as a leader

Second, list your goals in terms of financial rewards:

1. Financial security for yourself and family
2. Achievement of wealth to some degree
3. Making some fast money by building up a computer business venture and then selling it
4. The start of a computer business empire

Keep in mind that there are no bad goals per se; so choose your goals honestly and they will form the basis of your planning to reach them.

LIFESTYLES CONSIDERATIONS

There are certain benefits, or trappings, if you will, that go with business success. The large home with swimming pools, tennis court and a staff of servants is one. Others are the fine car, boat, airplane, etc. There is the ability to travel in style anywhere on the earth, and the clothes, jewelry and other status symbols that the successful entrepreneur enjoys. When you make your list of personal goals you can also make up a list of these material things that you would enjoy having and even make timetables for the acquisition of each of them. It will give you something to shoot at in planning and operating the business.

DECISION POINT

Think about what you want and make a realistic estimate of how soon you want them. This gives you a set of personal goals and a timeframe for reaching them.

Make a list on a separate sheet of paper for your goals, then put it aside. But refer to it from time to time as a reminder of the reason you began this journey.

SETTING YOUR BUSINESS GOALS

The next step in your planning is setting your business goals. It is important to do this because you must decide if the goals you are setting for your computer business are compatible with your personal goals. Many times the new entrepreneur assumes that running a small business is a nine-to-five job, just like the one he or she had before, and that because he owns the business, he can take off whenever he wishes. Reality is quite different. Owning a small business is like owning a cow. It must be attended to daily, or it will die. A business owner puts in far longer hours than an employee, and vacations in the first few years are mostly wishful thinking. So, in making plans and setting business goals, you must assume that 12 to 16-hour working days are going to be commonplace, and the higher your business goals, the more time and work will be required.

In general terms, there are four stages to business success:

1. The break-even point
2. The survival point
3. The expansion point
4. The wealth-building point

There is a time frame required to reach these points, depending on the skill of the manager and the type of computer business. Again, in general terms, it takes less time to reach break-even in a small business that has a known market and known product or services. The time to reach the point where the business is going to survive is also somewhat less. But some types of businesses seldom go beyond those points. On the other hand, the new service, product or program will take longer to reach the break-even and survival point in most cases, but is far more apt to go past those points to expansion and wealth building.

Here is the definition of Goal Points.

THE BREAK-EVEN POINT

This is when the computer business is generating enough income to pay all of its costs of doing business, plus enough salary to the owner so he can continue to run the business without dipping into savings or other sources of income to maintain a modest standard of living. As a rule, this is only a matter of months in well-planned and managed computer business, but in some cases, such as marketing a new product, it can take two or three years.

THE SURVIVAL POINT

This is where the business is not only covering all the costs of the business, including a salary for the owners that maintains a respectable standard of living, but also gives the owners an acceptable return on investment. This usually takes a year or more, and it is the point at which 95 percent of all small businesses stop growing.

THE EXPANSION POINT

This is the point where the business is showing a gross cash increase (with commensurate profits) of 20 percent a year or more, and can command the borrowing capacity to carry on a sustained expansion of marketing either to new geographical areas (branch stores or offices) or to expand in the present market. This is the point where the entrepreneur starts managing his managers, rather than managing the business.

THE WEALTH-BUILDING POINT

This is the point where the expanding company either goes public with a stock issue or is merged with a larger company, and the entrepreneur turns his interest into marketable stock that would be worth seven or more figures if converted into cash.

In developing a realistic business plan, there is no precise way to create a timetable for reaching these goal points, but in the case of the first two, the entrepreneur has a built-in time limit. That is how long he can survive without having the business provide him enough personal income to maintain his standard of living.

In developing the business plan it is important for the entrepreneur to examine his assets and judge his staying power in terms of how long it will take for the business to provide him the personal cash flow he or she needs to keep food on the table and a roof overhead.

Your first and most immediate concern in planning is time. You must reach the survival point before your personal resources are exhausted. It is exactly like starting across a desert with a limited supply of food and water. The food and water, if properly managed, will last 10 days. If you can't reach a water hole by the tenth day, you are probably in trouble. You will start to weaken on the eleventh day and probably die on the twelfth. The food and water represent your available personal capital to keep going while the business develops into a source of income.

So, planning to reach break-even—where you don't have to put any more money in the business and can actually take some out—is the first step to your survival plan.

Then, the time it will take for the business to start paying you a salary that reflects your worth, and to give a return on investment, is more a matter of how long you want to sacrifice with a lower standard of living to keep the business going. There is no mathematical formula for making a precise estimate of this time; yet the planner need determine not only the time the business will take to reach these points, but also determine his position in being able to stay with it until it does.

SOME REASONS WHY SMALL BUSINESSES FAIL FAST

Why They Fail in 90 Days or Less:

1. The entrepreneur gambled on a bad idea without first determining who would buy what he was selling.
2. The founder went in on a shoestring without a provable plan for a fast buildup of cash flow to support lack of initial capital investment.
3. The founder "knifed and forked" up the business capital. Instead of using the capital to generate sales, it was used for personal draws, expensive trappings, prestige transportation, etc.
4. The failure of a promise to materialize—whether more capital from another source, a license for an exclusive product, a piece of equipment, or credit. A business was started on a promise, not a contract.
5. Chaos from indecision—changes of direction or putting off decisions that create chaos.

Location is the key. If there is a large enough population in a three to five-mile radius and not too much competition, then the concept is a definite go.

But, if you are going to market a new service, you've got to make a market survey to determine the demand, if any, and your potential market share.

If you want to know how to do market research on your own, there is a book that will give you the necessary information. It is titled, DO IT YOURSELF MARKET RESEARCH, written by George Edward Breen and published by McGraw Hill. You can probably borrow a copy through your local library (inter-library loan service) or buy one from your local book store.

It is important to do a feasibility study of some kind to be sure you are on solid ground.

THINKING ABOUT BUSINESS GOALS

Below, you will find your goal planner. You will note that there are two spaces under each goal point—one for your estimated time and one for the absolute time for break-even and survival. You will want to give some serious thought to both estimates. In most cases your estimated time is going to be optimistic because things never go as planned. There are always setbacks you can't foresee.

The absolute time is based on how much personal capital you have to sustain your living standard without a guaranteed paycheck. The business will contribute some income, and should increase from month to month, but to be on the safe side you should plan for at least six months of living out of your personal funds without taking a dime out of the business. If this is a problem, then you should plan to organize the business as a part-time venture, keeping your present source of income until break-even is reached. Most of the plans in this book can easily be operated part-time. Think about these points as you determine which businesses are best suited to you.

The second two goals are strictly long-range goals and are not important other than setting a future timetable. In most small business ventures, these would be 10 or more years in the future.

YOUR BUSINESS GOALS

1. To Reach the Break-Even Point—the time when the business no longer requires additional personal capital. It is paying its own way and providing a living wage for the entrepreneur.

Estimated Time: _____

Absolute Time: _____

2. To Reach the Survival Point—The time when the business is in a position to pay the entrepreneur a chosen (within reason) standard of living wage and provide a return on investment of at least the average in the industry. In short, the place where the entrepreneur is willing to continue the business or can sell it for a profit.

Estimated Time: _____

Absolute Time: _____

3. To Reach The Expansion Point—Where the business is producing sufficient profits in an expanding market which will allow it to expand its market share by increasing market coverage, introducing new products or increasing store or production capacity.

Long Range Goal: _____

4. To reach the Wealth-Building Point—Where a public stock offering is made, or the business merged with another business, resulting in the entrepreneur's interest being converted to cash or stock in seven or more figures.

Long Range Goal: _____

CHOOSING YOUR BUSINESS NAME

The entrepreneur starting a new venture in most lines of business should give serious thought to picking a name that will generate public recognition of what the company does. The cigar store wooden Indian of past years was a symbol that gave instant recognition. So did the barber pole. While it is true that some of the best-known business firms in America are named after people—"Macys," "Sears," "Wards," "Hewlett-Packard"—if they were new small businesses today, no one would know what business they were in. Imagine if you were coming from another country and saw the name "Sears;" it would mean nothing. When you start a new business, you have to remember there are 230 million people who have never heard of you or your business.

If you decide to use a family name, you should consider the problems of educating the public as to what business you are in when they see your name. As an example, if you came from another country and wanted to buy a hamburger and you looked in the phone book and found names such as "Wendys," "McDonalds," and "Burger King," you would know from the names that only one for sure had anything to do with hamburgers. If you consider that your name is going to be displayed many places—on the outside of envelopes, letterheads, listings in phone books and other directories, you have many places to tell people what business you are in. So, if you list "Ford Motor Company," Macy's Department Store," "Kraft Candy Company," etc., you are getting information across as to what you have to sell. This is not small matter for a new company. The market is large, you have tremendous competition for attention and anything that you do that causes confusion in the minds of your potential customers costs you business. Your business name should identify your product or service.

GENERIC NAMES

The generic name is often used by business firms—"Greyhound," "Royal," "Caterpillar," etc. In and of themselves they have no meaning to a potential buyer. As in the use of your family name, you should use the product or service name as well: "Greyhound Bus Company," "Royal Office Machines," "Caterpillar Tractor Company," "United Air Lines," etc. The best use of generic names is in an allegorical use. That is, "Greyhound" bus company runs fast. The "Caterpillar" tractor can crawl over anything. "Lightning Express" is the name for a trucking company.

THE INITIALS FOR A NAME

We have all heard of "IBM," "ITT," "RCA," "3M," "TRW" and the like. These are current favorites of large corporations that have many different businesses, or in some cases are simply the initials of their original titles. It may be a great idea for them, but it is a lousy idea for the small business entrepreneur for a couple of reasons. First, the initials can't tell prospective customers what business you are in. Second, they are hard to remember or keep straight. When you become a conglomerate, you can change to initials, but until then it is best to forget it.

CONTRIVED NAMES CAN BE USEFUL

The contrived name can be a good choice. It gives you a unique name, hopefully one that will be easy to remember and can be trademarked easily. "Manpower," "Burger King," "ComputerLand," "U-Haul"," etc. all indicate what is being sold. On the other hand, contrived names can also mean nothing in terms of what they represent. "Exxon," "K-Tel," "Safeway," etc. may mean something now because they represent large companies that have spent billions educating the public, but for the small business the best contrived name will be one that names the product or service.

It is important to go about choosing a name not for your own ego satisfaction, but to sell more goods or services. Every advantage you can get at the start is a plus and means you won't have to waste capital in educating of your prospects.

GEOGRAPHICAL NAMES

This is another favorite of many businesses and is a particular favorite of retailers. Examples are the "Seattle Furniture Store," "The Southwestern Savings and Loan," "Eastern Airlines," etc. The idea is to give your business some instant status by tying it to the name of a city, county or region.

YOUR CHOICES

In general terms you have five choices for a business name:

1. Your family name—Jones Company
2. Industry or product name—Jones Computer Consulting
3. Geographical name—Los Angeles Bookkeeping Service
4. Generic name—Inventory Services
5. Contrived name—Perfect Mates

Here are the points you want to consider in choosing the name:

1. It tells people what you have to sell
2. It is easy to pronounce
3. It is easy to remember
4. It is not offensive to anyone
5. It is legal for you to use it
6. It will wear well

I want to touch on the sixth point, wearing well. Too many new entrepreneurs spend a lot of time working on cutsie-pie names that they think will tickle people. For example, "Pee Wee Town," a children's shop, "Toys R Us," a toy franchise, "Fran's Fantastics," a dress shop. These names tend to cheapen the image of a business and seldom attract any attention. While "Toys R Us" has been a successful franchise, I would say it happened in spite of the name. You want a name that will stand the test of time, wear well in the community, and be something you won't find yourself becoming ashamed of.

Take some time in choosing your name, and look through phone book yellow pages for ideas. Make some lists and pick the one you like best.

OTHER CONSIDERATIONS IN CHOOSING A BUSINESS NAME

I don't intend to throw any more wrenches into your method of choosing a business name, but there are some further considerations you must think about. Most of the businesses included in this book require low start-up capital. What this means is that you want to take any steps you can in the beginning to save yourself money.

In choosing a business name, if you choose something other than your own name, it will cost you more. Extra expenses to using a fictitious name, or one that doesn't include your family name in it, are registering the name or filing a fictitious name report. This ensures that nobody else is already operating a business with the name you've chosen. It will require researching the name and paying fees to the city, county or state for the registration of the name, as well as publishing it in the legal section of the newspaper.

If you choose a fictitious name, you will also be required to get a new phone number under the new name at business rates, which are higher than consumer rates. But in doing this, you ensure a listing for your business in the local yellow pages. You will also need a business bank account under your new business name. What all this adds up to is additional start-up expenses for you.

On the other hand, if you decide to use your own name for your business, you'll be able to keep all the services already in your own name, including phones, bank accounts, utilities, etc. For example, if you decide to open an information research business, there is little reason to call it by anything other than your own name. "John Jones & Associates Research Services" is a good name for such a business. And it prevents the necessity of filing a fictitious name report.

In many of the business plans presented in this book, you'll find a short discussion about choosing a business name. In some cases I recommend you choose a fictitious name and in others I advise you to go with your own name. The ones for which you'll need a fictious name will cost more for you to get started in, but you'll be able to earn your initial investments over and over again by the increased exposure and understanding your fictitious name will create.

THE CHOICE OF LEGAL STRUCTURE FOR YOUR BUSINESS

When you start considering the structure of your business, you will have to make a decision as to the legal form of ownership. You have three choices—the sole proprietorship, the partnership, or the corporation. Each has advantages and disadvantages.

To some extent your choice may be dictated by your needs in organizing the business. If you need outside funds and perhaps extra help in managing it, then you should consider a partnership or corporation. If you can supply your own funds and supply all the management skills, then you will be better off to go it alone.

You will read in some books that a corporation will protect your present assets by limiting your liability for the debts of the corporation. In a small business this won't work. All lenders and suppliers who extend credit to small business corporations without a strong credit rating will require the owners to take personal liability for all corporate debts, so the corporation will not provide such protection.

In almost every case a small business should start either as a sole proprietorship or partnership in the formative and initial stages of development. The only real advantage a corporation would provide a new venture is some tax sheltering of income. If this need appears, a corporation can always be formed when required.

However, if you need to raise capital to fund the business start-up, the Sub-Chapter "S" corporation is an ideal business format on which to raise funds.

THE SOLE PROPRIETORSHIP

This format requires no special forms or agreements, other than those required by local licensing authorities. You get into business at once. You march to the beat of your own drum. You make all the decisions and have total control over business operations. All the profits are yours and you can move at your own speed.

The Advantages are:

1. Ease of getting started
2. Total control over the business
3. No sharing of the financial returns
4. Ease of changing course—expanding or closing up
5. Ability to take in a partner or incorporate later if you wish

But there are also disadvantages. You are alone, risking most or everything of what you now have, and if you should become ill or have an accident, the business could suffer or fail.

The Disadvantages are:

1. Everything you have is at risk
2. Illness or accident can wreck the business
3. Death can be a disaster for the family
4. There are few options for tax shelters
5. Credit line is restricted to your net worth
6. The pressure on you is constant—no management help

Except in cases of partnerships formed to provide more working capital, or in professional practices, the sole proprietorship is the best format for the new, small business.

In fact, most of the businesses presented in this book would best be suited as a sole proprietorship. It will, for the most part, be just you and your computer.

I have chosen to include extensive discussions of your other two options simply because I want you to make the choice based on a true understanding of all the business structures. You may find a business in this book that you consider better suited to a partnership or corporate structure from the very beginning. In that case, go with your choice. Or better yet, you may find after awhile that your business has expanded so that you need more information about taking on a partner or incorporating.

THE PARTNERSHIP

This is a legal entity formed by one or more persons who operate the business in a general partnership as co-owners. The partnership distributes its earnings to the partners, and each is responsible for paying his own taxes on the income.

The Advantages of Partnerships are:

1. More capital can be invested in the business
2. Responsibilities and work can be shared
3. More partners can be taken in without changing business format.
4. The Uniform Partnership Act gives partners protection in disputes.
5. More credit can be obtained
6. A larger volume of business can be managed without additional help or wage costs.

The Disadvantages are:

1. All partners in a general partnership are liable for the acts of all other partners
2. There is always an unequal contribution to profits that creates dissension among partners
3. Death or dispute can dissolve the partnership
4. One partner can force dissolution
5. Management by committee is difficult and often unsuccessful

In real life, partnerships are a hard way to go in non-professional operations. Personality conflicts crop up in many areas of business operations and, after a time, partners are operating under strained relationships. Partnerships in professional fields can work because each member is primarily doing business with his own clients, and shares-out are generally pro rata to income-in. What you have primarily is a sharing of expenses and not of income. But in other businesses the income comes from a common pot. It is a rare situation where all of the partners consider they have made equal contributions to the profit they will share. There is also a problem with working hours. One partner may be a married person and require weekends off with the spouse or children, so that the other may be put in the position of working longer hours and at inconvenient times. Another problem is that where duties are divided up and each partner is responsible for his own department or function, problems will occur when any action is taken by other partners that seem to infringe on that area. This is human nature and nothing anyone can do will change it.

CHOOSE A PARTNER WITH CARE

Remember when you are thinking about taking in a partner that it's much like getting married. You are going into a close relationship with another person and the financial welfare of each of you is at stake. There will be many pressures on each of you. The first test is to sit down together and make up your partnership agreement. You can use the outline at the end of this section. If you get into hassles over the agreement, you are going to be in trouble in the enterprise very quickly. The second test is to see if your partner can get along with your spouse; not because you will be socializing, but because you really don't need to go home at night and hear what a "no-good bum" your partner is.

The best answer is to write out the agreement so that the partnership can be dissolved without closing up the business. Make it possible for either partner to buy the other one out in some reasonable manner, and the decision of who goes and who stays is decided automatically if the time comes. It can be decided by a cut of the cards, a flip of the coin or which one makes the best offer to the other.

THE CORPORATION

This business format is something the new entrepreneur should stay away from until the business has reached the survival point. It is a complicated procedure. You can look at the checklist in the back of this section and see how many decisions you will have to make on a subject about which you know little.

In addition, the corporate format creates an incredible amount of paperwork. You have federal, state, county and city forms to file at regular intervals. You have to hold meetings, keep minutes of those meetings, maintain a complicated set of books, and pay higher fees and taxes in most states. Since a new venture is seldom a tax problem in its first year or two, the tax advantages of a corporation are of no value, and the expenses of maintaining it can be a problem. A corporate format for a sole proprietor is seldom anything more than a status symbol.

THE SPECIAL SITUATION

There are some start-up situations that call for the corporate format. If you have to raise capital—particularly seed capital—to get started, the Sub-Chapter S and Rule 1244 corporation are needed. Briefly, these two choices of corporate formation allow the seed capital investors to choose to take company losses as personal income losses to be deducted from their personal income. And in a later year, they can choose to have the corporation be taxed as a corporation and pass through dividends to them, or sell their stock and pay capital gains taxes. It is the corporate format designed to help the entrepreneur raise capital for new ventures.

The second situation is when you are in a business where you risk large damage suits. For instance, some examples are serving or selling food, drugs or a new product that could bring class action damage suits that would overwhelm your insurance. A corporate shield for your personal assets is good planning. While you will have insurance, if circumstances should cause judgments beyond your insurance protection, the corporate shield is your second line of defense. Most of the businesses listed in this book won't entail these kinds of problems, but you should still consider your position before choosing a structure.

The new, small business will not get any protection against debt with a corporation. Banks, major suppliers and others will require the corporate founders to take personal liability for debt until the corporation is sound enough financially to stand on its own.

One other point about corporations: if you are selling through agents in other states, you can be required by that state to pay income taxes on all business you do in the state or a percentage of your gross income from all sources. So be very careful about incorporating until you have examined the full costs.

TAKE GREAT CARE IN INCORPORATING

The primary purpose of a corporation should be to raise capital and protect the assets of the corporate owners. It does this by shielding them from liability for corporate debt and through tax reductions and tax-free benefits.

In order to make the corporate shield secure, you will need to take some steps to make sure there is a legal shield established. This comes both in the manner in which the business is incorporated and in how it is operated after incorporation.

You need good legal advice in both sequences. You need a lawyer who knows corporation law and can tell you exactly how to proceed to set up a valid corporate shield against personal liability.

You must follow those instructions to the letter. If you fail to hold the necessary meetings, keep the minutes, file the necessary papers or other procedures, another lawyer can sue you and prove your corporation was a sham, making your stockholders jointly and severally liable for corporate obligations.

You should also use the services of a qualified accountant to show you how to save money tax-wise when you incorporate, and when the best time to form the corporation is.

INCORPORATION DECISION

Below you will find the outline of decisions and steps you will have to take to form a corporation. It is important to remember you can do this after your business is operating and do it more or less tax-free. You will want to be clear in your mind as to the purposes of incorporation—what advantages you expect from it and how you will use it. If you need the corporation to raise seed capital, then consider the Sub-Chaper S Corporation, as it has the structure to appeal to investors and still provides the corporate shield.

The advantages of incorporation are:

1. Limited personal liability of stockholders
2. Tax advantages in corporate incomes
3. Business life is perpetual
4. Free transfer of interest through stock sales
5. Corporation does not have to allow public trading of stock—it can be closely held
6. Can acquire and operate other businesses through sale or transfer of stock.

The disadvantages are:

1. Difficulty of initial formation
2. Expense of initial formation
3. Obtaining credit—getting loans difficult for new business unless owners personally guarantee them
4. High degree of regulation by state and federal agencies

The corporation also offers the entrepreneur the vehicle with which to raise additional capital from a wide range of sources by selling stock rather than borrowing or selling assets.

THE SUB-CHAPTER S CORPORATION REQUIREMENTS

1. It cannot have more than 10 (15 in some cases) stockholders and all must consent to Sub-Chapter S declaration.
2. It can issue only one class of stock.
3. The stockholders must be individuals, estates, and in some cases, a voting trust.
4. It must be a domestic corporation with stockholders who are U.S. residents and cannot have over 80 percent foreign income.
5. No more than 20 percent of its income may be from rents, royalties, interest, dividends or so-called passive income.
6. It must be organized as a corporation before it can elect Sub-Chapter S status— using appropriate IRS tax forms.
7. Organization provisions should be included in the charter and bylaws.
8. It must qualify to act as a foreign corporation in order to do business in other states or to get rights to sell stock in other states.

Here Are The Steps To Incorporating:

1. Check availability of chosen name and reserve it.
2. Complete and execute pre-incorporation agreements.
3. Draft and file incorporation papers in chosen state.
4. Pay filing fee and organizational tax.
5. Hold first meeting to organize the corporation.
6. Get subscriptions to stock.

7. File the necessary papers.
   a. Obtain an agent for corporation.
   b. Statement of paid-in capital.
   c. Officer's oath.
   d. Local city or county filing.
8. Draft the by-laws.
9. Make sure it is legal to issue securities without special authorization.
10. Get stock certificates, corporate seal, stock register and minute book.
11. Hold meeting to elect directors.
12. Authorize issuing stock certificates and accept the stock subscriptions.
13. Receive payments from investors.
14. Authorize setting up of corporate bank account by a director's resolution authorizing deposit and withdrawal in the bank.
15. Set schedule for future meetings to meet legal requirements.

INCORPORATION OF A VENTURE

What you need to know before you file your papers:

1. The purposes of the corporation and business activities it will engage in.
2. The proposed name of the corporation, and a search to determine the legal right to use the name.
3. Name of incorporators, addresses and details as to age and present occupations.
4. Functions of the incorporators in the business operations—if any—and compensation to be paid.
5. Capital investment of each participant—what they are in-vesting as far as cash, property, equipment, patents, trademarks, inventory, etc. and how the value of each is adjusted.
6. Estimates of corporate profits for first 15 years.
7. How profits are to be divided by incorporators.
8. Where voting control will rest.
9. Whether any incorporators are getting employment contracts with the corporation, and what are they.
10. The state where incorporation will take place.
11. The capitalization of the corporation:
    a. Shall common shares be par or no par?
    b. How many shares will be authorized and issued?
    c. Will there be preferred stock?
12. If preferred shares are to be issued, make these decisions:
    a. Face value.
    b. Shall they be redeemable?
    c. Shall they be convertible into common?
    d. What dividend rate is guaranteed?
    e. Will it be cumulative?
    f. Will a sinking fund be maintained for dividends?
    g. If dividends not paid do holders get voting rights?

13. Considerations under which shares will be issued.
14. Whether shareholders have pre-emptive rights.
15. Kind of voting rights will be offered.
    a. Cumulative voting
    b. Quorum provisions for voting.
    c. Special meeting provisions.
    d. Annual meeting provisions.

ESSENSE OF A PARTNERSHIP AGREEMENT

Articles to be included:

Article I

The name and purpose of the partnership. The location of the business operation.

Article II

Duration of the partnership—usual statement is that it will continue until dissolved under terms of the agreement.

Article III

How capital is invested.

What form investment takes—cash or other assets?

How much contributed by each partner?

The firm will maintain a separate capital account for each partner.

The definition of what the partners consider to be capital contributions and what are expenses.

There will be an annual audit of physical assets and cash securities held by the firm, and individual capital accounts will be adjusted accordingly.

Article IV

Devotion of time to the firm.

What amount of time each partner will contribute to the business.

All compensation received by the partners for sales and services for the firm will be accounted for.

The length and number of vacations the partners will take.

If either is incapacitated, how his share in profits will be divided.

If a partner fails to give the time to the business that is required by this agreement—he will have to take the amount of compensation the other partners judge to be fair.

Article V

Management

Each partner shall have an equal voice in management. All management decision noted legated to each partner shall be decided by a majority of partners present at any meeting of partners of which all partners are aware of the time and place to be held.

Admission of new partners shall be made only by affirmative vote of a majority of all partners.

Decisions on expulsion of a partner shall be made only by unanimous vote of all partners.

Decisions to call meetings may be made by any partner, but the management partner shall schedule the regular meetings.

All partners must be notified of meetings times and places with reasonable time allowed to make necessary arrangements to attend.

A quorum shall be a majority of partners.

Day-to-day affairs directed by managing partner.

Carry out firm policies.

Hiring and firing of employees.

Control and training of employees.

Supervising records and office duties.

Handling or supervising collections and credit.

Scheduling and notifying of partner meetings.

Article VI

Open and maintain bank accounts by agreement of all partners. Two or more signatures on checks as agreed on by partners.

Article VII

Records and Accounts

An adequate partnership accounting system to be used.

All books and records open to all partners at all times.

Separate income account maintained for all partners.

Setting of the fiscal year date.

An outside auditor or accountant shall be used as directed by the partners.

Article VIII

Profits, Losses and Draws

Each partner shall receive a semi-monthly draw as agreed by all partners. Profits and losses shall be credited or debited to each partnership account each month.

All partners agree not to draw against their accounts if funds are not there—and to repay the partnership within 30 days for any excess draws. Repayment can also be made from future profits, and no draws can be made.

At the close of the fiscal year all profits will be distributed to all partners—less draws and borrowings of each partner.

Article IX

Limitations of Partners

No partner shall:

Borrow money in name of partnership without consent, or assign, transfer, release or adjust any claims or debts due the partnership except on payment-in-full.

Make, execute or deliver any assignment for benefit of creditors by bond, confession of judgement, guarantee, indemnity bond, surety bond or any contract to sell, lease or mortgage any part of partnership assets.

Make any purchase or expenditure not related to business operations in excess of $50 without consent of all partners. No partner shall engage in any other business or corporation other than passive investments not requiring business time.

Article X

Purchase of interests.

First Option to buy interest goes to other partners.

Set rule for retirement of partners.

Set purchase plan in case of partner death or incapacity. If other partners do not wish to purchase interest, set rules for purchase by outside party, along with acceptable minimum qualifications of purchaser. If no acceptable outside buyer can be found, the partnership is dissolved. Set time limit for dissolution to be triggered.

Valuing the Partnership Interest:

Value shall be sum of any unpaid loans due, partner's capital account, any balance in partner's income account, a given percentage of the accounts receivable at withdrawal date, less any obligation owed the partnership by withdrawing partner.

Set terms of payment of interest by the firm—giving time allowed to pay, method of payment and recourse in case default is made in payments. The withdrawing partner is to be held harmless from all past and present obligations of the firm, except for discovered fraud or error on part of the withdrawing partner.

Remaining partners shall have the right to sell the withdrawing partner's interest to a third party at their discretion.

All files and records are to remain with firm.

The remaining partners shall have the right to use the present name of the firm if they wish, even though it may contain the name of the withdrawing partner.

The withdrawing partner or his representative shall have the right to examine the books until full payment is made.

Set rules for each partner on how interest is to be repaid (and to whom) in case of death or incapacity.

Article XI

Continuation of the firm after dissolution.

When a partner withdraws according to the terms of the partnership agreement, the purchase partners shall continue operation of the firm until those interests are satisfied or shall pay him full amount due if business is discontinued.

Article XII

Expulsions

Set the rules for expulsion from a partnership. They can be fraud, violation of agreement, or personal actions that seriously affect the operation of the business. Expulsion can occur upon unanimous vote of other partners.

The remaining partners are obligated to pay full value of the expelled partner's interest at the price and terms stipulated in Article X.

Article XIII

Liquidation of Partnership

All matters in process to be completed or completion assumed by one or more partners with consent of customers if such consent is necessary.

Assets shall first be used to pay all debts, reserves for taxes, leases, etc. set up. Repayment to be made in the following order:

1. Repay any loans to partnership by partners.
2. Pay all net balances in capital accounts.
3. Distribute petty cash or other cash.
4. Determine who will maintain necessary records as required by law.

Article XIV

Admission of New Partners

All partners must agree on admission of new partners.

All partners must agree on financial requirements for the new partner: amount of cash to be invested, how much to be paid at once, whether notes can be issued for some part, how they are to be repaid, etc.

New partners are to become parties to the partnership agreement and bound by its obligation.

GETTING THE LICENSES AND PERMITS

Since the days of Rome the bureaucrats have been sticking it to the merchants. Operating on the "deep pocket" principle, they stick it to those who have money but no political clout. The fees and permits for operating businesses have been prime targets for the raising of funds.

The fee or permit payments you must make to start a business do not put one dollar in your pocket, nor provide you with any benefit over and above what you are entitled to as an individual taxpayer.

For that reason, it will pay the entrepreneur to do some shopping around concerning the need for various licenses and permits, and their costs. The bureaucrats who issue these are only interested in how much money they can extract from you—and will always quote the maximum rate if you ask them. You will find in most cases the clerk running the desk that takes the money has no idea of what the right permit or fee should be. They will not offer you any choices, and unless you ask for specific licenses and permits, you will get and pay for the ones that cost the most.

COST OF BUSINESS FORMATION

Sole Proprietor _____

Make a will _____

Partnership _____

Legal cost of partnership agreement _____

Registering agreement with county or state _____

Making of partner wills _____

Other costs _____

Incorporation _____

Search to determine legality of name use _____

Reserving name use with the state _____

Legal fees for preparing incorporation papers _____

Notary fees _____

Copying costs of incorporation papers _____

State license fees _____

State tax on capitalization _____

Other state fees or taxes _____

Legal fees for preparation of corporation by-laws _____

Other legal fees _____

Costs to register as a foreign corporation in other states _____

Costs of copying by-laws _____

Cost of corporate seal _____

Cost of printing stock certificates _____

Fees for registering corporation with city or county _____

Cost of a corporate agent _____

Cost of a transfer agent _____

Prepayment of taxes or fees _____

Other expenses _____

Total Expenses _____

LOCAL BUSINESS LICENSES

In almost every community the city clerks or county commissioners sell business licenses and permits as a fund raising venture. These are always raised first when the need for more funds arises, and in some cases new types of permits invented to get even more.

The first step is to get a list of their fees—what they charge for different types of businesses and professions, and then pick the type that costs the least.

For example, a friend was going to sell carbon paper in a large city. The license for a sales agency was $250 a year. The license for a peddler was $10 a year. I had a friend who ran a five million dollar a year business in the same city on a $10 peddler's license.

The point is not to be a sucker and pay for a high cost license if you can get by on a cheaper one. In most cases, the bureaucrats have no idea of what you are doing, all they need to know is that you have a business license. If they find out you have the wrong license you can always tell them that's what the clerk said you should have, and then get the higher priced one if they insist.

If you are not running a store you can probably operate without a license in most large cities until the business produces the cash flow to pay for the proper license.

The key is to get the list of their fees before you apply for the license, and apply for the one you picked and don't discuss the reasons with the clerk. If it's a peddler's license say you are going to be peddling something door-to-door or office-to-office.

SHOP YOUR TERRITORY

Another thing to do is to check out the permit and license fees in different areas or jurisdictions. In some places, you have to buy a license in an incorporated city, but no license in the county. So, if you can find a location in the county, you'll be better off. This may not be possible for a retail location, but if you are going to have an office or warehouse—then your location is not important from the standpoint of having customers come to you. This territory shopping is very important for high gross volume businesses where the city charges a percentage of gross volume as part of the license to do business. Often the permit will only be a few dollars, but you've taken in a partner who shares in your gross business from then on.

So, get a list of the costs of licenses and permits—how many you are required to have—and pick out those that cost the least and apply for them specifically.

THE FICTITIOUS FIRM NAME

Some states require that a business doing business in a name other than that of the owner must fill out a fictitious firm name application, and have it published in a newspaper of record for a period of issues or weeks. This establishes a record of who the owners of the businesses are, their addresses, etc. to allow businesses, credit agencies and financial institutions time to check out the new owners.

There are firms, or attorneys who handle this chore, and most papers qualified to publish legal ads have the necessary form. In metropolitan areas this filing and advertising can cost several hundred dollars if done by an agency or lawyer. However, if you check around in the county, you can find small, weekly papers who are legally entitled to publish these ads, and will run them for you for half or less of what city papers or legal papers charge.

If you use your own name as the title of the business, then you can eliminate this step. If you start a business without filing, you may not be able to open a bank account or sue on debts owed you, etc.

In some states, it is required that you renew publication of this fictitious firm name periodically. If you fail to do it, someone else can legally steal your business name, and you can no longer use it. That is another scam pushed through by newspaper publishers to suck money out of the pockets of small business, along with the bureaucrats. Be sure to make a note of when this refiling must be done so you won't forget. There is a great little racket in picking off the business names of owners who forget to refile, and selling them back for a nice ransom.

STATE LICENSES

Many skills and professions are licensed by states. This ranges from doctors, lawyers and CPA's to beauticians, contractors, insurance and real estate brokers, and salesmen, collection agents, etc.

In these situations the state may require the applicant to:

1. Pass an examination.
2. Furnish a bond or other security.
3. Meet certain prerequisites of experience or training without a test.
4. Furnish proof of good moral character.
5. File information on background and business methods of the founders—such as in franchise selling.
6. Furnish proof of financial responsibility.
7. Meet other qualifications.

These licenses are issued for a specified period of time (usually annually) and subject to cancellation for various breaches of conduct.

In cases where alcoholic beverages are sold, or a business deal in automobiles, cash registers, tobacco products, fireworks, etc., you also have to get state licenses. Be sure to check these out, as failure to get them can bring on stiff fines or closure of your business.

SALES TAX PERMITS

In all but a few states the seller of goods has to have a sales tax permit to sell to end-users, or a permit that allows him to exempt his sales from taxes in the case of wholesalers and those selling tax-exempt items.

There is usually no charge or a small fee for the permit and, in some cases, an advance deposit against future collection of taxes.

You remit your collected taxes to the state, usually on a quarterly basis.

You want to get this permit as soon as you start making purchases for your business. Wholesalers will not sell to you as a rule without a resale license number, or will charge you sales tax.

THE PRE-TAX DEPOSIT

Some states will require you to make an advance deposit on future sales when you apply for a permit. This is a legal scam to grab money from new businesses, to put the state in the position of having their cake and eating it too.

The best way to handle this problem is to tell the state you are going to be running a little hand-to-mouth business which will only do a few hundred dollars in business. This way you get the permit without a deposit.

One tip: in getting this permit, don't walk in wearing a thousand-dollar suit and Gucci loafers; go in wearing old clothes and look like you just came off the bread line. Remember, you are playing a game with these bureaucrats to conserve your start-up capital. Keep your seed capital out of the hands of the tax eaters as long as you can.

FEDERAL PERMITS

If you are going to have employees, you will have to apply for your employer identification number from the IRS. There is no charge and it puts you on the federal government's list as an employer. They will send you quarterly forms to fill out, listing your employees, and how much you paid them, how much you withheld for income tax and social security. Then you will have to deposit the withheld funds plus your own contributions through the bank.

It is best to have your bookkeeper or accountant handle the filling out of these forms and the filing of them with the fees, as well as those for the state, on the proper due dates.

POSTAL PERMITS

If you wish to take advantage of certain post office services, such as bulk mail, business reply postage, pre-sort first class postage rates, pre-cancelled stamps, etc., you will have to obtain a permit, for which there is an annual fee in most cases. These can be obtained at your local post office.

BUSINESS LICENSES AND PERMITS

You must approach the licensing of your business in a pragmatic manner. Pay what you need to pay to start operations and avoid paying anything until it is necessary. If you have to take some sort of test to be licensed, be sure you have allowed enough time for the results of the test to be certified and a license issued. You don't want to pay rent, utilities and other overhead while you are waiting for a state license to do business.

You will find a listing chart below that you can use to note all the permits and licenses you will need, along with the cost. List them and total them up so you will have your complete up-front costs for licenses and permits.

Use this form to get costs of licenses and permits and to compare costs in different locations.

Name of License or Permit	Issued By	Initial Cost	Annual Cost
Local Business License			
Fictitious Firm Name			
State Occupation			
Federal Employment No.			
Others			

SETTING UP YOUR BOOKKEEPING RECORDS

When you are ready to install your bookkeeping system, keep one thing in mind. Make it as simple and non-time-consuming as possible. While accurate records are vital to your operation, you don't need to spend hours of your time fooling with them.

If you have bookkeeping or accounting experience, then you can set up your own. If you are starting a simple cash in-cash out business with no accounts receivable and no large inventory—such as a small mail-order business—then you can go to the stationary store and pick up one of the stock systems they sell (Ideal or Dome are the two best-known). If you follow the instructions given in the books, you will have an adequate bookkeeping system.

HIRING THE ACCOUNTANT OR BOOKKEEPING SERVICE

If you are new to business, or are going to be involved in a great deal of work in creating business, then you should hire an accounting service to care for your records, make out and send in your tax forms, and give you monthly statements on how you are progressing.

The top of the profession is the CPA (Certified Public Accountant). He is the most expensive, and supposedly the most knowledgeable. A good many CPA offices are nothing more than computerized bookkeeping services, but they charge CPA rates. The work is done by so-called junior members of the firm, and you are expected to deliver and pick up your paperwork. Unless you are operating a complicated corporate setup, you really do not need a CPA.

THE BOOKKEEPING SERVICES

There are many good bookkeepers and services that the small business person can use, and use profitably. The bookkeeper is often listed as an accountant, and one with experience in working with small businesses is ideal. He understands the problems, knows what needs to be done and can handle the tax forms and paperwork for you. This person comes to your place of business to do his work on the books, then delivers your reports. You will find these people listed in the phone book under "Accountants" or "Bookkeeping Services."

It is important that the person you employ for this service be reliable and not have more clients than he or she can really handle. You want to remember that these people are not creative thinkers or skilled in all forms of tax law and sophisticated corporate tax shelters. They are technicians who know how to do the job you need done, and can help you in your planning by showing you where you are springing "profit leaks." You will have to keep certain daily records for them, and they will come in and either pick them up or do the work in your office. It will be a big help if the person you choose has had experience in the same line of business you are entering, or one very much like it. Interview more than one, and choose one who seems competent and, more important, who you will get along with on a personal basis.

COMPUTERIZED BOOKKEEPING SERVICES

These are usually computer-based services—something like the systems you buy at the stationary store. You keep certain forms and records, send them to the service, and they return computer printouts of the results. Operators of these services are almost always oversold in terms of personal service, so you won't get much personal advice or help as a rule. One point: stay away from the franchised small business consulting services. They put anyone with the franchise fee in business and sell a so-called consulting service along with bookkeeping services. Check with established small businesses in the area and get some names from them as a starting point. Also check with your banker. He or she may know of a good person or service. Always get references from the people you interview and check them out. And a final tip: when you are interviewing, ask them what types of businesses they now serve. Steer the conversation around to how well firms in that type of business are doing. See if the person tells you any war stories about his past or present accounts. Revealing what should be confidential information, even in a general way, means you do not need him doing your books.

Discuss costs completely—how much to set up the books, how much to balance them, how much to prepare tax reports, etc. Give the accountant an estimate of your volume and what you want to find out from your records. There is a list at the end of the chapter to help you decide this point.

THE SMALL COMPUTER SYSTEMS

This is another route you can go that will allow your computer to keep your inventory and other records on it.

There are a multitude of programs now available to assist you in this part of your business. To find the one right for you, read reviews in computer magazines and go to your local dealer for demonstrations. The resource section of this book will also direct you to many of the software packages you might consider investigating.

The advantage of going this route is that you will save money in the long run from not paying somebody else to do your bookkeeping. Plus, you will have a better understanding of how your business runs and how the numbers involved in it add up.

The computer system is not difficult to master, and it allows you to do your own books with the aid of part-time office help. You can still hire a service to do your taxes and tax reports. It is worth investigating these systems as part of your decision process in planning your record keeping.

THE EXPENSE BUDGET

The new entrepreneur will need some controls and guidelines as he or she begins operations. The most important job is to manage the capital and income so the business stays solvent and growth goals are met. The new business is going to be exposed to a lot of high pressure sales tactics to buy all manner of things that are guaranteed to increase business or business efficiency. The best way to control impulse buying is to have a budget for each function in which ongoing buying decisions are made—inventory, advertising, dues and subscriptions, office supplies and equipment, telephone, travel and entertainment, etc. Allocate funds month-to-month based on business volume, and stick to them. This makes it easy to say no and keep your expenses under control.

Set aside some time everyday to do your bookwork. Make it a time you won't be interrupted, then do all your number crunching, ordering and other paperwork then. Many small business operators find the morning hours the best time for this. Don't let paperwork pile up on you. Daily attention keeps the job manageable. Leave it undone for a few weeks and you'll never catch up.

The following checklists will give you starting points for your thinking about what you want from your record-keeping systems. Keep in mind that too much detail is as bad as too little.

SETTING UP RECORDS AND ACCOUNTS

What kind of records will you need?

1. How will sales be recorded?

Cash register tape.
Sales slips or written orders.
Contracts with customers.
Charge card slips.
Forms for telephone orders.
Purchase orders sent to you.
Entries on ledger cards.
Other.

2. How will purchases and payouts be recorded?

Issuing Purchase orders.
Use of voucher checks.
Signing contracts.
Receipts for cash purchases.
Receipts for payments on account with cash.
Slips to record petty cash withdrawals.
Method of recording owner cash withdrawals.
Method of recording owner or employee merchandise withdrawals.
Issuing promissory notes.
Method of recording barter or exchanges.

3. How to record refunds, discounts, shortages, customer exchanges.

Credits to an accountant.
Cash pay-outs
Check pay-outs.
Recording cash shortages and overages.
Goods exchanged by customers.
Bad checks.
Bad debts.

4. How to record deductible expenses.

On checks—how entered and noted.
Accounts journal.
Cash receipts.
Credit Card purchases.

5. How to record long-term and short-term liabilities:

Notes payable ledger.
Payment books.
Other
Method to record division of interest and principle for tax deductions.

6. How to track depreciation:

Record of items and rates of depreciation.
Type of depreciation taken.

7. How to record taxes due:

When due on the calendar.
Funds to be held or maintained for tax payments.
How and when payments are to be made.

8. How to handle payroll:

How often it will be met.
How deductions and withholding will be determined.
How payroll will be recorded.
How W-2 and other forms will be handled.

9. How inventory records will be maintained:

Setting up initial inventory records.
Records of inventory re-orders.
Method of value for accounting purposes—IFO or FIFO.
How often counted and checked.
How often shortages and overages will be handled.

10. How to complete financial statements:

Balance sheet—open for business—how often?
Cash flow statements—how often?
Financial ratio analysis—how often?
Tax reports—who prepares?

11. How to set up budgets:

Cash budget.
Financial budget.
Expense budget.
Sales budget.
Advertising budget.
Research and development budget.

12. How to maintain credit records and accounts:

Ledgers for accounts receivable.
Aging reports on accounts—how often?
System for triggering collection action.
System for and how accounts will be written off as bad debts.

What information do you want from your record keeping?

1. What income was received—what expenses incurred?
2. How do they compare with successful business operations?
3. How can expenses be reduced or eliminated?
4. How is the inventory: too high, too low, about right?
5. What are the assets/liabilities and net worth of this firm?

6. What is your return on investment?
7. What is the value of your non-liquid assets at this time?
8. How is cash flow?
9. How are your accounts being collected—average or better?
10. How productive is your staff?
11. Are your prices producing the best profit possible?

COST OF RECORDKEEPING

Item	Annual Cost
Cost of initial books and supplies	$
Accountant's charges to set up books	
Cost of accountant's services	
Cost of tax form preparation	
Cost of preparing payroll	
Cost of postage and duplication tax forms	
Other expenses	
Total pre-starting costs	
Total monthly costs	
Total annual costs	

NOTE:

Pre-starting costs are not considered business expenses for tax purposes, but a capital investment. If you use an accountant, have him arrange his work so that he is not finished, and does not bill you for services until after you have started business. Then it's fully deductible.

NOTE:

Divide annual costs by 12 to get monthly costs of starting expenses for record keeping.

BUYING YOUR BUSINESS PRINTING

One of the first purchasing decisions you will make is buying your printing—your letterheads, envelopes, business cards, invoices and business forms.

In the first blush of enthusiasm, and as an ego kick, a lot of new entrepreneurs spend too much money getting fancy artwork, paper and high-priced printing for these things. In some types of business it is worth the investment if your literature has to impress people in order to do more business, but in most businesses it is a waste of money.

Your job in organizing the business is to make your capital go as far as possible, so there is no point in spending money just to make yourself feel good.

There are firms who print for other printers—who produce high quality work at reasonable prices—as well as retail mail order printers who use stock formats and turn out very nice stationery at prices considerably lower than you would pay a local printer. And they print in small quantities as well.

If you want to get the lowest possible prices on your printing, here's a way to get price lists and catalogs from "trade printers" (printers who print for other printers). Get some note heads printed up at a local "quick printer" with your name and address at the top and with a line across the bottom of the page reading "printing broker." Use this to write to Graphic Arts Monthly, 600 5th Avenue, New York, NY 10019. This is a printers' trade magazine. Ask to be put on their mailing list. By checking advertising in their classified section and some display ads, you will find trade printers for everything from business cards to business forms.

For example:

Summit Thermography, 8171 S. Grant Way, Littleton, CO 80122. For printing of business cards, letterheads, etc., at about 50 percent less than printers charge.

U. S. Tag and Ticket Co., 2219 Robb St., Baltimore, MD 21218. For tags or tickets.

Label Art, 23 Riverside Way, Wilton, NH. For mailing labels, product labels, etc.

Nationwide Stock Business Forms, 75–7th Avenue, New York, NY 10011. For business forms, such as purchase orders, bills of lading, invoices, etc. They have over 75 stock designs to fit most needs.

Dexter Press, Rt. 303, West Nyack, NY 10094. For four-color catalog sheets.

There are many more in each category in the magazine. I found it easiest to call these firms on the phone. I told them I was a printing broker and would like their catalogs or prices, as I had accounts wanting the products they printed.

The advantage of using these firms is they are specialists in what they do. Plus, they produce a quality job at a reasonable price. The one problem is time. You must order far enough in advance to allow four to six weeks in some cases for your order to arrive.

If you don't want to go to that much trouble, then you can order a catalog from: Drawing Board, P. O. Box 505, Dallas, TX 75221. They are a retailer of all types of business printing in small quantities, and they do excellent work.

The advantage of doing business with these firms and others who sell by mail is that they achieve economies of scale. As a rule, they can charge less than local printers because they use stock forms, limited choices of type styles, and quantity runs on the presses to deliver a good product at a lower price.

If you are going to use local printers, then shop around. Check prices, the look of the shop, and quality of work. Almost all local printers are oversold from time to time. They sell more than they can produce in the promised time. The one thing you want to avoid is dealing with a printer who is always in that situation. His prices may be lower, but the problems become far worse than the savings are worth. These days, the quick printers can do most of what you need and are geared to getting out the work.

If you are going to buy artwork for your literature, and you talk to a couple of commercial artists who toss around estimates like $100 an hour or $500 for a small design, don't pay it. Put an ad in the paper under "Help Wanted" for an artist with the experience to draw what you need. You'll find all kinds of talented people who will do a good job at a more reasonable price.

If you are planning on printing some brochures and using a couple of colors, then write to: Champion Printing Co., P. O. Box 148, Ross, OH 45061. They will send you a pricing catalog that also has a short course in how to paste up your copy for proper reproduction.

If you take some time to develop your sources, particularly if your business calls for a lot of printed matter, you will save a considerable amount of money and get good quality work.

ITEM TO BE PRINTED	DATE REQUIRED	QUANTITY	PRICE

HOW TO SELECT YOUR INSURANCE COVERAGE

The need for insurance is obvious to any responsible person. Business insurance takes many forms, but the small business operator usually has a standard set of insurance needs that the industry is able to cover with one or two policies. It is a fairly simple matter to get the required coverage, which is offered by two types of agents.

First, the independent agent represents several insurance companies who offer varying types of policies. In some fields with a large number of businesses involved in it, there are companies that specialize in coverage for that particular industry. Often this is the best type of coverage, since it is offered by firms who know the business well and can offer a good deal of help in managing risk. If there is such a company, you can find out about it from your trade association, or someone else in the business. You can then locate the agent in your area that represents the company.

The second type of agent is the direct writer. This agent represents one company, as an employee. The company, not the agent, owns your account. The independent agent owns his own accounts, and can shift them from one company to another.

There is some argument about which type of agent is best—and cases can be made for both sides. But, the small business operator would, in general terms, be better off with an independent agent who is also a small business operator, than with a direct writer. You represent a valued account to your independent agent, but you represent peanuts to the company represented by the direct writer. In case you have a claim, the independent agent has a vested interest in seeing that the claim is settled to your satisfaction. The direct writer is an employee of the company and his interest is the company's interest. In claim disputes he will be on the side of the company.

The first step is to determine what you are going to be able to insure. The second step is to determine how much of it can you afford to insure.

To make this decision you must understand the nature of risk. There are two major types of risk with which you will be confronted: pure risk and speculative risk. Pure risk is the situation in which there is the possibility of loss, theft, a fire, sickness or death of the owner, flood, earthquake, etc. There is no way to anticipate timing or control of pure risk.

Speculative risk is that in which, there is the possibility of gain or loss, depending on the outcome of an event or situation. Gambling on a horse race, investing in a stock and opening a small business are speculative risks and, as a rule, cannot be insured.

Your insurance priorities will usually run in this order:

1. Business fraud and theft
2. Fire
3. Bad debts
4. Legal liability
5. Business interruption
6. Death or loss of key people
7. Natural disasters—flood, storm, earthquake, etc.
8. Obsolete products or processes

You can get some form of insurance against them all, but you probably cannot afford insurance of that magnitude. So you must cover the largest loss exposure first. And make sure that you buy enough to protect your business for up to 95 percent of possible personal liability. The way to get maximum amounts of coverage at affordable premiums is to self-insure some of the low- end items yourself by using deductible policies. That is, you agree to be liable up to $500, $1000, $5000, or whatever your insurance pays any amount over that. This enables you to buy higher amounts of insurance at the high end for maximum protection.

To find the proper agent, ask around among other small businesspeople in your area. See who they use or will recommend. If a name comes up more than once, you should contact that agent's office first and shop a few others before making your decision. If the agent knows business coverage, can make suggestions and show you how to get more coverage per dollar, that's the one you should go with.

ESSENTIAL COVERAGES

Your insurance program can be divided into two categories: the essential and the desirable coverages. The essential are fire insurance, liability insurance, automobile insurance, and worker's compensation. There are some points to consider in each of them. Here is a checklist:

FIRE INSURANCE

Make a note to add other perils—windstorm, hail, smoke, vandalism, explosion, flood and malicious mischief—to the policies. In most cases it can be done at quite a low cost.

Check out the comprehensive coverage policy—the all-risk policy to get broadest possible coverage at least cost. NOTE: The total premium is usually less on an all-risk policy than buying separate coverage.

Determine how your losses will be paid by the insurer. There are several ways it is done.

1. It may pay actual cash value on the property at the time of loss.
2. It may repair or replace the property with material of like value.
3. It may take over the remaining property and pay for all property (damaged and undamaged) in one lump sum.

Is there any need to insure property you don't own? One example is property left for repair or service. Or is there a need to insure a building on your property? If not, you can get a deduction on your premium payment.

Remember, you cannot over-insure and be paid an amount that exceeds the value of what was lost. Insurance companies combine to pay off only a percentage of the value of the loss. They do not pay full amounts independently.

You will need a special "floater" (additional coverage added to the policy) to recover the costs of losses of accounts records, bills, currency, deeds, evidences of debt, money and securites.

If you move out of a building you own and it remains vacant for 60 consecutive days, the standard fire policy suspends coverage unless there is a special endorsement to the policy cancelling this provision.

If you increase the fire hazard, such as by storing drums of gasoline, the insurance company may suspend your coverage even for losses not originating from the fire hazard.

After a loss you must use all reasonable means to protect the property from further loss, or risk having your coverage cancelled.

To recover losses, you must furnish within 60 days (unless the insurance company grants an extension) a complete inventory of damaged, destroyed and undamaged property, showing in detail quantities, costs, actual cash value and amount of loss claimed.

Note the clause in the policy that sets forth the method to be used to settle disputes over amounts of damage. It is important to have your agent explain this to you.

Note the cancellation terms. Usually either party may cancel on five days notice. The insured gets a refund of part of the premium paid.

Have the agent explain co-insurance to you. By putting a co-insurance clause in your contract which states that you agree to carry insurance equal to 80 percent to 90 percent of the value of the property, you can get a deduction on your premium payment.

LIABILITY INSURANCE

Be sure to carry enough liability—$1 million at least, and probably more in light of today's damage awards.

Be sure to notify the insurance company of any incident happening on your property or premises that might cause a future claim, no matter how petty it may seem.

Most liability policies now carry, in addition to bodily injuries, personal injuries such as libel and slander, etc. if they are specifically mentioned in the policy.

Remember: if you have employees or agents or independent contractors working in your behalf, you can be held liable for their actions in some circumstances. This risk is insurable—and necessary.

AUTOMOBILE INSURANCE

Make your policy cover employees, contractors and agents acting in your behalf, even if you don't own the car or truck they were in during an accident.

Five or more motor vehicles of any type used in a business under one ownership, and operated as a fleet, can usually qualify for a low-cost fleet policy for damage to the vehicles themselves as well as to people or property.

Carry as much collision deductible as you can in order to reduce premiums.

You should carry the uninsured motorist coverage and medical payments for all parties to an accident in your business policy.

You can also carry a floater on personal property stolen from a car or vehicle, but it is probably not worth the cost. This coverage is not standard in an auto policy.

WORKER'S COMPENSATION

Common law says employers must:

1. Provide a safe place to work
2. Hire competent fellow employees
3. Provide safe tools and equipment
4. Warn employees concerning any existing danger

If the employer fails to provide the above, he is liable for damages if a worker is injured or killed on the job. The worker's compensation insurance is needed to cover that risk.

As a rule, state law determines the level and type of benefits payable under worker's compensation policies. Check carefully to be sure you understand your obligations.

There are some exceptions to coverage of some employees. Have your agent explain these to you—who you must cover and who is not covered.

In some states you are not legally required to cover your employees under worker's compensation, but you may lose some of your legal defenses in lawsuits if you don't.

Rates for worker's compensation vary from one tenth of a percent to 25 percent of the payroll, depending on occupations. Be sure that all your employees are properly rated to make sure you are not over-paying premiums.

Worker's compensation rates can be reduced by keeping accident rates low—below average for your industry. So a good safety program can save money.

DESIRABLE INSURANCE COVERAGES

These coverages are not essential, but should be included if you can afford them. They will greatly improve your risk management and could save your business.

BUSINESS INTERRUPTION INSURANCE

You can purchase insurance to cover fixed expenses and normal profit if a fire or other natural disaster should make operating your business impossible.

If you have a key supplier or material source on which the operation of your business depends, you can purchase insurance to pay out fixed expenses and profits should the supplier be shut down by fire or other disaster.

The business interruption policy provides payments for amounts you spend to get back into operation.

There is also coverage available for increased costs due to partial interruption of your business. It can also include indemnification of losses due to failure or interruption of light, power, heat, gas or water that is furnished by a public utility.

CRIME INSURANCE

Burglary insurance has certain exclusions—accounts, valuable articles in a showcase window, and others. Be clear with the agent as to what they are.

In most cases, visible evidence, confirmed by a police investigation of forced entry, must be present in order to collect on burglary insurance.

A policy can be written to cover the contents of a safe, inventoried merchandise and damage incurred in the course of the burglary.

Robbery insurance protects you from loss of property, money and securites by force, trickery or threat of violence on or off your premises.

Investigate a comprehensive crime policy for small business that covers burglary, robbery and other types of loss by theft, including theft by employees.

If your location will be a "high risk area" where no commercial crime insurance is offered, check with the U.S. Department of Housing and Urban Development about their plan. There are others your agent should be able to tell you about.

GLASS INSURANCE

You can purchase a special glass insurance policy that covers all risk to plate glass windows, glass signs, motion picture screens, glass brick, glass doors, showcases, countertops and insulated glass panels.

Check to see if the glass policy covers not just the glass but the cost of lettering and ornamentation and the cost of boarding up when necessary.

After the glass is replaced, the same policy should continue without any premium increase for the period covered.

RENT INSURANCE

You can buy rent insurance to cover a lease obligation to pay rent should a property become unuseable due to fire or other disasters. If you own the property, you can insure loss of lease income due to fire or disaster.

There are also employee benefit insurance programs, such as group life insurance, health and disability, but these plans should come out of business income—not out of capital investment.

THE INSURANCE PROGRAM

Policy	Insurer	Term	Cost

YOUR INSURANCE PLAN

1. Cover your largest exposure first.
2. Use as high a deductible as you can afford.
3. Avoid duplication of insurance coverage.
4. Buy "package policies" if possible.
5. Review your program annually to be sure you are fully covered.
6. Write your insurance plan, listing what you need from insurance.
7. Select one agent with small business experience to handle it.
8. Keep complete records of your insurance policies, premiums paid, losses and loss recoveries.
9. Have your property appraised periodically by independent appraisers to prove your actual losses in case of disaster.
10. Do everything you can to reduce risk of loss.

HOW TO DO YOUR FORECASTING

Now we come to the most difficult subject for the new entrepreneur — forecasting. You must make an educated guess as to the amount of business you will do — how the cash flow will be generated and what expenses of operations will be. There is no way to be sure you have the right figures, but with a little research and some positive thinking you can come close enough to make sensible planning possible.

GROSS SALES PLANNING

The method of estimating gross sales, based on something other than personal optimism, is to use existing information as the base.

You can get the figures for your industry from local professional associations or the Department of Commerce Bureau of Census figures. What you want to find out is the rate of growth or decline in the gross sales industry-wide. This will give you a base figure of average increase or decrease in business for the industry. Next, you want to find out what the average industry customer spends per year. Then, you want to know how much is being spent in your trading area — and the rate of growth or decline in the population of the area. With this information you can determine the prospects for the growth or decline of your total market. Here's how it could work:

Industry figures show a 5 percent annual growth in sales of products or services over the past five years. The average customer spends $100 a year. Your trading area is increasing in population at the rate of 2 percent per year. The present volume of business in the trading area is $10 million dollars.

From these figures you can determine this: that the current year will see a 5 percent growth in sales in your area, or $500,000 in natural growth from the existing population.

CASH ON HAND

Months	1	2	3	4	5	6
Cash on Hand	5000	1000	-0-	-0-	-0-	240
Cash Sales	1200	1500	2000	2500	3000	3500
Credit Sales	4800	5500	7000	7500	9000	11,500
Credit Collect.	-0-	2400	4670	6120	7650	8200
Cash in Bank	6200	4900	6670	8620	10,650	11,940

DISBURSEMENTS

Fixed Expenses	1000	1000	1000	1000	1000	1000
Cost of Sales	600	700	900	1000	1200	1500
Inventory Buy	3600	4200	5400	6000	7200	9000
Total Cash Out	5200	5900	7300	8000	9400	11,500
Cash Balance	1000	− 1000	− 630	+ 620	+ 1250	+ 440
Total Cash Bal.	+ 1000	− 1000	− 1630	− 1010	+ 240	

By looking at this chart, you know you are going to need an additional $1,000 in the second month to pay your bills, and another $630 in the third month. After that, the cash flow gets into a positive amount and no additional funds are needed.

It is important to prepare a projected cash flow chart for your first year in business to determine your cash position. This projected cash flow will also help you if you need a loan before the business starts. It will tell loan officers or investors what you expect your business to do in its first months of operation.

PROJECTING EXPENSES

The final projection is your cost of doing business. This should be budgeted by the ratios of your industry. You can get these ratios from Dun & Bradstreet (operating ratios). Your projected gross volume of business gives you the figures to work with. You multiply the gross volume by your ratio figures to get your expense budgets.

For example, if your ratio for rent is five percent of gross, then taking the $75,000 estimated gross, we multiply it by 5 percent and find $3,750 is what we should pay for rent each year. But going back to your estimated average gross business, we recall that that was $107,000 and our rent should be predicted on that figure, as that is what we will be doing in our second year. So the rent budget should be $5,350, to give us the kind of location we need.

Thus, our first year's rent budget will be just over 7 percent of our gross. After you add in all other costs, you may find you will need additonal capital your first year to cover expenses. So project your fixed ratios, rent, utilities, advertising, etc. on the basis of an average gross business and arrange to supply the additional capital if necessary.

Use the chart at the end of this section to compute your projections for the first two years. These figures include the gross sales, cost of inventory and selling, expenses, the withdrawals by owners, and finally, the profit.

From those figures you can determine this—that the current year will see a 5 percent growth in sales in your area. That will be $500,000 as the area share of industry-wide growth. Then your population will grow 2 percent, which will add another $200,000 to the total market or $10,700,000.

Now, get the statistics from the Bureau of Census on the average volume of business done by firms in your line of business in the area. We'll say it is $100,000 a year. In the coming year they will do an average of $107,000.

Now you have an average gross volume figure for the business you are entering. To be on the safe side, you can estimate you will do 70 percent of the average volume your first year, or $75,000. That will be your sales target.

So, forecasting sales using existing figures is not all that difficult. The reason you want this figure is to show your banker when you are getting started, so you can keep him posted on your progress—and get a loan if and when you need it.

THE CASH FLOW FORECAST

This is critical because it will show you whether you will need additional capital and when. To make a cash flow forecast you need to estimate two things: your monthly sales, and your cash sales and credit sales. You will also have to know your fixed and selling expenses.

To make this forecast you need to break your total estimated volume of sales down into a monthly sales forecast. You will have some published figures to work with. Almost every business has a monthly percentage of total sales breakdown, either from the trade association or a trade magazine. It is also available for the more traditinal lines of business from the Bureau of Census. You can use these figures to estimate your monthly sales by multiplying each by total gross volume. Let's say the average for your first month in business is 8 percent and your estimated gross is $75,000. Eight percent of that is $6,000. If you are selling on credit, then you can also find the ratio of credit-to-cash sales in your industry from the same sources. Let's say it is over 20 percent cash and 80 percent credit.

Now we will do a cash flow chart for six months to see how our cash flow will come out. We will take an average of 8 percent per month to simplify the figuring, and have an 80 percent credit to 20 percent cash sales ratio. We will also estimate the industry average on collection of accounts. Nationwide it runs 50 percent within 30 days, 40 percent within 60 days, and 10 percent within 90 days. There will be some bad debts, but we won't estimate them for this chart.

Now you are ready to figure out how much capital you are going to need to put the business in operation and carry it to the break-even point.

Below, you will find a form that you can follow to determine exactly how much capital you will need. You will find the directions for using the form in the previous explanation of cash flow forecasting. If you have done the cost estimates as you went along, you have all the figures at hand. Just fill in the form and run your totals, and you have the information you need.

(YOUR COMPANY NAME)
PROJECTED INCOME
STATEMENT

	lst year	Sales	2nd Year	Sales
PROJECTIONS				
Gross receipt				
Cost of Sales				
Gross Profit				
EXPENSES:				
Employee wages				
Advertising				
Phone & utilities				
Repairs				
Professional fees				
Supplies				
Rent				
Freight				
Depreciation				
Interest				
Taxes and licenses				
Insurance				
Miscellaneous				
Total expenses				
Net profit before tax				
Less income taxes				
Net profit after tax				
Owner withdrawals				
Undistributed profit				

Other costs of doing business are included in each business plan under the Potential Income section. These expenses are particular to the business you intend to operate and should be include in the Expenses Section.

SECTION 5

Business Promotion and Marketing will give you all the information you will want to ensure a steady flow of customers through your door. It will teach you how to properly promote and market the business, how to tell the difference between advertising and promotion and how to get the most from both with the least amount of money. You'll also read about how to write display and classified ads that get read, how to get free publicity from local newspapers, how to handle direct mail, and how to use your telephone to sell your computer service.

SECTION FIVE

BUSINESS PROMOTION

WHY ADVERTISING AND PROMOTION?

Advertising and promotion are important for several reasons. The first is that advertising and promotion work together, and people who don't understand advertising almost never grasp the idea of promotion.

For our purposes, advertising is a sub-species of promotion. It is paid-promotion. You are paying someone directly to put your message out, instead of using other methods to have him get your message across.

Promotion is the business of making yourself and your business known to your potential customers, and getting those customers to come to you so you can sell them your service. There are more elegant definitions and more inclusive ones, but that is the meat of the matter.

It also tells you why you need to promote. Promotion brings you customers. Promotion builds up your business. Things that don't do that are not successful promotions.

THE GREAT AMPLIFIER

Promotion is an amplifier. It takes your message and makes it larger. In fact, it takes both you and your service and makes them larger in your community. If you have a good service, you will find that good promotion amplifies its values or benefits. If you have a bad service, that gets amplified too.

If your message is confused and poorly thought out, that confusion will be amplified. To promote successfully, you have to know who you want to reach and what you want to tell them.

Promotion also magnifies you personally. There are a lot of prominent people in any community whose prominence comes from owning a business which is successfully promoted. The promotions may not mention the owners at all, but they become known very quickly.

A good promotion scheme is like a big public address system. It magnifies everything that you feed into it, from messages to the sound of heavy breathing, while you try to make up your mind about what to say. There are a few people who know how to promote instinctively, but who do it badly because they don't understand how to use that instinct.

The thing that gets amplified most by promotion is money spent on advertising. A very small amount of money put into advertising, backed up by a well thought out promotion campaign, will be far more successful than the same amount of money in advertising with no promotion campaign.

In a sense, any business is already advertising, whether you have an item like that in your budget or not—or even if you don't have a budget. If you are in business, you have a certain amount of advertising. You have a sign and you have customers who will spread the word. You have that much at the very least.

Now, if you combine that with a good promotion campaign—even if you don't spend a cent on it—you will increase your effectiveness by 10 to 20 times!

That's a conservative figure, by the way. We know of cases where the amplification factor has gone as high as 100 or even more. (Above about 120 it gets hard to measure.) Our experience has shown that businesses that begin to promote skillfully, yet had done no advertising or promotion before, will experience an increase of between 25 to 40 times as many customers coming To them in the course of the first year's promotion. How many of those you convert into sales is up to you, but at least you've got them coming in.

Of course, if the business has been advertising or promoting previously, the increase won't be as large. However, it will still usually be substantial.

THE BOTTOM LINE

The bottom line is customers coming to you—people who are willing to spend money for whatever it is you have to sell. This is how you judge the success of any promotion plan.

We stress this because it tends to get forgotten for a lot of reasons. One of the reasons is that advertising and promotion are both games that have a fascination all their own.

The opposite of the business owner who doesn't advertise or promote is the person who is so hung up in the advertising and promoting that he forgets about running his business. He or she is convinced that the product or service doesn't really matter. All he needs is a good handle and a big advertising budget and he can sell anything.

A similar case is the person who finds the technical side of advertising so interesting, he doesn't really care if he's bringing in the customers or not. Most of the time he isn't, or if he is, he's not bringing in nearly the number he should be for what he is paying out. He can talk your ears off about demographics, cost per thousand and influencing the market mix. He's full of technical terms, and his business is virtually empty of customers.

IT IS NOT DIFFICULT

Our super-technical friend is the carrier of another myth: advertising and promotion are highly technical sciences that require a lot of support services, special skills and market research to use properly.

This is nonsense. True, if you're handling the advertising budget for General Motors, you need a great deal of special skill. In that case, the difference of a percentage point in your response figures can mean an enormous amount of money. For the small and medium-sized business, you do not need that kind of expertise. The "expertise" you need is largely a matter of a little knowledge and a fair amount of common sense. Anyone can learn to promote his computer business successfully and effectively. You don't need a lot of special help and you don't need a lot of money. You will need to put a little thought into it, especially in the beginning, and you will need to take action. But that is about the extent of the "difficulty" of promoting a computer business.

IT IS NOT EXPENSIVE

Another thing that tends to over-awe small business operators is the expense figures that get tossed out so casually by advertising salespeople. To them, $500 is barely worth looking at. To a small business person, it can be a month's profit.

The situation is even worse when you talk to an advertising agency. For reasons we'll discuss later, advertising agencies are under no compulsion to keep a close eye on their client's money, and they tend to spend it the way Congress spends taxes. A big company may be able to afford that sort of outlook, but a small one cannot.

The usual answer to complaints about the price of advertising is for the account executive to point out to you that you've got to spend money to make money, and to look at the "real cost per thousand" you are getting. This is usually done slowly, carefully and patiently, as if talking to a child.

As a result, most small business owners are convinced that a good advertising campaign, with its attendant promotion, is hopelessly out of their reach. They settle for either doing nothing, or buying an occasional spot on the radio or in the newspaper.

First off, it just isn't true that successful advertising and promotion has to cost you a bundle. If you do it right, it will cost you very little. In fact, you can put together a pretty good promotion campaign for next to nothing.

The trick is to know what you want and why you are spending money where you're spending it. An advertising agency has no real reason to hold costs down, and as far as the various account executives are concerned, the more you buy, the better. You can't expect effective advice on low-cost advertising and promotion from those sources. Almost everyone else you run into will have a similar attitude. A market researcher will tell you the way to cut your cost is to advertise more effectively — which is true — and that what you need is a good market survey, at a cost of several thousand dollars, of course.

The other trick is to recognize opportunities when you see them, and grab them. If you look, you will find that there are opportunities for successful promotions all around you. By knowing how to exploit them, you can make maximum use of the amplification effect and reap a harvest of customers coming through the door.

OH, THE EXPERTS!

By now you may have the idea that we don't have much use for experts in the fields of advertising and promotion. Actually, that's not true. We have a great deal of use for them and we are well aware of the tremendous contributions they have made. But we are also well aware that they think and deal in terms of large national corporations with enormous budgets to spend on advertising.

There are two reasons for this. In the first place, the large national corporations are the ones who keep the big advertising agencies afloat. They are the ones who spend the money for market research, product design and various promotional activities.

The big companies are the ones who have shaped modern advertising, and they have shaped it in their own image. When a college student studies advertising, he studies national advertising. At the end of four years he can tell you more than you want to know about running a campaign to introduce a new kind of soap, but next to nothing about getting customers for your computer business.

The second reason for the concentration is that it's always more interesting to do things on a large scale than a small one. If you're going to play with toy soldiers, you want to play with armies. Because the theoretical considerations are more important and tend to apply more generally, it's easier to draw up a computer model showing how the introduction of a new soap will go than it is to plan a campaign for a computerized service on a strict budget.

For these reasons the expert can be very useful. But if you're running a small business, you can't accept everything they tell you blindly and try to apply it. You'll not only go broke, you'll look awfully silly.

CAN YOU REALLY DO IT CHEAPLY?

A lot of people are amazed at the idea that they can do their promotion inexpensively.

Some of them flat-out won't believe it. When we explain our system and its costs, we almost always have someone ask if we really mean it!

Yes, we mean it, and, yes, you can do it. It's nice to have money, of course. If you've got a fair amount of money to spend, you can do some of the things we talk about much more gracefully and effectively, but most of them you can do without money and still get some results. What we mean by "a fair amount of money" will vary depending on several factors. These include the line of business you're in, the rates for advertising in your area, what your competition is like, and any unique circumstances you may have. However, even given an ideal budget—all the money you could want to spend—the total amount will still be relatively small. In fact, you can put together an "ideal" advertising and promotion and campaign for less than the cost of a single market survey.

IT'S UP TO YOU

So you have a choice. You can sit around and wait for customers to come to you or you can start them moving in your direction. The cost isn't much higher for one than another, but the difference in return is enormous.

There is a catch, of course. The catch is that you have to do it. It doesn't just happen; you have to make it happen. You will have to act in ways that will make it happen.

It isn't difficult, but it will be strange at first. You'll find yourself doing things you wouldn't normally do. But after awhile the strangeness will wear off and you'll probably discover you like what you are doing.

You will certainly find it is more profitable.

ADVERTISING IN GENERAL

Advertising is promotion you pay for—pay for directly, that is. The amount you pay is what determines how often your message is printed or broadcast and for how long or how big.

Paid advertising is the thing that gets multiplied by the multiplier of promotion. If you have a good paid advertising campaign going, its effectiveness will be enhanced by your promotions—and vice versa.

Advertising does not have to cost you an arm and a leg. In fact, if it is costing you parts of your body, then you're probably not doing it right. Effective advertising can cost a lot of money, but to be effective, it does not have to. If you make proper use of the multiplier effect you can keep your costs very low.

SPEND IT WHEN YOU NEED IT

Advertising is one thing you should never try to do cheaply. If your promotion plan calls for the use of a certain amount of advertising to get a message across, then for heaven's sake, use that much advertising. Don't try to save here. Spending some money is an integral part of your plan.

The trick in making effective use of advertising is to combine the best qualities of the miser and the spendthrift. You hoard your advertising budget until you need it, and then you spend it like there's no tomorrow, until you have spent enough to accomplish your goal. Then you go back to hoarding.

There is a certain trick to judging when to hoard and when to spend. The typical small business owner goes to one extreme or the other. Either he sets up a regular schedule of advertising and sticks to it come hell or high water, or he refuses to spend any money on advertising at all. A third possibility is related to the second. That is not spending nearly enough to do the job.

The trick is easy when you look at advertising as part of a promotion plan. You know what you are trying to do and you have a pretty good idea what you can accomplish with promotion. When you need help getting the message across, that's the time to open up the advertising budget.

A typical use for advertising is in getting news of a promotion to the public. The promotion is what is going to draw in the customers, but you've got to let them know it's going on. So you spend some advertising money to make sure people find out about it.

REGULAR ADVERTISING

Any advertising account executive you talk to will try to sell you on a regular advertising schedule. He will probably tell you that it's the way to keep your company's name in front of the public, and that is the way all the large companies do it. To clinch the argument, he will point out that you get a break on costs if you buy advertising in bulk.

All true, but with the exception of the last point, it's pretty much irrelevant for the typical small business. If you start totaling it up, you will quickly see that the costs of a continuous advertising campaign big enough to make an impression on your potential customers is more money than you have to spend.

It's true that large companies operate on the basis of an enormous amount of advertising. For most of them, it's one of the biggest items in their budget. But they don't spend that money because they like it, and they didn't start out spending that sort of money.

A big advertiser can't pick up on promotion opportunities as quickly as a small company can. He doesn't have the multiplication effect, so he has to advertise heavily. What's more, a big advertiser is large enough that he isn't troubled by the threshold effect that can kill a small advertiser.

ADVERTISING AND THE THRESHOLD

The fact is, all other things being equal, an advertising message must be exposed to the public a certain number of times to be effective. Yet the ways that cut the number of times the message must be exposed increase the cost. A full-page ad in the sports section of your Sunday newspaper will definitely cut the number of times you have to run a message to get sufficient response. But it will also shoot your advertising costs out of sight.

If you don't have X amount of dollars to spend on advertising, you usually can't get over the threshold and get your message across. What this means is that you must be more selective about the message you try to put across. The big advertiser can afford to cross that threshold every week just to keep his name before the public. You can't, so you need to plan the advertising part of your campaign accordingly.

REGULAR ADVERTISING AND RATE REDUCTIONS

Fine, but you still get a break on rates if you advertise frequently. You may want to plan your advertising to take advantage of those rate breaks. What you do not want to do is try to use that time to hammer home the same message.

Running the same 10 second spot on the radio three times a week for three months isn't going to do anything for your business unless you're a genius at promotion. Running the same 10-second spot 36 times in one week might get a message across nicely.

In most cases, you would get the same rate on both schedules. The difference is the first one piddles your money away; the second one approaches a useful frequency.

More important, let's say you don't run the same spot. Let's say you're planning on running a 10-second spot three times a week. But instead of running the same spot, "Jones Computerized Tax Service for all of your tax-time needs," tailor your messages every week to support your promotion campaign. You're still spread thin, but you have a much better chance of making an impact.

The reason is that you're not just trying to keep your name before the public. You are using your advertising to trigger your changing promotions. This is effective use of advertising dollars.

HEAD-TO-HEAD WITH THE BIG BOYS

There's another lesson here. Just because the big firms do something doesn't mean that you should. In fact, it can be an excellent reason not to do it.

Advertising and promotions are susceptible to a background noise factor. The more advertising there is, the louder you have to shout to be heard over the racket. If you're talking about advertising, that shouting is going to cost you money. By moving to a quieter environment, you can be heard more easily and cheaply.

Unless he has a world-beater of a promotion, a small computerized recipe service operator is foolish to advertise in the food section of a big city daily on a Wednesday. That's when every chain store in town will have rolled out it's heavy guns. The little guy is going to get lost in the forest of loss leaders and double-page ads.

On the other hand, he could run the same ad in a shopper for less money and probably get a better effect. His cost-per-thousand, or cost for every thousand people reached with the ad, would not be as good, but he would have a lot better chance of being read.

Regular advertising "to keep your name before the public" is the case par excellence of trying to beat the big boys at their own game. Most of the time they will swamp you.

In some cases the same thing will be true of loss-leader promotions. If Wednesday is the traditional day for loss leaders in your town, try shifting to Monday. Or try Saturday before noon.

If you decide that you want to run your promotion on the same day everyone else does, then put a lot of thought into making it so special that it will stand out no matter what the others do.

REINFORCE STRENGTH

To be successful, you need to keep experimenting. This is particularly true of promotions in general, and advertising in particular.

Try different media, different types of ads, different schedules and different promotions. You'll find that some will work better than others, for reasons no one understands.

For example, if you send out a direct mail piece, try sending your fliers in plain white envelopes with postage stamps rather than metered postage. And put the stamp on the envelope sideways.

You'll find it makes an appreciable difference in your returns. Why? No one knows. But it does.

When you get a winner, ride it for all it's worth. Plan on repeating the promotion or rerunning the ad. Increase the frequency if it's doing a good job for you. Keep pushing until you've milked it for everything you can. Then move on to something else.

PRUNE RUTHLESSLY

By the same token, when an ad is no longer producing for you, get rid of it. Some businesses will try to keep using the same advertisement for months or years. It worked pretty good once upon a time, and, besides, there's sort of a sentimental attachment to it after all these years.

Wrong. Keep an eye on the effectiveness of your advertising and prune out the weak ones. You should have something ready to replace it with when you need to.

You can prolong the life of an ad by fiddling with the concept. If it's for a newspaper, you can run it in a different size or specify placement in a different part of the paper. You might redesign it to extend its life.

EXPERIMENT CONSTANTLY

But sooner or later you are going to have to dump it, and the time to dump it is while it is still fairly popular, but definitely slipping.

The ideal method of handling your advertising is to have five or six things cooking at the same time. You may have one ad that's running in the local newspaper, another in the shopper, a third on the radio and a fourth going out in direct mail. All of them take a different approach to your basic theme.

This is a good method, but it's expensive. You will probably have to settle for experimenting in one medium at a time.

You can control your costs by using tests. If you do a direct mail ad, limit your mailing to, say, 1,000 pieces. This will let you know what sort of a response to expect. In the same way, if you want to use a new newspaper ad, try it out on a fairly small scale and see how it does.

Experimentation is important because it is the only way you can find out what your market is like. No two markets are ever exactly the same. This is a fact of life that large advertisers have to ignore. There is no way they can tailor their advertising for every neighborhood they operate in. You, on the other hand, can. This means you can make your advertising more effective than theirs.

This is fine, but in order to find out the characteristics of your market, you need to experiement. You need to find out what works and what doesn't.

DON'T BE AFRAID TO FAIL

Even the biggest companies make mistakes. Remember yours and keep track of them. A failed promotion may not produce the customers this time around, but it will help you know what will bring them in on the next round.

NEWS MEDIA AND PUBLIC RELATIONS

Putting together successful promotions means dealing with the news media. This is a very different proposition from buying advertising. The reporters and editors you need to deal with to get the free publicity that will help you put your promotion over, are not the same kind of people as the salespeople you buy your space from. In fact, you might want to think of them as representing entirely different organizations, because in large part they do.

THE BIG ADVERTISER MYTH

Let's dispel one piece of fiction right now. That is that all you have to do to get anything you want out of a newspaper or radio station is to advertise heavily with them.

Not only isn't it true, you can ruin your chances of getting anything out of the news departments if you approach them that way.

The amount of advertising you do with a paper or radio station does have an influence on how they view you, but it's an indirect influence in most cases. You can get the same sort of consideration in a variety of other ways that are much less expensive.

The newsroom and the advertising department are usually separate from one another in any but the smallest operations. Your contacts in one won't do much more than get you an introduction in the other.

What's more, there's a certain amount of antagonism between news and advertising in even the best-run operation. Having your friend, the ad salesman, introduce you to the news editor may not do anything but raise hackles.

The basic problem is that the people on the inside heavily resent the implication that they can be bought by a lot of advertising. If you're a big advertiser, things will go much smoother if you are careful not to give the impression you expect favors from the news side.

THE CARE AND FEEDING OF NEWSPEOPLE

The first thing you need is a contact on the news side, preferably someone who can do you a lot of good.

Who this might be will vary from paper to paper, depending in part on the size of the operation and the sort of material you want to plant. Usually a working reporter is better than an editor. The editor may make the assignments, but the reporters carry them out, and often suggest assignments of their own. If you're cozy with a reporter, it's easier to get him or her to give you a good write-up and argue it past the editor than it is for the editor to assign what is basically a puff piece to a reporter and have it come back as a good story. Reporters hate puff pieces unless they are the ones who suggested them to the editor.

It's not difficult to make friends with a reporter. They tend to be gregarious by nature and all over town by occupation.

On a highly departmentalized paper or radio station you should try to get someone on a general news beat or a feature assignment beat. Most of what you want to plant will fall into those categories.

One way to keep your contact on the newspaper happy is to feed him bits of information about news that you happen to run across. You'll quickly get a feel for what he is interested in and be able to develop a nice symbiotic relationship with him.

USING YOUR CONTACT

The important thing about using a contact on the local paper or station is to use him sparingly. Don't expect him to handle everything you want to get in. If you do, he'll soon get tired of you.

Plan on submitting press releases in the standard fashion on things like new employees, promotions, new product lines and similar happenings. Save your contact for the larger stuff, things that have an element of news value to them.

Give your contact as much warning as possible before springing something. It's considered very bad form to call him up at the last minute and ask him to come down to see what you've got. In fact, it's an excellent way to get ignored. To get maximum coverage, you may have to work your demonstration or whatever around his schedule. If you plan things with lots of advance warning, you minimize problems in this area.

Try to get your contact interested in what you're doing rather than just as news. If your contact finds the event intrinsically interesting, he'll be willing to push it to his editor.

MAKING UP A PRESS RELEASE

When you don't want to use your contact, you will need a press release to tell your story. This doesn't have to be anything fancy, but it should be written out with first things first.

The release should be typed and should have a name and telephone number somewhere to act as a further contact in case the paper or station wants more information. Handwritten releases are harder to read, and some editors and reporter won't bother with them.

If you are combining something that has already happened and something that will happen in the same release, lead with the future event.

Remember, you can only be sure of having the first one or two sentences read, so tell your story in those sentences. Then build on them in the body of the release.

Keep the release short. Unless it's a really polished job, you should never run more than two pages. One is better.

Get the release typed double-spaced on one side of the paper only. Make sure the ribbon is new enough to be easily legible.

Allow plenty of lead between the release and the event. A week is a good minimum and you may want to give even more time.

NEWS AND FREE ADVERTISING

Most editors hate free advertising. They are taught in journalism school that the place for advertising is in the commercial breaks or with the other paid ads, and they don't like to feel they are giving something away that they should be selling.

Since you're running a business and since what you're doing will obviously promote the business, you can expect the editors to look on your promotional events with a jaundiced eye. You're going to have to be prepared for this and know how to counter it.

The basic way to counter it is to have something that is also newsworthy. That is a slippery term, but for our purposes a rough definition would be something that is either: so unusual the editor feels compelled to run something about it anyway; or a cause so worthy he doesn't want to ignore it.

This is one of the basic rules of the game, and you simply have to be prepared for it. A lot of people don't understand this prejudice and get very upset when they cannot get publicity for their promotion because it looks like free advertising to the editor.

It's worthwhile to find out how the editors you have to deal with feel about this, and to plan your promotions with their prejudices in mind. Editors will vary tremendously on this point. Some have nothing at all against free advertising and others will do just about anything to avoid it.

If your local shopper runs news, it can be a good place to put promotions you can't get in anywhere else. Shoppers are often very lenient on free advertising.

PHOTOGRAPHS

Sometimes what you really need is a picture to run in the paper. If you do the work right, you may be able to get it.

However, unless your promotion is something very special, chances are that you won't. You can ask, but newspaper photographers are kept hopping and it's probable that one won't be available.

The obvious alternative is to provide your own picture. This can be done fairly easily. You might want to take it yourself, or you might get someone to do it for you.

There are a lot of freelance photographers around who are willing to take pictures for you for a few dollars a print. Get one who has his own darkroom and can make enlarged prints for you.

Newspapers almost never use color, and they don't like Polaroids because they cause reproduction problems. Also, stay away from cartridge-loading cameras of the instamatic type. The lenses in some of them are so poor they won't produce acceptable quality pictures.

If you are going to provide photographs, it's a good idea to check with the reporter or editor to see what they want. If they think the idea is particularly good, they may want you to bring the undeveloped film over for them to develop and use. Most of the time, they'll want to see the prints.

Try to find a photographer who knows what newspapers want in their pictures and can give it to you. Pictures that look perfectly good to you will often be rejected by the newspaper as being too dull. The journalism class of the local high school is a good place to go looking for photographers.

DEADLINES

Deadlines are an area where you can help yourself or hang yourself with no trouble at all. A news-gathering operation runs on a very definite schedule and anything that disrupts that schedule—other than major news events—gets brushed aside. That includes you, if you show up at the wrong time.

The first thing to do is find out when each of the newspapers in your area goes to press and what their deadlines are. Do the same thing for the radio and TV stations.

Generally, the closer you get to the deadline, the less time anyone on the operation is going to have for you. The best time to catch people is at the beginning of the cycle, and after the deadline has passed.

If your local newspaper is published in the afternoon, it will probably have a deadline right around noon. The reporters will go to lunch shortly after noon, and the editor will eat lunch after the pages have been put together—between 1:30 and 2:00 p.m. usually.

You can expect that from 10 a.m. on, everyone is going to be so busy, there won't be much time for you. If you need to talk to a reporter that day, try to catch him in the morning or when he comes back after lunch. The editor is the same way, but remember, he may go to lunch much later.

On a morning paper the press run is typically somewhere around midnight, and the deadline is 10 p.m. or so. Most reporters don't arrive at their desks until some time in the afternoon, although they may be busy in the morning collecting material.

Radio and television will vary greatly depending on how big the news staff is and how the operation is run. But here again, the rule is, the closer you get to deadline, the less time the reporters and editors will have for you.

YOUR MEDIA LIST

You need one other thing before you launch your media promotion campaign. That's a media list telling you what you're going to send where.

A media list is a list of all the newspapers, publications and radio stations in your area that may be able to do you some good. It should include the name of the person the press release or photographs should go too, and information on deadlines, etc. If you know something about the people who work in the newsroom, note that too. If a reporter on a paper is interested in flying, he's a natural contact if your promotion involves airplanes.

This information would be easy to keep if you possess a data base. A data base allows you to file the same information under a number of different headings. That way, you can designate such headings as subject, morning, evening, contact name, media, etc. Under each heading, you can then input complete information about each contact, where to call, name of paper or station, etc.

The list you compile is your basic tool when sending out press releases and deciding who to contact with what stories. Often, if a promotion doesn't appeal to one reporter or editor, it will appeal to another. But your batting average will go way up if you know who is partial to what.

If your promotion is clever and well-done, you may reach beyond your immediate goal. Every day the wire services move several hundred photographs and stories to newspapers all over the country. If a photo of your promotion is good enough and has enough human interest, it may make papers all over the country.

DISPLAY ADVERTISING AND HOW TO USE IT

Display advertising is probably the kind most frequently used by small business. This isn't a bad thing, since it offers a number of advantages. However, it is also the most frequently misused kind, and that is bad.

The first problem with display advertising is that it's so seductively easy to make up an ad. Supposedly, all you have to do is write down what you want to say and there's your message. If you have an understanding of how display advertising functions, you may have written a good ad. Since most people don't, they don't produce good ads.

The second problem is that display space is sold in very small blocks—too small to do anyone any good under most circumstances. But many people will buy only one of those blocks, or divide the space they have bought into a lot of blocks that are too small.

The unit of figuring display space is the column inch. This is an area one inch high and one column wide. Just how big that is in square inches will vary, depending on how many columns there are on each page.

Try an experiment. Take a ruler, a page from your newspaper, and a crayon or felt-tipped pen. Then mark out a space one column wide and one inch high. Not very big, is it?

A one-column-inch ad is going to get lost on any page. Yet there are a lot of people who think that putting in several one-inch ads is "advertising in the newspapers or magazines."

ART

Any illustrations, photos, etc. that go into an ad are known as "art." On some newspapers there is an additional charge for art work because of the extra steps involved. Others make no charge for it.

Generally, if you are going to use art of some sort, you will need a larger ad. Even a small illustration fills up a four-inch ad and doesn't leave much room for copy (your words).

You also need to exercise some care in choosing what you are going to reproduce. Photographs and other illustrations will usually have to be reduced to fit into your ad. Reduction tends to make art work appear darker and more crowded. You need good, clear originals to work from if you don't want to end up with a blob. If you have any doubts on this point, ask to see the reduced illustration before the ad is made up.

Most newspapers will have books of line drawings of almost anything you can imagine. The books, called "clip art books," will include all sorts of drawings of products, borders, seasonal and holiday symbols and other useful illustrations for ads. Check with the sales rep to see what is available.

LOGOS

A logo (short for logotype) is a visual symbol for your business. Most big businesses have them; most small businesses should too. A logo is a kind of visual shorthand that tells people it's you they are dealing with. It identifies your business. A well done one that is carried throughout your advertising will help build recognition.

If you have a logo, you should use it in your ads. Often it will be the only piece of art you will need.

In some cases, you can make a very effective ad just by using your logo and perhaps one line of additional copy with your address.

You will have to supply the logo for the display ads. The simplest way to do this is to have a printer reproduce it for you several times in different sizes. This is usually done by means of a special, very large camera most printers have. It shouldn't cost more than four or five dollars for each reproduction. You don't need many.

An offset newspaper can reproduce anything it can take a picture of. This has led some advertisers to cut out copies of their ads from one publication to use in others. Since the cost of putting the ad together is usually included in the cost of a newspaper ad, this has upset some publishers.

The publishers have begun fighting back by copyrighting the ads that appear in their publications. This doesn't actually prevent you from using the same design elsewhere, especially if you specified what you wanted in the ad, how it was to be arranged, the type faces, etc. What it does prevent is clipping an ad from one paper and having another paper copy it to use.

Check to see if the publication you are dealing with copyrights its ads, and stay out of trouble by not asking anyone to reproduce a copyrighted ad.

DISPLAY ADVERTISING SALESPEOPLE

Display ad salespeople are hired for their ability to sell advertising. This is worth noting because circumstances also often make them art directors for the people they sell advertising to as well. An ad sales rep may or may not be artistically talented enough to do a good job in designing ads. A lot of the time he won't even be sure of what his publication can or cannot do in the way of reproduction. It takes a brave one to prevent a customer from producing an ad that is so poorly designed it will actually hurt.

This is one area where you can't always depend on the other person knowing his business. Actually, his business is selling you advertising, not designing ads. He will usually be willing to help you in your design efforts but don't count on him being able to do a good job in this respect.

By the same token, ad sales reps are not advertising counselors. Asking one how often an ad should run or what to say in an ad will probably not give you an expert opinion, and it certainly won't give you an unbiased one.

With the exception of classified advertising (which we'll come to a little later) a one-inch ad is useless. Actually, it's worse than useless, since it costs you money for no results.

The minimum size for any ad ought to be four times that. You can arrange that space as either one column four inches deep or two columns two inches deep, but never try to use an ad smaller than that.

OVERCROWDING

A related mistake is to try to put too much into your ad. A crowded ad gets lost in itself. Don't try to put everything in the ad just because you think you have space. The truth is, you don't have space, unless you've taken a full page ad in a regular-size newspaper or other publication.

Keep your message simple and put it in large type if you've got space you don't need.

Never put type in your ad smaller than the body type of the publication. This will usually be between eight and 10 points in a newspaper. (A point is a seventy-second of an inch.) Ten-point type is a good minimum size.

However, don't use the same kind of type the newspaper uses for news. If you do that, it's easier for your ad to get lost. There are many different styles of type and the advertising sales rep will probably have a portfolio of typefaces (styles) for you to look at. Pick something that is different from the body type, but not too hard to read. Ask the sales rep for advice on this point if you're not sure.

CLASSIFIED ADS

Classified advertising is the most profitable part of a newspaper for the publisher. That should tell you something about the rates you're charged to advertise there.

Classified advertising can also pay big dividends to you as a user if you use it right. It is not the same as display advertising at all. Strategies for classifieds are very different.

WHO READS CLASSIFIED ADS

At one time or another almost everyone reads classified advertising. Some people read it every day, some people only when they are looking for something to buy.

There is the first difference between regular ads and classified ads. The person who is reading the display ads in a newspaper may not be interested in them at all. For him they may just be something that fills in the space between the baseball scores and

"Dear Abby." Even if he is interested, he may not be in the mood to buy something. A classified ad reader is interested in the advertising. If he wasn't, he would not be looking in that part of the newspaper. Typically, he is also just about half convinced to buy something. If he is thumbing through the classifieds, he is in a buying mood—a prime prospect, in other words.

GRAB 'EM

The big problem in using classifieds effectively is that you have to make your ad stand out from the hundreds of others on the page. Since you can't use different type or illustrations (at least not in most places), you have to use ingenuity.

In most cases the first word of the ad will be set in capitals. This should be your key word, the one that will do most of your selling.

Your key word often isn't what you think. If you were selling a house, for example, your ad would appear under the proper classification. If it's a house, you don't want to start with the word "HOUSE." The reader already knows the items under the "Houses for Sale" heading are houses, and you would have wasted your key word.

Instead, pick out the best feature and sell it. "FIREPLACE" or "SWIMMING POOL" is a good lead for a house ad.

GIVE 'EM A BARGAIN

Classified readers are very bargain-conscious. Try to give the impression that you are offering a bargain in what you're selling. Don't tell them you're giving them a bargain; that wastes words. Just offer a service or item at an exceptionally low price.

Car dealers are the masters of this technique. A lot of automobile ads will feature one or two vehicles at very low prices. The cars may be in bad mechanical condition, but the low price acts to draw people onto the lot.

This isn't even particularly dishonest. Most people are very realistic about expecting to get what they pay for. But they also know that someone else's junk might be their treasure.

DON'T GET CUTE

One of the biggest problems with classifieds right now is that many of the businesses that use them are suffering from a bad case of the "cuties". In their search for attention-grabbers, businesses have run ads with all sorts of weird heads. Right now real estate offices are the worst offenders. If you look at the "House for Sale" section you'll see that half the headings have no relation to the houses. In fact, at least one book has been published of nothing but cute lead-ins for real estate ads.

All these things violate the first principle of writing a good grabber. It has to be related to what follows.

The classic examples of violating this rule are the ads headed "SEX" in big letters, that start into a pitch that has nothing to do with sex at all. The readers look at the head and read the first few words of the copy. When they find out there is no relation between the two, they stopped reading, feeling as if they have been tricked and annoyed by it.

This is what happens with most "cutsie" heads. You not only don't get your message read, you create hostility in the reader.

PICKING YOUR NEWSPAPER

Most American towns and cities have only one, or at most two, major newspapers. Most people assume that if they are going to advertise in a newspaper, they will advertise in the major newspaper.

This doesn't have to be true, and sometimes it is not a good idea. If you look in the phone book of most medium-sized cities you will find a number of newspaper listed, more than you probably imagined.

Some of these will be shoppers, which we talk about in the next chapter. Others will be foreign language newspapers serving a specific ethnic community. Those you will probably want to ignore, unless the ethnic group represents a major market for you. A few of the others will be fading weeklies of only a few hundred circulation. At least one will probably be a legal newspaper read only by lawyers and business people. For some businesses, this will be a good place to advertise. It all depends on who your service is geared for.

But even after you finish eliminating all the obvious non-possibilities, you will still find at least one or two that represent viable alternatives. They may be weeklies or small dailies that serve suburban communities surrounding the city. Or, they may serve only part of the city itself.

If your potential customers come from an area served by one of these smaller newspapers, you may find you want to do a significant amount of your advertising there.

WHY A SMALL PAPER?

The major reason for using a small newspaper is cost. A major daily will give you a good cost-per-thousand figure, but in absolute terms the cost is going to be higher than the smaller paper.

This is partially due to a deliberate pricing strategy on the part of the small paper. The big daily puts a ceiling on what the small paper can charge for advertising.

Another important reason for using a small paper is the ability to target your market. If the area you get your customers from is about the same as the newspaper's circulation area, you know that your advertising is going where it will do you the most good. This can be especially important if you are using a heavy loss leader offering of some sort. With the small paper you know all your coupons are going into the area where your customers will come from. You won't have people from miles away stopping in to take advantage of your special and then never coming back.

Of course, there may be times when you will want to blanket the circulation area, and in those cases you will want the bigger paper. You need to weigh these considerations carefully before choosing your medium.

SHOPPERS

A shopper isn't exactly a newspaper. And from the standpoint of promotions, that's its biggest asset.

Shoppers are publications that look something like newspapers. They are printed once or twice a week and distributed free. They are mostly advertising with little or no editorial matter and a lot of classified ads. Regular newspapers hate them because they drain off advertising revenue. A lot of smart business people have come to love them, and you might too.

ADVERTISING ON THE CHEAP

One of the biggest attractions of a shopper is that it's a cheap medium to advertise in. Shoppers are strictly a low overhead medium. They don't have the big news staffs and big budgets of a regular newspaper. To pick up more customers, they pass their savings along to the people who buy advertising.

Another factor that holds the lid on the prices of ads in shoppers is the lack of national advertising. Shoppers do not have their circulation checked the way a regular newspaper does, so they can't prove how many copies are actually read. This means that national advertisers won't touch them. It also means their rates stay low.

Advertising rates are usually figured on the basis of how many people the advertiser will reach with his message. If there is no reliable way of knowing that, advertising rates practically have to stay low.

THE READY-TO-BUY AUDIENCE

It's true that there's no way of proving how many people actually read shoppers, but the very nature of the medium suggests that the ones who do are a good potential market.

Most shoppers are almost all classified ads. When you buy space in a shopper you will be aiming at a group of people who are more akin to your typical classified ad reader — ready to spend money and interested in a bargain.

You're not going to sell many Cadillacs to these people, but you might do a booming business in used Volkswagens.

On strictly readership terms, shoppers do not stack up well at all. In terms of readership by people who are in the mood to buy, they do very well indeed.

ADVERTISING TO TARGETS

In a large metropolitan area, shoppers can be a godsend. In all but the smallest communities there will be several editions of the shopper, each one covering a particular area. This lets you select the area you want to cover at a minimum cost.

It also lets you find out just where you are getting your business from. You can run slightly different promotions in two different shopper editions and see what the results are. If you are trying to draw business from all over the city, you can also use a rolling promotion. That is, you run your promotion in a different edition each week until you have covered the whole area.

PRESS RELEASES AND SHOPPERS

Another way to make good use of a shopper is for your press releases and other news-type announcements. Shoppers that use "news" at all will often bite on material that everyone else throws away.

Shoppers are not newspapers, and they are almost never edited to newspaper standards. The amount of space for news of any sort is limited and the amount of time and effort allowed to gather it and write it up is even more limited. If you present your release in ready-to-go form, the chances that the shopper will decide to pick it up are excellent.

Since shoppers have large circulations, and since many times the news content won't be changed even when the ads are, this can be a very effective way of reaching a lot of people.

Given the nature of shoppers, you cannot expect the staff to do any of the work for you. You have to have your material to them in good time, and you have to have it in a form they can use. Asking a shopper to send a photographer to cover something is wasted effort. However, if you are aware of their deadlines and make everything easy for them, you have a good chance of having the shopper staff pick up your item.

WRITING ADS FOR SHOPPERS

Most shoppers will take display ads as well as classifieds. Their rates will not be as high as for newspaper ads, but you probably won't get near the help you get from a newspaper advertising salesperson. Also, you will usually find the quality of reproduction is not as good.

If you choose to use display advertising in a shopper, you should remember that the people you are aiming at are the same sort of people you would aim a classified ad at. Your copy has to be written accordingly.

Whether classified or display ads, stress bargains. Try to have at least one outstanding deal you can put in each ad. The people you will be reaching will be very price-conscious, so you should be too.

Make your ads short and punchy. If you use classifieds, keep the ad under five lines long. Make maximum use of that first capitalized word.

If you use display ads, you still need to make them at least four column inches. Since most shoppers are tabloid size (half a regular newspaper page) or magazine size (one quarter of a regular newspaper page) your four-inch ad will get even more punch than it would in a regular newspaper.

Don't feel you have to stick to either display ads or classifieds. Switch them around depending on circumstances. You also might want to use three or four classifieds instead of one display ad. In a regular newspaper this is very poor technique, but in a shopper it can work very well. The reason is that a person who opens a shopper is going to read the classified ads whereas a person who opens a newspaper probably won't. If the shopper is thick (48 pages or more in an issue), then several classifieds will probably do the job better than one display ad since there is a larger likelihood that one of them will be encountered and read.

DIRECT MAIL TARGETS YOUR MARKET

Direct mail can be a very effective method of marketing most of the businesses in this book. What is direct mail? Well, it can be in the form of a letter or brochure or even disply ad. What makes it effective is that you include some method whereby your customer contacts you for more information about the product or service, whether by mail-in coupon or by phone.

Either way, you have a technique in which you are able to measure the effectiveness of your direct mail piece. In other words, you can count the number of coupons or phone calls you receive from a particular letter, brochure or ad.

DEVELOP A CUSTOMER PROFILE

Who is going to be interested in this offer you are planning to make? Will they be men or women, young or old, rich or poor, city, suburban or rural dwellers, highly educated or dropouts, etc.? In short, you want a "make sheet" on your prospect. You want to get to know him or her, to put that faceless future customer into terms you can understand. You'll want to put clothes on him, put him in a home or office, in his car, provide him with a family, a job and hobbies. You want to make him a living breathing person in your mind's eye. To put a face on him, use the features of someone similar you know or have met. And, presto! You have someone to aim at.

WRITE YOUR TARGET A LETTER

The first step in building your advertising plans is to write your target a letter about your product or service. Don't try to make it a structured sales letter. Just make it a long letter, like you would write a friend, telling everything you can think about the product. Be positive and honest. Go into as much detail as needed to get your point across. Stress all the benefits it will bring to your friend. This letter is going to be the raw material for your advertising and promotion efforts, so keep adding to it as thoughts occur.

WORKING WITH WORDS

Copywriting is carpentry with words. The words are the materials you use to construct a complete message that motivates the reader to a specific course of action.

There are three kinds of words that the copywriter has to build with. Action words (verbs) are the strength and positive tone words. Picture words (nouns) create vivid impressions in the reader's mind. Expander words (adjectives) are words that make the nouns come alive for the reader. The action words give movement and power to the phrases.

The action word is the key to the desires of the reader. Start, grow, learn, enjoy, win— are all things that describe desires. Pick the primary desire of your composite target, and use the appropriate action word at will get attention.

The picture words—business, roses, music—create pictures in the mind of the reader. To make those pictures more specific and desirable, you use expanders—beautiful roses, successful business, etc.

These three types of words are your ad copy builders, and you can use them in an almost unlimited combination of ways to create a positive reaction from your prospect.

WRITING YOUR COPY

One important thing to always remember is that the first 10 words of your copy are probably a great deal more important than the next 1,000. The reason is, if the first 10 words don't attract and hold the reader's attention, the next 1,000 are not going to be read. So, your first words and first paragraph must be carefully thought out, and written in such a fashion that it immediately "hooks" the reader's attention, and assures he will read further into the copy.

The narrative hook is a familiar device used by successful short story writers. It is the first paragraph that gets the reader involved enough to read the story:

> Kelly was grinning. His blue eyes winked merrily as he raised the gun slowly, aimed carefully, and shot me dead. Or so he thought.

That is the opening for a short mystery story. It immediately hooks the reader's curiosity and interest, and assures that he is going to go farther into the story. The short story is the hardest kind to write, because in 1,000 to 1,500 words it must establish character, conflict and conclusion—just like a novel that may run 50,000 words or more.

A direct mail letter is a short story with the title (your headline), a narrative hook (your opening paragraph), the story theme (your convincers), and a logical end (having the customer act on your offer).

FORMULA COPYWRITING

If you buy books on copywriting, you will almost invariably find a list of formulas, checklists or other mechanical methods of creating copy. In general, these are contrived gimmicks, used by people who have written successful sales letters, but that in reality have little value to someone setting out to write their own copy. By keeping in mind the short story formula, you will have the building blocks for writing a successful direct mail letter.

THE HEADING

If you have written that long letter about your product or service, you will find the substance for your headline in it. Look for the strong, positive benefit statements in it. The headline is the eye-catcher that will make your reader continue reading into the body of the copy.

Benefit statements include: "Increase your business by 40 percent," "Save yourself two days of work every month," or "Reduce production down-time."

These tell the reader how he will benefit directly by using your product or service.

THE HOOK

Once you have your headline written, your next most important and carefully planned step is to develop your hook. This is where you appeal to the reader's self interest, solve a problem, arouse curiosity, involve the reader instantly in the message.

The hook must arouse the reader's immediate empathy and self-interest in the first paragraph. Always lead with your ace. The strongest selling point about the product or service you offer should be the one featured in the hook paragraph. The greatest hook that you can develop is personal involvement.

NEWSLETTER

A newsletter customer drive might benefit by using your computer to insert personal names into the letters mailed out to potential subscribers. It might open like this: "It is a painful fact that the cost of living in Reno has gone up 20 percent in the last 10 years." That is the headline. This is the hook: "What that means to you, Mr. Jones, is that you have to be several times more astute in managing your affairs." This copy is particularly powerful, but by putting the potential subscriber's name and town in the letter, you involve him instantly in what you have to say, as well as in what you have to sell.

Keep in mind one very important psychological fact when you are writing advertising copy. People do not work for financial gain per se. They work for approval from their family, friends and neighbors. Money is the way they keep score, and the things money will buy is the object of it all.

When writing your letters, keep this "psychic income" very much in mind, as it has tremendous persuasive power.

Create the idea that you are selling something that winners use, and you will have an instant market.

Here are some benefit ideas to help you develop a hook paragraph:

.

1. Use time better
2. Get better job
3. Make more money
4. Save more money
5. Eliminate worry
6. Avoid embarrassment
7. More comfort
8. Better health
9. Personal popularity
10. Self confidence
11. Advancement
12. Security
13. Happiness
14. Personal power
15. Be up to date
16. Be a leader
17. Be creative
18. Resist domination
19. Become famous
20. Sex appeal

These are not all of them, but they are 20 pegs on which you can hang a hook to get readers involved in your copy.

Now, let's examine some successful narrative hooks that have been used in the past, to give you an idea and a feel of how they are written. Here is one that is a paraphrase on an opening paragraph used by one of the best-known magazines in the country in it's circulation solicitation letter.

> I don't know you personally, but I'll tell you this, the source of your name makes me know you are a very rare person in this America of ours.

This bit of flattery has made this letter one of the best pulling subscription letters ever written.

Too many copywriters insult instead of flatter in their openings. They set up an instant negative reaction in the reader. One example is:

> Do you know you are losing money by using antiquated (equipment, ideas, systems, etc.)

The reaction to this is, "Who in the hell are you to tell me I am using antiquated anything?" You are challenging the judgment of the individual using the equipment or process or whatever you are talking about. He purchased it, and he is using it, and he may not even like it, but he doesn't want anyone to tell him that he is a dummy.

Avoid negative approaches at all costs. Always be positive and always get the reader involved in a positive way in your opening paragraph.

THE CONVINCERS!

Now, assuming you have the attention-grabbing headline, and the good narrative hook to arouse instant reader curiosity and attention, you are ready to get down to the nitty-gritty of selling the product or service. This will be a series of convincers that create a positive reaction in the reader, taking him logically through the copy down to the point where you can ask him to send the order.

What you will want to include in the copy is to tell him what it is going to do for him, how it is going to do it for him, why it will do it for him, when it will do it for him, who it has been done for in the past, (this is where you include testimonials), and finally, tell him that now is the time to act.

There is one simple way to do this, and that is to make a list of all the reasons that people will not buy your product. Here is an example of such list:

1. Too expensive
2. Sounds too cheap
3. I'll wait awhile
4. I'll shop around
5. Buying by mail is too risky
6. What I have now is just as good
7. Takes too long to get here
8. I'll buy it at the local store
9. I don't really need it

If you build your letter properly, you can supply rebuttals to each of these reasons as you go through your copy. For example, let's take the "too expensive" reason for not buying. Here is a type of paragraph you might use in your copy to overcome that bit of resistance:

> The old saying: "You get what you pay for" has never been more true. Just think. You get (list the benefits) and an unqualified 100 percent guarantee. If you are not satisfied for any reason we will cheerfully refund your entire purchase price. Order today!.

SOME COPY TRICKS

There are some professional tricks to writing copy that keep it flowing, interesting and easy to read and understand.

The first thing is to keep your sentences short. If you have long sentences, try writing in the plural. You will find that by writing in the plural, you will use shorter sentences.

Another device that gives the copy flow is to use connectors in your pargraphs. These lead logically from one paragraph to the next and keep the reader interested in continuing. Here is a list of a few of them:

1. But that's not all
2. Now here is the most important part
3. And in addition
4. Better yet
5. You will understand why
6. More important than that
7. What is more
8. And one more thing
9. Now, for a limited time only

These connectors make a bucket brigade out of your copy, connecting one paragraph to the next, and swing the reader evenly onto the next thought.

When you have finished writing your copy, read it out loud. This is the quickest way to discover how readers will react to it.

Out of every 100 words, you should have 70 to 80 that are only one syllable long, or you are not using the proper words in your copy.

Another item to check is the number of "that's" you have in the letter. Eliminate as many as possible without losing the sense of the copy.

At the end of each body of copy you write, you should try to summarize the advantages you have outlined.

ASK FOR THE ORDER

The final piece of copy you write should state specifically what you want the reader to do. You want him to write a check, fill out the coupon, send the money, and you want him to do it now.

Don't beat around the bush, and don't use weak words like "I trust you," I hope you will," etc. Put in concrete terms exactly what you want him to do, such as "Write your check now and send it along with the coupon."

TESTIMONIALS

The use of testimonials is one of the strongest convincers you can use in writing copy. In every ad where you are asking for an order, you should try to work in some testimonials. You can either work them in throughout the copy, or use a separate box or space in the ad.

KEYING YOUR ADS

Keying is a very important function. It is a system that lets you know which publication is doing the best job for you by inserting a key number or code in the address in the ad. Each time an envelope arrives, by glancing at the address you can tell which key publication produced the inquiry or order.

The common way to key is to insert a number or letter series after the address. For example, in "Box 1234-A," the A is the key that identifies the source of any mail coming in from that ad. Another method is to use intials in your name: "J. J. Jones" for the first publication, "J. L . Jones" for the second and soon.

PROJECTING RETURNS

When you begin getting inquiries or orders from an ad, you can make a fairly accurate projection within a couple of weeks as to how many returns you will get, if you know how the magazines are circulated. The two forms of circulations are: subscription sent by mail, and newstand sales. If the publication is primarily circulation to paid subscribers, then all subscribers receive it at about the same time, and results will start and build rapidly. If the publication is primarily newsstand, then you have to allow time for the copies to be sold and read. This takes longer.

Taking your returns from the first day of either type of publication, you can project them like this: for a monthly magazine, your first week will produce six to 10 percent of the total returns within seven days after you receive the first order. By the end of the second week, 20 to 25 percent will be in, and the first month will produce just about half of the orders you will finally get. The other 50 percent will stretch out over a period of months, and in many cases you will still get returns two years later. But, by the sixth month after the ad ran, you'll have well over 90 percent of everything you are going to get.

Of course, these are not ironclad figures that work every single time. They will have some wide variations, but over a period of time they will pretty well average out at about these figures.

TELEPHONE SELLING

The opportunities of going into a business with a telphone as a sales method are many, and some are tremendously profitable.

The telephone sales method can reach almost anyone, anywhere, given the proper approach. This makes it much more effective, systematic type of sales for businesses.

DEVELOPING A SALES PITCH

The key to success or failure of any phone selling or survey program is in the "pitch" or sales talk that is used.

The best pitch is short and uses easily understandable terms with strong appeal to a basic human emotion. For example, "I love you. Will you marry me?" is a perfect example of such a pitch. In essense, all selling pitches are based on this theme.

The best telephone sales programs are not really selling at all, in the classic sense of the term. They are rather quick (Buddy can you spare a dime?) pitches designed to get a yes or no answer. The best telephone deal is a percentage game that will close a given number of orders per call list.

The key to the quick pitch is to give a logical reason why the prospect should buy, and ask for the order.

If you try to develop an intricate sales pitch that involves a long explanation of what is offered, then try to overcome the ensuing objections. Give the prospect alternate choices. If it takes over 20 to 30 seconds to reach the point where the order is asked for, you are in trouble.

OPEN UP WITH A GRABBER

The selling pitch should open up with an attention grabber. "Hello, how are you?" won't get it done. You have, at best, about 10 to 20 seconds of full attention from the person called. And to assure that you retain it, the opening line should grab and hold that needed attention.

Telephone selling is like chess in that respect—a strong opening is 75 percent of the game. Thus, if you were selling an office service, your grabber might be: "Good morning, sir. Our computer just discovered you were overcharged by 30 percent on your bookkeeping last year."

This has to arouse the interest of a business person long enough to get to the sales pitch.

Your opener, then, should be like a headline in the newspaper. It grabs the reader's attention long enough to get him to read or listen to the remainder of the pitch. The telephone caller should deliver the opening line in a strong, emphatic tone of voice, giving it a news quality.

THE WHO AND THE WHAT

The next lines of the pitch should give the party called the information about who is calling, whom they represent, and the purpose of the call.

For example, "This is John White with ABC Computerized Bookkeeping, and we feel every business person should know how badly he's being overcharged for payroll preparation. If you use an average amount each year, our computer checkout shows your overpayments amount to $543.49. I think you'll agree that this money would look better on your bottom line than on that of your present supplier."

At this point, you have the full attention of the person called. The best strategy to use at this point is to bring the potential customer into the pitch with a question that requires an affirmative answer. Getting the participation of the person called assures he will continue to pay attention.

In this case of the business person, the caller can ask what kind of bookkeeping system he uses. In the case of failure of the prospect to respond at this point, a demand for an answer could go like this: "is there any reason why you would not be interested in saving (amount of money quoted)?"

This question demands involvement and will get an "of course not" 95 percent of the time.

Always try to frame questions so that the answer is positive in terms of the offer to be made. People who, in effect, say yes once are more likely to say it again.

The total pitch takes only seconds. The pressure to buy is set up at once, and even a complicated subject like bookkeeping is handled quickly and simply. This type of pitch will have a high closing rate.

You can follow this type of formula when putting together your own phone selling pitches.

1. A grabber for the opening line
2. An introduction of the caller and a reinforcement of the opening line
3. A participation question to bring the person called into the pitch
4. Absolute proof of savings and a strong guarantee
5. A call to close

The pitch must be short, concise and believable. The key is to step it up so that there can be a minimum of objections and an easy decision. Any pitch that requires the phone people to high pressure the person called into an order will flounder quickly.

KEEP COMING BACK

The pitch is the business. It makes or breaks the deal, and you should spend all the time necessary developing it. Work out two or three variations of your pitch and test them in actual selling. Also remember this: there are no absolute rules in selling. You may be able to break any or all of them and make money. Never work inside boundaries that are simply arbitrary.

Try new things, even things that others say are impossible. If they think they are impossible, they won't be using them, and you may find a gold mine.

PITCH CHECKLIST

1. Use a grabber line
2. Identify yourself and your company
3. Reinforce your grabber line with a logical statement

4. Get an affirmative answer to a question
5. Get an absolute proof statement of advantage of your product or service to person called
6. Have a strong guarantee
7. Ask a buying question
8. Close
9. Objections—close again by asking buying question

YOUR MASTER FILE

Your master file is the source of your call sheets. You can put it on your computer and have call sheets printed out from it.

The file, at the start, will be just a collection of telephone numbers and names. But, as business develops, you will be able to add more pertinent information to each computer segment. This will include any additional information you can get, such as family names, other business names, things they purchased, things they turned down, how much paid, etc. As the file grows, you will be able to pull names of people or business firms who are known buyers of the kind of deal you are working on. This will enable you to start with a lot of fast sales, creating an immediate cash flow.

One item you should keep track of is the best calling time for each customer.

Here is a list of people in various fields and the best times to reach them by telephone:

Attorneys	after 3 p.m.
Clergy	not on weekends
Contractors	before 8 a.m. or after 5 p.m.
Dentists	before 9:30 a.m.
Druggists	between 1 p.m. and 3 p.m.
Executives	after 10:30 a.m.
Farmers	between 3 p.m. and 5 p.m.
Government officials	2 p.m. and 5 p.m.
Media people	between 2 and 4 p.m.
Printers	between 3 p.m. and 5 p.m.
Publishers	after 3 p.m.

Salespeople	between 9 a.m. and 11 a.m.
Secretaries	between 10 a.m. and 11 a.m.
Stockbrokers	after market closes
Merchants	after 10:30 a.m.

This file, when properly kept, can be worth many thousands of dollars and enable you to run fast, tightly controlled and highly profitable sales campaigns.

CRISS CROSS DIRECTORY

If at all possible when you start, work from a criss-cross directory. This is a directory where phone numbers are listed by street address rather than alphabetically. This enables you to contain your calls to areas where you are likely to get the best results and avoid those areas where it will largely be a waste of time.

If you don't have a criss-cross directory, get a list of prefixes from the phone company and place them in their geographical areas so you can work the best areas first.

GETTING THE DECISION MAKER

One of the major problems all phone sellers have is isolating the decision maker. This is the party who has the authority to say yes or no to the deal being offered.

In calling large companies, they are often isolated by secretaries, assistants, and the like who will fend off any selling deals. They will say something like, "put it in writing." Never call a big company asking who the boss is. (no matter what you are selling.) Instead, use this bit of vocal magic:

> This is Ms. White with the ABC Corporation, and we need specific instructions regarding the handling of your purchase orders for (service name). Please give me the name of the person who signs them for you, and his or her extension number.

If the phone worker says this in a positive, somewhat demanding tone of voice, the operator will assume that you have orders from them and are looking for some information about shipping, etc. The information will usually be given.

SECTION 6

Where and How To Get Money For Your Business will let you in on all the secrets you need to obtain your start-up capital. It will show you how to handle bankers, where to go if the banks turn you down, how to put together a solid business plan and financial statement, what to expect when obtaining a loan, and how to know when your business should start turning a profit.

SECTION SIX

BUSINESS FINANCING

GETTING THE MONEY YOU NEED

When you're in business, you're going to need money sooner or later. In fact, the chances are excellent you need it right now.

If you're in a small business, the chances are you're going to have trouble getting the money you need. You'll have to work harder and smarter to pry the financing you need out of the money sources.

Your trouble stems from two things. The first is the prejudice that most sources of money have against small businesses. The second is that one of the major differences between a small business and a big business is that the small business seldom knows how to ask for money effectively.

The prejudice against smallness in American capital markets is well known and all too well documented. The right way to ask for money is not well known. If you know how to go about getting money and where to go looking for it, you will find it is a lot easier to get than you ever imagined.

That's what this section is all about—finding and getting money.

BORROWING VS. EQUITY SALES

There are only two ways to get money for a business (aside from stealing it or having it given to you). You can borrow it and promise to pay it back later, or you can sell part of the business. A bank loan is the best known example of the first, and selling stock is a good example of the second.

In both cases the money costs you something. In the first case, that cost is called "interest." In the second case, the cost amounts to giving up part of the future profits of the business.

In addition to these so-called "direct" costs of borrowing, there are also likely to be indirect costs. For example, the bank you get your loan from is very likely to insist that you do your banking business there. They may also require that you conduct your business in a certain manner, such as not making any new inventory purchases without the bank's consent.

Equity financing also has indirect costs as well. It can cost you loss of control of the company or a reduction of your freedom to carry on the company's business. It will definitely cost you something in underwriter's fees if you decide to sell stock to the public. You will also find that you have to disclose a great deal more information about the way the company is run.

You need to be aware of these costs and think carefully about their effect on your business.

WHEN TO BORROW, WHEN TO SELL

There is a time in the life of a business when it's best to sell equity to raise capital, and there is a time when it's best to borrow. If you try to borrow when you should be selling, you'll find your difficulties enormously increased. Selling when you should be borrowing will also be more costly, and will mean giving up more of the business than you need to.

Generally speaking, a business that is just starting up will have to be financed with non-borrowed money. This means either money from you, or equity financing of some sort. As we'll see later, borrowed money is very difficult to come by when you don't have a track record.

Most lenders will not be willing to loan more than you or the other owners have invested in the business. They want to see some commitment on your part before they will advance any money.

It is possible to start a business entirely on other people's money, of course. We will discuss how to do it later in this section.

Generally, though, it will be an expensive proposition and more difficult to pull off. Consider the possibility of selling equity carefully.

WHAT KIND OF BUSINESS DO YOU HAVE, ANYWAY?

There are two different business strategies common today. Each one requires a different approach to financing. You should match your financing efforts with your game plan to get the best possible results from your efforts to raise money.

START SMALL—STAY SMALL

This is probably the most common approach in small businesses. You start a business with the idea that it will have a definite limit on its growth. Perhaps you're opening a computer school and you don't plan on having more than one school. You hope the school will expand and you hope that sales will grow, but the business is always going to be a one-unit operation.

This approach offers a lot of advantages. For one thing, by staying small you can keep a closer eye on the business and the market and you can move aggressively when you see an opportunity. Your control over the business is more direct and you can keep a tighter rein on overhead and inventory costs.

A "start small—stay small" operation probably will be pretty much a self-funding operation after you get it going. You may need trade credit and you may need short-term loans to balance out the business cycle, but you won't have to go looking for large infusions of capital. You are also likely to find that your overall start-up costs are smaller than for a business that plans to grow. Your own capital contribution becomes a bigger proportion of your capital needs.

A small business of this sort is easier to sell to small investors. Someone with a few thousand bucks is likely to be more attracted to this kind of operation because he or she can understand it. A growth-type setup often frightens small investors because they can see so many things that can go wrong. Bankers like these firms too—if they present themselves well.

START SMALL—GROW BIG

This is the opposite of a "start small—stay small" business. The idea here is to grow, grow, grow. Typically, a company like this starts with almost nothing, ploughs everything back into the business, and grows quickly. It needs large amounts of money right from the start, and as the business matures, it needs even more money. Typically, its value doubles every year or six months, and it has to scrape to meet every payroll.

These are the companies that make the big money. They also take big risks and need big capital. In fact, chronic capital problems are almost a hallmark of this sort of business.

These businesses are not favorites with bankers. They seem to be bottomless pits for capital. Worse, their ratios always look terrible because the company is growing so fast. Once these ventures get off the ground, they can usually secure bank loans, but for the first year or two the banks usually won't touch them no matter how good their sales figures are. Even when they do get bank loans, they have to coddle the banker to prevent him from getting nervous and pulling the rug out at a critical moment.

On the other hand, these companies are tailor-made for investors looking for a large capital gain. There are special firms of "venture capitalists" in this country that specialize in providing money to these fast-growing firms. In return, they get part of the action and a big profit when the company goes public or sells out.

Because these companies depend so heavily on outside capital, they must make special efforts to see that their financial statements look good. We'll discuss statement analysis and the various financial ratios later so that you'll know what lenders and investors are looking for. If you're running this kind of a company, you'll need to keep those figures before you and give them careful consideration in making business decisions. Often, the decisions that appear wrong from a strictly business point of view can turn out to be very right when the ability to obtain financing is taken into consideration.

THE FIRST STEP: HAVE A GOAL

The first step in being successful in the money market is the same as the first step in being successful in business. You've got to have a plan for your business that meshes with your personal goals.

If you don't have a clearly defined goal before you, it's difficult to draw up a business plan that will reflect what you want. If your goal is to retire at age 35 with $2 million in the bank, you would be dumb to start that computer school we talked about a moment ago. On the other hand, if you want something that will provide you with an adequate income and the possiblity of selling out at a healthy profit when you reach 55, the computer school might be just the trick.

Once you have a goal, you'll need a plan on how you're going to get there with your business.

THE SECOND STEP: HAVE A BUSINESS PLAN

Now you're going to need a plan to get you to that goal. Your plan should be as complete and accurate as you can make it. It should include projections of business over the next several years, how fast you expect the business to grow, even when you'll sell out as covered in Section 4.

This plan will serve two purposes. Not only is it going to help you in your planning, it's going to help you get the money you need to make the business a success.

INFORMATION: THE KEY TO FINANCING

The key to asking for money in the right way is information. If you don't have the information lenders or investors need (or think they need) to make a decision, you've got no hope of getting the money you need.

Recognizing what information will be needed and supplying it without being asked is also the mark of a good manager, something every lender and investor is looking for.

Most small businesspeople don't recognize this crucial fact. When they go in for a loan or when they look for investors they don't have enough information on hand. Some of them don't even know how much money they need or what they're willing to give up to get it. Frequently, the financial figures they have are incomplete.

Often, they don't have even simple financial statements worked up and can't answer questions about the specifics of the financial position of their business.

This is the sort of basic information lenders and investors need to see before they will look at a business. If you don't have it ready, you will have damaged your chances of getting that money.

PREPARING YOUR BUSINESS PLAN

When a company decides to sell stock nationally, it is required to file a prospectus showing particulars of its financial position and other important data. Copies of this prospectus have to be provided to all investors to let them see where the company stands.

This isn't a bad idea for a small business either. What you need is an accurate statement of where you are and where you're going in business. This information not only gives you a plan, it also gives you information you can use on the money markets.

Properly done, this business plan is a fairly large document. It is also going to cost a fair hunk of change to have it drawn up. For one thing, you will need the services of an accountant to draw up and analyze the financial data in it. You will also need to spend a fair amount of time putting it together. But the result will be something that will command respect and open doors for you.

The plan will include more than financial statements. It will also include a survey of your market, a statement of how you run your business and how you intend to expand your market share, a biography of you and your key people, and a lot of other information. It will also include budgets and projects for coming years.

If this is properly done, it will not only give you access to needed money, it will also provide you with an extremely valuable marketing tool to let you plan and prepare for your future growth. It can also force you to answer some important, but usually unasked, questions.

THE ELEMENTS OF YOUR BUSINESS PLAN

Every good business plan should contain the following information. Not all of it will be needed by every source of money, but all of them will want to see some of it.

Introduction

This is a one or two-page summary of what your business is all about: what sort of business it is, where it is located, the market you serve, what your volume is, what your sales are and what your profits are.

Table of Contents

As you will see, there's a lot of ground covered here. Your readers are going to want to be able to go right to the part they're interested in.

Capital Required

This goes right up front since it's the major area of concern to anyone reading this document. On the basis of your research and projections you should be able to come up with an accurate dollar amount and when you will need it.

You should also tell what the money will be used for. Exactly. Don't just put down something like "operating expenses" or "capital improvement." Spell it out. What kind of equipment are you going to buy? From whom? What operating expenses are you going to pay? Itemize them. How long will the money last? How does this tie into your overall plan? Get it complete and get it down on paper.

Financial Summary

This section will include a full set of financial statements and an explanation of them. This includes balance sheets, income statements and cash flow statements for the last three years (if you've been around that long). The statements should be set up in comparative form with the percentage changes worked out next to each item. This will be a big help to investors and loan analysts.

You should also include projected financial statements to cover the next year on a monthly basis and at least the following year on a quarterly basis. These represent your budget for that period of time. They will be looked at very carefully to see where you think you're going.

All this information should be fully explained. Your accountant will be able to tell you what areas are likely to be questioned. Put the answers to those questions in the explanations.

Operating History Of The Business

This should be a short but complete history of your operation: how long it has been in operation, how long in the present location, when it was incorporated, when it started new product lines, when it stopped handling old ones.

Directors or Limited Partners

Include brief biographies of anyone who owns part of the business but isn't directly involved in running it. The people who are reading this will be looking for people with business savvy on your board. Barring that, they'll want to be sure you don't have any built-in problems—like a former owner who was forced out of control and is still nursing his wounds while holding a seat on the board.

Yourself And Other Key People

Sound business management is valued almost as much as a good credit rating by lenders. They like to see companies being run by people with experience in the firm's line of work and a solid record of accomplishment.

Try to present yourself and your top people in that light. Sometimes it makes the difference between "yes" and "no" on a deal.

If you or your top people don't have any experience in the field, emphasize your experience in other lines of work. The important thing is to make yourself and your managers sound capable and competent.

You should also include the level of compensation for each member of your management team. This means not only salary, but stock options, etc. In a business that is just starting up, this is particularly important, because money sources will be looking for evidence of you or your employees "milking" the company. This will prevent you from getting outside money.

You should include information on life insurance policies carried by the company on all key people. This means the amount, company issuing, and possibly the policy numbers. Money sources like to see evidence of protection in case of the death or illness of a key person.

Outside Professional Help

This includes your attorney, your accountants, etc. You should include a very brief biography on each one as well as any other professionals, such as insurance agents, advertising agency, etc.

This is also a good place to mention your commercial banker (if you have one) and your investment banker (if you have one).

You should also indicate any fee arrangements you may have with these people (i.e., "contingency basis" or "retainer").

This information serves to nail you down more solidly in the eyes of the reader. If your accountant or attorney is well-known either locally or nationally, it will be taken as an indication of your solidity.

Major Products

If your major product is a secretarial service, then mention something about how you run your business and why it's better than most secretarial services.

Every company, no matter how small, needs this section. The people you are trying to get money from will know little or nothing about your business. If you expect their help, you're going to have to tell them something. A lot of businesspeople will ignore this step, feeling it's only for manufacturers. It's for everybody. As a computer business owner you handle a certain line of services. What those lines are will tell something about the kind of business you're running.

This section should also include a discussion of profit margins, warranty and delivery policies, repair work done, and other items that will help your reader understand how your business functions.

Market Being Serviced

This area is one that is most often neglected or ignored. It is one of the most important for two reasons. First, your money source is going to want to know what kind of market you are serving, to help estimate how well you are going to do. Is your market expanding or declining? What is the growth potential? Without information on questions like these, it's hard to understand the climate that a business is operating in. See Section 4.

The second reason is that your money source is going to feel that you need this kind of information yourself. If you don't have it, he's going to see that as a sign that you aren't a good manager. It will look like you are operating by the seat of your pants, and that always makes money people nervous.

A request for market information of this kind usually produces one of two responses. The first is a guess:

"Well, let's see. There are an average of 35,000 cars an hour going by here on the freeway. Let's say that one percent of them need gas. That's 350 cars an hour pulling into" — Wrong. That's a fallacious argument and the person making it knows it. What's more, anyone with any money knows it too.

The other response is usually to give up. It would costs thousands of dollars to have a market survey done and the small company doesn't have that kind of money.

A small company doesn't, but the banks, newspapers, and universities in the area do. What's more, they have done most of the work for you already.

Large lending institutions do constant business surveys evaluating business conditions and loan requests in their area. Newspapers do similar surveys to convince advertisers to advertise with them. Universities and colleges also do surveys to try to find out what's going on economically in their area. There's also the information about turn-ons, turn-offs and slow pays that utility companies have, the data from census files, and a host of other sources.

And it's all free for the digging.

Just what data you'll need to construct your market survey will depend on your service and to whom you're selling. The operator of a secretarial service will be interested mainly in the small businesses within a couple miles for his or her home base. He'll want to know the kinds of businesses, staff sizes, need for secretarials services, etc.

All that information is easily available from a demographic survey of a city done by the major newspaper or chamber of commerce.

In some cases, you'll even be getting the information from the very same bank you go back to later for the loan.

When you draw up your market survey, indicate the source of your data.

Competition Factors

Identify your competition in your report. Try to find out what proportion of the market each of your competitors has. If your product is secretarial services, what other similar businesses are located nearby? What sort of clientele do they serve? Who are your most direct competitors? Why do you think you can overtake them?

State of the Market

Every market for every product is either growing, standing pat ("mature"), or declining. Find out the state of your market. Again, you can use the figures from economic surveys over the last few years to show what's happening. Remember that the market may be growing in one area and declining in another. If that's the case, you may want to indicate it.

Expected Market Share

How much of the market do you want? What segment are you aiming at? Are you going to take in new customers in a growing market or are you going to have to take customers away from other businesses in a static or declining market?

Marketing Strategy

Indicate how you're going to go after your market. If you're selling secretarial services, are you trying to give your customers more quality for their money? Do you offer some services that your competitors don't?

Take a look at the market segments. A computer kit business can sell equipment to homeowners in different income brackets. It can also sell office systems to businesses. Break your market down into segments and indicate where and how you will make your marketing efforts.

Tell how you intend to sell your product. Will it be handled through the mail? Will you sell to walk-in customers? Door-to-door? What are your options and how do you intend to exercise them?

Financing Strategy

This is an important part of your overall marketing picture. It is doubly important because of its effect on your financial statements. Your reader is going to want to see something about how you plan to handle your credit sales. Will you use a credit card arrangement for retail sales? What will your payment terms be for the business? Are you planning on a liberal credit policy or a conservative one?

These are all decisions that will affect your ability to penetrate the market, and how fast you can turn your money over.

If you are planning on using a factoring or accounts receivable financing arrangement, indicate it here.

THE USES OF THE BUSINESS PLAN

A lot of information?

You better believe it. A well-done business plan can easily run 30 to 40 pages, and documents of 100 pages and more aren't unknown. It will also be expensive. Your accounting fees for drawing up and analyzing the financial statements will be considerable. If you value your time at anything, you will have a bundle of money invested here. You will have to get your plan printed if you're going to make effective use of it. (Do it on your printer or get 25 or so copies run off by a local quick print shop.) In short, you will have a fairly nice chunk of green tied up in this document by the time you get it done.

Your return on your investment will come in two ways. The first is going to be increased information about your own business. We'd be very surprised if, when you finish doing all this work, you don't have some new insights into your business and its place in the market.

The second will be more tangible. It will be money coming in the door from lenders and investors who will see you in a new light through this document. Not only are you telling them all about your business in this pile of information, you're also telling them something about yourself. You're saying that you're a competent businessperson who knows where you're going and how to get there. You're saying that you're someone who studies all the angles and learns the markets before moving. You're saying that you've got the kind of management talent it takes to succeed in a small business.

You're saying you're worth investing in or loaning money to.

Getting It Done For You

For a variety of reasons, you might not want to take on that much work yourself. You may not have the time left over from your business, or you may not feel you have the writing and research skills to handle the job.

It would cost a fortune to get this sort of thing done by a business consultant, but there is a way to get it done much cheaper.

Contact the business school at your local college or university and tell them what you want. Tell them you'll pay a student $100 or so to draw up this plan from the figures your accountant will provide. Stress how complete it needs to be, that it will cover more than just financial data, and stress that you want a professional job.

Chances are the schools will jump at the opportunity to provide you with someone. This sort of project is perfect for a business student. It teaches him or her the basics needed to do similar analyses after graduation. Not only that, it looks good when he or she goes looking for a job. And in most cases the student can get school credit through this internship.

You will probably get one of the top students the school has to work on the project. You may get more than that. We know of one businessman who went to his local college to get some help with his business plan, and ended up getting an entire class working on it for six weeks. The professor thought it was such a good idea he assigned an entire class of seniors to work on the plan.

SUBVERTING A BANKER TO GET THE MONEY YOU NEED

Subversion.

Sounds like something out of a spy novel, doesn't it? Burrowing from within, secret payoffs and all the rest.

It subversion is too melodramatic for you, try calling it "getting through to" or "establishing a relationship with" or "getting to know." Those are the terms that are usually used, but it still means the same thing: having your own man on the inside who will look after your interests and bend or break the rules to get you what you want.

Whatever you call it, it's the name of the game. In every major company and most of the minor ones, you'll find a master subverter, otherwise known as a "money man." He's the guy who's got the contacts with the money sources and can pry the funding out of them when the company needs them. In many ways he's the most important man in the company, since he's often the one who keeps the whole thing going. The guy may be the biggest flake around, but as long as he can keep the money coming in he's a major asset to the company.

No matter what a banker tells you when he turns you down for a loan, business loans are not cut-and-dried affairs made according to a strict list of criteria. It's obvious even to bankers that that won't work. There is considerable discretion in making any loan and that discretion is vested in two people: the commercial loan officer, whom you deal with, and the loan analyst, whom you'll never see.

Some banks also have a loan committee, but that tends to be guided by the other two people.

Of the pair, the commercial loan officer, or CLO, is the most important. If he is convinced that the loan is a good risk, then you are very likely to get it.

CLO's are human, and like any other human being they are susceptible to a variety of pressures. They can be flattered, beguiled, bribed (subtly), over-awed and generally influenced.

The rule is this: Find a CLO you can "get through to" (subvert) and play him for all he's worth. Once you've got him solidly in your corner, your money worries are largely over.

FINDING YOUR BANKER

Start early!

The worst time to go looking for a banker is when you need one. By the time you need one, you're going to be in trouble and bankers don't like businesspeople in trouble. They smell of risk to bankers.

Choosing your banker will require a certain amount of care on your part. The one you're looking for will have two outstanding characteristics. He will be able to approve a loan in the amount you're likely to need, and he's susceptible to the sort of pressure you can bring to bear.

You probably know about the importance of reciprocity and contact in building power. Since power is what you need here, you need reciprocity and contact. You should also be familiar with the techniques of making yourself visible in the community.

If you want that loan, you're going to have to apply those techniques.

As you move through the community, you'll meet a number of bankers. Just as you're looking for a loan, the bankers are looking for business for their banks. As you meet with them and talk to them, size them up. Since you're small, you'll probably need someone who's hungry. You're looking for a bright young banker who's trying to make a name for himself with the bank—a pusher, a go-getter, someone on the way up.

It helps if he's just a touch dishonest.

You'll probably find several likely prospects, since the type isn't all that rare today. Cultivate them all. Get to know them. Take them to lunch. Go golfing with them. You may not be able to write this off as a business expense, but it will be the best investment you'll ever make.

GATHERING INTELLIGENCE

Meanwhile, keep your antennae out for news about the banks in general. You need to know who's got money to loan. (Not all banks will—or at least not very much.) You need to know how each bank does business. Do they use a loan committee? What is the loan limit a CLO can authorize on his own hook? Does the bank have a reputation for being conservative or liberal in its lending policies? How tightly controlled are the CLO's?

Your accountant can give you some of this information. You can get other parts of it from listening to gossip around town. Another good source is someone in the commercial real estate field. You should cultivate at least one commercial real estate salesperson. He or she is very knowledgable about financial trends and business conditions in general.

By combining the information you've gotten on the banks with your evaluation of the bankers you've met, you should be able to narrow the field down to one best prospect. However, don't ignore the others. Keep up your contacts with all of them. Not only does this make it easier for you to fall back if your prime candidate goes sour, it will also keep your secondary bankers interested if the loan goes through. It offers a feeling of competition.

THE INDIRECT APPROACH

This takes time, of course—weeks or months in most cases. But it's time well spent. Once you've sold yourself to a banker, you can expect that to go on paying dividends for years to come.

Now you start your courtship in earnest. You don't have to become the banker's bosom buddy; in fact, too much closeness can hurt. What you do have to do is project an image of solidity, of someone who's going places fast. You want this banker to think you're the greatest guy who ever walked on the face of the earth.

The whole purpose of this part of the approach is to get the banker on your side. You are trying to sell yourself to him so that he'll buy the loan when you come in to ask for it. It's more important to sell yourself than the business, because the business is a tangible thing that can be reduced to facts and figures on paper. Those the loan analyst will handle. You, on the other hand, are an intangible. To evaluate you, the bank will have to rely on your contact's judgment.

THE DIRECT APPROCH—MAKING YOUR PITCH

Finally comes the day when you're ready to ask for the loan. You've got a pile of information your accountant put together for you, and you're going to the bank. You're not going in cold, of course. You sounded your buddy out more or less casually about the possibility of a loan, and you called ahead to make an appointment. Now you put it all on the line.

You might want to bring your accountant with you, particularly if you don't speak finance well. But the important thing you're taking into that meeting is yourself and your confidence. That's what you've got to sell.

Like any good pitch, your talk to the CLO should be positive and to the point. Stress the strong points of your company, show him how the money will increase your profits enormously, etc. Don't lie and don't fudge too much. Everything you say will probably be checked. If there are any problem areas, meet them squarely—and have good explanations worked up.

Above all, don't be hangdog about it. You're not just selling something, you're proposing a mutually profitable arrangement. You need enthusiasm from your banker. He's the one who's going to have to sell the deal inside the bank. Sell it to him and you're home free.

Your preliminary softening up will have made this an easy sell. Before you walk in there, the banker is already favorably impressed with you.

DOCUMENTATION: WHAT YOU'LL NEED

Even if the banker is completely in your pocket, you're going to need some paperwork to help him sell the loan to the other bankers.

Typically, you'll need to present a variety of material, including:

A brief history of your company.

A summary of your business facilities and other physical resources.

Resumes on yourself and any other key personnel. These should emphasize your ability to manage the company soundly and to make a profit.

A description of your business and the markets served.

Your strengths in the market, and general competitive conditions.

A current financial statement and possibly statements for one or two years previously so the bank can judge trends. These should be prepared by your accountant, and you can expect that any exceptions he notes will be studied carefully.

A statement of the purpose of the loan, including specifically what you'll use the money for, and what you can offer as security.

How you intend to repay the loan. If you're going to repay out of future profits, include a very specific cash flow forecast backed up with convincing reasons.

The availability of guarantees, either personal or from other people or businesses.

It all makes quite a package.

That package is one of the reasons small businesspeople fair so poorly with banks. If you come in without this sort of information at hand, it makes a poor impression on the banker. He knows that he'll need most or all of it to present to the powers that be. If he has to drag it out of you a piece at a time, he is not going to be impressed (you are "not businesslike") and will probably feel his time and effort is better spent elsewhere.

A neatly done up presentation makes a favorable impact. It makes him feel that here is someone who knows how to do business, and it also means less work for him.

Bone up with your accountant before the meeting so you can answer any questions he might have. The ability to come out with direct answers is also impressive.

THE IMPORTANCE OF IT ALL

Does all this hocus-pocus really increase your chances of getting a loan?

You'd better believe it! If your figures are terrible, of course, it probably doesn't make any difference what sort of presentation you make. The banker is no fool and he can't afford to be played for one, no matter how persuasive you are. On the other hand, the figures are seldom terrible. Usually they're just not so hot. The bank makes a lot of loans on not-so-hot figures. A good presentation really makes the difference in such a case.

WHAT YOU'RE SELLING

You're selling two things to the banker. One is yourself. If you've pre-sold that carefully, you'll have less trouble with the second part, which is the loan proper. The question your banker will have to answer is: can this person repay the loan in the manner he outlines?

This involves both your business and yourself. The more you can do to set his mind at ease about both, the better off you will be.

However, no matter how firmly you have the banker in your pocket, you must also sell the deal. The deal has got to look good, or you've got to be able to make it sound very good.

TERMS

Most people don't realize that terms and interest rates are both negotiable to some extent. When your loan is approved, you don't have to take the first deal that's offered, on the assumption it's all you'll get.

A loan approval is more like an agreement in principle than a specific bargain. If you proposed the terms, you'll be expected to stick to them. If the bank wants to set the terms, you can try to change them to your advantage.

When the bank agrees to make a loan, it is primarily agreeing that you are a good credit risk, at least up to whatever amount they have agreed to loan you. The terms the bank proposes will be the ones that the bank considers advantageous to itself. You can make counterproposals on any of the points, even the interest rates. Then both of you can dicker to arrive at something mutually agreeable.

Actually, the interest rate is likely to be the least objectionable subject of the loan agreement. You expected to pay something for the use of the money, didn't you? If you drew up your forecasts and repayment plan carefully, you should be confident of your ability to repay the loan.

The other requirements are the ones that are more likely to tie you down. These are much more easily negotiated than the interest rate (although that's negotiable too).

Probably the most objectionable requirements are those having to do with the control of the business. Some banks will want you to take in a partner, or if you're a corporation, put one of their nominees on your board of directors. Be especially wary of a bank that wants this kind of voice in running your business. An awful lot of small businesspeople have found themselves eased out of their own businesses by taking loans on these terms.

More common are requirements that have to do with the financial operation of your company. The bank will probably insist that you open a commercial checking account with them and keep a compensating balance in the checking account at all times. In effect, this is free money that the bank can loan out, and for you, it increases the effective interest rate on your loan. Once again, the amount of that compensating balance is decidedly negotiable.

You may also be required to maintain certain operating ratios. This may or may not be a disadvantage to you, depending on how you see the business operating in the future. Think this one through carefully.

If you've done a particularly good job of selling yourself to the banker, he may insist that the business take out "key-man" life insurance policies on you or your corporate officers. This isn't a bad thing to have anyway, but it's something that will cost you money right now.

DEALING WITH TERMS

The important thing to remember about the bank's proposed terms is that you don't have to accept them all. The fact that the bank is willing to even discuss loaning the money indicates they feel sure you're a good risk. Once that's been established, they are essentially jockeying for position. You can jockey right back.

Don't sign anything until you talk the bank's proposal over with your accountant, attorney and your key employees, if any. Make a counter-offer if you feel it's warranted. By being willing to negotiate, you can save a bundle of money — and possibly your business.

NEW BUSINESS

A new business has a special problem—no history. Since bankers are primarily interested in a business' history, it's extremely difficult to get a loan to start one. (Remember that puritanical banker deep inside who keeps saying businesses should start and grow on equity.)

If you have a track record, this isn't so bad. You might not be able to sell the business history, but you can sell yours as a successful manager. It also helps to have some very solid projections of expenses and income, although these will be regarded with suspicion.

How well a new business does at the bank will depend largely on how well your program of subversion has fared with the banker. Here you will need every scrap of help you can get. If the banker is convinced you're a real ball of fire, you might be able to sell your proposal.

There is another possibility. If you can find a business for sale that's engaged in the line of work you want to enter, you might consider buying it and using it as a shell for your new firm. In this way you can buy a track record and use it to swing the loan you need (or get a loan to buy the business). The problem is that the track record you buy probably won't be very good and the business is likely to be in debt already. On the other hand, if the bank you're dealing with is holding the paper and if the banker believes you're solid, you can probably make an even better deal.

All these are long shots. If you're starting a new business, resign yourself to having to get most of the capital you need either from your own resources, or from equity financing.

PRIVATE INVESTORS

Next to banks, private investors of one sort or another are the major source of long-term finance for small businesses, especially new small businesses.

Very often a private investor sets his priorities very differently than a bank. This can mean that a deal that has no attraction at all for a bank will look very good for a private investor.

RULE ONE: KNOW WHOM YOU'RE DEALING WITH

There are all sorts of private investors willing to loan businesses money. They range from friends and relatives of the businessperson, to professionals who make their money by making these loans, to Mafia members looking for a place to stash dirty money. Some private investors can be very good partners, and some of them are nothing but trouble. It is vitally important to know whom you're dealing with and what their motives are before you make a deal. There are some types of investors that are too expensive no matter how badly you need the money.

THE PROFESSIONALS: HARD TO GET, EASY TO DEAL WITH

Professional lenders are the easiest and most businesslike of all money sources to deal with. They are also the most cautious and the hardest to get money out of.

A professional will size you and your business up very carefully before he makes a loan, but that loan will usually be a solid, businesslike deal. There will be a contract with all the terms spelled out and you'll know what's due when and under what conditions. You may not appreciate the value of this until you've borrowed money from your brother-in-law and discovered that he thinks he's entitled to all sorts of privileges and freebies from your business.

You can expect to provide a professional lender with at least as much information as you'd give a bank. You can also expect to take anywhere from two weeks to three or four months to put a deal together with him.

THE PROFESSIONAL'S MOTIVATION

The professional's motive in making you a loan is simple: he wants to get a high return on his investment.

The absolute lowest rate anyone can borrow money from a bank is at the prime rate. Most people can't hope to borrow at that rate; they pay more. But if you as an investor go into a bank and ask to make an investment that will pay you the prime rate, or anything close to it, you'll be laughed out of the bank. There will be a spread of anything from two to four or five percent between what the bank pays depositors and what it charges even its best customers for the money.

If you go to nearly any other investment outfit, the story is going to be the same. The prime rate is a ceiling. It's very hard to find anyone who will pay that much on invested money.

There are a couple of ways around this through more or less conventional channels. One is to invest in equity—buy stocks, in other words. But in today's market, even stocks are not paying off that well. Besides, with stocks you make your money when you sell out, not from your dividends.

If a lender wants to do better than the prime rate, he's just about going to have to lend his money out directly. In any medium to large city, there are going to be a lot of people who are going to be willing to make loans.

HOW THE PROFESSIONAL SEES THE DEAL

For a professional lender the argument is quite simple. He will lend you the money you need at a mutually agreeable rate of interest in order to allow him to make a profit on the loan. He will look on his loan to your business as a fairly high-risk propositon. After all, you couldn't get what you wanted at the bank, could you? There must be something a little bit wrong.

When you deal with a professional lender, you have to expect this attitude. It will manifest itself in a very careful check of you and your business and in a demand for stringent guarantees. You will undoubtedly have to put up something for collateral, possibly everything. You will probably have to agree to submit monthly trial balances of your books to be audited regularly by his accountants. In short, you can expect to have the lender practically living in your pocket for the term of the loan.

PROTECTING YOURSELF

Some professional lenders are only interested in seeing that their money is protected and that they get paid on time. Others see lending you money as the first step in taking over your business. A professional can turn out to be a "shark" whose main interest is taking you for all you're worth. Since the guarantees and collateral you will have to give are considerable, the lender will be in a position to ruin you in very short order if he chooses to do so.

Because of this, it is extremely important that you find out everything you can about your would-be lender before the deal is closed. Find out what sort of reputation he has on these deals. See if you can talk to people who have borrowed money from him, and find out what their opinion is. Ask your attorney and accountant to find out what sort of reputation the lender has in their professions.

Another good place to check is the county courthouse and city courts. These places have records of all lawsuits filed. The records are cross-indexed by name of plaintiff and defendant, and they are public by law. You or your attorney can check those records to see if your prospect has been involved in lawsuits, and what the suits were about. If he was suing to foreclose on a loan or if someone was suing him because he foreclosed on them, it's a bad sign.

You should also feel comfortable with the lender and his methods of operation. If he's a hard driver and you're not, there's probably going to be friction.

FINDING A LENDER

This can be easier than you think. Many professionals advertise in newspaper classified ads or the financial section. Some are listed in the telephone book. Others will be known around the community by word-of-mouth. If you look around, ask around and keep your ears open, you'll probably get several prospects.

MAKING YOUR APPROACH

Approaching a lender of this sort is much like approaching your banker. Take your business plan—or parts of your business plan—under your arm, and make an appointment. Lay out to the lender how much you want, for how long, and why. Give him the financial statements and the other facts he asks for.

You will very quickly get one of two responses. The first is a flat no. If he's not interested, he'll let you know in no uncertain terms. If the turndown appears hedgy, though, you may have the beginnings of a yes.

Generally speaking, expressions of interest will be tentative. In part, this is because there are so many details that need to be negotiated. In part, this is because you're going into a real horse-trading situation and your opponent doesn't want to give away a strong position.

NEGOTIATING THE LOAN

This can be one of the most frustrating things you've ever done. Both you and the lender will be pushing for maximum advantage in a field where there are no rules other than a few state laws. There are a lot of things involved that can be traded back and forth to be balanced against each other. For example, if you offer more security, the lender might be willing to give a little on the interest rate. The discussions will go back and forth until you finally arrive at a generally acceptable figure and set of terms.

You will need your attorney and your accountant at your elbow all through the process. The ideal way to handle a deal like this would be for both of you to meet in a hotel room somewhere with your attorneys and accountants, and to stay there for 12 or 14 hours until you get a deal thrashed out. In practice, the process will be strung out over weeks. You'll meet, discuss matters, then one or both of you will have to confer with someone else on the deal. Then you'll meet again a few days later and repeat the process. In the middle of this, details you thought were settled months ago come unglued and have to be renegotiated.

INTEREST RATES AND PRIVATE LENDERS

You can expect to pay at least the prime rate to a private lender, and sometimes a good bit more. This isn't as bad as it sounds. A bank may lend you money at one percent or so above the prime rate, but you'll be required to maintain a compensating balance with them. If you figure that balance as money needed to get the loan, which it is, that loan will have cost you a good bit more than the interest rate that appears in the loan agreement.

With a private lender there is usually no such agreement. This is worth at least something when you conduct your negotiations.

FRIENDS, ASSOCIATES AND RELATIVES

Most small businesses get money from people the operator knows. This is especially true in the case of a business that is just starting up.

Loans from people you know can be either the easiest or the most difficult to handle. The level of business sophistication you'll be dealing with probably won't be very high and the formal terms of the loan may not be very severe. But you can find unwritten kickers on these loans that will turn your hair gray.

It is vitally important for your peace of mind and the survival of your business that you accept loans from friends, associates and relatives on the most businesslike basis possible. This means a formal loan agreement with a repayment schedule and a reasonable rate of interest. If you don't do this, you're letting yourself in for trouble later.

THE PROBLEM WITH BORROWING FROM PEOPLE YOU KNOW

The problem with borrowing money from people you know is that sometimes you have trouble telling where friendship or blood ends and business begins. Where the person has invested money in the business, it can be particularly difficult to make the personal/professional distinction and to make it stick. Failure to do so has killed a lot of promising businesses.

When you're negotiating the loan, everything is probably going to be easygoing and friendly. The lender is not likely to see any need for contracts or other legal documents. He'll say that your word is good enough for him and he trusts you. That may be true, but you'd better have a record somewhere of what it is your word was and what he is trusting you to do. Otherwise, the disagreements that arise may not only wreck a perfectly good friendship, but can end in court as well.

One point that you should always include in a loan from a relative is a subordination clause saying that the lender agrees to subordinate his claim on the business to any other creditors who may be specified later. If you don't have some sort of subordinate agreement, you will have trouble getting loans from banks and other sources. Bankers feel that having a debt outstanding to a relative is pretty much the same thing as owing money to yourself. They will usually insist that such debts be subordinated to their own. It's easier if you have gotten approval for the subordination in advance.

MINING THE PEOPLE YOU KNOW FOR MONEY

The first thing you need to do is sit down and draw up a list of the people you know who have money and who might be willing to lend it to you. This can be a very considerable list. You probably know other businesspeople in the community, people who are well-to-do or relatives with money they might be able to loan.

The list will often include some unlikely sources. We know of one middle-aged businessman who was able to pull his business through a bad time with the help of a rather large loan from a no-good nephew of his who was barely out of his teens. The kid had a very profitable drug dealing business on the side and was willing to loan his uncle some of the profits.

Also remember that even people who don't have a lot of cash around will often have other assets they can borrow on, or that they can turn into cash to help finance the business.

Once you've made up your list, you can start making your pitch. Talk to each of the people on your list individually and try to sell them on the idea of investing in your business. Lay out for them the interest you'll pay and the term the loan will run. Be prepared to answer questions ranging from the sophisticated to the silly. Stress the rate of return you can offer and explain what you need the money for and why. Don't lie about things like the safety of the investment or the terms of the loan. There are rather severe laws designed to protect unsophisticated investors, even if they are your relatives.

You may find that you'll get a few hundred here and a few thousand somewhere else, instead of getting it all at once. You may end up with a patchwork of small loans instead of the one big one you hoped for.

TAKING IT OUT IN TRADE

If you have a consumer business, you might consider letting your small lenders take it out in trade. Not only does this pay off the debt cheaply, it also promotes traffic for your business.

If you do decide to pay off your small lenders in trade, make sure you keep a record and make sure they understand that a record is being kept. It's important that everyone understands that you're repaying a loan, not just handing out free goodies.

There are two ways to repay a loan in trade. One is to let the lender have goods and services up to the value of the loan without additional payment. The other is to count only your profit and overhead as repayment and to charge him for the rest. If you're dealing with a large ticket item such as computer kits or home security equipment, the second is probably preferable from your point of view. On services, like bookkeeping or tax preparation, which do not require any additional money, the first way is generally best because there's no elaborate bookkeeping.

WHAT TO DO WHEN THE SQUEEZE GOES ON

When the squeeze really goes on, creative financing becomes a prime tool of survival. If you haven't faced a real squeeze brought on by lack of ready money, you haven't been in business very long.

Typically, a squeeze will be a temporary situation brought on by slow sales, problems with a supplier, unexpected expenses, or some other situation that drains all the money out of the business. Usually it will only last for a few days to three months, but it can kill you in that time if you can't come up with enough money to see you through. Squeezes are particularly common in small businesses that are just starting out. They don't have the track record to have access to bank loans, their capital is stretched tight anyway, and their relationships with their suppliers are still likely to be shaky. Under those circumstances even the most minor problems can snowball.

Beating the credit squeeze isn't easy. This is where the small business operator shows his ability and initiative to the utmost. You may find yourself forced to take breathtaking risks, make decisions on the spur of the moment that will keep you alive or break you, and generally live to the limit. You'll need to be alert and ready to move instantly to come through with your business intact.

IT CAN HAPPEN TO YOU

Good management is no guarantee you won't get squeezed. A successful business, a good relationship with your lenders, a strong reputation in the community, good credit rating—none of them will protect you. Lack of any of them can kill you when trouble hits, but they will seldom prevent trouble.

In most cases the trouble will not be of your own making. Oh, in an abstract sense a management specialist might be able to study your company's case history and say, "This is where you went wrong." But given the conditions small businesses have to operate under today, it is impossible for them to protect themselves adequately from some of the major dangers. If you had $1 million sitting in the bank, you could undoubtedly avoid the problem. But it's not a very realistic criticism of your business to fault you for not having that money.

GO LOOKING FOR TROUBLE

The best antidote to being sunk by unforeseen money problems is to foresee them. That and good management will pull you through a lot, or if it's obvious you can't pull through, it will allow you to fold gracefully and save whatever you can.

Figure out where you are weakest and what you can do to protect yourself. Is your business highly seasonal? What happens if the season is late in arriving—or never arrives at all? Are there things you can do that will allow you to pull through?

There are two basic kinds of squeeze: the small and the big. They can both be fatal, but the ways to handle them are quite different.

A small squeeze occurs when you must meet a sudden expense for a relatively small amount, say $1,000 or less, and you just don't have the money. It often happens that the money is needed quickly, and if you don't get it there will be an avalanche effect that will sink you. If one supplier cuts off credit, you can expect trouble with all your suppliers.

The trick here is to raise the relatively small amount of money you need for a relatively short period of time.

A big squeeze involves a major problem with the business. Say the customers haven't been coming in for weeks. Or your building just burned down. Or your largest customer has cancelled out.

CREDIT CARDS AND QUICK-FIX FINANCING

Credit cards are the consumer equivalent of trade financing. The customer buys from you, pays with a credit card, you submit the invoice and get your money in a few days. The customer pays the credit card company at the end of the month.

Like trade financing, you can use credit cards to pull you out of temporary holes. In fact, you can borrow $2,000 or more for up to six weeks at no interest on your credit cards.

If your business accepts credit cards, you have probably gotten or can get credit cards from the same company. Since you are in business, you will probably get the cards with $1,000 limits. If you accept both Visa and MasterCard, you'll have something close to a $2,000 total line of credit.

The next thing to do is to find out when the companies bill your account. Different accounts are billed at different times of the month to spread out the work. Typically, you can discover this by just calling up and asking. This works better if you use your business name.

Let's say your account is billed on the 19th for merchandise purchased in the previous month. This means that if you buy something on the first of the month you've got until the 18th of the next month to repay the money with no interest charges. That's better than a six-week loan at no interest.

Of course, you can't pay your trade suppliers with credit cards, but you can pay off a lot of incidental expenses with them, freeing money to pay suppliers.

A less ethical dodge is to enlist the aid of several friends with credit cards. They purchase merchandise or services from you on credit cards, you submit the invoices, and they then return the merchandise. The credit card company pays you for the merchandise, and you send through the cancellation notices. Typically, you will get 30 days or so to repay the company. You can find out the terms from your contract with the company.

BORROWING ON PERSONAL ASSETS

You can often raise money by borrowing on things you own personally. The classic example is the equity you've built up in your house. A second mortgage can allow you to convert that equity into ready cash, although at a higher interest rate than you paid on the first mortgage. The second-morgage route can be especially attractive in these days of rapidly rising real estate values, because the chances are excellent that your property has increased in value since you bought it. Even if you've paid off very little of your mortgage, you will find you've got a considerable amount of equity you can borrow against.

You can also borrow against your car, furniture and other assets. But before you do, ask yourself if you are really going to be able to meet the repayment schedule. If you think you might not be able to, you might want to go elsewhere for your money.

KNOW WHEN TO BAIL OUT

The methods we have outlined here will keep you afloat through a temporary money shortage. They will not make up for other serious deficiencies in the business. Remember that sooner or later all problems of a business manifest themselves as a money shortage. When you find yourself facing a cash crisis, ask yourself if the money problem is the cause or an effect.

There is no sense in going through some of the gyrations we have described here to raise money, if your basic problem is that the industry you're in is declining, or that your management is hopelessly inefficient, or that you're being swamped by bigger competitors. All these things will give you cash trouble, but all the cash in the world won't solve them.

All the maneuvers we have described will prejudice your financial position in one way or another. All the money will have to be paid back eventually, and if your problem is more than money, you'll be in just as bad shape when the time comes to pay the money back. If that is the case, you're better off winding up the business early and going on to something else. Remember, there is always something else for you to try just around the corner.

In these cases, the problem is deep-seated in the business. The thing that brings the crisis to a head can be quite small, but the problem itself is far-reaching and won't go away in a couple of weeks.

A small squeeze can be handled by raising some money quickly. A big one will either take a lot of money quickly, or some major alterations in the way you do business, or both.

Know what sort of trouble you are in. Look at it clearly and squarely. A lot of business owners have broken their hearts trying to slap bandages on major wounds to keep from bleeding to death. In the end all they had was a major wound covered with bandages and a company that bled to death anyway.

THE VALUE OF INSURANCE

Insurance is an important asset in a squeeze. Adequate fire or casualty insurance can protect you in the event of a major loss, and life insurance offers a source of easily borrowed money that can get you through a crisis.

You should figure your fire and casualty insurance on the basis of how much loss you are willing to assume yourself. Buying as much insurance as you can afford is a lousy policy. You might not be able to afford enough to keep your business going at all. In that case you might want to take out only a minimal policy to cover your creditors, or carry no insurance at all. The theory here is that the business will go under anyway in the event of a major loss (you're assuming all the loss), so there's no point in protecting your assets.

On the other hand, you may find that you're fully covered by insurance. Except in special cases, this isn't a good idea either. It costs a lot of money to carry 100 percent insurance on a business, and your chances of suffering a loss in any given year are relatively small. You're usually better off carrying enough insurance to allow you to restart the business in case of a total loss, but perhaps on a slightly smaller scale. This usually amounts to 50 percent to 70 percent of the value of the tangible assets.

However, it's very important to make arrangements to safeguard your business records in the event of a loss, either through insurance or storage of duplicate records, or both. This can make the difference between being able to continue or losing everything. Studies show that most businesses that fail as the result of a fire, flood, etc. don't go under as a result of the damage to their productive capacity. The thing that kills them is the loss of records. See Section 4 for more detailed information on insurance.

LIFE INSURANCE AS BUSINESS INSURANCE

Life insurance policies occupy an ambiguous place in discussing business finance. In one sense they are a total drain on the business. Year after year you pay out premiums, but get nothing back. In order to win, you've got to die. Worse, you've got have them to satisfy your creditors, and still worse, the government won't allow you to deduct the premium payments as a business expense.

All true, but a cache of "key-man" life insurance policies has a couple of very strong advantages for any small business.

The first advantage is that you can borrow money on them at a fairly low rate of interest. If you need money to get you through a squeeze, this can be an excellent source. What's more, you can usually determine when you will repay the principle. As long as the interest is paid, the company isn't too concerned.

The second advantage to key-man insurance is that in the event of the death or disability of yourself or a key officer, it will provide money to keep the business going. It's not unusual for a small business to fail because the owner gets sick and the creditors get nervous. If they know there's going to be a considerable sum of money available to back up the business in case that happens, they're less likely to press for payment.

STRETCHING OUT YOUR CREDIT

If you get into a squeeze and you have a loan at the bank, the first thing to do is go talk to your banker. Do not wait for him to come to you. You want to be able to go in and present the most positive picture you can. You want to be able to show him what has happened and why, and you want to be able to show him what you'll need in the way of help. If you need additional money, say how much. If you need your credit extended, tell him for how long.

If a bank has confidence in your ability as a manager, they will do almost anything to keep from forcing a business into bankruptcy. In the first place, they know they'll probably lose money if you go under. In the second place, they'd rather have a living potential customer than even the most asset-rich corpse.

Expect some hard questions from your banker. He will want precise answers and he will want the figures to back them up. As in getting a loan in the first place, you're better off over-estimating your needs (and telling him you're making an over-estimate) than trying to see what you can just barely scrape by on. Scraping by makes bankers nervous. What doesn't is business that's got a comfortable margin of cash on hand, even if it's borrowed.

The thing you need to avoid at all costs is having the banker decide that the situation is hopeless. Unfortunately, that's likely to be the conclusions he'll draw from looking at the hard figures. Bankers are great pessimists and never more so than when a business is in trouble. On the other hand, bankers also live in a paper world, and a rescue plan, even on paper, reassures them.

You will usually find you can make deals with your other creditors as well. This will involve calling them, explaining the situation, and asking for a change in terms. Here again, you need to be exact, if not as voluminous as you were with your banker. You need to tell them how much time you'll need and what terms you'll be able to repay them on.

Usually you will find your creditors are very understanding if they get the impression that you're actively working to get yourself out of trouble. The thing that they are most afraid of is having you throw up your hands and do nothing while the business just slides. This is a very common reaction to a crisis. Naturally it snarls things beyond hope of retrieval and is absolutely the worst thing you can do.

BUYING YOUR WAY OUT WITH GOVERNMENT MONEY

Like Christmas, taxes come but once a year. If you're like most business owners, you've been saving all year for tax time. That money can be used to get out of a squeeze quickly.

Property taxes are an excellent place to start. The typical business will pay several thousand dollars a year in property taxes. Typically, you'll make that payment in one lump sum, but accumulate the money through the rest of the year.

What happens if you take that money and apply it to your immediate business needs?

Nothing at first. Eventually your property can be sold for nonpayment of taxes, but that takes several years. Usually you will have a two or three year grace period and the opportunity to cancel the liability just by paying the back taxes and a penalty of eight to 10 percent a year or so. Where else can you borrow money at that rate?

During the first year or two the primary effect is going to be on your credit rating. It will drop when your creditors discover you haven't paid your taxes. If your payment of trade debts is good, you will probably not be affected too much.

If you want to protect your credit rating for several months you can file an appeal of your taxes. In most states this will be noted on the records and you will not be technically delinquent until you have finished the appeal process.

You can do a similar act with your federal and state income taxes, although for a shorter period of time. If you file your federal income tax return on time and do not send in the payment with it, it will be several months before you will have to pay. You can defer part of your taxes by filing a return that shows you owe only a small amount because you have taken some questionable deductions. The result will be a visit from the IRS, an audit and a notice of tax deficiency. But it typically takes six months to a year for this process to run its course.

Another possible source of money from tax funds is the withholding and social security taxes you are required to collect and submit, usually quarterly. But be very careful with this one. Failure to pay withholding will get your business padlocked posthaste. Make very sure you will have the money by the end of the quarter, or you may be out of business and in jail.

SECTION 7

The Reference Section lists software products that you can use for whatever business you've decided to succeed at. It also lists where to obtain the products. We've included a table of contents at the beginning of the list to refer you to those types of software that would best be suited for the business venture you intend to start.

SECTION 7

REFERENCE SECTION

In order to locate the resources that apply to your business, find the number and name of the business in the following list. Then refer to the section numbers that follow.

This is not by any means a complete list, but it has been our purpose throughout the entire book to at least get you started in the right direction to making your business plans a reality. The listings that are included in this section will give you a starting point in locating software and resources that will aid you in your quest.

No. 101 Executive Recruiting and Employment
Sections 3 and 4

No. 102 Computer Custom Diet Service
Section 5

No. 103 Computerized Custom Exercise Programs
Section 20

No. 104 Economic Forecasting
Sections 21 and 28

No. 105 Computer Tax Service
Section 2

No. 106 Tax Service Rental Plan
Section 2

No. 107 Computer Dating Service
Sections 3 and 4

No. 108 Multi-Level Computer Sales
Sections 7 and 19

No. 109   Sell Computerized Sales Leads
          Sections 7 and 19

No. 110   Typing Broker
          Section 7

No. 111   Computerized Formula Mix Service
          Section 9

No. 112   Computer Reminder Service
          Section 7

No. 113   Computer Roommate Service
          Sections 3 and 4

No. 114   Computerized Advertising Cost Newsletter
          Sections 13 and 24

No. 115   Computerized Press Release Service
          Sections 7 and 24

No. 116   Local Who's Who Directory
          Sections 7 and 24

No. 117   Computerized Collection Letter Service
          Sections 7 and 24

No. 118   Local Market Survey Service
          Sections 21 and 28

No. 119   Computer Handwriting Analysis Service
          Section 11

No. 120   Computerized Astrological Chart Service
          Section 17

No. 121   Computerized Bio-Rhythms Service
          Section 17

No. 122   Order Processing-Catalog and Mail Order Sales
          Sections 7 and 19

No. 123   Real Estate Listing Service
          Section 18

No. 124   Computerized Legal Forms Business
          Section 14

No. 125   Computerized Loan Package Service
          Section 8

No. 126   Specialty Locating Service
          Section 4

No. 127   Computerized Map Sales
          Section 23

No. 128   Pro-Formas for New Businesses
          Sections 8, 21 and 28

No. 129 Payroll Preparation Service
Section 16

No. 130 Lease or Buy Analysis Reports
Section 8

No. 131 Cost Estimates for Printers
Sections 13 and 24

No. 132 Rare Book Locator Service
Section 4

No. 133 Recipe Service for Gourmets
Section 5

No. 134 Vitamin Requirement Service
Section 5

No. 135 Computerized Energy Survey Service for Homes and Offices
Section 6

No. 136 SBA Financing Package Service
Section 8

No. 137 Establishing Business Values for Buyers and Sellers
Section 8

No. 138 Computerized Newsletter
Section 24

No. 139 New Business Plan Start-Ups Service
Section 8

No. 140 Sports Forecasting Business
Section 20

No. 141 Secretarial Service
Section 24

No. 142 Travel Planning Service
Section 23

No. 143 Computer School
Sections 26 and 27

No. 144 Computer Camps
Sections 26 and 27

No. 145 Computer Consulting
Sections 26 and 27

No. 146 Apartment Locating Service
Section 18

No. 147 House Rental Locating Service
Section 18

No. 148 Typesetting Service
Section 24

No. 149 Barter Club Service
Section 4

No. 150 Multi-Level Marketing and Record-Keeping
         Sections 7 and 19

No. 151 Sell Local Mailing Lists at $1 per Name
         Sections 7 and 19

No. 152 Computerized Classified Newspaper
         Sections 4 and 24

No. 153 Programming Games for Market
         Section 30

No. 154 Sell Stock Market Advice
         Sections 21 and 28

No. 155 Bookkeeping Service
         Section 1

No. 156 Used Personal Computer Broker
         Sections 4 and 27

No. 157 Customized Sales Letters for Salespeople
         Sections 7, 19 and 24

No. 158 Computerized Corporation Filing Service
         Section 25

No. 159 Custom Electronic Mailing System
         Section 25

No. 160 Computerized Music Systems
         Section 15

No. 161 Sell Custom Educational Programs
         Sections 26 and 27

No. 162 Foreign Language Instruction School
         Sections 26 and 27

No. 163 Information Research Service
         Sections 21 and 28

No. 164 Genealogy and Family Tree Service
         Section 10

No. 165 Home Tutoring for Children Business
         Section 26

No. 166 Personal Financial Statement Service
         Section 8

No. 167 Private Pilot Trip Planner
         Section 23

No. 168 Computer Kits
         Sections 4 and 27

No. 169 Poetry-Made-Easy Verse Business
         Section 4

No. 170 Start and Operate A Computer Club
Sections 7 and 19

No. 171 Custom Computer Poster Service
Section 11

No. 172 Software Exchange Service
Section 4

No. 173 Restaurant Pricing Service
Section 5

No. 174 Crossword Puzzle Design Business
Section 4

No. 175 Checkbook Balancing Service
Section 8

No. 178 Custom Loan, Annuity and Interest Calculations and Analysis Service
Section 8

No. 179 Personal Budget Management Consulting
Section 8

No. 180 Local Store Menu Planning Service
Section 5

No. 181 Coin and Stamp Collection Inventories and Values Service
Section 12

No. 183 Design and Sell Computer Programs for Farmers
Sections 2 and 30

No. 184 Personal Library Cataloguing Service
Section 12

No. 185 Computer Carpooling Service
Section 23

No. 186 Legal Research Service
Section 14

No. 187 Estate Planning Service
Sections 8 and 14

No. 189 Property Analysis Service
Sections 8 and 18

No. 190 Horse Race Handicapping Service
Section 20

No. 191 Accounts Payable Service
Section 1

No. 192 Keeping Stats for Little League Teams for Profit
Section 20

No. 193 Remodeling and New Construction Cost Estimate Service
Section 13

No. 194　Bowling Team Stats Service
　　　　　Section 20

No. 195　Teach Typing for Profit
　　　　　Sections 24 and 25

No. 196　Local Gardeners' Planting Times Newsletter
　　　　　Sections 2 and 4

No. 197　Sell Inventory Controls for Small Business
　　　　　Section 12

No. 198　Auto Trip Planning Service
　　　　　Section 23

No. 199　Investment Analysis Advisor
　　　　　Sections 8 and 28

No. 200　Home Security Systems Analysis Service
　　　　　Sections 4 and 13

No. 202　Local Computer Shows
　　　　　Sections 7, 19 and 27

No. 203　Computer Clubs for Kids for Profit
　　　　　Sections 7 and 19

No. 204　Accounts Receivables and Statement—Mailing Service
　　　　　Section 1

No. 206　Sell Computer Programming Courses
　　　　　Sections 24, 26, 27 and 30

RESOURCE SECTIONS

1. Accounting Software
2. Agriculture and Farming Software
3. Compatibility Analysis Software
4. Data Base Software
5. Diet, Food Service and Menu Planning Software
6. Energy Analysis Software
7. File List, Scheduling, Mailing and Membership Management Software
8. Financial Planning and Analysis Software
9. Formula References
10. Genealogy Software
11. Graphics Software
12. Inventory Control Software
13. Job Cost Software
14. Legal Services Software
15. Music Software
16. Payroll Software
17. Personality Analysis Software

18. Real Estate Software
19. Sales and Marketing Software
20. Sports Software
21. Statistical and Numbers Analysis Software
22. Tax Preparation Software
23. Travel and Transportation Software
24. Word Processing Software

SPECIAL RESOURCE SECTIONS

25. Communications Software
26. Computer-Aided Instruction Software
27. Computer Literacy Software
28. Information Network Data Bases
29. Operating Systems, Languages and Compilers Software
30. Program Creation Software

1. GENERAL ACCOUNTING SOFTWARE

The Accounting Partner
Star Software Systems
206 Gramercy Place
Suite 103
Torrance, CA 90901
(213)538-2511

Altos Accountant
Altos Computer Systems, Inc.
2641 Orchard Parkway
San Jose, CA 95134
(408)946-6700

Architectural Engineering Accounting System
Data Basics
11000 Cedar Road
Suite 110
Cleveland, OH 44106
(216)721-3400

Accounting Pearl
Pearlsoft Inc.
P.O. Box 638
Wilsonville, OR 97070
(503)682-3636

The Assistant Controller Series (Financial Reporting)
Lake Avenue Software
77 North Oak Knoll
Suite 105
Pasadena, CA 91101
(818)792-1844

Apartment Building Management System
Coleman Computer Services
187-02 Keeseville Avenue
St. Albans, NY 11412
(212)454-9833

Accountant's Client Write-Up System
Cyberan Software Inc.
11222 Richmond
Suite 140
Houston, TX 77082
(713)558-8090

Accountant's Pac I
Omni Software Systems, Inc.
146 North Broad Street
Griffith, IN 46319
(219)924-3522

Accountant's Pac II
Omni Software Systems, Inc.
146 North Broad Street Griffith, IN 46319
(219)924-3522

ACUITY Accounting Programs
Computer Cognition
225 West 30th Street
National City, CA 92050
(619)474-6745
(619)474-2010

+ ACCOUNT: General Ledger
Computer Software Consultants, Inc.
180 State Street
Binghamton, NY 13901
(607)722-3538

+ ACCOUNTS: Cash and Payables
Computer Software Consultants, Inc.
180 State Street
Binghamton, NY 13901
(607)722-3538

Datawrite
Accountants Microsystems Inc.
3633 136th Place SE
Bellevue, WA 98006
(206)643-2050

Certiflex Fixed Assets With Depreciation
Certiflex Systems
2526 Manana Drive
Dallas, TX 75220
(214)350-6641

Certiflex Client Write-Up
Certiflex Systems
2526 Manana Drive
Dallas, TX 75220
(214)350-6641

Crossfoot
Omni Software Systems, Inc.
146 North Broad Street
Griffith, IN 46319
(219)924-3522

Construction Master Accounting System
Data Basics
1000 Cedar Road
Suite 110
Cleveland, OH 44106
(216)721-3400

Client Billing System
High Technology Software Products, Inc.
P.O. Box 60406
1161 N.W. 23rd Street
Oklahoma City, OK 73146
(405)524-4359

General Ledger/SuperCalc Interface
Micro Business Applications, Inc.
12281 Nicollet Avenue South
Minneapolis, MN 55337
(612)894-3470

Great Western Software Order Entry
Great Western Software
P.O. Box 1645
Redondo Beach, CA 90278
(213)370-8338

General Ledger
Libra Programming
1954 East 7000 South
Salt Lake City, UT 84121
(899)453-3827
(801)943-2084

General Ledger
Microcomputer Consultants
P.O. Box 1377
Davis, CA 95617
(916)756-8104
(800)824-5952

General Ledger
Sorcim/US Micro Software
2195 Fortune Drive
San Jose, CA 95131
(408)942-1727

General Ledger
Zenith Data Systems
950 Milwaukee Avenue
Glenview, IL 60025
(312)391-8949

General Ledger—Accounts Receivable
Holman Data Products
2366 Lincoln
Oroville, CA 95965
(916)533-5992

General Ledger Accounting System
Univair Systems
9024 St. Charles Rock Road
St. Louis, MO 63114
(314)426-1099

General Ledger II System
International Micro Systems Inc.
6445 Metcalf
Shawnee Mission, KS 66202
(913)677-1137

General Ledger System
Cyberan Software Inc.
11222 Richmond
Suite 140
Houston, TX 77082
(713)558-8090

General Ledger System
Fargo Electronic Services, Inc.
7150 Shady Oak Road
Eden Prairie, MN 55344
(612)941-9470

General Ledger System
International Micro Systems Inc.
6445 Metcalf
Shawnee Mission, KS 66202
(913)677-1137

General Ledger
Eagle Enterprises
2375 Bush Street
San Francisco, CA 94115
(415)346-1249

General Ledger
Computer Agri Venture
105 South Third
St. Peter, MN 56082
(507)931-4075
(507)931-6060

Maxi Accountant
Scott Adams, Inc.
The Business Division
155 Sabal Palm Drive, P.O. Box 3435
Longwood, FL 32790
(305)862-6917

Membership Billing System
MBA Computer Services Inc.
3819 100 Street S.W.
Suite No. 6
Tacoma, WA 98499
(206)581-3262

Moneytrack
Fincom, Inc.
12401 W. Olympic
Los Angeles, CA 90064
(213)207-5330

Multi-Company Option
Micro Business Applications, Inc.
1281 Nicollet Avenue South
Minneapolis, MN 55337
(612)894-3470

Multi-Entity
Lake Avenue Software
77 North Oak Knoll
Suite 105
Pasadena, CA 91101
(818)792-1844

OCC-Accounts Payable
Occupational Computing Company, Inc.
31243 Via Colinas
Suite 107
Westlake Village, CA 91362
(818)991-5077

MONEYWORKS/GL
Northwest Computerworks, Inc.
9725 S.E. 36th Street
Suite 312
Mercer Island, WA 98040
(206)232-6343

MYTE MYKE General Ledger
MDS Associates, Inc.
P.O Box 108
385 N. Buffalo Road
Orchard Park, NY 14127
(716)662-6611

MONEYTRACK
Pacific Data Systems, Inc.
6090 Sepulveda Blvd.
Suite 300
Culver City, CA 90230
(213)559-8713
((800)343-9194

Journal Entry/Cash Disbursement Log
Mighty Byte Computer, Inc.
12629 North Tatum Blvd.
Suite 555
Phoenix, AZ 85032
(602)953-1317

Junior Ledger
Lake Avenue Software
7 North Oak Knoll
Suite 105
Pasadena, CA 91101
(818)792-1844

Lease Classification
Personal Software Company
P.O. Box 776
Salt Lake City, UT 84110
(801)943-6908

The Ledger
Westware, Inc.
2455 S.W. 4th Avenue
Ontario, OR 97914
(503)881-1477

MAI Integrated Accounting Software
MAI/Basic Four Business Products Corp.
601 San Pedro, N.E.
Albuquerque, NM 87108
(505)266-5811

MAPS/AP
Ross Systems Inc.
1860 Embarcadero Road
Palo Alto, CA 94303
(415)856-1100

MAPS/GL
Ross Systems Inc.
1860 Embarcadero Road
Palo Alto, CA 94303
(415)856-1100

MAS 80
MAS 80, Inc.
Box 109A-R2
Ottawa, KS 66067
(913)242-9414

MAXI ACCOUNTANT
Adventure International, Inc.
P.O. Box 3435
Longwood, FL 32750
(305)862-6917

The MBA Accountant
Micro Business Applications, Inc.
12281 Nicollet Avenue South
Minneapolis, MN 55337
(612)894-3470

MDS-Finance
Medical Data Service
P.O Box 740875
Dallas, TX 75374
(214)340-8336

Interactive Business System
Performance Engineered Programs
3970 Syme Drive
Carlsbad, CA 92008
(619)434-6023
(619)434-6024

RealWorld-Sales Analysis
RealWorld Corporation
Dover Road
Chichester, NH 03263
(603)798-5700
(800)255-1115

Solomon General Ledger
Computech Group Incorporated
Mainline Industrial Park
Lee Boulevard
Frazer, PA 19355
(215)644-3344

Solomon Fixed Assets
Computech Group Incorporated
Mainline Industrial Park
Lee Boulevard
Frazer, PA 19355
(215)644-3344

State of the Art General Ledger
State of the Art, Inc.
3183-A Airway Avenue
Costa Mesa, CA 92626
(714)850-0111

STI General Ledger System
Software Technology, Inc.
620 North 48th Street
Suite 120
Lincoln, NE 68504
(402)466-1997

Self-Training Series
BPI Systems, Inc.
3423 Guadalupe
Austin, TX 78705
(512)454-4677

Series 9000 Professional Time Accounting
Univair Systems
9024 St. Charles Rock Road
St. Louis, MO 63114
(314)426-1099

Series 9000 Super Ledger CLient Writeup
Univair Systems
9024 St. Charles ROck Road
St. Louis, MO 63114
(314)426-1099

Single Entry Ledger System
Universal Data Research, Inc.
2457 Wehrle Drive
Buffalo, NY 14221
(716)631-3011
(716)631-3012

Software Solutions
Compleat Systems
1914 Monongahela Avenue
P.O. Box 82561
Pittsburgh, PA 15218
(412)351-6755

Powerful Business Software
Distributed Computing Systems
157 S. Martha Street
P.O. Box 185
Lombard, IL 60148
(312)495-0121

Purchase Order System for Open Systems
Productive Computer Systems, Inc.
111 East Wacker Drive
Suite 2824
Chicago, IL 60601
(312)565-2244

Protime
Resource Systems Group
215 South Highway 101
Suite 112
Solana Beach, CA 92075
(619)755-1626

Quickstart Systems Accounting Systems
Lovett Associates
1089 185th Avenue, N.E.
Bellevue, WA 98008
(206)746-9007

RealWorld-General Ledger
RealWorld Corporation
Dover Road
Chichester, NH 03263
(603)798-5700
(800)255-1115

Public Accounting Business Management System
TOM Software
127 Southwest 156th Street
P.O. Box 66596
Seattle, WA 98166
(206)246-7022

PeachTree General Ledger for the Wang PC
Wang Laboratories, Inc.
One Industrial Avenue
Lowell, MA 01851
(800)225-0234
(617)256-1400

Professional Time Accounting
Micro Business Applications, Inc.
12281 Nicollet Avenue South
Minneapolis, MN 55337
(612)894-3470

The Professional Manager
Automate Computer Software
10,000 1H 10W, Suite 404
P.O. Box 290336
San Antonio, TX 78289
(512)694-4029

PeachPak 4
Peachtree Software Inc.
3445 Peachtree Road, N.E.
Eighth FLoor
Atlanta, GA 30326
(404)239-3000
(800)554-8900

ProBill II
COMPAL, Inc.
8500 Wilshire Blvd.
Beverly Hills, CA 90211
(213)652-2263

Preventative Maintenance System
Omni Software Systems, Inc.
146 North Broad Street
Griffith, IN 46319
(219)924-3522

Open Systems General Ledger
Open Systems, Inc.
430 Oak Grove
Minneapolis, MN 55403
(800)328-2276
(612)870-3515

P.A.C.E.
E.F. Haskell & Assoc., Inc.
1528 E. Missouri Ave.
Suite A-131
Phoenix, AZ 85014
(602)277-2534
(800)732-3688

Open Systems Fixed Assets
Open Systems, Inc.
430 Oak Grove
Minneapolis, MN 55403
(800)328-2276
(612)870-3515

PSS General Ledger System
Programming Services & Support, Inc.
1601 Caledonia Street
Suite B
Lacrosse, WI 54603
(608)781-3200

PC Client Accounting
Omni Software Systems, Inc.
146 North Broad Street
Griffith, IN 46319
(219)924-3522

PSSP—Professional Services Support Package
National Software Support Enterprises
3785 N.W. 82 Avenue
Suite 208
Miami, FL 33166
(305)594-0870

PTA—Professional Time Accounting
Frontier Software
(ASYST Design Services)
756 Bowling Green
Cortland, NY 13045
(607)756-8247

PUMA
Cougar Mountain Software, Inc.
2609 Kootenai
P.O Box 6886
Boise, ID 83707
(208)344-2540

The Write-Up Solution
Creative Solutions, Inc.
230 Collingwood
Suite 250
Ann Arbor, MI 48103
(313)995-8811

Versa Ledger II
Hand E Computronics, Inc.
50 North Pascack Road
Spring Valley, NY 10097
(800)431-2818
(914)425-1535

Vandata Business Package
Vandata
17544 Midvale Avenue North
Suite 107
Seattle, WA 98133
(206)542-7611

Time Accounting
BPI Systems, Inc.
3423 Guadalupe
Austin, TX 78705
(5012)454-4677

TKR III Time and Billing System
E.F. Haskell & Assoc., Inc.
1528 E. Missouri Ave.
Suite A-131
Phoenix, AZ 85014
(602)277-2534
(800)732-3688

TCS Total Accounting System
TCS Software, Inc.
6100 Hillcroft
Suite 600
Houston, TX 77081
(713)771-6000

TCS QNet
TCS Software, Inc.
6100 Hillcroft
Suite 600
Houston, TX 77081
(713)771-6000

Star's General Ledger
Star Software Systems
20600 Gramercy Place
Suite 103
Torrance, CA 90901
(213)538-2511

Star System Plus Legal Billing
Sunbear Systems
1095 Market Street
Suite 404
San Francisco, CA 94103
(415)986-3184

TBS General Ledger System
Theta Business Systems
1110 Sonora Avenue
Suite 106
Glendale, CA 91201
(818)242-7981
(818)442-7984

Super Ledger Client Write-Up
Univair Systems
9024 St. Charles Rock Road
St. Louis, MO 63114
(314)426-1099

Super-G/L General Ledger
Microcomputer Applications
3485 Mock Orange Court South
Salem, OR 97302
(503)364-1090

S.A.I.L. Business System
S.A.I.L. Systems
86 W. University, No. 14
Mesa, AZ 85201
(602)962-1876
(602)890-9143

RealWorld-LedgerLINK
RealWorld Corporation
Dover Road
Chichester, NH 03263
(603)798-5700
(800)255-1115

2. AGRICULTURE AND FARMING SOFTWARE

AG Planner
Countryside Date Inc.
718 North Skyline Drive
Suite 201
Idaho Falls, ID 83402
208-529-8576

AG/PAC
Wisconsin Microware Inc.
5201 Old Middleton Road
Madison, WI 53705
608-233-4459

AgDisk Budget Analysis
AgDisk/Harris Technical Systems
624 Peach Street
Box 80837
Lincoln, NE 68501
402-476-2811

AgDisk Crop Livestock Profit Protection
AgDisk/Harris Technical Systems
624 Peach Street
Box 80837
Lincoln, NE 68501
402-476-2811

AgDisk Crop Record Keeping
AgDisk/Harris Technical Systems
624 Peach Street
Box 80837
Lincoln, NE 68501
402-476-2811

AgDisk Financial Management Series One
AgDisk/Harris Technical Systems
624 Peach Street
Box 80837
Lincoln, NE 68501
402-476-2811

AgDisk Swine Record Keeping
AgDisk/Harris Technical Systems
624 Peach Street
Box 80837
Lincoln, NE 68501
402-476-2811

Beef in Production I
Savant Software Inc.
9124 Switzer
Shawnee Mission, KS 66214
913-222-0544

Beefup 3.01
St. Benedict's Farm
Box 366
Waelder, TX 78959
512-540-4814

Crop Management System
Pd Inc.
2750 N. Texas Street
Suite 110
Fairfield, CA 94533
707-442-0572

Crop Production
Ag Plus Software
906 South Main
Ida Grove, IA 51445
712-364-2135

Dairy Cattle Record Keeping System
Quinn, Gerald. H.
Consultant
32 Weatherstone Pkwy.
Marietta, GA 30067
404-971-4422

Dairy Herd Management Program
Dairy Management Associates
450 West 21st Street
Suite A
Merced, CA 95340
209-383-3955

Dairy-2
University of Maryland
Dept. of Agricultural Economics
Symons Hall
College Park, MD 20742
301-454-4848

Easi-Crop
Universal Software Associates, Inc.
606A West Arch
Searcy, AR 72143
501-268-3018

Easi-Data
Universal Software Associates, Inc.
606A West Arch
Searcy, AR 72143
501-268-3018

FARMCALC
Miracle Computing
313 Clayton Court
Lawrence, KS 66044
913-843-5863

Farm and Agribusiness Management
Summerville Enterprises Agricomputer Sr.
104 Broad Street SE
Aliceville, AL 35442
205-373-6383

Feed Formulation
Computer Agri Venture
105 South Third
St. Peter, MN 65082
507-931-4075

Harvest
Savant Software, Inc.
9124 Switzer
Shawnee Mission, KS 66214
913-888-0544

Micro-Crop
Micro-Crop, Inc.
8245 N.W. 53rd Street
Miami, FL 33166
305-594-2925

Mini-Max
Agricultural Software Consultants, Inc.
1706 Santa Fe
Kingsville, TX 78363
512-595-1937

Nutrition & Money Beef Feeding
Farm & Ranch Software
Rt. 1
Box 51A
Philip, SD 57567
605-386-4523

PDS-AGDATA
Progressive Data Services
207 S. Main Street
Winchester, IN 47394
317-584-0912

Pedigree 2.01
St. Benedict's Farm
Box 366
Waelder, TX 78959
512-540-4814

Professional Ration Package
Agricultural Computer Applications, Inc.
1320 Notre Dame Drive
Davis, CA 95616
916-756-8946

RMS-BEEF Ranch Management System
Computer Systems House
2525 South Main Street
Suite 18
Salt Lake City, UT 84115
801-483-1000

RMS-SHEEP Ranch Management System
Computer Systems House
2525 South Main Street
Suite 18
Salt Lake City, UT 84115
801-483-1000

3. COMPATIBILITY ANALYSIS SOFTWARE

CARS
Computer Development Specialists
P.O. Box 999
Centereach, NY 11720
516-732-2407

Personnel Agency Search System
Solid Software, Inc.
5500 Interstate North Parkway
Suite 501
Atlanta, GA 30328
800-554-4078

Personnel Agency Talent Bank
Executive Data Systems, Inc.
290 Interstate North
Suite 116
Atlanta, GA 30339

Search Manager
Hitech International, Inc.
4966 El Camino Real
Suite 101
Los Altos, CA 94022
415-949-0141

Career Network
Computer Search International
1500 Fulgrave Avenue
Baltimore, MD 21201

Computer-Assisted Research International
1501 Woodfield Rd.
Schaumberg, IL 60195

Computer Job Bank
The Direct Connection Company
P.O. Box 3497
Honolulu, HI 96811

Simulvision
P.O. Box 2382
La Jolla, CA 92038

4. DATABASE SOFTWARE

Version 2.00
GMS Software, Inc.
12 West 37th Street
New York, NY 10018
212-947-3590

DBASE II
Ashton-Tate
10150 W. Jefferson Blvd.
Culver City, CA 90230
213-204-5570

DBASE III
Ashton-Tate
10150 W. Jefferson Blvd.
Culver City, CA 90230
213-204-5570

PFS File
Software Publishing Corporation
1901 Landings Drive
Mountain View, CA 94043
415-962-8910

PFS Report
Software Publishing Corporation
1901 Landings Drive
Mountain View, CA 94043
415-962-8910

The Client Information System
Omni Software Systems, Inc.
146 North Broad St.
Griffith, IN 46319
219-924-3522

The 10 Base
Fox Research, Inc.
705 Corporate Way
Dayton, OH 45459
513-443-2238

1st Base
Desktop Software Corporation
228 Alexander Street
Princeton, NJ 08450
609-924-7111

AE Data Base Development Programs
Aquarius Enterprises
Computer Applications Division
801 Harbor Drive
Forked River, NJ 08731
609-693-0513

Aims
Aims + Plus
1701 Directors Blvd.
Austin, TX 78744
512-385-0702

Aladin
A. D.I. America
1215 Howe Avenue
Sacramento, CA 95825
916-925-2229

Quick File III
Apple Computer, Inc.
20525 Mariani Avenue
Cupertino, CA 95014
408-996-1010

RL-1 Relational Database
ABW Corporation
P. O. Box M1047
Ann Arbor, MI 48106
313-663-3011

RTFIL
Contel Information Systems
430 East West Highway, No 200
Bethseda, MD 20814
301-654-9120

Relational Database Application
Computing Things, Inc.
3021 S. E. 67th Avenue
Portland, OR 97206
503-774-0638

RBase 4000
Microrim
3380 146 Place S.E.
Bellevue, WA 98007
800-547-4000

SALVO
Software Automation, Inc.
14833 Proton Road
Dallas, TX 75234
214-392-2802

SST Data
Satellite Software International
288 West Center St.
Orem, UT 84057
801-224-8554

Sed Data Base Management System
Sed Software
Two Bala Plaza
Suite 300
Bala Cynwyd, PA 19004
215-668-0880

Selector V
Micro-Ap
7033 Village Parkway
Suite 206
Dublin, CA 94568
415-828-6697

PC Focus
Information Builders, Inc.
1250 Broadway
New York, NY 10001
213-736-4433

Please
Hayes Microcomputer Products, Inc.
5923 Peachtree Industrial Blvd.
Norcross, GA 30092
404-449-8791

Pascal Data Management System
Pascal & Associates
P. O. Box 350
Chapel Hill, NC 27514
919-942-1411

Personal Pearl
Pearlsoft, Inc.
P. O. Box 638
Wilsonville, OR 97070
503-682-3636

PhD Integrated Data Management
Micro Business Applications, Inc.
12281 Nicollet Avenue South
Minneapolis, MN 55337
612-894-3470

Pilar Database Management System
Micro Decisionware, Inc.
1695 386th Street
Boulder, CO 80301
303-443-2706

Powerbase
GMS Software, Inc.
12 West 37th Street
New York, NY 10018
212-947-3590

Practibase
PractiCorp. International, Inc.
The Silk Mill
4 Oak Street
Newton Upper Falls, MA 02164
617-965-9870

Practifile
PractiCorp. International, Inc.
The Silk Mill
44 Oak Street
Newton Upper Falls, MA 02164
617-965-9870

Quick File III
Apple Computer, Inc.
20525 Mariani Avenue
Cupertino, CA 95014
408-996-1010

Nomad II
D & B Computing Services
187 Dunbury Rd.
Wilton, CT 06897
203-762-2511

The NPL Information Management System
Digital Equipment Corp.
Professional Applications Group
150 Coulter Drive
Concord, MA 01742
617-264-1165

The NPL Information Management System
Desktop Software Corporation
228 Alexander St.
CN 5287
Princeton, NJ 08450
609-924-7111

Name Directory
Tartec International Inc.
P. O.Box 81
Comack, NY 11725
516-543-8790

Notebook
Digtal Marketing Corp.
2363 Boulevard Circle
Suite 6
Walnut Creek, CA 94595
415-938-2880

The Oficesmith
Officesmiths, Inc.
31 Cooper Street
Ottawa, Ontario K2P OG5
Canada
613-235-6749

**Omnifile-The Professional's
Information Management System**
SSR Corporation
1600 Lyell Avenue
Rochester, NY 14604
716-254-3200

Omnis 3 The Database Manager
Organizational Software Corporation
2655 Campus Drive
Suite 150
San Mateo, CA 94403
415-521-0222

PC Data Base for the Wang PC
Wang Laboratories, Inc.
One Industrial Avenue
Lowell, MA 01851
800-255-0234

Mag Base 1
Mag Software, Inc.
21054 Sherman Way
Suite 305
Canoga Park, CA 91303
818-883-3267

Mag Base 2
Mag Software, Inc.
21054 Sherman Way
Suite 305
Canoga Park, CA 91303
818-883-3267

Mag Base 3
Mag Software, Inc.
21054 Sherman Way
Suite 305
Canoga Park, CA 91303
818-883-3267

Maps DB
Ross Systems, Inc.
1860 Embacadero Rd.
Palo Alto, CA 94303
415-856-1100

MDBS III
Micro Data Base Systems, Inc.
Application Development Products
85W. Algonquin Rd. Suite 400
Arlington Heights, IL 60005
800-323-3629

MDBS EDA
Micro Data Base Systems, Inc
85 W. Alonquin Rd. Suite 400
Arlington Heights, IL 60005
800-323-3629

Metafile
Sensor-based Systems
1701 East Lake Avenue
Glenview, Il 60025
801-323-3731

Manager
Call Manager, Inc.
1961 Old Middlefield Way
Mountain View, CA 94040
415-964-5331

Intellient Database Machine
Britton Lee, Inc.
14600 Winchester Blvd.
Los Gatos, CA 95030
408-378-7000

Intuit
Nouenon Corporation
Suite 201
Alameda, CA 94501
415-521-2145

Key II
Lighthouse Software
P. O. Box 15
Hilton Head Island
Hilton Head, SC 29938
803-785-4949

Keyunit
Great Western Software
P.O. Box 1645
Redondo Beach, CA 90278
213-370-8338

Lan Datastore
Software Connections, Inc.
2041 Mission College Blvd.
Suite 135
Santa Clara, CA 95054
408-988-0300

List Key—The People Program
The Soft Place P. O. Box 7370
1439 East Garfield Avenue
Glendale, CA 91205
818-243-5111

ListKey—The People Program
The Soft Place
P. O. Box 7370
1439 East Garfield Avenue
Glendale, CA 92105
Glendale, CA 91205
818-243-5111

The List Master
Palace Software Co.
Rt. 1, Box 320
Moundsville, WV 26041
304-845-3905

Los File Retriever
Telephone Software Connection, Inc.
P. O. Box 6548
Torrance, CA 90504
213-516-9430

Lucid
Softerware, Inc.
20 Office Center
Suite 305
Fort Washington, PA 19304
215-628-0400

Informix
Relational Database Systems, Inc.
2471 E. Bayshore Rd.
Suite 60
Palo Alto, CA 94303
415-424-1300

IT
MichTron
6655 Highland Rd.
Pontiac, MI 48054
313-666-4800

Incredible Jack Of All Trades
Business Solutions, Inc.
60 East Main Street
P. O. Box 341
Kings Park, NY 11754
800-645-4513

Info 80 Application Development System
The Software Store
706 Chippewa Square
Marquette, MI 49855
906-228-7622

Info Gen
Info Pros, Inc.
2102 Business Center Drive
Irvine, CA 92715
714-851-8975

Info Reporter
Info Pros, Inc.
2102 Business Center Drive
Irvine, CA 92715
714-851-8975

Information Management
BPI Systems, Inc.
3423 Guadalupe
Austin, Texas 78705
512-454-4677

Information Master
High Technology Software Products, Inc.
P. O. Box 60406
16 N. W. 23rd Street
Oklahoma City, OK 73146
405-524-4359

Informational Data Base
Epcom, Inc.
3647 Fairmount Avenue
San Diego, CA 92105
619-283-6211

Infoscope I
Microstuf, Inc.
1845 The Exchange
Suite 140
Atlanta, GA 30339
404-998-3998

Infostar 1.6
Micro International Corp.
3 San Pablo Avenue
San Rafael, CA 94903
415-499-4024

FilePro Multi User
The Small Computer Co., Inc.
230 W. 41st St.
Suite 1200
New York, NY 10036
800-847-4740

File Pro Single User
The Small Computer Co.
230 W. 41st Street
Suite 1200
New York, NY 10036
800-847-4740

Fixed Disk Organizer
International Business Machines
P. O. Box 1328
Boca Raton, FL 33432
800-447-4700

Formula II
Dynamic Microproessor Associates
545 Fifth Avenue
New York, NY 10017
212-687-7115

Formula III
Allied Computer
255 West 98th Street
New York, NY 10025
212-222-5665 **Garbage Plus**
Simple Software
708 Hingham
Schaumburn, IL 60193
312-980-4760

Helix
Odesta
3186 Doolittle Drive
Northbrook, IL 60062
800-323-5432

Homefiler
Micro Lab
2699 Skokie Valley Road
Highland Park, IL 60035
312-433-7550

IBM Bundle
PractiCorp International, Inc.
The Silk Mill
44 Oak Street6
Newton Upper Falls, MA 02164
617-965-9870

Data Manager III
Micro Lab
2699 Skokie Valley Rd.
Highland Park, IL 60035
312-433-7550

Database III for Non-programmers
Applied Micro Management
2791 Interlaken Drive
Marietta, GA 30062
404-993-8802

Database Manager II—The Integrator
Alpha Software Corporation
30 B Street
Burlington, MA 01803
800-451-1018

Database Manager in Microsoft Basic
Tab Books, Inc.
P. O. Box 40
Blue Ridge Summit, PA 17214
800-233-1128

EZ Dbase
Blanton Software Service
4522 Briar Forest
San Antonio, TX 78217
512-657-0766

File It
Relational Database Systems, Inc.
2471 E. Bayshore Blvd.
Suite 60
Palo Alto, CA 94303
415-424-1300

File Clerk Reporter
Landrum Software, Inc.
P. O. Box 842
Palm City, FL 33490
305-286-1324

File Pro 16
The Small Computer Co.
230 W. 41st Street
Suite 200
New York, NY 10036
800-847-4740

File It
Swan Software
P. O. Box 206
Lititz, PA 17543
717-627-0504

File Pro CP/M
The Small Computer Co
230 W. 41st Street
Suite 1200
New York, NY 10036
800-847-4740

DB Pack II
Compu Draw Software House
1227 Goler House
Rochester, NY 14620
716-454-3188

Ddquery
Gemin Information Systems
5500 South Syracuse Circle
Englewood, CO 80111
303-773-1805

DMS II
Microline, Inc.
171 West Front Street
Tyler, TX 75702
214-591-3778

Data Ace
Computer Software Design, Inc.
1911 Wright Circle
Anaheim, CA 92806
714-634-9012

Data Base Manager System
Universal Data Research, Inc.
2457 Wehrle Drive
Buffalo, NY 14221
716-631-3011

Data Factory 6.0
Micro Lab
2699 Skokie Valley Rd.
Highland Park, IL 60035
312-433-7550

Custom File Data Base Management
Custom Data
P. O. Box 1408
Salt Lake City, Utah 84110
801-535-4350

Dard—All Purpose Personal Database
DAR Systems International
P. O. Box 4925
Berkeley, CA 94704

DARAD II Database System, Second Generation
DAR Systems International
P. O. Box 4925
Berkeley, CA 94704

DART
H. J. Hansen Company
330 East Northwest Highway
Mt. Prospect, IL 60056
312-870-8708

DATAFAX
Hewlett Packard Personal Software
3410 Central Expressway
Santa Clara, CA 95051
800-367-4772

DATASAFE
IMSI
633 Fifth Avenue
San Rafael, CA 94901
415-454-6500

DB Master Macintosh
Stoneware Incorporated
50 Belvedere Street
San Rafael, CA 94901
415-454-6500

DBPLUS
Software Banc
61 Massachusetts Avenue
Arlington, MA 02174
617-641-1235

Citation Fact Management
Eagle Enterprises
2375 Bush Street
San Francisco, CA 94115
415-346-1249

Condor20-1
Condor Computer Corp.
2051 S. State Street
Ann Arbor, MI 48104
800-221-8479

Condor 20-3 for the DEC Rainbow 100
Condor Computer Corp.
2051 S. State Street
Ann Arbor, MI 48104
800-221-8479

Condor 3
Hewlett Packard Personal Software
3410 Central Expressway
Santa Clara, CA 95051
800-367-4772

Condor I
Hewlett Packard Personal Software
3410 Central Expressway
Santa Clara, CA 95051
800-367-4772

Condor, Jr.
Condor Computer Corp.
2051 S. State Street
Ann Arbor, MI 48104
800-221-8479

Advanced DB Master
Stoneware Incorporated
50 Belvedere St.
San Rafael, CA 94901
415-454-6500

Advanced Report Generator
Mirage Concepts,Inc.
4055 W. Shaw NO 108
Fresno, CA 93711
209-227-8369

Apple NPL
Apple Computer Inc.
20525 Mariani Avenue
Cupertino, CA 95014
408-996-1010

Apple NPL
Apple Computer Inc.
20525 Mariani Avenue
Cupertino, CA 95014
408-996-1010

AppleFile III
Apple Computer Inc.
20525 Mariani Avenue
Cupertino, CA 95014
408-996-1010

**BDMADS Basic Data Manipulation
and Display System**
Cosmic
112 Barrow Hall
University of Georgia
Athens, GA 30602
404-542-3265

CIP The Concentric Information Processor
Concentric Data Systems, Inc.
18 Lyman Street
Westborough, MA 01581
617-366-1122

CBIMS
Tab Books, Inc.
P. O. Box 40
Blue Ridge Summit, PA 17214
800-233-1128

CCA Data Management System
CE Software
Division of Custom Electronics
238 Exchange Street
Chicopee, MA 01013
413-592-4761

Smart Set
Innovative Software, Inc.
9300 W. 110th Street
Suite 30
Overland Park, KS 66210
913-383-1089

Softdoc
Learning Tools, Inc.
686 Massachusetts Avenue
Cambridge, MA 02139
617-864-8086

Sphere Product Family
Kinch Computer Company
425 Mitchell Street
Ithaca, NY 14850
607-273-0222

T Mate Flash PC
CMDS
P. O. Box 386
Harrisonburg, VA 22801
703-828-6357

THOR
Fastware, Inc.
200 Freeway Drive East
East Orange, NJ 07018
800-372-2345

TIM IV
Innovative Software, Inc.
9300 W. 110th Street
Suite 30
Overland Park, KS 66210
913-383-1089

Unify
Unify Corporation
9570 S.W. Barbur Blvd., No 303
Portland, Or 97219
503-245-6585

Unicorn
Guardian Automated Systems, Inc.
Liberty Building—Suite 600
420 Main Street
Buffalo, NY 14202
716-842-6410

Unifile
Univair Systems
9024 St. Charles Rock Rd.
St. Louis, MO 63114
314-426-1099

5. DIET, FOOD SERVICE and MENU PLANNING SOFTWARE

Nodvill Diet Program
Nodvill Software
24 Nod Road
Ridgefield, CN 06877
203-431-6449

Dietivities 2-1
Progressive Programming
11016 Irwin Avenue S
Bloomington, MN 55437
612-888-7658

Dietmate Weight Loss Predictor
American Dataware, Inc.
P.O. Box 2771
Reston, VA 22090

Healthdisk
Shep Field, Jr.
910 Tyrell Street
Raleigh, NC 27609
919-782-6528

Nutritional Program
Allied Systems Co.
P.O. Box 245
Trona, CA 93562
619-372-5355

Best of Wok Talk
Software Toolworks
15233 Ventura Blvd.
Suite 1118
Sherman Oaks, CA 91403
818-986-4885

Dinner on a Disk
The Computerized Shopper
960 San Antonio Avenue
Suite 5
Palo Alto, CA 94303
415-856-7467

Dinner on a Disk
Homemaker Software
683 Towie Way
Palo Alto, CA 94306
415-856-7467

Micro Cookbook
Virtual Combinatics
P.O. Box 755
Rockport, MA 01966
617-546-6553

What's for Dinner
Software Toolworks
15233 Ventura Blvd.
Suite 1118
Sherman Oaks, CA 91403
818-986-4885

Recipe File
Comm-Data Computer House, Inc.
P.O. Box 325
Milford, MI 48042
313-685-0113

Kitchen Planner
Sav-Soft Products
P.O. Box 24898
San Jose, CA 95154
408-978-1048

Computer Chef Recipe File
Software Toolworks
15233 Ventura Blvd.
Suite 1118
Sherman Oaks, CA 91403
8128-986-4885

The Pizza Program
Gourmet Software
671 Eden Avenue
San Jose, CA 95117
408-866-0887

The Model Diet
Softsync, Inc.
14 East 34th Street
New York, NY 10016
212-685-2080

6. ENERGY ANALYSIS SOFWARE

Solarsoft Energy Design Series
Solarsoft, Inc.
Box 124
Snowmass, CO 81654
303-927-4411

Sunheat 1
Solartek
RD No.1
P.O. Box 255A
West Hurley, NY 12491
914-679-5366

Software Tools for Regulation
The Boston Systems Group
5609 Stearns Hill Rd.
Waltham, MA 02154
617-891-3986

Solar Energy for the Home
Instant Software
Rt. 101 & Elm Street
Peterborough, NH 03458
800-258-5473

7. LIST MANAGEMENT, SCHEDULING, MAILING and MEMBERHSIP MANAGEMENT SOFTWARE

Membership Billing
MBA Computer Services
4810 112th St., S.W.
Tacoma, WA 98499
(206)584-6308

Membership Management System
Davidson and Associates
609 Grove Oak Place, No. 12
Rancho Palos Verdes, CA 90274
(213)378-7826

Membership Manager
Hitech International, Inc.
4966 El Camino Real
Suite 101
Los Altos, CA 94022
(415)949-0141

Method-80 System
ERB Software
P.O. 58713
Houston, TX 77258
(713)485-7436

Microbiz Fund Raiser
Micro Business Consulting
111 S. Locust
Visalia, CA 93291
(209)625-4597

Non-Profit Collection (N-P COLL)
Automated Accounting Systems
1025 Howell Drive
Vinton, VA 24179
(703)890-3446

Non-Profit General Ledger (N-P GL)
Automated Accounting Systems
1025 Howell Drive
Vinton, VA 24179
(703)890-3446

Not-for-Profit Operations Management System
TOM Software 127 Southwest 156th St.
Seattle, WA 98166
(206)246-7022

AA Computer Systems Employee Scheduling
AA Computer Systems
19301 Ventura Blvd.
Suite 203
Tarzana, CA 91356
(213)708-3917

Databook II
Digital Marketing Corporation
2363 Boulevard Circle
Suite 6
Walnut Creek, CA 94595
(800)826-2222

Appointments/Scheduler
Market Software
P.O. Box 2392
Secaucus, NJ 07094
(212)627-1293

Calendar
Compleat Systems
1914 Monongahela Avenue
Pittsburgh, PA 15218
(412)351-6755

Calendar 1
Clear Systems
607 Ashland Avenue
Suite A
Santa Monica, CA 90405
(213)394-7740

Tickler System
Stanford Bank Systems Inc.
P.O. Box 181
Salem, IL 62881
(618)548-5148

BENCHMARK Mail List Manager
Metasoft Corporation
6509 West Frye Road
Suite 12
Chandler, AZ 85224
(602)961-0003
(800)621-1908

BISYBASE
IMSI
633 Fifth Avenue
San Rafael, CA 94901
(415)454-7101

Bluebush Speed File
BlueBush Incorporated
379 St. Mary's Place
Santa Clara, CA 95051
(408)244-1631
(408)244-1632

Bulk Mailer
Satori Software
5507 Woodlawn Avenue
Seattle, WA 98103
(206)633-1469

Address Book
Market Software
P.O Box 2392
Secaucus, NJ 07094
(212)627-1293

ZyINDEX Professional
Zylab Corporation
233 East Erie
Chicago, IL 60611
(312)642-2201

DATAHANDLER
Miller Microcomputer Services
61 Lake Shore Road
Natick, MA 01760
(617)653-6136

DATAHANDLER-PLUS
Miller Microcomputer Services
61 Lake Shore Road
Natick, MA 01769
(617)653-6136

Catalyst
Stone & Associates
7910 Ivanhoe Avenue
Suite 319
La Jolla, CA 92037
(800)624-2262
(619)459-9173

Client List
Navic Software
Box 14727
North Palm Beach, FL 33408
(305)627-4132
(800)327-2133

Client Lists & Labels
Data Easy
Data Consulting Group
12 Skylark Drive, No. 18
Larkspur, CA 94939
(415)927-0990

Clo$e (Computer Logic for $ales Efficiency)
Adler Computer Technology
21777 Ventura Blvd.
Suite 228
Woodland Hills, CA 91364
(818)703-0350

Computer Cat
Colorado Computer Systems, Inc.
3039 West 74th Avenue
Westminster, NC 80030
(303)426-5880

PLUS DESKTOP
Computer Software Consultants, Inc.
180 State Street
Binghamtom, NY 13901
(607)722-3538

DataManagr
Vector Graphic, Inc.
500 North Ventu Park Road
Thousand Oaks, CA 91320
(805)499-5831
(800)235-3547

E-Mail Management (E-MAILMGT)
CobraSoft, Inc.
13543 Hawthorne Blvd.
Suite 203
Hawthorne, CA 90250
(213)644-1135
(213)644-1136

EAZYFILE
Miracle Computing
313 Clayton Court
Lawrence, KS 66044
(913)843-5863

EAZYMAIL
Miracle Computing
313 Clayton Court
Lawrence, KS 66044
(913)843-5863

EZ-MAILIST
Blanton Software Service
4522 Briar Forrest
San Antonio, TX 78217
(512)657-0766
(512)341-8801

EZ-SPEED Record Management System
TOM Software
127 Southwest 156th Street
P.O. Box 66596
Seattle, WA 98166
(206)246-7022

EasyFiler
Sorcim/IUS Micro Software
2195 Fortune Drive
San Jose, CA 95131
(408)942-1727

Eureka!
Disco-Tech
Division of Morton Technologies
600 B Street, P.O. Box 1659
Santa Rosa, CA 95402
(707)523-1600

MailMerge
Zenith Data Systems
950 Milwaukee Avenue
Glenview, IL 60025
(312)391-8949

Mailer
Maurizi Associates
1344 Fitch Way
Sacramento, CA 95825
(916)486-2993

Mailing
COMPAL, Inc.
8500 Wilshire Blvd.
Beverly Hills, CA 90211
(213)652-2263

Mailing List Management System
International Micro Systems, Inc.
6445 Metcalf
Shawnee Mission, KS 66202
(913)677-1137

Mailing List Programs
Brock's
1226 Booth Street
Howell, MI 48843
(517)546-1075

Mailing List System
Fargo Electronic Services, Inc.
7150 Shady Oak Road
Eden Prairie, MN 55344
(612)941-9470

Mailing List and Business Letters
MicroPro International Corporation
33 San Pablo Avenue
San Rafael, CA 94903
(415)499-4024
(415)499-4022

Mailstar I
Sapana Micro Software
1305 South Rouse
Pittsburg, KS 66762
(316)231-5023

Memory Finder
Hes Ware
150 North Hill Drive
Brisbane, CA 94005
(415)468-4111

Merge'n Print/Mailing Label and Datafiler
MBS Software
12729 N.E. Hassalo Street
Portland, OR 97230
(503)256-0130
(503)228-9402

Post Master
High Technology Software Products, Inc.
P.O. Box 60406
1161 N.W. 23rd Street
Oklahoma City, OK 73146
(405)524-4359

PowerIndex
Beaman Porter, Inc.
Pleasant Ridge Road
Harrison, NY 10528
(914)967-3504

Query!2
Hoyle & Hoyle Software, Inc.
716 S. Elam Avenue
Greensboro, NC 27403
(919)378-1050

Quick File III
Apple Computer, Inc.
20525 Mariani Avenue
Cupertino, CA 95014
(408)996-1010

Rabbit Base 20
PractiCorp International Inc.
The Silk Mill
44 Oak Street
Newton Upper Falls, MA 02164
(617)965-9870

Sales CTRL
Computer Task Group, Inc.
800 Delaware Avenue
Buffalo, NY 14209
(716)882-8000

Sapana:Cardfile
Sapana Micro Software
1305 South Rouse
Pittsburg, KS 66762
(316)231-5023

SeekEasy
Correlation Systems
81 Rockinghorse Road
Rancho Palos Verdes, CA 90274
(213)833-3462

Solomon Address Mail List
Computech Group Incorporated
Mainline Industrial Park
Lee Boulevard
Frazer, PA 19355
(215)644-3344

Speedtrieve
Assurance Software Products, Inc.
92 Wyckoff Street
Brooklyn, NY 11201
(212)834-1279

Database 3
Holliday Software
4807 Arlene Street
San Diego, CA 92117
(619)292-7766

Database Manager
Mirage Concepts, Inc.
4055 W. Shaw, No. 108
Fresno, CA 93711
(209)227-8369

Database Manager II-The Integrator
Alpha Software Corporation
30 B Street
Burlington, MA 01803
(617)229-2924
(800)451-1018

Desk Organizer
Conceptual Instruments
4730 Warrington Avenue
Philadelphia, PA 19143
(215)726-7856

Diskette Librarian
International Business Machines
P.O. Box 1328
Boca Raton, FL 33432
(800)447-4700
(800)447-0890

Tims
Sugar Software
2153 Leah Lane
Reynoldsburg, OH 43068
(614)861-0565

Timsmail
Sugar Software
2153 Leah Lane
Reynoldsburg, OH 43068
(614)861-0565

Universal Mailing List
Computer Barn
P.O. Box 6388
319 Main Street, No. 2
Salinas, CA 93912
(408)757-0788
(408)663-5665

VisiFile
VisiCorp Personal Software
2895 Zanker Road
San Jose, CA 95134
(408)946-9000

WORD.EX
Supplemental Software
1825 Westcliff Drive
Suite 116
Newport Beach, CA 92660

WP Sorter
Satellite Software International
288 West Center Street
Orem, UT 84057
(801)224-8554
(800)321-5906

PC File Utilities
Data Easy
Data Consulting Group
12 Skylark Drive, No. 18
Larkspur, CA 94939
(415)927-0990

PC Names & Notes
Data Easy
Data Consulting Group
12 Skylark Drive, No. 18
Larkspur, CA 94939
(415)927-0990

PC Ultimate Mailer
Data Easy
Data Consulting Group
12 Skylark Drive, No. 18
Larkspur, CA 94939
(415)927-0990

PSS Mailing Lable System
Programming Services & Support, Inc.
1601 Caledonia Street
Suite B
Lacrosse, WI 54603
(608)781-3200

Palantir Filer
Palantir Software
7701 Wilshire Place Drive
Suite 110
Houston, TX 77040
(713)520-8221
(800)368-3797

Personal Card File
Hewlett-Packard Personal Software
3410 Central Expressway
Santa Clara, CA 95051
(800)367-4772

Phi Beta Filer
Scarborough Systems, Inc.
25 North Broadway
Tarrytown, NY 10591
(914)332-4545

Multiple Labels
Applied Professional Software
30 E. Huntland Drive
Suite 111
Austin, TX 78752
(512)452-3538

8. FINANCIAL PLANNING and ANALYSIS SOFTWARE

Collection Cartoons
123 Fourth Street, N.W.
Charlottesville, VA 22901

Abacus Software
P.O. Box 7211
Grand Rapids, MI 49510
616-241-5510

Apparat, Inc.
4401 S. Tamarac Pkway.
Denver, CO 80237
303-741-1778

Arrays, Inc.
Continental Software
11223 S. Hindry Ave.
Los Angeles, CA 90045
213-410-9466

Atari, Inc.
1272 Borregas Avenue
Sunnyvale, CA 94086
408-745-2000

Best Programs, Inc.
5134 Leesburg Pike
Alexandria, VA 22302
703-931-1300

BPI Systems, Inc.
3424 Guadalupe
Austin, TX 78705
512-454-4677

Computer Ed.
1002 Brookes Avenue West
San Diego, CA 92103
619-291-4344

Computer Tax Service
P.O. Box 7915
Incline Village, NV 89450
702-832-1001

Computerized Management Systems
1039 Caldiz Dr.
Simi, CA 93065
805-526-0151

Computerware
P.O. Box 668
Encinitas, CA 92024
619-436-3512

Creative Software
50 N. Pascack Road
Spring Valley, NY 10977
800-745-1655

Decision Support Software
1300 Vincent Place
McLean, VA 22101
703-442-7900

Douthett Software
200 W. Douglas
Suite 930
Wichita, KA 67202
316-262-1040

Dow Jones & Company,Inc.
P.O. Box 300
Princeton, NJ 08540
609-452-2000

Dynacomp, Inc.
1427 Monroe Avenue
Rochester, NY 14618
716-442-8960

E.E.Comstock
Rt. 2 P.O. Box 26
Pt. Washington, FL 32454
904-231-4332

Ensign Software
7337 Northview
Boise, ID 83704
208-378-8086

Financier, Inc.
P.O. Box 670
Westboro, MA 01851
617-366-0950

Firefighter Software/Practical Peripherals
31245 La Baya Drive
Westlake Vill., CA 91362
213-991-8200

Futurehouse, Inc.
P.O. Box 3470
Chapel Hill, NC 27514
919-967-0861

Hesware
150 N. Hill Dr.
Brisbane, CA 94005
415-468-4111

High Technology Software Products, Inc.
P.O. Box 60406
Oklahoma City, OK 73146
405-524-4359

Howard W. Sams & Co., Inc.
4300 W. 62nd Street
Indianapolis, IN 46206
317-298-5400

IBM
P.O. Box 1328
Boca Raton, FL 33432
800-447-4700

Innosys, Inc.
2150 Shattuck Avenue
Berkeley, CA 94704
415-843-8122

International Microcomputer Software, Inc.
633 5th Avenue
San Rafael, CA 94901
415-454-7101

International Tri Micro
1010 N. Batavia
Suite G
Orange, CA 92667
714-771-4038

Lumen Systems, Inc.
P.O. Box 9893
Englewood, NJ 07631
201-592-1121

Micro-Art Programmers
173 Birch Avenue
Cayucos, CA 93430
805-995-2329

Modular Turnkey Systems, Inc.
State Rte. 1
P.O. Box 60
Jessieville, AR 71949
501-984-5424

Monogram
8295 S. La Cenega Blvd.
Inglewood, CA 90301
213-215-0529

Peachtree Software, Inc.
3445 Peachtree Road, N.E.
Atlanta, GA 30326
800-554-8900

Powersoft, Inc.
P.O. Box 157
Pitman, NJ 08071
609-589-5500

Rak Electronics
P.O. Box 1585
Orange Park, FL 32067
904-264-6777

Reichert Digital Systems
29 Blazier Rd.
Warren, NJ 07060
201-469-3854

Scarborough Systems, Inc.
25 N. Broadway
Tarrytown, NY 10591
914-332-4545

SDE Software
2463 McCready Avenue
Los Angeles, CA 90039
213-661-2031

Silent Butler Software
1423 E. Alameda Avenue
Burbank, CA 91501
213-846-7571

Silversoft
906 N. Main
Wichita, KS 67203
316-262-1040

Softquest
P.O. Box 3456
McLean, VA 22103
703-281-1621

The Software Guild
2935 Whipple Road
Union City, CA 94587
415-487-5200

Spectrum Software
690 W. Fremont Avenue
Suite A
Sunnyvale, CA 94087
408-738-4387

Sundex Software
3000 Pearl Street
Boulder, CO 80301
303-440-3600

Tandy Corp./Radio Shack
1800 One Tandy Center
Fort Worth, TX 76102
817-390-3935

Taranto & Associates, Inc.
P.O. Box 6073
San Rafael, CA 94903
800-227-2868

Timeworks, Inc.
P.O. Box 321
Deerfield, IL 60015
312-942-9200

Total Software, Inc.
1555 3rd Avenue
Walnut Creek, CA 94596
415-943-7877

Turning Point Software
11A Main Street
Watertown, MA 02172
617-923-4441

Wizard of OSZ
9614C Cozycraft Avenue
Chatsworth, CA 91311
213-709-6202

Desktop Broker
C.D. Anderson
300 Montgomery St.
Suite 440
San Francisco, CA 94104
800-822-2222

Market Analyst
Anidata
7200 Westfield Avenue
Pennsauken, NJ 08110
609-663-8123

Oscar
ATS Software, Inc.
90 John St.
New York, NY 10038
212-227-5731

Micro PMS
The Boston Company
One Boston Place
Boston, MA 02106
617-722-7939

Window on Wall Street
Bristol Financial Systems, Inc.
23 Bristol Place
Wilton, CT 06897
203-834-0040

Opval
Calc Shop, Inc.
P.O. Box 1231
W. Caldwell, NJ 07007
201-228-9139

CompuServe Information Service
CompuServe
5000 Arlington Centre Blvd.
Columbus, OH 43220
614-457-8650

Compu Trac Programs
Compu Trac, Inc.
1021 9th Street
New Orleans, LA 70115
504-895-1474

Stockcraft
Decision Economics, Inc.
14 Old Farm Road
Cedar Knolls, NJ 07927
201-539-6889

Market Analyzer
Dow Jones & Co.
P.O. Box 300
Princeton, NJ 08540
800-257-5114

9. FORMULA REFERENCES

A Handbook of Laboratory Solutions
M.H. Gabb, W.E. Latcham
1968

Harry's Cosmeticology
Revised by J.B. Wilkinson
1973

Concise Chemical and Technical Dictionary
Edited by H. Bennett
1974

Flavor Technology
Henry B. Heath
1978

A Formulary of Paints and Other Coatings
Compiled by Michael and Irene Ash
1978

A Formulary of Cosmetic Preparations
Compiled by Michael and Irene Ash
1977

The Chemical Formulary Series
Edited by H. Bennett

A Formulary of Detergents and Other Cleaning Agents
Michael and Irene Ash
1980

Practical Formulas for Hobby or Profit
edited by Henry Goldschmiedt
1973

Concise Paint Technology
J. Boxall
1977

Dyes and Their Intermediates
E.N. Abrahart
197

Encyclopedia of Surfactants
Michael and Irene Ash
Vol. I, 1980, Vol. II, 1981, Vol. III, 1981

Household and Industrial Chemical Specialties
L. Chalmers, revised by P. Bathe

Lange's Handbook of Chemistry, Twelfth Edition
Edited by John A. Dean
1978

The Analysis of Detergents and Detergent Products
G.F. Longman
1975

The Chemist's Companion
A.J. Gordon
1973

10. GENEALOGY SOFTWARE

Commsoft
655 Maybell Avenue
Palo Alto, CA 94306
415-493-2184

Family Reunion
Personal Software Company
P.O. Box 776
Salt Lake City, UT 84110
801-943-6908

Family Tree
Mich Tron
6655 Highland Road
Pontiac, MI 48054
313-666-4800

Family Tree
Personal Software Company
P.O. Box 776
Salt Lake City, UT 84110
801-943-6908

11. GRAPHICS SOFTWARE

4-POINT GRAPHICS
IMSI
633 Fifth Avenue
San Rafael, CA 94901
(415)454-7101

Apple Flasher
Crow Ridge Associates, Inc.
P.O. Box 1
New Scotland, NY 12127
(518)765-3620

Apple II Business Graphics
Apple Computer, Inc.
20525 Mariani Avenue
Cupertino, CA 95014
(408)996-1010

Applegraphics
Apple Computer, Inc.
20525 Mariani Avenue
Cupertino, CA 95014
(408)996-1010

Artchart
Color Terminals Inc.
189 E. Big Beaver Road
Troy, MI 48083
(313)528-2787

Artist
Sunshine Computer Software Co.
1101 Post Oak Blvd.
Suite 90493
Houston, TX 77056
(713)552-0949

Banner Maker
Telephone Software Connection, Inc.
P.O. Box 6548
Torrance, CA 90504
(213)516-9430

Banner Printer
Reynolds, Raymond L.
384 Hyacinth Street
Fall River, MA 02720
(617)673-4968

Bar Graph Generator
Data Easy
Data Consulting Group
12 Skylark Drive, No. 18
Larkspur, CA 94939
(415)927-0990

C-Graphics
Kern Publications
433 Washington Street
P.O. Box 1029
Duxbury, MA 02331
(617)934-0445

CLM COGO
CLM Systems, Inc.
3654 Gandy Blvd.
Tampa, FL 33611
(813)831-7090

ChartStar
MicroPro International Corporation
33 San Pablo Avenue
San Rafael, CA 94903
(415)499-4024

Chartgraphics/Artgraphics
Xybion Corporation
240 Cedar Knolls Road
Cedar Knolls, NJ 07927
(201)538-5111

Chartpak-64
Abacus Software
P.O. Box 7211
Grand Rapids, MI 49510
(616)241-5510

Charts Unlimited
Graphware, Inc.
5084 Mosiman Road
Middletown, OH 45042
(513)424-6733

Color Graphic Printer Package
Dragonfly Software
729 Westview Street
Philadelphia, PA 19119

Color Magic
Brightbill-Roberts and Co. Ltd.
Suite 421, University Bldg.
120 E. Washington Street
Syracuse, NY 13202
(315)474-3400

Commodore 64 Graphic & Sound Programming
Tab Books Inc.
P.O. Box 40
Blue Ridge Summit, PA 17214
(800)233-1128

Creative Graphics
Accupipe Corporation
222 West Lancaster Avenue
Paoli, PA 19301
(215)296-7376

Curve II CRT
West Coast Consultants
1775 Lincoln Blvd.
Tracy, CA 95376
(209)835-1780

Curve Three-D
West Coast Consultants
1775 Lincoln Blvd.
Tracy, CA 95376
(209)835-1780

Curvefit
West Coast Consultants
1775 Lincoln Blvd.
Tracy, CA 95376
(209)835-1780

DICOMEDIA Micro 2
DICOMED Corporation
9700 Newton Avenue
Minneapolis, MN 55431
(612)887-7100

DaVinci II
Professional Research Consultants Inc.
12832 Augusta Avenue
Omaha, NE 68144
(402)330-5433

Dazzle Draw
Broderbund Software
17 Pual Drive
San Rafael, CA 94903
(415)479-1170

Designer's Toolkit
Apple Computer, Inc.
20525 Mariani Avenue
Cupertino, CA 95014
(408)996-1010

Designer-3D
Kern Publications
433 Washington Street
Duxbury, MA 02331
(617)934-0445

Diagraph by Computer Support Corp.
Hewlett-Packard Personal Software
3410 Central Expressway
Santa Clara, CA 95051
(800)367-4772

The Direc/Tree
Micro-Z Company
Box 2426
Rolling Hills, CA 90274
(213)377-1640

EASYGRAF
Miracle Computer
313 Clayton Court
Lawrence, KS 66044
(913)843-5863

Ed-A-Sketch Graphics Editor
Software Toolworks
15233 Ventura Blvd.
Suite 1118
Sherman Oaks, CA 91403
(818)986-4885

Energraphics
Enertronics Research Inc.
150 North Meramec
St. Louis, MO
(800)325-0174

Enhanced Business Graphics
Strobe, Inc.
897-5A Independence Ave.
Mountain View, CA 94043
(800)451-8108

FINGRAPH
Digital Equipment Corporation
Professional Applications Group
150 Coulter Drive
Concord, MA 01742
(617)264-1165

Flowchart
Sunshine Computer Software Co.
1101 Post Oak Blvd.
Suite 9-493
Houston, TX 77056
(713)552-0949

Fontrix 1.1
Data Transforms, Inc.
616 Washington Street
Suite 106
Denver, CO 80203
(303)832-1501

Fontrix 2.0
Data Transforms, Inc.
616 Washington Street
Suite 106
Denver, CO 80203
(303)832-1501

Forecast Plus
Walonick Associates
5624 Girard Avenue South
Minneapolis, MN 55419
(612)866-9022

GRAPHIT
Miracle Computing
313 Clayton Court
Lawrence, KS 66044
(913)843-5863

Giant Graphics
Telephone Software Connection, Inc.
P.O. Box 6548
Torrance, CA 90504
(213)526-9430

Grafiti
MichTron
6655 Highland Road
Pontiac, MI 48054
(313)666-4800

Grafix Partner
Brightbill-Roberts and Co. Ltd.
Suite 421, University Bldg.
120 E. Washington Street
Syracuse, NY 13202
(315)474-3400

GraphPlan
Hewlett-Packard Personal Software
3410 Central Expressway
Santa Clara, CA 95051
(800)367-4772

Graphics for the IBM
Kern Publications
433 Washington Street
Duxbury, MA 02331
(617)934-0445

GraphicMaster
Tid Bit Software
P.O. Box 5579
Santa Barbara, CA 93150
969-5834

Graphicom
MichTron
6655 Highlands Road
Pontiac, MI 48054
(313)666-4800

Graphics Applications System
Avant-Garde Publishing Corp.
P.O. Box 30160
Eugene, OR 97403
(503)345-3043

Graphics Programs for IBM PC
Tab Books Inc.
P.O Box 40
Blue Ridge Summit, PA 17214
(800)233-1128

Graphics Wizard III
Micro Lab
2699 Skokie Valley Road
Highland Park, IL 60035
(312)433-7550

Graphics in "C" Library With Source
Solution Systems
45-L Accord Park
Norwell, MA 02061
(617)871-5435

Graphmagic
Brightbill-Roberts and Co. Ltd.
Suite 421, University Bldg.
120 E. Washington Street
Syracuse, NY 13202
(315)474-3400

IBM Graphing Assistant
International Business Machines
P.O. Box 1328
Boca Raton, FL 33432
(800)447-4700

IBM PC Graphics
Tab Books Inc.
P.O. Box 40
Blue Ridge Summit, PA 17214
(800)233-1128

The Illustrator
Island Graphics
1 Harbor Drive
Sausalito, CA 94965
(415)332-5400

Insta-Graph
Microsci
2158 South Hathaway
Santa Ana, CA 92705
(714)241-5600

JOYDRAW
Miracle Computing
313 Clayton Court
Lawrence, KS 66044
(913)843-5863

Laser Shapes
Scarborough Systems, Inc.
25 North Broadway
Tarrytown, NY 10591
(914)332-4545

MacGraphics
Tab Books Inc.
P.O. Box 40
Blue Ridge Summit, PA 17214
(800)233-1128

12. INVENTORY CONTROL SOFTWARE

Absolut Business and Inventory Management System
Absolut Software
2001 Beacon Street
Boston, MA 02146
(617)277-0610
(800)ABS-UNIX

BACS-Order and Inventory System
American Business Systems, Inc.
3 Littleton Road
Westford, MA 01886
(617)692-2600

BPI Inventory Control System
Apple Computer, Inc.
20525 Mariani Avenue
Cupertino, CA 95014
(408)996-1010

Bill of Materials Package for Open Systems
Productive Computer Systems, Inc.
111 East Wacker Drive
Suite 2824
Chicago, IL 60601
(312)565-2244

Business Accounting—Inventory Management
Peachtree Software, Inc.
3445 Peachtree Road, N.E.
Eighth Floor
Atlanta, GA 30326
(404)239-3000
(800)554-8900

BACS—Order and Inventory System
American Business Systems, Inc.
3 Littleton Road
Westford, MA 01886
(617)692-2600

BACS-Point of Sale System
American Business Systems, Inc.
3 Littleton Road
Westford, MA 01886
(617)692-2600

BPI Inventory Control System
Apple Computer, Inc.
20525 Mariani Avenue
Cupertino, CA 95014
(408)996-1010

Bake Sheet and Inventory
Digitz, Inc.
3015 Hillsborough Street
Raleigh, NC 27607
(919)828-5227
(919)828-5112

Bill of Material
Computer Detailing Corporation
301 York Road
Warminster, PA 18974
(215)675-4831

Bill of Materials Package for Open Systems
Productive Computer Systems, Inc.
111 East Wacker Drive
Suite 2824
Chicago, IL 60601
(312)565-2244

Business Accounting—Inventory Management
Peachtree Software Inc.
3445 Peachtree Road, N.E.
Eighth Floor
Atlanta, GA 30326
(800)554-8900

Coins
Compu-Quote
6914 Berquist Ave.
Canoga Park, CA 91307
(213)348-3662

Coinminder II
Mitchell Software Associates
699 Oregon Avenue
Palo Alto, CA 94301
(408)263-7155
(415)328-2177

CYMA Inventory
CYMA Corporation
2160 East Brown Road
Mesa, AZ 85203
(602)835-8880

Carpet Inventory
Micros Illuminated
Box 745
Olney, TX 76374
(817)873-4550

Certiflex Bill of Materials Inventory
Certiflex Systems
2526 Manana Drive
Dallas, TX 75220
(214)350-6641

Certiflex Inventory Control
Certiflex Systems
2526 Manana Drive
Dallas, TX 75220
(214)350-6641

Desktop Inventory Manager
Rocky Mountain Software Systems
1280C Newell Avenue
Suite 1292
Walnut Creek, CA 94596
(415)680-8378

Easy Business Inventory Control
Information Unlimited Software
2401 Marinship Way
Sausalito, CA 94965
(415)331-6700

Full-Screen Inventory With MRP
Computer Systems Consultants
1454 Latta Lane
Conyers, GA 30207
(404)483-1717

HAI-LINE Inventory
Holland Automatic U.S.A, Inc.
3400-D West MacArthur Blvd.
Santa Ana, CA 92704
(714)641-2844

HARDISK Accounting Series—Inventory
Great Plains Software
1701 38th Street, S.W.
Fargo, ND 58103
(701)281-0550

HP 150 Inventory Control by BPI
Hewlett-Packard Personal Software
3410 Central Expressway
Santa Clara, CA 95051
(800)367-4772

ICAS—Inventory Control
Infoware Systems Inc.
P.O. Box 22487
Denver, CO 80222
(303)740-6071

Inventory
COMPAL, Inc.
8500 Wilshire Blvd.
Beverly Hills, CA 90211
(213)652-2263

Stockroom Manager
Navic Software
Box 14727
North Palm Beach, FL 33408
(800)327-2133

The Store Manager
High Technology Software Products, Inc.
P.O. Box 60406
1161 N.W. 23rd Street
Oklahoma City, OK 73146
(405)524-4359

Symbtrak
Advanced Business Technology, Inc.
1180 Coleman Avenue
San Jose, CA 95110
(408)275-9880

TBS Order Entry With Inventory Control, Billing & Sales Analysis
Theta Business Systems
1110 Sonora Avenue
Suite 106
Glendale, CA 91201
(818)242-7981

Versa Inventory
H and E Computronics, Inc.
50 North Pascack Road
Spring Valley, NY 10097
(800)431-2818

Warehouse Manager
Organic Computing
96 Caddo Peak
Joshua, TX 76058
(817)295-3802

Purchase Order Control V1
Data Easy
Data Consulting Group
12 Skylark Drive, No. 18
Larkspur, CA 94939
(415)927-0990

Purchase Order Control V2 Data Easy
Data Consulting Group
12 Skylark Drive, No. 18
Larkspur, CA 94939
(415)927-0990

RealWorld Inventory Control
RealWorld Corporation
Dover Road
Chichester, NH 03263
(800)255-1115

RealWorld Order Entry
RealWorld Corporation
Dover Road
Chichester, NH 03263
(800)255-1115

Retail Inventory & Billing
Alpine Data
635 Main Street
Montrose, CO 81401
(303)249-1400

Small Business Inventory
Data Soft of New Hampshire
22 Stevens Avenue
Merrimack, NH 03054
(603)424-5217

Software Solutions
Compleat Systems
1914 Monongahela Avenue
P.O. Box 82561
Pittsburgh, PA 15218
(412)351-6755

COINS
Compu Quote
6914 Berquist Avenue
Canoga Park, CA 91307
213-348-3662

Coinminder II
Mitchell Software Associates
699 Oregon Avenue
Palo Alto, CA 94301
408-263-7155

13. JOB COST SOFTWARE

Photo Offset Printing Cost Estimator
Pasadena Technology Press
3543 E. California Blvd.
Pasadena, CA 91107
(213)795-9460

Reach and Frequency
Mediasoft Inc.
6161 N. May Ave.
Suite 2004
Oklahoma City, OK 73112
(405)842-8165

TVCPP Analysis: TV Media Buyer/Seller CPP Calculations
North Country Computer Services
R.R. No. 2, Box 198
Cornish, NH 03745
(603)675-6433

Tracker
Design Consultants
24522 Quad Park Lane
Mt. Clemens, MI 48043
(313)792-0772

Application Interpreter-l, AI/1
Construction Estimating Company
1713 Sutter Street
Vallejo, CA 94590
(707)552-5476

Audit
Micro Craft, Inc.
2007 Whitesburg Drive
Huntsville, AL 35801
(205)534-4190

HARDISK Accounting Series-Job Cost With Cost Estimating
Great Plains Software
1701 38th St., S.W.
Fargo, ND 58103
(701)281-0550

Business Accounting—Job Costing
Peachtree Software Inc.
3445 Peachtree Road, N.E.
Eighth Floor
Atlanta, GA 30326
(800)554-8900

Job Accounting System
International Micro Systems Inc.
6445 Metcalf
Shawnee Mission, KS 66202
(913)677-1137

Job Cost
BPI Systems, Inc.
3423 Guadalupe
Austin, TX 78705
(512)454-4677

Job Cost Accounting
Fargo Electronic Services, Inc.
7150 Shady Oak Road
Eden Prairie, MN 55344
(612)941-9470

Job Costing
Libra Programming
1954 East 7000 South
Salt Lake City, UT 84121
(800)453-3827

Jobcost Accounting
Computer Guidance and Support
P.O Box 620127
Littleton, CO 80162
(303)973-4035

ALEC
Rockware
P.O. Box 8526
La Crescenta, CA 91214
(818)957-8187

Crystal Estimating
Software Resource Center
3100 Broadway
Suite 203
Boulder, CO 80302
(303)443-5528

Expert-Plus
Decision Science Software, Inc.
P.O. Box 7876
Austin, TX 78746
(512)926-4527

Monitor
The Clements Company
936 Alice Lane
Menlo Park, CA 94025
(415)321-1617

Netcon I/Netcon II
PPMCS
1309 East 132nd Street
Burnsville, MN 55337
(805)644-1418

On Time
MicroComputer Specialists Inc.
18 Lyman Street
Westboro, MA 01581
(617)366-1200

PMS-II
North America MICA, Inc.
1772 Sorrento Valley Road
Suite 100
San Diego, CA 92121
(619)481-6998

PeachPlan
Peachtree Software Inc.
345 Peachtree Road, N.E.
Eighth Floor
Atlanta, GA 30326
(800)554-8900

Peachtree Job Costing for the Wang PC
Wang Laboratories, Inc.
One Industrial Avenue
Lowell, MA 01851
(800)225-0234

Solomon Job Costing
Computech Group Incorporated
Mainline Industrial Park
Lee Boulevard
Frazer, PA 19355
(215)644-3344

Construction Cost Estimating
Caldwell Software
514 Peralta Avenue
San Francisco, CA 94110
(415)824-4315

Construction Estimating System
Computer Services
P.O. Box 702
Fairmont, NC 28340
(919)628-8727

Construction Management Information System
Construction Data Control, Inc.
6140 Northbelt Parkway
Suite A
Norcross, GA 30071
(404)448-4722

The Edge
The Edge
P.O Box 149
San Luis Obispo, CA 93406
(805)544-1077

ICAS—Job Costing
Infoware Systems Inc.
P.O. Box 22487
Denver, CO 80222
(303)740-6071

Job Cost
BPI Systems, Inc.
3423 Guadalupe
Austin, TX 78705
(512)454-4677

Jobcost
Gemini Information Systems
5500 South Syracuse Circle
Englewood, CO 80111
(303)773-1805

MEDALLION Job Cost
Timberline Systems, Inc,.
7180 S.W. Fir Loop
Portland, OR 97223
(503)684-3660

P.A.C.E. (Prompt, Accurate Cost Estimator)
High Technology Software Products, Inc.
P.O Box 60406
1161 N.W. 23rd Street
Oklahoma City, OK 73146
(405)524-4359

Quick $
Construction Computing
Box 2066
Kansas City, KS 66110
(913)596-2113

14. LEGAL SERVICES SOFTWARE

Unilaw Legal Case Management
Guardian Automated Systems, Inc.
Liberty Building-Suite 600
420 Main Street
Buffalo, NY 14202
(800)472-4600

Business Agreements
MichTron
6655 Highland Road
Pontiac, MI 48054
(313)666-4800

California Legal Systems: Corporations
Matthew Bender and Co., Inc.
P.O. Box 2329
San Francisco, CA 94126
(800)821-2232

California Legal Systems: Domestic Relations
Matthew Bender and Co., Inc.
P.O. Box 2329
San Francisco, CA 94126
(800)821-2232

California Legal Systems: Personal Injury
Matthew Bender and Co., Inc.
P.O. Box 2329
San Francisco, CA 94126
(800)821-2232

California Legal Systems: Probate
Matthew Bender and Co., Inc.
P.O. Box 2329
San Francisco, CA 94126
(800)821-2232

California Legal Systems: Wills & Trusts
Matthew Bender and Co., Inc.
P.O. Box 2329
San Francisco, CA 94126
(800)821-2232

Datalit/PC
DLC Company
6341 South Troy Circle
Suite E
Englewood, CO 80111
(30)790-8193

Deltax System
Deltax Corporation
P.O. Box 1780
Orem, UT 84057
(810)225-3614

Docket
Micro Craft, Inc.
2007 Whitesburg Drive
Huntsville, AL 35801
(205)534-4190

ESTAX 100
Professional Data Corporation
6449 Goldbranch Rd.
Columbia, SC 29206
(803)771-8880

Fiduciary Accountant
Institute for Paralegal Training
1926 Arch Street
Philadelphia, PA 19103
(215)567-4800

Illinois Legal Systems: Corporation
Matthew Bender and Co., Inc.
P.O. Box 2329
San Francisco, CA 94126
(800)821-2232

Illinois Legal Systems: Domestic Relations
Matthew Bender and Co., Inc.
P.O. Box 2329
San Francisco, CA 94126
(800)821-2232

Illinois Legal Systems: Wills & Trusts
Matthew Bender and Co., Inc.
P.O. Box 2329
San Francisco, CA 94126
(800)821-2232

Key-Doc Document Indexing & Retrieval
RTG Data Systems
1003 Wilshire Blvd.
Suite 202
Santa Monica, CA 90401
(213)451-3662

Lawman W3
Davies, A.E.
Box 1854
Ojai, CA 93023
(805)646-9731

Lawsearch
Direct Aid, Inc.
P.O. Box 4420
Boulder, CO 80306
(303)442-8080

Legalmaster
Computer Software for Professionals
1615 Broadway
Suite 308
Oakland, CA 94612
(415)444-5316

Legaltime II
American Business Automation, Inc.
Corporate Center
Hartford, CT 06103
(203)249-7036

Litigation Manager
Automated Legal Systems Inc.
1926 Arch Street
Philadelphia, PA 19103
(215)567-4800

Litigator
Institute for Paralegal Training
1926 Arch Street
Philadelphia, PA 19103
(215)567-4800

Litigator
Micro Craft, Inc.
2007 Whitesburg Drive
Huntsville, AL 35801
(205)534-4190

PC Cylaw
Cybernetics Resource Corporation
10 Maple Street
Port Washington, NY 11050
(212)961-4307

Profit Lawyer
TJS Data Systems, Inc.
2120 Wicker Avenue
Suite F
Schereville, IN 46375
(219)322-7000

Quick Tax Legal Time and Billing
Accounting Technologies Inc.
319 Clawson Street
Staten Island, NY 10306
(212)351-6143

ReadAble Document Analyzer
Solution Systems
45-L Accord Park
Norwell, MA 02061
(617)871-5435

Recruit
Institute for Paralegal Training
1926 Arch Street
Philadelphia, PA 19103
(215)567-4800

Texas Legal Systems: Family Law
Matthew Bender and Co., Inc.
P.O. Box 2329
San Francisco, CA 94126
(800)821-2232

Unilaw Legal Accounting
Guardian Automated Systems, Inc.
Liberty Building — Suite 600
420 Main Street
Buffalo, NY 14202
(800)472-4600

15. MUSIC SOFTWARE

AlphaSyntauri Synthesizer
Syntauri Corp.
3506 Waverly St.
Palo Alto, CA 94306
415-494-1017

Basic Guitar 1
Digtal Concept Systems, Inc.
4826 Bucknell
Suite 201
San Antonio, TX 78249
512-692-1201

Composer
Computer Software Associates, Inc.
50 Teed Drive
Randolph, MA 02368
617-527-7510

Comprehensive Music Publisher Royalty Reporting System
Topaz Systems, Inc.
17 Lawson Lane
Ridgefield, CT 06877
203-797-2323

Edumusic
Europro, Inc.
129 Saratoga
Petaluma, CA 94952
707-763-9700

Kaleido-Sound
Passport Designs, Inc.
116 North Cabrillo Highway
Half Moon Bay, CA 94019
415-726-0280

Music Box Composer
Alceon Computer Resources
P. O. Box 6286
Stanford, CA 94305
415-326-2511

Music Teacher
Instant Software
Rt.101 & Elm St.
Peterborough, NH 03458
603-924-9471

Music Sounds Using RF Interference
Florida Creations Dept. L
P. O. Box 16422
Jacksonville, FL 32245
305-631-5568

16. PAYROLL SOFTWARE

AA Computer Systems Payroll
A Computer Systems
19301 Ventura Blvd.
Suite 203
Tarzana, CA 91356
213-708-3917

After The Fact Payroll
Omni Software Systems, Inc.
146 North Broad Street
Griffith, IN 46319
219-924-3522

The Assistant Controller Series Payroll System
Lake Avenue Software
77 North Oak Knoll
Suite 105
Pasadena, CA 91101
818-792-1844

BPI Payroll System
Apple Computer, Inc.
20525 Mariani Avenue
Cupertino, CA 95014
408-996-1010

Versa Payroll
Hand E Computronics, Inc.
50 North Pascack Road
Spring Valley, NY 10097
800-431-2818

Solmon Payroll
Computech Group Incorporated
Mainline Industrial Park
Lee Boulevard
Frazer, PA 19355
215-644-3344

SolidPay
Solid Software, Inc.
2625 Cumberland Parkway
Suite 250
Atlanta, GA 30339
404-433-0823

Super P/R Payroll
Microcomputer Applications
3485 Mock Orange Court South
Salem, OR 97302
503-364-1090

Stars Payroll
Star Software Systems
20600 Gramercy Place
Suite 103
Torrance, CA 90901
213-538-2511

TBS Payroll Systems
Theta Business Systems
1110 Sonora Avenue
Suite 106
Glendale, CA 91201
818-242-7981

State of the Art Payroll
State of the Art, Inc.
3183 A Airway Avenue
Costa Mesa, CA 92626
714-850-0111

Peachtree PeachPay Payroll for the Wang PC
Wang Laboratories, Inc.
One Industrial Avenue
Lowell, MA 01851
800-225-0234

Payroll Costing
Libra Programming
1954 East 7000 South
Salt Lake City, UT 84121
800-453-3827

Restaurant Payroll
Fisher Business Systems
1010 Huntcliff Trace
Suite 22150
Atlanta, GA 30338
404-587-1717

Payware Payroll System
Computer Products International
3225 Danny Park
Metairie, LA 70002
504-455-5330

Post Facto Payroll
Delta Software Co.
3436 Mendocino Avenue
Santa Rosa, CA 95401
707-544-3425

RealWorld Payroll
RealWord Corporation
Dover Road
Chichster, NH 03263
603-798-5700

17. PERSONALITY ANALYSIS SOFTWARE

Computerware
4403 Manchester Avenue Suite 102
P. O. Box 668
Encinitas, CA 92024
619-436-3512

Bio Charts
Aladdin Software
1001 Colfax Street
Danville, IL 61832
217-443-4611

Biorhythm
Modtec
4144 N. Via Villas
Tucson, AZ 85719
602-293-5186

Astro Scope
Ags Software
P. O. Box 28
Orleans, MA 02653
617-255-0510

Astrocalc
Zephyr Services
306 S. Homewood Avenue
Pittsburg, PA 15208
412-247-5915

Horoscopics
Zephyr Services
306 S. Homewood Avenue
Pittsburg, PA 15208
412-247-5915

Professional Chart Services
Maltrix Software Inc.
315 Marion Avenue
Big Rapids, MI 49307
616-796-2483

Sex O Scope
AGS Software
P. O. Box 28
Orleans, MA 02653
617-255-0510

Superprogram
AGS Software
P. O. Box 28
Orleans, MA 02653
617-255-0510

18. REAL ESTATE SOFTWARE

PlanEas Offer Evaluation Models
Analytic Associates
4817 Browndeer Lane
Rolling Hills Estates, CA 90274
213-541-0418

PlanEas Partnership Models
Analytic Associates
4817 Browndeer Lane
Rolling Hills Estates, CA 90274
213-541-0418

AMS RealStar Client Follow Up
AMS RealStar, Inc.
P. O. Box 22415
Denver, Co 80222
303-695-1300

AMS RealStar Real Estate
AMS RealStar, Inc.
P. O. Box 22415
Denver, CO 80222
303-695-1300

APR Loan Analysis
Realty Software
1926 South Pacific Coast Highway
Suite 29
Redondo Beach, CA 90277
213-372-9419

Acquisition & Disposition Analysis
Berge Software
1200 Westlake Avenue North
Suite 612
Seattle, WA 98109
206-284-7610

All 9 Real Estate Modules Package
Realty Software
1926 South Pacific Coast Highway
Suite 229
Redondo Beach, CA 90277
213-372-9419

Client Prospecting
Micro Venture
2111 Business Center Drive
Suite 220
Irvine, CA 92715
714-975-0963

Commercial Finance
Berg Software
1200 Westlake Avenue North
Suite 612
Seattle, WA 98109
206-284-7610

DPS 11 Analysis and Finance
National Real Estate Exchange, Inc.
P. O. Box 475
Maitland, FL 32751
305-647-6739

DPS 12 Supercash Cash Flow Analysis
National Real Estate Exchange, Inc.
P. O. Box 475
Maitland, FL 32751
305-647-6739

Depreciation Amortization Schedule
Executive Data Systems
290 Interstate North
Suite 16
Atlanta, GA 30339
800-272-3374

Financial Analysis System Volume 1
Valuation Systems Company
Galleria Tower One
7130 S. Lewis Street, Suite E235
Tulsa, OK 74136
918-496-7655

Financial Analysis System Volume 2
Valuation Systems Company
Galleria Tower One
7130 S. Lewis St., Suite E-235
Tulsa, OK 74136
918-496-7655

Home Purchase
Realty Software
1926 South Pacific Coast Highway
Suite 229
Redondo Beach, CA 90277
213-372-9419

How To Make Good Investments
The Wizards
P. O. Box 7118
The Woodlands, TX 77387
713-367-6438

Income Property Analysis
Realty Software, Inc.
1926 South Pacific Coast Highway
Suite 229
Redondo Beach, CA 90277
213-372-9419

Investment Property Model
Kustom Software
665 Pacific View Dr.
San Diego, CA 92109
619-483-7119

Loan Pak
Crownsoft Applications, Inc.
Buckingham Commons
P. O. Box 96
Furlong, PA 18925
215-794-3272

Land & Leasing Analysis
Berge Software
1200 Westlake Avenue North
Suite 612
Seattle, WA 98109
206-284-7610

Leasead
Decisonex, Inc.
1200 Post Road East
Westport, CT 06880
203-765-3338

Loan Amortization Program
Comtronic Systems
31620 121st Avenue S.E.
Auburn, WA 98002
206-735-2916

Loan Amortization Schedule
Realty Software
1926 South Pacific Coast Highway
Suite 229
Redondo Beach, CA 90277
213-372-9419

Loan Amortization Schedule
Western Properties Investment Company
P. O. Box 9602
Marina Del Rey, CA 90295
213-823-4844

Loansales Purchase
Realty Software
1926 South Pacific Coast Highway
Suite 229
Redondo Beach, CA 90277
213-372-9419

MLCS PC Mortgage Lending Control System
Symbolics Financial Systems, Inc.
1740 N. Collins Blvd.
Richardson, TX 75081
214-238-5750

Mortage Maker
Navic Software
Box 14727
North Palm Beach, FL 33408
800-327-2133

Pandex
Decisionex, Inc.
1200 Post Road East
Westport, CT 06880
203-226-7424

Property Listings and Comparables
Realty Software
1926 South Pacific Coast Highway
Suite 229
Redondo Beach, CA 90277
213-372-9419

Property Sales
Realty Software
1926 South Pacific Coast Highway
Suite 29
Redondo Beach, CA 90277
213-372-9419

The Prospector
Scorpion Systems, Inc.
214 W. Patrick Street
Frederick, MD 21701
301-663-0539

Qual Pac
Creative Business Computer Systems, Inc.
6731 Red Road
Coral Gables, FL 33143
305-666-7970

RAP Residential Appraisal Processor
United Systems Corporation
60 East Baseline Rd.
Suite B-7
Tempe, AZ 85282
602-831-9363

REAP
Dominion Financial Projection
2551 Almeda Avenue
Norfolk, VA 23513
804-855-2398

Real Estate Accounting
MicroVenture
2111 Business Center Drive
Suite 220
Irvine, CA 92715
714-975-0963

Real Estate Aids
JKR Software & Systems
606 Welsh Place
Fayetteville, NC 38303
919-867-8597

Real Estate Analysis
Century Software Systems
1875 Century Park East
Suite 1730
Century City, CA 90067
213-879-5911

19. SALES AND MARKETING SOFTWARE

Art of Negotiating
Experience in Software, Inc.
2039 Shattuck
Suite 401
Berkeley, CA 64704
415-644-0694

Big Print
ATC Software
Rt. 2, Box 448
Estill Springs, TN 37330
615-976-9759

Easy Sales Pro
Sorcim/IUS Micro Software
2195 Fortuna Drive
San Jose, CA 95131
408-942-1727

The Forty-Niner
Excalibur Systems, Inc.
1512 Katella Avenue
Anaheim, CA 92805
714-385-1211

ICAS-Purchase Orders
Infoware Systems, Inc.
P.O. Box 22487
Denver, CO 80222
303-740-6071

ICAS-Sales Analysis
Infoware Systems, Inc.
P.O. Box 22487
Denver, CO 80222
303-740-6071

ICAS-Sales Commissions
Infoware Systems, Inc.
P.O. Box 22487
Denver, CO 80222
303-740-6071

ICAS-Sales Orders
Infoware Systems, Inc.
P.O. Box 22487
Denver, CO 80222
303-740-6071

MARKIS
Softworks, Inc.
7700 Old Branch Avenue
Clinton, MD 20735
301-868-4221

MYTE MYKE Sales Analysis
MDS Associates, Inc.
P.O. Box 108
Orchard Park, NY 14127
716-662-6611

On Line Order Entry With Inventory Control
Univair Systems
9024 St. Charles Rock Road
St. Louis, MO 63114
314-426-1009

Open Systems Sales Order Processing
Open Systems, Inc.
430 Oak Grove
Minneapolis, MN 55403
800-328-2276

Order Entry
COMPAL, Inc.
8500 Wilshire Blvd.
Beverly Hills, CA 90211
213-658-8863

PeachTree Sales Invoicing for the Wang PC
Wang Laboratories, Inc.
One Industrial Avenue
Lowell, MA 01851
617-256-1400

Prospect Tracking
MicroPro International Corporation
33 San Pablo Avenue
San Rafael, CA 94903
415-499-4024

The Prospector
Executive Data Systems, Inc.
290 Interstate North
Suite 116
Atlanta, GA 30339
800-272-3374

The Prospector
Scorpion Systems, Inc.
214 W. Patrick Street
Frederick, MD 21701
301-633-0539

Prospects
ATC Software
Rt. 2, Box 448
Estill Springs, TN 37330
615-967-9159

Quotation and Price Book System
Microcomputer Technology Systems
3759 West 170th Street
Torrance, CA 90504
213-329-6463

REDATA
REDATA
59 Middlesex Turnpike, SR 300
Bedford, MA 01730
617-275-0355

Sales Order Entry
Micro Business Applications, Inc.
12281 Nicollet Avenue South
Minneapolis, MN 55337
612-894-3470

Sales Planner
National Microware
2102 Business Center Dr.
Suite 110
Irvine, CA 92715
714-752-2344

Sapana Cardfile
Sapana Micro Software
1305 South Rouse
Pittsburg, KS 66762
316-231-5023

Solomon Sales Analysis
Computech Group Inc.
Mainline Industrial Park
Lee Boulevard
Frazer, PA 19355
215-644-3344

Stepped Multiple Regression
Anthion Software Group
6202 Damask Avenue
Los Angeles, CA 90056
213-293-0718

Order Entry and Invoicing With Catalog
Nepenthe Programs
44 Third Avenue, Suite F
Chula Vista, CA 92010
619-425-5501

Send for Free Catalog
Ensign Software
7337 Northview
Boise, ID 83704
208-378-8086

B.I.S. Sourceware—Order Entry System
Budget Infosytems, Inc.
607 N. E. Highway Ten
Blaine, MN 55434
612-786-5545

Distributor Ordering System
Richal Enterprises, Ltd.
607 Holmes Avenue
Placentia, CA 92670
714-528-7523

EZ Mainsales
Data Consulting Group
Software Dept L
87 Bounty Drive, No. EE203
Foster City, CA 94404
415-349-4001

Fulfilment I
Sunward Systems, Inc.
655 W. Irving Park Rd.
Suite 5203
Chicago, IL 60613
312-935-5702

Master Pac 100
H & E Computronics, Inc.
50 N. Pascack Rd.
Spring Valley, NY 10097
800-431-2818

Order Entry
Compal, Inc.
8500 Wilshire Blvd.
Beverly Hills, CA 90211
213-652-2263

A Stat 79
Rosen Grandon Associates
7807 Whittier St.
Tampa, FL 33617
813-985-4911

BIS Sourceware—Sales Analysis Module
Budget Infosytems, Inc.
607 N. E. Highway Ten
Blaine, MN 55343
612-786-5545

Creative Graphics
Accupipe Corporation
222 W. Lancaster Avenue
Paoli, PA 19301
215-296-7376

Microstat
Edosoft
P. O. Box 68602
Indianpolis, IN 46268
215-296-7376

Stepped Multiple Regression
Anthion Software Group
6202 Damask Avenue
Los Angeles, CA 90056
213-294-8058

Survey Analyst
Survey Technology Corp.
934 Pearl, Suite D
Boulder, CO 80302
303-449-7824

The Survey System
Creative Research Systems
1864 Larkin Street
San Francisco, CA 94109
415-771-0912

20. SPORTS SOFTWARE

Pro/Pik
Pro Systems
6561 Gillis Drive
Suite 333
San Jose, CA 95120
408-997-1776

SCOREKEEPER, HOUSE MANAGER
Microsystems
72014 87th Avenue, S.E.
Mercer Island, WA 98040
206-232-1513

Sports Statistics I
Educational Data Systems, Inc.
4661 Pinewood Drive East
Mobile, AL 36618
205-342-6021

TOP SCOUT: Football
Athletic Information Systems
8843 E. Altadena
Scottsdale, AZ 85260
602-991-5029

TOP SCOUT: Basketball
Athletic Information Systems
8843 E. Altadena
Scottsdale, AZ 85260
602-991-5029

Win At the Races
System Design Lab
2612 Artesia Blvd.
Suite B
Redondo Beach, CA 90278
213-374-4471

College Football
System Design Lab
2612 Artesia Blvd.
Suite B
Redondo Beach, CA 90278
213-374-4471

Football Scouting Report
Precision Prototypes
410 East Roca
Refugio, TX 78377
512-526-4758

The Gold Edition
System Design Lab
2612 Artesia Blvd.
Suite B
Redondo Beach, CA 90278
213-374-4471

Gambler's Edge Computing
250 Richards Rd.
Suite 254
Kansas City, MO 64116

Marathon Software
Dept. S
P.O. Box 1349
Jacksonville, TX 75766
214-586-8282

Phenom Sportsware
215 Catherine Street
Scotia, NY 12302

Generic Computer Products
P.O. Box 790
Department CID
Marquette, MI 49855

Dog Handicapper
Alfred Camisa
7615 Glenbrook Court
Pleasanton, CA 94566

Football Forcaster
Instant Software
Rt. 101 & Elm Street
Peterborough, NH 03458
800-258-5473

NFL Prognosticator
Instant Software
Rt. 101 & Elm Street
Peterborough, NH 03458
800-258-5473

NFL Speed Calculations
Pro Systems
6561 Gillis Drive
Suite 333
San Jose, CA 95120
408-997-1776

PONY-PICK/SULKY
Bonjoel Enterprises, Inc.
P.O. Box 2180
Des Plaines, IL 60018
312-297-2921

Handicapper
GolfSoft, Inc.
10333 Balsam Lane
Eden Prairie, MN 55344
612-941-2172

Horse Handicappper
Alfred Camisa
7615 Glenbrook Ct.
Pleasanton, CA 94566

League Bowl-24
Briley Software
P.O. Box 2913
Livermore, CA 94550
415-455-9139

League Reservations
Market Computing, Inc.
210 15th Avenue, S.W., Dept.L
Puyallup, WA 98371
206-848-9276

League Scheduling
Market Computing, Inc.
201 15th Avenue, S.W., Dept.L
Puyallup, WA 98371
206-848-9276

League Standings
Market Computing, Inc.
201 15th Avenue, S.W., Dept.L
Puyallup, WA 98371
206-848-9276

League Bowl-24
Briley Software
P.O. Box 2913
Livermore, CA 94550
415-455-9139

League Bowl-36
Briley Software
P.O. Box 2913
Livermore, CA 94550
415-455-9139

**Baseball Stats Package for
Manager, Coach and Fan**
Steve Lent
215 Catherine Street
Scotia, NY 12302
518-346-3924

Bowler's Information System
All-Pro Information Systems
P.O. Box 271
Dept. JAL
Plainfield, IN 46168
317-839-0283

Bowling Data System 2.0
Rainbow Computing, Inc.
19517 Business Center Drive
Northridge, CA 91324
213-349-0300

Bowling League Secretary
Instant Software
Rt. 101 & Elm Street
Peterborough, NH 03458
800-258-5473

Bowling League Secretary
Mighty Byte Computer, Inc.
12629 North Tatum Blvd., Suite 555
Phoenix, AZ 85032

Bowling Secretary
Brock Computer Services
1226 Booth Street
Howell, MI 48843
517-546-1075

Baseball Stats
Compustat Data Services
906 W. Sierra
Santa Ana, CA 92707
714-540-5529

Life Expectancy
Data Systems
2214 West Iowa Street
Chicago, IL 60622
312-235-2699

Computer Running Log
Homesoft
P. O. Box 6254
Salt Lake City, UT 84106
801-534-5604

Inshape
DEG Software
11999 Katy Freeway
Suite 150
Houston, TX 77079
800-231-0627

Healthaide
Knossos, Inc.
422 Redwood Avenue
Corte Madera, CA 94925
415-924-8528

Sante
Scaramouche
1425 Shirley Place
Mt. Vernon, WA 98273
206-428-0441

21. STATISTICAL and NUMBERS ANALYSIS SOFTWARE

Micro-Dynamo
Addison-Wesley Publishing Company
One Jacob Way
Reading, MA 01867
617-944-3700

Survey Analyst
Survey Technology Corp.
934 Pearl
Suite D
Boulder, CO 80302
303-449-7824

dCAMP-Finance, Organizer, Schedule Polling
PoliComp Associates, Inc.
P.O. Box 13822
Tallahassee, FL 32317
904-386-5128

Number Cruncher Statistical system
865 East 400 North
Kaysville, UT 84037

A-Stat
Rosen Grandon Assoc.
7807 Whittier Street
Tampa, FL 33617

Human System Dynamics
9010 Reseda Blvd.
Northridge, CA 91324

VisiCorp
2895 Zanker Road
San Jose, CA 95134

Desk Top Computer Software
303 Potrero Street
Santa Cruz, CA 95060

Conduit
P.O. Box 388
Iowa City, IA 52244

Wadsworthy Electronic Pub. Co.
Statler Office Building
20 Park Plaza
Boston, MA 02116

1-2-3
Lotus Development Corporation
161 First Street
Cambridge, MA 02141
800-343-5414

ABS 86
Altos Computer Systems, Inc.
375 E. Trimble Road
San Jose, CA 95131
800-538-7872

Altos Executive Financial Planner
Altos Computer Systems, Inc.
375 E. Trimble Road
San Jose, CA 95131
800-538-7872

BIZPACK
The Virginia Company
P.O. Box 2167
Christiansburg, VA 24073
703-382-4135

BMDP Statistical Software
BMDP Statistical Software, Inc.
Suite 6, Box 750, Route 3 Center
Maryland Route 3 South
Millersville, MD 21108
301-987-6822

BPT (Business Planning Tool)
Softstar, Inc.
13935 U.S. 1, Juno Square
Juno Beach, FL 33408
305-627-5511

Bottom Line Strategist for the DEC Rainbow 100
Ashton-Tate
9929 W. Jefferson Blvd.
Culver City, CA 92030
213-204-5570

Business Analysis
Instant Software
Rt. 101 & Elm Street
Peterborough, NH 03458
800-258-5473

Business Analytical Review Using VisiCalc
Spreadsoft Div. of Execsystems
P.O. Box 192
Clinton, MD 20735
301-856-1180

Business Planner
Duosoft Corporation
1803 Woodfield Drive
Savoy, IL 61874
217-356-7542

CalcStar for the DEC Rainbow 100
MicroPro International Corporation
33 San Pablo Avenue
San Rafael, CA 94903
415-499-1200

The Context MBA
Context Management Systems
23808 Hawthorne Blvd., Suite 101
Torrance, CA 90505
213-378-8277

Dow Jones Market
Dow Jones & Company
P.O. Box 300
Princeton, NJ 08540
800-352-8500

ENCORE!
Ferox Microsystems
1701 N. Ft. Myer Drive
6th Floor
Arlington, VA 22209
703-841-0800

EasyPlanner
Information Unlimited Software
2401 Marinship Way
Sausalito, CA 94965
415-331-6700

Forecasting
Programmed Press
2301 Baylis Avenue
Elmont, NY 11003
516-775-0933

HOMECALC
SIM Computer Products
Lee Park Office Complex
1100 East Hector St.
Whitemarsh, PA 19428
215-825-4250

Market Counselor
Capital Management Systems
3800 W. 17th Avenue
Denver, CO 80204
303-595-9998

Money Decisions
Eagle Software Publishing, Inc.
993 Old Eagle School Road
Suite 409
Wayne, PA 19087
215-964-8660

Multiplan
International Business Machines
P.O. Box 1328
Boca Raton, FL 33432
800-447-4300

Multiplan
Microsoft Consumer Products
400 108th Avenue, N.E.
Suite 200
Bellevue, WA 98004
206-454-1315

OptiCalc
Savant Corporation
P.O. Box 440278
Houston, TX 77244
800-231-9900

PeachCalc Electronic Spreadsheet
Peachtree Software, Inc.
3445 Peachtree Road, N.E.
Atlanta, GA 30326
404-239-3000

PerfectCalc
Perfect Software, Inc.
702 Harrison Street
Berkeley, CA 94710

Portable Spreadsheets
American Micro Products, Inc.
705 N. Bowser, No.121
Richardson, TX 75081
214-238-1815

Proof
MicroSPARC, Inc.
P.O. Box 325
Lincoln, MA 01773
617-259-9710

Statistical Analysis
Century Software Systems
1875 Century Park East
Suite 1730
Century City, CA 90067
213-879-5911

SuperCalc
Sorcim Corporation
2310 Lundy Avenue
San Jose, CA 95131
408-942-1727

THE FUNDAMENTAL INVESTOR
Savant Corporation
P.O. Box 440278
Houston, TX 77244
800-231-9900

THE TECHNICAL INVESTOR
Savant Corporation
P.O. Box 440278
Houston, TX 77244
800-231-9900

TK!Solver
Wang Laboratories, Inc.
One Industrial Avenue
Lowell, MA 01851
800-225-0234

Tax Planning, Real Estate Investment
Disko Courageous Corporation
No.1 Shimmering Oak Court
Chico, CA 95926
916-345-3721

22. TAX PREPARATION SOFTWARE

Quick Tax After-The-Fact Payroll
Accountng Technologies, Inc.
319 Clawson Street
Staten Island, NY 10306
212-351-6143

Quick Tax Amortization
Accounting Technologies, Inc.
319 Clawson Street
Staten Island, NY 10306
212-351-6143

Quick Tax Client Write-Up
Accounting Technologies, Inc.
319 Clawson Street
Staten Island, NY 10306
212-351-6143

Quick Tax Federal 1040 Tax Professional
Accounting Technologies, Inc.
319 Clawson Street
Staten Island, NY 10306
212-351-6143

Quick Tax Federal 1120 Corp. Tax Package
Accounting Technologies, Inc.
319 Clawson Street
Staten Island, NY 10306
212-351-6143

Quick Tax IL, KS MO & OH Tax Program
Accounting Technologies, Inc.
319 Clawson Street
Staten Island, NY 10306
212-351-6143

Quick Tax NJ Personal Tax Res & Non-Res
Accounting Technologies, Inc.
319 Clawson Street
Staten Island, NY 10306
212-351-6143

Business Tax Package
Accounting Plus Software, Inc.
P.O. Box 2619
Sarasota, FL 33578
800-872-1040

Silent Butler
Silent Butler
1423 East Alameda Avenue
Burbank, CA 91501
213-846-7571

Tax Preparer
Howard Software Services
8008 Girard Avenue
Suite 310
La Jolla, CA 92037
619-454-0121

Tax Shelter
Navic Software
Box 14727
North Palm Beach, FL 33048
800-327-2133

"C" Corporation Tax Generator
Omni Software Systems, Inc.
146 North Broad Street
Griffith, IN 46319
219-924-3522

Embassy Institute Tax Practice Library
The Embassy Institute
1001 Jefferson Plaza
Suite 112
Wilmington, DE 19801
302-654-6688

Estate Tax Plan
Aardvark/McGraw-Hill
1020 North Broadway
Milwaukee, WI 53211
414-225-7500

Federal Income Tax
E-Z Tax Computer Systems, Inc
5 Eagle View Court
Monsey, NY 10952
914-356-7780

ESTAX 100
Professional Data Corporation
6449 Goldbranch Rd.
Columbia, SC 29206
803-782-5376

Quick Tax Accountant Time & Billing
Acounting Technologies,Inc.
319 Clawson Street
Staten Island, NY 10306
212-351-6143

Massachusetts State Personal Income Tax
E-Z Tax Computer Systems, Inc.
5 Eagle View Court
Monsey, NY 10952
914-356-7780

Master Tax Programming
CPAIDS
1061 Fraternity Circle
Kent, OH 44240
216-678-9015

New Jersey Personal Income Tax
E-Z Tax Computer Systems, Inc.
5 Eagle View Court
Monsey, NY 10952
914-356-7780

Corporate 1120 Tax
E-Z Tax Computer Systems, Inc.
5 Eagle View Court
Monsey, NY 10952
914-356-7780

Quick Tax New York Personal Tax
Accounting Technologies, Inc.
319 Clawson Street
Staten Island, NY 10306
212-351-6143

Quick Tax AR, IN, PA, VA, MD Tax Packages
Accounting Technologies, Inc.
319 Clawson Street
Staten Island, NY 10306
212-351-6143

PC Tax Planner
Omni Software Systems, Inc.
146 North Broad Street
Griffith, IN 46319
219-924-3522

- PC/Taxcut
Best Programs
5134 Leesburg Pike
Alexandria, VA 22302
800-368-2405

New York Resident Personal Income Tax
E-Z Tax Computer Systems, Inc.
5 Eagle View Court
Monsey, NY 10952
914-356-7780

Standard Tax Programming
CPAIDS
1061 Fraternity Circle
Kent, OH 44240
216-678-9015

TAXPRO
Contract Services Associates
706 S. Euclid
Anaheim, CA 92802
714-635-4055

Tax Decisions
Eagle Software Publishing, Inc.
993 Old Eagle School Road
Suite 409
Wayne, PA 19087
215-964-8660

Tax Deferred Exchange
Realty Software
1926 South Pacific Coast Highway
Suite 229
Redondo Beach, CA 90277
213-372-9419

The Tax Machine
Accountants Microsystems, Inc.
3633 136th Place SE
Bellevue, WA 98006
206-643-2050

Tax Manager
Micro Lab
2699 Skokie Valley Road
Highland Park, IL 60035
312-433-7550

Tax Mini-Miser
Sunrise Software, Inc.
36 Palm Court
Menlo Park, CA 94025
415-441-2351

Tax Preparer
Howard Software Services
8008 Girard Avenue
Suite 310
La Jolla, CA 92037
619-454-0121

Taxpack
Alpine Data
635 Main Street
Montrose, CO 81401
303-249-1400

The 1040 Solution
Creative Solutions, Inc.
230 Collingwood
Suite 250
Ann Arbor, MI 48103
313-995-8811

Tax Advantage
Arrays, Inc./Continental Software
11223 South Hindry Avenue
Los Angeles, CA 90045
213-410-3977

Softax-Preparer's Version
Design Trends Ltd.
P.O. Box G
Wilton, CT 06897
800-243-4358

Softax-Professional Version
Design Trends Ltd.
P.O. Box G
Wilton, CT 06897
800-243-4358

1040 System
Omni Software Systems, Inc.
146 North Broad Street
Griffith, IN 46319
219-924-3522

23. TRAVEL and TRANSPORTATION SOFTWARE

AGCYMGT
CobraSoft, Inc.
13543 Hawthorne Blvd.
Suite 203
Hawthorne, CA 90250
(213)644-1135
(213)644-1136

AUTO-Pool
Star Point Technology
4730 Grannan Way
Placerville, CA 95667
(916)621-1393

Aircraft Approach Simulator
Sprott, Professor J.C.
5002 Sheboygan, N. 207
Madison, WI 53705
(608)273-0627

Aviation Department Management System
Aviaton Analysis, Inc.
P.O. Box 3570
Carson City, NV 89702
(702)246-5023

Aviation Flight Planner
Sprott, Professor J.C.
5002 Sheboygan, No. 207
Madison, WI 53705
(608)273-0627

Aviation Software Volumes 1-5 S. Gilman
574 East 87th Street
Brooklyn, NY 11236
(212)531-3276

Easi-Truck
Universal Software Associates, Inc.
606A West Arch
Searcy, AR 72143
(501)268-3018
(501)268-3048

Flight Plan Helper
Leland Young Company
P.O. Box 4127
Bay Pines, FL 33504
(803)961-7371

Flight Planner
Master Planner Inc.
302 Whispering Hills Drive
Victor, NY 14564
(716)924-2704

Flight Planning Aids
The Teaching Assistant
22 Seward Drive
Huntington Station, NY 11746
(516)499-8397

Pilot Flight Planner
Master Planner Inc.
302 Whispering Hills Drive
Victor, NY 14564
(716)924-2704

RNAV3 Navigator (West or Northeast)
Briley Software
P.O. Box 2913
Livermore, CA 94550
(415)455-9139

Roadsearch
Columbia Software
5461 Marsh Hawk Way
P.O. Box 2235
Columbia, MD 21045
(301) 997-3100

Roadsearch-Plus
Columbia Software
5461 Marsh Hawk Way
P.O. Box 2235
Columbia, MD 21045
(301)997-3100

Routeplanner
Columbia Software
5461 Marsh Hawk Way
P.O Box 2235
Columbia, MD 21045
(301)997-3100

Sunrise and Sunset
Telephone Software Connection, Inc.
P.O. Box 6548
Torrance, CA 90504
(213)516-9430
(213)516-9432

Transportation System
Collins Systems Inc.
4605 Lankershim Blvd.
Suite 421
North Hollywood, CA 91602
(818)506-4501

Travel Agency Accounting System
Agency Mgmt. Services Inc.
1902 Leland Drive
Suite 4
Marietta, GA 30067
(404)955-2392

24. WORD PROCESSING SOFTWARE

3-16 Word Processor
Qaz International Systems Corp.
59 East Cunningham Drive
Palatine, IL 60067
(800)323-6556
(312)358-3783

AMS-RealStar Word Processing
AMS-RealStar, Inc.
P.O. Box 22415
DenvEr, CO 80222
(303)695-1300

Altos Executive Word Processor
Altos Computer System, Inc.
2641 Orchard Parkway
San Jose, CA 95134
(408)946-6700

Apple Speller III
Apple Computer, Inc.
20525 Mariani Avenue
Cupertino, CA 95014
(408)996-1010

Apple Writer
Apple Computer, Inc.
20525 Mariani Avenue
Cupertino, CA 95014
(408)996-1010

Apple Writer II
Apple Computer, Inc.
20525 Mariani Avenue
Cupertino, CA 95014
(408)996-1010

Apple Writer III
Apple Computer, Inc.
20525 Mariani Avenue
Cupertino, CA 95014
(408)996-1010

Arabic/English Word Processor
Economic Insights
416 Hungerford Drive
Suite 216
Rockville, MD 20850
(301)294-2660
(301)294-2666

BENCHMARK Spelling Checker
Metasoft Corporation
6509 West Frye Road
Suite 12
Chandler, AZ 85224
(602)961-0003
(800)621-1908

BENCHMARK Word Processor
Metasoft Corporation
6509 West Frye Road
Suite 12
Chandler, AZ 85224
(602)961-0003
(800)621-1908

Bank Street Speller
Broderbund Software
17 Paul Drive
San Rafael, CA 94903
(415)479-1170

Bank Street Writer
Broderbund Software
17 Pual Drive
San Rafael, CA 94903
(415)479-1170

Bibliography
Digital Marketing Corporation
2363 Boulevard Circle
Suite 6
Walnut Creek, CA 94595
(415)938-2880
(415)947-1000

CMPR Text File Compare Program
Harlan S. Hersey Inc.
106 Quaker Drive
West Warwick, RI 02893
(401)822-0176

CT-OS WP/Spell/LP
Compu-Tome Inc.
234 East Colorado Blvd.
Pasadena, CA 91101
(818)796-9371

Colortext
Jupiter Island Corporation
14 Rock Lane
Berkeley, CA 94708
(415)526-5265

CorrectStar
MicroPro International Corporation
33 San Pablo Avenue
San Rafael, CA 94903
(415)499-4024
(415)499-4022

CrystalWriter
Syntactics
3333 Bowers Avenue
Suite 145
Santa Clara, CA 95051
(408)727-6400
(800)626-6400

Insta-Writer
Microsci
2158 South Hathaway
Santa Ana, CA 92705
(714)241-5600

Jack 2
Business Solutions Inc.
60 East Main Street
P.O. Box 341
Kings Park, NY 11754
(800)645-4513
(516)269-1120

KWIX 2.0 Key Word Index for Scripsit
Skylink Software
3705 S. George Mason Drive
Suite 2411-S
Falls Church, VA 22041
(703)578-3940

LEX Word Processing System
SofTest, Inc.
555 Goffle Road
Ridgewood, NJ 07450
(201)447-3901

LEX-11
EEC System Inc.
327/E Boston Post Road
Sudbury, MA 01776
(617)443-5106

Lazy Writer
Alphabit Communications, Inc.
13349 Michigan Avenue
Dearborn, MI 48126
(313)581-2896

Letter Writer
Astro-Star Enterprises
5905 Stone Hill Drive
Rocklin, CA 95677
(916)624-3709

LexiCom
MicroSPARC/Nibble, Inc.
10 Lewis Street
P.O. Box 325
Lincoln, MA 01773
(617)259-9710
(617)259-9039

MAILMAKER
Signature Software Corporation
615 West Gray
Houston, TX 77019
(713)526-0909
(713)526-1889

Mailer
Maurizi Associates
1344 Fitch Way
Sacramento, CA 95825
(916)486-2993

Megawriter
Megahaus Corporation
5703 Oberlin Drive
San Diego, CA 92121
(619)450-1230

MemoMaker
Hewlett-Packard Personal Software
3410 Central Expressway
Santa Clara, CA 95051
(800)367-4772

Merge 'n Print/Mailing Label and Datafiler
MBS Software
12729 N.E. Hassalo Street
Portland, OR 97230
(503)256-0130
(503)228-9402

MicroSpell
Trigram Systems
3 Bayard Road
Suite 66
Pittsburgh, PA 15213
(412)682-2192

Mini Word Processor
Coleman Computer Services
187-02 Keeseville Avenue
St. Albans, NY 11412
(212)454-9833

Multimate
MultiMate International Corporation
52 Oakland Avenue North
East Hartford, CT 06108
(203)522-2116
(800)842-8676

NewWord
Rocky Mountain Software Systems
1280C Newell Avenue
Suite 1292
Walnut Creek, CA 94596
(415)680-8378

Office Writer
Office Solutions Inc.
5708 Odana Road
Madison, WI 53719
(608)274-5047

D.A.T.A. 3500-Word Processing System
TOM Software
127 Southwest 156th Street
P.O. Box 66596
Seattle, WA 98166
(206)246-7022

DB Master Business Writer
Stoneware Incorporated
50 Belvedere Street
San Rafael, CA 94901
(415)454-6500

DIGIspell Dictionary and Spelling Checker
ATS Data Processing Inc.
1101 North 9th Avenue
Pensacola, FL 32501
(904)433-7578

DIGItext
ATS Data Processing Inc.
1101 North 9th Avenue
Pensacola, FL 32501
(904)433-7578

DWA's Em-U-Print
Koch Industries
P.O. Box 812
Northbrook, IL 60062
(312)228-0590

Data Base Manager (DBM) Report Writer II
Universal Data Research, Inc.
2457 Wehrle Drive
Buffalo, NY 14221
(716)631-3011
(716)631-3012

Docu-Power!
Computing!
2519 Greenwich Street
San Francisco, CA 94123
(415)567-1634
(415)346-0625

EDM-The Programmable Editor
The Alternate Source
704 North Pennsylvania Avenue
Lansing, MI 48906
(517)482-8270
(517)482-8271

EUREKA! Disk Cataloger
Mendocino Software Company, Inc.
Dept. LM
P.O. Box 1564
Willits, CA 95490
(707)459-9130

EZ Script
Blanton Software Service
4522 Briar Forest
San Antonio, TX 78217
(512)657-0766
(512)341-8801

EZ Script Plus
Blanton Software Service
4522 Briar Forest
San Antonio, TX 78217
(512)657-0766
(512)341-8801

Easy Writer 1.15
International Business Machines
P.O. Box 1328
Boca Raton, FL 33432
(800)447-4700
(800)447-0890

EasyWriter
Information Unlimited Software
2401 Marinship Way
Sausalito, CA 94965
(415)331-6700

Volkswriter Scientific
Lifetree Software
411 Pacific Street
Suite 315
Monterey, CA 93940
(408)373-4718
(408)373-4904

WES
W B Systems
137 Main St.
Westerly, RI 02891
(401)596-1811

WSSORT
Nugget Software Inc.
P.O. Box 440979
Aurora, CO 80044
(303)755-1481

Word Commander 64
MMG Micro Software
P.O. Box 131
Marlboro, NJ 07746
(201)431-3472
(201)972-1266

Word Exec
Signature Software Corporation
615 West Gray
Houston, TX 77019
(713)526-0909
(713)526-1889

25. COMMUNICATIONS SOFTWARE

Bulletin Board
Micro Lab
2699 Skokie Valley Rd.
Highland Park, IL 60035
312-433-7550

Coaxxsus
IE Systems, Inc.
112 Main St.
Newmarket, NH 03857
603-659-5891

Connect
Vector Graphic, Inc.
500 North Venture Park Rd.
Thousand Oaks, CA 91320
805-499-5831

Cross Talk XVI
Microstuf, Inc.
1845 The Exchange
Suite 140
Atlanta, GA 30339
404-998-3998

Data Capture
Southeastern Software
7743 Briarwood Drive
New Orleans, LA 70128
617-865-3435

Ecom-International
Add Engineering Corp.
21738 South Avalon Blvd.
Carson, CA 90745
213-327-6208

Easy Link Instant Mail Manager
Kensiton Microwave, Ltd
251 Park Avenue South
New York, NY 10010
212-475-5200

Forum-80
Forum-80 Headquarters
7600 East 48th Terrace
Kansas City, MO 64129
816-921-9439

IBM Personal Communications Manager
International Business Machines
P.O Box 1328
Boca Raton, FL 33432
800-447-4700

In Basket
Guardian Automated Systems, Inc.
Liberty Building—Suite 600
420 Main Street
Buffalo, NY 14202
716-842-6410

In Search
Menlo Corporation
4633 Old Ironsides Drive
Suite 400
Santa Clara, CA 95060
408-986-0200

Infocmom Infohost
Infoservices, Inc.
1728 Montreal Circle No. 22
Tucker GA 30084
404-938-9960

Micro-Sna-3270
Micro-Integration, Inc.
P. O. Box 335
Friendsville, MD 21531
301-746-5888

Micro-Sna-3770
Micro-Integration, Inc.
P. O. Box 335
Friendsville, MD 21531
301-746-5888

Micro Courier for the Apple III
Apple Computer, Inc.
20525 Mariani Avenue
Cupertino, CA 95014
408-996-1010

MacPhone
Intermatrix
547 Satsuma Avenue
North Hollywood, CA 91601
818-509-0474

The Market Link
Smith Micro Software, Inc.
P. OBox 7137
Huntington Beach, CA 92615
714-964-0412

MTerm
Mich Tron
6655 Highland Rd.
Pontiac, MI 48054
313-666-4800

Micro EZ Link
Advanced Micro Techniques
1291 East Hillsdale Blvd.
Suite 210
Foster City, CA 94404
415-349-9336

Smarterm 100
Persoft, Inc.
2740 Ski Lane
Madison, WI 53713
608-273-6000

Micro TLX
Advanced Micro Techniques
1291 East Hillsdale Blvd.
Suite 210
Foster City, CA 94404
415-349-9336

Micro SNA 3270
IE Systems, Inc.
12 Main St
P. O. Box 359
Newmarket, NH 03857
603-659-5891

Move It
Woolf Software Systems, Inc.
6754 Eton Avenue
Canoga Park, CA 91303
818-703-8112

Pro/Communiations for the DEC Pro Series 300
Digital Equipment Corporation
4 Mount Royal Avenue
Marlboro, MA 01752

Poly BSC 3270
Polygon Associates, Inc.
1024 Executive Parkway
St. Louis, MO 63141
314-576-7709

Poly BSC RJE
Polygon Associates, Inc.
1024 Executive Parkway
St. Louis, MO 63141
314-576-7709

Poly-Com
Polygon Associates, Inc.
1024 Executive Parkway
St. Louis, MO 63141
314-576-7709

Poly TRM/VT
Polygon Associates, Inc.
1024 Executive Parkway
St. Louis, MO 63141
314-576-7709

Poly XFR
Polygon Associates, Inc.
1024 Executive Parkway
St. Louis, MO 63141
314-576-7709

Powernet
Beam Porter, Inc.
Pleasant Ridge Rd.
Harrison, NY 10528
914-967-3504

Smarterm 125
Persoft, Inc.
2740 Ski Lane
Madison, WI 53713
608-273-6000

Smartem 400
Persoft, Inc.
2740 Ski Lane
Madison, WI 53713
608-273-6000

Softerm 1
Softronics, Inc.
3639 New Getwell
Suite 10
Memphis, TN 38118
901-683-6850

Softerm 2
Softronics, Inc.
3639 New Getwell
Suite 10
Memphis, TN 38118
901-683-6850

SpedtrmIII
Astral Image
812 B Street
Studio A
San Rafael, CA 84801
415-453-6213

Supercom Telecommunications Utility
The Software Store
706 Chippewa Square
Marquet, MI 49855
906-228-7622

Tcom
Zentek Marketing Corporation
308 1/2 South State St.
Third Floor, Dept. L
Ann Arbor, MI 48104
314-761-6100

TelMerge
Micro Pro International Corporation
33 San Pablo Avenue
San Rafael, CA 94903
415-499-4022

Telephone Utilities
Telephone Software Connection, Inc.
P. O. Box 6548
Torrance, CA90504
213-516-9430

TermExec
Exec Software
201 Waltham St.
Lexington, MA 02173
617-862-3170

26. COMPUTER-AIDED INSTRUCTION SOFTWARE

MARCK
280 Linden Ave.
Branford, CT 06405
(203)481-3271

Edutek Corporation
415 Combridge, No. 14
Palo Alto, CA 94306
(415)325-9965

Academic Skill Builders
Developmental Learning Materials
P.O. Box 4000
Allen TX 75002
(800)527-4747

Random House, School Division
400 Hahn Road
Westminster, MD 21157
(800)638-6460

Aladdin Software
1001 Colfax St.
Danville, IL 61832
(217)443-4611

Edufun! Division of Milliken Publishing
1100 Research Blvd.
St. Louis, MO 63132
(314)991-4220

United ProCom Systems
8459 Courthouse Blvd. Court
Inver Grove Heights, MN 55075
(612)457-6129

Little Bee Educational Programs
P.O. Box 262
Massillon, OH 44646
(216)832-4097

Learning Well
200 South Service Rd.
Roslyn Heights, NY 11577
(800)645-6564

Gessler Educational Software
900 Broadway
New York, NY 10003
(212)673-3113

I WIMS Computer Consulting
6723 E. 66th Place
Tulsa, OK 74133
(918)492-9036

Right On Programs
27 Bowdon Rd.
Greenlawn, NY 11740
(516)271-3177

Instant Software
Rt. 101 & Elm St.
Peterborough, NH 03458
(800)258-5473

Microcomputer Software Systems Inc.
4716 Lakewood Drive
Metairie, LA 70002
(504)887-8527

International Business Machines
P.O Box 1328
Boca Raton, FL 33432
(800)447-4300

Dorsett Educational Systems, Inc.
Box 1226
Norman, OK 73070
(405)288-2300

The Jay Gee Programming Company
7185 Blue Hill Drive
San Jose, CA 95129
(408)257-7795

H.C. Ward
P.O. Box 3412
Deland, FL 32720
(904)789-4654

Educational Software and Design
P.O. Box 2801
Flagstaff, AZ 86003
Russian Software
Box 36, 1744 W. Devon Road
Chicago, IL 60626

Storybooks of The Future
P.O. Box 4447
Santa Clara, CA 95054
(415)386-5184

Brainbank, Inc.
220 Fifth Avenue (408)
New York, NY 10001
(212)686-6565

Bob Baker Software
5845 Topp Court
Carmichael, CA 95608
(916)972-1931

Reader's Digest Services, Inc.
Microcomputer Software Division
Pleasantville, NY 10570
(914)241-5738

John Wiley & Sons Inc.
605 Third Avenue
New York, NY 10158
(212)850-6000

Data Systems
2214 W. Iowa
Chicago, IL 60622
(312)235-2699

Eduware Services, Inc.
28035 Dorothy Drive
Agoura Hills, CA 91301
(213)706-0661

Swiftware-Dolphin Software Corp.
318 Country Club Road
Newton, MA 02159
(617)332-2776

Rockroy Inc.
7721 E. Gray Road
Scottsdale, AZ 85260
(602)998-1577

Conduit (The University of Iowa)
P.O. Box 388
Iowa City, IA 52244
(319)353-5789

Computer Software Curriculum
1604 Limestone Trail
Fort Worth, TX 76134
(817)293-2282

SchoolHouse Software
290 Brighton Road
Elk Grove, IL 60007
(312)526-5027

Creative Publications
3977 East Bayshore Road
Palo Alto, CA 94303
(415)968-3977

Microcomputer Software Systems, Inc.
4716 Lakewood Drive
Metairie, LA 70002
(504)887-8527

Spin-A-Test Publishing Company
404L Old Orchard Ct.
Danville, CA 94526
(415)837-4532

Notable Software
P.O. Box 1556, Dept. LI
Philadelphia, PA 19105

Sublogic Communications Corporation
713 Edgebrook Drive
Champaign, IL 61820
(217)359-8482

TSC/Houghton Mifflin
P.O. Box 683
Hanover, NH 03755
(603)448-3838

J & S Software
140 Reid Avenue
Port Washington, NY 11050
(516)944-9304

SoftArt Software
P.O. Box 417
Carver, MA 02330
(617)866-2103

George Earl Software
1302 S. Gen McMullen
San Antonio, TX 78237
(512)434-3618

Morgan Computing Co., Inc.
104 N. Central Expressway
Suite 210
Dals, TX 75231
(214)739-5895

Davidson and Associates
6069 Grove Oak Place, No. 12
Rancho Palos Verdes, CA 90274
(213)378-7826

Regena
P.O Box 1502
Cedar City, UT 84720
(801)586-0157

Computer Software Associates, Inc.
50 Teed Drive
Randolph, MA 02368
(617)527-7510

Europro, Inc.
129 Saratoga
Petaluma, CA 94952
(70)763-9700

Computrickx, Inc.
129 Saratoga
Petaluma, CA 94952
(707)763-9700

SouthWest EdPsych Services, Inc.
P.O Box 1870
Phoenix, AZ 85001
(602)253-6528

Math Progams
Milton Bradley Company
43 Shaker Road
East Longmeadow, MA 01028
(413)525-6411

Telephone Software Connection, Inc.
P.O. Box 6548
Torrance, CA 90504
(213)516-9430

DeZoysa Enterprises
P.O Box 170
Keyport, NJ 07735

27. COMPUTER LITERACY SOFTWARE

1-2-3-Advanced Features
Micro Video Learning Systems, Inc.
119 West 22nd St.
New York, NY 10011
212-255-3108

1-2-3-An Introduction
Micro Video Learning Systems, Inc.
119 West 22nd St.
New York, NY 10011
212-255-3108

AB Cenes
Banbury Brooks Acorn Software
353 W. Lancaster
Wayne, PA 19807
215-964-9103

Apple Co Pilot
Apple Computer, Inc.
20525 Mariani Avenue
Cupertino, CA 95014
408-996-1010

Apple II Basic
Tab Books, Inc.
P. O. Box 40
Blue Ridge Summit, PA 17214
800-233-1128

Apple Super Pilot
Apple Computer, Inc.
20525 Mariani Avenue
Cupertino, CA 95014
408-996-1010

Arithmagic Addition
Banbury Books
353 W. Lancaster
Wayne, PA 19807
215-964-9103

Arithmagic Counting
Banbury Books Acorn Software
353 W. Lancaster
Wayne, PA 19807
215-964-9103

Arithmagic Subtraction
Banbury Books Acorn Software
353 W. Lancaster
Wayne, PA 19807
215-964-9103

The Author Computer Authoring System
Raptor Systems, Inc.
324 South Main St.
Stillwater, MN 55082
612-430-2980

The Author Plus
Raptor Systems Inc.
Stillwater, MN 55082
612-430-2980

Basic
Emerson & Stern Associates
2-Bit Software
13674 Boquita Drive
P. O. Box 2036
Del Mar, CA 92014
612-481-3242

Basic Tutor Series
Educational Courseware
67A Willard Street
Hartford, CT 06105
203-247-6609

Beginning PC Basic
Europ, Inc.
P. O. Box 390605
Mountain View, CA 94039
408-248-9700

Blue Chip I
Micro Courseware Corporation
4444 Geary Blvd. Suite 300
San Francisco, CA 94118
415-751-5223

The Computer Survival Guide
Micro Video Learning Systems
119 West 22nd St
New York, NY 10011
212-255-3108

Computers and Communications
International Business Machines
P. O. Box 1328
Boca Raton, FL 33432
800-447-4700

Cordatumsal
Cordatum, Inc.
4720 Montgomery Lane
Bethesda, MD 20814
301-652-5424

DOS Made Easy
QED Information Sciences, Inc.
QED Plaza
P. O. Box 181
Wellesley, MA 02181
800-343-4848

Eazy Learn
Miracle Computing
3132 Clayton Court
Lawrence, KS 66044
913-843-5863

The First Book of the IBM PC
Tab Books, Inc.
P. O. Box 40
Blue Ridge Summit, PA 17214
717-794-2191

Fun Games & Graphics for the Apple
Tab Books, Inc.
P.O. Box 40
Blue Ridge Summit, PA 17214
800-233-1128

Fundamentals Of IBM PC Assembly Language
Tab Books, Inc.
P. O. Box 40
Blue Ridge Summit, PA 17214
717-794-2191

How To Operate the Apple IIe
Fliptrack Learning Systems
999 Main Street
Suite 200
Glen Ellyn, IL 60137
312-790-1117

How To Operate The Apple IIe Using Pro-Dos
Fliptrack Learning Systems
999 Main Street
Suite 200
Glen Ellyn, IL 60137
312-790-1117

How To Operate the IBM PC and Portable PC
Fliptrack Learning Systems
999 Main Street
Suite 200
Glen Ellyn, IL 60137
312-790-1117

How to Operate the IBM PCjr.
Fliptrack Learning Systems
999 Main Street
Suite 200
Glen Ellyn, IL 60137
312-790-1117

How to Operate The IBMXT
Fliptrack Learning Systems
999 Main Street
Suite 200
Glen Ellyn, IL 60137
312-790-1117

Teach Yourself PC DOS on the IBM PC
Deltak Microsytems, Inc.
1751 Diehl Rd.
Naperville, IL 60566
800-282-5586

Teach Yourself Series
Deltak Microsytems, Inc.
1751 Diehi Rd.
Naperville, IL 60566
800-282-5586

Teach Yourself Visiword on the IBM PC
Deltak Microsystems, Inc.
1751 Diehi Rd.
Naperville, IL 60566
800-282-5586

Teach Yourself Wordstar on the IBM PC
Deltak Microsystems, Inc.
1751 Diehi Rd.
Naperville, IL 60566
800-282-5586

Teach Yourself DBase II on the IBM PC
Deltak Microsystems, Inc.
1751 Diehi Rd.
Naperville, IL 60566
800-282-5586

Teach Yourself DBase II on the IBM PC Extended
Deltak Microsystems, Inc.
1751 Diehi Rd.
Napervile, Il
800-282-5586

Turtle Tot
Harvard Associates, Inc.
260 Beacon Street
Somerville, MA 02143
617-492-0660

Using & Programming the Commodore 64
Tab Books, Inc.
P. O. Box 40
Blue Ridge Summit, PA 17214
800-233-1128

Using & Programming the IBM PC jr.
Tab Books, Inc.
P. O. Box 40
Blue Ridge Summit, PA 17214
800-233-1128

Using & Programming the Macintosh
Tab Books, Inc.
P. O. Box 40
Blue Ridge Summit, PA 17214
800-233-1128

28. INFORMATION NETWORK DATA BASES

NEWSNET
NewsNet Inc.
945 Haverford Road
Bryn Mawr, PA 19010
800-345-1301

Knowledge Index
Dialog Information Services, Inc.
3460 Hillview Avenue
Palo Alto, CA 94304
415-858-3785

Bibliographic Retrieval Services
1200 Route 7
Latham, NY 12110
518-783-1161

Nielsen Business Services
A.C. Nielsen Co.
Nielson Plaza
Northbrook, IL 60062
312-498-6300

ADP Network Services, Inc.
175 Jackson Plaza
Ann Arbor, MI 48106
313-769-6800

Boeing Computer Services, Inc.
7990 Gallows Court
Vienna, VA 22180
703-827-4603

BRS (Bibliographic Retrieval Services)
1200 Route 7
Latham, NY 12110
800-833-4707

BRS/After Dark
1200 Route 7
Latham, NY 12110
800-833-4707

BRS/Executive Information Service
John Wiley & Sons, Inc.
One Wiley Drive
Somerset, NJ 08873
201-469-4400

CBD Online
United Communications Group
8701 Georgia Ave. Suite 800
Silver Spring, MD 29010
301-589-8875

Chase Econometrics/Interactive Data
486 Totten Pond Road
Waltham, MA 02154
617-890-1234

Citishare
850 Third Avenue
New York, NY 10043
212-572-9600

CompuServe Executive Information Service
P.O. Box 20212
Columbus, OH 43220
614-457-8600

The Computer Company
P.O. Box 6987
Richmond, VA 23230
804-358-2171

Comshare
P.O. Box 1588
Ann Arbor, MI 48106
313-994-4800

Control Data Corp./Business Information Services
P.O. Box 7100
Greenwich, CT 06836
203-622-2000

Cornell University Computer Services
G-02 Uris Hall
Ithaca, NY 14853
607-256-4981

Data Resources Inc.
1750 K St., N.W., 9th Floor
Washington, D.C. 20006
202-862-3700

Delphi
3 Blackstone Street
Cambridge, MA 02139
800-544-4005

Dialog Information Retrieval Service
3460 Hillview Avenue
Palo Alto, CA 94304
800-227-1927

Dow Jones News/Retrieval
Dow Jones & Co. Inc.
P.O. Box 300
Princeton, NJ 08540
800-257-5114

Dun & Bradstreet Corporation
299 Park Avenue
New York, NY 10171
212-593-6800

General Electric Information Services Co.
401 N. Washington Street
Rockville, MD 20850
301-340-4000

GML Information Services
594 Marrett Road
Lexington, MA 02173
617-861-0515

I.P. Sharp
Box 418, Exchange Tower
2 First Canadian Place
Toronto, Ontario Canada
416-443-2381

Infonet
Computer Sciences Corp.
650 North Sepulveda Blvd.
El Segundo, CA 90245
213-6715-0311

Innerline
95 W. Algonquin Road
Arlington Heights, IL 60005
800-323-1321

Interactive Market Systems
19 W. 44th Street
New York, NY 10036
800-223-7942

ITT Dialcom Inc.
1109 Spring Street
Silver Spring, MD 20910
301-588-1572

29 OPERATING SYSTEMS, LANGUAGES and COMPILERS SOFTWARE

Apple Computer, Inc.
20525 Mariani Avenue
Cupertino, CA 95014
408-996-1010

Apple SuperPILOT Log
Apple Computer, Inc.
20525 Mariani Avenue
Cupertino, CA 95014
408-996-1010

Applesoft BASIC
Apple Computer, Inc.
20525 Mariani Avenue
Cupertino, CA 95014
408-996-1010

The Assembler
MicroSPARC/Nibble, Inc.
P.O. Box 325
Lincoln, MA 01773
617-259-9710

BASIC 09
Microware Systems Corporation
1886 N.W. 114 Street
Des Moines, IA 50322
515-224-1929

BASIC Compiler
MMG Micro Software
P.O. Box 131
Marlboro, NJ 07746
201-431-3472

BASIC Compiler
SofTech Microsystems, Inc.
16875 West Bernardo Drive
San Diego, CA 92127
619-451-1230

BASIC by Microsoft
Hewlett-Packard Personal Software
3410 Central Expressway
Santa Clara, CA 95051
800-367-4772

BAZIC
Micro Mike's, Inc.
3015 Plains Blvd.
Amarillo, TX 79102
806-372-3633

BI-280/286
Control-C Software, Inc.
6441 S.W. Canyon Court
Portland, OR 97221
503-297-7153

BSO/C Compiler
Boston Systems Office, Inc.
469 Moody Street
Waltham, MA 02254
617-894-7800

BSO/PASCAL Compiler
Boston Systems Office, Inc.
469 Moody Street
Waltham, MA 02254
617-894-7800

Billings Operating System
Billings Computer Corporation
18600 East 37th Terrace
Independence, MO 64057
816-373-0000

C Compiler
Microware Systems Corporation
1866 N.W. 114 Street
Des Moines, IA 50322
515-224-1929

C Executive
JMI Software Consultants, Inc.
P.O. Box 481
Spring House, PA 19477
215-628-0840

X/80 "C" Compiler
Software Toolworks
15233 Ventura Blvd.
Suite 1118
Sherman Oaks, CA 91403
818-986-4885

C/80 MATHPAK Floats and Longs
Software Toolworks
15233 Ventura Blvd.
Suite 1118
Sherman Oaks, CA 91403
818-986-4885

C80 Compiler
Zeighty Data Systems
P.O. Box 28355, 6/0 JC
Columbus, OH 43228
614-279-8271

C86 C Language
Computer Innovations, Inc.
980 Shrewesbury Avenue
Tinton Falls, NJ 07724
201-530-0995

MasterFORTH
MicroMotion
12077 Wilshire Blvd.
Suite 506
Los Angeles, CA 90025
213-821-4340

Micro Works Color FORTH
The Micro Works
P.O. Box 1110
Del Mar, CA 92014
619-942-2400

Microsoft PC BASIC Compiler for the Wang PC
Wang Laboratories, Inc.
One Industrial Avenue
Lowell, MA 01851
800-225-0234

Miniac
Shai Microcomuputers, Ltd.
P.O. Box 2137
Del Mar, CA 92014
619-755-7940

Multi-FORTH
Creative Solutions, Inc.
4701 Randolph Road
Suite 12
Rockville, MD 20852
301-984-0262

NCA-The BASIC Not-A-Compiler
Joe McConnell Assoc.
630 Second
Ann Arbor, MI 48103
313-662-3569

Nevada COBOL
Ellis Computing
3917 Noriega Street
San Francisco, CA 94121
415-753-0186

Nevada FORTRAN
Ellis Computing
3917 Noriega Street
San Francisco, CA 94121
415-753-0186

OS-9
Microware Systems Corporation
1866 N.W. 114 Street
Des Moines, IA 50322
515-224-1929

PASCAL
Mich Tron
6655 Highland Road
Pontiac, MI 48054
313-666-4800

PASCAL by Microsoft
Hewlett-Packard Personal Software
3410 Central Expressway
Santa Clara, CA 95051
80-367-4772

PC COBOL Compiler for the Wang PC
Wang Laboratories, Inc.
One Industrial Avenue
Lowell, MA 01851
800-225-0234

PC FORTRAN Compiler for the Wang PC
Wang Laboratories, Inc.
One Industrial Avenue
Lowell, MA 01851
800-225-0234

PC PASCAL Compiler for the Wang PC
Wang Laboratories, Inc.
One Industrial Avenue
Lowell, MA 01851
800-225-0234

PC/FORTH
Laboratory Microsystems, Inc.
P.O. Box 10430
Marina Del Rey, CA 90295
213-306-7412

CC-86
Control-C Software, Inc.
6441 S.W. Canyon Court
Portland, OR 97221
503-297-7153

COBOL by Microsoft
Hewlett-Packard Personal Software
3410 Central Expressway
Santa Clara, CA 95051
800-367-4772

COBOL-86 Compiler
Zenith Data Systems
950 Milwaukee Avenue
Glenview, IL 60025
312-391-8949

Catalog Search
Telephone Software Connection, Inc.
P.O. Box 6548
Torrance, CA 90504
213-516-9430

Compiled BASIC by Microsoft
Hewlett-Packard Personal Software
3410 Central Expressway
Santa Clara, CA 95051
800-367-4772

30. PROGRAM CREATION SOFTWARE

1802 Cross Assembler XASM18
Avocet Systems, Inc
804 South State Street
Dover, DE 19901
800-448-8500

3270 Emulator
Zenith Data Systems
950 Milwaukee Avenue
Glenview, IL 60025
312-391-8949

4-1-1
Select Information Systems, Inc.
919 Sir Frances Drake Blvd.
Kentfield, CA 94904
415-459-4003

6502 Cross-Assembler XASM-65
Avocet Systems, Inc.
804 South State Street
Dover, DE 19901
800-448-8500

6502-6809 Translator
Computer Systems Consultants
1454 Latta Lane
Conyers, GA 30207
404-483-1717

6800 Cross-Assembler XASM68
Avocet Systems, Inc.
804 South State Street
Dover, DE 19901
800-448-8500

6800-6809 & 6809 PIC Translators
Computer Systems Consultants
1454 Latta Lane
Conyers, GA 30207
404-483-1717

68000 Cross-Assembler XMAC68K
Avocet Systems, Inc.
804 South State Street
Dover, DE 19901
800-448-8500

6809 Cross-Assembler XASM09
Avocet Systems, Inc.
804 South State Street
Dover, DE 19901
800-448-8500

8048 Cross-Assembler XASM48
Avocet Systems, Inc.
804 South State Street
Dover, DE 19901
800-448-8500

8051 Cross-Assembler XASM51
Avocet Systems, Inc.
804 South State Street
Dover, DE 19901
800-448-8500

8505 Cross-Assembler XASM85
Avocet Systems, Inc.
804 South State Street Dover, DE 19901
800-448-8500

80C Disassembler
The Micro Works
P.O. Box 1110
Del Mar, CA 92041
619-942-2400

A.B.C.
Breakthrough Software
505 San Marin Drive
Nevato, CA 94947
415-898-1919

ADU-Application Development Utilities
Frontier Software
756 Bowling Green
Cortland, NY 13045
607-756-8247

AID Quality Assurance System
Applied Information Developers
823 Commerce Drive
Oak Brook, IL 60521
312-654-3030

ASMB-18 Cross-Assembler
Ashley, Allen
395 Sierra Madre Villa
Pasadena, CA 91107
213-793-5748

Diskovery
Micro Mantic Computer
541 N.E. McWilliams Road
Bremerton, WA 98310
206-377-9267

EAZYLEARN
Miracle Computing
313 Clayton Court
Lawrence, KS 66044
913-843-5863

EDM—The Programmable Editor
The Alternate Source
704 North Pennsylvania Avenue
Lansing, MI 48906
517-482-8270

About the author . . .

Robert H. Morrison, is a professional entrepreneur, who has started and operated over 100 small business ventures, and became a multi-millionaire in the process. His education came from doing—not schooling. He is not a multi-millionaire because he writes best selling books—he made his fortune doing what he writes about.

He is the author of "Why S.O.B.'s Succeed and Nice Guys Fail in a Small Business" which has sold over 400,000 copies to date. He owns Financial Information Exchange, a bank, office buildings, and a half million dollar home—all made by using the ideas and techniques he writes about. He has owned and operated supermarkets, cattle ranches, motels, building supply stores, accounting services, was the original founder of Dial-A-Horoscope, has been in several manufacturing enterprises, was a dealer in luxury yachts, a notary public supply company, several successful mail order companies and a home construction company. His wide and varied experiences in small businesses are refined and presented in this book. It is a trail blazed in the school of hard knocks for others to follow and achieve their goals in life.

Books by Robert H. Morrison:

Why S.O.B.'s Succeed & Nice Guys Fail in A Small Business
Divorce Dirty Trick
The Greedy Bastard's Business Manual
Promoter's Gold
New Venture Planner
Contracting Out
How To Get Blood From A Turnip
How To Win, Delay, Reduce Or Eliminate Lawsuits For Money Without A Lawyer
How To Survive And Prosper In The Next American Depression, War Or Revolution
How To Sell Every Word You Write
Tax Navigation
The Fraud Reports
Getting Money For Your Business
How To Make Yourself, Your Product, Or Your Company Famous
How To Steal A Business